INTRODUCTION
TO THE
CRIMINAL JUSTICE SYSTEM

By

HAZEL B. KERPER, J.D.
Of the Wyoming, California and Texas Bars

CRIMINAL JUSTICE SERIES

ST. PAUL, MINN.
WEST PUBLISHING CO.
1972

Library of Congress Catalog Card Number: **79–181453**

Kerper Intro.Crim.Justice MTB
2nd Reprint—1973

DEDICATION

To my husband, with whom I practiced law, and to our daughters, who had to put up with two lawyers as parents.

PREFACE

This book is not a law book, but a book about the law. It is written for the beginning student in law enforcement, criminology and corrections, sociology, social welfare, government, and urban affairs who needs an understanding of the criminal law as a means of social control. Because it gives an over-view of the criminal justice process, the book is also valuable to law students who all too often complete their legal education without consideration of the criminal justice system *as a system*, though such consideration could well preface their in-depth study of the law. The book is also written for the practitioner in criminal justice and for the reader who as professional and citizen must take part in the coming reform of the criminal justice system. He will find in the text the answers to many of his common questions about the way the criminal law goes about its important task of protecting society by apprehending, convicting, and, hopefully, rehabilitating the offender.

The reader or student who seeks a general knowledge of the criminal justice system can obtain this from the text only. The footnotes have been added to cite the leading cases and to reference the appropriate statutory provisions of four of the largest states—New York, Illinois, California, and Texas. The footnotes provide examples of contrasting statutory law and supply supplemental study materials for the student whose professional goals may suggest a more thorough examination of the criminal law and the correctional process.

The study of the law can be interesting, stimulating, exciting, revealing, and frustrating. Law is a social institution, and like all social institutions, it is imperfect. Nevertheless, with all its imperfections—and they are many and growing—the law day after day performs its main functions of settling disputes, controlling authority, and shoring-up the foundations of ordered liberty. In this essential task of social control, the criminal law plays an important part. To introduce the process and the people involved in the American criminal justice system is the purpose of this book.

December, 1971

H. B. K.

*

SUMMARY OF CONTENTS

APPENDICES

TABLE OF CONTENTS

APPENDICES

†

INTRODUCTION
TO THE
CRIMINAL JUSTICE SYSTEM

Part One

THE NATURE OF CRIME AND CRIMINAL RESPONSIBILITY

INTRODUCTION TO PART ONE

Every citizen should understand how the criminal justice system works. The criminal justice system is the institution charged with direct responsibility for the prevention and control of crime. Each year millions of people are victims of crime. Two million men and boys, and an increasing number of women and girls, are sent each year to adult or juvenile institutions as perpetrators of crime. It is almost impossible to estimate the dollar cost of crime. Crime affects the quality of life of every American.

Knowledge of how the criminal justice system operates is essential to all those who work in the system. Law enforcement officers, probation and parole officers, employees of correctional institutions, and of course, lawyers and judges cannot do their own particular job properly unless they know what happens to the offender between arrest and return to the free society. Welfare workers, truant officers, teachers, mental health workers, and doctors, though not directly employed in law enforcement and corrections, are constantly involved in one aspect or another of the criminal justice system. Charitable organizations work with offenders' families. Foster parents provide homes for children who are wards of the juvenile court. Junior Leagues and

The League of Women Voters undertake studies of court operation and investigate detention homes for young offenders. The Jaycees have chapters in penitentiaries. The National Association of Manufacturers in its STEP program trains offenders, both in and out of prison, for useful work in industry and business. Members of Congress and of the Legislature of all fifty states are constantly concerned with the problems of crime and delinquency and must shape the laws which guide the operation of the criminal justice system in the United States. The courts, from the Supreme Court to the Justice of the Peace Court in a small rural precinct, judge offenders within the constitutional guarantees of due process. Every parent is concerned with how successfully the criminal justice system controls the drug problem; every retail merchant with the detection and prosecution of shop-lifting. All of these persons must of necessity inform themselves about the operation of the social institution directly charged with protecting society and rehabilitating the offender.

The criminal justice system is a part of the larger institution of the law. Before we can understand how the criminal justice system works, we must look at the functions and limitations of the law and the historical development of the criminal law as a part of the larger legal system. We must consider the nature of crime, the legal concepts of criminal responsibility and the elements of the major crimes against persons and property, as these are basic to an understanding of the criminal justice process. We must also acquire a legal vocabulary and acquaint ourselves with important legal definitions in order to improve our communication. In this endeavor, the Glossary at the back of the book will prove helpful.

Chapter I

WHAT IS LAW?

To answer the question "What Is Law?" we must first consider the character of a society, its organization, its social norms, the methods it has chosen to transmit these norms, and the nature of the sanctions it imposes for their violation. We will examine the need for social control, and the different means by which social control is accomplished in a society. We will determine that law is one means of social control and attempt to differentiate it from other means of social control employed in a society.

LAW AS A MEANS OF SOCIAL CONTROL

The need for social control comes about whenever men begin to live together in groups. Social control introduces order into the society and the element of *predictability* into social relations. If I can predict that you will drive down the right side of the road, I can safely drive in the other direction on the right side of the road. If I were not able to predict your behavior, at least most of the time, I would either drive erratically myself attempting to guess where you would be driving, or I would stay off the road to avoid a head-on collision with injury and possible death. Because there are rules (in this case, laws) which prescribe the method of driving on a public highway, the behavior of both of us is controlled and we are both able to use the public highways most of the time in safety.

There are many means by which the society controls the behavior of the individual. Law is only one of these means. It is easy to identify other means of social control, or, to state it another way, the means by which the individual is induced to conform his behavior to the needs and desires of the group. Morals, mores, ethics, culture, tradition, habit, manners, fashion, to name a few, affect and even determine how the individual behaves. Most Americans use the fork in the right hand. When they want to cut meat, they shift the fork to the left hand and pick up the knife with the right. Englishmen and Frenchmen keep the fork in the left hand and do not have to keep shifting the fork from right hand to left. (It is said that American intelligence agents operating in foreign countries often give themselves away when they absent-mindedly use the fork in the right hand.) Thus, the *manners* and *habits* of Americans, Englishmen, and Frenchmen determine how they behave at the table, just as the current *fashions* in their respective countries will largely determine what they wear. In the famous battle between mini-skirt and midi-skirt, American women successfully defied the French fashion houses.

The *morals* of the group have tremendous influence on the behavior of the individual. The enforcement of moral codes is usually associated with religious beliefs and practices. The divorce rate among Catholics is lower than the divorce rate among many other religious groups. Orthodox Jews observe strict dietary restrictions. Seventh Day Adventists go to church on Saturday and keep their places of business open on Sunday. Other religious sects wear distinctive clothing. In every case, the individual who is identified with one or the other of the groups behaves differently than he would behave if he were not a member of that particular group. The group norms have controlled his behavior.

The *code of ethics* of doctors, lawyers, peace officers, teachers, and welfare workers determines how they will relate to their clients, other professionals in their own group, and the clients and professionals in the other groups. A doctor will not knowingly accept a patient who is being treated by another doctor except on a referral basis. Lawyers must not consult directly with the clients of other lawyers. Welfare workers are non-authoritarian in their contacts with clients; police officers impose authority. The professional behavior of the individual is thus guided by the ethical code of the group to which he belongs. This affects the relationships of the professional to his patient or client, which in turn affects the behavior of the patient or client toward the particular professional, and toward other professionals in the other groups.

Each of you can think of many examples of how morals, mores, ethics, culture, tradition, habit, manners, and fashion affect your own behavior and that of your friends and determine or influence the way you interact with each other and with other individuals and groups. Let us now consider how the individual is induced or persuaded to act according to group norms and expectations. This consideration will throw light on the question of how law differs from other means of social control and permit us to arrive at a definition of law.

The Informal Decision Making Process. Let us suppose that Johnny is the new boy in the sixth grade. He has just moved to a big city school from a school in a small country town. To make his problem more serious, he enters school six weeks after school has started. Johnny, like every normal boy, wants to be accepted by his classmates, and particularly he wants to be accepted by the "in-group."

Now begins a period of what the sociologist calls "testing." Johnny looks over the other boys in the class to try to find out who is in the group he wants to belong to. He picks out one of the boys and says "hello" to him on the playground. At lunch, he offers his dessert to another member of the group. At the same time the boys in the in-group and other boys and groups of boys are looking over Johnny. They notice the way he looks, the kind of clothes he wears, how he behaves toward the teacher, and how he throws a ball. They find out where he lives and what kind of car his family drives. They soon learn how much money he has in his pockets. They listen to his speech, determine that he is not a Mexican-American, but nevertheless talks "funny." This process of information gathering and decision making goes on for a considerable period of time during which Johnny has no way of knowing whether or not he is going to make it into the in-group.

If the in-group finds Johnny acceptable, one of the boys, usually the recognized leader of the group, will make overtures toward Johnny. He will be invited into the games, allowed to sit in a certain section of the school bus, or permitted to buy treats during recess. If they do not find him acceptable, none of these things will happen, and Johnny must settle for membership in a lesser group, or in extreme cases, will not be admitted to membership in any group.

How was Johnny's ultimate fate determined? Just what aspects of Johnny's looks, speech, behavior, skills, or family status got him into the in-group or kept him out? For that matter, what about Johnny admitted him to any other group, or kept him out of all the groups? Who made the decisions? When were they made? Was a vote taken? Did one boy, or several boys, refuse him membership in the group? If no vote was taken, who said what to whom that produced the decision to admit or reject Johnny? Maybe nobody actually *said* anything to anybody, yet Johnny was excluded from the group. How was the group decision arrived at?

If you think about it a while, you will realize that it is very difficult to answer any of the questions. Certainly Johnny will never get the answers, nor will his parents, nor the teacher, nor the principal. A social investigator would have difficulty in getting the answers. No boy in the in-group may be able to tell how the decision about Johnny was made. One may say he got the idea that Mike, the leader of the group, didn't like Johnny, or he will say that "Most of the guys just didn't want him around." Pressed for information on whether Mike or the other boys *said* they didn't want Johnny around, the answer, more often than not, will be "Nobody talked about it. I could tell they didn't like him." This will be a true statement. Without saying a word, Mike may have moved every time Johnny sat down beside him, Peter refused the offered dessert, and Jake deliberately dropped the ball thrown by Johnny. The signs were given, the signs were read, and the group decision arrived at. Nobody, least of all Johnny, will ever know just how nor why the decision was made. No appeal is provided for.

In the case of Johnny, the group punished Johnny by refusing him membership in the group. Putting it another way, it imposed negative sanctions on Johnny for his failure to meet the standards of the group, though exactly what those standards were would be very difficult to determine. The group could, of course, have rewarded Johnny by admitting him to the group, since this was something he wanted very much. In either case, it would be very difficult to say why and how the decision was made and almost impossible to identify who made it.

The decision-making process in most groups is similarly informal and difficult to identify and describe. The members of the Country Club may hold a formal vote to admit or reject the new couple in town, but the reasons why any member voted for or against their admission would be hard to learn. A mother's disapproval of her child's behavior may be expressed in words or indicated by a frown and a refusal of cookies. A group may express its decision in words or just fail to act, and give no reasons. Groups give rewards and mete out punishments to individuals by informal means, unguided by rules of decision making, and often largely unaware of the factors which really shape the decisions. When the group is aware of the reasons for its decisions, it very often refuses to verbalize them even within the group, particularly if the decision is a negative one or would give rise to a suspicion of arbitrariness or prejudice. Thus, an individual may be informally punished by a group for a "crime" which neither he nor the members of the group can identify. It is sufficient that he fails in some way to measure up to the standards of the group. Conversely, an individual may be rewarded by a group for behavior which neither he nor the group could readily point to as deserving of group acceptance.

The Decision Making Process in the Law. The decision-making process in the law is very different. In the first place, the law seldom rewards an individual for obeying the law. True, the individual who conforms his conduct to the dictates of the law may reap an incidental reward in that he is not arrested and called into court to answer for his behavior. But this is only incidental, and the law does not consider that in failing to apply sanctions it has rewarded the law-abiding citizen. The law imposes largely negative sanctions, and concerns itself with transgressors against the law. But unlike the other means of social control, the reasons for the application of negative sanctions are clearly identifiable in the law, the persons who will make the decisions are determined by their official positions, the nature and extent of the sanctions which may be applied are set out, and the decision-making process is governed by rules. What is even more important, all of these matters are determined *in advance*, and the offender against the law can ascertain in advance of his offense what conduct is unlawful, who will decide on his guilt or innocence, the limits of the punishment that he may receive, and the conditions under which he will be judged and sentenced.

Law is distinguishable from all other means of social control because the reasons for decision, the place of decision, the rules which govern decision making, and the limits of the sanctions are set out in advance. The individual knows before he undertakes the alleged act where, how, by whom, and under what conditions he will be judged. He knows what conduct has been declared illegal, and the limits of the punishments he may suffer. Usually, he has an appeal.

The social institution particularly charged with the decision-making process in the law is the *courts.* Thus, we can arrive at a definition of law which distinguishes law from all other means of social control.

Definition of Law. *Law is a formal means of social control that involves the use of rules that are interpreted and are enforceable by the courts of a political community.*[1] We will discuss other elements in the definition later on. The important word right now is *courts.*

Rules of Procedure. The decision-making process in courts of law is governed by rules, called rules of procedure. In the criminal law, the rules of procedure are set out in the United States Constitution, the constitutions of the various states, the acts of Congress, the statutes passed by the state legislatures, in decisions of courts, and in rules adopted by the courts themselves. The Bill of Rights, which is the name given to the first ten amendments of the United States Constitution, is largely concerned with setting up rules of procedures in criminal cases, and every state constitution has a similar "bill of rights." The United States Constitution also provides that the trial of all criminal cases must be held in the state or territory where the offense was committed, before a court *chosen in advance* to try such cases. This provision makes it clear that the founders of our nation placed great store on identifying in advance the courts empowered to make decisions in criminal cases and on setting up rules to guide that decision making. Today, all persons deeply concerned about the preservation of individual rights and liberties pay constant attention to the reasons for the application of criminal sanctions and the way in which the decisions to impose such sanctions are made by the courts.

LAW AND SOCIAL VALUES

The law, as do other means of social control, molds the behavior of the individual by imposing sanctions for failure to conform to group norms and expectations. We must now consider how

1. F. James Davis, Henry H. Foster, Jr., C. Ray Jeffery, E. Eugene Davis, *Society And The Law*, New York: The Free Press of Glencoe, 1962, p. 41.

the norms set out in the law can be distinguished from those imposed by morals, for example, or by custom and tradition. We must also consider the relative importance of the different means of social control in controlling the behavior of the individual. This will bring us to another element in our definition of law—that law is interpreted and enforced by the courts of a *political community*.

Social Values Expressed in the Customs and Traditions of a Society. All rules made by a society to insure social control are based upon value judgments made by that society. The society must identify the needs of the society which must be protected if the society is to survive. This usually requires the additional determination of which needs come first. If only some of the needs can be met, or if the needs cut up against each other, priorities must be set. For example, a society cannot have maximum order and maximum individual freedom at the same time. It must make the value judgment of how much order will be sacrificed for individual freedom and how much individual freedom will be sacrificed for order.

The needs for food, shelter, and some degree of order are common to all societies. Thus, very primitive societies make rules to protect the food supply and against destroying the shelter. Killing another member of the tribe is also prohibited. Anthropologists tell us that almost all societies very early make rules to protect the blood lines. These rules govern family formation and sexual relations, and are both affirmative and negative in that they require some forms of union and prohibit others. For example, in ancient Egypt, the Pharaoh was required to marry his sister; marriage of brother and sister was prohibited to all other members of the society. So prevalent are the social taboos against sexual relationships among persons closely related by blood, that incest, not murder, is considered to be the most universal crime in human society.

Once having made the value judgments that form the basis of its rules, the society must develop a method for passing on knowledge about the rules to the younger members of the group and insuring their acceptance. The society must also decide what degree of deviance from the rules will be tolerated by the group and what sanctions will be applied to the individual whose conduct exceeds the limits set by the group. All societies make these decisions. In all societies a degree of deviancy which threatens the existence of the group will rarely be tolerated. In primitive societies, the most common punishment was banishment from the group—ostracism being equivalent, under the conditions of most primitive societies, to a sentence of death. All societies devise means of inculcating in the individual the values and norms of the group and informing him about the limits to behavior set by the group. In primitive societies the usual means were custom and tradition. In more complex societies, more formal means have been developed. The goal in all cases is social control. The means vary from society to society. In modern societies the process by which the values and norms of a society are transmitted to the individual is called *socialization.*

It is very difficult to determine when "law" in its modern sense appears in a social group. Rules of behavior are not synonymous with law. Rules in primitive societies treat with matters which are of general concern to the society, and the content of the rules resembles law. Nevertheless, the rules of primitive societies lack many characteristics that we associate with law and a legal system. Primitive societies do not have formal institutions of government, a legislature, legal officials and courts and, as we have seen, the courts are what distinguishes law from other means of social control.

The Meaning of a Political Community. A political community according to Weber involves "forcible maintenance of orderly dominion over a territory and its inhabitants." [2] A political community controls a territory, and its right to control the territory is recognized by other political communities. If we think of the Jewish people before and after the establishment of the state of Israel, we can understand the distinction between a community and a political community. During the Diaspora, the Jewish people in country after country maintained themselves as a community, bound together by shared religious beliefs, customs, and traditions. They considered themselves a community, and were recognized by others, including governments, as a community. However, it was not until the Jews established the state of Israel and began to control a territory that they became a *political* community.

Law in its modern sense is enforced by a political community. Law "involves a systematic and formal application of force by

2. Max Weber, *Law in Economy and Society,* ed. by Max Rheinstein, Cambridge, Mass.: Harvard University Press, 1954, p. 338.

the state in support of explicit rules of conduct."[3] The word "state" in this definition means the same thing as "political community," for "the state is the supreme political community."[4] The significance is that while rules are enforced by family or group, law is enforced by government itself; if necessary, by all of the forces of government, including the armed forces.

Social Values Expressed in the Laws of a Society. In the development of a society, some rules become law; others do not. Some of the norms of the society become a part of the formal, coherent statement of rules and process that we call law; others remain in the realm of morals, manners, custom, and tradition. Some values of the society are enforced by the state through its courts which are supported by the maximum power of the state, if necessary; other values are enforced, if at all, by informal group controls and by group sanctions which have behind them only the power of the particular group, which cannot call upon the assistance of the state. The interesting questions are: What rules are raised to the dignity of law, and which are not? What values of the state are important enough that they can be enforced by the courts and the armed forces while others must continue to depend upon group pressures and informal sanctions? In the process of socialization of the individual, which is more important—the law, supported as it is by the full power of the state, or group rules expressed in moral codes, custom, and tradition, enforced by informal sanctions such as group disapproval or ejection from the group?

The question as to what rules and values are expressed as laws is easier to answer than the question about the relative importance of law in the socialization process. In general, a society tends to give the dignity of law to those values about which it feels most deeply and concerning which it is in the greatest agreement. The so-called "common law crimes" are a good example.

American law is derived from English law; our system of law is referred to as the "Anglo-American system of law." Long before the colonies broke away from England, and indeed long before it became the custom to have the crimes defined in written statutes enacted by legislative bodies, certain acts were declared to be crimes under the common law. These common law crimes

3. Robert Redfield, "Primitive Law," *University of Cincinnati Law Review*, Vol. 33 (1964), pp. 3–22.

4. Davis, Foster, Jeffery, Davis, *op. cit.* p. 45.

included treason, murder, arson, rape, robbery, burglary, and theft. We can readily see that the majority of the people in any civilized society, and probably the majority in many primitive societies as well, would agree that the behavior defined by those common law crimes constituted a threat to the very existence of the society, and therefore should be prohibited. Moreover, few would deny that the conduct prohibited by the common law crime is conduct about which most people feel very deeply. In other words, almost everybody is strongly against treason, murder, arson, rape, robbery, burglary, and theft.

While it is generally true that the rules which become law are those about which people feel the most strongly and concerning which they are in the greatest agreement, a moment's reflection will demonstrate that this would be hard to prove by an examination of modern penal codes. Today, literally hundreds of crimes are on the books which only a few people feel strongly about. There are many additional laws which people may feel strongly about but about which they are not in general agreement. (For example, Sunday closing laws; laws prohibiting sale by the drink of alcoholic beverages; laws declaring abortion and the use of marijuana to be crimes, and the like.) This situation has come about because for years Americans have had difficulty in distinguishing crime from sin. Moreover, many groups have attempted to impose their own morality upon the whole society by using the criminal law. (It is interesting to note that most laws covering "immoral" behavior, exclusive of the immoral behavior prohibited in the common law crimes, are directed at the "immoral" behavior of *others*.)

Though the statement about the relationship between law, strong feelings, and general consensus in the society is incapable of proof in modern penal systems, the assertion nevertheless states a truth about the law. Whenever people feel strongly about a social value and are in general agreement about it, it is very apt to be enacted into law, and the law is easy to enforce. The more the people disagree about the value, the more they consider the rule to be trivial and unimportant, the harder it is to enact it into law, and if enacted, the harder it is to enforce. When whole groups of people, as distinguished from the occasional or even frequent individual violator, systematically disobey or ignore a law, we speak of "patterned evasion." Continued patterned evasion usually brings about a change in the law.

The Importance of Law in the Socialization Process. We now come to the question about the importance of law in the socialization process. Do people conform their behavior to the norms and expectations of the society because they are afraid of the law, or because they want the approval of the group? Which is more effective in changing the individual's behavior—the punishments prescribed in the law or the informal sanctions imposed by the group whose acceptance he seeks? Some scholars, pointing to the fact that crime continues in spite of legal sanctions, maintain that the law is of minor importance in molding the individual's values and behavior. "After all," they say, "pickpockets picked pockets at public hangings of pickpockets."

Other students of human behavior state that while it is easy to identify those who ignore the edicts of the law and whose behavior the law has obviously not controlled, it is impossible to point out those who do conform their behavior to the social norms because of the law. Proving the negative fact that law often does not succeed in its task of controlling behavior is easy enough. It is much more difficult to prove the affirmative fact that the law has probably worked surprisingly well. There are certainly more law-abiding citizens than there are law violators.

It is not easy to reconcile these points of view, nor to prove either of them wrong. We seldom suspend the rule of law, so we really don't know what would happen in our society if we did. Certain events, however, have furnished a few clues. During the Boston police strike that brought Calvin Coolidge to national attention and ultimately to the Presidency, the city of Boston was in a shambles within hours after the police left the streets. Robbery, burglary, assault, rape, and other violent crimes increased many fold. Citizens were afraid to be on the streets; many locked themselves in their houses and refused to venture forth. Racketeers, hoodlums, and just plain criminals from all over the eastern seaboard, and later from all parts of the country swarmed into Boston to take advantage of the fact that its citizens were without police protection. It was then that Calvin Coolidge, Governor of Massachusetts, declared the police strike itself illegal. "There is," he said, "no right to strike against the public safety." In recent years, a police strike in one of the Canadian cities produced a similar result. A dramatic increase in all types of crime followed immediately upon the withdrawal of the police from the streets of the city of Montreal.

The Boston and Montreal police strikes demonstrated beyond any doubt that law as symbolized by the police is a deterrent to antisocial acts. Another conclusion also seems justified. The role of law in the socialization process is more important in a complex society than it is in a simple or primitive society. When the individual lives closely within family and tribe, when he depends directly on their support for food and shelter, when earning their disapproval means ostracism and death, the pressures on him to conform to the values and norms of the group are powerful indeed. On the other hand, family and peer group pressures are not so great upon the individual who makes his living working for an impersonal corporation, whose social contacts are largely with strangers, and who can find anonymity in the city no matter what antisocial behavior he wants to indulge in. The limits, if any, on his social conduct must come from the law. Because he can so easily avoid family and peer group pressures, he will modify his behavior only when he is afraid of being picked up and punished by the law.

FUNCTIONS OF THE LAW

We have defined law as a formal means of social control and distinguished it from other means of social control by the unique character of its decision-making process. We will now consider some of the functions and limitations of law.

It is difficult to arrive at a satisfactory list of the functions of the law. The following are the most obvious:

1. Keeping the peace
2. Preventing and punishing illegal conduct
3. Resolving value conflicts in the society
4. Settling disputes
5. Allocating authority among different governmental and social agencies
6. Making "rules for the rulers."

Keeping the Peace. In keeping the peace, the law functions to maintain order in the society. No society can continue to exist without a certain degree of order. In a complex society, we traditionally look to the law to keep, and if necessary, impose order. This ties in with the distinction we have previously made between law and rules—law is supported by the entire force of the state. It follows that the entire force of the state can be brought to bear to maintain or impose order. This peace keeping function of the law is so well known that the phrase "law and order" could almost be written as a single word "lawandorder." It is also significant that law enforcement officers are commonly called "peace officers."

Preventing and Punishing Illegal Conduct. Preventing and punishing illegal conduct is another important assignment of the law. Police officers prevent criminal conduct by their mere presence in an area. They also apprehend law violators and take them before the courts for determination of guilt or innocence. The sanctions imposed are carried out in jails, penitentiaries, or juvenile correctional institutions or by specialized agencies such as probation departments and parole boards. These correctional institutions and agencies are a part of the criminal justice system.

Resolving Value Conflicts in the Society. Law plays an important part in resolving value conflicts in the society. Different groups in a society have different values, as a result of which their views differ on what conduct is a threat to the society and should therefore be illegal. These value conflicts come to a head in the legislature when the passage or change of a law is being considered. For example, the proposal may be that the use of marijuana be legalized. In legislative committees, on the floor of the senate and house, in the news media, the pros and cons will be exhaustively discussed, sometimes quietly, more often, heatedly. Ultimately, the legislature will adopt one or the other of the opposing points of view, or a compromise will be arrived at. This choice of the legislature is expressed in the law, which must be passed by both houses and signed by the Governor. In the case of marijuana, the legislature may do nothing, thus keeping in effect all of the existing laws; it may remove possession and use of marijuana from the list of crimes and thus legalize its use; or it may simply reduce the penalty on the use of marijuana, which represents a kind of compromise between the conflicting positions.

Of course, the controversy about marijuana does not automatically end when the law is passed or left unchanged, nor do all the people suddenly share the same value judgment about its use.

Nevertheless, the law as passed or left unchanged, expresses the dominant value judgment about the use of marijuana at that time and place. The significant thing is that, once the law is passed or left unchanged, most people will abide by it, and the entire force of the government can be brought to bear to enforce it. The "patterned evasion" we mentioned earlier may, of course, occur. If tomorrow the values of the minority become the majority values, the law will then change. The changed law will again represent the dominant value judgment about marijuana at that time and place.

Settling Disputes. A major contribution of the law is in settling disputes. The courts spend all their time in settling disputes, in some cases disputes between individual and individual, or between the individual and the state. In the criminal law, we see the dispute as being between the individual and the state. If there were no laws and courts to settle private disputes, it would be almost impossible to keep order in the society. Every man with a grievance against his neighbor would undertake to get even. Fights would result, which would probably be joined in by family and kin of both parties. The result would be to damage the whole society as the disputes kept widening to take in more and more people and as the energy of the people became devoted to fighting each other instead of to the production of goods or protection of the state as a whole. As we will see later, this situation at one time actually occurred, which led to the development of the criminal law.

By providing a forum for the settlement of disputes the law provides a "safety valve" for the society. In the course of any single day, the courts of the United States hand down hundreds of decisions which establish the rights and responsibilities of conflicting parties. The remarkable thing is that once the decision has been handed down, both parties abide by it. Only rarely does a disgruntled litigant take up arms against his opponent or against the judge rendering the decision. In settling disputes, the law functions to keep the peace, prevent and punish illegal conduct, and to preserve the energy of the people for productive pursuits.

Allocating Authority Among Different Governmental and Social Agencies. The law is charged with allocating authority among different governmental and social agencies. The people of the society make choices about how they are to be governed, and in a complex society they express these choices in law. The basic form of government is set out in the constitution, which means that it can be changed only by constitutional amendment, a rather difficult thing to accomplish. By means of statutes passed from time to time as the society grows and changes, other agencies of government come into being.

It is easy to understand how law allocates authority among different governmental and social agencies if we think of the *new* governmental agencies that have come into existence in the last few years, or will be required in the near future. Examples are agencies charged with responsibility to control air traffic, deal with airplane hijackers, prevent pollution of our air and water, provide increased driving safety in automobiles, control sales of drugs and cure drug addiction, make decisions about organ transplants, and put a man on the moon. As will be discussed in greater detail later, law is not a static thing. It is a social institution that is constantly changing as the organization and values of the society change. This changing aspect of the law is particularly well illustrated in this area where its responsibility is to allocate authority among different governmental and social agencies.

Making Rules for the Rulers. Another important function of the law is to make rules for the conduct of persons in authority. When we say we believe in the rule of law, not men, we are expressing the fact that we insist that our rulers must be governed by law. No official of the federal government and no state official in the United States has unlimited power. In our constitutional and statutory law we spell out what the President or the chief executive of a state can and cannot do; what the Congress or the legislature can and cannot do; what the federal and state courts can and cannot do.

Because the colonists at the time of the Revolution had had particularly bad experiences with courts they refused to ratify the Constitution until the first ten amendments were added. These first ten amendments, which comprise the "Bill of Rights," set out in great detail the rules governing the courts and the legal system, particularly in the area of criminal law. Not only the federal government, but every state, has its "bill of rights" which sets out the rules that protect the citizen in his encounters with the criminal justice system. Law is distinguished from other means of social control, not only by the fact that the decisions are made by courts set up in advance, but also by the fact that the courts must make their decisions according to rules of procedure also established in advance, and set out in the law.

Pound's Jural Postulates. We have previously established the fact that in general the values of a society expressed in the law are those about which the society feels the most strongly and about which it has reached the greatest concensus. Roscoe Pound, in attempting to set forth the basic functions of the law, addressed himself to these values, and in his *Jural Postulates* set forth a concise statement of the interests to be recognized and secured by the law. He began with the statement, "In a civilized society men must be able to assume: * * *" and went on to analyze the interests which a man living in a political community should be able to expect the law to secure. We will set forth here Pound's Jural Postulates, and then give examples of the specific ways in which the law, particularly the criminal law, attempts to protect those interests by making their violation a crime. The protection of these interests is a major function of the law.

In civilized society men must be able to assume:

I. That others will commit no intentional aggressions upon them.

II. That they may control for beneficial purposes what they have discovered and appropriated to their own use, what they have created by their own labor, and what they have acquired under the existing social and economic order.

III. That those with whom they deal in the general intercourse of society will act in good faith and hence

(a) will make good reasonable expectations which their promises or other conduct reasonably create;

(b) will carry out their undertakings according to the expectations which the moral sentiment of the community attaches thereto;

(c) will restore specifically or by equivalent what comes to them by mistake, or the failure of the presupposition of a transaction, or other unanticipated situation whereby they receive at another's expense what they could not reasonably have expected to receive under the actual circumstances.

IV. That those who engage in some course of conduct will act with due care not to cast an unreasonable risk of injury upon others.

V. That others who maintain things or employ agencies, harmless in the sphere of their use but harmful in their normal action elsewhere, and having a natural tendency to cross the boundaries of their proper use, will restrain them or keep them within proper bounds.[5]

Postulate I.

In a civilized society men must be able to assume that others will commit no intentional aggressions upon them.

The criminal law punishes any kind of intentional injury inflicted upon one man by another. If death results, the offense is one of the homicide offenses punishable by imprisonment for life, or a term of years, or in some cases by death. If the victim does not die, the offender may be guilty of aggravated assault if serious injury is inflicted, or of simple assault if the injury is minor. Robbery, which involves the taking of property from the person of another by putting him in fear, is punishable by long terms of imprisonment, and if a weapon is used, by death in some states. As we shall see hereafter, intentional (willful, voluntary) aggression, and injury inflicted needlessly, are both punished more severely than injury inflicted negligently. Accidental injury may be non-culpable (non-punishable) in the criminal law.

Postulate II.

In a civilized society men must be able to assume that they may control for beneficial purposes, what they have discovered or appropriated to their own use, what they have created with their own labor, and what they have acquired under the existing social and economic order.

The law's protection of private property carries out this postulate. Thus, a man is guilty of one of the theft offenses if he takes property in possession (control) of another man. It is a crime to steal the following kinds of property: a wild horse which a man has tamed and keeps in his corral for his use; water which a man has dammed to be diverted to his fields; gold or oil which a man has discovered and legally claimed; a sled which a man has built

5. Roscoe Pound. *Jurisprudence.* St. Paul, Minnesota: West Publishing Co., 1959, Vol. 1, pp. 367–456.

with his own labor; a machine a man has invented; or property which a man has inherited under the laws of inheritance. These are merely examples of property protected by the laws against theft—stealing almost any kind of private personal property is punishable under the criminal law. Legal remedies are also provided for the illegal taking or use of real property.

Postulate III.

> In a civilized society men must be able to assume that those with whom they deal in general intercourse of society will act in good faith and hence (a) will make good reasonable expectations which their promises or other conduct reasonably create; (b) will carry out their undertakings according to the expectations which the moral sentiment of the community attaches thereto; (c) will restore specifically, or by equivalent, what comes to them by mistake, or the failure of the presupposition of a transaction, or other unanticipated situation whereby they receive at another's expense what they could not reasonably have expected to receive under the actual circumstances.

In carrying out the principles expressed in Postulate III(a) the law makes it a crime to sell stock in a "salted" mine. It is also a crime to pass a bad check. A check is a promise to pay a certain sum. When the maker of the check defaults in his promise because the check is returned for lack of funds, he has committed an offense against the law. Some states permit an action for breach of promise. If a man by his promises and conduct leads a young lady to believe that he intends marriage, if he thereafter refuses to do so, the law will not require that he marry her, but will require that he pay damages for his broken promise. If he gets her consent to sexual intercourse by a promise of marriage, he may be guilty of the crime of "Seduction."

The law protects the interests stated in Postulate III(b) by requiring that people who marry each other do not commit adultery; that a man support his wife or be liable for non-support; that a mother and father support their children if they are able, or be liable for criminal neglect; that places of business close on Sunday; that persons refrain from blasphemy in public, etc. Laws governing sexual conduct express the moral sentiments of the community and impose standards of sexual conduct upon the individual. The violation of these laws may lead to criminal sanctions.

In accordance with Postulate III(c), a person is required to return to the owner money he finds, if the owner can be located; a merchant is required to return the down payment on the refrigerator if he cannot deliver the refrigerator. An owner of real estate, under certain circumstances, may be required to pay for a road built on his premises by mistake, if he knew a mistake was being made and said nothing while the work was performed.

Postulate IV.

> In a civilized society men must be able to assume that those who engage in some course of conduct will act with due care not to cast an unreasonable risk of injury upon another.

The criminal law imposes responsibility for both reckless and negligent conduct which injures another. An officer may use deadly force to arrest an offender only when his own life or the life of an innocent victim is in danger; the law thus imposes upon him a duty of due care of the offender's life in all other circumstances. Failure to exercise that care may make the officer liable for criminal homicide. Traffic laws place heavy responsibility upon the driver of an automobile to use it in a manner that will not injure another. Driving while intoxicated, reckless driving, and in some cases merely negligent driving, can lead to criminal sanctions, and civil remedies are also available to the person injured. When we study the elements of the major crimes, we will see that the nature of the unlawful act, i. e., whether performed purposefully, knowingly, recklessly, or negligently, affects the severity of the sanctions which may be imposed by the criminal law.

Postulate V.

> In a civilized society men must be able to assume that others who maintain things or employ agencies harmless in the sphere of their use but harmful in their normal action elsewhere, and having a natural tendency to cross the boundaries of their proper use, will restrain them or keep them within proper bounds.

We will see in the law of arson that a man who is lawfully burning off the weeds on his own land may be guilty of negligent burning if he lets the fire escape to his neighbor's land. A man impounding water in a reservoir will be liable to his neighbor if the walls of the reservoir give way and the released water drowns his neighbor's chickens. A circus must take extreme precautions that the wild animals do not get loose and cause injury to persons or property. A crop duster must be careful that the wind does not take his poison spray into a neighboring area where another man's bee hives are located. The United States Government may be liable for sheep killed by a poisonous nerve gas which escapes its storage tank.

LIMITATIONS OF THE LAW

Law in a society is one means by which subgroups and persons in the society are influenced to conform to group norms and expectations. The law protects the values of the society and the social interests important to the society. The law sets out the rules for determining the guilt or innocence of the transgressor, and establishes the agencies of punishment and correction. Since law is a social institution, it functions imperfectly and is subject to limitations.

Law Cannot Guarantee Conformity by Itself. A limitation of the law is that it cannot guarantee conformity by itself. The most the law can do is to formally express the dominant values of the society and carry out the social agreement about the penalties to be imposed on individuals and groups who refuse to conform their conduct to the dictates of the law.

Law is Dependent upon Other Social Institutions. Another limitation of the law is that it is dependent upon other social institutions. To be effective, law needs the assistance of non-legal social institutions such as the family, the church, and the school. Law must depend upon these institutions to assist in the socialization process. The family, the church, the school transmit the values of the society to the individual, and teach him to distinguish "right" from "wrong" according to the definitions of the society. Law alone could not accomplish these things. The whole system of law would break down were it charged with the sole responsibility of turning every child into a law-abiding citizen.

Law Cannot Itself Control Conduct. Law is also limited because it cannot of itself control conduct. Law can enunciate the dominant value of the society that marriages should be preserved, but it cannot prevent marriages from breaking up. Law, therefore, seldom makes the attempt to compel two people to live together, and further recognizes its limitations in this area by providing for divorce. There are laws against adultery, prostitution, and the like, but the law of and by itself cannot prevent adultery and prostitution. The most that can be said is that the law generally operates in support of morality and that the possibility of legal sanctions may provide controls that reinforce those imposed by church and family.

Law is Dependent Upon Proof of Facts. Another limitation of law is that it must be applied to concrete factual situations, and facts are difficult to come by. We attempt in our adversary system, where we "choose up sides" so to speak, to provide a method for getting the facts and finding the truth. For many reasons completely out of the control of the law, this is not easy to do, and sometimes cannot be done at all. Witnesses die, disappear, move away. People on the witness stand lie about, distort, misrepresent, mistake, or forget the facts. Defendants are prevented by ignorance, poverty, or lack of legal representation, from producing the evidence in their favor. The syndicate buys off the witness or arranges for him to disappear or change his story. The law is frustrated in its search for the truth by social conditions over which it has no control, and circumvented by every method that can be devised in the mind of man who for his own reasons does not want the truth to prevail. The result is that the successful application of the law is limited by the difficulty in getting at the facts.

Law Changes Slowly. Many people maintain that another limitation of the law is that it changes slowly. Other people see this as one of the definite advantages that the law has over other means of social control. The people who see law as changing too slowly point out that desirable social goals are often prevented or delayed because of outmoded laws. Those holding the opposite view call attention to the undesirable results that would be sure to follow if law changed every year, as does fashion. The fact that law is a relatively stable force in a changing society is thus seen by some as a limitation on the law, by others as one of the great plus values of the law.

LAW AS A SOCIAL INSTITUTION

In our discussion of the functions and limitations of the law, we have established the fact that law is a social institution, changing as society changes. Many people, unfortunately, do not have this concept of the law. Even lawyers speak of "finding" the law as though it were just a matter of going to the correct place and bringing back the rule that should be applied to the case. Whether law moves too slowly as believed by some, or just fast enough, as believed by others, law does "move" in the sense that it is constantly changing. From one place to another, from one generation to another, and even from one day to another, law makes new rules and abandons old ones. The functions the law performs enlarge as the society grows, or contract as the society removes some facet of social control from the law. Today, the law is charged with preventing abortion; tomorrow, an abortion may concern only the woman and her doctor. The law must constantly adapt itself to new values suddenly important to the society, or meet the problems presented by advances in science and technology. In an era of organ transplants, law must arrive at a new and more precise definition of death. In the age of computers, it must protect the consumer from false credit information and loss of reputation. It is the eternal genius of the law that it is able to successfully adapt itself to changes in the society while continuing to be one of its most stable institutions.

KINDS OF LAW

Before we leave our general discussion of the law, let us talk briefly about *kinds of law*. This is another way of saying that we can distinguish different aspects of the law. By breaking the whole subject of the law into parts, we can make it easier to understand.

Criminal and Civil Law. The title to this book indicates that we are going to devote our attention to the area of the law called the criminal justice system. If the book bore the title, "Introduction to the Legal System," we would have to give like attention to civil law and procedure. *Criminal law* has to do with crimes, and as we shall see, crimes are illegal acts which are punished by fine and imprisonment. Only the state, acting through the courts, can impose fines or send a man to prison. *Civil law,* on the other hand, has to do with such things as contracts, wills, inheritance, marriage, divorce, adoption and the like, and with private injuries which are called "torts." The remedy for a private injury is damages recovered in the courts, and payable to the party injured. Fines, on the other hand, are paid to the state; sometimes the law provides that fines go into a special fund, as for example, a school fund. The victim of a crime does not have a right to the fine. Because of such differences one of the major dichotomies in the law is between *civil law* and *criminal law.* When we talk about the act which brings the law into operation, we distinguish between a *crime,* which is a public injury and is punished in a criminal court, and a *tort,* which is a private injury redressed in a civil court.

Law and Equity. A distinction is sometimes made between *law* and *equity.* This distinction arose at a time in the history of Anglo-American law when the law had developed a great deal of rigidity. As a result, the law could not always provide justice. A kind of special court came into being referred to as the "court of the King's conscience." The king appointed some trusted person to be the "chancellor" in charge of this special court. The chancellor very often, though not aways, was a clergyman. The special purpose of the court was to provide justice or "equity" when the law courts were unable to do so. The "court of the King's conscience" was first known as the "chancellor's court," and then because of its duty to act fairly and with equity, as the "equity court," or "court of equity." The distinction between law courts and equity courts has in modern times been largely done away with, though technical differences between law and equity are still of some importance to lawyers.

Substantive and Procedural Law. Law is also classified into *substantive law* and *procedural law.* In the criminal law, the statutes which define the crimes and set out the punishments are found in the penal code and are a part of the substantive law of crimes. The statutes which set out the rules which must be followed in investigating crimes, apprehending the offender, and determining his guilt or innocence are set out in codes of criminal procedure and constitute the procedural law, or the law of criminal procedure. In general, from substantive law we determine the basic law of crimes and punishments. Procedural law regulates how we must go about enforcing the basic law. Substantive law tells us "what it is"; procedural law tells us "how to do it."

Statutory and Case Law. In the Anglo-American system of jurisprudence, the law is "made" in acts of the legislative body (Congress and Legislatures of the fifty states, town councils), and also in decisions of courts, both state and federal. We therefore speak of *statutory law* and *case law*, the one referring to statutes passed by Congress and the legislatures; the other referring to rules announced in the decisions of courts. This does not mean that statutory law and case law are entirely separated; on the contrary, there is constant interaction between statutory and case law. For example, the legislature may pass a law which is susceptible to more than one meaning. It falls upon the courts to decide what the legislature meant. Other times, decisions announced by the courts may require action by the legislature. For example, after the Supreme Court of the United States decided that a child is entitled to representation by counsel in a juvenile court, the legislature of Texas passed a statute requiring parents who could afford attorneys to provide an attorney for their child, and also providing for the appointment of an attorney at state expense if the parents could not afford to employ one. Before a lawyer answers an important question put to him by his client, he "briefs," i. e., investigates, both the statutory and case law.

Common Law. The Common Law, sometimes referred to as the "Common Law of England," constitutes the basic legal rules and concepts which the colonists brought over to America from England and which they incorporated into their statutory and case law, expanding and adopting it to their different conditions. Other states, as they came into the Union, also incorporated the common law into their systems of law. The Common Law of England is a body of legal principles which developed in England after the Norman Conquest. Prior to 1066, there was no clear-cut differentiation between customs, religion, morality and law. The Normans, however, wanted unity and system (this made governing easier), and they also wanted to know what was going on. They began sending representatives of the Norman king to every part of England, and the one thing they always did was to look in on any trials that were taking place. The king's representatives not only checked up on things, they also carried news and information from one place to another. If a dispute was settled in one county or shire by applying a certain principle, the traveling representative of the king mentioned this in the next county or shire where a similar matter was being considered. The result of all this was that the legal principles being applied began to be similar, or common, in all parts of England. Thus, the terms "Common Law of England," and "Common Law."

As early as 1270, a common and continuous record of legal practice was kept in the Year Books, which were a kind of handbook of legal principles used by the early judges and barristers. These were the first written records of the common law. Around 1765, William Blackstone gave the first lectures on law in an English University, and published a book on law called *Blackstones Commentaries,* which was one of the first textbooks of English law.

The genius of the common law was that it could adapt itself to the extremely varied conditions of the English colonies, dominions, and dependencies around the world, including the colonies in America. Thus the principles developed in the common law became the basic law of all of the United States.

Because the common law was largely case law, developed in the decisions of judges in actual cases being tried before them, the words "case law" and "common law" are often used interchangeably. We often contrast *statutory law* and *common law,* though today it is more accurate to say *statutory law* and *case law.* Common law, as the term is correctly used in the United States, means the basic principles developed in England from the time of the Norman Conquest to the date of the American Revolution.

Law Classified According to Subject Matter. We can also classify law according to subject matter. This is the way law is classified in law schools and in bar examinations. Students of the law study are examined over criminal law and procedure, contracts, torts, civil procedure, wills and estates, tax law, commercial law, constitutional law, and other special subjects. Whenever a client walks into a lawyer's office with a problem, one of the first things the lawyer must do is to determine into what area of the law the problem falls. Of course, some legal problems involve more than one area of the law.

There are other classifications in the law which we will consider later on. Crimes, for example, are divided into felonies and misdemeanors, or into capital and noncapital offenses. Crimes are also classified as crimes against property and crimes against persons. Courts are divided into federal and state courts, upper and lower courts, trial and appellate courts, and so on.

Our purpose in distinguishing different kinds of law by classifying law in several ways is to increase ease of understanding. To increase understanding is, of course, the purpose of any classification.

Chapter II

WHAT IS A CRIME?

The definition of crime always involves a dual problem of behavior (acts) and value judgments of the society. As stated by Vold: "Crime always involves both human behavior (acts) and the judgment or definition (laws, customs, mores) of fellow human beings as to whether specific behavior is appropriate and permissible, or is improper and forbidden. Crime and criminality lie in the area of behavior that is considered improper and forbidden. There is, therefore, always the dual problem of explanation—that of accounting for the behavior, *as behavior,* and equally important, accounting for the *definitions* by which specific behavior comes to be considered crime or non-crime." [1]

DEFINITIONS OF CRIME

There are many definitions of crime. One writer defines a crime as a "voluntary and intentional violation by commission or omission, by a legally competent person, of a legal duty that commands or prohibits an act for the protection of society, punishable by judicial proceedings in the name of the state." [2] The author then goes on to identify the elements of a crime as (1) the voluntary and intentional commission of an act or conduct by (2) a person legally capable of performing such an act, (3) the existence of a law commanding or prohibiting that act or conduct, (4) the existence of a law that prescribed punishment for the act or conduct (5) which is enforceable by the state.[3]

The Penal Code of California defines a crime as:

> A crime of public offense is an act committed or omitted in violation of a law forbidding or commanding it, and to which

1. George C. Vold, *Theoretical Criminology.* New York: Oxford Press, 1958, pp. 40–41.
2. M. Cherif Bassiouni, *Criminal Law and Its Processes.* Springfield, Illinois: Charles C. Thomas, Publisher, 1969, p. 50.
3. *Ibid.*

is annexed, upon conviction, either of the following punishments:

1. Death;
2. Imprisonment;
3. Fine;
4. Removal from office; or,
5. Disqualification to hold and enjoy any office of honor, trust, or profit in this State.[4]

A simple definition of crime, which we will adopt here, is that *a crime is an offense against the state punishable by fine or imprisonment.* Although this definition does not set out alternative types of conduct that may constitute a crime nor include all the forms of punishment which may be imposed, it points out the essential nature of crime, i. e., that a crime is an *offense against the state.*[5] A crime is a violation of duties due the whole community considered as such and can be punished only by the state. The sanctions of fine and imprisonment cannot be imposed by a civil court or in a civil action (we shall later note some exceptions in the area of juvenile offenses).

Crimes and Torts. A *crime*, which is a public injury, is distinguished from a *tort*, which is a private injury. Crimes, regardless of their classification, are always offenses against the state, and are prosecuted by the state. A tort is a private injury for which the injured party can obtain redress in a civil action.

A single act may be both a crime and a tort. In other words, the person committing the act may simultaneously violate the duties he owes to the whole community and inflict private injury

4. West's Annotated California Penal Code, § 15.

See also, McKinney's N.Y.Penal Law, § 10.00, (6): "'Crime' means a misdemeanor or a felony."

In Kansas a crime is defined as follows: "The terms 'crime,' 'offense,' and 'criminal offense' when used in this or any other statute shall be construed to mean any offense, as well misdemeanor or felony, for which any punishment by imprisonment, or fine, or both may by law be inflicted." Kansas Statutes, Annotated, 21–128.

In Arizona a crime is defined as follows: "A crime or public offense is an act committed or omitted in violation of the law forbidding or commanding it, and to which is annexed, upon conviction, the punishment of death, imprisonment, fine, removal from office, or disqualification to hold any office of honor, trust, or profit in this state." Arizona Revised Statutes, § 13–101.

5. *Corpus Juris Secundum*, St. Paul, Minn.: West Publishing Company, Vol. 22, p. 1.

on another. If A attacks B without provocation and puts out B's eye, the state will punish A in a criminal action and fine him, imprison him, or both. The victim B, in a civil action, can recover money damages from A for the personal injury he suffered in losing an eye. A's unprovoked attack was an offense against the state, hence a crime. At the same time, it inflicted injury on the individual B, and was a tort against B. In the criminal action against A, the state (not B) would be the plaintiff, and the form of the action would be (for example) State of Wyoming v. A. The remedy sought in this action would be the fine or imprisonment of A. In the civil action against A, B (not the state) would be the plaintiff, and the form of the action would be B v. A. The remedy sought in the civil action would be money damages to be paid by A to B. We can distinguish the criminal action from the civil action in two ways: (1) by the remedy sought, and (2) by the character of the plaintiff, i. e., the state or an individual.

Offenses. In many states an act or omission is criminally punishable if it was punishable under the common law of England.[6] In other states, however, it is expressly provided by statute that no act or omission is criminal or punishable unless it is made such by constitutional provision or state statute.[7] The words "positive law" are sometimes used to refer to statutory law as distinguish-

6. Florida follows the common law of England in relation to crimes. The statute provides, "The common law of England in relation to crimes, except so far as the same relates to the modes and degrees of punishment, shall be in full force and effect in this state where there is no existing provision by statute on the subject." *Adkins, Florida Criminal Law and Procedure, Annotated,* § 775.01.

7. States which hold this view include California, Georgia, Indiana, Iowa, Kansas, Michigan, Minnesota, Missouri, New York, Ohio, Oregon, and Texas.

Smith-Hurd Illinois Annotated Statutes, Chapter 38, Criminal Law and Procedure, Sec. 1-3: Applicability of Common Law. No conduct constitutes an offense unless it is described as an offense in this Code or in another statute of this State.

McKinney's N.Y.Penal Law, § 5.05, Note 2: "Common Law Crimes. There is no longer any common law crime in this state. People v. Knapp, 1912, 206 N.Y. 373, 99 N.E. 841. See also, Darrow v. Family Fund Soc., 1889, 116 N.Y. 537, 22 N.E. 1093; People v. Beintner, 1918, 168 N.Y.S. 945; 1910, Op.Atty. Gen. 386. All common-law crimes have been abolished not only for the advantage of those individuals who might be charged with offenses, but also for the benefit of the people of the state. People v. Fein, 1944, 292 N.Y. 10, 53 N.E.2d 374."

See also, fn. 8, *infra.*

ed from common law.[8] In all jurisdictions the legislation must, either by statutory definition or by resort to rules of the common law, so define an offense that its elements are capable of being understood by a reasonable person.[9]

The word "crime" is derived from the Latin word "crimen" which means "offense." Hence, the word "offense" is often used synonymously with the word "crime," [10] though the word offense may sometimes have a little broader meaning than the word crime and may be used to mean any fault. Persons who violate criminal laws are called "offenders." They are also referred to as "criminals," though many persons maintain that the word "criminal" should be applied only to a convicted criminal and not to a person merely suspected or accused of a crime. In this book we will use the words crime and offense, and the words criminals and offenders, interchangeably.

HISTORICAL DEVELOPMENT OF THE CONCEPT OF CRIME

It is interesting to know that originally all crimes were torts; in other words, all injuries were originally considered to be private injuries.[11] In the early history of the law, the state (in those days represented by the king) did not concern itself with punishing wrongs except those directed against the state, such as treason. In the case of A putting out the eye of B, it was B's responsibility to "get even," which he often did by trying to put out the

8. Vernon's Penal Code of the State of Texas, Annotated, Article 47: Offenses. An offense is an act or omission forbidden by positive law, and to which is annexed, on conviction, any punishment prescribed in this Code.

9. Wm. E. Burby, *Law Refresher: Criminal Law and Procedure*, 1969, Fourth Edition. St. Paul, Minnesota: West Publishing Company, 1969.

10. Smith-Hurd Ill.Ann. Stat. ch. 38, § 2–12: Offense means a violation of any penal statute of this State. See also, fn. 8, *supra*. Vernon's Texas Penal Code, Ann.

McKinney's N.Y.Penal Law, § 10.00, (1) and (6): Definitions. Offense means conduct for which a sentence to a term of imprisonment or to a fine is provided by any law of this state or by any law, local law or ordinance of a political subdivision of this state, or by any order, rule or regulation of any governmental instrumentality authorized by law to adopt the same. "Crime" means a misdemeanor or a felony.

11. Davis, Foster, Jeffery, Davis, *op. cit.*, ch. 8.

eye of A. In many societies, not only was it B's responsibility to punish A, it was also the responsibility of all of B's family or kin to see that the damage done to B was punished. Sometimes, under such circumstances, A could not be found, so it became the custom to "get even" by putting out the eye of any one of A's family or kin who could be located. A blood feud developed in which every member of B's family was seeking to avenge B on any one in A's family they could find. Since A's family couldn't be expected to be happy about this, the result often was that everyone in A's family was trying to inflict injury on everyone in B's family. Famous feuds like that of the Hatfields and the McCoys in the Kentucky mountains could wipe out entire families on both sides.

Feuding was costly in terms of lives and property; it also destroyed the peace of the community. The king didn't like either situation very much. The king saw that he was losing a lot of good soldiers because his subjects were killing each other off. So the king took over the right and the responsibility of punishing offenders. The king said in effect, "If one citizen inflicts an injury on another, the injured party must report it to me, and I will take care of punishing the wrongdoer." Conduct which resulted in injury to one of the king's subjects was declared to be an offense against the king's peace. The action brought against the offender was brought in the king's name. To this day, a crime is seen to be an offense against the "king's peace," although today the king has been replaced by the state. In Texas, every criminal complaint, after setting out the offense, ends with the words "against the peace and dignity of the State of Texas."

Not only the king, but the individuals concerned began to realize that blood feuds were an extremely unsatisfactory way of settling arguments. The payment of compensation gradually replaced feuding. If a man stole a cow, he or his family were entitled to get a cow back from the thief. If the thief had killed the stolen cow, and had no cow at the time of the action, then, after the invention of money, the victim could collect from the thief in money the value of the cow. The king noticed this exchange of money and decided he ought to get some of it for himself. So he not only decided the punishment due the thief for breaking the king's peace, he also required that the thief or his family pay him money. The compensation for the cow went to the owner of the cow, but the fine went to the king. This was the origin of our modern system of fines in criminal cases. To go back to our earlier example, when B sues A in a civil action for putting out his eye, the money damages are paid to B. But if A is fined in a criminal action for putting out the eye of B, the fine goes to the state.

One author sums up the historical development of the notion of "crime" in this way: "The concept of criminal law emerged only when the custom of private vengeance was replaced by the principle that the community as a whole is injured when one of its members is harmed. Thus the right to act against a wrongdoing was, indeed, granted to the state as the representative of the people." [12]

ELEMENTS OF A CRIME

At least in theory, every crime contains several elements. These include: (1) a law defining the crime, which is to say a law commanding or prohibiting the act; (2) a material element called the *actus reus;* (3) a mental element called the *mens rea;* (4) an injury or result; (5) a causal relationship between the act or conduct and the injury or result; and (6) a prescribed penalty. Actually, we cannot distinguish all of these elements in every crime. Crimes of chiefly regulatory nature do not require a *mens rea;* the mere commission of the act may be sufficient to constitute the crime.[13]

The *actus reus,* the *mens rea,* the nature of the required injury, and to some extent the degree of causal connection between act and injury vary from crime to crime. The penalty, of course, also varies from crime to crime or, as in the Model Penal Code formulation, from one class of crimes to another.

12. Richard Quinney, *Crime and Justice in Society,* Boston: Little, Brown and Company, 1969, p. 5.

13. McKinney's N.Y.Penal Law, § 15.10: The minimal requirement for criminal liability is the performance by a person of conduct which includes a voluntary act or the omission to perform an act which he is physically capable of performing. If such conduct is all that is required for commission of a particular offense, or if an offense or some material element thereof does not require a culpable mental state on the part of the actor, such offense is one of "strict liability." If a culpable mental state on the part of the actor is required with respect to every material element of an offense, such offense is one of mental culpability.

The Law Defining the Crime. One of the aims of the law is to regulate conduct among men and prevent acts which cause harm to others or to the society as a whole. As we have seen, only the most important values of the society reach the dignity of law, and hence not all transgressions of one man upon another are the concern of the law. In developing a body of criminal law, a society must first decide what acts are harmful to the society and therefore should be prohibited. It must likewise decide when a failure to act is harmful to the society, and hence acting should be required. Having made the judgment as to the harmfulness of the act, or failure to act, the society must then determine whether the harm is great enough or of sufficient importance to prohibit (or require) it in the law. If the act is to be prohibited or required by the law, it must be carefully defined so individuals in the society can know in advance what conduct is prohibited or required. The society must also determine the penalties to be imposed upon the individual who engages in the harmful conduct. If there is no definition of the illegal act, and no penalty is prescribed, there is no crime.

These principles of the law are set up in three legal maxims. (A legal maxim is a statement of a legal principle or rule.) The first maxim is *Nullum Crimen Sine Lege,* which translates from the Latin as "No Crime Without Law." The second, *Nulla Poena Sine Lege,* states the proposition "No Punishment Without Law." The third, "No Crime Without Punishment," is expressed in Latin as *Nullum Crimen Sine Poena.* Together these three maxims state a fundamental fact about crime, which is that crime *is an offense defined by the law and for which the law prescribes punishment.* Both the definition of the crime and a prescribed punishment are necessary elements of the crime.

These legal maxims give rise to certain other principles that have to do with the nature and elements of crime. When no law prohibits certain conduct, such conduct cannot be made criminal *after* its occurrence. (The Constitution of the United States and the constitutions of most of the states expressly forbids *ex post facto* laws,[14] i. e., in criminal law, laws that make certain conduct a crime *after* the conduct takes place.) These maxims also require that a law defining a crime must be precise, so that the individual may be able to determine *in advance* what conduct is

14. Constitution of the United States of America, Article I, Section 9 (3).

prohibited or required. A statute defining a crime, says The United States Supreme Court, must be "sufficiently explicit to inform those who are subject to it what conduct on their part will render them liable to penalties.[15]

The criminal laws of the United States are found in the Constitution of the United States, the constitutions of the respective states, the common law offenses, the statutes enacted by the Congress or the legislature of the respective states, and in municipal ordinances.

The Actus Reus. The word *actus* means simply an act or an action. An act means something done which produces an effect. *Reus* means the criminal actor, or the person committing the criminal act. In criminal law, *actus reus* means the criminal act or wrongful conduct (as defined in the law) committed by the offender that gives rise to the criminal action. The *actus reus* is the *material element* of the crime, and varies from crime to crime.

The *actus reus* may be either a positive act, or a failure to act when a duty to act is imposed by law; thus, it may be either a *commission* or an *omission.* A person who gives poison to another with intent to cause his death commits a crime by an act of *commission.* A person who withholds medicine from a dying person, which it is in his power to provide, with the intent to cause the death of that person, commits a criminal act by *omission.* Where the law imposes a duty to act, failure to act may be a crime to the same extent that acting against the prohibition of the law may constitute a crime.[16]

The Mens Rea. The word *mens* means mind. *Mens rea* in the criminal law means the state of mind of the actor, or his intent.

15. Whitney v. California, 274 U.S. 357, 47 S.Ct. 641, 71 L.Ed. 1095 (1927), reh. gr. 269 U.S. 538, 46 S.Ct. 120, 70 L.Ed. 400.

16. McKinney's N.Y.Penal Law, § 15.00: **Culpability; definitions of terms**

The following definitions are applicable to this chapter:

1. "Act" means a bodily movement.
2. "Voluntary act" means a bodily movement performed consciously as a result of effort or determination, and includes the possession of property if the actor was aware of his physical possession or control thereof for a sufficient period to have been able to terminate it.
3. "Omission" means a failure to perform an act as to which a duty of performance is imposed by law.
4. "Conduct" means an act or omission and its accompanying mental state.

The *mens rea* is the necessary *mental element* of the crime. An old legal axiom says, "An act does not make the doer of it guilty, unless the mind be guilty; that is, unless the intention be criminal." The intent and the act must both concur to constitute a major crime; thus, both the *actus reus* and the *mens rea* are necessary elements of a crime.

There are many definitions of *mens rea* besides the ones given above.[17] *Mens rea* has been held to mean a guilty mind; a guilty or wrongful purpose; a criminal intent. Some definitions distinguish between the general and specific state of mind, or between general and specific intent.

General intent is a general criminal state of mind, or intent to do a wrongful act, or, as it is said, "a state of mind bent on the commission of an offense or any deviation from standard conduct which, without regard for others, may expose 'anybody' to harm, even without any specific intent as to the object or consequence of such conduct."[18] *Specific intent* is mental determination to produce a given result. The definitions of some crimes require a specific intent. For example, to constitute the crime of burglary, the breaking and entering must be with the specific intent to commit a felony or theft, or otherwise as set out in the statute.

17. McKinney's N.Y.Penal Law, § 15.00. (6.): "Culpable mental state" means "intentionally" or "knowingly" or "recklessly" or with "criminal negligence," as these terms are defined in section 15.05. [See fn. 33, 35, 38, 40 *infra* for the definitions.]

§ 15.15. **Construction of statutes with respect to culpability requirements.**

1. When the commission of an offense defined in this chapter, or some element of an offense, requires a particular culpable mental state, such mental state is ordinarily designated in the statute defining the offense by use of the terms "intentionally," "knowingly," "recklessly," or "criminal negligence," or by use of terms, such as "with intent to defraud" and "knowing it to be false," describing a specific kind of intent or knowledge. When one and only one of such terms appears in a statute defining an offense, it is presumed to apply to every element of the offense unless an intent to limit its application clearly appears.

2. Although no culpable mental state is expressly designated in a statute defining an offense, a culpable mental state may nevertheless be required for the commission of such offense, or with respect to some or all of the material elements thereof, if the proscribed conduct necessarily involves such culpable mental state. A statute defining a crime, unless clearly indicating a legislative intent to impose strict liability, should be construed as defining a crime of mental culpability.

18. Bassiouni, *op. cit.*, p. 66.

The mental condition of the offender, determined by whether he inflicts the injury purposely, knowingly, recklessly, or negligently, is also part of the *mens rea.* We shall discuss these factors in the chapter on the nature of criminal responsibility.

The *mens rea,* as does the *actus reus,* varies from crime to crime. When we study the elements of the major crimes in a succeeding chapter, we will see that the *actus reus* in robbery is the taking of personal property belonging to another from his person by threats or putting him in fear. The *mens rea* is the intent of the robber to appropriate the property to his own use and deprive the owner of the same. The *actus reus* of the offense of Passing Counterfeit Money is passing the money from the offender to another; the *mens rea* is the knowledge of the offender that it is counterfeit, and his intent to defraud.

An Injury or Result. Except for the regulatory crimes where it is often difficult to identify the injury, a crime involves a wrong or an injury inflicted by the offender on another. The injury may be inflicted directly upon the whole society, as in the offense of treason, or the injury may be inflicted upon an individual, and because of its nature considered to be an injury to the society. (Refer back to the discussion of the historical development of the concept of crime.) The nature of the injury may determine the nature of the crime. For example, if a person intentionally assaults another and kills him, the crime is murder. If he inflicts serious bodily harm, the crime is aggravated assault. If the injury is minor, the crime is simple assault. For the reason that the nature of the injury often determines the offense, many scholars insist that the nature of the injury is the most important element of the crime. Other scholars point out that some crimes do not even require an injury. Criminal conspiracy, for example, may be committed though no injury is actually inflicted. All that is required is that the injury be planned and intended and that some *overt* (open, specific) act be taken by one of the conspirators in furtherance of the conspiracy. Under such a statute, four people who plot together to blow up an R.O.T.C. building may be equally guilty of criminal conspiracy if one of them has gone out and purchased the material to make the bomb, though they are apprehended before the bomb is made, and before the building is blown up.

As we will see hereafter, the nature of the injury or potential injury to the victim is of great importance in the fixing of the statutory penalties and in determining the actual sentence of the wrongdoer. Generally, a wrong or injury must be proved as an element of a crime.

A Causal Relationship Between the Act or Conduct and the Injury or Result. The law says that before criminal sanctions can be imposed, the offender's conduct must constitute the "proximate cause" of the injury or result. This means that the conduct of the offender, operating in a natural and continuous sequence, must produce the injury or result. There must also be a showing that without the offender's conduct, the harm or injury would not have occurred.

The determination of causation is not always easy. Sometimes an intervening event will break the chain of causation. A man may assault his wife and inflict only a minor injury. He takes her to a hospital, where an incompetent doctor performs an unnecessary operation from which she dies. Is the husband guilty of killing his wife? Suppose the wife, by careless attention to the injury, permits it to get infected and she dies as a result of the infection. Is the husband guilty of murder or manslaughter? Suppose as a result of the blow, the wife falls in a contaminated place. Dirt gets into the minor wound inflicted by her husband and she dies from infection. Did he cause her death? Suppose A inflicts a mortal wound upon B, but before B dies of that wound, C inflicts a wound upon B from which he dies. Who is to be charged with B's death?

Resolution of questions such as these is very difficult. All of the circumstances must be taken into account. Whenever the actor's conduct is the direct, proximate, or determining cause of the resulting injury to the victim, the actor is criminally liable. Where other circumstances intervene, the question is: "Was the injury inflicted by the actor sufficient to cause the result had the intervening factor not occurred?" If the consequences of the actor's conduct followed in the natural and probable course of events, he is criminally liable for the result. If the consequences, on the other hand, were beyond his control and not a natural or probable consequence of his act, he is not criminally liable for the result.

The Model Penal Code sets out the causal relationship between conduct and result as follows:

Section 2.03. Causal Relationship Between Conduct and Result; Divergence Between Result Designed or Contemplated and Actual Result or Between Probable and Actual Result.

(1) Conduct is the cause of a result when:

(a) it is an antecedent but for which the result in question would not have occurred; and

(b) the relationship between the conduct and result satisfies any additional causal requirements imposed by the Code or by the law defining the offense.

(2) When purposely or knowingly causing a particular result is an element of an offense, the element is not established if the actual result is not within the purpose or the contemplation of the actor unless:

(a) the actual result differs from that designed or contemplated, as the case may be, only in the respect that a different person or different property is injured or affected or that the injury or harm designed or contemplated would have been more serious or more extensive than that caused; or

(b) the actual result involves the same kind of injury or harm as that designed or contemplated and is not too remote or accidental in its occurrence to have a (just) bearing on the actor's liability or on the gravity of his offense.

(3) When recklessly or negligently causing a particular result is an element of an offense, the element is not established if the actual result is not within the risk of which the actor is aware or, in the case of negligence, of which he should be aware unless:

(a) the actual result differs from the probable result only in the respect that a different person or different property is injured or affected or that the probable injury or harm would have been more serious or more extensive than that caused; or

(b) the actual result involves the same kind of injury or harm as the probable result and is not too remote or accidental in its occurrence to have a (just) bearing on the actor's liability or on the gravity of his offense.

(4) When causing a particular result is a material element of an offense for which absolute liability is imposed by law, the element is not established unless the actual result is a probable consequence of the actor's conduct.

A Prescribed Penalty. The need for a prescribed penalty, as we have seen, is derived from the ancient legal maxim, "No Crime Without Punishment." [19] If the conduct is not defined as criminal, or if defined as criminal, no penalty is attached, the conduct is not a crime. The penalty is an integral part of the crime.[20] At one time, the author, then an assistant prosecuting attorney, attempted to convict a man for practicing medicine without a license. The statutes of the state specifically prohibited practicing medicine without a license. There was no question but that the accused was performing operations, prescribing medicines, and the like, and that he had no license to do so. The entire case was before the jury when the prosecutor discovered that nowhere in the statute prohibiting practicing medicine without a license was a penalty provided for. The law made it illegal to practice medicine without a license, but said not a word about what would happen to anyone who did! The result was that the jury was instructed to bring in a verdict for the defendant. No penalty, no crime! (Because of the unfavorable publicity, the "doctor" left the community and no further proceedings were instituted against him. At the following session, the Legislature of Wyoming added a penalty clause to the statute.)

CLASSIFICATION OF CRIMES

Crimes are classified according to whether they are *mala in se* or *mala prohibita,* as to whether they are infamous or non-infamous, according to the penalty affixed, and according to the social harm inflicted. They may be classified as statutory and com-

19. This principle is sometimes stated in the statutes. See Vernon's Texas Penal Code, Ann., Art. 3: "In order that the system of penal law in force in this State may be complete within itself, and that no system of foreign laws, written or unwritten, may be appealed to, it is declared that no person shall be punished for any act or omission, unless the same is made a penal offense, and a penalty is affixed thereto by the written law of this State."

20. Redding v. State, 165 Neb. 307, 85 N.W.2d 647 (1957).

mon law crimes, major and petty crimes, violent or non-violent crimes, or federal and state crimes.

Offenses Mala In Se and Mala Prohibita. An offense which is *mala in se* is a crime which is inherently wrong, or wrong of itself. Offenses which are *mala prohibita* are wrong because prohibited, though not inherently wrong. Offenses *mala in se* are felonies and breaches of the public order which injure persons and property, or which outrage public decency and morality. The regulatory crimes make up the bulk of the crimes which are merely *mala prohibita.* Driving a car fast is not, of itself, wrong and a racing driver on a race track may go as fast as he can. Driving too fast on a public highway is prohibited because it is apt to result in injury to others. Setting fire to one's own house is not inherently wrong, but injury caused to another's house by the spreading fire is of itself wrong. Setting fire to the house for the purpose of collecting the insurance is both morally wrong and prohibited by law. Making a lot of noise in one's own home is not inherently wrong, but keeping the neighbors awake at 2:00 a. m. is an offense against the laws relating to public order.

The crimes defined in the common law are crimes which were *mala in se* and represented a prohibition of acts which the society considered dangerous to itself and hence inherently wrong. As we shall see, in modern law crimes *mala in se* are also *mala prohibita* since they are defined and their punishment fixed in the positive (statutory) law.

Infamous and Non-infamous Crimes. The word "infamous" means "without fame and good report," and was applied at common law to certain crimes upon the conviction of which a person became incompetent to testify as a witness, upon the theory that a person would not commit so heinous a crime unless he was so depraved as to be unworthy of credit * * *.[21] The word "infamous" as applied to a crime had more to do with the nature of the punishment which might be imposed than with the nature of the act. Thus, any crime for which the punishment of imprisonment in a penitentiary could be imposed was an "infamous crime." The importance of the distinction between infamous and non-infamous crimes is emphasized by the fact that in some jurisdic-

21. *Blacks Law Dictionary*, Revised Fourth Edition, St. Paul, Minn.: West Publishing Company.

tions civil death is imposed with conviction for an infamous crime. Civil death deprives a person of the right to vote and hold public office.[22]

The infamous crimes are the felonies: arson, bigamy, bribery, burglary, deviate sexual conduct, forgery, incest or aggravated incest, kidnapping or aggravated kidnapping, murder, perjury or subornation of perjury, rape, robbery, sale of narcotics, and theft-larceny.[23]

Infamous crimes are often said to possess "moral turpitude," which has been defined as "An act of baseness, vileness, or depravity in the private and social duties which a man owes to his fellow men, or to society in general, contrary to the accepted and customary rule of right and duty between man and man." [24] In California, moral turpitude is defined as "conduct contrary to justice, honesty, modesty, or good morals." [25]

Felonies and Misdemeanors. In most states, a felony is any offense for which the penalty may (not must) be death or imprisonment in the penitentiary (a jail is not a penitentiary); all other offenses are misdemeanors.[26] In other states, a felony is an of-

22. Bassiouni, *op. cit.*, p. 49.

23. *Ibid.*

24. Traders & General Ins. Company v. Russell, 99 S.W.2d 1079 (Tex.Civ.App.1937), error dism.

25. Marsh v. State Bar of California, 210 Cal. 303, 291 P. 583 (1930).

26. Smith-Hurd Ill.Ann.Stat. ch. 38,

§ 2-7. "Felony" means an offense punishable with death or by imprisonment in the penitentiary.

§ 2-8. "Forcible felony" means treason, murder, voluntary manslaughter, rape, robbery, burglary, arson, kidnaping, aggravated battery and any other felony which involves the use or threat of physical force or violence against any individual.

§ 2-11. "Misdemeanor" means any offense other than a felony, and includes conduct prohibited by a statute which provides no penalty for its violation.

Vernon's Ann.Texas Penal Code, Art. 47: An offense is an act or omission for bidden by positive law, and to which is annexed, on conviction, any punishment prescribed in this Code. An offense which may—not must—be punishable by death or by confinement in the penitentiary is a felony; every other offense is a misdemeanor. Felonies are either capital or not capital. An offense for which the highest penalty is death is a capital felony. Offenses are divided into felonies and misdemeanors.

McKinney's N.Y.Penal Law:

§ 10.00(2). "Traffic infraction" means any offense defined as "trafic infraction" by section one hundred fifty-five of the vehicle and traffic law.

§ 10.00(3). "Violation" means an offense, other than a "traffic infraction," for which a sentence to a term of imprisonment in excess of fifteen days cannot be imposed.

fense for which the penalty may be imprisonment for a year or more; all other offenses being misdemeanors. Some states have an offense category called infractions or violations.[27] Under the United States Criminal Code, offenses punishable by death or imprisonment for a term exceeding one year are felonies. Thus, felonies are distinguished in some states according to the *place* where the punishment takes place; in other states and the federal government, by the *length* of the sentence. The distinction is usually based upon the penalty prescribed by statute, or the penalty which *may* be affixed. In California, however, the sentence *actually given* determines the nature of the offense.[28]

It has been said that the word "felony" is derived from two old English words, the word "fee" which meant land, and "lon" which meant forfeiture. Forfeiture of the land was considered to be a punishment of extreme severity and, in English law, "attainder" (the infliction of direct punishment without judicial determination) usually included taking the land of the offender. Although the United States Constitution prohibits Bills of Attainder (a prohibition applicable to both the federal and state governments),[29] the association of the word felony with severe punishment continues to this day. A felony in all states is a more serious offense than a misdemeanor, and carries a more severe punishment.

Felonies are referred to as "major crimes" and misdemeanors as "petty crimes;" thus the distinction between major and petty crimes. This distinction has much to do with the organization of the criminal court system, as we shall see hereafter.

§ 10.00(4). "Misdemeanor" means an offense, other than a "traffic infraction," for which a sentence to a term of imprisonment in excess of fifteen days may be imposed, but for which a sentence to a term of imprisonment in excess of one year cannot be imposed.

§ 10.00(5). "Felony" means an offense for which a sentence to a term of imprisonment in excess of one year may be imposed.

§ 10.00(6). "Crime" means a misdemeanor or a felony.

West's Ann.Cal.Penal Code, § 16:

Crimes and public offenses include:

1. Felonies;
2. Misdemeanors; and
3. Infractions

§ 17(a): A felony is a crime which is punishable with death or by imprisonment in the state prison. Every other crime or public offense is a misdemeanor except those offenses that are classified as infractions.

27. *Ibid.* (West's Ann.Cal.Penal Code, § 16.)

Ibid. (McKinney's N.Y.Penal Law, § 10.00(2), (3).)

28. People v. Brown, 52 Cal.App.2d 428, 126 P.2d 406 (1942).

29. U.S.Const. Art. I, § 9(3) (federal), § 10(1) (state).

Classification According to Social Harm Inflicted. Crimes are sometimes classified as offenses against the person, offenses against property, offenses against morality and decency, offenses against public peace and tranquility, and offenses against the administration of governmental functions. Using a similar standard, crimes may be divided into violent and non-violent crimes, the crimes of violence carrying the greater penalty. Crimes which inflict physical injury, or involve a threat of physical injury, are violent crimes; offenses such as forgery, embezzlement, theft (other than from the person), and the like are non-violent crimes, though they may be felonies.

Common Law Crimes. As we have seen, the common law was a body of law developed in England from the time of the Norman Conquest to the date of the American Revolution. Much of this common law found its way into the constitutions and statutory law of the colonies and principles of the common law are enunciated in the United States Constitution. The common law made a distinction between felonies (forcible felonies) and misdemeanors. The felonies were the more serious offenses for which the usual penalty was death or banishment. A forcible felony was a felony committed with the use of force. The common law felonies included Treason, Voluntary Manslaughter, Aggravated Battery, Murder, Rape, Battery, Kidnapping, Burglary, Arson, Larceny from the Person.

Model Penal Code Classification of Crimes. The Model Penal Code establishes three basic classifications of crimes—felonies, misdemeanors, and petty misdemeanors. As is usual, these classifications are based upon the relative degree of seriousness of the criminal offense. Felony offenses are then divided into three degrees, felonies in the first degree, felonies in the second degree, and felonies in the third degree. The felony in the first degree is the most serious and carries the highest penalty.[30] The provisions of the *Model Penal Code* are as follows:

Section 1.04. Classes of Crimes—Violations.

(1) An offense defined by this code or by any other statute of this State, for which a sentence of (death or of) imprison-

30. The American Law Institute, *Model Penal Code, Proposed Official Draft*, Philadelphia, Pennsylvania, The Executive Office, The American Law Institute, May 4, 1962 (Hereafter referred to as MPC).

ment is authorized, constitutes a crime. Crimes are classified as felonies, misdemeanors or petty misdemeanors.

(2) A crime is a felony if it is so designated in this Code or if persons convicted thereof may be sentenced (to death or) to imprisonment for a term which, apart from an extended term, is in excess of one year.

(3) A crime is a misdemeanor if it is so designated in this Code or in a statute other than this Code enacted subsequent thereto.

(4) A crime is a petty misdemeanor if it is so designated in this Code or in a statute other than this Code enacted subsequent thereto or if it is defined by a statute other than this Code which now provides that persons convicted thereof may be sentenced to imprisonment for a term of which the maximum is less than one year.

(5) An offense defined by this Code or by any other statute of this State constitutes a violation if it is so designated in this Code or in the law defining the offense or if no other sentence than a fine, or fine and forfeiture or other civil penalty is authorized upon conviction or if it is defined by a statute other than this Code which now provides that the offense shall not constitute a crime. A violation does not constitute a crime and conviction of a violation shall not give rise to any disability or legal disadvantage based on conviction of a criminal offense.

(6) Any offense declared by law to constitute a crime, without specification of the grade thereof or of the sentence authorized upon conviction, is a misdemeanor.

(7) An offense defined by any statute of this State other than this Code shall be classified as provided in this Section and the sentence that may be imposed upon conviction thereof shall hereafter be governed by this Code.

In the Model Penal Code pattern, the penalties for the crimes are set out in tables of penalties. All offenses classified as first degree felonies would be subject to the same sentencing provisions; all second degree felonies to the same penalties, and so on, according to the classification of the offense. A further discussion of punishments under the *Model Penal Code* will be found in a succeeding chapter.

The Model Penal Code Project. Since we will be mentioning the Model Penal Code quite often, this is a good time to learn something about it. The Model Penal Code was developed by the American Law Institute. A group of lawyers and judges interested in improvement of the criminal law worked for several years in writing the Code. Their purpose was to arrive at a simpler and more consistent statement of the criminal law, and to work out a model which each state could use, if it wished, whenever it undertook to revise or modernize its criminal law. There was no intention that every state would adopt all the provisions of the Model Penal Code. The Code was just what is said it was—a model only.

Many states have used the Model Penal Code as a reference when revising their criminal codes. If your state has revised its criminal law recently, the chances are that the revision committee adopted many of the patterns and much of the language of the Model Code. We will keep referring to it because the language used in the Model Penal Code is often easier to understand than more complicated language which appears in many state codes. For another reason, as more and more states use the Model Penal Code as a pattern for their own statutes on the criminal law, prior knowledge of the general provisions of the Model Code will prove to be very useful to students and practitioners in law enforcement.

Delinquent Acts. A distinction is also made between *crimes* committed by adults and *delinquent acts* committed by juveniles. An offense which would be a crime if committed by an adult, is called a "delinquent act" when committed by a juvenile. The reason for this is that society hesitates to label a juvenile as a "criminal" no matter what the character of his illegal behavior.

Organized Crime. We also hear of *organized crime.* Organized crime is a business enterprise which has been defined as economic enterprises organized for the purpose of conducting illegal activities and which when they operate legitimate ventures, do so by illegal methods. Organized crime can be distinguished from ordinary crime which is an offense committed by an individual and not part of a continuing course of criminal conduct carried on with others for profit. An "ordinary murder" usually represents the culmination of unhappy personal relationships between the offender and the victim, or an "ordinary murder" may take place in the course of committing another felony such as robbery. A murder by the Mafia does not necessarily involve personal ill will;

the objective is to get the store owner to pay "protection money" or to prevent another operator from "muscling in" on the numbers racket, or to punish a member of the group who has broken the code of "Omerta" (silence) about the activities of the group. The purpose of the murder is largely economic and a part of an organized and continuing business based on an illegal activity. The most common "business" of the syndicates (a name given to the criminal organizations) are gambling, prostitution, and traffic in drugs.

The FBI List of Criminal Offenses. The Federal Bureau of Investigation classifies offenses according to the following list of offenses and definitions:

1. *Criminal homicide.* (a) Murder and non-negligent manslaughter: all willful felonious homicides as distinguished from deaths caused by negligence. Excludes attempts to kill, assaults to kill, suicides, accidental deaths, or justifiable homicides. Justifiable homicides are limited to: (1) the killing of a person by a peace officer in line of duty; (2) the killing of a person in the act of committing a felony by a private citizen. (b) Manslaughter by negligence: any death which the police investigation establishes was primarily attributable to gross negligence of some individual other than the victim.

2. *Forcible rape.* Rape by force, assault to rape and attempted rape. Excludes statutory offenses (no force used—victim under age of consent).

3. *Robbery.* Stealing or taking anything of value from the person by force or violence or by putting in fear, such as strong-arm robbery, stickups, armed robbery, assault to rob, and attempt to rob.

4. *Aggravated assault.* Assault with intent to kill or for the purpose of inflicting severe bodily injury by shooting, cutting, stabbing, maiming, poisoning, scalding, or by the use of acids, explosives, or other means. Excludes simple assault, assault and battery, fighting, etc.

5. *Burglary—breaking or entering.* Burglary, housebreaking, safecracking, or any unlawful entry to commit a felony or a theft, even though no force was used to gain entrance and attempts. Burglary followed by larceny is not counted again as larceny.

6. *Larceny—theft* (except auto theft). (a) Fifty dollars and over in value; (b) under $50 in value. Theft of bicycles, automobile accessories, shoplifting, pocket-picking, or any stealing of property or article of value which is not taken by force and violence or by fraud. Excludes embezzlement, "con" games, forgery, worthless checks, etc.

7. *Auto theft.* Stealing or driving away and abandoning a motor vehicle. Excludes taking for temporary use when actually returned by the taker or unauthorized use by those having lawful access to the vehicle.

8. *Other assaults.* Assault and attempted assaults which are not of an aggravated nature.

9. *Arson.* Willful or malicious burning with or without intent to defraud. Includes attempts.

10. *Forgery and counterfeiting.* Making, altering, uttering or possessing, with intent to defraud, anything false which is made to appear true. Includes attempts.

11. *Fraud.* Fraudulent conversion and obtaining money or property by false pretenses. Includes bad checks except forgeries and counterfeiting.

12. *Embezzlement.* Misappropriation or misapplication of money or property entrusted to one's care, custody or control.

13. *Stolen property; buying, receiving, possessing.* Buying, receiving, and possessing stolen property and attempts.

14. *Vandalism.* Willful or malicious destruction, injury, disfigurement or defacement of property without consent of the owner or person having custody or control.

15. *Weapons; carrying, possessing.* All violations of regulations or statutes controlling the carrying, using, possessing, furnishing, and manufacturing of deadly weapons or silencers and attempts.

16. *Prostitution and commercialized vice.* Sex offenses of a commercialized nature and attempts, such as prostitution, keeping bawdy house, procuring or transporting women for immoral purposes.

17. *Sex offenses* (except forcible rape, prostitution, and commercialized vice). Statutory rape, offenses against

chastity, common decency, morals, and the like. Includes attempts.

18. *Narcotic drug laws.* Offenses relating to narcotic drugs, such as unlawful possession, sale or use. Excludes Federal offenses.

19. *Gambling.* Promoting, permitting, or engaging in gambling.

20. *Offenses against the family and children.* Nonsupport, neglect, desertion, or abuse of family and children.

21. *Driving under the influence.* Driving or operating any motor vehicle while drunk or under the influence of liquor or narcotics.

22. *Liquor laws.* State or local liquor law violations, except "drunkenness" (class 23) and "driving under the influence" (class 21). Excludes Federal violations.

23. *Drunkenness.* Drunkenness or intoxication.

24. *Disorderly conduct.* Breach of the peace.

25. *Vagrancy.* Vagabondage, begging, loitering, etc.

26. *All other offenses.* All violations of state or local laws except classes 1–25.

27. *Suspicion.* Arrests for no specific offense and released without formal charges being placed.

28. *Curfew and loitering laws (juveniles).* Offense relating to violation of local curfew or loitering ordinances where such laws exist.

29. *Runaway (juvenile).* Limited to juvenile taken into protective custody under provisions of local statutes as runaways.[31]

The Index Crimes. Seven of the more serious of the listed offenses are referred to as the Index Crimes. These crimes are murder, non-negligent manslaughter, forcible rape, robbery, aggravated assault, burglary, larceny $50 and over, motor vehicle theft. These Index Crimes are used by the Federal Bureau of Investigation to gather and report crime statistics for the United States.

31. Federal Bureau of Investigation, U. S. Department of Justice, *Uniform Crime Reports For The United States, 1966,* Washington, D.C.: U. S. Government Printing Office, 1966, pp. 55–56.

CRIMINAL RESPONSIBILITY

We have seen that in order to have a crime we must have a criminal act. We will now consider what *kinds of acts* give rise to criminal responsibility. If a driver of an automobile has a heart attack and before he can stop the car runs over a child and kills it, did he commit a criminal act? If another man during an attack of epilepsy makes violent movements of his arms and legs and inflicts injury on a person near him, is this the kind of guilty conduct that gives rise to a criminal action? If a woman is taking care of her child when the house catches on fire and she is unable to get into the bedroom to save the child, is she guilty of any crime? It is easy to see that not all acts which inflict injury upon another are guilty or punishable. In the eyes of the law, some acts are culpable, or blameworthy, and thus subject to punishment and other acts are non-culpable and are not blameworthy, and hence not subject to punishment.

In general, criminal liability is based only upon conduct which includes a voluntary act or the omission to perform an act which the actor was physically able to perform.[32] In the case of the man running over the child, or the epileptic causing injury to a person near him, the acts which precipitated the injury were involuntary, and hence non-culpable. (We assume of course that the man did not know he was subject to heart attacks and had not been warned not to drive a car.) The act of the woman was not criminal unless it can be shown that she could have saved the child with no danger to herself and deliberately failed to do so.

The Legal Concept of Culpability. In addition to the requirement of a voluntary act, four concepts are needed to describe the kinds of culpability (or blameworthiness) that may be deemed sufficient to constitute a criminal act—that are sufficient, in other words, to make the doer subject to punishment by the state in application of the criminal statutes. These concepts are *purpose*, *knowledge*, *recklessness*, and *negligence*. It is by no means easy to distinguish between these terms and to apply them correctly to the acts of persons charged with a criminal offense. Some of the best definitions are to be found in the *Model Penal Code, Sec. 2.02,* entitled "General Requirements of Culpability."

32. McKinney's N.Y.Penal Law, § 15.10: The minimal requirement for criminal liability is the performance by a person of conduct which includes a voluntary act or the omission to perform an act which he is physically capable of performing.

See also, fn. 13, *supra.*

Acting Purposely.[33] A person acts with respect to a material element of an offense purposely if his conduct meets the following requirements:

(i) if the element involves the nature of his conduct or a result thereof, it is his conscious object to engage in conduct of that nature or to cause such a result; and

(ii) if the element involves the attendant circumstances, he is aware of the existence of such circumstances or he believes or hopes that they exist.[34]

Let us suppose that A shoots at his enemy E, but by mistake, he kills his friend F. Under this definition did A act purposely in killing his friend? The answer is "yes." Though he did not intend to kill his friend, he did intend to kill his enemy, so his conduct was purposeful *as far as the act was concerned.* He intended to engage in conduct (shooting) that would cause the result (killing a person), and under such circumstances he cannot claim that he is not guilty because his purpose was to kill his enemy, not his friend. The test of acting purposely is applied to the intent to do the act, not the intent to produce the particular result that followed the act.[35]

Acting Knowingly.[36] A person acts knowingly with respect to a material element of the offense, according to the Model Penal Code if his conduct meets with the following requirements:

(i) if the element involves the nature of his conduct or the attendant circumstances, he is aware that his conduct is of that nature or that such circumstances exist; and

33. The New York statute uses the word "intentionally," which is defined as follows: "A person acts intentionally with respect to a result or to conduct described by a statute defining an offense when his conscious objective is to cause such result or to engage in such conduct." McKinney's N.Y.Penal Law, § 15.05(1).

The Illinois statute defines intent as follows: "A person intends, or acts intentionally or with intent, to accomplish a result or engage in conduct described by the statute defining the offense, when his conscious objective or purpose is to accomplish that result or engage in that conduct." Smith-Hurd Ill.Ann.Stat., ch. 38, § 4-4.

34. MPC 2.02(2) (b).

35. New York defines "knowingly" as follows: "A person acts knowingly with respect to conduct or to a circumstance described by a statute defining an offense when he is aware that his conduct is of such nature or that such circumstance exists." McKinney's N.Y.Penal Law, § 15.05(2).

36. The Illinois Code defines "knowledge" as follows: "A person knows, or acts knowingly or with knowl-

(ii) if the element involves a result of his conduct, he is aware that it is practically certain that his conduct will cause such a result.[37]

A person who passes a counterfeit $10 bill is guilty of no crime if he does not know the bill is counterfeit. However, if he knows the bill is counterfeit, and uses it to pay for the gas he has just bought at the filling station, he has committed the offense of passing counterfeit money, which is a crime. In the one case he *knowingly* passed the bogus money, in the other case the required element of knowledge was missing.

Acting Recklessly.[38] A person acts *recklessly* with respect to a material element of an offense when he consciously disregards a substantial and unjustifiable risk that the material element exists or will result from his conduct. The risk must be of such nature and degree that, considering the nature and purpose of the actor's conduct and the circumstances known to him, its disregard in-

edge of: (a) The nature or attendant circumstances of his conduct, described by the statute defining the offense, when he is consciously aware that his conduct is of such nature or that such circumstances exist. Knowledge of a material fact includes awareness of the substantial probability that such fact exists. (b) The result of his conduct, described by the statute defining the offense, when he is consciously aware that such result is practically certain to be caused by his conduct. Conduct performed knowingly or with knowledge is performed wilfully, within the meaning of a statute using the latter term, unless the statute clearly requires another meaning." Smith-Hurd Ill. Ann.Stat. ch. 38, § 4–5.

37. MPC 2.02(2) (b).

38. New York defines "recklessly" as follows: "A person acts recklessly with respect to a result or to a circumstance described by a statute defining an offense when he is aware of and consciously disregards a substantial and unjustifiable risk that such result will occur or that such circumstance exists. The risk must be of such nature and degree that disregard thereof constitutes a gross deviation from the standard of conduct that a reasonable person would observe in the situation. A person who creates such a risk but is unaware thereof solely by reason of voluntary intoxication also acts recklessly with respect thereto." McKinney's Penal Law, § 15.05(3).

The definition of "recklessness" in Illinois is as follows: "A person is reckless or acts recklessly, when he consciously disregards a substantial and unjustifiable risk that circumstances exist or that a result will follow, described by the statute defining the offense; and such disregard constitutes a gross deviation from the standard of care which a reasonable person would exercise in the situation. An act performed recklessly is performed wantonly, within the meaning of a statute using the latter term, unless the statute clearly requires another meaning." Smith-Hurd Ann.Stat. ch. 38, Crim.Law & Proc., § 4–6.

volves a gross deviation from the standard of conduct that a law-abiding person would observe in the actor's situation.[39]

This definition is particularly difficult to apply in practice, since it involves a decision of what is "gross deviation from the standards of conduct that a law-abiding person would observe under the circumstances." Thus, a decision must be made as to what the standards of conduct of a law-abiding person would have been under the particular circumstances, and a further decision made that the accused grossly deviated from those standards. In spite of the difficulty of applying the test, it is nevertheless possible to give some examples of reckless conduct. A man fires a gun in a crowded dance hall, throws large firecrackers into a group of children, drives 80 miles an hour in a school zone, or drops heavy timbers from the roof of a building along a city street without in any way attempting to protect the people on the sidewalk below. Such recklessness is culpable, and if someone is injured, the person who engages in such conduct is held responsible for the injury and is answerable to the criminal law.

Acting Negligently. The fourth kind of culpability is *negligence.*[40] This is the most difficult standard of all to apply in the law. Acting negligently is distinguished from acting purposely, knowingly, or recklessly in that it does not involve a state of awareness. A person may not be aware that he was creating a risk to the life or safety of another, yet if he *should have known* that he was creating such a risk, and a person is killed or injured, he will be held criminally liable. The Model Penal Code says that * * *. "The risk must be of such a nature and degree that the actor's failure to perceive it, considering the nature and

39. MPC 2.02(3) (c).

40. The New York statute refers to "criminal negligence," which is defined as: "A person acts with criminal negligence with respect to a result or to a circumstance described by a statute defining an offense when he fails to perceive a substantial and unjustifiable risk that such circumstance exists. The risk must be of such nature and degree that the failure to perceive it constitutes a gross deviation from the standard of care that a reasonable person would observe in the situation." McKinney's Penal Law, § 15.05(4).

Illinois statutes define negligence as follows: "A person is negligent, or acts negligently, when he fails to be aware of a substantial and unjustifiable risk that circumstances exist or a result will follow, described by the statute defining the offense; and such failure constitutes a substantial deviation from the standard of care which a reasonable person would exercise in the situation." Smith-Hurd AnnStat. ch. 38, § 4-7.

purpose of his conduct and the circumstances known to him, involves a gross deviation from the standard of care that a reasonable person would observe in the actor's situation." [41]

Negligent acts which injure others sometimes are due to the fact that the actor may not care about other people's interests and just fails to pay attention to them. He may be punished by the law for his failure to pay such attention if his lack of attention or awareness causes death or injury to another. An example would be the driver of an automobile who fails to keep a proper look-out when crossing an intersection, or deliberately fails to slow down when he sees children playing in the street, or drives on the super-highway knowing that he is liable to sudden loss of consciousness from a brain injury.

While the Model Penal Code, as do the criminal codes of the United States and of the fifty states, imposes criminal liability upon acts that are negligent and reckless as well as those that are done knowingly and purposely, the punishment provided for is usually less for negligent and reckless acts than for knowing and purposeful acts, unless, of course, the reckless acts were so grossly and obviously reckless that a high degree of culpability is imposed. Both crimes and punishments are "graded," with more severe punishments for major offenses done knowingly and purposely and less severe penalties for minor offenses done recklessly or negligently. Both the nature of the conduct and the nature of the injury affect the penalty which is imposed for criminal conduct.

The Yardstick of the Law. We are now going to turn our attention to the yardstick of the law—the legal concept of the reasonable man. Wags have it that there is no such thing as a "reasonable woman."

Recklessness and negligence may, under certain circumstances, give rise to criminal liability. The standard given in the Model Penal Code for recklessness is "a gross deviation from the standard of conduct that a *law-abiding* (italics supplied) person would observe in the actor's situation." [42] Negligence is defined as involving "a gross deviation from the standard of care that a *reasonable person* (italics supplied) would observe in the actor's situation.[43] According to the Code, the actor is judged against

41. MPC 2.02(2) (d).

42. MPC 2.02(2) (c).

43. MPC 2.02(2) (d).

See also McKinney's N.Y.Penal Law, § 15.05(4), fn. 40 *supra*.

the standards of a law-abiding person (in the case of recklessness) or a reasonable person (in the case of negligence). The significance of this is that a person is not held to the highest possible level of conduct in judging whether or not his act is criminal nor permitted to avoid responsibility if his conduct falls below the required standard.

The usual yardstick of the law is that of the "reasonable man." To avoid liability, at least for negligence, a person is expected to do under the circumstances what the reasonable man would do, or perform according to the standards of the "average person" or the "ordinary prudent person," or "a man of ordinary temperament." The word "law-abiding" is a slightly longer yardstick applied in the Model Penal Code to measure recklessness.

Suppose a man is driving down the street and a child darts in front of his car. How are we to determine whether or not the man was reckless or negligent, and so criminally and civilly answerable for the death of the child? We will apply the standard of the reasonable man. If a person of extraordinarily fast reflexes could have swerved and missed the child, we will not require extraordinarily fast reflexes from our driver. But if an average man, paying attention to his driving, having his car under control, being able to observe the child at a sufficient distance, could have stopped and not hit the child, and our driver did not stop, then he is at least negligent according to the yardstick of the law. His conduct fell below the required standard. If he was driving 80 miles an hour in a school zone, or just "took a chance" that no child would be in his path, his conduct is reckless according to our legal standard. Not only did his conduct fall below the expected standard, there was an element in his conduct of not caring about the life and safety of others.

Obviously, it is not easy to determine exactly what conduct is reasonable, negligent, or reckless under the circumstances. The jury, made up of "ordinary men" hears the evidence and decides on the basis of all the evidence whether or not the driver did or did not do all that a reasonable man could be expected to do under the circumstances. Its verdict is rendered accordingly—"not guilty" if his conduct met the standard; "guilty" if his conduct failed to measure up. The "reasonable man" is the yardstick of the law; the decision as to whether a particular individual on a particular occasion met the standard is made by his fellow "reasonable men."

THE HIERARCHY OF PENALTIES

We have seen that the concept of criminal culpability involves blame for deviation from social norms. Criminal culpability is first of all predicated upon the commission of an act which the society has defined as a crime. To fully understand how society feels about a certain act, we must look not only to the act and the social definition which declares it to be blameworthy but to the penalties which the society imposes for its commission. We demonstrated this close relationship in a previous chapter where we noted "no penalty, no crime." Let us therefore turn our attention to the matter of punishments prescribed for criminal behavior, attempting first to develop a "hierarchy of penalties" and then to consider the objectives and the moral justification for punishment. This will lead us to a consideration of the factors which may excuse from criminal responsibility or mitigate the punishment.

As you know, some offenses carry very high penalties—life imprisonment, or even death. Other offenses carry relatively mild penalties—a short stay in jail or a small fine. If I ask you how these penalties are determined, you will say, "By the legislature," and this will be a correct answer. But, how does the legislature decide what criminal conduct will be severely punished by the society and what criminal conduct will be given a relatively light punishment? Is there any general pattern to be found in the way crimes are punished? Can we, for example, make a list which would show that certain kinds of crimes are apt to carry severe punishment, certain others less severe punishment, and still others very minor punishments? Saying, "Felonies have severe punishments, and misdemeanors have lighter punishments," won't help us any. That would be going around in a circle, for we have already learned that felonies and misdemeanors are distinguished by the severity of the punishment (imprisonment in prison being considered more severe than imprisonment in jail). We would still have to ask the question, "Why is certain conduct classified as a felony and certain other conduct classified as a misdemeanor?"

To make our list we will have to get at the *reason* some kinds of conduct are punished more severely than other kinds. What we are asking is why the value judgments of the society are that some behavior is a threat to society and other behavior is not.

Punishments prescribed by the legislature reflect the value judgments of the society concerning the seriousness of different kinds of criminal behavior. If we were to start at the top of the list with the kinds of criminal conduct that carry the most severe penalties and go on down our list to the criminal conduct which carries the lowest penalties, we would be constructing a "hierarchy of penalties." "Hierarchy" means going from top to bottom or bottom to top like going down or up a ladder.

At the very top of our ladder—the crimes carrying the highest penalties—we would find treason, murder, and kidnapping. These three offenses carry the death penalty in many states. In some states, armed robbery and rape would be at the top of the ladder; in such states, armed robbery and rape are both punishable by death. In other states, armed robbery and rape would be on the second rung of the ladder, with maximum penalties of life imprisonment, or a long term of years. Going on down the ladder, we would find assault below murder, robbery below armed robbery, burglary below robbery, day-time burglary below night-time burglary, and so on. Most traffic offenses, except while intoxicated, would be on one of the lower rungs. Parking in front of a fire hydrant would be apt to carry a very small fine and be very near the bottom of the ladder.

One thing we would surely notice. Almost without exception, offenses against persons carry higher penalties (and hence would be nearer the top of the ladder) than offenses against property (which would appear on lower rungs of the ladder.) This tells us that the society considers crimes against persons more serious (more of a threat to the society) than crimes against property. We would also notice that *the greater the damage or potential damage to the victim, the higher the penalty is apt to be.* Thus murder, which causes the death of the victim, will be punished more severely than an assault in which the victim is injured, but not killed. In the offense of armed robbery, property is taken from the *person* of the victim, at gun point, or because of some other threat used by the robber. The potential danger to the victim is thus very great. When the robber is not armed, the chances of injury to the victim are less; hence robbery is not punished as severely as armed robbery. The offense of burglary is defined as breaking and entering into a house or other structure with intent to commit a felony or a theft. Because people live in private residences and are usually home at night, there is more chance that a person will be hurt during the burglary of a private residence at night than the burglary of a locked garage in the day-time. The night-time burglary carries a longer prison sentence than the day-time burglary.

If you were to set out the "hierarchy of penalties" for crimes committed in your state, your list would not look exactly like the one we have described here. People of different states make different value judgments as to what conduct should be punished more or less severely. Also, for many reasons, the penalty patterns get "skewed." For example, if a state is suffering from an unusually large number of day-time burglaries and the number of night-time burglaries is decreasing, the legislature may increase the penalty on day-time burglary without changing the penalty on night-time burglary. In that particular state, at a particular time, the usual test of damage or potential damage to the victim would not explain the differences in the penalties. Nevertheless, the rule generally is that *the greater the damage or potential damage to the victim of a criminal act, the higher will be the statutory penalty.*

Some offenses, like possession and sale of narcotics, and the so-called "victimless crimes": such as gambling, prostitution, and the like, are difficult to place on the rungs of the ladder. The tendency is for drug penalties to be high, gambling penalties rather low. What we learn from this is that the society considers drug usage as potentially very damaging to the user. By setting high penalties, the legislature hopes to prevent, or at least reduce, the sale and use of dangerous drugs and thus protect the people in the society from the effects of such use.

The Statutory Penalties. In the ordinary case, the statute defining the crime fixes the permissible penalties.[44] The penalty for kidnapping in California, for example, is set out as follows: "Kidnapping is punishable by imprisonment in the state prison not less than one nor more than twenty-five years."[45] To find the permissible penalty for any particular offense committed in your state, you will have to consult the Penal Code. The Model Penal Code does not fix penalties crime by crime. Instead, it

44. California, Texas, and Illinois follow the pattern of fixing penalties crime by crime.

45. West's Ann.Cal.Codes, Penal, § 208.

classifies all crimes into categories and then fixes the penalty according to the category into which the crime falls.[46]

Authorized Punishments Under the Model Penal Code. The permissible punishment for any offense under the Model Penal Code is determined first by the category into which the offense falls—first, second, or third degree felony, misdemeanor, or petty misdemeanor. The Code sets out both an "Ordinary Term" and an "Extended Term" and establishes criteria for imposing the extended term which have to do with such things as whether or not the defendant has a prior conviction of a felony, is a persistent offender or a professional criminal, or the defendant is a dangerous, mentally abnormal person whose commitment for an extended term is necessary for the protection of the public.[47]

MODEL PENAL CODE
TABLE OF AUTHORIZED PUNISHMENTS
FOR ADULT OFFENDERS *

CLASSIFICATION OF THE CRIME	ORDINARY TERM	EXTENDED TERM	MAXIMUM FINE
Felony of the first degree	1–10 yr. minimum Life maximum (6.06)†	5–10 yr. minimum Life maximum (6.07)	$10,000 (6.03)
Felony of the second degree	1–3 yr. minimum 10 yr. maximum (6.06)	1–5 yr. minimum 1–10 yr. maximum (6.07)	$10,000 (6.03)
Felony of the third degree	1–2 yr. minimum 5 yr. maximum (6.06)	1–3 yr. minimum 5–10 yr. maximum (6.07)	$5,000 (6.03)
Misdemeanors	No minimum 1 yr. maximum (6.08)	1 yr. minimum 3 yr. maximum (6.09)	$1,000 (6.03)
Petty misdemeanors	No minimum 30 day maximum (6.08)	6 mo. minimum 2 yr. maximum (6.09)	$500 (6.03)

* All punishments of imprisonment suggested by the Model Penal Code are based on the use of the indeterminate sentence.

† Numbers in parentheses indicate section of Model Penal Code in which standard is set out.

46. The classification in New York contains eight categories and the penalty is fixed according to the category of the crime. See McKinney's Penal Law.

§ 55.05 Classifications of Felonies and Misdemeanors.

1. Felonies. Felonies are classified, for the purpose of sentence, into five categories as follows:
   (a) Class A felonies;
   (b) Class B felonies;
   (c) Class C felonies;
   (d) Class D felonies; and
   (e) Class E felonies.

2. Misdemeanors. Misdemeanors are classified, for the purpose of sentence, into three categories as follows:
   (a) Class A misdemeanors;
   (b) Class B misdemeanors; and
   (c) Unclassified misdemeanors.

47. MPC 7.03.

MODEL PENAL CODE
TABLE OF PUNISHMENT FOR YOUNG ADULT OFFENDERS (AGES 16–21)*

SPECIALIZED CORRECTIONAL TREATMENT	SPECIAL TERM
Authorized where any sentence exceeds 30 days. To be served in a special youth facility with emphasis on individualized correction and rehabilitative treatment.	May be given in lieu of any authorized punishment in any felony case. No minimum 4 yr. maximum May be given where such special term is adequate for correction and rehabilitation and will not jeopardize the protection of the public.

* Section 6.05, Model Penal Code.

THE OBJECTIVES OF PUNISHMENT

The Classical School of Criminology. You will remember that we constructed our hierarchy of penalties according to the damage or potential damage to the victim; the penalty prescribed was roughly equivalent to the harm done. This notion is also expressed in the phrase, "The punishment should fit the crime," which is the philosophy of punishment which characterizes what is known as the "Classical School of Criminology."

The man whose name is associated with the Classical School of Criminology was an Italian, Beccaria. In an age when punishments for crimes were left largely to the whims of those in authority, he proposed a system of graded punishments that would match the harm done to the victim. We can argue that "An eye for an eye, a tooth for a tooth" can be interpreted not only to justify retribution for crime, but also can be interpreted as setting a limit on punishments. An eye for an eye, not an eye for a tooth, or a life for an eye. A definition of "equal justice" might then be that the punishment should equal the harm. This was in essence a theory of retribution.

The Positivist School of Criminology. Somewhat later, another Italian by the name of Lombroso thought he had discovered the "born criminal" whom he could identify by certain "stigmata" or physical signs. When it was proved that "stigmata" were as prevalent in the halls of Oxford as they were in the Rome jails, the idea of a "criminal type" lost favor. Nevertheless Lombroso succeeded in shifting attention from the crime to the criminal.

The theory came into being that "punishment should fit the criminal." Thus was born the idea that rehabilitation of the offender should be the objective of criminal sanctions.

The two doctrines "punishment should fit the crime" and "punishment should fit the criminal" came into immediate conflict, for it is obviously not possible to consistently do both. There was also the matter of protection of society, which did not fit neatly into either of the two theories, yet was certainly a consideration in imposing punishment for deviant behavior.

In an effort to find an acceptable "theory of punishment" let us, therefore address ourselves to the fundamental questions. Why does society impose punishment on the individual who deviates from its norms? What does society hope to accomplish with punishment? What moral justification is there for punishment?

Criminologists say that the objectives of criminal sanctions are:

1. Retribution
2. Incapacitation
3. Deterrence
4. Rehabilitation

Retribution. The word retribution means "something for recompense." "An eye for an eye, a tooth for a tooth," interpreted as a command to punish the offender has been acceptable in our culture since Biblical times. It is also a natural human reaction. People who get hurt, hurt back. One has only to read the daily papers to realize that punishments for crimes which are currently upsetting the citizenry are drawing heavy penalties. Juries in one city in Texas have been returning sentences of over 100 years against a drug pusher. Juries reflect the social judgments very accurately, and there is little doubt but that society is upset about the drug problem. Society's retribution is against the drug seller since it has no other means of obtaining "recompense."

Restitution means returning to the victim what he has lost. In the case of personal injury or death, this is almost impossible to do. How do you repay a man for the loss of an eye? Also, because most offenders are without property, it is very difficult to obtain value restitution to the victim. Revenge then becomes the only means of restitution—the only way to "even things up," or obtain something for recompense.

Incapacitation. Incapacitation means to make a person incapable of doing something. Imprisonment makes it impossible or difficult for the offender to repeat his transgression. Of course a man incarcerated in a state prison can injure an officer, or steal from the prison commissary or his fellow prisoners, but the fact of his being in prison keeps him away from the rest of us. We send men to prison to make it difficult, if not impossible, for them to continue to harm the society. In primitive societies, the same result was reached by banishment. The malefactor was ejected from the tribe. We can no longer banish an offender from our society by physically ejecting him from the country—that has been declared to be unconstitutional—but we still practice a form of banishment when we put an inmate in solitary confinement, or keep him out of certain jobs after his release. Banishment has always been considered to be one of the most severe forms of punishment, as few men can live without the contact and support of the group. Today we rely heavily upon incapacitation—imprisonment—as a form of punishment. As long as the offender is incarcerated, we have banished him from our midst.

Deterrence. When society punishes a wrong-doer, one of its main objectives is deterrence. There are two aspects to deterrence. When we punish A, we want to deter A from committing additional offenses, not only during his period of incapacitation, but after he gets out. We strongly believe that punishment brings about changes in the behavior of the person punished. We also expect another kind of deterrence—we believe that punishing A will deter B. What we say is "If B sees A punished for stealing, then he will be afraid of being punished in a similar way, and will refrain from stealing."

As to whether or not punishment acts as a deterrent in these ways there is much controversy. Not all agree that punishing A will deter A, let alone that punishing A will deter B. In our first chapter we talked about pickpockets picking pockets while watching the hanging of pickpockets. "This proves," say many, "that punishing A never deters B." But as we have already pointed out, this conclusion does not necessarily follow. Certainly X number of pickpockets went on picking pockets in the crowd around the gallows, and hence were obviously not deterred by the punishments going on. But not all the persons around the gallows picked pockets. They were deterred by *something*. How many were deterred from picking pockets by the sight of pickpockets being hanged? This we never know. We catch and count only those who were not deterred. The deterrent value of punishment is very difficult to prove or disprove.

Rehabilitation. The objective of criminal sanctions that we like to emphasize today is that of rehabilitation[48] of the offender. "The punishment should fit not only the crime, but the criminal," we say. We thus have programs of treatment and resocialization in our prisons and in our institutions for juveniles, and we have developed community-based treatment such as probation and parole. We have criminologists attempting to determine the causes of criminal behavior, and psychologists researching ways to change it. We need to keep the goal of rehabilitation in mind throughout our entire correctional system, because the way a police officer arrests a man, and the treatment he receives in court, may have a lot to do with how successful we are going to be in his rehabilitation.

It is obvious, of course, that the stated goals of criminal actions may be in conflict in any particular case. If the crime is a heinous one, the goal of revenge demands a strong punishment, yet the particular offender may be one who could be rehabilitated in a relatively short period of time. The crime committed may be relatively minor, but the offender a psychopath. It is notoriously difficult to reform a psychopath. And so it goes. Our goals cut up against each other, so we often choose one to the detriment of the other. This creates confusion in our statutes about crime, in the authority we give to police officers, in the way we handle the offender during trial, and especially in the way we treat him after conviction. A sentence almost always represents a kind of compromise. Our different objectives have been put in the basket, so to speak, and what comes out depends on how much of each objective we put in. What we put into the basket will vary from place to place and from time to time. The result is that we seldom know just what goal, or goals, we are trying to achieve in the case of any individual upon whom we impose criminal sanctions.[49]

48. That this objective has existed for some time is demonstrated by the State of Oregon, which in 1859 put these words into its Constitution: "Laws for the punishment of crime shall be founded on principles of reformation, and not of vindictive justice."

49. The stated objectives of modern criminal codes include the objectives we have discussed. For example:

Smith-Hurd Ill.Ann.Stat. ch. 38, § 1–2. General Purposes

THE MORAL JUSTIFICATION FOR PUNISHMENT

There is also a moral dilemma posed by the imposition of punishments by the society on the individual, which we will now consider.

Early Notions About the Causes of Wrongdoing. In the early development of social norms and the imposition of punishment for deviation from those norms, it was believed that a man offended against the social rules because (1) he had a bad depraved mind, or because (2) he was possessed of evil spirits. In either event, punishment was obviously justified. No moral question was presented by the punishment of a man with a bad and depraved mind who deliberately transgressed against the society. If the cause of the wrongful act was that the man was possessed of evil spirits, he clearly had permitted them to usurp his will, and anyway punishing him severely was the best way to free him from them. Thus, early punishments sought both to inflict pain for the depraved mind and to exorcise the evil spirits. With the development of more advanced moral codes, a more logical justification for punishment was sought. This justification was found in the

The provisions of this Code shall be construed in accordance with the general purposes hereof, to:

(a) Forbid and prevent the commission of offenses;

(b) Define adequately the act and mental state which constitute each offense, and limit the condemnation of conduct as criminal when it is without fault;

(c) Prescribe penalties which are proportionate to the seriousness of offenses and which permit recognition of differences in rehabilitation possibilities among individual offenders;

(d) Prevent arbitrary or oppressive treatment of persons accused or convicted of offenses.

McKinney's N.Y.Penal Law, § 1.05. General Purposes.

The general purposes of the provisions of this chapter are:

1. To proscribe conduct which unjustifiably and inexcusably causes or threatens substantial harm to individual or public interests;
2. To give fair warning of the nature of the conduct proscribed and of the sentence authorized upon conviction;
3. To define the act or omission and the accompanying mental state which constitute each offense;
4. To differentiate on reasonable grounds between serious and minor offenses and to prescribe proportionate penalties therefor; and
5. To insure the public safety by preventing the commission of offenses through the deterrent influence of the sentences authorized, the rehabilitation of those convicted, and their confinement when required in the interests of public protection.

concept of "free will," which almost immediately was challenged by "determinism."

Free Will and Determinism. At the heart of the moral justification for punishment is the idea that every man is possessed of "free will;" that he is, in other words free to make choices. The doer of a criminal act, according to this view, always has the choice between doing the act and not doing it. If he chooses to do it knowing it is wrong, he should be held responsible for his acts.

The deterministic position, on the other hand, is that the acts of an individual are "determined" by his prior life experiences and that at any given moment he really has no power of choice. He will act, or not act, according to psychic determinants of which he is largely unaware and over which he has little or no voluntary control. According to this view, there is no justification for punishing a man for an act over which he has no control.

If we go back to our discussion of objectives of punishment, it is easy to see that the determinist would see the objective of "punishment" chiefly in terms of rehabilitation of the offender. Deterrence would be an objective only to the extent that "treatment" could modify the results of the life experience of the individual and thus change his behavior. In truth, the determinist would reject the word "punishment," making a distinction between "punishment," which involves deliberate infliction of pain, and "penalty," which means the unpleasant natural or social results of certain behavior.

The philosopher of free will, on the other hand, would accept the rightness of retribution, see the need for incapacitation of the wrong-doer, and approve a system of penalties that takes into consideration not only the nature of the act but the amount of harm done. Those who strongly support free will would maintain that the general application in the criminal law of the doctrine of determinism would result in a situation where no individual is held responsible for his conduct no matter how much injury he inflicts on another and no matter how great the danger to the society.

During the nineteenth century, the arguments on free will and determinism raged hard and heavy in the learned journals. It finally became an accepted fact that "The law believes in free will." In a case decided in 1968, Justice Wright of the Circuit

Court of Appeals for the District of Columbia states the position of law:

> In the long-standing debate over criminal responsibility, there has always been a strong conviction in our jurisprudence that to hold a man criminally responsible his actions must have been voluntary, the product of a "free will." In deciding responsibility for crimes, therefore, the law postulates a "free will" and then recognizes known deviations. Thus the postulate can be undermined in certain areas where there is a broad consensus that free will does not exist.[50]

Long before the days of Freud, the *mens rea* was an essential element of all common law crimes. The law refused to impose a criminal penalty without a criminal intent. As a result, the existence of the guilty mind had to be affirmatively shown. The moral justification for punishment was thus found in postulating free will and insisting upon proof of the guilty mind. Together they made the actor blameworthy and thus subject to the application of criminal sanctions.

The law also found in the condition of mind of the actor, grounds for excusing him entirely from criminal responsibility—one of the recognized "deviations" from the postulate of free will mentioned by Judge Wright. And in cases where the actor was not granted full immunity from responsibility, he could be found guilty of a lesser offense or be benefited by mitigation of his punishment. Before studying these in detail, let us briefly discuss the forms of punishment, since these were directly related to the severity of punishment and represented the value judgments of the society as to "degrees of blameworthiness" of the offender.

FORMS OF PUNISHMENT

Punishments During the Middle Ages. The punishments of the Middle Ages were corporal—branding, flogging, mutilation, and execution. At the time the American colonies broke away from England, there were over 200 felonies under English law, and all

50. Salzman v. United States, 131 U.S.App.D.C. 393, 405 F.2d 358 (1968).

felonies were capital offenses. Many of the felonies of that period are today considered misdemeanors, or even minor misdemeanors. Eighty percent of executions were for property offenses. Executions were public affairs, attended by huge crowds, and carried out as cruelly as possible.[51]

Another much used form of punishment was transportation of convicts to overseas colonies. Certain of the American colonies were populated almost entirely by felons fleeing the harsh punishments of the motherland. (The great insistence on including the Bill of Rights in the Constitution came in large part from such colonists.) The American Revolution almost created a crisis in English justice. Temporarily there was no place to send the "banished" convicts—and no place for the fugitive from that "justice" to flee to. The opening up of Australia helped to solve the problem.

Modern Forms of Punishment. Imprisonment had existed much earlier than the eighteenth century, but early imprisonment was only for the purpose of retaining a prisoner for trial. It was later, in America, that imprisonment became the usual form of legal punishment. One of the earliest prisons was established in Pennsylvania by the Quakers, for humane reasons. The good Quakers believed that if a man were confined in solitary confinement, and permitted to meditate upon his sins without cease, he would be rehabilitated. Though in those early prisons no cruel treatment was permitted, the "Pennsylvania system" unfortunately did not result in rehabilitation of the offender. Instead there was rampant suicide and mental illness among the inmates.

Today's punishments still include capital punishment, which is legal in all but nine of the states.[52] Imprisonment in a state

51. Davis, Foster, Jeffery and Davis, *op. cit.*, p. 272.

52. The following states have completely abolished capital punishment: West Virginia, Iowa, Oregon, Michigan, Alaska, Hawaii, Minnesota, Maine, and Wisconsin.

Vermont, Rhode Island, North Dakota retain the death penalty for treason, North Dakota and Rhode Island retain the death penalty for murder by a prisoner serving a life sentence. New Mexico maintains it for murder of a prison guard on duty, of a prison official, or of more than one person.

New York retains the death penalty for persons guilty of killing a police officer who is acting in line of duty, and for prisoners under a life sentence who murder a guard or inmate while in confinement or while escaping from confinement.

The rest of the states, including Texas, California, and Illinois, and the federal government, may impose the death penalty for a selected list of

penitentiary "*as* but not *for* punishment," is the most frequent disposition of the convicted man. Other penalties include fines, terms of probation, and confinement in jail. Within the prison, "treatment" can include solitary confinement, and in one or two states, flogging. Deprivation of privileges is the most used method of control within the modern prison community.

CONDITIONS OR CIRCUMSTANCES WHICH MAY EXCUSE FROM CRIMINAL RESPONSIBILITY OR MITIGATE PUNISHMENT

The law recognizes certain factors or circumstances which may excuse from criminal responsibility, reduce the grade of the offense, or mitigate the punishment.[53] Criminal responsibility must be based upon a voluntary act, and acts which are not voluntary are usually not culpable. Thus, the requirement of voluntary act is one of the first considerations in determining criminal responsibility. Other excusing or mitigating factors are identified as insanity and incompetency; intoxication; ignorance or mistake; duress and consent; entrapment; justification; [54] and limitation of actions.

offenses which may include murder, kidnapping, rape, and armed robbery (Texas).

United States Department of Justice, Bureau of Prisons, *National Prisoner Statistics*, Number 45, August 1969.

53. New York distinguishes between defenses involving lack of criminal responsibility such as infancy or mental disease or defect (Art. 30) and defenses involving lack of culpability such as justification, duress, and entrapment (Art. 33). See McKinney's Penal Law.

54. West's Ann.Cal.Penal Code, § 26: All persons are capable of committing crimes except those belonging to the following classes:

One — Children under the age of fourteen, in the absence of clear proof that at the time of committing the act charged against them, they knew its wrongfulness.

Two — Idiots.

Three — Lunatics and insane persons.

Four — Persons who committed the act or made the omission charged under an ignorance or mistake of fact, which disproves any criminal intent.

Five — Persons who committed the act charged without being conscious thereof.

Six — Persons who committed the act or made the omission charged through misfortune or by accident, when it appears that there was no evil design, intention, or culpable negligence.

Seven — Married women (except for felonies) acting under the threats, command, or coercion of their husbands.

Requirement of a Voluntary Act. A general principle of responsibility is that criminal liability is based on conduct which includes a voluntary act or the omission to perform an act of which the actor is physically capable.[55] Therefore, acts which are not voluntary are generally not culpable. The Model Penal Code states the proposition as follows:

Section 2.01 Requirement of Voluntary Act; Basis of Liability; Possession as an Act.

(1) A person is not guilty of an offense unless his liability is based on conduct which includes a voluntary act or the omission to perform an act of which he is physically capable.

(2) The following are not voluntary acts within the meaning of this Section:

(a) a reflex or convulsion;

(b) a bodily movement during unconsciousness or sleep;

(c) conduct during hypnosis or resulting from hypnotic suggestion;

(d) a bodily movement that otherwise is not a product of the effort or determination of the actor either conscious or habitual.

Age (Infancy). In the early history of the law, all persons who committed an act defined as a crime were held to be equally guilty before the law. Neither age, sex, nor unsoundness of mind could be offered as an excuse, and neither were these factors generally considered in mitigation of punishment. One of the first departures from this view came after the Church declared that a child under seven could not be guilty of sin. It followed as a natural conclusion that if a child under seven could not be guilty of sin, neither could he be guilty of a crime. The rule relieving the very young child from criminal responsibility found its way from the

Eight — Persons (unless the crime be punishable with death) who committed the act or made the omission charged under threats or menaces sufficient to show that they had reasonable cause to and did believe their lives would be endangered if they refused.

55. McKinney's N.Y.Penal Law, § 15.10: The minimal requirement for criminal liability is the performance by a person of conduct which includes a voluntary act or the omission to perform an act which he is physically capable of performing.

Smith-Hurd Ill.Ann.Stat. ch. 38, § 4–1: A material element of every offense is a voluntary act, which includes an omission to perform a duty which the law imposes on the offender and which he is physically capable of performing.

church courts to the Courts of the King's Bench, and into the Common Law. As a part of the common law, it is the almost universal rule in the United States.

From the ages of seven to fourteen, a child could be held criminally responsible only if it were affirmatively established that he understood the nature and quality of his act and knew it was wrong. To state the common law rule another way, infants below the age of fourteen were presumed incapable of committing a crime, but for persons between the ages of seven and fourteen the presumption was deemed rebuttable. That is, if it could be affirmatively shown that the child between the ages of seven and fourteen was capable of understanding the nature and quality of the act and was capable of distinguishing right from wrong, he could be held criminally responsible. Below the age of seven, the presumption that the child was incapable of committing a crime could not be rebutted.

The presumption that an infant is incapable of committing a criminal offense rests on the grounds that a person of tender years is incapable of distinguishing right from wrong, and may be too young to be able to form the necessary intent. If he is unable to form the necessary intent, the required *mens rea* cannot be proved.

Later, the age of seven was raised by statute in many states; the minimum age in Illinois, for example, is 13 years.[56] Below that age a child cannot be convicted of a crime no matter what acts he commits.

A child who commits an offense which if committed by an adult would be a felony or misdemeanor is not for reasons of age immune from the intervention of the law. A child under seven

56. Smith-Hurd Ann.Stat. ch. 38, § 6–1: No person shall be convicted of any offense unless he had attained his 13th birthday at the time the offense was committed.

In New York a person less than sixteen years is not liable for criminal conduct. See McKinney's Penal Law, § 30.00: "A person less than sixteen years old it not criminally responsible for conduct.

In California, the age is fourteen years. See West's Ann.Cal.Penal Code § 26: All persons are capable of committing crimes except those belonging to the following classes: One—Children under the age of fourteen, in the absence of clear proof that at the time of committing the act charged against them, they know its wrongfulness.

In Texas, the age is fifteen years except for the crime of perjury. See Vernon's Texas Ann.Penal Code, Art. 30, Sec. 1: No person may be convicted of any offense, except perjury, which was committed before he was 15 years of age; and for perjury only when it appears by proof that he had sufficient discretion to understand the nature and obligation of an oath.

(or the established minimum age for criminal responsibility in the particular state) who commits an offense may be taken under the protection of the law as a dependent or neglected child, or be subject to the delinquency jurisdiction of the juvenile court. This protection may extend to removing him from his parents and placing him in a home for dependent and neglected children or incarcerating him in a juvenile correctional institution.

The child over the minimum age for criminal responsibility but under seventeen years of age (or whatever age is established by juvenile delinquency statutes) may be declared to be a juvenile delinquent and placed in the custody of the state agency charged with the care of delinquent children. The "juvenile court age" is established by statute in each state, usually in the Act creating the juvenile court. A child of juvenile court age who commits an offense which if committed by an adult would be a felony or a misdemeanor is subject to the jurisdiction of the juvenile court. He may be adjudicated (deemed to be) a delinquent child. Once adjudicated a delinquent, he may be kept under the supervision of the court or the youth authority until he reaches the age of twenty-one or beyond. Juvenile court jurisdiction and the juvenile court process is discussed in detail in succeeding chapters.

The excusing of young children from criminal responsibility should not be confused with reducing punishment inflicted on children nor with the establishment of a special court to hear cases involving juveniles. Both of these events came about, but much later in the development of the law. As late as the middle of the 19th century, a boy of thirteen was hanged in the United States for stealing a small sum. It was not until 1900 that the first juvenile court was established in Chicago.

Insanity. Although the law included a mental element (the *mens rea*) in the definitions of the common law crimes, it was slow in deciding just *what* conditions of the mind would entirely excuse from criminal responsibility. That certain conditions of the mind should excuse was agreed upon quite early—arriving at definitions of the excusing states of mind was a different matter altogether, and much more difficult. Even after "insanity" was accepted as a condition which negated culpability, what constituted insanity was the central problem. To this day the law is trying to arrive at an acceptable definition of insanity, or more precisely, an acceptable definition of the unsoundness of mind that will relieve the actor from responsibility for his criminal act.

Always remember that insanity is a *legal* and not a medical term. Insanity is, therefore, defined by law and not by medicine.

The Wild Beast Test. About the middle of the eighteenth century, a rule developed which was called the "Wild Beast Test." It said, in effect, "that to escape punishment, the madman must be so deprived of understanding so as to know what he was doing no more than a wild beast would." Persons excused by this rule were the so-called "raving maniacs." Lesser states of mental disorder were not deemed sufficient to excuse from criminal responsibility.

The M'Naghten Case. In the year 1843, a man by the name of M'Naghten shot and killed a man named Drummond. M'Naghten was suffering from a delusional psychosis and thought he was being persecuted by certain of the King's ministers, including Sir Robert Peel. (Sir Robert Peel established the first modern police system in England, which is why English policemen are called "Bobbies.") M'Naghten, when he shot at Drummond, thought he was shooting at Peel.

M'Naghten was tried and acquitted of the offense, the jury finding him not guilty by reason of insanity. Because both Drummond and Peel were popular figures in the government of that day, and because an attempt on the Queen's life had been made shortly before the Drummond killing, the acquittal of M'Naghten raised a great public outcry. The House of Lords then posed a series of questions to the Judges of the Queen's Bench concerning the nature and extent of the unsoundness of mind which would excuse the commission of a felony of this sort (murder). The answer given by the House of Lords states the famous "M'Naghten Rule," which is the rule followed today in the courts of most of the states of the United States to define the condition of mind which will excuse from criminal responsibility.[57]

57. Texas and California are among the states that follow the McNaghten Rule. See Vernon's Ann.Texas Penal Code, Art. 34: No act done in a state of insanity can be punished as an offense. No person who becomes insane after he committed an offense shall be tried for the same while in such condition. No person who becomes insane after he is found guilty shall be punished while in such condition. Art. 35: The rules of evidence known to the common law as to the proof of insanity shall be observed in all trials where that question is an issue.

See West's Ann.Cal.Penal Code, § 26: All persons are capable of committing crimes except those belonging to the following classes: * * * Three—Lunatics and insane persons.

The M'Naghten Rule. To excuse from responsibility, said the Lords, "It must be clearly proved that, at the time of committing the act, the party accused was laboring under such a defect of reason, from disease of the mind, as not to know the nature and quality of the act he was doing, or, if he did know it, that he did not know it was wrong." Thus rule is variously referred to as the "test of the intellect," or the "test of reason," or the "right and wrong test."

Irresistible Impulse Test. The M'Naghten Rule did not prove to define insanity to everyone's satisfaction. It ignored the emotions, said many, and man's actions are determined as much, or more, by his emotions than by his intellect. Gradually, in a series of cases, the "Irresistible Impulse Test" came into being, usually applied along with the M'Naghten Rule. This text excused from criminal responsibility "where, while the mental perception is unimpaired, the mind is powerless to control the will; that while its unhappy subject knows the right, and desires to pursue it, some mysterious and uncontrollable impulse, compels him to commit the wrong." This test was called "the test of the emotions." It is used, along with the M'Naghten Rule, as the test of insanity in about seventeen states.

The Durham Case. The Durham Rule was an attempt to update the tests of criminal responsibility in the light of the knowledge derived from modern psychology and psychiatry. It was announced in Durham v. U. S.[58] Monte Durham had had a long history of criminal activity and also a long history of mental illness that had resulted in several different periods of hospitalization in the St. Elizabeth's Hospital in the District of Columbia. He was 26 years old when, with two companions, he broke into a house. He was convicted by the trial court and appealed to the Circuit Court of Appeals for the District of Columbia. Judge Bazelon sent the case back for a retrial and told the trial court to apply what became known as the "Durham Rule" in the determination of Durham's criminal responsibility. (Durham ultimately pleaded guilty to a lesser offense and served a year in prison.)

The Durham Rule. The Durham rule says that "the accused is not criminally responsible if his unlawful act was the product of mental disease and defect." While the rule was meant to be a

58. Durham v. United States, 94 U.S. App.D.C. 228, 214 F.2d 862 (1954).

great step forward in arriving at a test for the unsoundness of mind that will negate criminal culpability, the test did not find favor with the courts. The Durham Rule is used in the District of Columbia, in Maine, in New Hampshire (somewhat modified), and in Puerto Rico. It is referred to as "the product test."

The Model Penal Code Rule. The test for criminal responsibility suggested by the Model Penal Code is a modernized form of the M'Naghten and the Irresistible Impulse test. By substituting "appreciate" for "know," it indicates a preference for the view that a sane offender must be emotionally as well as intellectually aware of the significance of his conduct. It also requires only a "substantial" incapacity, thereby eliminating references in some older cases to "complete" destruction of the normal capacity of the defendant.

Section 4.01 Mental Disease or Defect Excluding Responsibility.

(1) A person is not responsible for criminal conduct if at the time of such conduct as a result of mental disease or defect he lacks substantial capacity either to appreciate the criminality (wrongfulness) of his conduct or to conform his conduct to the requirements of the law.

(2) As used in this Article, the terms "mental disease or defect" do not include an abnormality manifested only by repeated criminal or otherwise anti-social conduct.

Section 4.02 Evidence of Mental Disease or Defect Admissible When Relevant to Element of the Offense; (Mental Disease or Defect Impairing Capacity as Ground for Mitigation of Punishment in Capital Cases).

(1) Evidence that the defendant suffered from a mental disease or defect is admissible whenever it is relevant to prove that the defendant did or did not have a state of mind which is an element of the offense.

The Model Penal Code rule is followed in an increasing number of states,[59] sometimes as an acceptable alternative to M'Nagh-

59. The New York statute reads as follows:

1. A person is not criminally responsible for conduct if at the time of such conduct, as a result of mental disease or defect, he lacks substantial capacity to know or appreciate either:

(a) The nature and consequence of such conduct; or

(b) That such conduct was wrong.

ten, and in several of the federal circuits. It is possible that the responsibility of an offender who commits a state crime may be determined by a different rule than the defendant who commits a federal crime in the same city or town.

We could use many pages in discussing the pros and cons of the different definitions of insanity. Psychiatrists quite generally disapprove of the M'Naghten Rule, which the majority of lawyers and judges believe is still the best. However, an extensive discussion of insanity as a defense is more appropriate to more advanced books on criminal justice. We will do better to go on to a brief discussion of other factors which may excuse from criminal responsibility, or which will reduce the grade of the offense or mitigate punishment.

Incompetency. Whenever a certain state of mind is an element of the offense, a condition of mind which would render the accused incapable of that state of mind may be sufficient to reduce the grade of the crime or to mitigate punishment. This is true though the condition of mind of the defendant may be insufficient to entirely relieve him from criminal responsibility. Thus, unsoundness of mind (incompetency) which would not meet the test of insanity, and intoxication, may reduce a first degree murder charge to a second degree murder charge, or make imposition of the death penalty unlikely. An element of first degree murder is "premeditation" or "malice aforethought." Unsoundness of mind or drunk-

2. In any prosecution for an offense, lack of criminal responsibility by reason of mental disease or defect, as defined in subdivision one of this section, is a defense. McKinney's Penal Law, § 30.05.

The Illinois statute reads as follows:

(a) A person is not criminally responsible for conduct if at the time of such conduct, as a result of mental disease or mental defect, he lacks substantial capacity either to appreciate the criminality of his conduct or to conform his conduct to the requirements of law.

(b) The terms "mental disease or mental defect" do not include an abnormality manifested only by repeated criminal or otherwise antisocial conduct. Smith-Hurd Ill. Ann.Stat. ch. 38, § 6-2.

The Model Penal Code test and its variations are leading the trend away from M'Naghten in legislatures and state and federal courts. See, e. g., Conn.Gen.Stat.Ann. § 53-13; Smith-Hurd Ill.Ann.Stat. ch. 38, § 6-2; Md.Ann.Code art. 59, § 9 (a); Mo.Stat.Ann. §§ 552.010, 552.-030; Mont.Laws 1967, ch. 196, § 95-501; Minn.Stat.Ann. § 609.07; 13 Vt. Stat.Ann. §§ 4801, 4802; United States v. Freeman, 357 F.2d 606 (2d Cir. 1966); United States v. Currens, 290 F.2d 751 (3d Cir. 1961); United States v. Chandler, 393 F.2d 920 (4th Cir. 1968); Blake v. United States, 407 F.2d 908 (5th Cir. 1969); United States v. Shapiro, 383 F.2d 680 (7th Cir. 1967).

enness may be of a sufficient degree to make it doubtful, or improbable, that the defendant deliberately planned and committed the homicide, thus the *mens rea* for first degree murder has not been proved.

Unsoundness of Mind. The Model Penal Code rule on this subject is addressed particularly to the effect unsoundness of mind (always remembering that we are talking about less than insanity) will have upon the imposition of the death penalty. The rule is as follows:

> **Section 4.02 Evidence of Mental Disease or Defect Admissible When Relevant to Element of the Offense; (Mental Disease or Defect Impairing Capacity as Ground for Mitigation of Punishment in Capital Cases).**
>
> (2) Whenever the jury or the court is authorized to determine or to recommend whether or not the defendant shall be sentenced to death or imprisonment upon conviction, evidence that the capacity of the defendant to appreciate the criminality (wrongfulness) of his conduct or to conform his conduct to the requirements of law was impaired as a result of mental disease or defect is admissible in favor of sentence of imprisonment.

Intoxication. The general rule is usually stated "drunkenness is no excuse," which means that intoxication will seldom completely exonerate an actor from responsibility for his criminal act. Intoxication does not of itself constitute mental disease, and only when intoxication is so severe as to meet the test of "insanity" will it amount to a full defense. This is particularly true of voluntary intoxication.

There are situations, however, when intoxication may make it doubtful or improbable that the defendant could harbor the necessary state of mind which is an element of the crime.[60] We

60. The Illinois provision is: "A person who is in an intoxicated or drugged condition is criminally responsible for conduct unless such condition either:

(a) Negatives the existence of a mental state which is an element of the offense; or

(b) Is involuntarily produced and deprives him of substantial capacity either to appreciate the criminality of his conduct or to conform his conduct to the requirements of law." Smith-Hurd Ann.Stat. ch. 38, § 6–3.

will see hereafter, for example, that "intent to commit a felony or a theft" must accompany breaking and entering to constitute the crime of burglary. If the accused is shown to have been so drunk that he did not know what he was doing when he broke into the house, and could not have had it in his mind to commit a felony or theft, he may be guilty only of Breaking and Entering and not of Burglary. His intoxication has reduced the grade of the crime.

As can be surmised, the law on the subject of intoxication is complicated, particularly now that the suggestion is that alcoholism is a "disease." The Model Penal Code has attempted to formulate some rules on the subject.

Section 2.08 Intoxication.

(1) Except as provided in Subsection (4) of this Section, intoxication of the actor is not a defense unless it negatives an element of the offense.

(2) When recklessness establishes an element of the offense, if the actor, due to self-induced intoxication, is unaware of a risk of which he would have been aware had he been sober, such unawareness is immaterial.

(3) Intoxication does not, in itself, constitute mental disease within the meaning of Section 4.01.

(4) Intoxication which (a) is not self-induced or (b) is pathological is an affirmative defense if by reason of such intoxication the actor at the time of his conduct lacks substantial capacity either to appreciate its criminality (wrongfulness) or to conform his conduct to the requirements of law.

(5) *Definitions.* In this Section unless a different meaning plainly is required:

(a) "intoxication" means a disturbance of mental or physical capacities resulting from the introduction of substances into the body;

The New York statute on the effect of intoxication upon liability provides: Intoxication is not, as such, a defense to a criminal charge; but in any prosecution for an offense, evidence of intoxication of the defendant may be offered by the defendant whenever it is relevant to negative an element of the crime charged. McKinney's Penal Law, § 15.25.

(b) "self-induced intoxication" means intoxication caused by substances which the actor knowingly introduces into his body, the tendency of which to cause intoxication he knows or ought to know, unless he introduces them pursuant to medical advice or under such circumstances as would afford a defense to a charge of crime;

(c) "pathological intoxication" means intoxication grossly excessive in degree, given the amount of the intoxicant, to which the actor does not know he is susceptible.

Ignorance or Mistake. Under certain circumstances ignorance or mistake may be a sufficient defense to relieve the defendant from criminal responsibility.[61] The Model Penal Code provision is:

Section 2.04 Ignorance or Mistake.

(1) Ignorance or mistake as to a matter of fact or law is a defense if:

(a) the ignorance or mistake negatives the purpose, knowledge, belief, recklessness or negligence required to establish a material element of the offense; or

(b) the law provides that the state of mind established by such ignorance or mistake constitutes a defense.

(2) Although ignorance or mistake would otherwise afford a defense to the offense charged, the defense is not available if the defendant would be guilty of another offense had the situation been as he supposed. In such case, however, the ignorance or mistake of the defendant shall reduce the grade and degree of the offense of which he may be convicted to those of the offense of which he would be guilty had the situation been as he supposed.

61. The New York statute reads in part as follows:

1. A person is not relieved of criminal liability for conduct because he engages in such conduct under a mistaken belief of fact, unless:

(a) Such factual mistake negatives the culpable mental state required for the commission of an offense; or

(b) The statute defining the offense or a statute related thereto expressly provides that such factual mistake constitutes a defense or exemption; or

(c) Such factual mistake is of a kind that supports a defense of justification as defined in article thirty-five of this chapter. McKinney's Penal Law, § 15.20. See fn. 65 *infra*.

Duress and Consent. A person may be excused from criminal responsibility if he acts under duress or if the victim consents to the criminal act.[62] The Model Penal Code states the general rule as follows:

Section 2.09 Duress.

(1) It is an affirmative defense that the actor engaged in the conduct charged to constitute an offense because he was coerced to do so by the use of, or a threat to use, unlawful force against his person or the person of another, which a person of reasonable firmness in his situation would have been unable to resist.

(2) The defense provided by this Section is unavailable if the actor recklessly placed himself in a situation in which it was probable that he would be subjected to duress. The defense is also unavailable if he was negligent in placing himself in such a situation, whenever negligence suffices to establish culpability for the offense charged.

(3) It is not a defense that a woman acted on the command of her husband, unless she acted under such coercion as would establish a defense under this Section. (The presumption that a woman, acting in the presence of her husband, is coerced is abolished.)

(4) When the conduct of the actor would otherwise be justifiable under Section 3.02, this Section does not preclude such defense.

Section 2.10 Military Orders.

It is an affirmative defense that the actor, in engaging in the conduct charged to constitute an offense, does no more than execute an order of his superior in the armed services which he does not know to be unlawful.

62. McKinney's N.Y.Penal Law, § 35.35:

1. In any prosecution for an offense, it is an affirmative defense that the defendant engaged in the proscribed conduct because he was coerced to do so by the use or threatened imminent use of unlawful physical force upon him or a third person, which force or threatened force a person of reasonable firmness in his situation would have been unable to resist.

2. The defense of duress as defined in subdivision one of this section is not available when a person intentionally or recklessly places himself in a situation in which it is probable that he will be subjected to duress.

Section 2.11 Consent.

(1) *In General.* The consent of the victim to conduct charged to constitute an offense or to the result thereof is a defense if such consent negatives an element of the offense or precludes the infliction of the harm or evil sought to be prevented by the law defining the offense.

(2) *Consent to Bodily Harm.* When conduct is charged to constitute an offense because it causes or threatens bodily harm, consent to such conduct or to the infliction of such harm is a defense if:

(a) the bodily harm consented to or threatened by the conduct consented to is not serious; or

(b) the conduct and the harm are reasonably foreseeable hazards of joint participation in a lawful athletic contest or competitive sport; or

(c) the consent establishes a justification for the conduct under Article 3 of the Code.

(3) *Ineffective Consent.* Unless otherwise provided by the Code or by the law defining the offense, assent does not constitute consent if:

(a) it is given by a person who is legally incompetent to authorize the conduct charged to constitute the offense; or

(b) it is given by a person who by reason of youth, mental disease or defect or intoxication is manifestly unable or known by the actor to be unable to make a reasonable judgment as to the nature or harmfulness of the conduct charged to constitute the offense; or

(c) it is given by a person whose improvident consent is sought to be prevented by the law defining the offense; or

(d) it is induced by force, duress or deception of a kind sought to be prevented by the law defining the offense.

Entrapment. Entrapment is a defense to criminal responsibility that arises not from the condition of the accused or from the character of his act, but from an act committed by another, in this case a public law enforcement official.[63] To constitute "entrapment" a person who *otherwise would not have committed the act* must have been persuaded or influenced to commit it by a public law enforcement official. The law recognizes the defense of entrapment as a matter of public policy—the policy being that the officers of the law should not themselves promote crime. The Model Penal Code provisions are:

Section 2.13 Entrapment.

(1) A public law enforcement official or a person acting in cooperation with such an official perpetrates an entrapment if for the purpose of obtaining evidence of the commission of an offense, he induces or encourages another person to engage in conduct constituting such offense by either:

(a) making knowingly false representations designed to induce the belief that such conduct is not prohibited; or

(b) employing methods of persuasion or inducement which create a substantial risk that such an offense will be committed by persons other than those who are ready to commit it.

(2) Except as provided in Subsection (3) of this Section, a person prosecuted for an offense shall be acquitted if he proves by a preponderance of evidence that his conduct occurred in response to an entrapment. The issue of entrapment shall be tried by the Court in the absence of the jury.

(3) The defense afforded by this Section is unavailable when causing or threatening bodily injury is an element of the offense charged and the prosecution is based on conduct causing or threatening such injury to a person other than the person perpetrating the entrapment.

63. McKinney's N.Y.Penal Law, § 35.40: In any prosecution for an offense, it is an affirmative defense that the defendant engaged in the proscribed conduct because he was induced or encouraged to do so by a public servant, or by a person acting in cooperation with a public servant, seeking to obtain evidence against him for purpose of criminal prosecution, and when the methods used to obtain such evidence were such as to create a substantial risk that the offense would be committed by a person not otherwise disposed to commit it. Inducement or encouragement to commit an offense means active inducement or encouragement. Conduct merely affording a person an opportunity to commit an offense does not constitute entrapment.

"Entrapment" must be distinguished from "encouragement" or from "setting a trap" to catch a suspect.[64] An officer may use several methods to encourage or trap a guilty person, including pretending to be a victim, without giving rise to the defense of entrapment. When a narcotics agent poses as a member of the "hippie" community, and offers to buy narcotics from a pusher or other person ready and willing to sell, this is encouragement but not entrapment. The important question is, "In whose mind did the idea for the offense originate?" If an *otherwise innocent* person is induced by the officer to commit an offense, the defense of entrapment will lie. If the officer merely makes it easier for a person to commit an offense which he has made up his own mind to commit, there is no entrapment, and no relief from criminal responsibility for the offender.

Justification. Certain otherwise criminal acts may be free of criminal responsibility because they were justified. Injuries inflicted upon another in self defense, in defense of others, or in defense of property may be justified and non-culpable depending upon the circumstances and the law of the particular state.[65]

64. Conduct merely affording a person an opportunity to commit an offense does not constitute entrapment. McKinney's Con.Laws of N. Y., Ann., Penal, fn. 63, *supra.*

65. The New York statute on justification reads as follows:

The use of physical force upon another person which would otherwise constitute an offense is justifiable and not criminal under any of the following circumstances:

1. A parent, guardian or other person entrusted with the care and supervision of a minor or an incompetent person, and a teacher or other person entrusted with the care and supervision of a minor for a special purpose, may use physical force, but not deadly physical force, upon such minor or incompetent person when and to the extent that he reasonably believes it necessary to maintain discipline or to promote the welfare of such minor or incompetent person.

2. A warden or other authorized official of a jail, prison or correctional institution may, in order to maintain order and discipline, use such physical force as is authorized by the correction law.

3. A person responsible for the maintenance of order in a common carrier of passengers, or a person acting under his direction, may use physical force when and to the extent that he reasonably believes it necessary to maintain order, but he may use deadly physical force only when he reasonably believes it necessary to prevent death or serious physical injury.

4. A person acting under a reasonable belief that another person is about to commit suicide or to inflict serious physical injury upon himself may use physical force upon such person to the extent that he reasonably believes it necessary to thwart such result.

5. A duly licensed physician, or a person acting under his direction,

Some jurisdictions draw a distinction between justification and excuse, which is not important to our discussion here.

Self defense is a legal privilege available in defense of one's own person; in defense of the person of others; and (with certain restrictions) in defense of one's own property and the property of others. Self-defense means that a person may use force

may use physical force for the purpose of administering a recognized form of treatment which he reasonably believes to be adapted to promoting the physical or mental health of the patient if (a) the treatment is administered with the consent of the patient or, if the patient is a minor or an incompetent person, with the consent of his parent, guardian or other person entrusted with his care and supervision, or (b) the treatment is administered in an emergency when the physician reasonably believes that no one competent to consent can be consulted and that a reasonable person, wishing to safeguard the welfare of the patient, would consent.

6. A person may use physical force upon another person in defending himself or a third person, in defending property, in making an arrest or in preventing an escape, as hereafter prescribed in this article. McKinney's Penal Law, § 35.10.

The Illinois statutes on justification provide:

§ 7–1. A person is justified in the use of force against another when and to the extent that he reasonably believes that such conduct is necessary to defend himself or another against such other's imminent use of unlawful force. However, he is justified in the use of force which is intended or likely to cause death or great bodily harm only if he reasonably believes that such force is necessary to prevent imminent death or great bodily harm to himself or another, or the commission of a forcible felony.

§ 7–2. A person is justified in the use of force against another when and to the extent that he reasonably believes that such conduct is necessary to prevent or terminate such other's unlawful entry into or attack upon a dwelling. However, he is justified in the use of force which is intended or likely to cause death or great bodily harm only if: (a) the entry is made or attempted in a violent, riotous, or tumultuous manner, and he reasonably believes that such force is necessary to prevent an assault upon, or offer of personal violence to, him or another then in the dwelling, or (b) he reasonably believes that such force is necessary to prevent the commission of a forcible felony in the dwelling.

§ 7–3. A person is justified in the use of force against another when and to the extent that he reasonably believes that such conduct is necessary to prevent or terminate such other's trespass on or other tortious or criminal interference with either real property (other than a dwelling) or personal property, lawfully in his possession or in the possession of another who is a member of his immediate family or household or of a person whose property he has a legal duty to protect. However, he is justified in the use of force which is intended or likely to cause death or great bodily harm only if he reasonably believes that such force is necessary to prevent the commission of a forcible felony. Smith-Hurd Ill.Ann.Stat. ch. 38.

upon another when he reasonably believes such force is necessary to protect himself or others from bodily harm or to protect his property or the property of another from destruction or loss. An important distinction is made between the use of *deadly force* and *non-deadly force*; the right to use deadly force being severely restricted.[66]

66. Typical statutory provisions are as follows:

McKinney's N.Y.Penal Law.

§ 35.15: 1. Except as provided in subdivisions two and three of this section, a person is justified in using physical force upon another person in order to defend himself or a third person from what he reasonably believes to be the use or imminent use of unlawful physical force by such other person, and he may use a degree of force which he reasonably believes to be necessary for such purpose; except that deadly physical force may not be used unless the actor reasonably believes that such other person is (a) using or about to use unlawful deadly physical force, or (b) using or about to use physical force against an occupant of a dwelling while committing or attempting to commit a burglary of such dwelling, or (c) committing or about to commit a kidnapping, robbery, forcible rape or forcible sodomy.

2. Notwithstanding the provisions of subdivision one of this section, a person is not justified in using deadly physical force upon another person if he knows that he can avoid the necessity of using such force with complete safety (a) by retreating, except that the actor is not required to retreat (i) if he is in his dwelling and was not the initial aggressor, or (ii) if he is a peace officer or a private person assisting him at his direction, and was acting pursuant to section 35.30, or (b) by surrendering possession of property to a person asserting a claim of right thereto, or (c) by complying with a demand that he abstain from performing an act which he is not obligated to perform.

3. Notwithstanding the provisions of subdivision one of this section, a person is not justified in using physical force if (a) with intent to cause physical injury or death to another person, he provoked the use of unlawful physical force by such other person, or (b) he was the initial aggressor, except that his use of physical force upon another person under such circumstances is justifiable if he withdraws from the encounter and effectively communicates to such other person his intent to do so, but the latter notwithstanding continues or threatens the use of unlawful physical force, or (c) the physical force involved was the product of a combat by agreement not specifically authorized by law.

§ 35.20: A person in possession or control of premises, as that term is defined in section 140.00, or a person who is licensed or privileged to be thereon, is justified in using physical force upon another person when and to the extent that he reasonably believes it necessary to prevent or terminate what he reasonably believes to be the commission or attempted commission of a criminal trespass by such other person in or upon such premises; but he may use deadly physical force under such circumstances only (a) in defense of a person as prescribed in section 35.15, or (b) when he reasonably believes it necessary to prevent what he reasonably believes to be an attempt by the trespasser to commit arson.

In the simplest situation, a person has a right to kill another (use deadly force) to protect his own life if he reasonably believes that this amount of force is necessary to prevent death or great bodily harm. The same standard is applied to a person who kills in defense of another who is in imminent danger of death or great bodily harm. A person may also use deadly force, in many states, to prevent the commission of a violent (forcible) felony on himself or another, whether or not the felony would actually result in death or severe bodily injury [67] (to prevent rape, for example). An officer may use deadly force (kill another) when a felon is resisting arrest and the life of the officer or an innocent person is in danger, though his use of force must not

§ 35.25: A person is justified in using physical force upon another person when and to the extent that he reasonably believes it necessary to prevent what he reasonably believes to be an attempt by such other person to commit larceny or criminal mischief involving property; but he may use deadly physical force under such circumstances only in defense of a person as prescribed in section 35.15.

Also see fn. 65, *supra*, Smith-Hurd Ill.Ann.Stat.

67. In Illinois a person may not use force in resisting arrest. Smith-Hurd Ill.Ann.Stat. ch. 38, § 7–7: (a) A person is not authorized to use force to resist an arrest which he knows is being made either by a peace officer or by a private person summoned and directed by a peace officer to make the arrest, even if he believes that the arrest is unlawful and the arrest in fact is unlawful.

In Texas, using force to resist an unlawful arrest is upheld under Vernon's Ann.Texas Penal Code, Art. 1224: Homicide is justifiable also in the protection of the person or property against any other unlawful and violent attack besides those mentioned, and in such cases all other means must be resorted to for the prevention of the injury, and the killing must take place while the person killed is in the very act of making such unlawful and violent attack, and any person interfering in such case in behalf of the party about to be injured is not justified in killing the aggressor unless the life or person of the injured party is in peril by reason of such attack upon his property. * * * Note 25. Force Used in Resisting Arrest. A citizen is authorized to stand upon his individual rights and oppose force to force in the prevention of an attempted wrong, and when he is threatened with unlawful arrest, he may not only use force, but can increase that force even to the killing of his adversary, if necessary to prevent the attempted wrong. Ross v. State, 10 Tex.App. 455, 38 Am.Rep. 643 (1881). A party may meet unnecessary force with force, but cannot take the arresting officer's life, unless it is necessary or apparently necessary in defense of himself. Condron v. State, 69 Tex.Cr.R. 513, 155 S.W. 253 (1913). Where an illegal arrest is attempted or made, the person illegally restrained may use such force as appears to him to be reasonably necessary to prevent the illegal arrest or to free himself. Grafft v. State, 134 Tex.Cr.R. 30, 113 S.W.2d 546 (1938).

endanger the life of another (as where an officer shoots on a crowded street). An officer generally has no right to use deadly force on a misdemeanant or a felon who is merely trying to escape, unless the law specifically permits it.[68]

68. McKinney's N.Y.Penal Law, § 35.30:

1. Except as provided in subdivision two of this section, a peace officer is justified in using physical force upon another person when and to the extent that he reasonably believes it necessary:

(a) to effect an arrest or to prevent the escape from custody of a person whom he reasonably believes to have committed an offense, unless he knows that the arrest is unauthorized; or

(b) to defend himself or a third person from what he reasonably believes to be the use or imminent use of physical force while effecting or attempting to effect such an arrest or while preventing or attempting to prevent such an escape.

2. A peace officer is justified in using deadly physical force upon another person for a purpose specified in subdivision one of this section only when he reasonably believes that such is necessary:

(a) to defend himself or a third person from what he reasonably believes to be the use or imminent use of deadly physical force; or

(b) to effect an arrest or to prevent the escape from custody of a person whom he reasonably believes (i) has committed or attempted to commit a felony involving the use or threatened use of deadly physical force, or (ii) is attempting to escape by the use of a deadly weapon, or (iii) otherwise indicates that he is likely to endanger human life or to inflict serious physical injury unless apprehended without delay; provided that nothing contained in this paragraph shall be deemed to constitute justification for reckless or criminally negligent conduct by such peace officer amounting to an offense against or with respect to innocent persons whom he is not seeking to arrest or retain in custody.

7. A guard or other peace officer employed in a detention facility, as that term is defined in section 205.00, is justified in using physical force when and to the extent that he reasonably believes it necessary to prevent the escape of a prisoner from such detention facility.

Smith-Hurd Ill.Ann.Stat. ch. 38, § 7–5:

(a) A peace officer, or any person whom he has summoned or directed to assist him, need not retreat or desist from efforts to make a lawful arrest because of resistance or threatened resistance to the arrest. He is justified in the use of any force which he reasonably believes to be necessary to effect the arrest and of any force which he reasonably believes to be necessary to defend himself or another from bodily harm while making the arrest. However, he is justified in using force likely to cause death or great bodily harm only when he reasonably believes that such force is necessary to prevent death or great bodily harm to himself or such other person, or when he reasonably believes both that: (1) such force is necessary to prevent the arrest from being defeated by resistance or escape; and (2) the person to be arrested has committed or attempted a forcible felony or is attempting to escape by use of a deadly weapon, or otherwise indicates that he will endanger human life or inflict great bodily harm unless arrested without delay.

(b) A peace officer making an arrest pursuant to an invalid warrant is justified in the use of any force which he would be justified in using if the warrant were valid, unless he knows that the warrant is invalid.

In Texas, the law as to use of deadly force by the officer is found in the definition of "justifiable homicide." See Vernon's Ann. Texas Penal Code, Art. 1210: "Homicide by an officer in the execution of lawful orders of magistrates and courts is justifiable when he is violently resisted and has just grounds to fear danger to his own life in executing the order." Art. 1211: "The officer is justifiable though there may have been an error of judgment on the part of the magistrate or court, if the order emanated from a proper authority."

An officer as well as any other person is justified in using deadly force. See Vernon's Ann. Texas Penal Code, Art. 1221: Homicide is permitted in the necessary defense of person or property, under the circumstances and subject to the rules herein set forth. Art. 1222: Homicide is justifiable when inflicted for the purpose of preventing murder, rape, robbery, maiming, disfiguring, castration, arson, burglary and theft at night, or when inflicted upon a person or persons who are found armed with deadly weapons and in disguise in the night time on premises not his or their own, whether the homicide be committed by the party about to be injured or by another in his behalf, when the killing takes place under the following circumstances:

1. It must reasonably appear by the acts or by words coupled with the acts of the person killed that it was the purpose and intent of such person to commit one of the offenses above named.

2. The killing must take place while the person killed was in the act of committing the offense, or after some act done by him showing evidently an intent to commit such offense.

3. It must take place before the offense committed by the party killed is actually completed, except that in case of rape the ravisher may be killed at any time before he has escaped from the presence of his victim, and except also in the cases hereinafter enumerated.

4. Where the killing takes place to prevent the murder of some other person, it shall not be deemed that the murder is completed so long as the offender is still inflicting violence, though the mortal wound may have been given.

5. If homicide takes place in preventing a robbery, it is justifiable if done while the robber is in the presence of the one robbed or is flying with the property taken by him.

6. In cases of maiming, disfiguring or castration, the homicide may take place at any time while the offender is mistreating with violence the person injured, though he may have completed the offense.

7. In case of arson the homicide may be inflicted while the offender is in or at the building or other property burnt, or flying from the place before the destruction of the same.

8. In cases of burglary and theft by night, the homicide is justifiable at any time while the offender is in the building or at the place where the theft is committed, or is within reach of gunshot from such place or building.

9. When the party slain in disguise is engaged in any attempt by word, gesture or otherwise to alarm some other person or persons and put them in bodily fear.

In California, the limits on the right to use force are to be found in the case law.

The use of non-deadly force is permitted in less serious circumstances and in a wider variety of situations.[69] Thus, an officer may shoot to disable a fleeing (non-resisting) felon, under circumstances that would not justify the use of deadly force.

The use of force must be reasonable. Therefore, if the aggressor takes flight or otherwise clearly indicates that he intends to stop his aggression, the victim is precluded from continuing to inflict injury upon him, and an officer's right is limited to the use of non-deadly force. In some states, the test of "reasonableness" imposes upon the victim the duty to retreat, if by retreating he can protect himself and avoid the necessity of injuring the wrong-doer.[70] Under the rule of retreat, a person must retreat until his "back is against the wall," or until he can no longer retreat before resorting to the use of force. Whether or not this rule is applied is often determined by whether or not the intended victim is in his own home. If he is in his own home, he may stand his ground and is not bound to retreat.[71] An early New York case stated the rule that, "It is not now, and never has been the law, that a man assailed in his own dwelling, is bound to retreat * * *. He is under no duty to take to the fields and highways, a fugitive from his own house." [72] The thrust of recent legislation and case law in New York, however, has been to require retreat except in one's own dwelling and in defense of one's own life.[73] Retreat is required before force can be used merely to protect property, and a person coming to the defense of another (as in the case of a citizen's arrest) who inflicts unreasonable harm upon the aggressor does so at his own peril.[74]

69. See fn. 67, *supra*, Vernon's Ann. Texas Penal Code, Art. 1224.

70. See fn. 66, *supra*, McKinney's N.Y.Penal Law, § 35.15(2).

Retreat is not necessary in Texas. See Vernon's Ann.Texas Penal Code, Art. 1225: The party whose person or property is so unlawfully attacked is not bound to retreat in order to avoid the necessity of killing his assailant.

71. Brown v. United States, 256 U.S. 335, 41 S.Ct. 501, 65 L.Ed. 961 (1921). In this case Justice Holmes said that a person attacked "may stand his ground and if he kills he has not exceeded the bounds of lawful self defense."

72. People v. Tomlins, 213 N.Y. 240, 107 N.E. 496 (1914). See, however, McKinney's N.Y.Penal Law, § 35.15 (2), fn. 66, *supra*.

73. See fn. 66, *supra*, McKinney's N.Y.Penal Law, § 35.15(2).

74. See fn. 66, *supra*, McKinney's N.Y.Penal Law, § 35.15(1).

People v. Young, 11 N.Y.2d 274, 229 N.Y.S.2d 1, 183 N.E.2d 319 (1962).

Texas, on the other hand, stands firmly on the doctrine that a man's home is his castle, and specifically negates the duty to retreat.[75]

In this introductory work, we cannot go into all of the circumstances under which the use of force may be justified and thus relieve from criminal responsibility. The law differs in details from state to state. Your penal code and the decisions in your state will tell you what constitutes justification or excuse for certain otherwise blameworthy acts.

The Model Penal Code sets out the following general principles of justification:

Section 3.01 Justification an Affirmative Defense; Civil Remedies Unaffected.

(1) In any prosecution based on conduct which is justifiable under this Article, justification is an affirmative defense.

(2) The fact that conduct is justifiable under this article does not abolish or impair any remedy for such conduct which is available in any civil action.

Section 3.02 Justification Generally: Choice of Evils.

(1) Conduct which the actor believes to be necessary to avoid a harm or evil to himself or to another is justifiable, provided that:

(a) the harm or evil sought to be avoided by such conduct is greater than that sought to be prevented by the law defining the offense charged; and

(b) neither the Code nor other law defining the offense provides exceptions or defenses dealing with the specific situation involved; and

(c) a legislative purpose to exclude the justification claimed does not otherwise plainly appear.

(2) When the actor was reckless or negligent in bringing about the situation requiring a choice of harms or evils or in appraising the necessity for his conduct, the justification afforded by this Section is unavailable in a prosecution for any offense for which recklessness or negligence, as the case may be, suffices to establish culpability.

75. See fn. 70 *supra*, Vernon's Ann. Texas Penal Code, Art. 1225.

Section 3.03 Execution of Public Duty.

(1) Except as provided in Subsection (2) of this Section, conduct is justifiable when it is required or authorized by:

(a) the law defining the duties or functions of a public officer or the assistance to be rendered to such officer in the performance of his duties; or

(b) the law governing the execution of legal process; or

(c) the judgment or order of a competent court or tribunal; or

(d) the law governing the armed services or the lawful conduct of war; or

(e) any other provision of law imposing a public duty.

(2) The other sections of this Article apply to:

(a) the use of force upon or toward the person of another for any of the purposes dealt with in such sections; and

(b) the use of deadly force for any purpose, unless the use of such force is otherwise expressly authorized by law or occurs in the lawful conduct of war.

(3) The justification afforded by Subsection (1) of this Section applies:

(a) when the actor believes his conduct to be required or authorized by the judgment or direction of a competent court or tribunal or in the lawful execution of legal process, notwithstanding lack of jurisdiction of the court or defect in the legal process; and

(b) when the actor believes his conduct to be required or authorized to assist a public officer in the performance of his duties, notwithstanding that the officer exceeded his legal authority.

Section 3.05 Use of Force for the Protection of Other Persons.

(1) Subject to the provisions of this Section and of Section 3.09, the use of force upon or toward the person of another is justifiable to protect a third person when:

(a) the actor would be justified under Section 3.04 in using such force to protect himself against the injury he believes to be threatened to the person whom he seeks to protect; and

(b) under the circumstances as the actor believes them to be, the person whom he seeks to protect would be justified in using such protective force; and

(c) the actor believes that his intervention is necessary for the protection of such other person.

(2) Notwithstanding Subsection (1) of this Section:

(a) when the actor would be obliged under Section 3.04 to retreat, to surrender the possession of a thing or to comply with a demand before using force in self-protection, he is not obliged to do so before using force for the protection of another person, unless he knows that he can thereby secure the complete safety of such other person; and

(b) when the person whom the actor seeks to protect would be obliged under Section 3.04 to retreat, to surrender the possession of a thing or to comply with a demand if he knew that he could obtain complete safety by so doing, the actor is obliged to try to cause him to do so before using force in his protection if the actor knows that he can obtain complete safety in that way; and

(c) neither the actor nor the person whom he seeks to protect is obliged to retreat when in the other's dwelling or place of work to any greater extent than in his own.

Section 3.06 Use of Force for the Protection of Property.

(1) *Use of Force Justifiable for Protection of Property.* Subject to the provisions of this Section and Section 3.09, the use of force upon or toward the person of another is justifiable when the actor believes that such force is immediately necessary:

(a) to prevent or terminate an unlawful entry or other trespass upon land or a trespass against or the unlawful carrying away of tangible, movable property, provided that such land or movable property is, or is believed by the actor to be, in his possession or in the possession of another person for whose protection he acts; or

(b) to effect an entry or re-entry upon land or to retake tangible movable property, provided that the actor believes that he or the person by whose authority he acts or a person from whom he or such person derives title was unlawfully dispossessed of such land or movable property and is entitled to possession, and provided, further, that:

(i) the force is used immediately or on fresh pursuit after such dispossession; or

(ii) the actor believes that the person against whom he uses force has no claim of right to the possession of the property and, in the case of land, the circumstances, as the actor believes them to be, are of such urgency that it would be an exceptional hardship to postpone the entry or re-entry until a court order is obtained.

(2) *Meaning of Possession.* For the purposes of Sub-section (1) of this Section:

(a) a person who has parted with the custody of property to another who refuses to restore it to him is no longer in possession, unless the property is movable and was and still is located on land in his possession;

(b) a person who has been dispossessed of land does not regain possession thereof merely by setting foot thereon;

(c) a person who has a license to use or occupy real property is deemed to be in possession thereof except against the licensor acting under claim of right.

(3) *Limitations on Justifiable Use of Force.*

(a) *Request to desist.* The use of force is justifiable under this Section only if the actor first requests the person against whom such force is used to desist from his interference with the property, unless the actor believes that:

(i) such request would be useless; or

(ii) it would be dangerous to himself or another person to make the request; or

(iii) substantial harm will be done to the physical condition of the property which is sought to be protected before the request can effectively be made.

(b) *Exclusion of trespasser.* The use of force to prevent or terminate a trespass is not justifiable under this Section if the actor knows that the exclusion of the trespasser will expose him to substantial danger of serious bodily harm.

(c) *Resistance of lawful re-entry or recaption.* The use of force to prevent an entry or re-entry upon land or the recaption of movable property is not justifiable under this Section, although the actor believes that such re-entry or recaption is unlawful, if:

(i) the re-entry or recaption is made by or on behalf of a person who was actually dispossessed of the property; and

(ii) it is otherwise justifiable under paragraph (1) (b) of this Section.

(d) *Use of deadly force.* The use of deadly force is not justifiable under this Section unless the actor believes that:

(i) the person against whom the force is used is attempting to dispossess him of his dwelling otherwise than under a claim of right to its possession; or

(ii) the person against whom the force is used is attempting to commit or consummate arson, burglary, robbery or other felonious theft or property destruction and either:

(1) has employed or threatened deadly force against or in the presence of the actor; or

(2) the use of force other than deadly force to prevent the commission or the consummation of the crime would expose the actor or another in his presence to substantial danger of serious bodily harm.

(4) *Use of Confinement as Protective Force.* The justification afforded by this Section extends to the use of confinement as protective force only if the actor takes all reasonable measures to terminate the confinement as soon as he

knows that he can do so with safety to the property, unless the person confined has been arrested on a charge of crime.

(5) *Use of Device to Protect Property.* The justification afforded by this Section extends to the use of a device for the purpose of protecting property only if:

(a) the device is not designed to cause or known to create a substantial risk of causing death or serious bodily harm; and

(b) the use of the particular device to protect the property from entry or trespass is reasonable under the circumstances, as the actor believes them to be; and

(c) the device is one customarily used for such a purpose or reasonable care is taken to make known to probable intruders the fact that it is used.

(6) *Use of Force to Pass Wrongful Obstructor.* The use of force to pass a person whom the actor believes to be purposely or knowingly and unjustifiably obstructing the actor from going to a place to which he may lawfully go is justifiable, provided that:

(a) the actor believes that the person against whom he uses force has no claim of right to obstruct the actor; and

(b) the actor is not being obstructed from entry or movement on land which he knows to be in the possession or custody of the person obstructing him, or in the possession or custody of another person by whose authority the obstructor acts, unless the circumstances, as the actor believes them to be, are of such urgency that it would not be reasonable to postpone the entry or movement on such land until a court order is obtained; and

(c) the force used is not greater than would be justifiable if the person obstructing the actor were using force against him to prevent his passage.

Section 3.07 Use of Force in Law Enforcement.

(1) *Use of Force Justifiable to Effect an Arrest.* Subject to the provisions of this Section and of Section 3.09, the use of force upon or toward the person of another is justifiable when the actor is making or assisting in making an arrest

and the actor believes that such force is immediately necessary to effect a lawful arrest.

(2) *Limitations on the Use of Force.*

(a) The use of force is not justifiable under this Section unless:

(i) the actor makes known the purpose of the arrest or believes that it is otherwise known by or cannot reasonably be made known to the person to be arrested; and

(ii) when the arrest is made under a warrant, the warrant is valid or believed by the actor to be valid.

(b) The use of deadly force is not justifiable under this Section unless:

(i) the arrest is for a felony; and

(ii) the person effecting the arrest is authorized to act as a peace officer or is assisting a person whom he believes to be authorized to act as a peace officer; and

(iii) the actor believes that the force employed creates no substantial risk of injury to innocent persons; and

(iv) the actor believes that:

(1) the crime for which the arrest is made involved conduct including the use or threatened use of deadly force; or

(2) there is a substantial risk that the person to be arrested will cause death or serious bodily harm if his apprehension is delayed.

(3) *Use of Force to Prevent Escape From Custody.* The use of force to prevent the escape of an arrested person from custody is justifiable when the force could justifiably have been employed to effect the arrest under which the person is in custody, except that a guard or other person authorized to act as a peace officer is justified in using any force, including deadly force, which he believes to be immediately necessary to prevent the escape of a person from a jail, prison, or other institution for the detention of persons charged with or convicted of a crime.

(4) *Use of Force by Private Person Assisting an Unlawful Arrest.*

(a) A private person who is summoned by a peace officer to assist in effecting an unlawful arrest, is justified in using any force which he would be justified in using if the arrest were lawful, provided that he does not believe the arrest is unlawful.

(b) A private person who assists another private person in effecting an unlawful arrest, or who, not being summoned, assists a peace officer in effecting an unlawful arrest, is justified in using any force which he would be justified in using if the arrest were lawful, provided that (i) he believes the arrest is lawful, and (ii) the arrest would be lawful if the facts were as he believes them to be.

(5) *Use of Force to Prevent Suicide or the Commission of a Crime.*

(a) The use of force upon or toward the person of another is justifiable when the actor believes that such force is immediately necessary to prevent such other person from committing suicide, inflicting serious bodily harm upon himself, committing or consummating the commission of a crime involving or threatening bodily harm, damage to or loss of property or a breach of the peace, except that:

(i) any limitations imposed by the other provisions of this Article on the justifiable use of force in self-protection, for the protection of others, the protection of property, the effectuation of an arrest or the prevention of an escape from custody shall apply notwithstanding the criminality of the conduct against which such force is used; and

(ii) the use of deadly force is not in any event justifiable under this Subsection unless:

(1) the actor believes that there is a substantial risk that the person whom he seeks to prevent from committing a crime will cause death or serious bodily harm to another unless the commission or the consummation of the crime is prevented and that the use of such

force presents no substantial risk of injury to innocent persons; or

(2) the actor believes that the use of such force is necessary to suppress a riot or mutiny after the rioters or mutineers have been ordered to disperse and warned, in any particular manner that the law may require, that such force will be used if they do not obey.

(b) The justification afforded by this Subsection extends to the use of confinement as preventive force only if the actor takes all reasonable measures to terminate the confinement as soon as he knows that he safely can, unless the person confined has been arrested on a charge of crime.

Section 3.11 Definitions.

In this Article, unless a different meaning plainly is required:

(1) "unlawful force" means force, including confinement, which is employed without the consent of the person against whom it is directed and the employment of which constitutes an offense or actionable tort or would constitute such offense or tort except for a defense (such as the absence of intent, negligence, or mental capacity; duress; youth; or diplomatic status) not amounting to a privilege to use the force. Assent constitutes consent, within the meaning of this Section, whether or not it otherwise is legally effective, except assent to the infliction of death or serious bodily harm.

(2) "deadly force" means force which the actor uses with the purpose of causing or which he knows to create a substantial risk of causing death or serious bodily harm. Purposely firing a firearm in the direction of another person or at a vehicle in which another person is believed to be constitutes deadly force. A threat to cause death or serious bodily harm, by the production of a weapon or otherwise, so long as the actor's purpose is limited to creating an apprehension that he will use deadly force if necessary, does not constitute deadly force;

(3) "dwelling" means any building or structure, though movable or temporary, or a portion thereof, which is for the time being the actor's home or place of lodging.

LIMITATION OF ACTIONS

Statutes of limitations prescribe the time within which a criminal action may be commenced, and thus puts a time limit upon criminal responsibility. The time is usually counted from the date of the offense to the date of filing the indictment or formal complaint and varies from offense to offense. One offense, murder, customarily has no time limit, but other serious offenses may also be relieved from limitation.[76]

The idea behind statutes which limit the time within which a criminal may be prosecuted for his offense is that a man should not have to live a long time under threat of criminal action. Also, if trials are delayed too long, witnesses die and disappear, evidence is lost, parties move away, and many other things happen that make getting at the truth very difficult. It is therefore of interest to the society, as well as the accused, to hold criminal trials promptly and get them over with.[77]

It will serve no good purpose to set out here the specific time limits for a list of offenses. The limits vary widely in different states. Usually, however, the time limit for felonies is longer than that for misdemeanors, and for serious felonies longer than for less serious felonies.

The offense for rape is an exception. Usually the time limit for beginning a prosecution for rape is very short—often one year. If the prosecution is not brought within one year, the case "outlaws," i. e., because of the passage of time, the state loses its right

76. Smith-Hurd Ill.Ann.Stat. ch. 38, § 3–5:

(a) A prosecution for murder, manslaughter, treason, arson, or forgery may be commenced at any time.

(b) Unless the statute describing the offense provides otherwise, or the period of limitation is extended by Section 3–6, a prosecution for any offense not designated in Subsection (a) must be commenced within 3 years after the commission of the offense if it is a felony, or within one year and 6 months after its commission if it is a misdemeanor.

Vernon's Ann. Texas Code of Criminal Procedure, Art. 12.04: An indictment for any other felony may be presented within three years from the commission of the offense, and not afterward; except murder, for which an indictment may be presented at any time.

77. Do not confuse limitations of actions and the right to a speedy trial. The statutes of limitations have to do with the time permitted to elapse between the date of the offense and the date of the indictment or information. The right to a speedy trial is concerned with the period between indictment or information and trial.

to punish the offender. The reason for the short time limit on rape is that the charge of rape is particularly devastating to the accused. Even before conviction, the charge alone may cause him to lose his job, be dismissed from public office, and denied social acceptance. If he is innocent of the offense, his need for prompt vindication is acute. The law also seems to feel that any woman who brings a charge of rape should be required to do so promptly—it is not the kind of thing that she should have to live with or be able to hold over the head of the man for an extended length of time. The proof of rape becomes difficult as time passes; the guilty rapist should not be permitted to be at large to commit other similar offenses; the community has an interest in the prompt settlement of such cases because of the ill will they cause, etc. All of these arguments result in a relatively short statute of limitations for this particular offense.

Time Limitations Under the Model Penal Code. The Model Penal Code has attempted to simplify the various time limitations for bringing criminal actions. It provides, as do the laws of most states, that a prosecution for murder may be commenced at any time. The Model Penal Code provision is:

> **Section 1.06 Time Limitations.**
>
> (1) A prosecution for murder may be commenced at any time.
>
> (2) Except as otherwise provided in this Section, prosecutions for other offenses are subject to the following periods of limitation:
>
> > (a) a prosecution for a felony of the first degree must be commenced within three years after it is committed;
> >
> > (b) a prosecution for any other felony must be commenced within two years after it is committed;
> >
> > (c) a prosecution for a misdemeanor must be commenced within two years after it is committed;
> >
> > (d) a prosecution for a petty misdemeanor or a violation must be commenced within six months after it is committed.

The time limitations on criminal actions in your state will be found in the statutes relating to criminal law and procedure. Some of the provisions have to do with "tolling" the statute of limitations. "Tolling" means "stopping the clock." Under certain conditions, the time within which an action may be brought will be extended. The usual reason is that the defendant cannot be found. He leaves the state or conceals himself to avoid arrest and prosecution. Or the defendant may be serving a prison sentence in another state for another crime. The provisions for "tolling" the statutes of limitations permit the time that the defendant cannot be found or is not available to stand trial to be "dropped out" of the time calculations.[78]

Let us suppose Z commits a robbery in your state and the time limitation for commencing the action against him is fixed in the statute at five years. The offense is committed on June 1, 1962. The defendant stays in the community and can be located but he is not arrested and charged with the offense. On June 1, 1964, he disappears. He cannot be found until June 1, 1970, when he again shows up in your state—he may even come back into the county where the offense occurred. Since the time from June 1, 1962 to June 1, 1970, is more than five years, you might suppose that the action against Z had "outlawed," i. e., that prosecution of the offense is now barred by the running of the statute of limitations. This would not be true. The time from June 1, 1964, when Z left the state, until June 1, 1970, when he returned, would be dropped out of the time calculation. In most states, a felony action could be commenced against Z any time before June 1, 1973—two years of the statute running from June 1, 1962 to June 1, 1964; three years running from June 1, 1970, to June 1, 1973; five years in all—the total time provided for in the statute.

In some states, under the circumstances of Z, the law provides that the action must be brought within a shorter time after the accused returns to the state, as for example, within a year of his return. In any event, the absence of the defendant from the state "tolled" the running of the statute of limitations and extended the

78. The Illinois statutory provision is typical. See Smith-Hurd Ann. Stat. ch. 38, § 3-7: The period within which a prosecution must be commenced does not include any period in which:

(a) The defendant is not usually and publicly resident within this State; or

(b) The defendant is a public officer and the offense charged is theft of public funds while in public office; or

(c) A prosecution is pending against the defendant for the same conduct, even if the indictment or information which commences the prosecution is quashed or the proceedings thereon are set aside, or are reversed on appeal.

time within which the action could be commenced against him after he returned. The Model Penal Code provision is:

Section 1.06 Time Limitations.

(6) The period of limitation does not run:

(a) during any time when the accused is continuously absent from the State or has no reasonably ascertainable place of abode or work within the State, but in no case shall this provision extend the period of limitation otherwise applicable by more than three years; or

(b) during any time when a prosecution against the accused for the same conduct is pending in this State.

In the preceding two chapters we have discussed the legal concepts of criminal responsibility, and the objectives and form of punishment. We have seen that the law recognizes facts and circumstances which may excuse the actor from criminal responsibility. Age, insanity, involuntary act, ignorance or mistake, duress, and entrapment may make an otherwise criminal act nonculpable. Unsoundness of mind less than insanity and intoxication may serve to mitigate punishment. The statutes of limitations set up a time barrier for criminal responsibility except for the crime of murder or other serious offenses.

Chapter III

ELEMENTS OF THE MAJOR CRIMES

CRIMES AGAINST THE PERSON

We have seen that the basic definition of a crime involves an act (behavior) coupled with the judgment of the society that it is wrong. Society must then go on to specify the kinds of behavior that are considered wrong, and affix a penalty according to the degree to which the behavior is considered a threat or injury to the society. The society must also define "wrong" and "wrongness."

In the case of the major crimes, the necessary element of "wrongness" is that the offender have a "guilty mind." To constitute a major crime, we must not only have the *actus reus*—behavior that is illegal because the society considers it wrong—we must also have the *mens rea*—the actor must have had an intent to do wrong. There are many phrases used to express *mens rea*, such as "guilty mind," "criminal intent," "malice," "deliberate intent to inflict injury," "scienter," and so on. When a defendant seeks to escape criminal responsibility on the grounds of insanity, the test usually applied is the "right and wrong test." The famous M'Naghten rule says that to be held criminally responsible, the person must have understood "the nature and quality of his act, and that it was wrong."

What is right and what is wrong is, of course, a value judgment of the society, just as who is and who is not a wrongdoer is also a value judgment of the society. In the laws passed by the legislature, society sets out its value judgments as to what behavior is to be considered wrong. In the verdict of the jury or the decision of the trial judge, society decides who is or who is not a wrongdoer.

The acts of the legislature which define the crimes [1] also include society's value judgments on degrees of wrongness—the fact that

1. In some states the rule is that no act or omission is criminal or punishable unless expressly made so by statute. The states following this rule include California, Georgia, Indiana, Iowa, Kansas, Michigan, Minnesota, Missouri, New York, Ohio, Oregon, and Texas. All federal crimes are crimes only by statutory definition. There are no federal common law crimes.

some conduct is more harmful to the society than other conduct. The criminal laws therefore set out the permissible punishments for each crime, usually providing both a minimum and maximum penalty. In the sentencing process, the judge or jury decides upon the punishment that is appropriate to the particular offender, always, of course, within the limits (value judgments) expressed by the society in the statutes which define the crimes and fix the penalties.

In the process of defining "wrongness," a distinction is often made between acts which are *malum in se*—wrong in themselves—and acts which are *malum prohibitum*—wrong because they are prohibited. Acts which inflict serious bodily injury on another, such as murder, assault, rape, kidnapping, and the like, as well as acts against the rights of property, such as robbery, burglary, and theft, are *malum in se*. An act *malum in se* is deemed to be morally wrong, and is said to be characterized by "moral turpitude," i. e., wrong-doing according to the common moral values of the society. An act such as parking in front of a fire hydrant, or failing to sack the garbage properly for its pickup by the sanitation department, or disturbing the neighbors by too much noise at a party, are merely *malum prohibitum*, and do not constitute "moral turpitude."

Many acts which are *malum in se* are also *malum prohibitum*, for the criminal law specifically forbids the acts which the majority of the society considers morally wrong. The more complex a society becomes, the more regulations it takes to keep the society functioning, the more kinds of behavior become *malum prohibitum*. Society's definition of what acts should be prohibited by the law changes from time to time. Dumping wastes in a river or stream has not up to recent times been considered an offense against the society, and was thus not an act which was *malum prohibitum*. As our interest in preserving our environment increases, more kinds of behavior that adversely affect the environment will become *malum prohibitum*. Of course, other kinds of behavior that are now *malum prohibitum* may not in the future be so considered. An example might be possession and use of marijuana. Even behavior which many people now consider as *malum in se* as well as *malum prohibitum*—for example, abortion, may not be defined as wrong in the criminal law of the '70s.

The value judgments of society change and the kinds of behavior permitted to the individual likewise change. This means that the definitions of crime vary from time to time and place to place. There are certain acts such as treason, murder, incest, rape, robbery, burglary, and theft of valuable personal property, that almost all modern societies during most periods of their history have considered wrong. These acts were declared by the early English Common Law—before the time when crimes were defined in the statutes passed by the legislature—to be wrong.[2] The crimes of a serious character which involve conduct almost every member of a society would agree to be wrong, and which were defined as crimes early in the development of English law, are called the "Common Law Crimes." Because the statutory law has changed or introduced new elements into the definitions of these early crimes, there is no exact agreement as to what offenses should be included in a list of the Common Law crimes.[3] For that reason, in this chapter we use the term "major crimes."

The crimes we will study are felonies. In the early law, *all* felonies were punishable by death. In modern law, felonies are offenses punishable by death or by confinement in a penitentiary for a specified length of time. As we have seen, the exact definition of a felony varies from state to state. Whatever the exact definition, felonies are considered to be serious or "major" crimes. In our study of the particular crimes, we will refer to the definitions of the Model Penal Code and include the statutes of some of the larger states. The definition of any crime varies in details from jurisdiction to jurisdiction, but the formulations of the Model Penal Code resulted from a dedicated effort to arrive at fair and

2. Even in states which provide that no act is criminal unless it is made such by state statute, resort may be had to the rules of common law to aid in statutory interpretation. For example, in Minnesota, resort was had to the common law concept of unity of husband and wife to absolve a wife of the crime of larceny of her husband's property, and the words "every person" as used in the statute were held not to include the wife. State v. Arnold, 182 Minn. 313, 235 N.W. 373 (1931).

3. The common law felonies included the following forcible felonies, i. e., felonies committed with the use of force: treason; voluntary manslaughter; aggravated battery; murder; rape; battery; kidnapping; burglary; arson; larceny from the person. Many other offenses were also felonies at common law, the punishment for which was death. Breach of the peace was a common law misdemeanor, and included various kinds of misconduct classified today as disorderly conduct, breach of the peace, rout, riot, etc.

accurate statements of crimes, punishments, and criminal responsibility. As more and more states use the Model Penal Code in revisions of their criminal law, the formulations of the Code will tend to become standard throughout the United States. You must understand, of course, that you will need to go to the Penal Code of your own state to determine exactly what are the necessary elements of the major offenses in your state. A study of the statutes of your state will inform you, as to any particular offense, of the major differences between the elements set out in the Model Penal Code provisions or in the statutes of the representative states and the elements required in the laws of your state.

THE HOMICIDE OFFENSES

The word homicide comes from the Latin noun "homo" which means "man," and a Latin verb meaning "to kill, or cause the death of." Homicide is therefore defined as "the killing of one human being by the act, agency, procurement, or culpable omission of another." [4]

Not all homicides are crimes, which is another way of saying that not all killings of one human being by another are blameworthy. The death of the victim may be due to accident or misfortune, for which no blame attaches, and thus be excusable. Or the killing, though intended, may be under circumstances considered justifiable by the law. When defining non-culpable homicides, some states label all such homicides as "excusable homicides." Others label all non-blameworthy homicides "justifiable homicides." Still other states make a distinction between excusable and justifiable homicides,[5] although both are alike in being non-culpable and thus non-criminal.

4. Vernon's Ann.Texas Penal Code, Art. 1201.

McKinney's N.Y. Penal Law, § 125.00.

California and Illinois have no general statutory definition of homicide.

5. The Texas law distinguishes between justifiable homicide Vernon's Ann.Texas Penal Code, (Arts. 1207–1227) and excusable homicide (Art. 1228). Excusable homicide is when the death of a human being happens by accident or misfortune, though caused by the act of another who is in the prosecution of a lawful object by lawful means.

The Elements of Criminal Homicide. Criminal homicide is culpable homicide. The elements of culpable homicide are

1. The death of a human being,
2. Caused without justification or excuse by the unlawful act of another human being.

These two elements together are referred to as the *corpus delicti* of criminal homicide.[6]

The elements of death of a human caused without justification or excuse by the unlawful act of another human being are essential elements of all of the homicide offenses. Typically, however, criminal homicide is divided into degrees which reflect both the extent of the injury to the victim inherent in the criminal act and the degree to which the offender can be said to have had a "guilty mind." The greater the potential injury to the victim, and the more guilty the mind of the offender, the higher the homicide offense and the greater the punishment. A typical classification of the homicide offenses is shown in Figure 1.[7]

6. *Corpus delicti* means "the body of the crime," or the material substance upon which the criminal act was committed. In the case of homicide, the *corpus delicti* is the body of the victim who has been killed by the unlawful act of another human being. The words *corpus delicti* do not refer only to the human victim of a homicide. The *corpus delicti* of arson is the building unlawfully burned; of theft, the stolen property appropriated to the use of the thief; of forgery, the instrument unlawfully forged and passed; and so on.

In California, the dead body need not be produced; death can be established by circumstances. The People v. Thomas R. McMonigle, 29 Cal.2d 730, 177 P.2d 745 (1947).

7. The Texas classification of homicides does not follow the typical pattern. Justifiable and excusable homicide are defined, followed by a definition of the misdemeanor offenses of homicide by negligence, and murder is the name given all homicide offenses which are not justifiable, excusable, or which do not amount to negligent homicide. The two degrees of murder are distinguished in statutory jury instructions. Homicide by negligence is of two kinds, in first degree, "such as happens in the performance of a lawful act," and second degree, "that which occurs in the performance of an unlawful act." Vernon's Ann.Texas Penal Code, Arts. 1230, 1231, 1238. An unlawful act is defined as (1) such acts as by the penal law are called misdemeanors; and (2) such acts, not being penal offenses, as would give just occasion for a civil action. If the intent is to commit a felony, as when one is in the execution of or in attempting to execute an act made a felony by law shall kill another, though without any apparent intention to kill, the offense does not come within the definition of negligent homicide. Art. 1241.

Murder is defined by Art. 1256 as follows: "Whoever shall voluntarily kill any person within this State shall be guilty of murder. Murder shall be distinguished from every other species of homicide by the

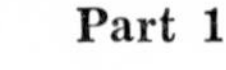

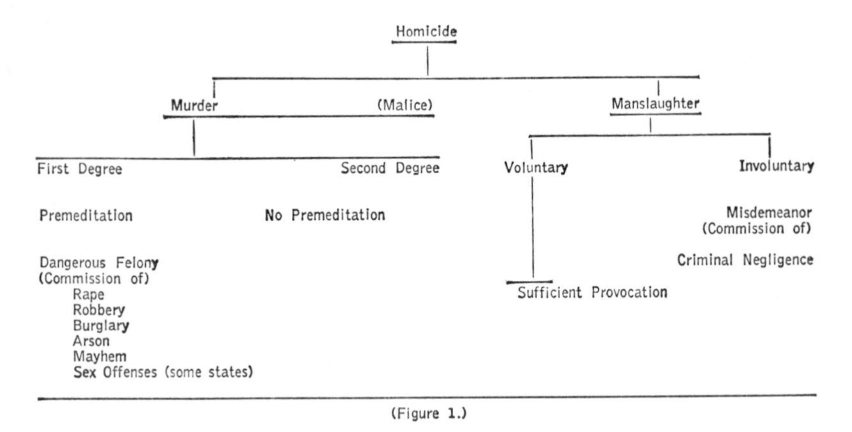

(Figure 1.)

The above chart is taken from Wm. E. Burby, Law Refresher, Criminal Law and Procedure, Fourth Edition. St. Paul, Minn.: West Publishing Company, 1969.

Murder. The deliberate, premeditated killing of another human being is murder, the highest form of criminal homicide.[8] Many

absence of circumstances which reduce the offense to negligent homicide or which excuse or justify the killing." Murder with malice and murder without malice are distinguished in the instructions to the jury. The instructions to the jury are that murder without malice is a "voluntary homicide committed without justification or excuse under the immediate influence of a sudden passion arising from an adequate cause, by which it is meant such cause as would commonly produce a degree of anger, rage, resentment, or terror in a person of ordinary temper sufficient to render the mind incapable of cool reflection."

8. Deliberation, premeditation, and willfulness may be inferred from the circumstances. The People v. Arthur R. Eggers, 30 Cal.2d 676, 185 P.2d 1 (1947), cert. den. 333 U.S. 858, 68 S.Ct. 728, 92 L.Ed. 1138, reh. den. 333 U.S. 870, 68 S.Ct. 786, 92 L.Ed. 1147.

West's Ann.Cal.Penal Code, § 187: Murder is the unlawful killing of a human being, with malice aforethought.

§ 188: Such malice may be express or implied. It is express when there is manifested a deliberate intention unlawfully to take away the life of a fellow creature. It is implied, when no considerable provocation appears, or when the circumstances attending the killing show an abandoned and malignant heart.

§ 189: All murder which is perpetrated by means of a bomb, poison, lying in wait, torture, or by any other kind of willful, deliberate and premeditated killing, or which is committed in the perpetration of, or attempt to perpetrate, arson, rape, robbery, burglary, mayhem, or any act punishable under Section 288, is murder of the first degree; and all other kinds of murders are of the second degree. As used in this section, 'bomb' includes any device, substance, or preparation, other than fixed ammunition or fireworks regulated under Part 2 (commencing with Section 12500) of Division 11 of the Health and Safety Code, which is designed to cause an explosion and is capable of causing death or serious bodily injury.

§ 190: Every person guilty of murder in the first degree shall suffer death, or confinement in the state prison for life, at the discretion of the court or jury trying the same, and the matter of punishment shall be determined as provided in Section 190.1, and every person guilty of murder in the second degree is punishable by imprisonment in the state prison from five years to life.

Smith-Hurd Ill.Ann.Stat. ch. 38, § 9–1: **Murder.**

(a) A person who kills an individual without lawful justification commits murder if, in performing the acts which cause the death: (1) he either intends to kill or do great bodily harm to that individual or another, or knows that such acts will cause death to that individual or another; or (2) he knows that such acts create a strong probability of death or great bodily harm to that individual or another; or (3) he is attempting or committing a forcible felony other than voluntary manslaughter.

(b) Penalty. A person convicted of murder shall be punished by death or imprisonment in the penitentiary for any indeterminate term with a minimum of not less than 14 years. If the accused is found guilty by a jury, a sentence of death shall not be imposed by the court unless the jury's verdict so provides in accordance with Section 1–7(c) (1) of this Code.

McKinney's N.Y.Penal Code, § 125.25: A person is guilty of murder when:

1. With intent to cause the death of another person, he causes the death of such person or of a third person; except that in any prosecution under this subdivision, it is an affirmative defense that:

   (a) The defendant acted under the influence of extreme emotional disturbance for which there was a reasonable explanation or excuse, the reasonableness of which is to be determined from the viewpoint of a person in the defendant's situation under the circumstances as the defendant believed them to be. Nothing contained in this paragraph shall constitute a defense to a prosecution for, or preclude a conviction of, manslaughter in the first degree or any other crime; or

   (b) The defendant's conduct consisted of causing or aiding, without the use of duress or deception, another person to commit suicide. Nothing contained in this paragraph shall constitute a defense to a prosecution for, or preclude a conviction of, manslaughter in the second degree or any other crime; or

2. Under circumstances evincing a depraved indifference to human life, he recklessly engages in conduct which creates a grave risk of death to another person, and thereby causes the death of another person; or

3. Acting either alone or with one or more other persons, he commits or attempts to commit robbery, burglary, kidnapping, arson, rape in the first degree, sodomy in the first degree, sexual abuse in the first degree, escape in the first degree, or escape in the second degree, and, in the course of and in furtherance of such crime or of immediate flight therefrom, he, or another participant, if there be any, causes the death of a person other than one of the participants; except that in any prosecution under this subdivision, in which the defendant was not the only participant in the underlying crime, it is an affirmative defense that the defendant:

   (a) Did not commit the homicidal act or in any way solicit, request, command, importune, cause or aid the commission thereof; and

states label such a deliberate premeditated murder "Murder in the First Degree" to distinguish it from murder in the heat of passion, but without legally sufficient provocation, which will be termed "Murder in the Second Degree." The penalty for Murder in the First Degree is usually death or life-imprisonment; for Murder in the Second Degree, a term of years less than life. Texas, as we have seen, distinguishes two types of murder, the higher degree being "Murder with Malice," including in the definition both deliberate, premeditated murder, and murder in the heat of passion without sufficient legal provocation. Homicide in the heat of passion caused by legally sufficient provocation is "Murder without Malice." [9] Other states have different terminology and

(b) Was not armed with a deadly weapon, or any instrument, article or substance readily capable of causing death or serious physical injury and of a sort not ordinarily carried in public places by law-abiding persons; and

(c) Had no reasonable ground to believe that any other participant was armed with such a weapon, instrument, article or substance; and

(d) Had no reasonable ground to believe that any other participant intended to engage in conduct likely to result in death or serious physical injury.

Vernon's Ann.Texas Penal Code, Art. 1256: Whoever shall voluntarily kill any person within this State shall be guilty of murder. Murder shall be distinguished from every other species of homicide by the absence of circumstances which reduce the offense to negligent homicide or which excuse or justify the killing. See fn. 6 *supra.*

9. Vernon's Ann.Texas Penal Code, Art. 1257b: In all cases tried under the provisions of this Act, it shall be the duty of the court to define "malice aforethought" and shall apply that term by appropriate charge to the facts in the case and shall instruct the jury that unless from all the facts and circumstances in evidence the jury believes the defendant was prompted and acted with his malice aforethought, they cannot assess the punishment at a period longer than five years; provided, however, that no offense committed prior to the taking effect of Chapter 274 of the General Laws of the 40th Legislature of 1927, shall be affected hereby whether an indictment has been returned or not, but in every such case the offender may be proceeded against and punished under the law as it existed prior to the taking effect of said act, the same as if said act had not been passed.

Art. 1257c: In all cases tried under the provisions of this Act it shall be the duty of the Court, where the facts present the issue of murder without malice, to instruct the jury that murder without malice is a voluntary homicide committed without justification or excuse under the immediate influence of a sudden passion arising from an adequate cause, by which it is meant such cause as would commonly produce a degree of anger, rage, resentment, or terror in a person of ordinary temper sufficient to render the mind incapable of cool reflection, and in appropriate terms in the charge to apply the law to the facts as developed from the evidence.

different classifications of murder, or have a single definition of murder.[10]

Regardless of the particular terminology used, the highest degree of murder is characterized by a deliberate, purposeful killing of another human being. A deliberate act which has as its purpose the taking of the life of another is a very dangerous act and the potential injury to the victim is great. Also, such a deliberate and planned act shows a very depraved and guilty mind, with none of the elements such as sudden passion or unplanned event which may characterize a lesser degree of homicide.

The Felony Murder Rule. The state of mind of the offender is such an important element in determining the degree of culpability that under some circumstances a killing which is not done deliberately or purposely may nevertheless constitute the highest degree of murder—First Degree Murder, Murder with Malice—whatever it is called in the particular state. Thus, a burglar may enter a room at night only to take the jewelry, and without the slightest intention of killing the occupant of the room. He may have agreed with his confederates waiting outside that "there will be no shooting." He may not even carry a weapon. But suppose after he enters the room, the occupant wakes up and reaches for a gun. The burglar gets the gun first and shoots and kills the occupant. The laws says that the burglar, under these circumstances, is guilty of the highest degree of murder.[11]

The way the law reasons is this: The burglar entered the house with the intent to commit a felony. This intent amounted to malice, a guilty mind, criminal intent—the *mens rea.* The fact that the burglar's guilty intent was only to take the jewelry will not be heard in defense of the killing. He entered with "malice," i. e., the intent to commit one crime. He cannot use this to excuse himself for the crime which actually occurred. True, he did not plan the killing, but it happened in the course of carrying out his original felonious purpose. The law says that the criminal intent which originally was directed toward committing a theft will be transferred to the killing which actually took place. The

10. West's Ann.Cal.Penal Code, § 189. See fn. 8 *supra.*

McKinney's N.Y.Penal Law, § 125.25. See fn. 8 *supra.*

Smith-Hurd Ill.Ann.Stat. ch. 38, § 9–1. See fn. 8 *supra.*

11. A killing occurring during the commission of a burglary is murder in the first degree. The People v. Fallie Sutton, 17 Cal.App.2d 561, 62 P.2d 397 (1936).

thief will be deemed to have deliberately done what he actually did do—namely, kill the occupant. This rule is called the "felony murder rule."

The effect of this rule is that the intent directed toward the commission of one felony will transfer to the felony actually committed, and the highest penalty which can be assessed against the offense actually committed may be imposed on the offender. A murder which takes place under these circumstances is sometimes given the special label of "felony murder," though this does not mean this is the only homicide which is a felony. In this sense, "felony murder" means a murder committed in the course of perpetrating another felony.

Manslaughter. Homicides which are the result of reckless, as opposed to purposeful acts, may, depending on the degree of recklessness, constitute a lower level of homicide than murder, and homicides by negligence, the lowest culpable homicide of all. Reckless homicides which are not so reckless as to manifest a callous disregard of human life, and negligent homicides, are commonly called "manslaughter." Some states distinguish first and second degree manslaughter. Others use a different terminology altogether. Texas, as we have seen, labels the two lowest homicide offenses "Homicide by Negligence in the Second Degree" and "Homicide by Negligence in the First Degree," and has no offense called "Manslaughter." [12]

California has three manslaughter offenses—voluntary manslaughter, involuntary manslaughter, and manslaughter in driving a motor vehicle.[13] A killing upon a sudden quarrel or in the

12. Vernon's Ann.Texas Penal Code, Arts. 1224 to 1255, repealed 1927.

13. West's Ann.Penal Code, § 192: Manslaughter is the unlawful killing of a human being, without malice. It is of three kinds:

1. Voluntary—upon a sudden quarrel or heat of passion.

2. Involuntary—in the commission of an unlawful act, not amounting to felony; or in the commission of a lawful act which might produce death, in an unlawful manner, or without due caution and circumspection; provided that this subdivision shall not apply to acts committed in the driving of a vehicle.

3. In the driving of a vehicle—

(a) In the commission of an unlawful act, not amounting to felony, with gross negligence; or in the commission of a lawful act which might produce death, in an unlawful manner, and with gross negligence.

(b) In the commission of an unlawful act, not amounting to felony, without gross negligence; or in the commission of a lawful act which might produce death, in an unlawful manner, but without gross negligence.

This section shall not be construed as making any homicide in the driving of a vehicle pun-

heat of passion is voluntary manslaughter and is distinguished from murder in that murder involves a deliberate killing. No deliberate killing is voluntary manslaughter. Also, in the case of voluntary manslaughter, the defendant must have acted with legal provocation. Lack of legal provocation would transform the offense into second degree murder. Involuntary manslaughter covers the situation where death results from the commission of an unlawful act not amounting to a felony.

New York distinguishes between manslaughter in the first degree and manslaughter in the second degree and has an offense category called Criminally Negligent Homicide.[14] A person may be guilty of Criminally Negligent Homicide in New York if he did not have a specific intent to violate the law.[15]

ishable which is not a proximate result of the commission of an unlawful act, not amounting to felony, or of the commission of a lawful act which might produce death, in an unlawful manner.

14. McKinney's N.Y. Penal Law, § 125.20: A person is guilty of manslaughter in the first degree when:

1. With intent to cause serious physical injury to another person, he causes the death of such person or of a third person; or

2. With intent to cause the death of another person, he causes the death of such person or of a third person under circumstances which do not constitute murder because he acts under the influence of extreme emotional disturbance, as defined in paragraph (a) of subdivision one of section 125.25. The fact that homicide was committed under the influence of extreme emotional disturbance constitutes a mitigating circumstance reducing murder to manslaughter in the first degree and need not be proved in any prosecution initiated under this subdivision; or

3. He commits upon a female pregnant for more than twenty-four weeks an abortional act which causes her death, unless such abortional act is justifiable pursuant to subdivision three of section 125.05.

Manslaughter in the first degree is a Class B felony.

§ 125.15: A person is guilty of manslaughter in the second degree when:

1. He recklessly causes the death of another person; or

2. He commits upon a female an abortional act which causes her death, unless such abortional act is justifiable pursuant to subdivision three of section 125.05; or

3. He intentionally causes or aids another person to commit suicide.

Manslaughter in the second degree is a Class C felony.

§ 125.10: A person is guilty of criminally negligent homicide when, with criminal negligence, he causes the death of another person.

Criminally negligent homicide is a Class E felony.

15. For example, in one case the landlord was convicted of manslaughter because of the inability of two of his tenants to escape from his building which was not provided with adequate fire protection as required by law. People v. Nelson, 309 N.Y. 231, 128 N.E.2d 391 (1955).

Illinois recognizes the offense of voluntary manslaughter and offenses called Involuntary Manslaughter and Reckless Homicide.[16]

Model Penal Code Definitions of Criminal Homicide. The elements of criminal homicide, according to the Model Penal Code, are (1) purposely, knowingly, recklessly, or negligently (2) causing the death of (3) another human being. Elsewhere the Code defines a human being as "a person who has been born and is alive." The grade or degree of the offense depends on whether the homicide was committed purposely, recklessly, or negligently.

The Model Penal Code provisions are as follows:

Section 210.1 Criminal Homicide.

(1) A person is guilty of criminal homicide if he purposely, knowingly, recklessly, or negligently causes the death of another human being.

16. Smith-Hurd Ill.Ann.Stat. ch. 38, § 9.2:

(a) A person who kills an individual without lawful justification commits voluntary manslaughter if at the time of the killing he is acting under a sudden and intense passion resulting from serious provocation by:

(1) The individual killed, or

(2) Another whom the offender endeavors to kill, but he negligently or accidentally causes the death of the individual killed.

Serious provocation is conduct sufficient to excite an intense passion in a reasonable person.

(b) A person who intentionally or knowingly kills an individual commits voluntary manslaughter if at the time of the killing he believes the circumstances to be such that, if they existed, would justify or exonerate the killing under the principles stated in Article 7 of this Code, but his belief is unreasonable.

(c) Penalty. A person convicted of voluntary manslaughter shall be imprisoned in the penitentiary from one to 20 years.

§ 9.3:

(a) A person who kills an individual without lawful justification commits involuntary manslaughter if his acts whether lawful or unlawful which cause the death are such as are likely to cause death or great bodily harm to some individual, and he performs them recklessly.

(b) If the acts which cause the death consist of the driving of a motor vehicle, the person may be prosecuted for reckless homicide or if he is prosecuted for involuntary manslaughter, he may be found guilty of the included offense of reckless homicide.

(c) Penalty.

(1) A person convicted of involuntary manslaughter shall be imprisoned in the penitentiary from one to 10 years.

(2) A person convicted of reckless homicide shall be fined not to exceed $1,000 or imprisoned in a penal institution other than the penitentiary not to exceed one year, or in the penitentiary from one to 5 years, or both fined and imprisoned.

(2) Criminal homicide is murder, manslaughter or negligent homicide.

Section 210.2 Murder.

(1) Except as provided in Section 210.3(1) (b), criminal homicide constitutes murder when:

(a) it is committed purposely or knowingly; or

(b) it is committed recklessly under circumstances manifesting extreme indifference to the value of human life. Such recklessness and indifference are presumed if the actor is engaged or is an accomplice in the commission of, or an attempt to commit, or flight, after committing or attempting to commit robbery, rape or deviate sexual intercourse by force or threat of force, arson, burglary, kidnapping or felonious escape.

(2) Murder is a felony of the first degree (but a person convicted of murder may be sentenced to death, as provided in Section 210.6).

Section 210.3 Manslaughter.

(1) Criminal homicide constitutes manslaughter when:

(a) it is committed recklessly; or

(b) a homicide which would otherwise be murder is committed under the influence of extreme mental or emotional disturbance for which there is reasonable explanation or excuse. The reasonableness of such explanation or excuse shall be determined from the viewpoint of a person in the actor's situation under the circumstances as he believes them to be.

(2) Manslaughter is a felony of the second degree.

Section 210.4 Negligent Homicide.

(1) Criminal homicide constitutes negligent homicide when it is committed negligently.

(2) Negligent homicide is a felony of the third degree.

The grading of the homicide offense in the Model Penal Code as murder, manslaughter, or negligent homicide is based upon a logical pattern arrived at according to the character of the act and state of mind of the offender, i. e., whether the accused acts purposely, recklessly, or negligently. The Code also brings within its grading scheme factors which have commonly differentiated degrees of homicide—for example the difference between deliberate, premeditated (cold blooded murder) and murder committed in the heat of passion upon sufficient provocation (hot blooded murder). Society has always considered "cold blooded murder" to be deserving of maximum punishment while tending toward a lenient penalty for murder in the heat of passion.

Sentencing for the Homicide Offenses Under the Model Penal Code. The Model Penal Code goes further than the statutes of most states in setting out the factors which must be taken into consideration in sentencing. The state statutes set out minimum and maximum penalties, but are relatively silent on the criteria to be used in arriving at the sentence in a particular case. Thus a judge or jury sentencing for a homicide offense may sentence to death with few criteria to guide them. The Model Penal Code, on the other hand, not only sets out general criteria for sentencing but provides specific criteria to be taken into consideration in homicide offenses where the penalty may be death.

The Code provides for the death penalty for murder under *aggravating circumstances.* These include murder committed by a convict under sentence of imprisonment; murder by a defendant previously convicted of another murder or felony involving the use of threat of violence; murder in escaping or resisting lawful arrest; a multiple murder; murder for pecuniary gain; or a murder which was especially heinous or cruel.[17] (This is an alternative formulation of Article 210.6. The principle formulation provides for sentencing for murder as a first degree felony which carries a maximum penalty of life imprisonment.)

The Code also sets out certain *mitigating circumstances* which will prevent the death penalty and serve to reduce the sentence. These mitigating circumstances include: that the defendant has no significant prior criminal record; that the murder was committed when defendant was under the influence of extreme mental or emotional disturbance; that the victim consented to the homicidal act; that the murder was committed under circumstances which the defendant believed to provide a moral justification for his conduct; that the defendant was an accomplice in a murder committed by another and his participation in the act was relatively minor; that at the time of the murder the capacity of the

17. MPC 210.6(3).

defendant to appreciate the criminality (wrongfulness) of his conduct or to conform his conduct to the requirements of the law was impaired as a result of mental disease or defect or intoxication; and the youth of the defendant at the time of the crime.[18]

ASSAULT

The assault (often called Assault and Battery) offenses are also crimes against the person. They differ from the homicide offenses in that death does not result. The crime of assault in modern times is seen as a protection of people from the fear of receiving bodily harm at the hands of another. Assault offenses are usually graded according to the amount of injury inflicted upon the victim and according to whether or not a dangerous weapon was used.

Elements of the Offense of Assault. The elements of the offense of assault, or assault and battery, are:

1. Conduct of a kind to create in the victim fear of receiving bodily harm;
2. By a person who has the apparent present ability to carry out the threat, and who intends to commit the offense;
3. Which results in bodily harm to the victim.

To constitute an assault there must be commencement of an act which if not prevented would produce a battery. A battery is the unlawful and unauthorized infliction of bodily harm to the person of another, or the unlawful touching of the person of another with a wrongful or injurious purpose and without his consent. A touching is unlawful if done in anger, revenge, rudeness, or in a hostile manner.

Intent was required by common law and could be inferred from express malice or wantonness, defined as conscious disregard of the human interest of the victim. Modern statutes dispense with the strict requirement of proving intent, or impute intent from the nature of the act of the perpetrator.

Bodily harm as referred to in assault means any unauthorized, unlawful physical conduct or touching.

18. MPC 210.6(4).

In California, assault is defined as an "unlawful attempt coupled with a present ability to commit a violent injury on the person of another." [19]

Some states combine the offense of assault with the intent to commit a specific crime, as assault with intent to commit murder, assault with intent to commit rape, and so on.

In California, the additional assault offenses are called assault by prisoner, assault by a public officer without necessity, assault on executive and judicial officers, assault with caustic chemicals, assault with a deadly weapon or force likely to produce injury, assault with intent to commit rape, sodomy, mayhem, robbery, or grand larceny, assault with intent to commit enumerated fel-

19. West's Ann.Cal.Penal Code, § 240.

See also, Vernon's Ann.Texas Penal Code, Art. 1138: The use of any unlawful violence upon the person of another with intent to injure him, whatever be the means or the degree of violence used, is an assault and battery. Any attempt to commit a battery, or any threatening gesture showing in itself or by words accompanying it, an immediate intention, coupled with an ability to commit a battery, is an assault.

Art. 1147: An assault or battery becomes aggravated when committed under any of the following circumstances:

(1) When committed upon an officer in the lawful discharge of the duties of his office, if it was known or declared to the offender that the person assaulted was an officer discharging an official duty.

(2) When committed in a Court of Justice, or in any place of religious worship, or in any place where persons are assembled for the purpose of innocent amusement.

(3) When the person committing the offense goes into the house of a private family and is there guilty of an assault and battery.

(4) When committed by a person of robust health or strength upon one who is aged or decrepit.

(5) When the instrument or means used is such as inflicts disgrace upon the person assaulted, as an assault or battery with a whip or cowhide.

(6) When a serious bodily injury is inflicted upon the person assaulted.

(7) When committed with deadly weapons under circumstances not amounting to an intent to murder or maim.

(8) When committed with premeditated design, and by the use of means calculated to inflict great bodily injury.

(9) When committed by an adult male upon the person of a female or child or by an adult female upon the person of a child. * * *

(10) When committed with a knife under circumstances not amounting to an intent to murder or maim.

Assaults with intent to commit other offenses are separate offenses. They include assaults with intent to maim, disfigure, or castrate; to murder; to rape; to rob; and in attempting burglary. See Vernon's Ann.Texas Penal Code, Art. 1159–1165. Proof is of the assault coupled with an intention to commit the other offense. See Art. 1165.

onies, and assault with intent to commit murder. The definition of some of these offenses is set out below.[20]

Aggravated Assault. Some states aggravate assault according to the amount of injury received, thus aggravated assault would be an assault which inflicts serious bodily injury.[21] Other states aggravate assault according to whether a deadly weapon is used [22] or the perpetrator is in disguise. Sometimes the character of the assault is determined by the position held by the victim, as where the victim was a school teacher and the assault occurred on the school grounds.[23] Aggravated assault is a felony, and carries a higher punishment than a simple assault.

Simple Assault. An assault which is not an aggravated assault is a simple assault. An attack on another which causes bodily injury of a kind not included in the definition of "serious bodily injury" is a simple assault. As we have seen, any unlawful touching of one person by another is an assault, though most actions of assault are those in which some actual injury, however minor, has occurred, or the offender has attempted by physical means to put another in fear of imminent serious bodily harm. Simple

20. West's Ann.Penal Code, § 217: Assault With Intent to Commit Murder. Every person who assaults another with intent to commit murder, is punishable by imprisonment in the State Prison not less than one nor more than fourteen years.

§ 220: Every person who assaults another with intent to commit rape, the infamous crime against nature, mayhem, robbery, or grand larceny, is punishable by imprisonment in the State Prison not less than one year nor more than twenty years.

§ 221: Every person who is guilty of an assault, with intent to commit any felony, except an assault with intent to commit murder, the punishment for which assault is not prescribed by the preceding section, is punishable by imprisonment in the State Prison not exceeding 15 years, or in a county jail not exceeding one year, or by fine not exceeding five hundred dollars ($500), or by both.

21. MPC 210.0(3): Serious bodily injury means bodily injury which creates a substantial risk of death or which causes serious, permanent disfigurement, or protracted loss or impairment of the function of any bodily member or organ.

Marshall v. State, 34 Tex.Cr.R. 22, 36 S.W. 1062 (1894).

22. MPC 210.0(4): Deadly weapon means any firearm, or other weapon, device, instrument, material or substance, whether animate or inanimate, which in the manner it is used or is intended to be used is known to be capable of producing death or serious bodily injury.

In some states, such an offense is a separate offense called "Assault With a Deadly Weapon."

23. Lorenson, "Aggravated Assault in West Virginia." 62 *W.V.L., Rev.*, 319 (1960).

State v. Kuchmak, 159 Ohio St. 363, 112 N.E.2d 371 (1953).

assault is a misdemeanor, or, as in the Model Penal Code, a petty misdemeanor.

The assault offenses in Illinois are defined in Art. 12 "Bodily Harm," and consist of Assault, Aggravated Assault, Battery, and Aggravated Battery.[24]

24. Smith-Hurd Ann.Stat. ch. 38, § 12–1: Assault. (a) A person commits an assault when, without lawful authority, he engages in conduct which places another in reasonable apprehension of receiving a battery. (b) Penalty. A person convicted of assault shall be fined not to exceed $500.

§ 12–2: Aggravated Assault. (a) A person commits an aggravated assault, when, in committing an assault, he:

(1) Uses a deadly weapon; or

(2) Is hooded, robed or masked, in such manner as to conceal his identity; or

(3) Knows the individual assaulted to be a teacher or other person employed in any school and such teacher or other employee is upon the grounds of a school or grounds adjacent thereto, or is in any part of a building used for school purposes; or

(4) Knows the individual assaulted to be a supervisor, director, instructor or other person employed in any park district and such supervisor, director, instructor or other employee is upon the grounds of the park or grounds adjacent thereto, or is in any part of a building used for park purposes.

(b) Penalty. A person convicted of aggravated assault shall be fined not to exceed $1,000 or imprisoned in a penal institution other than the penitentiary not to exceed one year, or both.

§ 12–3: Battery. (a) A person commits battery if he intentionally or knowingly without legal justification and by any means, (1) causes bodily harm to an individual or (2) makes physical contact of an insulting or provoking nature with an individual. (b) Penalty. A person convicted of battery shall be fined not to exceed $500 or imprisoned in a penal institution other than the penitentiary not to exceed 6 months, or both.

§ 12–4: Aggravated Battery. (a) A person who, in committing a battery, intentionally or knowingly causes great bodily harm, or permanent disability or disfigurement commits aggravated battery and shall be imprisoned in a penal institution other than the penitentiary not to exceed one year or in the penitentiary from one to 10 years.

(b) A person who, in committing a battery, either:

(1) Uses a deadly weapon; or

(2) Is hooded, robed or masked, in such manner as to conceal his identity; or

(3) Knows the individual harmed to be a teacher or other person employed in any school and such teacher or other employee is upon the grounds of a school or grounds adjacent thereto, or is in any part of a building used for school purposes; or

(4) Knows the individual harmed to be a supervisor, director, instructor or other person employed in any park district and such supervisor, director, instructor or other employee is upon the grounds of the park or grounds adjacent thereto, or is in any part of a building used for park purposes; commits aggravated battery and

The related offenses are Reckless Conduct,[25] Intimidation,[26] and Compelling Confession or Information by Force or Threat.[27] Dueling is one of the bodily harm offenses,[28] as is Tattooing a Minor.[29]

Assault in New York is defined in degrees as assault in the third degree, assault in the second degree, and assault in the first degree,[30] and several special assault offenses are recognized.[31]

shall be imprisoned in a penal institution other than the penitentiary not to exceed one year or in the penitentiary from one to 5 years.

(c) A person who administers to an individual or causes him to take, without his consent or by threat or deception, and for other than medical purposes, any intoxicating, poisonous, stupefying, narcotic or anesthetic substance commits aggravated battery and shall be imprisoned in a penal institution other than the penitentiary not to exceed one year or in the penitentiary from one to 5 years.

25. Smith-Hurd Ill.Ann.Stat. ch. 38, § 12.5.

26. *Ibid*, § 12.6.

27. *Ibid*, § 12.7.

28. *Ibid*, § 12.8.

29. *Ibid*, § 12.10.

30. McKinney's Penal Law, § 120.00: A person is guilty of assault in the third degree when:

1. With intent to cause physical injury to another person, he causes such injury to such person or to a third person; or
2. He recklessly causes physical injury to another person; or
3. With criminal negligence, he causes physical injury to another person by means of a deadly weapon or a dangerous instrument.

Assault in the third degree is a Class A misdemeanor.

§ 120.05: A person is guilty of assault in the second degree when:

1. With intent to cause serious physical injury to another person, he causes such injury to such person or to a third person; or
2. With intent to cause physical injury to another person, he causes such injury to such person or to a third person by means of a deadly weapon or a dangerous instrument; or

   With intent to prevent a peace officer from performing a lawful duty, he uses physical injury to such peace officer; or
4. He recklessly causes serious physical injury to another person by means of a deadly weapon or a dangerous instrument; or
5. For a purpose other than lawful medical or therapeutic treatment, he intentionally causes stupor, unconsciousness or other physical impairment or injury to another person by administering to him, without his consent, a drug, substance or preparation capable of producing the same.
6. In the course of and in furtherance of the commission or attempted commission of a felony, other than a felony defined in article one hundred thirty, or of immediate flight therefrom, he, or another participant if there be any, causes

31. See note 31 on page 122.

Model Penal Code Definition of Assault. The Model Penal Code divides the assault offenses into (1) Simple Assault, which is a misdemeanor, unless committed in a fight or scuffle entered into by mutual consent, in which case it is a petty misdemeanor; and (2) Aggravated Assault, which involves serious bodily injury or attempts to cause serious bodily injury, inflicted purposely or with the higher degree of recklessness, and attempts purposely or knowingly to cause bodily injury to another with a deadly weapon. Aggravated Assault is either a second or third degree felony depending on the circumstances. The Code also defines assault offenses called "Recklessly Endangering Another Person," which includes pointing a firearm at another person whether or not the actor believed the firearm to be loaded, which is a misdemeanor, and "Terroristic Threats," which is a third degree felony.

Section 211.1 Assault.

(1) *Simple Assault.* A person is guilty of assault if he:

(a) attempts to cause or purposely, knowingly or recklessly causes bodily injury to another; or

(b) negligently causes bodily injury to another with a deadly weapon; or

physical injury to a person other than one of the participants.

Assault in the second degree is a Class D felony.

§ 120.10: A person is guilty of assault in the first degree when:

1. With intent to cause serious physical injury to another person, he causes such injury to such person or to a third person by means of a deadly weapon or a dangerous instrument; or
2. With intent to disfigure another person seriously and permanently, or to destroy, amputate or disable permanently a member or organ of his body, he causes such injury to such person or to a third person; or
3. Under circumstances evincing a depraved indifference to human life, he recklessly engages in conduct which creates a grave risk of death to another person, and thereby causes serious physical injury to another person; or
4. In the course of and in furtherance of the commission or attempted commission of a felony or of immediate flight therefrom, he, or another participant if there be any, causes serious physical injury to a person other than one of the participants.

Assault in the first degree is a Class C felony.

31. Menacing (see § 120.15), reckless endangerment in the second degree (see § 120.20), reckless endangerment in the first degree (see § 120.-25), promoting a suicide attempt (see §§ 120.30, 120.35).

(c) attempts by physical menace to put another in fear of imminent serious bodily harm.

Simple assault is a misdemeanor unless committed in a fight or scuffle entered into by mutual consent, in which case it is a petty misdemeanor.

(2) *Aggravated Assault.* A person is guilty of aggravated assault if he:

(a) attempts to cause serious bodily injury to another, or causes such injury purposely, knowingly or recklessly under circumstances manifesting extreme indifference to the value of human life; or

(b) attempts to cause or purposely or knowingly causes bodily injury to another with a deadly weapon.

Aggravated assault under paragraph (a) is a felony of the second degree; aggravated assault under paragraph (b) is a felony of the third degree.

Section 211.2 Recklessly Endangering Another Person.

A person commits a misdemeanor if he recklessly engages in conduct which places or may place another person in danger of death or serious bodily injury. Recklessness and danger shall be presumed where a person knowingly points a firearm at or in the direction of another, whether or not the actor believed the firearm to be loaded.

Section 211.3 Terroristic Threats.

A person is guilty of a felony of the third degree if he threatens to commit any crime of violence with purpose to terrorize another or to cause evacuation of a building, place of assembly, or facility of public transportation, or otherwise to cause serious public inconvenience, or in reckless disregard of the risk of causing such terror or inconvenience.

RAPE AND OTHER SEXUAL OFFENSES

We learned in the chapter entitled "What is a Crime?" that some of the first rules of a developing society are in the interest of preserving the purity of the blood, which means regulations as to marriage and sexual intercourse. Because the rules about intercourse, both within and without marriage and family formation, are peculiarly culture-based, rules of sexual behavior vary widely from culture to culture and in points of time. Sexual conduct has also always been of paramount concern to religious groups, resulting in most societies in a close and difficult relationship between law and morals.

It would be fair to say that at the present time ideas about sexual intercourse are in the process of change in the American culture. Offenses covering homosexuality, sexual relationships between consenting unmarried adults, deviant sexual acts, and the like, are being redefined in many states and there is great social pressure for continued redefinition. The Model Penal Code reflects many of these changing ideas.

Elements of the Offense of Rape. Traditionally, the crime of rape involves these elements:

1. sexual intercourse by a male with a female who is not his wife;
2. against her will; and
3. compelled by force or threat; or
4. performed upon an unconscious female or a drugged or intoxicated female, who was unable to resist.[32]

32. Rape is defined in Illinois as follows: Smith-Hurd Ill.Ann.Stat. ch. 38, § 11.1. Rape.

(a) A male person of the age of 14 years and upwards who has sexual intercourse with a female, not his wife, by force and against her will, commits rape. Intercourse by force and against her will includes, but is not limited to, any intercourse which occurs in the following situations:

(1) Where the female is unconscious; or

(2) Where the female is so mentally deranged or deficient that she cannot give effective consent to intercourse.

(b) Sexual intercourse occurs when there is any penetration of the female sex organ by the male sex organ.

(c) Penalty. A person convicted of rape shall be imprisoned in the penitentiary for *an* indeterminate term with a minimum of not less than one year.

In New York, rape offenses are classified as Rape in the Third Degree, Rape in the Second Degree, and Rape in the First Degree:

McKinney's Penal Law, § 130.25. Rape in the third degree. A male is guilty of rape in the third degree when:

1. He engages in sexual intercourse with a female who is incapable of consent by reason of some factor other than being less than seventeen years old; or

The penalty for rape in many states is death or life imprisonment, or any term of years less than life.

At common law, any male who had reached the age of puberty was capable of committing rape. Certain state statutes require

2. Being twenty-one years old or more, he engages in sexual intercourse with a female less than seventeen years old.

Rape in the third degree is a Class E felony.

§ 130.30. Rape in the second degree.

A male is guilty of rape in the second degree, when being eighteen years old or more, he engages in sexual intercourse with a female less than fourteen years old.

Rape in the second degree is a Class D felony.

§ 130.35. Rape in the first degree.

A male is guilty of rape in the first degree when he engages in sexual intercourse with a female:

1. By forcible compulsion; or
2. Who is incapable of consent by reason of being physically helpless; or
3. Who is less than eleven years old.

Rape in the first degree is a Class B felony.

In California, the statute reads as follows: West's Ann.Penal Code, § 261. Rape defined. Rape is an act of sexual intercourse, accomplished with a female not the wife of the perpetrator, under either of the following circumstances:

1. Where the female is under the age of eighteen years;
2. Where she is incapable, through lunacy or other unsoundness of mind, whether temporary or permanent, of giving legal consent;
3. Where she resists, but her resistance is overcome by force or violence;
4. Where she is prevented from resisting by threats of great and immediate bodily harm, accompanied by apparent power of execution, or by any intoxicating narcotic, or anaesthetic substance, administered by or with the privity of the accused;
5. Where she is at the time unconscious of the nature of the act, and this is known to the accused;
6. Where she submits under the belief that the person committing the act is her husband, and this belief is induced by any artifice, pretense, or concealment practiced by the accused, with intent to induce such belief.

In Texas, the statute reads as follaws: Vernon's Ann.Texas Penal Code, Art. 1183: Rape. Rape is the carnal knowledge of a woman without her consent obtained by force, threats or fraud; or the carnal knowledge of a woman other than the wife of the person having such carnal knowledge with or without consent and with or without the use of force, threats or fraud, such woman being so mentally diseased at the time as to have no will to oppose the act of carnal knowledge, the person having carnal knowledge of her knowing her to be so mentally diseased; or the carnal knowledge of a female under the age of eighteen years other than the wife of the person with or without her consent and with or without the use of force, threats or fraud; provided that if she is fifteen years of age or over the defendant may show in consent cases she was not of previous chaste character as a defense.

that the male must have attained a certain age (usually 14 years) before he can be charged with the offense, or physical ability to commit the act must be affirmatively proved.[33] The age of the female was 10 years at common law; over the age of 10 years, she was capable of giving consent. Since an element of the crime was that the sexual intercourse be against the will of the female, consent to the act by the female did away with an essential element of the offense.

Force is a necessary element of the crime of rape, though no particular amount of force need be used. However, the force must exist in the form of physical violence or threats leading to violence to induce the female to be physically subjected to the male.

Generally, a high order of proof is required to convict a man of rape; the unsupported testimony of the victim is usually not enough. The reason is that the crime is considered to be a heinous one, and one which is not infrequently charged for reasons of revenge or ill-will. The states which do not require corroborating testimony nevertheless require the testimony given by the prosecutrix in a rape case be "clear and convincing." Statutes of limitations on rape are often very short. The action must be brought promptly, usually within a year from the date of the offense. In spite of these safeguards, many legal scholars believe that innocent men are convicted of rape.

Statutory Rape. Statutory Rape is often a separate offense,[34] or sexual intercourse with a female under a specified age may be

33. West's Ann.Cal.Penal Code, § 262: When Physical Ability Must be Proved. No conviction for rape can be had against one who was under the age of fourteen years at the time of the act alleged, unless his physical ability to accomplish penetration is proved as an independent fact, and beyond a reasonable doubt.

34. Smith-Hurd Ill.Ann.Stat. ch. 38, § 11–4. Indecent Liberties with a Child.

(a) Any person of the age of 17 years and upwards who performs or submits to any of the following acts with a child under the age of 16 commits indecent liberties with a child:

(1) Any act of sexual intercourse; or

(2) Any act of deviate sexual conduct; or

(3) Any lewd fondling or touching of either the child or the person done or submitted to with the intent to arouse or to satisfy the sexual desires of either the child or the person or both.

included in the general definition of the offense.[35] It differs from the crime of rape in that (a) force or threats are not a necessary element and (b) the commission of the offense depends solely on the *age* of the victim. The laws of the various states vary widely as to the age below which any sexual intercourse with a female not his wife makes a male guilty of statutory rape.[36] In many states the age is as high as 18 years. This means that technically any male who has sexual intercourse with a female below 18 years of age who is not his wife, whether or not she consents to the intercourse, is guilty of statutory rape. The actual age of the female controls, no matter how old she looks or pretends to be.

As strange as it may seem, some females are in state penitentiaries convicted of the crime of rape. A woman found guilty of this offense has helped a male to rape another female—the usual situation being when an older woman assists a man in introducing a girl into a life of prostitution.

While almost all persons in a society abhor the forceful violation of a female and are in accord with severe penalties for rape of a very young child, not all persons believe that the male should be deemed guilty of a crime because of intercourse with a consenting female, particularly if the male and female are about the same age. In the Model Penal Code, only intercourse by force or

(b) It shall be an affirmative defense to indecent liberties with a child that:

(1) The accused reasonably believed the child was of the age of 16 or upwards at the time of the act giving rise to the charge; or

(2) The child is a prostitute; or

(3) The child has previously been married.

(c) Penalty. A person convicted of indecent liberties with a child shall be imprisoned in the penitentiary from one to 20 years.

35. See fn. 32, *supra*, West's Ann. Cal.Penal Code, § 261.

36. In Oregon and Alaska, the statutory age is 16; in Kentucky, 12; in California and Texas, 18; in Illinois, 16. In New York, the degree of the crime increases in proportion to the youthfulness of the victim and the age of the defendant. It is first degree rape for a male of any age to have sexual intercourse with a female under the age of 11. A male over 18 commits second degree rape if he has intercourse with a female under 14. A male over 21 who has sexual intercourse with a female under 17 can be found guilty of third degree rape. See fn. 32, *supra*, McKinney's N.Y. Penal Law, §§ 130.25, 130.30, 130.35. In Texas, where the statutory age is 18, the defendant may show by way of defense concerning a female between 15 and 18 years of age that she was not of previous chaste character. See fn. 32, *supra*, Vernon's Ann.Texas Penal Code, Art. 1183.

with an unconscious or drugged woman, or with a female who is less than ten years old, is defined as rape. The crime in the Code is classified as a felony in the second degree, which limits the ordinary penalty to ten years unless serious bodily harm is inflicted upon the victim, in which case the offense is a felony in the first degree. The offense which is now called "Statutory Rape," in most states is a felony of the third degree and is called Corruption of Minors and Seduction in the Model Penal Code. The distinguishing feature of the Model Penal Code definition is that the female must be less than 16 years old and the male be at least four years older than the female.

Other Sexual Offenses. The Codes of all of the representative states define many sexual offenses in addition to rape. In New York the list includes Sexual Misconduct, Consensual Sodomy, first, second, and third degree Sodomy, and Sexual Abuse in the first, second, and third degree. California has offenses entitled: Abduction for Marriage or Defilement; Inveiglement or Enticement of an Unmarried Female Under Eighteen for Purposes of Prostitution; Abduction or Procurement by Fraudulent Inducement for Prostitution; Sale of Female for Immoral Purposes; Pimping; Pandering; Seduction Under Promise of Marriage; Cohabitation and Adultery, as well as Bigamy, Incest, and Crimes Against Nature. Illinois identifies the offenses of Deviate Sexual Conduct; Deviate Sexual Assault; Indecent Liberties with a Child; Contributing to the Sexual Delinquency of a Child; Adultery; Fornication; Public Indecency; Incest; Bigamy; Prostitution; Pimping; Pandering; Patronizing a Prostitute; and Obscenity. Texas defines similar sex offenses, the Sodomy statute being so extremely broad in the conduct prohibited that it was successfully challenged as to its Constitutionality in a three-judge decision in the United States District Court for the Northern District of Texas.[37]

A mere reading of the list of sexual crimes illustrates the point we have already made—a society expresses in the law its values regarding sexual conduct.

37. The appeal to the United States Supreme Court was dismissed. Pruett v. Texas, 402 U.S. 939, 91 S.Ct. 1601, 29 L.Ed.2d 108 (1971). The Supreme Court held that the sodomy statute was constitutional, the decision of the three judge federal court to the contrary notwithstanding. The Supreme Court pointed out that the federal district court decision was not binding on the state until the highest court of the state was afforded the opportunity of ruling on the legislation.

Model Penal Code Provisions Relating to Sexual Offenses. The pertinent provisions of the Model Penal Code are as follows:

Section 213.1 Rape and Related Offenses.

(1) *Rape.* A man who has sexual intercourse with a female not his wife is guilty of rape if:

(a) he compels her to submit by force or by threat of imminent death, serious bodily injury, or extreme pain or kidnapping, to be inflicted on anyone; or

(b) he has substantially impaired her power to appraise or control her conduct by administering or employing without her knowledge drugs, intoxicants or other means for the purpose of preventing resistance; or

(c) the female is unconscious; or

(d) the female is less than 10 years old.

Rape is a felony of the second degree unless (i) in the course thereof the actor inflicts serious bodily injury upon anyone, or (ii) the victim was not a voluntary social companion of the actor upon the occasion of the crime and had not previously permitted him sexual liberties, in which cases the offense is a felony of the first degree. Sexual intercourse includes intercourse per os or per anum, with some penetration however slight; emission is not required.

(2) *Gross Sexual Imposition.* A male who has sexual intercourse with a female not his wife commits a felony of the third degree if:

(a) he compels her to submit by any threat that would prevent resistance by a woman of ordinary resolution; or

(b) he knows that she suffers from a mental disease or defect which renders her incapable of appraising the nature of her conduct; or

(c) he knows that she is unaware that a sexual act is being committed upon her or that she submits because she falsely supposes that he is her husband.

Section 213.2 Deviate Sexual Intercourse by Force or Imposition.

(1) *By Force or Its Equivalent.* A person who engages in deviate sexual intercourse with another person, or who

causes another to engage in deviate sexual intercourse, commits a felony of the second degree if:

(a) he compels the other person to participate by force or by threat of imminent death, serious bodily injury, extreme pain or kidnapping, to be inflicted on anyone; or

(b) he has substantially impaired the other person's power to appraise or control his conduct, by administering or employing without the knowledge of the other person drugs, intoxicants or other means for the purpose of preventing resistance; or

(c) the other person is unconscious; or

(d) the other person is less than 10 years old.

Deviate sexual intercourse means sexual intercourse per os or per anum between human beings who are not husband and wife, and any form of sexual intercourse with an animal.

(2) *By Other Imposition.* A person who engages in deviate sexual intercourse with another person, or who causes another to engage in deviate sexual intercourse, commits a felony of the third degree if:

(a) he compels the other person to participate by any threat that would prevent resistance by a person of ordinary resolution; or

(b) he knows that the other person suffers from a mental disease or defect which renders him incapable of appraising the nature of his conduct; or

(c) he knows that the other person submits because he is unaware that a sexual act is being committed upon him.

Section 213.3 Corruption of Minors and Seduction.

(1) *Offense Defined.* A male who has sexual intercourse with a female not his wife, or any person who engages in deviate sexual intercourse or causes another to engage in deviate sexual intercourse, is guilty of an offense if:

(a) the other person is less than (16) years old and the actor is at least (4) years older than the other person; or

(b) the other person is less than 21 years old and the actor is his guardian or otherwise responsible for general supervision of his welfare; or

(c) the other person is in custody of law or detained in a hospital or other institution and the actor has supervisory or disciplinary authority over him; or

(d) the other person is a female who is induced to participate by a promise of marriage which the actor does not mean to perform.

(2) *Grading.* An offense under paragraph (a) of Subsection (1) is a felony of the third degree. Otherwise an offense under this section is a misdemeanor.

Sexual conduct heretofore defined as an offense is eliminated from the criminal definitions in the Code, provided the conduct is between consenting adults. Almost any kind of sexual conduct between husband and wife is removed in the Code from the purview of the law, and homosexual acts between consenting adults are no longer defined as criminal conduct. Penalties for sexual offenses are in general reduced.

Whether or not these changes will be accepted generally by the people of the various states remains to be seen. You will find in your penal code a substantial list of sexual offenses which reflect the previous, and perhaps the present, views of the people about what kinds of sexual relationships and sexual behavior should be prohibited by the society.

ROBBERY

Robbery, which is one of the theft offenses, and hence a crime against property, is also a crime against the person. The factor which peculiarly characterizes the offense of robbery and distinguishes it from other theft offenses is that the property is unlawfully taken from the person or the immediate presence of another by threatening him or putting him in fear. Robbery is a serious felony because the risk of injury to the victim is great; in some states the penalty for armed robbery may be death.

The Elements of the Offense of Robbery include

1. an unlawful taking;
2. of personal property;
3. from the person or presence of another;
4. by threat or putting in fear;
5. with intent to deprive the owner of the property and
6. with the intent to put the property to the use or benefit of the taker.

Essentially the crime of robbery constitutes an unlawful and unauthorized taking of the property of another against his will and without his consent. The crime involves the dual elements of larceny and assault. Therefore the taking must be from the person or from his presence. "From his presence" has been held to mean (a) within his reach; (b) within his control; (c) within his observation; and (d) within his inspection.[38]

Any amount of force necessary to induce the owner to part with his property is a sufficient force. Threats must be of physical violence [39] and the fear must be "of such a nature as in reason and common experience induce a person to part with his property against his will, and to put him, as it were, under the temporary suspension of the power of exercising his will through the influence of the terror impressed." [40] Sudden snatching of property (as a woman's purse) is not robbery, if there is no struggle and no injury done to the person.[41] The necessary elements of threat or putting in fear is absent.

The intent of the crime of robbery is the same as the intent of the crime of larceny. The intent to take the property temporarily, if the taking is from the person and accomplished by threats or putting him in fear, is sufficient, and it is not necessary that the robber intend to permanently deprive the owner of his property. Escape with the loot is not necessary to complete the crime of robbery.[42]

38. O'Donnell v. People, 224 Ill. 218, 79 N.E. 639 (1906).

39. If property is obtained by threats other than threats of physical violence, as for example, by threats to charge a person with a crime, the offense is not Robbery but Extortion.

40. Steward v. People, 224 Ill. 434, 79 N.E. 636, 639 (1906).

41. State v. Holmes, 317 Mo. 9, 295 S.W. 71, 58 A.L.R. 652 (1927).

42. People v. Clark, 70 Cal.App.2d 132, 160 P.2d 553 (1945).

In New York robbery is classified as an offense against property and is defined as forcible stealing. Force or fear must be employed. The intent must be to permanently or virtually permanently appropriate the property or deprive the owner of its use, which is distinguished from the "borrowing" type of intent to obtain temporary use or cause temporary loss. The offense is divided in this state into third degree, second degree, and first degree robbery. (The New York Penal Code employs the "ascending" system of presenting degree crimes; the usual pattern is the "descending" system which defines the highest degree of the offense first.) The first degree robbery offense in New York is similar to "aggravated robbery" offenses in other states.[43]

In Texas, the two degrees of robbery are distinguished by whether or not a firearm or other deadly weapon is used or exhibited. Armed robbery may carry the death penalty.[44] Texas defines the related offense labeled "Acquisition of Property by Threats," [45] an offense labeled "Extortion" in some states.

Illinois also classifies robbery as an offense against property and states that "a person commits robbery when he takes property from the person or presence of another by the use of force or by threatening the imminent use of force." [46] The higher grade of offense is armed robbery.[47]

43. McKinney's N.Y.Penal Law, § 160.00: Robbery is forcible stealing. A person forcibly steals property and commits robbery when, in the course of committing a larceny, he uses or threatens the immediate use of physical force upon another person for the purpose of:

1. Preventing or overcoming resistance to the taking of the property or to the retention thereof immediately after the taking; or
2. Compelling the owner of such property or another person to deliver up the property or to engage in other conduct which aids in the commission of the larceny.

§ 160.05: A person is guilty of robbery in the third degree when he forcibly steals property.

Robbery in the third degree is a Class D felony.

§ 160.10: A person is guilty of robbery in the second degree when he forcibly steals property and when he is aided by another person actually present.

Robbery in the second degree is a Class C felony.

44. Vernon's Ann.Texas Penal Code, Art. 1408.

45. *Ibid.*, Art. 1409. (Texas classifies Robbery as a crime against property.)

46. Smith-Hurd Ill.Ann.Stat. ch. 38, § 18–1. The penalty for Robbery is imprisonment in the penitentiary from one to 20 years.

47. *Ibid.*, § 18–2.

Robbery in California is included in the chapter of the Penal Code entitled "Of Crimes Against the Person," and is defined as "the felonious taking of personal property in the possession of another, from his person or immediate presence, and against his will, accomplished by means of force or fear." [48]

Model Penal Code Definition of Robbery. The Model Penal Code distinguishes between the robbery offenses according to whether bodily injury is intended or inflicted.

Section 222.1 Robbery

(1) *Robbery Defined.* A person is guilty of robbery if, in the course of committing a theft, he:

(a) inflicts serious bodily injury upon another; or

(b) threatens another with or purposely puts him in fear of immediate serious bodily injury; or

(c) commits or threatens immediately to commit any felony of the first or second degree.

An act shall be deemed "in the course of committing a theft" if it occurs in an attempt to commit theft or in flight after the attempt or commission.

(2) *Grading.* Robbery is a felony of the second degree, except that it is a felony of the first degree if in the course of committing the theft the actor attempts to kill anyone, or purposely inflicts or attempts to inflict serious bodily injury.

You will note that a person is guilty of robbery under the Model Penal Code definitions if (1) in the course of committing a theft, he (2) inflicts serious bodily injury on another, or (3) commits or threatens to commit any felony of the first or second degree. A man who induces a woman to give him her money under threat of raping her, or gets a man to give him money under threat of raping his wife, would be examples under (c). To fully understand the crime of robbery as set out in the Model Penal Code we also have to know what constitutes a "theft." The offense of theft is discussed in considerable detail in a succeeding section.

48. West's Ann.Calif.Codes, Penal, § 211.

Chapter IV

ELEMENTS OF THE MAJOR OFFENSES

CRIMES AGAINST PROPERTY

Before we begin the study of the offenses against property,[1] let us consider some necessary definitions and concepts, such as the differences between real and personal property, and the meaning of ownership and possession.

Real and Personal Property. Since only personal property is subject to theft, we must distinguish between real and personal property. *Real property* is land, and whatever is affixed to the land. *Personal property* is all other property. Real property is normally unmovable; personal property is normally movable.

It is possible to convert real property into personal property and vice versa. If a house is taken off the land and put on a trailer for moving, it has been changed from real property to personal property. Crops growing on the land are real property; once they are cut, they are personal property. Oil still in the ground is real property; when it is pumped out of the ground and put in storage tanks, it is personal property. A lavatory is personal property as long as it is in the crate; when it is installed in a bathroom, it has become real property; when taken from the wall, it is personal property again. A pile of lumber is personal property; when it has been built into a house, or a garage, or a store affixed to the land, it is real property. A mobile home is usually personal property, but if permanently affixed to a foundation, it may become real property.

In the typical code definitions, land and what is permanently affixed to it are not subject to theft; the offenses for "taking" a house or land belonging to another have such names as "trespass" and "criminal trespass." But property attached to the land which can be removed with relative ease, such as crops, and thus converted into personal property, are subject to theft, although sometimes the offenses are spelled out separately to avoid any question as to whether growing crops may be stolen.

1. We have, of course, already discussed robbery which is sometimes classified as a crime against property.

Two Meanings of "Personal Property." In the law, personal property subject to theft means any property that is a "thing" (as distinguished from "a right," such as a right to privacy) and is normally movable. The opposite of personal property in this context is real property. *Do not* confuse the word "personal" which means ownership by an individual with the word "personal" which means movable property. The opposite of personal property, meaning ownership, is public property.

There is public real property and public personal property; and personal real property and personal personal property. The post office is public real property; the mail truck is public personal property. A house is personal (or privately owned) real property; a car is personal (or privately owned) personal property. There are two meanings of "personal," one having to do with the nature of the property, the other having to do with the character of the ownership. When we use the words "personal property" in setting out the elements of offenses such as burglary, robbery, and theft, we are referring to the *nature of the property*, not the character of the ownership.

Ownership and Possession. Robbery is a crime against possession. This means that a person who takes the property of another by threats or putting in fear may be guilty of robbery even though the victim does not own the property. Suppose Mary loans a diamond necklace to Susie to wear to a party. M, a masked man, takes the necklace from Susie at the party. The masked man is guilty of robbing Susie even though she did not own the necklace. This would also be true even though Susie had "borrowed" the necklace from Mary without Mary's knowledge, or even if Susie had stolen the necklace from Mary.

An *owner* of property is the one who has title to the property or is the proprietor of it. The *possessor* of property is one who has control and custody over it. Of course, the owner and the possessor may be the same person; this is the usual case as to personal property. Possession may be actual—the thing is under the immediate physical control of the proprietor; or it may be constructive—where the owner who has title and is usually in physical possession of the property is temporarily absent, or has given the actual physical custody to another. You do not lose possession of your furniture when you leave the house to go to class, nor of your car when you park it. You would be considered in constructive possession of your furniture if a thief enters the house and moves it out, or steals your parked car.

In the theft statutes, the words owners and possessors may be used interchangeably. If the statute says the taking is unlawful if it is made "with the intent to deprive the owner of the use or value thereof," this will be interpreted to mean both the person who has title and the person in possession. In our example, Mary, who is the true owner, and Susie, the person in possession, are the owners of the necklace, since the word "owner" is taken to include the person in possession, having care, control, and management of the property at the time though the owner who has title was not present. The reverse is also true. If the statute says the taking is unlawful if it is, "with intent to deprive the person in possession of the use or value thereof," both Mary and Susie will be said to be the person in possession thereof—Susie because she is in actual possession of the necklace, and Mary because she has constructive possession of the necklace as holder of the title.

Because of these definitions, it is possible for a robber to be guilty of robbery even though the person in possession of the article taken has himself stolen the property. It is possible to steal from a thief if the offender being charged is not the owner of the property and has no right to it superior to that of the thief. Thus M, the masked man, would be guilty of robbing Susie even if Susie had stolen the necklace from Mary.

An Owner May Steal His Own Property. Under some circumstances, it is possible for an owner to steal his own property, as for example, when he has parted with possession of it to another. If you own a Ford truck and rent it to James for a period of two weeks to move his furniture from one place to another, and James pays the rental to you, or is bound to pay the rental, you cannot just go "take" the truck from James. If you do, you are guilty of theft, and if you took it from James at gun point or by threats, of robbery. You are the owner of the truck, but James has lawful possession of it under agreement from you. Because robbery (and also theft) is a crime against possession, you can be guilty of robbery when your intent is to take back property which you own, if you have given lawful possession of it to another and he is using the property in accordance with the agreement, and you take the property from his presence by threats or putting him in fear. In the case of the truck, if James rented the truck to John and he had no right to do so, you could take your own truck from John without being guilty of an offense, though use of force might render you liable for assault. Of course, you might get into a civil suit with both James and John if there is dispute about the agreement.

BURGLARY

The element that distinguishes burglary from the other offenses against property is that the crime of burglary involves a breaking and entering of a structure, or as this is phrased in the Model Penal Code, "a criminal intrusion."

Burglary at Common Law. At common law the offense of burglary consisted of (1) breaking into and entering; (2) a residence; (3) in the nighttime; (4) with intent to commit a felony. Under the statutes of most states, this definition of burglary has been considerably broadened.[2] The modern offense of burglary can be committed if any kind of structure is broken into and entered (it no longer need be just a house where people live), it can take place in the daytime, and the intent can be to commit a misdemeanor theft as well as a felony. The old common law offense, however, still remains in the statutes of many states as a separate offense, carrying a higher penalty.

Building or Structure. Almost any kind of building or structure can be burglarized, no matter what it is made of. A tent can be

2. Vernon's Ann.Texas Penal Code, Art. 1391.

In California, burglary is defined as follows: Every person who enters any house, room, apartment, tenement, shop, warehouse, store, mill, barn, stable outhouse or other building, tent, vessel, railroad car, trailer coach as defined by the Vehicle Code, vehicle as defined by said code when the doors of such vehicle are locked, aircraft as defined by the Harbors and Navigation Code, mine or any underground portion thereof, with intent to commit grand or petit larceny or any felony is guilty of burglary. West's Ann.Penal Code, § 459.

Burglary is divided into degrees (§ 460):

1. Every burglary of an inhabited dwelling house, trailer coach as defined by the Vehicle Code, or building committed in the nighttime, and every burglary, whether in the daytime or nighttime, committed by a person armed with a deadly weapon, or who while in the commission of such burglary arms himself with a deadly weapon, or who while in the commission of such burglary assaults any person, is burglary of the first degree.
2. All other kinds of burglary are of the second degree. * * *

burglarized, so can a mobile home, so can a store, a barn, a shed, a garage, a cocktail lounge, or a bank. If an edifice of any material has walls and is covered, it is probably within the definition of structures that can be burglarized. An early case had difficulty with a kind of storage shed used to store cotton. The offender claimed it was a box because the offense of breaking open and stealing the contents of a box is a lesser offense than burglary. The prosecutor claimed the container of the cotton was a house (i. e., structure) which under the law was subject to burglary. The court decided with the prosecutor. Whatever the structure looked like that the cotton was stored in, it was a building or structure and not merely a box.

California has decided that the following types of structures are a building or structure within the definition of burglary: a service station,[3] a powder magazine dug into the side of a hill with a door at the opening,[4] and a popcorn stand.[5] Illinois held that an outdoor telephone booth permanently attached to concrete slabs is a building which can be burglarized.[6]

The following structures have also been held to be subject to burglary: a sheriff's office; a shed; a show window attached to a store; a stockroom, the walls of which were made of wire and beaverboard; a tent; a cabin constructed on an automobile chassis; a church.[7]

An open corral is probably not a "structure" which can be burglarized; neither is a haystack, a fenced garden, nor a tennis court. An offender entering illegally on any such premises and taking the horses, the hay, the cucumbers, or the tennis net, is guilty of theft, but not of burglary, even though he forces a gate, or climbs a fence, in the process. The following have been held not to be the kind of "house" building or structure that can be

3. People v. Fred Pettinger, 94 Cal. App. 297, 271 P. 132 (1928).

4. People v. Alphonse Buyle, 22 Cal. App.2d 143, 70 P.2d 955 (1937).

5. People v. John L. Burley, 26 Cal. App.2d 213, 79 P.2d 148 (1938).

6. People v. Goins, 66 Ill.App.2d 251, 213 N.E.2d 52 (1965).

7. The Illinois statute includes among the structures that may be burglarized a building, housetrailer, watercraft, aircraft, motor vehicle, railroad car, or any part thereof. Smith-Hurd Ill.Ann.Stat. ch. 38, § 19–1.

The criminal trespass statutes in New York make it an offense to knowingly enter or remain unlawfully in or upon premises, McKinney's N.Y. Penal Law, § 140.05, or unlawfully upon real property which is fenced or otherwise enclosed, § 140.10.

burglarized: a car;[8] the header box on a harvesting machine; a railroad car; a portable structure used for storing dynamite and referred to as a "box;" and a portable oil rig doghouse.

Many states do not define burglary of a private residence at night as a separate offense, but merely impose a higher penalty if the offense is at nighttime and of a residence where people live. This is the approach in the Model Penal Code where burglary of a dwelling of another at night is a higher degree of felony than other burglary.

Night and nighttime are usually defined, as they are in the Model Penal Code, to mean the period between thirty minutes past sunset and thirty minutes before sunrise.

Elements of the Offense of Burglary. The modern offense of burglary contains the following elements:

1. a breaking and entering;
2. of a building or structure;
3. with intent to commit a felony or theft.[9]

The *actus reus* of burglary is the breaking and entering of the building belonging to another. The *mens rea* is the intent to commit a felony or theft. Thus, it is burglary to enter a building for the purpose of committing arson, or rape, to steal an article with a value over the sum defined in that state as a felony theft, or to steal an article defined in that state as merely a misdemeanor theft.[10]

8. But a motor vehicle is included in the Illinois statute. See fn. 7, *supra*.

The New York criminal trespass statutes make it an offense to remain unlawfully in or on certain "non-dwelling," such as fenced or enclosed real property, or "premises." See fn. 7, *supra*.

9. The New York code reads: "with intent to commit a *crime* therein." [Italics supplied] McKinney's N.Y. Penal Law, §§ 140.20, 140.25, 140.30.

10. See fn. 2, *supra*, West's Ann.Cal. Penal Code, § 459.

Smith-Hurd Ill.Ann.Stat. ch. 38, § 19–1:

(a) A person commits burglary when without authority he knowingly enters or without authority remains within a building, housetrailer, watercraft, aircraft, motor vehicle as defined in the Illinois Motor Vehicle Law, approved July 11, 1957, as amended, railroad car, or any part thereof, with intent to commit therein a felony or theft. This offense shall not include the offenses set out in Section 4–102 of the "Illinois Motor Vehicle Law," as heretofore or hereafter amended.

(b) Penalty. A person convicted of burglary shall be imprisoned in

Breaking and Entering. Breaking is usually defined to mean the use of any force to get into a building and entering means putting

the penitentiary for any indeterminate term with a minimum of not less than one year.

Possession of burglary tools is a separate offense set out in § 19–2.

The New York Penal Code defines in its customary "ascending" order, three degrees of burglary:

McKinney's Penal Law, § 140.20: A person is guilty of burglary in the third degree when he knowingly enters or remains unlawfully in a building with intent to commit a crime therein. Burglary in the third degree is a Class D felony.

§ 140.25: A person is guilty of burglary in the second degree when he knowingly enters or remains unlawfully in a building with intent to commit a crime therein, and when:

1. In effecting entry or while in the building or in immediate flight therefrom, he or another participant in the crime:
   (a) Is armed with explosives or or a deadly weapon; or
   (b) Causes physical injury to any person who is not a participant in the crime; or
   (c) Uses or threatens the immediate use of a dangerous instrument; or
2. The building is a dwelling and the entering or remaining occurs at night.

Burglary in the second degree is a Class C felony.

§ 140.30: A person is guilty of burglary in the first degree when he knowingly enters or remains unlawfully in a dwelling at night with intent to commit a crime therein, and when, in effecting entry or while in the dwelling or in immediate flight therefrom, he or another participant in the crime:

1. Is armed with explosives or a deadly weapon; or
2. Causes physical injury to any person who is not a participant in the crime; or
3. Uses or threatens the immediate use of a dangerous instrument.

Burglary in the first degree is a Class B felony.

There are also three degrees of criminal trespass:

§ 140.05: A person is guilty of criminal trespass in the third degree when he knowingly enters or remains unlawfully in or upon premises. Criminal trespass in the third degree is a violation.

§ 140.10: A person is guilty of criminal trespass in the second degree when he knowingly enters or remains unlawfully in a building or upon real property which is fenced or otherwise enclosed in a manner designed to exclude intruders. Criminal trespass in the second degree is a Class B misdemeanor.

§ 140.15: A person is guilty of criminal trespass in the first degree when he knowingly enters or remains unlawfully in a dwelling. Criminal trespass in the first degree is a Class A misdemeanor.

A great many theft related offenses are separately defined in New York. See §§ 165.00 to 165.65.

Vernon's Ann.Texas Penal Code, Art. 1389: The offense of burglary is constituted by entering a house by force, threats or fraud, at night, or in any manner by entering a house at any time, either day or night, and remaining concealed therein, with the intent in either case of committing a felony or the crime of theft.

Art. 1390: He is also guilty of burglary who, with intent to commit a felony or theft, by breaking, enters a house in the daytime.

any part of the body or any instrument into the building with intent to steal. A man may be a burglar if he inserts a coat hanger through an open window and with it picks up the watch on the dresser. He may be a burglar if he forces the latch on a screen door, or gets himself into the house through any unusual opening, such as the chimney.[11] He may be a burglar if he shoots into a house, for this too is an entry.[12]

11. Entering a store through the public entrance during business hours, with intent to commit a larceny is burglary in California. The use of force by breaking is not necessary to constitute the offense. People v. Michael Barry, 94 Cal. 481, 29 P. 1026 (1892).

12. The Texas Code defines entry and breaking as follows:

Vernon's Ann.Texas Penal Code, Art. 1392: Entry defined. The "entry" into a house includes every kind of entry but one made by the free consent of the occupant, or of one authorized to give such consent; it is not necessary that there should be any actual breaking to constitute burglary, except when the entry is made in the daytime.

Art. 1393: Entry further defined. The entry is not confined to the entrance of the whole body; it may consist of the entry of any part for the purpose of committing a felony or theft, or it may be constituted by the discharge of fire-arms or other deadly missile into the house, with intent to injure any person therein, or by the introduction of any instrument for the purpose of taking from the house any personal property, although no part of the body of the offender should be introduced.

Art. 1394: Breaking. By "breaking," as used in this chapter, is meant that the entry must be made with actual force. The slightest force, however, is sufficient to constitute breaking; it may be by lifting the latch of a door that is shut, or by raising a window, the entry at a chimney, or other unusual place, the introduction of the hand or any instrument to draw out the property through an aperture made by the offender for that purpose.

The New York definitions applicable to the offense of burglary are as follows:

McKinney's Penal Law, § 140.00: The following definitions are applicable to this article:

1. "Premises" includes the term "building," as defined herein, and any real property.

2. "Building," in addition to its ordinary meaning, includes any structure, vehicle or watercraft used for overnight lodging of persons, or used by persons for carrying on business therein. Where a building consists of two or more units separately secured or occupied, each unit shall be deemed both a separate building in itself and a part of the main building.

3. "Dwelling" means a building which is usually occupied by a person lodging therein at night.

4. "Night" means the period between thirty minutes after sunset and thirty minutes before sunrise.

5. "Enter or remain unlawfully." A person "enters or remains unlawfully" in or upon premises when he is not licensed or privileged to do so. A person who, regardless of his intent, enters or remains in or upon premises which are at the time open to the public does so with license and privilege unless he defies a lawful order not to enter or remain, personally com-

The Intent to Commit a Felony or Theft. The intent, *mens rea,* is essential to the crime of burglary. At common law the intent had to be to commit a felony; modern statutes have broadened this to include theft, and, as in New York, to include any crime. Suppose a man gets very drunk and decides to leave the party and go home. He lives in one of a row of houses that look pretty much alike, inside and out. He goes to a house, finds the screen door latched, forces a latch, opens the door and goes to sleep on the couch. Later on, he gets up to go back to the party and noticing a watch on the table, decides he had better take his watch with him. *But he is in the wrong house.* Is he guilty of burglary? The answer is "No." If these facts are really true, and the jury believes them, he has not committed the offense of burglary because the necessary intent was lacking. He didn't enter the house with intent to steal; he thought it was his own house. He didn't steal the watch, he thought it was his own watch. However, under the circumstances above, the man is guilty of an offense called "Breaking and Entering," because that crime does not require an intent to commit a felony or theft. That offense is complete when a person illegally enters the premises of another, regardless of his "intent." [13] Offenders and most court personnel speak of "B & E." "B & E" stands for the offense of "Breaking and Entering." A prisoner who is charged with burglary is usually glad to "cop out" to "B & E" because Breaking and Entering is a less serious offense. The Model Penal Code labels this offense "Criminal Trespass." [14]

municated to him by the owner of such premises or other authorized person. A license or privilege to enter or remain in a building which is only partly open to the public is not a license or privilege to enter or remain in that part of the building which is not open to the public. A person who enters or remains upon unimproved and apparently unused land, which is neither fenced nor otherwise enclosed in a manner designed to exclude intruders, does so with license and privilege unless notice against trespass is personally communicated to him by the owner of such land or other authorized person, or unless such notice is given by posting in a conspicuous manner.

13. It is generally not necessary that the prosecution establish what crime the intruder intended to commit. Intent may be inferred from the facts and circumstances. McCourt v. People, 64 N.Y. 583 (1876); People v. Oliver, 4 A.D.2d 28, 163 N.Y.S. 2d 235, affirmed 3 N.Y.2d 684, 171 N.Y.S.2d 811, 148 N.E.2d 874.

14. The New York criminal trespass statutes do not require an intent, the requirement is only to knowingly enter and remain unlawfully. See fn. 10, *supra*, §§ 140.05, 140.10, 140.15. The burglary offenses re-

Burglary and Another Offense Committed at the Same Time. In most states, an offender can be held guilty of both the offense of burglary and any other offense he commits after entry.[15] Let us suppose the offender breaks and enters a house intending to steal a $5.00 ring that he particularly wants. *Circumstance 1.* He steals the $5.00 ring. He is guilty of both burglary and misdemeanor theft. *Circumstance 2.* He steals a $600.00 ring in place of, or in addition to the $5.00 ring. He is guilty of burglary and felony theft. *Circumstance 3.* He doesn't steal anything, but he is attracted to the young girl in the house and rapes her. He is guilty of both burglary and rape. The offender can, and will be charged not only with the burglary, but with the offense actually committed, and he can be sentenced to a term in prison for each offense.

The Model Penal Code proposes a change in this rule by providing that a person may not be convicted both for burglary and for the offense which it was his purpose to commit after the burglarious entry, unless the additional offense constituted a felony of the first or second degree. Under the Model Code, given *Circumstance 1* above, the burglar could be charged only with the burglary but not with the misdemeanor theft. Theft under the Model Code is either a felony of the third degree or a misdemeanor. The rule under *Circumstance 2* above would change and the offender could only be charged with the burglary, since theft over $500.00 is a third degree felony only. Under *Circumstance 3* above, since the rape would be a first degree felony under the Model Penal Code, the Code would make no change in the pres-

quire an "intent to commit a crime." See fn. 10, *supra*, §§ 140.20, 140.25, 140.30.

In Texas and in many other states the "B & E" offenses are usually to be found in city ordinances and are misdemeanors.

15. Burglary and Larceny are distinct offenses. People v. Arthur Snyder, 74 Cal.App. 138, 239 P. 705 (1925).

The Texas statute makes the offense committed in the burglary a separate offense. Vernon's Ann.Texas Penal Code, Art. 1399: If a house be entered in such manner as to be burglary, and the one guilty of such burglary shall after such entry commit any other offense, he shall be punished for burglary and also for whatever other offense is so committed.

The Illinois rule is that one who commits burglary and larceny may be sentenced for both. People v. Saxton, 400 Ill. 257, 79 N.E.2d 601 (1948), cert. den. 335 U.S. 835, 69 S. Ct. 25, 93 L.Ed. 387, cert. den. 338 U.S. 944, 70 S.Ct. 424, 94 L.Ed. 582.

Indictments in New York recognize two offenses, as for example in an indictment charging third degree burglary and first degree grand larceny. People v. Travato, 309 N.Y. 382, 131 N.E.2d 557 (1955).

ent rule, and the offender could be prosecuted and punished for both burglary and rape.

Model Penal Code Provisions. The Burglary offenses as defined in the Model Penal Code are as follows:

Section 221.1 Burglary.

(1) *Burglary Defined.* A person is guilty of burglary if he enters a building or occupied structure, or separately secured or occupied portion thereof, with purpose to commit a crime therein, unless the premises are at the time open to the public or the actor is licensed or privileged to enter. It is an affirmative defense to prosecution for burglary that the building or structure was abandoned.

(2) *Grading.* Burglary is a felony of the second degree if it is perpetrated in the dwelling of another at night, or if, in the course of committing the offense, the actor:

(a) purposely, knowingly or recklessly inflicts or attempts to inflict bodily injury on anyone; or

(b) is armed with explosives or a deadly weapon.
Otherwise, burglary is a felony of the third degree.

An act shall be deemed "in the course of committing" an offense if it occurs in an attempt to commit the offense or in flight after the attempt or commission.

(3) *Multiple Convictions.* A person may not be convicted both for burglary and for the offense which it was his purpose to commit after the burglarious entry or for an attempt to commit that offense, unless the additional offense constitutes a felony of the first or second degree.

Section 221.2 Criminal Trespass.

(1) *Buildings and Occupied Structures.* A person commits an offense if, knowing that he is not licensed or privileged to do so, he enters or surreptitiously remains in any building or occupied structure, or separately secured or occupied portion thereof. An offense under this Subsection is a misdemeanor if it is committed in a dwelling at night. Otherwise it is a petty misdemeanor.

(2) *Defiant Trespasser.* A person commits an offense if, knowing that he is not licensed or privileged to do so, he

enters or remains in any place as to which notice against trespass is given by:

(a) actual communication to the actor; or

(b) posting in a manner prescribed by law or reasonably likely to come to the attention of intruders; or

(c) fencing or other enclosure manifestly designed to exclude intruders.

An offense under this Subsection constitutes a petty misdemeanor if the offender defies an order to leave personally communicated to him by the owner of the premises or other authorized person. Otherwise it is a violation.

(3) *Defenses.* It is an affirmative defense to prosecution under this Section that:

(a) a building or occupied structure involved in an offense under Subsection (1) was abandoned; or

(b) the premises were at the time open to members of the public and the actor complied with all lawful conditions imposed on access to or remaining in the premises; or

(c) the actor reasonably believed that the owner of the premises, or other person empowered to license access thereto, would have licensed him to enter or remain.

THEFT AND RELATED OFFENSES

Theft is the general term which denotes the unlawful taking by one person of the property of another. If the theft is from the person or his immediate possession and is by threatening the victim or putting him in fear, the offense is robbery. If the theft is the intent of the offender who breaks and enters the building of another, the offense is burglary. The term larceny is also applied generally to the theft offenses. Thus, in some states there is felony theft and misdemeanor theft, depending upon the value of the property taken. In New York, the higher grade of offense is grand theft. In other states, the value distinguishes grand larceny from petty larceny, or grand larceny from larceny. The value which distinguishes the higher theft offense, usually a felony, from the lower theft offense, usually a misdemeanor, varies from state to state. In some states a value as low as $50.00 is sufficient to constitute the higher grade of offense and felony theft may be charged as "Theft Over $50.00" and referred to as "Theft Over Fifty." The value necessary to constitute a felony theft in your state can be determined from the statutes.[16] In these days of inflation, the value in felony theft, like the price of everything else, has gone up. The Model Penal Code makes theft in excess of $500.00 a felony; theft of a lesser amount is a misdemeanor or petty misdemeanor.

Elements of the Offense of Theft. The necessary elements of the offense of theft are:

1. An unlawful taking;
2. Of personal property;
3. Of another;
4. From his possession or the possession of someone holding the same for him;
5. Without his consent;
6. With intent to deprive the owner of the value of the same; and
7. With intent to appropriate the property to the use or benefit of the person taking it.[17]

16. In Texas, the value is $50; in New York, $250; in Illinois, $150; in California, the value varies according to the nature of the item stolen.

17. Smith-Hurd Ill.Ann.Stat. ch. 38, § 16–1: A person commits theft when he knowingly:

(a) Obtains or exerts unauthorized control over property of the owner; or

(b) Obtains by deception control over property of the owner; or

(c) Obtains by threat control over property of the owner; or

(d) Obtains control over stolen property knowing the property to have been stolen by another or under such circumstances as would reasonably induce him to believe that the property was stolen, and

(1) Intends to deprive the owner permanently of the use or benefit of the property; or

(2) Knowingly uses, conceals or abandons the property in such manner as to deprive the owner permanently of such use or benefit; or

(3) Uses, conceals, or abandons the property knowing such use, concealment or abandonment probably will deprive the owner permanently of such use or benefit.

Penalty. A person first convicted of theft of property not from the person and not exceeding $150 in value shall be fined not to exceed $500 or imprisoned in a penal institution other than the penitentiary not to exceed one year, or both. A person convicted of such theft a second or subsequent time, or after a prior conviction of any type of theft, shall be imprisoned in the penitentiary from one to 5 years. A person convicted of theft of property from the person or exceeding $150 in value shall be imprisoned in the penitentiary from one to 10 years.

McKinney's N.Y.Penal Law, § 155.05:

1. A person steals property and commits larceny when, with intent to deprive another of property or to appropriate the same to himself or to a third person, he wrongfully takes, obtains or withholds such property from an owner thereof.

2. Larceny includes a wrongful taking, obtaining or withholding of another's property, with the intent prescribed in subdivision one of this section, committed in any of the following ways:

   (a) By conduct heretofore defined or known as common law larceny by trespassory taking, common law larceny by trick, embezzlement, or obtaining property by false pretenses;

   (b) By acquiring lost property. * * *

   (c) By committing the crime of issuing a bad check, as defined in section 190.05;

   (d) By false promise. * * *

   (e) By extortion. * * *

§ 155.25: A person is guilty of petit larceny when he steals property. Petit larceny is a Class A misdemeanor.

Grand larceny is divided into three degrees. When value of the property exceeds $250 and is taken in the ways specified in the statute, the offense is grand larceny in the third degree (§ 155.30); if the value exceeds $1,500, the offense is grand larceny in the second degree (§ 155.35); grand larceny in the first degree is described in § 155.40 as follows: A person is guilty of grand larceny in the first degree when he steals property and when the property, regardless of its nature and value, is obtained by extortion committed by instilling in the victim a fear that the actor or another person will (a) cause physical injury to some person in the future, or (b) cause damage to property, or (c) use or abuse his position as a public servant by engaging in conduct within or related to his official duties, or by failing or refusing to perform an official duty, in such manner as to affect some person adversely. Grand larceny in the first degree is a Class C felony.

In Texas, theft is defined as the fraudulent taking of corporeal personal property belonging to another from his possession, or from the possession of some person holding the same for him, with intent to deprive the owner of the value of the same, and to appropriate it to the use or benefit of the person taking. Vernon's Texas Penal Code, Ann., Art. 1410.

Felony theft is the theft of property of the value of fifty dollars or over and is punished by confinement in the penitentiary not less than two nor more than ten years. (Art. 1421).

Misdemeanor theft is the theft of property under the value of fifty dollars and over the value of five dollars, punishable by imprisonment in jail not exceeding two years and a fine not exceeding five hundred dollars; theft of property of the value of five dollars or under is punished by a fine not exceeding two hundred dollars. (Art. 1422).

Conversion by a bailee is a separate offense (Art. 1429), as is receiving stolen property. (Art. 1430).

California has some 28 sections in Chapter 5 of the Penal Code (West's Ann.Cal.Penal Code) entitled Larceny (Theft). Forgery, counterfeiting, and similar offenses appear in Chapter 4. Embezzlement, Chapter

The New York definitions applying to larceny set out below are helpful to our discussion and should be noted.[18]

6, contains some 15 sections covering special circumstances of fraudulent appropriation of property by a person to whom it has been entrusted. Extortion, False Impersonation and Cheats cover two additional chapters, and fraudulent insolvencies by corporations and other Fraud in their management make up Chapter 13. Various forms of theft offenses cover 462 pages of West's Annotated California Codes. The need for the Model Penal Code consolidation of the theft offenses is illustrated by the proliferation of theft-related offenses in the California Code. Only a few of the main provisions appearing in Chapter 5 (Larceny-Theft) are set out here:

§ 484. **Theft defined.** (a) Every person who shall feloniously steal, take, carry, lead, or drive away the personal property of another, or who shall fraudulently appropriate property which has been entrusted to him, or who shall knowingly and designedly, by any false or fraudulent representation or pretense, defraud any other person of money, labor or real or personal property, or who causes or procures others to report falsely of his wealth or mercantile character and by thus imposing upon any person, obtains credit and thereby fraudulently gets or obtains possession of money, or property or obtains the labor or service of another, is guilty of theft. * * *

§ 486. **Theft; degrees.** Theft is divided into two degrees, the first of which is termed grand theft; the second, petty theft.

§ 487. **Grand theft defined.** Grand theft is theft committed in any of the following cases:

1. When the money, labor or real or personal property taken is of a value exceeding two hundred dollars ($200); provided, that when domestic fowls, avocados, olives, citrus or deciduous fruits, nuts and artichokes are taken of a value exceeding fifty dollars ($50); provided, further, that where the money, labor, real or personal property is taken by a servant, agent or employee from his principal or employer and aggregates two hundred dollars ($200) or more in any 12 consecutive month period, then the same shall constitute grand theft.

2. When the property is taken from the person of another.

3. When the property taken is an automobile, fire-arm, horse, mare, gelding, any bovine animal, any caprine animal, mule, jack, jenny, sheep, lamb, hog, sow, boar, gilt, barrow or pig.

§ 488. **Petty theft defined.** Theft in other cases is petty theft.

Grand theft is a felony, petty theft is a misdemeanor punishable by fine or jail sentence. (See § 490.)

18. McKinney's N.Y.Penal Law, § 155.00:

Larceny; definitions of terms. The following definitions are applicable to this title:

1. "Property" means any money, personal property, real property, thing in action, evidence of debt or contract, or any article, substance or thing of value.

2. "Obtain" includes, but is not limited to, the bringing about of a transfer or purported transfer of property or of a legal interest therein, whether to the obtainer or another.

3. "Deprive." To "deprive" another of property means (a) to withhold it or cause it to be withheld from

Property Subject to Theft. The early law had trouble deciding what kinds of property were subject to theft. In most states, real property is not subject to theft, but property affixed to the land which can be easily removed is. Thus, hay, grain, garden produce, fruit on the trees, and all kinds of agricultural products are, according to the law in most states, subject to theft. Under the Model Penal Code definitions, all kinds of property are subject to theft, including real estate and services.

What Constitutes Taking. What constitutes a taking also presented problems to the law. Suppose a man has a satchel of money on the table which belongs to him. Another man, B, bigger and heavier, knowing that the money is not his, comes up to man A and says, "That is my money. Don't touch it." Rather than risk a fight with B, man A walks away from the satchel to go to get the police. The police get back to the room before man B has even touched the satchel. Has B "stolen" the satchel? Some early cases said "No." There has been no theft because there has been no "asportation," i. e., taking or carrying away. Many states passed statutes which said that to constitute "taking," it is not necessary that the property be removed any distance from

him permanently or for so extended a period or under such circumstances that the major portion of its economic value or benefit is lost to him, or (b) to dispose of the property in such manner or under such circumstances as to render it unlikely that an owner will recover such property.

4. "Appropriate." To "appropriate" property of another to oneself or a third person means (a) to exercise control over it, or to aid a third person to exercise control over it, permanently or for so extended a period or under such circumstances as to acquire the major portion of its economic value or benefit, or (b) to dispose of the property for the benefit of oneself or a third person.

5. "Owner." When property is taken, obtained or withheld by one person from another person, an "owner" thereof means any person who has a right to possession thereof superior to that of the taker, obtainer or withholder.

A person who has obtained possession of property by theft or other illegal means shall be deemed to have a right of possession superior to that of a person who takes, obtains or withholds it from him by larcenous means.

A joint or common owner of property shall not be deemed to have a right of possession thereto superior to that of any other joint or common owner thereof.

In the absence of a specific agreement to the contrary, a person in lawful possession of property shall be deemed to have a right of possession superior to that of a person having only a security interest therein, even if legal title lies with the holder of the security interest pursuant to a conditional sale contract or other security agreement.

* * *

the place of taking; it is sufficient that it has been in the possession of the thief.[19] In other words, it is sufficient if the thief has had dominion over the satchel, which deprived the owner of free control over it, no matter how short the time. Under the circumstances above, B is guilty of theft today in most states, but would not have been guilty at common law.

Unlawful Taking. To constitute theft there not only has to be a taking but the taking must be unlawful. Thus, generally a person cannot be guilty of taking property he honestly believes to be his. (We have already set out certain circumstances under which a man can take his own property, as when an owner has parted with lawful possession of his property and may be guilty of stealing it if he takes it from the person who has rightful possession of it.) The law also had trouble with the crime of theft in situations where the original possession was lawful, as where a person obtained rightful possession of property and *then* decided to convert it to his own use.

Suppose you take your car into a garage to be repaired. A workman in the garage takes the radiator out of your car and puts it in his own, putting his radiator in your car. The garage and the workman were lawfully in possession of your car since

19. Vernon's Ann.Texas Penal Code, Art. 1412: *Asportation not necessary.* To constitute "taking" it is not necessary that the property be removed any distance from the place of taking; it is sufficient that it has been in the possession of the thief, though it may not be moved out of the presence of the person deprived of it; nor is it necessary that any definite length of time shall elapse between the taking and the discovery thereof; if but a moment elapse, the offense is complete.

In New York, to "appropriate" property means to exercise control over it * * * permanently or for so extended a period or under such circumstances as to acquire the major portion of its economic value, or dispose of the property for benefit of oneself or a third person. See fn. 18, *supra*, § 155.00(4).

In Illinois, the crime of theft can be committed when a person knowingly "obtains or exercises unauthorized control over property of the owner," See fn. 17, *supra*, § 16–1(a), but the intent must be to permanently deprive him of the use and benefit. See fn. 17, *supra*, § 16–1(d). Permanently deprive is defined in Smith-Hurd Ill.Ann.Stat. ch. 38, § 15–3 as follows: As used in this Part C, to "permanently deprive" means to: (a) defeat all recovery of the property by the owner; or (b) deprive the owner permanently of the beneficial use of the property; or (c) retain the property with intent to restore it to the owner only if the owner purchases or leases it back, or pays a reward or other compensation for its return; or (d) sell, give, pledge, or otherwise transfer any interest in the property or subject it to the claim of a person other than the owner.

you drove it into the garage yourself. Did this exchanging of radiators amount to an unlawful taking? Or suppose you put your fur coat in storage, and during the late summer the owner of the store takes the coat out of storage and lets his wife wear it to Alaska. Did he unlawfully take the coat?

The law finally decided that, under circumstances similar to those above, there had, indeed, been an unlawful taking. In some states, a theft by a person who has original lawful possession of the property is a separate offense called "theft by a bailee," or "conversion by a bailee."[20] In other states, the offense is brought within the general definition of theft; in such states, taking by unlawful means, a taking by false pretext, or a taking after originally receiving lawful possession, are all unlawful taking under the general statute and no separate offenses are identified.

Do not confuse the word bailee with the word *bail.* A "bailee" in the law is a person who receives possession of an article from another for a specific purpose. Thus, a truck driver transporting tires is a bailee of the tires; a railroad hauling coal is a bailee of the coal; the merchant storing the fur coat, the garage man repairing the car, the cleaner possessing the clothes for the purpose of cleaning them, are all bailees. Bail, of course, means money or property put up to enable a person to be free of custody pending trial and a form of guarantee that the accused will be available for trial. A theft committed by a person free on bail is a theft by a person out on bail—it is not "theft by a bailee."

Theft in the Model Penal Code. The pattern of the theft offenses set out in the Model Penal Code is quite different from the usual

20. Vernon's Ann.Texas Penal Code, Art. 1429: *Conversion by a bailee.* Any person having possession of personal property of another by virtue of a contract or hiring or borrowing, or other bailment, who shall without the consent of the owner, fraudulently convert such property to his own use with intent to deprive the owner of the value of the same, shall be guilty of theft, and shall be punished as for theft of like property.

West's Ann.Cal.Penal Code, § 560: Any bailee, as defined in Section 7102 of the Uniform Commercial Code, who issues or aids in issuing a document of title, or any person who secures the issue by a bailee of a document of title, or any person who negotiates or transfers for value a document of title knowing that the goods for which such document is issued have not been actually received by such bailee or are not under his control at the time of issuing such receipt shall be guilty of a crime and upon conviction shall be punished for each offense by imprisonment not exceeding five years or by a fine not exceeding five thousand dollars ($5,000) or by both.

theft statutes. All kinds of property, including real property, are made subject to theft. Related theft offenses are distinguished by the character of the unlawful taking used, as Theft by Deception, Theft by Extortion; or the character of the property taken, as Theft of Property Lost, Mislaid, or Delivered by Mistake; Theft of Services; or Theft by Failure to Make Required Disposition of Funds Received. In some states such special offenses are given different labels, as "Extortion," "Embezzlement," and the like.[21]

21. Related theft offenses defined separately in New York include misapplication of property; unauthorized use of a vehicle; unlawful use of secret scientific material; theft of services; fraudulently obtaining a signature; jostling, fraudulent accosting; fortune telling; criminal possession of stolen property in three degrees. (See McKinney's Penal Law, § 165.00 to 165.65.) Offenses involving fraud (Title K) defines three degrees of forgery, three degrees of criminal possession of a forged instrument, and three degrees of unlawfully using slugs. (See § 170.00 to § 170.60.)

California defines separately Forgery and Counterfeiting, Embezzlement, Extortion, False Personation, and Cheats. This pattern is common to many other states as well. The following selected California titles and definitions are illustrative of the theft offenses as they may appear in a typical code.

West's Ann.Cal.Penal Code, § 470: *Forgery, intent; documents of value; counterfeiting seal; uttering; falsification of records.* Every person who, with intent to defraud, signs the name of another person, or of a fictitious person, knowing that he has no authority so to do, to, or falsely makes, alters, forges, or counterfeits, any charter, letters patent, deed, lease, indenture, writing obligatory, will, testament, codicil, bond, covenant, bank bill or note, post note, check, draft, bill of exchange, contract, promissory note, due bill for the payment of money or property, receipt for money or property, passage ticket, trading stamp, power of attorney, or any certificate of any share, right, or interest in the stock of any corporation or association, or any controller's warrant for the payment of money at the treasury, county order or warrant, or request for the payment of money, or the delivery of goods or chattels of any kind, or for the delivery of any instrument of writing, or acquittance, release, or receipt for money or goods, or any acquittance, release, or discharge of any debt, account, suit, action, demand, or other thing, real or personal, or any transfer or assurance of money, certificate of shares of stock, goods, chattels, or other property whatever, or any letter of attorney, or other power to receive money, or to receive or transfer certificates of shares of stock or annuities, or to let, lease, dispose of, alien, or convey any goods, chattels, lands, or tenements, or other estate, real or personal, or any acceptance or indorsement of any bill of exchange, promissory note, draft, order, or any assignment of any bond, writing obligatory, promissory note, or other contract for money or other property; or counterfeits or forges the seal of handwriting of another; or utters, publishes, passes, or attempts to pass, as true and genuine, any of the above-named false, altered, forged, or counterfeited matters, as above specified and described, knowing the same to be false, altered, forged, or counterfeited, with intent to prejudice, damage, or defraud any person; or who, with intent to defraud, alters, corrupts, or falsifies any record of any will, codicil, conveyance, or other instrument, the record of which is by law evidence, or any record of any judgment of a court or the return of any officer to any process of any court, is guilty of forgery.

§ 471. *Forgery; false entries in records or returns.* Every person who, with intent to defraud another, makes, forges, or alters any entry in any book of records, or any instrument purporting to be any record or return specified in the preceding section, is guilty of forgery.

§ 473. *Forgery; punishment.* Forgery is punishable by imprisonment in the State prison for not less than one year nor more than fourteen years, or by imprisonment in the county jail for not more than one year.

§ 474. *Forgery; telegraph or telephone messages; intent; punishment.* * * *

§ 475. *Possession or receipt of forged bills and notes; intent; possession of blank bills and notes; intent; punishment.* * * *

§ 475a. *Possession of completed check, money order or traveler's check with intent to defraud.* * * *

§ 476. *Making, possessing, uttering, etc., fictitious instruments; intent; punishment.* * * *

§ 476a. *Checks, drafts, or orders on banks; insufficient funds; intent to defraud; punishment; presumption from protest; credit defined; partial validity.*

(a) Any person who for himself or as the agent or representative of another or as an officer of a corporation, willfully, with intent to defraud, makes or draws or utters or delivers any check, or draft or order upon any bank or depositary, or person, or firm, or corporation, for the payment of money, knowing at the time of such making, drawing, uttering or delivering that the maker or drawer or the corporation has not sufficient funds in, or credit with said bank or depositary, or person, or firm, or corporation, for the payment of such check, draft or order and all other checks, drafts or orders upon such funds then outstanding, in full upon its presentation, although no express representation is made with reference thereto, is punishable by imprisonment in the county jail for not more than one year, or in the state prison for not more than 14 years.

(b) However, if the total amount of all such checks, drafts, or orders that the defendant is charged with and convicted of making, drawing, or uttering does not exceed one hundred dollars ($100), the offense is punishable only by imprisonment in the county jail for not more than one year, except that this subdivision shall not be applicable if the defendant has previously been convicted of a violation of Section 470, 475, or 476 of this code, or of this section of this code, or of the crime of petty theft in a case in which defendant's offense was a violation also of Section 470, 475, or 476 of this code or of this section or if the defendant has previously been convicted of any offense under the laws of any other state or of the United States which, if committed in this State, would have been punishable as a violation of Section 470, 475, or 476 of this code or of this section of this code or if he has been so convicted of the crime of petty theft in a case in which, if defendant's offense had been committed in this State, it would have been a violation also of Section 470, 475, or 476 of this code, or of this section. * * *

The object of the Model Code was to bring all "stealing" offenses into a set of related offenses under the general title "Theft."

§ 477. *Counterfeiting; coin, bullion, nuggets, etc.; uttering or passing counterfeited items; intent.* * * *

§ 478. *Counterfeiting; punishment.* Counterfeiting is punishable by imprisonment in the State Prison for not less than one nor more than fourteen years.

§ 479. *Counterfeit coin, bullion, etc.; possession or receipt; intent; punishment.*

§ 480. *Counterfeiting; making or possessing dies, plates, etc.; punishment; destruction of dies, etc.* Every person who makes, or knowingly has in his possession any die, plate, or any apparatus, paper, metal, machine, or other thing whatever, made use of in counterfeiting coin current in this State, or in counterfeiting gold dust, gold or silver bars, bullion, lumps, pieces, or nuggets, or in counterfeiting bank notes or bills, is punishable by imprisonment in the State Prison not less than one nor more than fourteen years; and all such dies, plates, apparatus, paper, metal, or machine, intended for the purpose aforesaid, must be destroyed. (Enacted 1872)

§ 480. *Sending of letter to newspaper signed with name of another.* Every person who signs any letter addressed to a newspaper with the name of a person other than himself and sends such letter to the newspaper, or causes it to be sent to such newspaper, with intent to lead the newspaper to believe that such letter was written by the person whose name is signed thereto, is guilty of a misdemeanor. (Added by Stats. 1963)

§ 481. *Railroad or steamship tickets; counterfeiting, forging or altering; uttering; intent to defraud; punishment.* * * *

§ 482. *Railroad or steamship tickets; cancellation; restoration to original appearance; intent; punishment.* * * *

§ 483. *Common carrier tickets, etc.; sale to person not entitled to use.*

§ 503. *Embezzlement defined.* Embezzlement is the fraudulent appropriation of property by a person to whom it has been intrusted.

§ 521. *Punishment of Extortion committed under color of official right.* Every person who commits any extortion under color of official right, in cases for which a different punishment is not prescribed in this Code, is guilty of a misdemeanor.

§ 528. *Marrying under false personation.* Every person who falsely personates another, and in such assumed character marries or pretends to marry, or to sustain the marriage relation towards another, with or without the connivance of such other, is guilty of a felony.

Illinois identifies theft by lessee, theft of lost or mislaid property, and theft of labor or services separately. Thefts practices are also handled separately. See Smith-Hurd Ill. Ann.Stat. ch. 38, §§ 17-1 and 17-2.

Texas also has a great many separate theft offenses, the usual classification being according to the type of property stolen, as stealing domesticated animals (Vernon's Texas Penal Code, Ann., Art. 1419); of agricultural products (Art. 1426); of cotton and cotton seed (Art. 1426a); of citrus fruits (Art. 1426b); of wool, mohair, or edible meat (Art. 1426c); of record books or filed papers (Art. 1427).

Section 223.1 Consolidation of Theft Offenses; Grading Provisions Applicable to Theft Generally.

(1) *Consolidation of Theft Offenses.* Conduct denominated theft in this Article constitutes a single offense embracing the separate offenses heretofore known as larceny, embezzlement, false pretense, extortion, blackmail, fraudulent conversion, receiving stolen property, and the like. An accusation of theft may be supported by evidence that it was committed in any manner that would be theft under this Article, notwithstanding the specification of a different manner in the indictment or information, subject only to the power of the Court to ensure fair trial by granting a continuance or other appropriate relief where the conduct of the defense would be prejudiced by lack of fair notice or by surprise.

(2) *Grading of Theft Offenses.*

(a) Theft constitutes a felony of the third degree if the amount involved exceeds $500, or if the property stolen is a firearm, automobile, or other motor-propelled vehicle, or in the case of theft by receiving stolen property, if the receiver is in the business of buying or selling stolen property.

(b) Theft not within the preceding paragraph constitutes a misdemeanor, except that if the property was not taken from the person or by threat, or in breach of a fiduciary obligation, and the actor proves by a preponderance of the evidence that the amount involved was less than $50, the offense constitutes a petty misdemeanor.

(c) The amount involved in a theft shall be deemed to be the highest value, by any reasonable standard, of the property or services which the actor stole or attempted to steal. Amounts involved in thefts committed pursuant to one scheme or course of conduct, whether from the same person or several persons, may be aggregated in determining the grade of the offense.

(3) *Claim of Right.* It is an affirmative defense to prosecution for theft that the actor:

(a) was unaware that the property or service was that of another; or

(b) acted under an honest claim of right to the property or service involved or that he had a right to acquire or dispose of it as he did; or

(c) took property exposed for sale, intending to purchase and pay for it promptly, or reasonably believing that the owner, if present, would have consented.

(4) *Theft from Spouse.* It is no defense that theft was from the actor's spouse, except that misappropriation of household and personal effects, or other property normally accessible to both spouses, is theft only if it occurs after the parties have ceased living together.

Section 223.2 Theft by Unlawful Taking or Disposition.

(1) *Movable Property.* A person is guilty of theft if he takes, or exercises unlawful control over, movable property of another with purpose to deprive him thereof.

(2) *Immovable Property.* A person is guilty of theft if he unlawfully transfers immovable property of another or any interest therein with purpose to benefit himself or another not entitled thereto.

Section 223.3 Theft by Deception.

A person is guilty of theft if he obtains property of another by deception. A person deceives if he purposely:

(a) creates or reinforces a false impression, including false impressions as to law, value, intention or other state of mind; but deception as to a person's intention to perform a promise shall not be inferred from the fact alone that he did not subsequently perform the promise; or

(b) prevents another from acquiring information which would affect his judgment of a transaction; or

(c) fails to correct a false impression which the deceiver previously created or reinforced, or which the deceiver knows to be influencing another to whom he stands in a fiduciary or confidential relationship; or

(d) fails to disclose a known lien, adverse claim or other legal impediment to the enjoyment of property which he transfers or encumbers in consideration for the property obtained, whether such impediment is or is not valid, or is or is not a matter of official record.

The term "deceive" does not, however, include falsity as to matters having no pecuniary significance, or puffing by statements unlikely to deceive ordinary persons in the group addressed.

Section 223.4 Theft by Extortion.

A person is guilty of theft if he obtains property of another by threatening to:

(a) inflict bodily injury on anyone or commit any other criminal offense; or

(b) accuse anyone of a criminal offense; or

(c) expose any secret tending to subject any person to hatred, contempt or ridicule, or to impair his credit or business repute; or

(d) take or withhold action as an official, or cause an official to take or withhold action; or

(e) bring about or continue a strike, boycott or other collective unofficial action, if the property is not demanded or received for the benefit of the group in whose interest the actor purports to act; or

(f) testify or provide information or withhold testimony or information with respect to another's legal claim or defense; or

(g) inflict any other harm which would not benefit the actor.

It is an affirmative defense to prosecution based on paragraphs (b), (c), or (d) that the property obtained by threat of accusation, exposure, lawsuit or other invocation of official action was honestly claimed as restitution or indemnification for harm done in the circumstances to which such accusation, exposure, lawsuit or other official action relates, or as compensation for property or lawful services.

Section 223.5 Theft of Property Lost, Mislaid, or Delivered by Mistake.

A person who comes into control of property of another that he knows to have been lost, mislaid, or delivered under a mistake as to the nature or amount of the property or the identity of the recipient is guilty of theft if, with purpose to deprive the owner thereof, he fails to take reasonable measures to restore the property to a person entitled to have it.

Section 223.7 Theft of Services.

(1) A person is guilty of theft if he obtains services which he knows are available only for compensation, by deception or threat, or by false token or other means to avoid payment for the service. "Services" includes labor, professional service, telephone or other public service, accommodation in hotels, restaurants or elsewhere, admission to exhibitions, use of vehicles or other movable property. Where compensation for service is ordinarily paid immediately upon the rendering of such service, as in the case of hotels and restaurants, refusal to pay or absconding without payment or offer to pay gives rise to a presumption that the service was obtained by deception as to intention to pay.

(2) A person commits theft if, having control over the disposition of services of others, to which he is not entitled, he diverts such services to his own benefit or to the benefit of another not entitled thereto.

Section 223.8 Theft by Failure to Make Required Disposition of Funds Received.

A person who obtains property upon agreement, or subject to a known legal obligation, to make specified payment or other disposition, whether from such property or its proceeds or from his own property in equivalent amount, is guilty of theft if he deals with the property obtained as his own and fails to make the required payment or disposition. The foregoing applies notwithstanding that it may be impossible to identify particular property as belonging to the victim at the time of the actor's failure to make the required payment or disposition. An officer or employee of the government or of a financial institution is presumed: (i) to know any legal obligation relevant to his criminal liability under this Section, and (ii) to have dealt with the property as his own if he fails to pay or account upon lawful demand, or if an audit reveals a shortage of falsification of accounts.

Motor Vehicle Theft. Theft of motor vehicles is one of the theft offenses. In some states, motor vehicle theft is covered by the theft offenses defined in the Penal Code;[22] in other states, motor vehicle theft statutes appear in the Motor Vehicle Code.[23] The words "motor vehicle" includes automobiles, airplanes, motorcycles, or other motor-propelled vehicle.

Removing engine numbers, selling or offering for sale a motor vehicle without the engine number, attempting to obtain a license on a stolen motor vehicle or one with the engine number removed, transferring used cars without complying with the regulations set up in the law, offering a car for sale without having the proper certificate, altering a certificate of title, offenses having to do with liens on motor vehicles, constitute related offenses. These usually are to be found in the Motor Vehicle Code. Transporting stolen vehicles across a state line is a federal offense, set out in the United States Code.[24]

Model Penal Code Provisions. Thefts of motor vehicles are included in the general theft offense designated in the Model Penal Code "Theft by Unlawful Taking or Disposition." You will remember that the approach to the theft offenses in the Code is to define them according to the character of the unlawful taking. The Code provisions are as follows:

> **Section 223.2 Theft by Unlawful Taking or Disposition.**
> (1) *Movable Property.* A person is guilty of theft if he takes, or exercises unlawful control over, movable property of another with purpose to deprive him thereof.

Receiving Stolen Property. The Model Code identifies the separate offense of "Receiving Stolen Property," as do the statutes of most states.[25] The necessary elements of this offense are (1) that the property was stolen and (2) that the person receiving it knew it was stolen. The Model Penal Code also contains a provision, common to the provisions in most states, that a person engaged in the business of buying or selling goods is under certain circumstances *presumed* to know that property was stolen, as when a dealer is found in possession of stolen property on sepa-

22. Vernon's Ann.Texas Penal Code, Art. 1410, 1424, 1431–1437.

23. West's Ann.Cal.Vehicle Code, § 10851.

24. *Transportation of Stolen Vehicles.* Whoever transports in interstate or foreign commerce a motor vehicle or aircraft, knowing the same to have been stolen, shall be fined not more than $5,000 or imprisoned not more than five years, or both. 18 U.S.C.A. § 2312.

25. Vernon's Ann.Texas Penal Code, Art. 1430.

rate occasions and buys property for less than it is worth. This kind of provision makes it easier to convict pawnshops and similar places generally thought to "fence" stolen property, since the defendant will have to put in evidence to show that he didn't know the property was stolen. The effect of a presumption of this sort is to put the burden of producing some evidence against the presumption on the defendant.

Model Penal Code Provisions Relating to Receiving Stolen Property. The Model Penal Code provisions are as follows:

Section 223.6 Receiving Stolen Property.

(1) *Receiving.* A person is guilty of theft if he receives, retains, or disposes of movable property of another knowing that it has been stolen, or believing that it has probably been stolen, unless the property is received, retained, or disposed with purpose to restore it to the owner. "Receiving" means acquiring possession, control or title, or lending on the security of the property.

(2) *Presumption of Knowledge.* The requisite knowledge or belief is presumed in the case of a dealer who:

(a) is found in possession or control of property stolen from two or more persons on separate occasions; or

(b) has received stolen property in another transaction within the year preceding the transaction charged; or

(c) being a dealer in property of the sort received, acquires it for a consideration which he knows is far below its reasonable value.

"Dealer" means a person in the business of buying or selling goods.

New York has three degrees of an offense called "Criminal Possession of Stolen Property." [26]

In Illinois, receiving stolen property is contained in the general theft offense.[27]

26. McKinney's N.Y.Penal Law, §§ 165.40, 165.45, 165.50.

27. Smith-Hurd Ill.Ann.Stat. ch. 38, § 16.1. People v. McCormick, 92 Ill.App.2d 6, 235 N.E.2d 832 (1968).

Unauthorized Use of Automobiles. The law had trouble in deciding upon the offense committed by a person who takes an automobile, motorcycle, motorboat, or other vehicle merely for the "ride." [28] Some states include the offense within the definition of theft, but provide for a lesser penalty (a fine only) if the vehicle is returned to the owner before any prosecution for the offense begins.[29] Some states have a special offense called "Unauthorized Use of Motor Vehicles," [30] or "Joy Riding." [31] The Model Penal Code makes the offense a misdemeanor, or no offense at all if the actor can show that he reasonably believed that the

28. In Illinois, evidence that a service station operator took another's automobile for the purpose of going to get coffee and who returned it to the service station was held to be insufficient to convict him of larceny of the motor vehicle. People v. De Stefano, 23 Ill.2d 427, 178 N.E. 2d 393 (1961).

29. Vernon's Ann.Texas Penal Code, Art. 1424: *Voluntary Return.* If property taken under such circumstances as to constitute theft be voluntarily returned within a reasonable time, and before any prosecution is commenced therefor, the punishment shall be a fine not exceeding one thousand dollars.

30. McKinney's N.Y.Penal Law, § 165.05. A person is guilty of unauthorized use of a vehicle when:

1. Knowing that he does not have the consent of the owner, he takes, operates, exercises control over, rides in or otherwise uses a vehicle. A person who engages in any such conduct without the consent of the owner is presumed to know that he does not have such consent; or
2. Having custody of a vehicle pursuant to an agreement between himself or another and the owner thereof whereby he or another is to perform for compensation a specific service for the owner involving the maintenance, repair or use of such vehicle, he intentionally uses or operates the same, without the consent of the owner, for his own purposes in a manner constituting a gross deviation from the agreed purpose; or
3. Having custody of a vehicle pursuant to an agreement with the owner thereof whereby such vehicle is to be returned to the owner at a specified time, he intentionally retains or withholds possession thereof, without the consent of the owner, for so lengthy a period beyond the specified time as to render such retention or possession a gross deviation from the agreement.

31. West's Ann.Cal.Penal Code, § 499b, is the "joyride" statute of the Code. Specific intent is not an element of the offense defined under this section. However, prosecution under Section 503 of the California Motor Vehicle Code, though it does not require an intent to steal, does require an intent to temporarily or permanently deprive the owner of the possession of the motor vehicle. The offense under Section 503 is committed when the taking or driving away is accompanied by the lack of consent of the owner and by the intention to temporarily deprive the owner of title or possession of the vehicle. People v. Lawrence Zervas, 61 Cal.App.2d 381, 142 P.2d 946 (1943).

owner of the vehicle would have consented to his using it had he known of it. The Model Penal Code Provisions are as follows:

Section 223.9 Unauthorized Use of Automobiles and Other Vehicles.

A person commits a misdemeanor if he operates another's automobile, airplane, motorcycle, motorboat, or other motor-propelled vehicle without consent of the owner. It is an affirmative defense to prosecution under this Section that the actor reasonably believed that the owner would have consented to the operation had he known of it.

ARSON

Arson, at common law, was the unlawful burning of the dwelling house belonging to another. As in the case of burglary, the statutory definitions extend the behavior prohibited by the common law, and arson now includes the willful burning of any structure belonging to another, and under some circumstances to the burning of one's own property.[32] A related offense, called

32. Smith-Hurd Ill.Ann.Stat. ch. 38, § 20–1: A person commits arson when, by means of fire or explosive, he knowingly:

(a) Damages any real property, or any personal property having a value of $150 or more, of another without his consent; or

(b) With intent to defraud an insurer, damages any property or any personal property having a value of $150 or more.

Property "of another" means a building or other property, whether real or personal, in which a person other than the offender has an interest which the offender has no authority to defeat or impair, even though the offender may also have an interest in the building or property.

Penalty. A person convicted of arson shall be imprisoned in the penitentiary for any indeterminate term with a minimum of not less than one year.

A special offense of possession of explosives or incendiary devices may carry a severe penalty. § 20–2: Whoever possesses, manufactures or transports any explosive compound, timing or detonating device for use with any explosive compound or incendiary device and either intends to use such explosive or device to commit any offense or knows that another intends to use such explosive or device to commit any offense for which one of the possible penalties is imprisonment in the penitentiary shall be imprisoned in the penitentiary from one to 20 years.

New York identifies three degrees of arson. McKinney's Penal Law, § 150.05:

1. A person is guilty of arson in the third degree when he reck-

lessly damages a building by intentionally starting a fire or causing an explosion.

2. In any prosecution under this section, it is an affirmative defense that no person other than the defendant had a possessory or proprietary interest in the building.

Arson in the third degree is a Class E felony.

§ 150.10:

1. A person is guilty of arson in the second degree when he intentionally damages a building by starting a fire or causing an explosion.
2. In any prosecution under this section, it is an affirmative defense that (a) no person other than the defendant had a possessory or proprietary interest in the building, or if other persons had such interests, all of them consented to the defendant's conduct, and (b) the defendant's sole intent was to destroy or damage the building for a lawful and proper purpose, and (c) the defendant had no reasonable ground to believe that his conduct might endanger the life or safety or another person or damage another building.

Arson in the second degree is a Class C felony.

§ 150.15: A person is guilty of arson in the first degree when he intentionally damages a building by starting a fire or causing an explosion, and when (a) another person who is not a participant in the crime is present in such building at the time, and (b) the defendant knows that fact or the circumstances are such as to render the presence of such a person therein a reasonable possibility.

Arson in the first degree is a Class B felony.

Vernon's Ann.Texas Penal Code, Art. 1304: "Arson" is the wilful burning of any house included within the meaning of the succeeding article of this chapter.

Art. 1305: A "house" is any building, edifice, or structure enclosed with walls and covered, whatever may be the material used for building.

Art. 1306: The burning is complete, when the fire has actually communicated to a house, though it may be neither destroyed nor seriously injured.

West's Ann.Cal.Penal Code, § 447a: Any person who willfully and maliciously sets fire to or burns or causes to be burned or who aids, counsels or procures the burning of any trailer coach, as defined in Section 635 of the Vehicle Code, or any dwelling house, or any kitchen, shop, barn, stable or other outhouse that is parcel thereof, or belonging to or adjoining thereto, whether the property of himself or of another, shall be guilty of arson, and upon conviction thereof, be sentenced to the penitentiary for not less than two or more than 20 years.

Burning of other buildings and of public buildings carries the same penalty. (See § 448a.)

The punishment for unlawful burning of personal property is not less than one nor more than three years. (See § 449a.)

Unlawful burning of bridges, tents, stacks of hay and grain, box, telephone and telegraph poles, etc., of a value of $25 or over carries a penalty of from one to ten years. (See § 449b.)

Burning of crops has the same penalty. (See § 449c.)

Burning with intent to defraud insurers is a separate offense carrying a penalty of one to five years. (See § 450a.)

variously "Willful Burning," "Unlawful Burning of Personal Property," covers the willful burning of personal property such as piles of lumber, stacks of hay and grain, woodland grass and prairie belonging to another, bridges, fences, cars, boats, and the like. Under some circumstances, this offense, like arson, may be committed when an owner willfully burns his own property.

The Elements of the Offense of Arson. The usual elements of the offense of Arson are:

1. willful burning;
2. of a building or structure;
3. belonging to another; or
4. structure belonging to oneself if,
    (a). it is insured,
    (b). it is in a city or populated place; or
    (c). a person is injured or real personal property belonging to another is burned as a result of the setting of the fire.

The *actus reus* of arson is the burning; the *mens rea* is that the burning be done willfully.

A structure is usually defined as any edifice enclosed with walls and covered, whatever the material used. Frequently a higher penalty is imposed for burning an "occupied structure," which includes any building commonly used and occupied as a home, store, etc., whether or not anyone is actually in it at the time of the fire.

In New York, "building" is defined in the arson statutes as follows:

> As used in this article, "building," in addition to its ordinary meaning, includes any structure, vehicle or watercraft used for overnight lodging of persons, or used by persons for carrying on business therein. Where a building consists of two or more units separately secured or occupied, each unit shall not be deemed a separate building.[33]

33. McKinney's N.Y.Penal Law, § 150.00.

Texas uses the word "house" and defines it as follows: A "house" is any building, edifice, or structure inclosed with walls and covered, whatever may be the material used for building. Vernon's Ann.Texas Penal Code, Art. 1305.

Burning of personal property is covered by offense entitled "Other Wilful Burning." Arts. 1317–1329.

To constitute a *burning*, it is not necessary that the building burn down or even that it be severely damaged—if the fire is "communicated" to the building, that is sufficient. No particular method of setting the fire is required to constitute the offense. An explosion which damages a building comes within the definition of arson in most states, though the statutes may make this a different offense or provide a higher penalty.

Burnings Excluded From the Offense of Arson. Since the *mens rea* of arson is a willful burning, accidental fire-setting is usually not included. However, "accidental" fire-setting under circumstances that amount to a reckless disregard of the lives and property of others, may be deemed "willful." Burning of one's own property does not usually constitute arson. However, burning of one's own property can be arson under the circumstances already set out, i. e., if (a) the property is insured, (b) is in a city or populated area, (c) the fire causes damage to the person or real or personal property of another.[34] The statutes also often specifically exclude from the offense of arson the blowing up or burning of a structure for the purpose of saving another house from fire. The situation in mind here is where firemen or others blow up a building to provide a fire-break and thus prevent the fire from spreading to substantial sections of a city or town.

The Model Penal Code definitions of Arson are similar to the traditional definitions. The Code also sets up the related offenses of Causing or Risking Catastrophe and Criminal Mischief. The offense of Causing or Risking Catastrophe covers behavior dangerous to others in addition to burning, such as causing a flood, releasing poisonous gas, etc. The offense of Criminal Mischief covers the negligent (as opposed to the willful or reckless)

In Illinois, the offense of arson is committed when the damage is to any real or personal property. See fn. 32, *supra*, Smith-Hurd Ill.Ann. Stat. ch. 38, § 20–1.

See fn. 32, *supra*, West's Ann.Cal. Penal Code, § 447a.

See also, People v. Fisher, 51 Cal. 319 (1876).

34. Vernon's Ann.Texas Penal Code, Art. 1311: The owner of a house may destroy it by fire or explosion without incurring the penalty of arson, except in the cases mentioned in the succeeding article.

Art. 1312: When a house is within a town or city, or when it is insured, or when there is within it any property belonging to another, or when there is apparent danger by reason of the burning thereof, that the life or person of some individual, or the safety of some house belonging to another will be endangered, the owner, if he burn the same, is guilty of arson.

damage of property of another by various means, including fire and explosion.

Model Penal Code Provisions. The provisions of the Model Penal Code defining Arson are as follows:

Section 220.1 Arson and Related Offenses.

(1) *Arson.* A person is guilty of arson, a felony of the second degree, if he starts a fire or causes an explosion with the purpose of:

(a) destroying a building or occupied structure of another; or

(b) destroying or damaging any property, whether his own or another's, to collect insurance for such loss. It shall be an affirmative defense to prosecution under this paragraph that the actor's conduct did not recklessly endanger any building or occupied structure of another or place any other person in danger of death or bodily injury.

(2) *Reckless Burning or Exploding.* A person commits a felony of the third degree if he purposely starts a fire or causes an explosion, whether on his own property or another's, and thereby recklessly:

(a) places another person in danger of death or bodily injury; or

(b) places a building or occupied structure of another in danger of damage or destruction.

(3) *Failure to Control or Report Dangerous Fire.* A person who knows that a fire is endangering life or a substantial amount of property of another and fails to take reasonable measures to put out or control the fire, when he can do so without substantial risk to himself, or to give a prompt fire alarm, commits a misdemeanor if:

(a) he knows that he is under an official contractual, or other legal duty to prevent, or combat, the fire; or

(b) the fire was started, albeit lawfully, by him or with his assent, or on property in his custody or control.

(4) *Definitions.* "Occupied structure" includes a ship, trailer, sleeping car, airplane, or other vehicle, structure or place adapted for overnight accommodation of persons or

for carrying on business therein, whether or not a person is actually present. Property is that of another, for the purposes of this section, if anyone other than the actor has a possessory or proprietory interest therein. If a building or structure is divided into separately occupied units, any unit not occupied by the actor is an occupied structure of another.

Section 220.2 Causing or Risking Catastrophe.

(1) *Causing Catastrophe.* A person who causes a catastrophe by explosion, fire, flood, avalanche, collapse of building, release of poison gas, radioactive material or other harmful or destructive force or substance, or by any other means of causing potentially widespread injury or damage, commits a felony of the second degree if he does so purposely or knowingly, or a felony of the third degree if he does so recklessly.

(2) *Risking Catastrophe.* A person is guilty of a misdemeanor if he recklessly creates a risk of catastrophe in the employment of fire, explosives or other dangerous means listed in Subsection (1).

(3) *Failure to Prevent Catastrophe.* A person who knowingly or recklessly fails to take reasonable measures to prevent or mitigate a catastrophe commits a misdemeanor if:

(a) he knows that he is under an official, contractual or other legal duty to take such measures; or

(b) he did or assented to the act causing or threatening the catastrophe.

Section 220.3 Criminal Mischief.

(1) *Offense Defined.* A person is guilty of criminal mischief if he:

(a) damages tangible property of another purposely, recklessly, or by negligence in the employment of fire, explosives, or other dangerous means listed in Section 220.2(1); or

(b) purposely or recklessly tampers with tangible property of another so as to endanger person or property; or

(c) purposely or recklessly causes another to suffer pecuniary loss by deception or threat

(2) *Grading.* Criminal mischief is a felony of the third degree if the actor purposely causes pecuniary loss in excess of $5,000, or a substantial interruption or impairment of public communication, transportation, supply of water, gas or power, or other public service. It is a misdemeanor if the actor purposely causes pecuniary loss in excess of $100, or a petty misdemeanor if he purposely or recklessly causes pecuniary loss in excess of $25. Otherwise criminal mischief is a violation.

In the past two chapters we have discussed the most common of the major crimes. Homicide, Assault, and Rape are classified as crimes against the person. Robbery is a crime against both persons and property. Burglary, Theft, Motor Vehicle Theft, and Arson are crimes against property.

In terms of frequency of occurrence, burglary is the most common crime. The incidence of robbery is considered an important indication of the social health of a modern society, i. e., the rise or fall of robbery offenses is deemed to indicate the degree to which a nation or state is, or is not, law-abiding.

As we have seen, in reporting crime statistics nation-wide, the Federal Bureau of Investigation uses the seven so-called "Index Crimes." These crimes are Murder; Non-Negligent Manslaughter; Forcible Rape; Robbery; Aggravated Assault; Burglary; Larceny $50.00 and Over; and Motor Vehicle Theft. The Uniform Crime Reports prepared by the Bureau show that crimes against persons exceed crimes against property by a ratio of almost 9 to 1.[35] Crimes of violence, which include robbery, make up approximately 13 percent of the Index.[36] You will note that of the crimes discussed in the past two chapters, arson and simple assault are not included in the Index Crimes.

35. President's Commission on Law Enforcement and Criminal Justice, *The Challenge of Crime in a Free Society*, Washington: U. S. Government Printing Office, 1967, p. 18.

36. *Ibid.*

Part Two

THE CRIMINAL JUSTICE PROCESS

INTRODUCTION TO PART TWO

The criminal justice system is the system by which society identifies, accuses, tries, convicts, and punishes offenders against the norms of the society expressed in the law. As we have seen, only certain norms of a society become embodied in its law. The criminal justice system, therefore, is not concerned with the enforcement of non-legal norms nor with the imposition of non-legal sanctions.

The criminal justice system is a *system* which involves interacting parts and is a *process* through which the offender moves in *stages*. If we follow the transgressor from suspicion of having committed an offense to ultimate release, we can easily identify the stages through which he passes—from investigation and arrest, to formal accusation, to trial, to conviction, to sentencing, to incarceration in a penal institution, to parole or mandatory release.

Of course, not everyone who starts through the system goes all the way through it. For many reasons, a suspect may never be arrested. The officer may be unable to develop enough evidence to support an arrest. The evidence, though sufficient to support an arrest, may not be sufficient to support the formal charge in an indictment or information. If he is indicted, the evidence may be insufficient to support conviction. If convicted, he may be allowed to be free on probation and not be sent to a penitentiary. If he is sent to the penitentiary, he may earn "good time" and be released quite early. Or he may be paroled, which means that he will serve part of his sentence under supervision in the community. Under any of these circumstances, the accused has not gone completely through the system which includes serving his full sentence in the penitentiary and final discharge.

A man may also by-pass the system at some point, and then re-enter it. For example, he may successfully appeal his conviction, have one conviction set aside, be re-tried, again convicted, and re-sentenced—in which case he will move again through the system in the usual way. He may also re-enter the system by committing a new offense and go through the entire process a second time. In such a case he is said to be a recidivist, or a repeater.

The criminal justice system may be likened to an assembly line in an automobile factory (though it is not even remotely as efficient as an assembly line). The offender, like the car, is on a moving belt. As he passes from station to station, different people do different things to him until ultimately he comes out at the end of the line a convicted man who has, hopefully, been "corrected" and is now ready to be discharged from the system. If he "makes it" without further trouble, he has, in effect, passed the final inspection and can function successfully in the "free world." The man, like the car, may drop off the assembly line at many points and never get clear to the end. He may be taken off the line temporarily and then be put back on it. He may get entirely through the line, but by committing a new offense, flunk the final inspection. So he is "called back by the factory," taken out of circulation, and started again through the line.

Unfortunately, many practitioners in law enforcement and corrections never understand the criminal justice system *as a system.* There is often little effective communication between parts of the system that must work constantly and closely together. Police officers, for example, complain (but not usually to the probation officers) that when they take juvenile offenders to the juvenile court, the court releases them so fast that "the kids beat us home." The probation officers reply (but seldom directly to the police officers) that "Home was the best place for the boy, and besides we have no other place to put him—the detention home is full, the institution for boys is full, and probation case loads are impossibly high." Because of this lack of communication and understanding and because obstacles along the line keep increasing, the criminal justice system is in danger of breaking down. If we go back to our assembly line analogy, it is obvious that if the line breaks or slows down at any one point, production ultimately stops. The cars ahead of the break-down point may be completed, but the cars behind pile up. The same thing happens in the criminal justice system. Let us consider a few examples.

The Supreme Court in its decision in Gideon v. Wainwright[1] in 1963 decreed that the right to be represented by a lawyer at a criminal trial is a constitutional right. As a result, over 4,000 inmates of the Florida prison system had to be re-tried. About 2,000 of them were not re-convicted and were set free. Florida had empty beds in its prisons for the first time in many years, and abandoned plans for constructing a new penal institution. County jails overflowed and there was no money for moving and guarding prisoners awaiting new trials. The relationship between county and state officials reached a new low. Thus, the requirement of counsel in a criminal trial was immediately felt along the entire criminal justice system of that state, and of other states as well.

When the percentage of guilty pleas declined in the District of Columbia, the average time lapse between arrest and conviction increased drastically. When counsel was required to be present at a line-up, the time needed in the station house expanded, and the investigatory parts of the criminal justice system slowed down. The *Gault* case[2] drastically altered juvenile court practices and procedures. Whenever a new requirement is introduced at any point in the criminal justice system, the movement of the accused through the system is slowed down or halted. If "warnings" must be given by the police, and the accused taken an extra time before the magistrate, the arrest and booking process takes longer. If additional questions must be asked of prospective jurors, the trial slows down. If pre-sentence reports are mandatory, additional time elapses between conviction and sentence. If the legislature cuts the "good time" allowance in the prison system, almost all of the inmates remain longer in prison. And so on.

The American Bar Foundation recently undertook a series of studies to find out how the criminal justice system actually works. Known as *The American Bar Foundation's Administration of Criminal Justice* series, the studies clearly demonstrated that no practitioner in the criminal justice system can any longer properly perform his own job unless he has a clear understanding of

1. Gideon v. Wainwright, 372 U.S. 335, 83 S.Ct. 792, 9 L.Ed.2d 799 (1963).

2. In re Gault, 387 U.S. 1, 87 S.Ct. 1428, 18 L.Ed.2d 527 (1967).

the entire process through which the offender moves from investigation to ultimate release. The studies also demonstrated that when changes are made in one part of the system, or the process is modified along any of its points, the effect is felt throughout the entire system.

General observations about the Criminal Justice System in the United States which appeared in an American Bar Foundation Report are worthy of quoting here:

> Four general observations may be made about the system of criminal justice in the United States. First, the system deals with an enormous number of cases, so high indeed as to constitute a chronic condition of system overload.
>
> Second, the system is pervaded by official discretion, that is, the power of individual judgment within general legal bounds. In part discretion is an administrative defense to system overload; in part it is an infusion of considerations of fairness or expediency into a system designed to assess guilt on formal legal premises; in part it is an inevitable feature of a criminal law system that must deal with conduct from first degree murder to parking violations and all shades within these extremes.
>
> Third, the administrative organization for dealing with crime and criminals is balkanized in the extreme. There are four functional components in the criminal law system: police, prosecution, judiciary, and corrections. In neither the United States as a whole nor in any single state is there common administrative supervision over these components, although there are points of common administration between some pairs of them in most states. Moreover, each one of these functional components may itself be divided jurisdictionally into parallel units. For example, in some localities there are county police (i. e., sheriffs' offices) and city police systems operating in the same geographical area; a county prosecutor and a city attorney prosecutor's office; a superior court for the trial of felonies, and a parallel, but independently operated, magistrate's court for hearing misdemeanors; and a division of correctional administration between local government, which handles probation and the administration of jail detention, and state government, which administers the prisons and parole supervision services.

> And finally, the quality of the personnel and facilities serving the system varies enormously from jurisdiction to jurisdiction. Such states as California and Wisconsin are conspicuously above the average in these respects. On the other hand, in many states, the personnel and facilities for the administration of criminal justice show the effects of long-term inadequacy of public support.[3]

The criminal justice process is the sequence of steps taken from the initial contact of the offender with the law until he is released back into a free society. The chart on the following page is a graphic representation of the criminal justice process. The process in no state is exactly like the one depicted on the chart, nor will the names of the steps in the system necessarily be the same. The chart, nevertheless, is an excellent composite of the procedures in the many states and in the federal system, and gives an accurate overview of the criminal justice process in the United States. The second chart gives information on the time required to complete each step of the process for a typical jurisdiction.

3. American Bar Foundation, *Criminal Justice in the United States*, Chicago: American Bar Foundation, 1967.

A general view of The Criminal Justice System *

This chart seeks to present a simple yet comprehensive view of the movement of cases through the criminal justice system. Procedures in individual jurisdictions may vary from the pattern shown here. The differing weights of line indicate the relative volumes of cases disposed of at various points in the system, but this is only suggestive since no nationwide data of this sort exists.

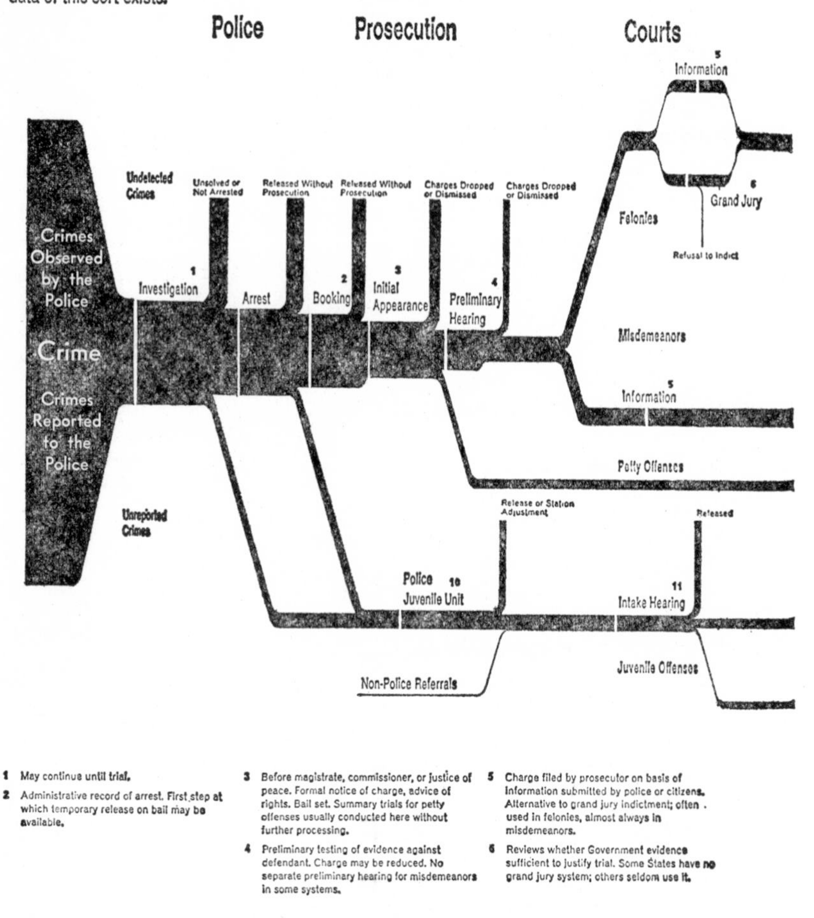

* THE PRESIDENT'S COMMISSION ON LAW ENFORCEMENT AND ADMINISTRATION OF JUSTICE: THE CHALLENGE OF CRIME IN A FREE SOCIETY 7–12 (1967)

[159Z]

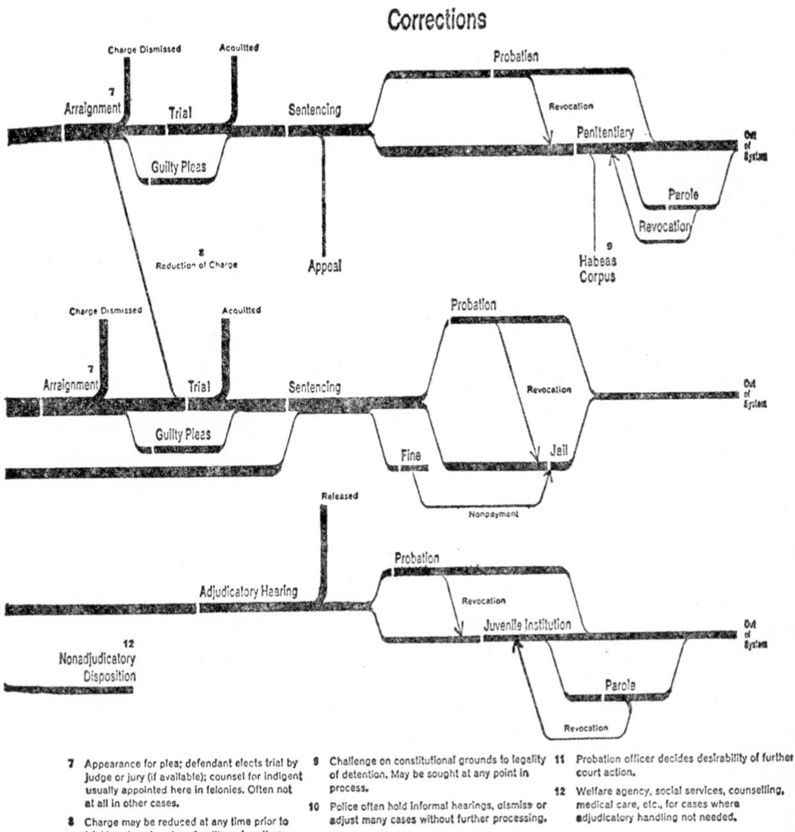

7 Appearance for plea; defendant elects trial by judge or jury (if available); counsel for indigent usually appointed here in felonies. Often not at all in other cases.

8 Charge may be reduced at any time prior to trial in return for plea of guilty or for other reasons.

9 Challenge on constitutional grounds to legality of detention. May be sought at any point in process.

10 Police often hold informal hearings, dismiss or adjust many cases without further processing.

11 Probation officer decides desirability of further court action.

12 Welfare agency, social services, counselling, medical care, etc., for cases where adjudicatory handling not needed.

[157Z]

TASK FORCE REPORT: SCIENCE AND TECHNOLOGY 40–42. NUMBER OF DAYS BETWEEN STEPS IN PROCESSING OF FELONY DEFENDANTS — 1965 (District of Columbia)

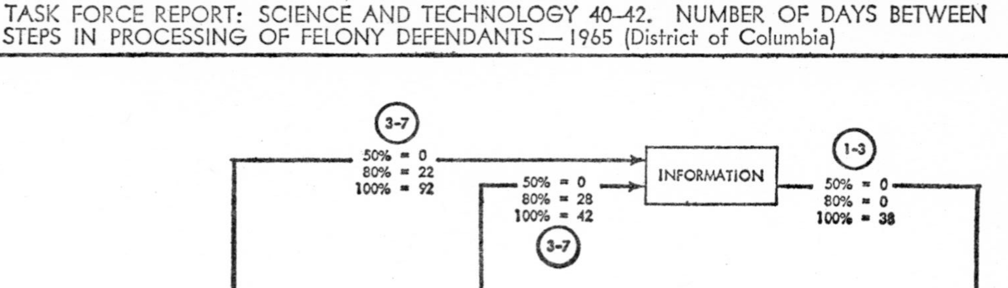
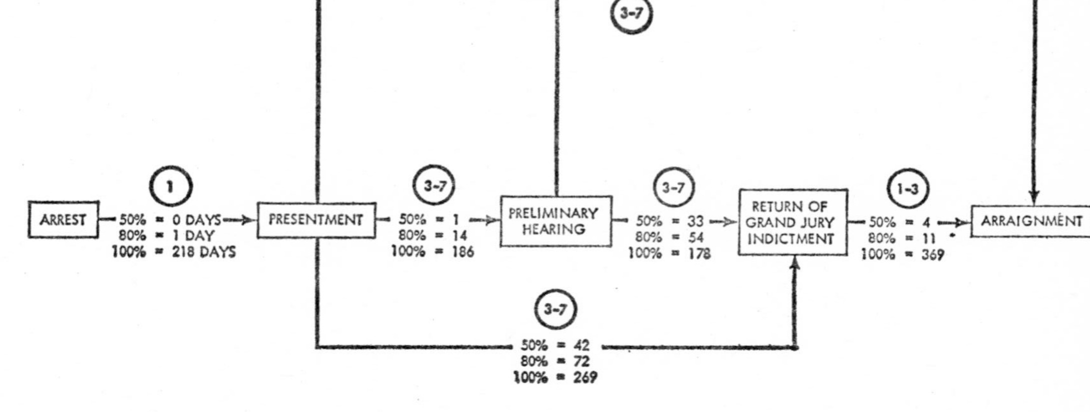

○ = Maximum number of days recommended by the Administration of Justice Task Force.

50% = 50th percentile. 50% of the defendants had times which exceeded the value shown.

80% = 80th percentile. 20% of the defendants had times which exceeded the value shown.

100% = The maximum time observed.

[160Z]

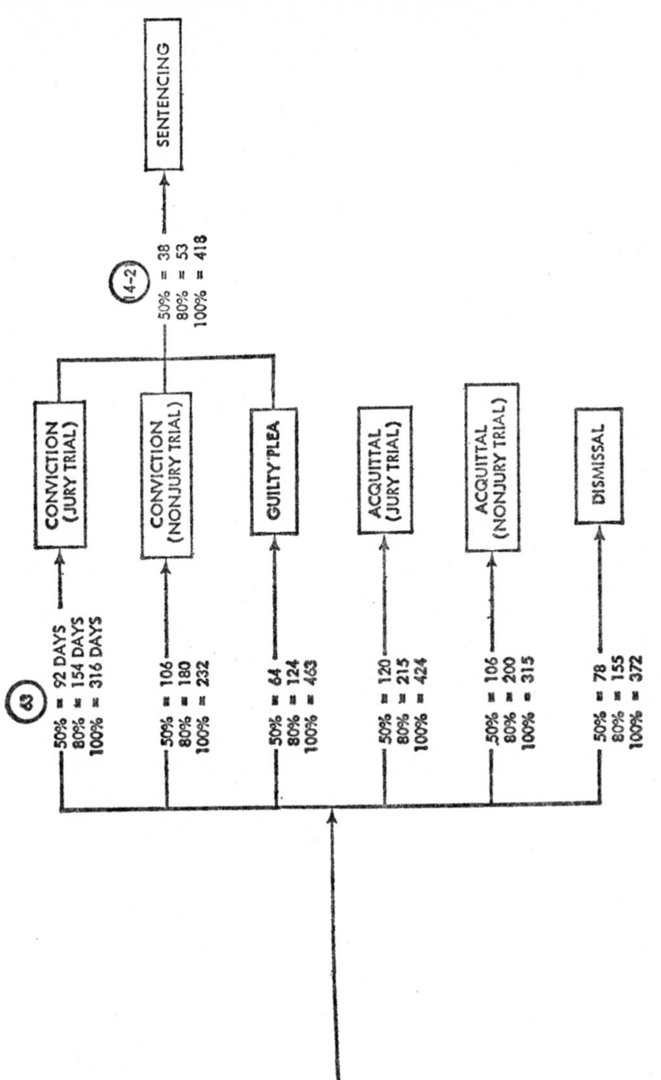

[158Z]

If you will look at the chart, you will see named in large black letters at the top the major parts of the criminal justice system—*Police*, *Prosecution*, *Courts*, and *Corrections*. Follow along the top horizontal lines to trace the steps of a felon through the criminal justice process from investigation until he is out of the system. The vertical lines above and below the main line show some of the ways he can drop out of the system, or by-pass parts of the process. The arrested offender may drop out because he is not indicted or convicted. He may be found guilty only of a misdemeanor and drop down into the misdemeanor process represented by the second horizontal line of the chart. If he receives probation, he may by-pass the penitentiary. Parole may shorten his stay in the penitentiary but revocation of parole take him back in. A successful appeal may either drop him out of the system or send him back to begin again at the point of trial. And so on.

The second horizontal line from the top has to do with misdemeanor offenses; the third with petty offenses, and the bottom line traces the juvenile court process.

The decision-making process in the law, we decided, is distinguished from informal decision-making processes in other means of social control by the existence of *courts*, so we defined law as "a formal means of social control that involves the use of rules that are interpreted, and are enforceable, by the courts of a political community." It is proper, therefore, that we begin our detailed study of the criminal justice system and the criminal justice process with the criminal courts. Juvenile courts are technically not criminal courts, but because they process juvenile offenders against the law, we will include them as a part of the criminal justice system. But first we must learn some of the basic concepts of the law and increase our legal vocabulary.

Chapter V

SOME BASIC CONCEPTS OF THE CRIMINAL LAW

In this chapter we will consider some concepts of the criminal law which are basic to our understanding of how the criminal justice system works. Many of these concepts apply as well to civil law, but since our major concern here is criminal justice, we will focus on their application in criminal law.

THE ADVERSARY SYSTEM

The Anglo-American system of law is an adversary system. This is to say that we conduct our legal decision making process by means of "choosing up sides" and staging a contest. In the criminal law, the state, the plaintiff, is on one side and the accused, the defendant, is on the other. The victim is on the state's side, or perhaps it is better to say that the state is on the victim's side. The contest is staged, however, between the state and the accused.

A contest in which the whole power of the state is arrayed against a single defendant hardly looks like a fair fight, of which fact the Founding Fathers were acutely aware. The guarantees and protections for the accused which they wrote into the Constitution and the Bill of Rights were for the express purpose of evening up the contest. Notice of the charges, representation by counsel, a public and impartial trial before a jury of his peers, were important safeguards accorded the defendant. He was also protected against being forced to testify against himself, and his papers and effects were made immune from unreasonable searches and seizures. Moreover, the accused was presumed to be innocent until proved guilty, and the state required to prove his guilt, not just by the weight of the evidence, but *beyond a reasonable doubt*. The provision against double jeopardy limited the contest to one bout; if the state lost in its first contest because the defendant was acquitted, it did not get a second chance to bring him to trial for the same offense.

Because it was felt that the constitutional protections and other procedural safeguards that developed in both the statutory and case law insured that the accused would receive a fair trial, the adversary system was accepted as the very best way to get at the truth. Thus, in every criminal case there is the plaintiff, the state, pitted against the defendant, the accused, before an impartial judge who acts as kind of a referee. The victim, called the prosecuting witness, assists the state in the presentation of the case. The rules of the contest are known to all parties in advance, and the judge sees to it that they are followed. Each side does its best to "win" by bringing in all the evidence in its favor and trying to discredit the evidence produced by the other side. Thus we have examination and cross-examination of witnesses. The arguments of counsel point out how strong the evidence is on their side and how weak and improbable the evidence is on the other side. Guilt or innocence must be determined from the evidence presented at the trial. And although the right to appeal is not a constitutional right, all of the states and the federal government have provided a method by which any defendant found guilty may appeal his conviction. On the other hand, if he is found innocent, there is no appeal granted the state that could overthrow the verdict of not-guilty or bring the accused back for another trial for the same offense.

Not all legal systems employ the adversary method of getting at the truth. In the Continental system of law, for example, the state is supposed to satisfy itself as to the guilt of the accused *before* it brings him to trial. Thus, when the trial begins he is presumed to be guilty, and must prove himself innocent. He is not judged by a jury of his peers, but by one or more judges appointed by the state. Even in England, which uses a trial system much like our own, the judge may "sum up" against the accused. This may almost amount to instructing the jury to bring in a verdict of guilty. A judge in the United States cannot comment on the weight of the evidence or the trustworthiness of witnesses. The facts are for the jury to decide.

In the United States, we set the rules to even up the contest, then by means of examination and cross-examination and arguments of counsel, each side presents its own case in the most favorable possible light. It is then up to the jury to decide what they consider to be the truth, and to render its verdict accordingly. As a further protection to the accused, the verdict in criminal cases must be unanimous, which means that all of the jurors must agree that the defendant is guilty before there can be conviction. If the jurors fail to agree, there is a "hung jury" and the defendant may be tried again. Usually, however, a hung jury results in the dismissal of the charge against him.

Advantages of the Adversary System. The advantages of the adversary system have been summed up as follows: It insures due process and a fair hearing to the accused and provides him with a lawyer who represents him exclusively and is his champion at all times. The trial serves the psychological needs of the participants, the spectators, and the community—the theory here is that a trial is a kind of safety-valve for public indignation against offenders. Probably the most important feature of the adversary system is that it leaves the moral judgment of guilt or innocence to the community—the community, in such case, being represented by the jurors.[1] However, not all people agree with this summation and there are those who advocate that we abolish the adversary system. Just what we would substitute is not clear.

THE CASE

Before there can be a case, there must be a controversy. In the criminal law the controversy is between the state, representing all the people as well as the victim, and the accused. A criminal case is therefore entitled: State of Wyoming v. John Jones; The People of the State of California v. Peter Smith; or The Commonwealth of Massachusetts v. Mary Williams. (The letter "v" stands for "versus," which means "against.")

The Controversy. In our system of jurisprudence a court will *not* hear a pretended or "sham" case, nor except in a few states will it give advisory opinions in advance of an actual dispute. It would be useless to go to a court and say, "If I do so and so, and somebody else does thus and thus, and we get into an argument about it, how will you decide?" After the "one man, one vote" rule was announced by the United States Supreme Court, several state legislatures attempted something like this. They said, "If

1. Davis, Foster, Jeffery & Davis, *op. cit.*, pp. 99–100.

we reapportion our state in such and such manner, will it be approved by the Court?" The Supreme Court answered, "*After* you have adopted a plan of reapportionment, we will tell you whether or not we approve."

Since a court will not hear a case when there is no controversy, if the controversy ends for any reason after the legal process has begun, no decision will be rendered. If during the trial a defendant dies, the trial will end. If during the trial someone else confesses to the crime, the trial will end. In civil cases some change in the status of one of the parties may terminate a case. For example, Adam Clayton Powell, a member of the House of Representatives from a New York district, had a suit pending for the purpose of reinstating him to the official positions in the Congress he had held before he was expelled from the House. He had been re-elected after the expulsion and allowed to resume his seat, but was not given the offices he had previously held. While his case on this matter was pending before the court, he was defeated for re-election. His case, in the words of the law, had thus become "moot." The court could not restore him to Congress, thus it would be useless to decide whether or not he had been illegally deprived of his special offices.

Standing. Not only must there be a controversy between real parties, the parties must have standing to sue. The doctrine of standing means that there is no justiciable controversy unless the party appearing in court shows that the conduct complained of by him invades or will invade a private substantive legally protected interest. The legal concept of standing keeps a citizen from coming into court to enforce or protect a "general principle" in which he has no personal and direct interest. Thus, a minister of the gospel has been held not to have "standing" to intervene in a case involving the right of a woman to have an abortion, or to prevent a certain hospital from performing abortions. Merely because the religious beliefs of his church are that abortion is sinful and should be prohibited by law does not give the minister the private substantive legally protected interest which will enable him to be a party in the suit or entitle him to present his arguments to the court. However, parties who have an identical interest in a pending controversy are sometimes permitted to intervene. The Supreme Court, for example, often gives leave to a state to file an "amicus curiae" (friend of the court) brief. Though the suit in Gideon v. Wainwright involved only the action of Florida in denying Gideon the right to counsel, many states appeared in that case as "friends of the court" to urge that the states not be required to provide counsel to the indigent defendant in a felony trial.

The Meaning of "Moot." The word "moot" means a sham or a pretense; thus, a pretended case, as opposed to a real one, is a "moot case." Law students practice trial procedures in a "moot court," so called because they are using pretended cases, not real ones, or if they actually reenact a real case, it is after it has been decided and hence no real controversy still exists. A moot case is defined as "one which seeks to get a judgment on a pretended controversy, when in reality there is none, or a decision in advance about a right before it has actually been asserted or contested, or a judgment upon some matter which, when rendered, for any reason, cannot have any practical legal effect upon a then existing controversy." [2]

Levels of Proof

We could draw a line representing a continuum of belief from complete doubt (no belief at all) to absolute certainty. Since the purpose of proof is to create belief, we could on the same line represent a continuum of proof from no proof to proof beyond all doubt.

Figure 1.

Complete doubt	Absolute certainty
No proof	Proof beyond all doubt

Continuum of Belief and Proof

Except for absolute certainty and thus proof beyond all doubt, which the law never requires and could not achieve, the legal process at different stages is concerned with several different levels of proof. At each stage in the criminal justice process there is the question of whether or not there is enough evidence to carry the process forward, and the degree of certainty required to act varies from stage to stage. In the criminal law, we can identify mere suspicion, reasonable belief, probable cause, preponderance of the evidence, and beyond a reasonable doubt as levels of proof, and certain levels of proof are required to support certain official actions in the criminal justice process.

2. Ex Parte Steele, 162 F. 694, 701 (D.C.Ala.1908).

Suspicion. Mere suspicion is sufficient to initiate an investigation of circumstances which may constitute an offense. The officer's suspicion may be aroused by things he has seen or heard or matters that have been reported to him.

Reasonable Belief. The officer who can show a reasonable belief based upon facts and circumstances perceived by the five senses (a mere "hunch" is not enough) that a crime has been committed has the authority to stop and question, and stop and frisk any individual who may be involved or who may have knowledge of the event. This means he can approach the individual and ask him his name and his business in the neighborhood. If the answers are unsatisfactory or there are other circumstances which contribute to a reasonable belief by the officer that a crime has been or is about to be committed, he may frisk the individual for weapons. A frisk is a search but differs from a complete search in that a frisk is accomplished by patting down the outer clothing and does not include examining pockets, inner clothing, and the like unless there is a bulge indicating a weapon, in which case the officer may remove the weapon wherever it is found.

Probable Cause. An officer may arrest, or a search warrant may be issued, upon probable cause, which means reasonable grounds to believe that a crime has been committed and that the accused committed it. A grand jury may return an indictment against an offender upon a finding of probable cause, or a magistrate may bind him over for trial after a preliminary hearing which discloses probable cause.

"Probable cause" has been defined in a leading decision by the United States Supreme Court, as follows:

> Probable means more than a mere suspicion and exists when facts and circumstances in knowledge of the officers and within which they had reasonable trustworthy information are sufficient in themselves to warrant a man of reasonable caution in the belief that an offense has been committed or is being committed.[3]

Probable cause is thus a quantum of proof sufficiently strong to warrant a reasonable belief that the accused has committed or is committing a crime. It is an important standard because it war-

3. Brinegar v. United States, 338 U.S. 160, 69 S.Ct. 1302, 93 L.Ed. 1879 (1949), reh. den. 338 U.S. 839, 70 S.Ct. 31, 94 L.Ed. 513.

must meet a level of proof which is "beyond a reasonable doubt." In the Continental system, the accused on trial is presumed to be guilty; thus, the burden of proving his innocence is on the accused. He doesn't have to prove his innocence beyond a reasonable doubt, but he does have to prove it by a preponderance of the evidence. In the United States, the burden of proof is on the State in a criminal action and the accused does not have to prove his innocence. (In a civil case, the burden of proof is on the plaintiff or the person seeking to establish the claim.)

"Burden of proof" is defined in Black's Law Dictionary as follows: "The necessity or duty of affirmatively proving a fact or facts in dispute on an issue raised between the parties in the cause." In a criminal case, the issue is the guilt or innocence of the defendant.

There are two meanings of the words "burden of proof," (1) the duty to establish the truth of the claim by the required weight of evidence (in a criminal case, beyond a reasonable doubt), which is sometimes called the "burden of the evidence;" and (2) the duty of producing evidence as the case progresses, called the burden of going forward with the evidence, or simply, "the burden of going forward."

The Duty of Establishing the Truth of the Claim. In a criminal action, the state has the burden of proving every material element of the offense beyond a reasonable doubt. This ultimate burden of the evidence never shifts, and if the state fails to prove any of the material elements of the offense beyond a reasonable doubt, the defendant is entitled to an acquittal.

The term burden of proof is not to be confused with the term "*prima facie* case." A *prima facie* case is one which is sufficient to establish the facts *if no evidence to the contrary is offered.* The burden of proof, on the contrary, means that the state must establish the material elements of the offense by the weight of all of the evidence, after the jury has duly considered all circumstances in the case and the testimony of the witnesses for both sides, including the opportunity of witnesses for observation of the facts, their interest in the case, their demeanor on the stand, and other circumstances. To meet its burden of proof, the evidence must indicate clearly that the state is entitled to the verdict because the greater amount of credible evidence sustains the allegations of the state as to the defendant's guilt of the offense.

The Burden of Going Forward With The Evidence. Though the burden of proof in a criminal action is always in the last resort upon the state and never shifts, it may be necessary as the case progresses for the defendant to put in evidence favorable to his side. Whenever the state has brought one side of the scale of evidence way down, the defendant has to do something to balance it up again. If the state presents a *prima facie* case (one that is good as it stands), then the defendant must introduce some evidence to disprove the state's case. The presumption that a man is sane is a form of evidence which the defendant can only counterbalance by putting in some proof of lack of mental capacity. Similarly, whenever the evidence at a particular time is favorable to the defendant, the state must go forward with the evidence by producing additional evidence in favor of the state. This duty is called the "burden of going forward with the evidence," and may pass from party to party as the case proceeds, though the ultimate duty to prove the case beyond a reasonable doubt rests with the state throughout the criminal trial.

DUE PROCESS

In discussing the adversary system, we mentioned that the Constitution gives to the accused certain protections for the purpose of evening-up his contest with the state. We discussed levels of proof and saw that in the sequence of steps from suspicion to conviction the law requires an ever increasing degree of proof before the state may take the next step toward the conviction of the accused, thus giving further protection to the accused. The myriad protection of the accused guaranteed in the Constitution of the United States and in the Constitutions of all of the states as well, are summed up in a legal concept known as "due process." The Fifth Amendment to the United States Constitution requires due process before the federal government can convict a man of an offense against the law. The Fourteenth Amendment to the Constitution says "No state shall deprive any person of life, liberty, or property, without due process of law." Just what constitutes "due process" in a particular case depends upon the facts in the case, the federal and state constitutional and statutory guarantees, the interpretation applied to those guarantees in the decisions of courts, particularly the United States

Supreme Court, and also to the values which the society desires to preserve and enforce at any given time or place. Due process is a *process*. The word "process" implies movement and change. Thus, the definitions of what constitutes due process expand and change.

The Bill of Rights. The words "by the law of the land" appeared in the Magna Charta (1215) and are considered to be the first written statement in Anglo-American law of the concept we now refer to as "due process." In Article 39 of the Magna Charta the King promised that: "No free man shall be arrested, or imprisoned, or disseized, or outlawed, or exiled, or in any way molested; nor will we proceed against him unless by the lawful judgment of his peers or by the law of the land." The words in the United States Constitution are "due process," and these are the words used in the constitutions of many of the states. Other states have kept the original phraseology "due course of the law of the land," or simply, "due course of law."

When the thirteen original colonies "pooled their sovereignty" to form the union, they were determined to preserve from federal encroachment the liberties which they considered essential to free men. When the original draft of the Constitution did not specifically guarantee these liberties, they refused to ratify it. It was not until the first ten Amendments were added to the basic document of government that the new nation could come into being. Because they guaranteed such important rights, these first ten Amendments to the United States Constitution have since been referred to as the "Bill of Rights."

At this time you should carefully read the first ten Amendments to the United States Constitution, which can be found in the back of the book. Note that Amendment I deals with freedom of religion, speech and press, and the right to peaceably assemble and petition the government for a redress of grievances. Amendment II guarantees the right of the people to keep and bear arms, at least in connection with a "well regulated militia." Amendment III prohibits a practice which had brought injury and inconvenience to the colonists—the quartering of soldiers in private homes. Amendments IV, V, and VI have to do with the criminal process. Amendment VII refers to civil cases but also provides that the decision on facts in a case shall be left to the jury. Amendment VIII provides for bail and protects against cruel and unusual punishments. Amendments IX and X are concerned with preserving to the states the rights not delegated to the federal government.

You will find the phrase "due process" in the Fifth Amendment "* * * nor shall (any person) be deprived of life, liberty, or property, without due process of law * * *"

The first ten Amendments were originally seen as applying *only* to the federal government. The original colonists were not apprehensive about securing their basic rights from violation by their state governments, which they could control. Since they were not at all sure they could secure these rights from a powerful and remote central government, they insisted that the Constitution itself guarantee these basic liberties. This they accomplished by prohibiting certain acts to the federal government. It is important to remember that the first ten Amendments originally applied only to the federal government. Some of the problems that have since arisen in the relationships between the federal and state governments, and particularly between the federal and state courts in the application of the criminal law, have their origin in the fact that the Amendments were not at first applicable to the states.

In 1868, during the Civil War, Amendments XIII, XIV, and XV were added to the Constitution. The Fourteenth Amendment was to prove to be the one which most profoundly affected the criminal law and the relationship between the federal and state courts. The second sentence in that amendment begins, "No *state*" and continues "shall make or enforce any law which shall abridge the privileges or immunities of citizens of the United States; nor shall *any state* [italics supplied] deprive any person of life, liberty, or property, without due process of law; nor deny to any person within its jurisdiction the equal protection of the law."

The Incorporation Argument. The impact of the Fourteenth Amendment was not immediately felt after its adoption in the criminal law of the states. However, it was soon noted that the Constitution now required "due process" not only of the federal government but of the states as well. Gradually, certain restrictions that had originally applied only to the federal government were held to be binding also upon the states. The question finally became, "Does the Fourteenth Amendment make applicable to the states all of the provisions of the Bill of Rights?" Stated another way, the question was, "Does the Fourteenth Amendment incorporate the Bill of Rights and make all of the provisions of the Bill of Rights binding upon the states?"

The attempt to find the answer to this question has proved to be a most difficult one, and even today it cannot be answered with a simple "yes" or "no." Several positions on the question have been assumed by different justices of the Supreme Court and legal scholars. There are those who answer the question, "Yes, the Fourteenth Amendment did incorporate all the provisions of the Bill of Rights and made them binding on the states." Those holding this position go on to say, "A democratic government requires that state criminal procedures become uniform in these important aspects, and that federal procedures be followed by the states." Another position says, "No, the Fourteenth Amendment did not incorporate the Bill of Rights." From this position it follows that the states should be free to work out their own criminal law and procedures so long as they do not violate the fundamental notions of fairness implicit in the concept of ordered government. Other justices and scholars took positions based on "selective incorporation," which meant that they believed that some, but not all, of the provisions of the Bill of Rights were made applicable to the states by the Fourteenth Amendment.

We cannot here analyze the different positions in detail nor comment pro and con upon their merits. Suffice it to say that the "Criminal Law Revolution" has seen a dramatic increase in the frequency with which the Supreme Court of the United States has made the provisions of the Bill of Rights binding upon the states. However, this by no means has resulted in state criminal procedures which are exactly like those of the federal government nor made the criminal laws of one state exactly like those of all of the sister states.

Due Process Rights of the Accused. The following are among the most fundamental of the due process rights guaranteed the accused in a criminal proceeding:

1. The right against unreasonable searches and seizures.
2. The right to be informed of his Constitutional rights whenever suspicion focuses upon him.
3. The right to remain silent, or the right against self-incrimination.
4. The right to counsel (a lawyer) at every critical stage of the criminal proceeding.

5. The right to reasonable notice of the nature of the charges against him.
6. The right to be heard, i. e., have his day in court.
7. The right to confront the witnesses against him.
8. The right to a fair trial in a fair tribunal (court) before an impartial judge.
9. The right to trial by jury for all except petty offenses.
10. The right to a speedy and public trial.
11. The right against double jeopardy, or the right not to be tried twice for the same offense.

The right to examine the record of the proceedings is sometimes included as one of the fundamental rights necessary for due process, but there are recognized exceptions to this right.

The right to appeal a criminal conviction is given to the convicted defendant in most states, and if provided for, must be made available to all defendants on an equal basis. Thus, counsel on appeal will be appointed for and transcripts furnished to an indigent defendant. However, the right to appeal is *not* considered a fundamental right guaranteed by the Constitution or the principles of due process.[5]

1. **The Right Against Unreasonable Searches and Seizures.** This guarantee is contained in the Fourth Amendment to the United States Constitution. It protects an individual against unreasonable searches and seizures of his person, his property, or his papers and effects. Since an arrest is a seizure of the person, this right protects the individual from unlawful arrest.

The Fourth Amendment does not protect the individual against all searches and seizures, but only against *unreasonable* searches and seizures. It is not easy to say which searches and seizures are unreasonable, and which are not. The Fourth Amendment contemplates that both arrests and searches shall be by warrant, based upon probable cause, but arrests and searches without warrant are, under certain circumstances, considered reasonable. Thus, not all warrantless searches and seizures are prohibited by the Constitution. As we shall see in Part II, an officer may arrest without warrant for a felony and (in most states) for a misdemeanor committed in his presence. A lawful arrest supports

5. In re Gault, 387 U.S. 1, 87 S.Ct. 1428, 18 L.Ed.2d 527 (1967).

a reasonable search without a warrant. The procedure known as "stop and frisk" has been held to be a reasonable search and seizure under certain circumstances,[6] though no probable cause for arrest exists at the time.

To determine whether or not a search or seizure is reasonable, each case must be considered on its own merits according to the guidelines set down by the United States Supreme Court, and the highest appellate courts of the states. A few rules can be stated: (1) Whenever reasonably possible, the police officer must secure a search warrant before he conducts a search. A search warrant is issued by a magistrate and can only be issued upon a showing of "probable cause" that the individual has committed some offense. Probable cause is more than suspicion, but less than certainty. (2) An arrest must also be based upon warrant issued by a magistrate after a showing of probable cause, unless an offense was committed in the presence of the officer or he has been informed of a felony by a reputable person and there is no opportunity to get a warrant, or to prevent the escape of the offender or the destruction of evidence. We will discuss these points more fully in the chapter on Investigation and Accusation.

2. **The Right to be informed of His Constitutional Rights Whenever Suspicion Focuses Upon Him.** This is sometimes called the "Right to the Miranda Warning." The United States Supreme Court in the landmark case of Miranda v. Arizona [7] declared that an accused must be informed of his Constitutional rights whenever suspicion focuses upon him. There are four parts to the Miranda Warning; the police officer must cover all points. The officer must warn the accused (1) that he has a right to remain silent; (2) that if he does talk, what he says may (will) be used against him; (3) that he has a right to counsel (a right to have an attorney represent him), and that he has the right to have counsel present at all questioning; (4) that if he cannot afford counsel, one will be provided for him at state expense. Most police officers these days read the Warning to the suspect from a printed card which they carry in their pockets. This is to make sure that they don't miss part of it, because if they do, it may jeopardize the conviction of the accused.

6. Terry v. Ohio, 392 U.S. 1, 88 S.Ct. 1868, 20 L.Ed.2d 889 (1968).

7. Miranda v. Arizona, 384 U.S. 436, 86 S.Ct. 1602, 16 L.Ed.2d 694 (1966), reh. den. 385 U.S. 890, 87 S.Ct. 11, 17 L.Ed.2d 121.

3. **The Right to Remain Silent.** The Fifth Amendment to the United States Constitution declares "No person shall * * * be compelled in any criminal case to be a witness against himself." This guarantee is referred to as the right to remain silent or the right against self-incrimination. This right protects the accused against being compelled to convict himself "out of his own mouth," and does away with forced confessions. Because of this guarantee, a defendant cannot be made to take the stand at his own trial. No comment may be made by the prosecution about the defendant's failure to take the stand in his own behalf, and no inferences can be drawn against the defendant because he refuses to testify for himself.[8]

4. **The Right to Counsel at Every Critical Stage of the Criminal Proceedings.** The Sixth Amendment to the United States Constitution declares that "In all criminal prosecutions, the accused shall enjoy the right to * * * have the Assistance of Counsel for his defence." This guarantee was originally interpreted to mean the right to counsel *of his own choosing,* and was not held to guarantee to an indigent defendant a right to counsel at state expense. In a series of important decisions, the United States Supreme Court gave to indigent defendants the same rights to counsel enjoyed by more affluent defendants, requiring that if the accused was too poor to employ his own counsel, one must be furnished him at state expense.[9] The Court has identified the "critical stages" of a criminal proceeding to include: trial of poor and ignorant defendant in a capital case;[10] trial in a non-capital felony case;[11] during interrogation at the station house;[12] during interrogation whenever suspicion has focused on the defendant;[13] during any time when the defendant was in custody and not free to leave the presence of the officer;[14] during the line-up (or show-

8. Griffin v. California, 380 U.S. 609, 85 S.Ct. 1229, 14 L.Ed.2d 106 (1965), reh. den. 381 U.S. 957, 85 S.Ct. 1797, 14 L.Ed.2d 730.

9. Griffin v. Illinois, 351 U.S. 12, 76 S.Ct. 585, 100 L.Ed. 891 (1956), reh. den. 351 U.S. 958, 76 S.Ct. 844, 100 L.Ed. 1480.

10. Powell v. Alabama, 287 U.S. 45, 53 S.Ct. 55, 77 L.Ed. 158 (1932).

11. Gideon v. Wainwright, 372 U.S. 335, 83 S.Ct. 792, 9 L.Ed.2d 799 (1963), on remand 153 So.2d 299 (Fla.).

12. Escobedo v. Illinois, 378 U.S. 478, 84 S.Ct. 1758, 12 L.Ed.2d 977 (1964).

13. Miranda v. Arizona, 384 U.S. 436, 86 S.Ct. 1602, 16 L.Ed.2d 694 (1966), reh. den. 385 U.S. 890, 87 S.Ct. 11, 17 L.Ed.2d 121.

14. Orozco v. Texas, 394 U.S. 324, 89 S.Ct. 1095, 22 L.Ed.2d 311 (1969), on remand 442 S.W.2d 376 (Tex).

up);[15] at the preliminary hearing;[16] at arraignment;[17] at entry of plea of guilty;[18] at the time of sentencing;[19] at a probation revocation hearing;[20] on appeal;[21] in juvenile delinquency proceedings.[22]

In Minnesota, the right to counsel has been extended to a parole revocation hearing.[23] The right to counsel in misdemeanor cases with felony length prison sentences has been upheld,[24] but the Supreme Court has declined to review cases where a state failed to provide counsel in misdemeanor cases carrying relatively short jail sentences.

The decision in Gideon v. Wainwright [25] was made retroactive by the Supreme Court. The result was that all persons in custody who had been convicted of a felony without aid of counsel had to be given new trial. In the state of Florida alone, some 4,000 felons were entitled to a new trial; some 2,000 convicted persons obtained their release because a new conviction could not be obtained. The fact that *Gideon* was made retroactive is indicative of the importance the court places upon the Constitutional guarantee of the right to counsel, a right which has been called the "most pervasive right of the accused."

5. **The Right to Reasonable Notice of the Nature of the Charges Against Him.** The Sixth Amendment to the United States Constitution reads in part as follows:

> In all criminal prosecutions, the accused shall enjoy the right to a speedy and public trial, by an impartial jury of the

15. United States v. Wade, 388 U.S. 218, 87 S.Ct. 1926, 18 L.Ed.2d 1149 (1967).

16. Coleman v. Alabama, 399 U.S. 1, 90 S.Ct. 1999, 26 L.Ed.2d 387 (1970). White v. Maryland, 373 U.S. 59, 83 S.Ct. 1050, 10 L.Ed.2d 193 (1963), conformed to 231 Md. 533, 191 A.2d 237.

17. Hamilton v. Alabama, 368 U.S. 52, 82 S.Ct. 157, 7 L.Ed.2d 114 (1961), on remand 273 Ala. 504, 142 So.2d 868.

18. Moore v. Michigan, 355 U.S. 155, 78 S.Ct. 191, 2 L.Ed.2d 167 (1957).

19. Townsend v. Burke, 334 U.S. 736, 68 S.Ct. 1252, 92 L.Ed. 1690 (1948).

20. Mempa v. Rhay, 389 U.S. 128, 88 S.Ct. 254, 19 L.Ed.2d 336 (1967).

21. Douglas v. California, 372 U.S. 353, 83 S.Ct. 814, 9 L.Ed.2d 811 (1963), reh. den. 373 U.S. 905, 83 S.Ct. 1288, 10 L.Ed.2d 200.

22. In re Gault, 387 U.S. 1, 87 S.Ct. 1428, 18 L.Ed.2d 527 (1967).

23. Warren v. Michigan Parole Board, 23 Mich.App. 754, 179 N.W. 2d 664 (1970).

24. Patterson v. Warden, 372 U.S. 776, 83 S.Ct. 1103, 10 L.Ed.2d 137 (1963).

25. 372 U.S. 335, 83 S.Ct. 792, 9 L. Ed.2d 799 (1963), on remand 153 So. 2d 299 (Fla.).

> State and District wherein the crime shall have been committed * * * and to be informed of the nature of the accusation; to be confronted with the witnesses against him; to have compulsory process for obtaining witnesses in his favor; and to have the Assistance of Counsel for his defense.[26]

The provisions of the Sixth Amendment, and similar provisions in the constitutions of the states, require that the accused be informed of the reason for his arrest; that he be shown a copy of the arrest warrant and of the complaint; that he be served with a copy of the information or indictment; and that he be personally present at the arraignment to enter his plea. The complaint, information or indictment must set forth in plain language of what offense the accused is charged, and give the date when he is supposed to have committed the offense. Unless he waives the right, the complaint, information, or indictment must be read to the accused in open court before he is required to answer the charges.

As part of the right to be informed of the nature of the charges against him, the federal statutes and the laws of many states require that when the accused is taken into custody he must be taken "immediately" or "without unnecessary delay," before a magistrate.[27]

A magistrate is a judge. Just who is a magistrate is determined by the laws of the state. Usually, judges of municipal courts, justices of the peace, and judges of county courts are magistrates. Judges of courts of record and appellate court judges may also be magistrates. In the federal system, all of the judges are magistrates, as are the United States Magistrates (formerly United States Commissioners).

26. Constitution of the United States of America, Sixth Amendment.

27. McNabb v. United States, 318 U.S. 332, 63 S.Ct. 608, 87 L.Ed. 819 (1943), reh. den. 319 U.S. 784, 63 S. Ct. 1322, 87 L.Ed. 1727.

Mallory v. United States, 354 U.S. 449, 77 S.Ct. 1356, 1 L.Ed.2d 1479 (1957).

Smith-Hurd Illinois Ann.Stat., ch. 38, § 109–1.

Vernon's Ann.Texas C.C.P. arts. 15.16–15.17.

McKinney's N.Y. CPL 120.90.

West's Ann.Cal.Penal Code § 825: The defendant must in all cases be taken before the magistrate without unnecessary delay, and, in any event, within two days after his arrest, excluding Sundays and holidays; * * *.

In practice, lower court judges and justices of the peace perform the duties of a "committing magistrate," and the initial appearance of the accused before a magistrate is before one of these lower court judges.

The duty of the magistrate is to determine the identity of the accused to make sure that he is the person meant to be charged, and to inform the accused of the charges against him. The magistrate again informs the accused of his Constitutional rights (repeating the Miranda Warning) and adds information about his rights to a preliminary hearing or other rights given him by the law of the state.

In all cases where notice to the accused is required, this notice must be given sufficiently in advance to enable the defendant to prepare his plea or defense, except that no prior notice need be given of the filing of the complaint or the issuance of the warrant of arrest or search. An accused may sometimes be arrested on a warrant which the police officer does not have in his possession. As soon as it is received, however, a copy must be delivered to the accused.

6. **The Right to be Heard.** The right to be heard is derived from the Sixth Amendment rights of the accused to have compulsory process for obtaining witnesses in his favor. This right permits (but does not require) the accused to testify for himself, and to speak in mitigation of punishment at the time of sentencing. The accused is granted a hearing on revocation of probation, and by statute or in practice is usually granted such a hearing on revocation of parole. The First Amendment gives all persons a right of access to the courts as a part of their right to "petition the Government for a redress of grievances." [28]

7. **The Right to Confront the Witnesses Against Him.** The Sixth Amendment guarantee of the right to confront witnesses against him gives the accused the right to face his accuser and to cross examine witnesses against him. It protects him against the introduction of hearsay (secondhand) evidence, except in certain well recognized situations. When the accused knows the character of the evidence against him, he can prepare his defense, and refute the testimony against him if it is not true. The right to confront a witness includes the right to cross-examine him.

28. Constitution of the United States of America, First Amendment.

In the *Gault* case, the right to confront the witnesses against him was declared to be a Constitutional right of a juvenile.[29] In that case, Gerald Gault had been taken into custody by the juvenile court for making lewd telephone calls to a Mrs. Cook. Mrs. Cook did not appear at the hearing. The sheriff testified to what Mrs. Cook told him about the improper telephone calls. In reversing the adjudication of delinquency, the United States Supreme Court held that Gerald had been denied his Constitutional right to confront the witnesses against him.[30]

In a case decided in 1970, the United States Supreme Court held that a defendant who disrupts the court proceedings waives his right to confrontation. He may be forcibly removed from the court room and the trial may proceed without him until such time as he is willing to conduct himself in a proper manner.[31]

8. **The Right to a Fair Trial.** The right to a fair trial in a fair tribunal is a basic requirement of due process.[32] A defendant who cannot obtain a fair trial in the jurisdiction in which the offense occurred is entitled to a change of venue,[33] i. e., has a right to have the trial transferred to a court where an impartial jury can be impaneled. This right extends to misdemeanor cases.[34]

Fair trial means that a verdict must be based upon evidence developed during the trial,[35] and not from outside sources. Press releases or other activities of the news media which render a fair trial impossible may lead to a reversal of a conviction.[36] As a result of the fair trial/free press controversy, the American Bar Association has adopted strict standards [37] for the press and for court officials to prevent "trial by newspaper" and to protect the

29. In re Gault, 387 U.S. 1, 87 S.Ct. 1428, 18 L.Ed.2d 527 (1967).

30. *Ibid.*

31. A. L. Dutton, Warden v. Evans, 400 U.S. 74, 91 S.Ct. 210, 27 L.Ed. 2d 213 (1970).

32. In re Murchison, 349 U.S. 133, 75 S.Ct. 623, 99 L.Ed. 942 (1955).

33. Rideau v. Louisiana, 373 U.S. 723, 83 S.Ct. 1417, 10 L.Ed.2d 663 (1963), on remand 246 La. 451, 165 So.2d 282.

34. Groppi v. Wisconsin, 400 U.S. 505, 91 S.Ct. 490, 27 L.Ed.2d 507 (1971).

35. American Bar Association Project on Minimum Standards for Criminal Justice, *Standards Relating to Fair Trial and Free Press*, New York: Office of Criminal Justice Project, Approved Draft, 1968.

36. Sheppard v. Maxwell, 384 U.S. 333, 86 S.Ct. 1507, 16 L.Ed.2d 600 (1966).

37. See fn. 35 *supra.*

Constitutional guarantee of a fair trial. The presumption of innocence, the rejection of hearsay evidence, the right to cross-examination of witnesses, to subpoena witnesses in his own behalf, and the requirement of proof beyond a reasonable doubt are all part of the guarantee of a fair trial. (A subpoena is a court order to a witness to appear in court.)

An accused may challenge a prejudiced juror, and remove from the case a judge before whom he cannot receive a fair trial. Certain restrictions are placed upon a prosecutor in the interest of giving the defendant a fair and impartial trial.

9. **The Right to Trial by Jury.** This provision of the Sixth Amendment has been held to insure the accused of a right to be tried by jury except for petty offenses.[38] (The provision however, does not fix the number of persons on a jury, though traditionally the number is twelve in felony cases.) The accused may waive his right to a trial by jury except in capital cases. Many states do not permit a waiver if the death penalty is to be requested by the prosecution; thus, only a jury can sentence a man to death in many states.

10. **The Right to a Speedy and Public Trial.** The Constitutional guarantee of the right to a speedy and public trial provided a protection against the old "star chamber" proceedings where an accused could be spirited away and tried in secret in a place remote from his family and friends. Trials in the United States are open to the public. The press cannot be excluded from a trial though the number of reporters admitted can be adjusted to the size of the court room and the rights of others to attend the trial. Since the decision in the *Sheppard*[39] case, courts have been admonished against turning a trial into a public spectacle with the use of TV cameras, and other news media devices. The judge has the authority to exclude spectators who disrupt a trial, and may order the bailiff to forcibly eject anyone disturbing the decorum of the court, including the defendant, as we have seen.

The right to a speedy trial is receiving more and more attention from the courts as the back-log of cases builds up in the trial

38. District of Columbia v. Clawans, 300 U.S. 617, 57 S.Ct. 660, 81 L.Ed. 843 (1937).

A sentence of six months or less in jail seems to be the dividing line, the defendant being entitled to a jury trial if the permissible penalty exceeds six months.

39. Sheppard v. Maxwell, 384 U.S. 333, 86 S.Ct. 1507, 16 L.Ed.2d 600 (1966).

courts, as well as the appellate courts.[40] Sometimes, delays in trials are sought by the defendants who hope to obtain an advantage from the passage of time (witnesses die or move away, their memory of events is less clear, etc.). A majority of the delays, however, are attributable to the fact that the courts are overburdened with cases awaiting disposition.[41]

The right to a speedy trial is now being accorded inmates against whom a detainer has been filed. A detainer is a kind of "hold order" against an inmate, requested by another jurisdiction. A man may commit an offense in Louisiana and flee to Florida, where he commits another offense. Florida convicts him for the offense committed in Florida and incarcerates him in its Raiford Penitentiary. Louisiana learns that he is in prison in Florida and sends word to the Director of the Division of Corrections in Florida that they want to pick him up when he is released from prison in Florida. The request to hold is called a "detainer," and until recently, a man could be held under detainer for the entire period of his incarceration. Recent decisions, however, require that the jurisdiction requesting the detainer make formal request for the return of the inmate to the requesting state for trial—thus affording the accused a speedy trial on the charge giving rise to the detainer. If the state filing the detain-

40. The Florida Supreme Court has adopted rules that require that a person charged with a felony be tried within 180 days from the date he was taken into custody. A person charged with a misdemeanor must be tried in 60 days. If the defendant is not brought to trial within the required time, he may file a motion before the appropriate court and have the charges against him dismissed. Before dismissal, the trial court must determine that the person has been continuously available for trial.

The rule in New Mexico is that all persons charged with crimes are to be brought to trial within six months after they are charged or indicted, or the case will be dismissed. Extensions can be granted only by the State Supreme Court, a Supreme Court Justice, or a judge designated by the Supreme Court.

41. In California, time limits are set out for each stage of a felony prosecution. Beginning with arrest, arraignment takes place in two court days; the preliminary hearing, no less than 2 nor more than 5 days after the arraignment; the District Attorney has 15 days within which to file the information; arraignment in superior court must be held within 60 days; at least one day is allowed after arraignment for plea; the trial date is set within 30 days of plea; the defendant is brought to trial within 60 days (or the case is dismissed); and judgment must be pronounced within 21 days (extended 10 days for motions or probation report) after finding of guilt. (See Allen P. Bristow, John B. Williams, *A Handbook in Criminal Procedure and the Administration of Justice, Revised Edition.* Beverly Hills: Glencoe Press, 1966, pp. 118–119.)

er fails to make arrangements for the trial, the case against the inmate must be dismissed and the detainer is no longer recognized by the state which has the inmate in custody.[42]

11. **The Right Against Double Jeopardy** is the right not to be tried twice for the same offense. If a man is acquitted of a crime, he cannot be tried again for the same crime. This guarantee is contained in the Fifth Amendment to the United States Constitution, which reads in part:

> * * * nor shall any person be subject for the same offense to be twice put in jeopardy of life nor limb.

Just what constitutes "jeopardy" is a complex legal question which is beyond the scope of this introductory text. In general, a man has been put in jeopardy if the trial has proceeded to the stage of hearing witnesses. However, a man may be retried after a trial which ends in a hung jury (a jury which cannot agree on a verdict), and this does not constitute double jeopardy. Nor does a second trial after a reversal on appeal constitute double jeopardy.

The Meaning of Due Process. We will discuss other due process rights as we consider the criminal justice process in detail. Before we leave the subject of due process, let us focus again on what "due process" means. One of the most eloquent definitions was given by Justice Frankfurter:

> "Due Process," unlike some legal rules, is not a technical conception with a fixed content unrelated to time, place, and circumstances. Expressing as it does in its ultimate analysis, respect enforced by law for that feeling of just treatment which has been evolved through centuries of Anglo-American constitutional history and civilization, "due process" cannot be imprisoned within the treacherous limits of any formula. Representing a profound attitude of fairness between man and man, and more particularly between the individual and government, "due process" is compounded of history, reason, the past course of decisions, and stout confidence in the strength of the democratic faith which we possess. Due process is not a mechanical instrument. It is not a yardstick. It is a process.[43]

42. See discussion of detainers, *infra.*

43. Joint Anti-Fascist Refugee Committee v. McGrath, 341 U.S. 123, 71 S.Ct. 624, 95 L.Ed. 817 (1951).

JURISDICTION

Before we can continue our study in the criminal justice process and particularly before we begin our discussion of the criminal court system, we must understand the concept of *jurisdiction*. As regards the criminal courts, *jurisdiction* means *the inherent power of a court to hear a case.* Just as crimes and punishments are "graded," so are criminal courts—there are "higher courts" and "lower courts." The powers of a particular court are set out in the constitution or legislative act that created the court. The jurisdiction of the United States Supreme Court is set out in the United States Constitution and in Acts of Congress. The jurisdiction of the other federal courts is set out in the Acts of Congress. The jurisdiction of the criminal courts in your state is set out in your state constitution and in the Acts of your legislature.

An important thing to remember is that *no court in the United States has unlimited jurisdiction.* Even the Supreme Court of the United States can hear only certain kinds of cases. The courts of a state cannot try cases outside the state. A juvenile court cannot try persons over the juvenile age (usually 16 or 17) who are charged with criminal behavior; the adult criminal court in the same city may not be able to hear cases involving juvenile misconduct. And so on. *Every* court is granted the power to hear some kinds of cases and denied the right to hear other kinds of cases.

We will study the jurisdiction of the criminal and juvenile courts in considerable detail in succeeding chapters. In this chapter we will learn the meaning of jurisdiction and consider the ways in which the jurisdiction of a criminal court may be limited.

Limitations on Criminal Court Jurisdiction. Criminal courts are limited in various ways as to the cases that may come before them for disposition. The most common limits on court jurisdiction are the following:

1. geographical boundaries—federal, state, district, county, municipality, precinct.
2. the nature of the proceeding—trial (hearing witnesses and argument of counsel, impaneling juries), or appellate (reviewing cases on the record coming up from a lower court). The authority to try the case is called

original jurisdiction. The authority to review cases coming up from lower courts is called appellate jurisdiction.

3. the nature of the case—civil, criminal, juvenile.
4. the nature of the subject matter—felony or misdemeanor, cases involving taxation, probate of wills, traffic offenses, etc.
5. the extent of the punishment—jail or prison, fines over or under $100, etc.
6. the character of the parties—juveniles or adults, citizens of the same state or of different states, ambassadors and other public officials, etc.

A single court may be subject to several of these limitations at the same time. Thus, the jurisdiction of a justice of the peace may be limited to the county or precinct; the justice may have authority to try cases with fines under $100 but no authority to try cases involving fines over $100 or a jail term. The judge presiding may have the power to conduct preliminary hearings in criminal cases involving adults, but no power to hear cases involving juvenile offenses. As another example, the circuit Courts of Appeals of the United States hear appeals in criminal cases arising in their circuit and involving a federal offense, but cannot conduct the original trial of an offender against the laws of any state.

Exclusive and Concurrent Jurisdiction. If only one court has the power to hear a case, we say that it has *exclusive jurisdiction* over that case. When more than one court can hear a case, the courts are said to have *concurrent jurisdiction.*

VENUE

Since more than one court may have the power to try a particular kind of case, how do we determine which court will actually hear the case? For example, all superior courts in a state may have the power to try criminal cases involving felonies. Which one of these courts will try a particular case? The answer lies in another legal concept—*venue.*

Definition of Venue. *Venue* comes from a French word meaning "neighborhood." *Venue* as a legal concept means *place of trial.*

A basic tenet of our criminal law is that criminal actions should be tried in the place (neighborhood) where the offense occurred. One of the abuses that drove many of the colonists from England was a legal practice known as the "Star Chamber." The Star Chamber was a court where an investigation and trial could take place at any time and any place, provided only that the proper officers of the King were in charge.[44] Prior to the American Revolution, an English subject could be picked up in the dead of night, transported to a secret place where his family and friends could not find him, tried without aid of counsel, convicted and punished—all in secret, and at a point remote from where his offense was alleged to have been committed. Provisions in the United States Constitution put an end to this practice in America. The Constitution provides that all criminal trials must take place in the state or territory where the offense occurred. The exact words in Article II, Sec. 2 of the Constitution are:

> The trial of all Crimes, except in Cases of Impeachment, shall be by jury; and such Trial shall be held in the State where the said Crimes shall have been committed; but when not committed within any State, the Trial shall be at such Place or Places as the Congress may by Law have directed.

The Sixth Amendment makes the requirement even more specific:

> In all Criminal Prosecutions, the accused shall enjoy the right to a speedy and public trial, by an impartial jury *of the state and district wherein the crime shall have been committed, which district shall have previously ascertained by law* * * [Italics supplied.]

Because of this Constitutional provision and the legal concept of venue, an offense committed in Iowa must be tried in Iowa, and one committed in Wyoming must be tried in Wyoming. A

44. *Black's Law Dictionary, 4th Ed.*, p. 433. *Court of Star Chamber.* This was an English court of very ancient origin, but new-modeled by St. 3. Hen. VII, c. 1, and 21 Hen. VIII, c. 20, consisting of divers lords, spiritual and temporal, being privy counsellors, together with two judges of the courts of common law, without the intervention of any jury. The jurisdiction extended legally over riots, perjury, misbehavior of sheriffs, and other misdemeanors contrary to the laws of the land; yet it was afterwards stretched to the asserting of all proclamations and orders of state, to the vindicating of illegal commissions and grants of monopolies; holding for honorable that which it pleased, and for just that which it profited, and becoming both a court of law to determine civil rights and a court of revent to enrich the treasury. It was finally abolished by St. 16 Car. I, c. 10, to the general satisfaction of the whole nation.

criminal offense committed in your state must be tried in your state, and a federal offense in the federal district court in the district where the offense occurred.

Many state constitutions have expanded this notion of venue and require that a criminal trial must be held in the county or district where the offense occurred. Provisions are made for unusual situations, as for example, where a man in Florida shoots across the border and kills another man in Georgia, or an offense happens so close to a county line that it is impossible to tell on which side of the line the offense occurred, or when there is a "continuing" offense, as when a man drives through several counties of a state in a stolen automobile. You may obtain information concerning the venue requirements in your state from your state statutes. These requirements determine where a particular criminal action will be tried in your state.

Change of Venue. An interesting thing about venue is that it can be changed. Under certain circumstances, a trial may be moved from the place where the offense occurred and held in another place. The usual reason for changing the venue of a trial is because the defendant feels that he cannot get a fair trial in the place where the offense occurred.

In most states, change of venue can be requested only by the defendant.[45] In other states, change of venue can also be requested by the prosecuting attorney as well.[46] In a few states, the judge may change the venue "on his own motion," which means that he can transfer the trial to another place if he feels that either the defense or the prosecution cannot obtain a fair trial in the original location; no request need be made by either of the parties.[47] No matter which party requests it, the decision to grant or deny a change of venue is made by the judge.

Jurisdiction has to do with power, venue with place, and limitations of actions (which we considered in Chapter II), with time. Together these concepts tell us as to a criminal case what court has the power to try it, the place where it will be tried, and the time within which the action must be brought.

45. This is the situation in Illinois. Smith-Hurd Ann.Stat. ch. 38, § 114.-6.

46. A change of venue may be requested in New York upon application of the defendant or the District Attorney. McKinney's N.Y. CPL 230.20.

47. Texas permits prosecution and defense to grant change of venue, and judge may grant on his own motion. Vernon's Ann.Code of Criminal Procedure, Art. 31.01.

Chapter VI

THE CRIMINAL COURTS

In the United States we have a "dual court system." By this is meant, we have a system of state courts, and a system of federal courts. With reference to crimes, the state courts prosecute state crimes, and the federal courts prosecute federal crimes. State crimes are declared to be such by the legislatures of the states; federal crimes are declared to be such by Acts of Congress. A single act may constitute both a state and a federal crime, and (with increasing limitation imposed by recent court decisions) an offender may be tried and punished for the same act by both a state and federal court.

THE DUAL COURT SYSTEM

When the thirteen original colonies declared their independence from England, each of them had an existing court system and an existing body of criminal law. The court systems were patterned on the English court system and their criminal law incorporated much of the Common Law of England.

To create the United States, the thirteen colonies "pooled their sovereignty." In so doing, they gave up certain rights and privileges, but also (in the Ninth and the Tenth Amendments) retained all other rights and privileges that they did not expressly give up. Thus, though they established a United States Supreme Court, they kept their own supreme courts, and their court systems. The framers of the Constitution did not create a federal court *system* in the document itself. All that the Constitution said about a federal court system (the Supreme Court alone was not a judicial system) was to give Congress the power to create one. As we shall see, Congress later exercised this power.

There is nothing in the nature of federalism that demands two court systems. Canada, for example, has a Supreme Court of the Dominion of Canada, and there are court systems in each of the Provinces. There is, however, no system of lower Dominion courts, which makes for a much simpler situation in respect to the courts of Canada than exists in the United States.

Two separate judicial systems, state and federal, came into existence in the United States when Congress passed the Federal Judiciary Act of 1789 (amended extensively in 1925). With that Act, Congress created two levels of lower (i. e., under the Supreme Court) federal courts—United States District Courts and United States Circuit Courts of Appeals (now the United States Courts of Appeals). The original states, nevertheless, retained their own court systems, and as new states came into the Union they came in with complete court systems. Thus, what we really have in the United States today are one federal court system and fifty independent state court systems. However, the fifty state court systems are referred to collectively as the "state court system," and the courts of the federal government make up the "federal court system." We thus have state courts and federal courts and a "dual court system."

Jurisdiction of the Federal and State Courts in Criminal Cases. The jurisdiction (power) of the federal and state courts overlap in some details, as we shall see, but basically the federal courts are empowered to hear criminal cases only when the act complained of has been declared a crime by Congress. The state courts have power to try all state offenses.

When President Kennedy was killed in Dallas, Texas, only a District Court of Dallas County, Texas, had the power to try Lee Harvey Oswald. At that time, Congress had not declared that killing the President was an offense against the United States. Therefore, no court in the federal system had authority to convict and sentence President Kennedy's assassin. Since that time, Congress has made killing or attempting to kill the President or Vice-President of the United States a federal offense. If another such tragedy occurs in the United States, both a federal district court and a trial court in the state where the offense occurs will have authority to try and punish the killer. In all probability, only one court would try the assassin—whether it would be a federal or state court we cannot at this point say with certainty. This would depend on whether the Act of Congress declaring the federal offense "pre-empted" the right of the state to act in the same matter. This is a technical legal question that could only be finally resolved by the United States Supreme Court.

Of all criminal cases, approximately 85 per cent are heard in state courts, about 15 per cent in the federal courts.

KINDS OF COURTS

Before we can discuss the court systems in detail we must identify certain kinds of courts.

Trial Courts. A court that has authority to try a case is a *trial court.* This court impanels a jury, hears the evidence and the arguments of counsel, receives the verdict, and sentences the defendant. Such a court has *original jurisdiction* of a case.

Appellate Courts. A court that reviews cases which have originally been tried in a trial court, is called an appeals court or an *appellate court,* and is said to have *appellate jurisdiction.*

Courts of Record. A court of record is a court whose decisions are reviewed *on the record.* This means, when an appeal is taken from the decision of a court of record, the appellate court does not hear the testimony of witnesses and the arguments of counsel over again. Instead it reads the written transcript (or record) of what went on in the trial and bases its findings and decision on the record.

The decisions of the court of last resort of a state when reviewed by the United States Supreme Court are reviewed on the record. In this sense, the highest court of a state is a court of record.

Intermediate courts of appeal (i. e., below the court of last resort) of a state are courts of record. All courts which try felonies and most courts which try serious misdemeanor cases (those carrying possible jail sentences) are courts of record. Other courts, such as justice of the peace courts and municipal courts, are not courts of record. This means that if an appeal is taken from the decision of a justice of the peace, the whole case will be tried over again in the higher court just as though no previous trial had taken place. Since the appeals from a justice of the peace cannot be heard on the record, and the higher court will certainly re-try the case, a justice of the peace court is not a court of record. The statutes of the state declare which courts are, and which are not, courts of record.

THE FEDERAL COURT SYSTEM

The federal court system consists of the United States Supreme Court, the Courts of Appeals (known until 1948 as the Circuit Courts of Appeals), and the United States District Courts. Only the Supreme Court was established by the Constitution; the other courts were established by Acts of Congress. The United States Districts Courts are trial courts; the Courts of Appeals are appellate courts. The Supreme Court is also essentially an appellate court though it is given "original jurisdiction" to hear controversies between states and cases involving foreign ambassadors and ministers.

There is only one Supreme Court which sits in Washington, D. C. The United States is divided into eleven Circuits, with the District of Columbia comprising the 11th Circuit. The circuits were established geographically. United States Judicial Circuits are made up as follows:

1st Circuit—Maine, New Hampshire, Massachusetts, Rhode Island, Puerto Rico

2nd Circuit—New York, Vermont, Connecticut

3rd Circuit—Pennsylvania, New Jersey, Delaware

4th Circuit—West Virginia, Virginia, North Carolina, South Carolina, Maryland

5th Circuit—Texas, Louisiana, Mississippi, Alabama, Georgia, Florida, Canal Zone

6th Circuit—Ohio, Kentucky, Tennessee, Michigan

7th Circuit—Wisconsin, Illinois, Indiana

8th Circuit—North Dakota, South Dakota, Nebraska, Missouri, Arkansas, Iowa, Minnesota

9th Circuit—Washington, Oregon, California, Nevada, Arizona, Idaho, Montana, Alaska, Hawaii

10th Circuit—Wyoming, Utah, Colorado, New Mexico, Kansas, Oklahoma

11th Circuit—District of Columbia

Each state has one or more federal districts. Wyoming, a small state, makes up a single federal district, and has only one District Court, though the court sits, on occasion, in different parts of the state. Texas, a large state geographically and in population, has four federal districts, called the Northern District of Texas, the Western District of Texas, the Eastern District of Texas, and the Southern District of Texas.[1] A case filed in the federal court in Dallas would be entitled "In the United States District Court for the Northern District of Texas." A legal directory or an Almanac will give you information on the number of federal districts in your state and the particular district into which your town or city falls.

There are more federal judges than there are circuits and districts. From time to time, Congress increases the number of judgeships. As of Fall, 1970, there were 97 circuit judges in the eleven circuits. There were 337 district judgeships, including five new California judgeships which went into effect in September, 1966. During the Nixon administration, 61 additional federal judgeships were created. All federal judges are appointed by the President and confirmed by the Senate. They hold office "during good behavior," which for all practical purposes means "for life." They can be removed from office only by impeachment.

Jurisdiction of the United States Supreme Court. Article III of the Constitution, called the "Judiciary Clause," vests original jurisdiction in the Supreme Court in only a few kinds of cases. The most important of these are suits between two states. For example, when Colorado and California disputed the water rights to the Colorado River, original (trial) jurisdiction was vested in the United States Supreme Court. Article III also extends to the Court "judicial power" over all cases arising under the Constitution, federal laws, and treaties. This jurisdiction, however, is appellate only; that is, limited to review of decisions from lower courts and, according to the Constitution, subject to "such exceptions and regulations as Congress shall make."

In 1925, an Act passed by the Congress made the appellate jurisdiction of the Supreme Court largely discretionary, which meant that the Court was obligated to hear only a few kinds of cases. As to other cases coming before it, it could review them

1. New York has four federal districts similarly designated. Pennsylvania is divided into the Eastern, Middle, and Western districts; Illinois into Northern, Eastern, and Southern; Wisconsin into the Western and Eastern; California into the Northern, Southern, Eastern, and Central districts. Arizona makes up a single federal district, as does New Mexico and some of the other states with small populations.

or not, as the court saw fit. Two kinds of appeals taken from a state court are included in these which the Supreme Court is obligated to hear: (a) where a federal statute has been held unconstitutional; and (b) where a state statute has been unsuccessfully challenged as being unconstitutional. The Supreme Court is also obligated to hear appeals from decisions of a three-judge federal court which has declared a state law unconstitutional as repugnant to the United States Constitution.[2] Similar appeals may be taken to the Supreme Court from the federal Courts of Appeals, and the Supreme Court is bound to hear them.

The majority of cases reviewed by the Supreme Court are in the exercise of its discretionary rather than its obligatory jurisdiction. These cases are not, strictly speaking, "appeals," since they reach the court by way of *Writ of Certiorari* which is a writ of review issued by the Court itself commanding a lower court to "send up the record" of a case for its consideration. A defendant who has been convicted in a state trial court, and who has had his appeal denied in the highest appellate court of the state, may petition the Supreme Court for a *Writ of Certiorari*. The Supreme Court may grant or deny the petition since it has the right to hear the case, or not to hear it, as it chooses. If it decides to review the case, the Court will send down to the highest state court (or in some instances to a lower state court "of last resort") for all the proceedings in the case. The Supreme Court will then consider the case "on the record" and render its decision.

Review of State Court Decisions by the Supreme Court. It must be clearly understood that the United States Supreme Court does *not* have the right to review all the decisions of state courts in criminal cases. *Certiorari* will lie *only* in cases where a federal statute has been construed or a *federal* constitutional right of the defendant has allegedly been infringed. The criminal cases which are heard in the United States Supreme Court are those in which the accused has successfully raised a "federal question." Usually, the accused is claiming that one or more of his due process rights have been denied him during the state criminal process. In

2. A three-judge district court consisting of three district or court of appeals judges must be impaneled to pass on the constitutionality of state legislation before injunctions may be issued. Appeals from decisions of three-judge district courts is directly to the Supreme Court and is a matter of right.

Gideon v. Wainwright,[3] the defendant claimed that by not having an appointed attorney during his trial when he was too poor to employ one, he had been denied his federal constitutional right to be represented by counsel. The Supreme Court agreed with him. In United States v. Wade,[4] the claim was that the federal constitutional rights of the accused had been violated when he did not have his attorney present at the police line-up. Again the court agreed with the petitioner. In countless other cases, however, the Supreme Court refuses to consider the claims of the petitioner, or finds against him. The court hears only about two percent of the cases which are presented to it and only about 15 percent of these cases are decided "on the merits." [5]

It can easily be seen that not every convicted offender can have his case reviewed by the United States Supreme Court, though it sometimes (but not always) happens that the decision in one case will have the effect of making new trials necessary for other defendants who during their trip through the state system were deprived of the same constitutional right. The defendant always hopes that a new trial will result in an acquittal and his release from custody. That hope is often a slim one. In the majority of new trials, the defendant is again convicted, and goes back to prison to serve the same, or even an extended, sentence.

The Courts of Appeals. The United States Courts of Appeals (prior to 1948 called the Circuit Courts of Appeals), are appellate courts similar to the highest appellate courts in the state systems. Criminal appeals may be taken from a United States District Court to the Court of Appeals of the circuit where the trial court is situated. The Appeals Court may affirm the decision of the District Court, or reverse it and send the case back for a new trial. Criminal appeals to the United States Supreme Court from the Courts of Appeals may be taken in certain cases involving federal constitutional questions or cases involving the constitutionality of statutes.

The United States District Courts. The United States District Courts are the trial courts of the federal system. A federal crime

3. Gideon v. Wainwright, 372 U.S. 335, 83 S.Ct. 792, 9 L.Ed.2d 799 (1963), on remand 153 So.2d 299.

4. United States v. Wade, 388 U.S. 218, 87 S.Ct. 1926, 18 L.Ed. 1149 (1967).

5. "The Supreme Court's Role in the Federal System." *Congressional Quarterly Service*, CQ Guide, Fall, 1966, pp. 68–73.

must be tried in the district or state where the crime was committed. As we have seen, this guarantee was written into the United States Constitution by its framers, who had had experience with "Star Chamber" proceedings in England where a man could be spirited away, interrogated, tried and convicted in secret, completely beyond the help of his family and friends. The Constitutional guarantee also applies to state crimes, which must be tried in the state where committed.

Behavior which has been declared by Congress to be an offense against the United States constitutes a federal crime, but by no means is all criminal behavior a federal offense. Of the total criminal cases heard in the United States in any one year, over 85 per cent of them are heard in state courts. Offenses which occur in subject areas in which the federal government has a paramount interest are usually defined as crimes against the United States. Theft from interstate shipments, taking a stolen automobile across state lines, robbery of a national bank or a federally-insured state bank, counterfeiting, stealing from or interfering with the mails, destroying federally-owned property, selling liquor upon which the federal tax has not been paid (i. e., "moonshining"), and the like, are some common federal crimes. Offenses which occur on land owned by the United States, as on a military post, an Indian reservation, or in a National Park, are likewise federal crimes.

The Federal Bureau of Investigation is the agency charged by Congress with investigating federal crimes. Contrary to popular belief, the F.B.I. has no authority to investigate purely state crimes unless the agents are invited into the case by the state law enforcement officials. The F.B.I. enters kidnapping cases, for example, whenever there is any evidence that the kidnapper or the victim has crossed a state line. In this particular crime, the parties often operate on a "presumption" that there has been movement across state lines before anyone really knows whether it is true or not. Because of the excellent assistance that the F.B.I. can give in kidnapping cases, this "presumption" is acted upon to get the F.B.I. into the case as soon as possible.

United States Magistrates. United States Magistrates (formerly called United States Commissioners)[6] occupy a place in the federal system similar to that of the justice of the peace in most of

6. The Federal Magistrates Act, 18 U.S.C.A. § 3060.

the state systems. The Magistrates issue warrants of arrest and search warrants, arraign defendants on complaints, fix bail, hold preliminary hearings, and try minor offenses if the defendant does not elect to be tried in the federal District Court. With certain exceptions, a minor offense is one punishable by imprisonment not to exceed one year and a fine not to exceed $1,000.[7]

Only a few of the Commissioners (now Magistrates) are full-time officers; the great majority work at other jobs or operate businesses in the town where they serve. They earn no salary, their only compensation is from fees; over 30 per cent are not lawyers. The suggestion is that this office be abolished and that the duties of the Magistrates be performed by a federal judge. If distances to the District Court were too great, some of the duties could be performed by a state judge.

Trial Procedures in Federal Courts. Trial procedures in criminal cases are very similar in the federal and state courts. The person accused of a federal felony is taken before a United States Magistrate (formerly Commissioner), where he is informed of his rights and the nature of the charge against him. A federal grand jury hears evidence about the case and if probable cause is established, returns an indictment, or formal charge, against the offender. He is then taken before a federal judge for arraignment, where the charges are again read to him and he enters his plea of guilty or not guilty; (he may also plead *nolo contendere*, "no contest," which as far as the criminal case is concerned is equivalent to a plea of guilty). If he pleads not guilty, he is entitled to a trial by jury. If convicted and sentenced to imprisonment, he will serve his sentence in a federal prison or correctional institution. If the conviction is for a misdemeanor, the sentence may be served in a local jail approved by the United States Bureau of Prisons.

STATE COURT SYSTEMS

The court systems of the various states vary in detail. No two states have exactly the same courts with exactly similar jurisdiction. However, in most states, three levels of courts can be distinguished. At the lower level are one or more trial courts

7. President's Commission on Law Enforcement and the Administration of Criminal Justice. *Task Force Report, The Courts*, p. 36.

whose jurisdiction is limited by city or county boundaries and by restrictions as to type of case, amount of fine, etc. With respect to criminal cases, these courts try petty offenses and misdemeanors. Above the lower courts are higher trial courts with general jurisdiction. In the criminal court system these courts are felony courts and may also try serious misdemeanors, or misdemeanors involving official misconduct. These courts usually serve a district or circuit made up of more than one county or are courts who have general trial jurisdiction in large metropolitan areas. At the uppermost level are appellate courts with little or no trial jurisdiction. There may be only one higher appellate court in a state—usually called the supreme court of the state [8] —or a state may have intermediate or specialized appeals courts in addition to the supreme court, or whatever its highest court is called.[9] The lower courts are usually called justice of the peace courts, municipal courts, or simply "lower courts." New York has local criminal courts called variously a city court, a town court, a village court, a district court, a recorder's court, a municipal court, and a police court. The higher courts are called district courts, circuit courts, superior courts, courts of common pleas, and the like.[10] The supreme court of a state is re-

8. The appellate tribunal which is the court of last resort bears different names in different states. In Kentucky, Maryland, the District of Columbia, and New York, the name is "Court of Appeals." In Virginia and West Virginia, it is known as the "Supreme Court of Appeals." In Connecticut, the name is "Supreme Court of Errors;" in Massachusetts and Maine, the "Supreme Judicial Court." In Texas, the Court of Criminal Appeals is the court of last resort in criminal cases. In the other states, the court of last resort is known as the Supreme Court. *Black's Law Dictionary*, 4th Revised Ed.

9. In California, the intermediate appeals courts are called District Courts of Appeals; in Illinois, the Appellate Court. In Texas, appeals are taken from the Court of Civil Appeals to the Supreme Court of Texas, but the Court of Criminal Appeals is the court of last resort in criminal cases. In Wyoming, appeals go from the District Court of the Judicial District in and for a named county to the Wyoming Supreme Court.

10. The Kansas Court system consists of the supreme court, district courts, county courts, probate courts, small debtors courts, Court of Common Pleas (in certain counties), and magistrates courts (in certain counties).

North Dakota names its courts the supreme court, the district courts, the county courts, the courts of County Justices, and there may be courts created by law for cities and villages.

In New York, a court of general jurisdiction in the City of New York is called the Court of General Sessions of the County of New York; the courts of special sessions are misdemeanor courts; the

ferred to as the supreme court; lower appellate courts are called appellate courts or appeals courts or may have a special name, such as the Texas Court of Criminal Appeals or the California Court of Appeals.

The Lower Courts. Justice of the peace courts are the most common and best known of the lower courts. The justice court usually has county-wide jurisdiction, though the jurisdiction of any one court may be limited to smaller geographical divisions, such as a precinct. The urban courts are called municipal courts, city courts, corporation courts (meaning the courts of an incorporated town or city), or have special names, such as recorders courts, magistrates courts, court of special sessions, traffic courts, etc. Their trial jurisdiction is usually limited to minor offenses occurring within the city limits, though a few city courts, such as the Detroit Recorders Court, can try any offenses, misdemeanor or felony, occurring within the city limits. County courts with jurisdiction above that of the justice courts are sometimes included in the designation of "lower courts" though they may be courts of record. They usually do not possess felony jurisdiction, but have authority to try "higher" misdemeanors and impose jail sentences as well as fines.

In addition to the geographical limitations, the jurisdiction of the lower courts is limited as to the kinds of cases they may dispose of. Limitations may be by classification of the offense as

supreme court is a court of statewide general jurisdiction.

Texas has the Court of Criminal Appeals, district courts, criminal district courts, county courts, county courts at law, justice of the peace courts, and municipal courts (formerly called corporation courts).

The highest court in Pennsylvania is the supreme court. A commonwealth court hears cases by or against the Commonwealth. The superior court is an appellate court which hears cases not appealable to the supreme court or the commonwealth court. The court of general jurisdiction is the Court of Common Pleas. Inferior courts are called community courts, justice of the peace and magistrate courts. In Philadelphia there are the Philadelphia Municipal Court and the Philadelphia Traffic Court.

The criminal courts in California are the supreme court, the district courts of appeals, the superior courts, justice courts, municipal courts.

Thus, the court of general criminal jurisdiction is called in California the Superior Court; in Illinois, the Circuit Court; in Texas, the District Court or the Criminal District Court; in New York, Superior Court (the supreme court or a county court); in Pennsylvania and the District of Columbia, the Court of Common Pleas; and in the City of Detroit, the Recorders Court.

misdemeanor or petty misdemeanors, or to misdemeanors punishable by fine only, or to offenses the maximum permissible fine for which is $200, and so on. Certain lower courts also have specialized jurisdiction, such as traffic courts, or courts dealing solely with violations of city ordinances. Within their geographical and other jurisdictional limits, lower courts have the power to try and dispose of cases coming before them.

Magistrates. One thing most of these lower courts have in common is that the judges of these courts are declared by law to be magistrates. A magistrate is a judicial officer with power to issue arrest and search warrants, inform accused persons of their rights, arraign defendants who are pleading to misdemeanors (and sometimes those pleading to felonies), fix bail, and in some cases, hold preliminary hearings.[11] A preliminary hearing determines whether or not there is probable cause to charge a defendant with a felony. In some states this function is also performed by a grand jury, and formal indictment can come only from the grand jury. In other states, no grand jury indictment is required, and a magistrate (usually a Justice of the Peace) is given the power to determine whether or not the accused shall be "bound over" to the felony court for trial. In the federal system, the United States Magistrates (formerly Commissioners) serve this function.

It is difficult to make any statement that would apply to all lower courts. Generally, however, the lower courts process felony cases up to the point of preliminary hearing, and misdemeanor and petty offense cases through trial and ultimate disposition. In all states, the jurisdiction of the lower courts is fixed in the constitution or statutes of the state. You will need to go to your own state laws to identify the lower courts in your state and learn the limits on their powers.

The Lower Courts a Disgrace to the Nation. Many sincere people believe that the lower courts in the United States are a disgrace to the nation. The judges are seldom lawyers, may have no training whatsoever in the law, and most are paid by a fee system which encourages questionable practices and abuse of au-

11. Who are magistrates is determined by the laws of the state. Judges of courts of record are magistrates, as are other designated officials such as mayors and recorders of incorporated towns or villages.

thority. The President's Commission on Law Enforcement and Administration of Criminal Justice has this to say:

> * * * These courts operate with the most meager facilities, with the least trained personnel, and with the most oppressive workload. Practices by judges, prosecutors and defense counsel which would be condemned in the higher courts may still be found in these courts. The most dedicated persons working there are frustrated by huge caseloads, and they lack opportunity to screen and prepare cases carefully or to deal with the problems posed by individuals brought to the bar of justice. No program of crime prevention will be effective without a massive overhaul of the lower criminal courts.[12]

The most frequent recommendation is that the entire lower court system be abolished, and that all criminal prosecutions be conducted in a single court manned by judges of equal status. Complete unification of all criminal courts, with a central court administration, is also strongly recommended.

The Trial Courts. At the intermediate level in the court system are the highest trial courts, which are courts of record with general jurisdiction. One such court may serve more than one county, in which case they may be called district or circuit courts. There may be several such courts in a large metropolitan area. In most non-urban areas, such a court will try both civil and criminal cases. In heavily populated areas, one or more of such courts will handle criminal cases only. In New York, the felony court is called a Superior Court (the supreme court or a county court); in Illinois, the Circuit Court. In Texas, the court with general trial jurisdiction is called a District Court; the courts trying criminal cases only are called Criminal District Courts. Because they are the highest trial courts, these courts are called or referred to as Superior Courts, as in California and New York. (The word "superior" is also often used simply to mean "higher.") In Washington, D. C., the court at this level is called the Court of Common Pleas, an old English name for courts of general jurisdiction.

The jurisdiction of the superior courts usually begins where the jurisdiction of the lower courts leaves off, though certain seg-

12. *Task Force Report, The Courts,* p. 29.

ments of jurisdiction may overlap. If a lower court is given the power to hear misdemeanors where the fine does not exceed $200, the jurisdiction of the higher court will include all misdemeanors involving a fine over $200 or a jail sentence, and will in addition include exclusive jurisdiction over felonies. Higher trial courts usually have appellate jurisdiction from the lower courts. Thus, a decision of the Justice of the Peace can be set aside by the trial court having general jurisdiction, or even a county court if it is "higher" than the justice court. Since the justice court is not a court of record, there will be a trial *de novo* (a second trial) in the higher court, and the judge of the higher court may render his decision without regard to the decision of the Justice of the Peace.

Superior courts are characterized by having broad power, usually limited only at the lower end to protect them from having to hear petty offenses and disputes, with rather extensive territorial jurisdiction or a large urban caseload. They are commonly referred to as "courts of general jurisdiction." The judges of such courts are lawyers. The courts follow formal procedures, and in the criminal law, try the serious offenses.

The State Appellate Courts. There is no Constitutional right to appeal a case, but all of the states have provided courts of review with authority to reverse or modify the decisions of either civil or criminal trial courts. Of course, the appeal courts can, and most frequently do, affirm the decisions of the trial court. Because the decisions of the trial courts are reviewed by the courts of appeal *on the record*, the trial courts are "courts of record." The record is a complete transcript of all that went on in the trial court, including pleadings filed, pleas entered by the defendant (if a criminal case), testimony of witnesses (as taken down by a court reporter), rulings of the court, and sometimes arguments of counsel. Very often the decision of the appeals court is to send the case back to the trial court for a new trial with instructions to modify its procedures or rulings in accordance with the decision of the appellate court.[13]

The Importance of Appellate Decisions. We have previously mentioned that in the Anglo-American legal system the law is

13. As we have seen, some states provide for only one court of appeal above the courts of general jurisdiction; other states have two levels of appellate courts.

made by the legislature and the decisions of courts. A decision of an appellate court not only disposes one way or another of the particular case appealed, it also "settles" the law of that state on the legal points necessarily decided in the case.

For example, Peter Green, who has been convicted of illegal possession of marijuana, may appeal his case on the grounds that the marijuana found in his car was obtained as a result of an illegal search and seizure, in which case it should not have been admitted in evidence against him. He will point out that he was given a ticket for missing a boulevard stop, but was not arrested. He pulled over willingly when he heard the siren, and was standing quietly outside his car when the officer decided to search it. He will claim that under such circumstances, the officers have no right whatsoever to search the glove compartment of his car. If the appeals court agrees with him, his case will be sent back for a new trial, and if the prosecutor feels that he cannot convict him without the evidence of the seized marijuana, the case against him will be dismissed. The decision of the appellate court not only serves to end the case against Peter Green, it also decides the law of the state concerning similar searches of automobiles. The rule will be that the traffic violation of missing a boulevard stop for which the driver is given a summons and not arrested will not support a search of his car without a warrant, particularly when the driver was standing quietly outside the car when the search took place.

As a result of the Peter Green decision, police officers will not generally attempt to search the car of a driver to whom they have given only a summons for missing a boulevard stop. However, suppose that under almost the same circumstances, they search the car of John Black. When John Black is tried, his lawyer will move during his trial not to admit into evidence the marijuana found in Black's car, and will cite the Peter Green case as "precedent." If John Black is being tried in the same state, the trial judge will rule in his favor since the Peter Green case has settled the law of that state and must be followed. If for some reason, John Black is nevertheless convicted, and appeals his case, the appellate court would refer back to the Peter Green case and reverse his conviction.

STARE DECISIS

This all comes about because of a doctrine of law known as *stare decisis,* which is Latin for "to abide by, or adhere to decided cases." The policy of the law is to follow previously decided cases and not to disturb a settled point, or, as it is said, to decide similar cases similarly. When a court has once laid down a principle of law as applicable to a certain state of facts, it will adhere to that principle, and apply it to all future cases where the facts are substantially the same, regardless of whether the parties are the same. This doctrine also requires that once the highest court of a state has announced a legal principle, all the courts in the state must follow that principle in similar cases unless and until it is overruled by the United States Supreme Court or is reversed by the highest court of the state in some future decision. The doctrine of *stare decisis* is sometimes called the "rule of precedent," because a rule of law announced in one case becomes a precedent to guide the decision in a subsequent similar case. It is grounded on the theory that security and certainty in the law require accepted and established legal principles upon which people can rely in conducting their affairs.

Legal Reasoning. "The basic pattern of legal reasoning," says an authority, "is reasoning by example." It is reasoning from case to case. It is a three-step process described by the doctrine of precedent in which a proposition descriptive of the first case is made into a rule of law and then applied to a next similar situation. The steps are these: similarity is seen between cases; next the rule of law inherent in the first case is announced, then the rule of law is made applicable to the second case.[14]

Precedent and *stare decisis* do not mean that a principle of law once announced in an appellate court never changes. Legal principles change as society and its values change. We have seen, for example, that a change in the rule about the constitutional right to counsel at a criminal trial released 4,000 Florida inmates for new trials and resulted in the complete release of over 2,000 of them. Such a drastic change in legal principles does not happen often, and even less frequently does such a change affect cases tried before the new rule is announced.

14. Edward H. Levi, *An Introduction to Legal Reasoning,* Chicago: The University of Chicago Press, 1948.

The point to be remembered here is that the rule of precedent based on the doctrine of *stare decisis* makes the opinions of appellate courts "binding" on the trial courts in their state, and will usually be followed in similar cases by the appellate court itself until changes in the statutory law or reasons of justice require that a different principle be announced. A much more difficult point is to determine the degree to which the decisions of federal courts are "binding" on state courts, and vice versa.

Relationship Between The State Courts and The Lower Federal Courts. The first fact to remember about the state courts and the lower federal courts is that the lower federal courts (the Courts of Appeals and the District Courts) are *not* "over" the state courts. No direct appeals can be taken from any state court to a lower federal court. (Criminal cases which reach lower federal courts from state courts get into these federal courts by way of writ of habeas corpus, which we will study in the succeeding chapter.) What is even more important, no state court is bound by the doctrine of *stare decisis* to follow a decision made by a lower federal court or principle or precedent established by such a court. As a matter of fact, no lower federal court is bound to follow the precedent of federal courts outside its own circuit. (By lower federal courts is meant the United States District Courts and the United States Courts of Appeals. The term does not, of course, include the United States Supreme Court.) As to the duty of a lower federal court to follow the decisions of state courts, the rule is stated as:

> " * * * federal courts are required to follow the law of the state with respect to construction of state statutes as determined by the highest courts of the state; their decisions are *stare decisis* and must be followed irrespective of federal courts' opinions concerning what the law ought to be, but with respect to the pronouncement of other state courts, federal courts are not so bound and may conclude that the decision does not truly express state law." [15]

That the lower federal courts are *not* "over" the state courts is a difficult point for many laymen to comprehend because the general impression is that the federal court system represents a sys-

15. The statement is from Kehaya v. Axton, 32 F.Supp. 266, 268 (D.C.N.Y.1940) as quoted in *Black's Law Dictionary*, 4th Revised Edition, under the definition of *stare decisis*.

tem of courts whose decisions control or are "higher" than the decisions of state courts, which is not true. The rule is stated as:

> The Supreme Court of the United States has appellate jurisdiction over federal questions arising either in state or federal proceedings, and by reason of the supremacy clause [of the Constitution], the decisions of that court on national law have binding effect on all lower courts whether state or federal. On the other hand, because lower federal courts exercise no appellate jurisdiction over state tribunals, decisions of lower federal courts are not conclusive on state courts * * *.[16]

Even when a three-judge federal court declares a state statute unconstitutional as repugnant to the United States Constitution, the state courts are not bound to follow the federal court interpretation until the Supreme Court of the United States affirms the judgment of the three-judge court.

The State Courts and the United States Supreme Court. The *only* federal court whose decisions are binding on the state courts is the United States Supreme Court, which in the Constitution is given the paramount authority "in all Cases, in Law and Equity, arising under this Constitution, the Laws of the United States, and Treaties made, or which shall be made, under their authority."[17]

This means that the United States Supreme Court has in criminal cases the "last word" as to whether or not the defendant in the case before it has been accorded all of his due process rights as granted to him by the Constitution and the Bill of Rights as interpreted by the Supreme Court itself. In addition, the principles of law announced by the United States Supreme Court, under the doctrine of *stare decisis* and of the "supremacy clause"[18] in the Constitution, are binding upon all state courts as to all federal questions.

16. Lawrence v. Woods, 432 F.2d 1072 (7th Cir. 1970).

17. U. S. Constitution, Art. III.

18. The "supremacy clause" of the United States Constitution reads as follows:
"This Constitution and the Laws of the United States which shall be made in Pursuance thereof; and all Treaties made, or which shall be made, under the Authority of the United States, shall be the supreme Law of the Land; and the Judges in every state shall be bound thereby; any Thing in the Constitution or Laws of Any State to the Contrary notwithstanding." Art. V, § 2.

When the United States Supreme Court decided in Gideon v. Wainwright [19] that being represented by counsel during a felony trial was a basic constitutional right of all offenders, the decision not only required that the defendant Gideon be given a new trial in which he was represented by counsel, it also served to give new trials to all inmates in the prisons of Florida—and all the other states—who had been tried and sentenced without proper representation. It should be noted, however, that only a few of the decisions of the United States Supreme Court have a retroactive effect. In the usual situation, the new rule is applied only from the date of the decision forward. Which decisions have retroactive effect and which do not is determined by the Supreme Court itself on the basis of the nature of the right, the extent to which the previous rule has been relied upon, the effect a change in the rule would have upon the administration of justice, and other factors.

It is very important for the student and practitioner in criminal justice to correctly understand the powers possessed by different courts, the limitations on their powers, and the degree to which the decisions of one court are binding upon another. It is also important to remember that no court, even the United States Supreme Court, has unlimited jurisdiction, and that the powers of all courts are determined in the constitution or legislative act that created them.

JUVENILE COURTS

Strictly speaking, we should not include juvenile courts in a chapter entitled "Criminal Courts." The juvenile court is not a criminal court, though it has many characteristics of a criminal court. Neither is the juvenile court an ordinary civil court, though it is called a civil court and appeals from its decisions are taken to a court of civil appeals. The juvenile court is a *special statutory court* that has among its responsibilities hearing and disposing of cases of juveniles who offend against the criminal law or who transgress against other rules specifically set forth for juveniles. Since juveniles are not "convicted," but are

19. Gideon v. Wainwright, 372 U.S. 335, 83 S.Ct. 792, 9 L.Ed.2d 799 (1963), on remand 153 So.2d 299 (Fla.).

declared to be delinquent children in need of the care and protection of the court, the power of the juvenile court to deal with such children is its "delinquency jurisdiction." A juvenile court is usually also vested with authority to hear cases concerning dependent and neglected children whose condition is such that the intervention of a court is necessary for their care and protection. This invokes the "dependency jurisdiction" of the juvenile court. Our discussion will be limited to the delinquency jurisdiction of the juvenile court since this is the power of the juvenile court to judge and treat the young offender against the law.

The Development of Separate Institutions for Juveniles. You will remember that the early law imposed criminal responsibility on all persons who committed an offense regardless of age, sex, or mental condition. When the church declared that no child under seven could be guilty of sin, the King's court went along with the same rule and did not hold a child under seven criminally liable. However, children over seven were treated exactly as adults—they were tried in the same courts and suffered the same punishments—if it could be shown (from ages 7–14) that they understood the nature and quality of their act and that it was wrong.

As society became more enlightened, people became upset over the severe punishments inflicted upon children. As a result, though children continued to be tried in adult courts, they were gradually exempted from the more severe punishments. At about the same time, the church and private individuals established institutions for the care of homeless children, which on occasion admitted children who had transgressed against the law. These institutions, though far from ideal by our standards, were a great improvement over the prisons of the same period. Later special institutions for young offenders were established by the state itself, and were given names which reflected the main purpose of the institutional programs. The very earliest were called "Workhouses" because the object of the institution was to see that the errant child did useful work. Later, they were named "Reform Schools" to reflect the newly articulated purpose of reform. When it was decided that one of the best ways to reform a young offender was to teach him a trade, the juvenile institutions became "Industrial Schools." Today, institutions for children who have been adjudicated delinquent are usually called "Training Schools" or simply "Schools." This is partly because almost all such institutions have complete educational programs and are accredited schools, but also because the name "school" reflects the fact that the institutions are places for care and treatment, and not for punishment.

The First Juvenile Court. The less severe punishments and the special institutions were a great step forward in the treatment of juvenile offenders. However, adult criminal courts that applied the same standards of accountability to young offenders, and followed the procedures used in the adult criminal courts, continued to hand down what many people considered to be unconscionable sentences against juveniles. It was also felt that many children did not need to be sent to an institution; they could be "reformed" right in their own communities if given the proper care and direction. The movement for a special court to handle juvenile cases was begun by women Settlement House workers in the city of Chicago. The Settlement Houses were charitable organizations devoted to the welfare of immigrants who came into this country, helping them to find homes and jobs and ways to learn the new language. In this work, the good ladies witnessed many instances of unreasonably harsh treatment of young offenders. The women got the support of the Chicago Bar, and in 1900, the first juvenile court was established in Cook County, Illinois. Gradually, other states set up this new court. Wyoming, in 1945, was the last state in the Union to add juvenile courts to its court system.

The Doctrine of Parens Patriae. The philosophy of this new court was unlike that of any other court in history, though it had some resemblance to the old "Court of the King's Conscience." The Chancellor's Courts of early England had often intervened on behalf of fatherless children to require accountings of their money from their guardians and in other ways to protect their interests. The doctrine of the law was that the king had the right and duty to do this because he was "the father of his country." The Latin phrase *parens patriae* means "father of his country," and this doctrine and this phrase became associated with the new court.

The jurisdiction of the juvenile court rested upon the doctrine of *parens patriae*—the duty of the state to protect its children. The purpose of this court was not to judge and punish the child for his misbehavior but to provide for him the care and treatment he needed to grow up into a useful and law abiding citizen. If the child's own parents failed or neglected to train him properly, then the state had a duty to take the place of his parents. This new juvenile court would act toward the errant child "as a kind and loving father."

Since the stated objective of this court was to provide the conditions under which the child brought before it could grow up as a useful citizen, the right of the court to act with respect to the child did not depend upon his having committed an act which, if committed by an adult, would be a crime. The state had a duty to protect the child against other kinds of harmful acts as well. The juvenile court was thus given the power to declare a child delinquent, and so take him under its protection, for such things as habitual truancy, frequenting places of ill repute, keeping bad company, and engaging in conduct harmful to himself or others.

Because the philosophy of the juvenile court was treatment and not punishment, the proceedings in the court tended to be relaxed and informal. As time went on, the procedures diverged more and more from those in an adult criminal court. In 1968, the decision of the United States Supreme Court in the case of In re Gault [20] extended certain due process safeguards to the juvenile offender. As a result, the adjudicatory (guilt finding) stage in a juvenile court now closely resembles trial procedures in a criminal court. However, the dispositional (sentencing) alternatives of the juvenile court are much greater than those of a criminal court, and as we have mentioned before, appeals from the decisions of a juvenile judge are heard by a court of *civil* appeals.

Delinquency Defined. Juvenile delinquency refers to the failure of children and youth to meet certain obligations expected of them by the society in which they live.[21] The Children's Bureau, a federal agency, uses the following definition of delinquency in its reports:

> Juvenile delinquency cases are those referred to courts for acts defined in the statutes of the State as the violation of a state law or municipal ordinance by children or youth of juvenile court age, or for conduct so seriously antisocial as to interfere with the rights of others or to menace the welfare of the delinquent himself or of the community. This

20. In re Gault, 387 U.S. 1, 87 S.Ct. 1428, 18 L.Ed.2d 527 (1967).

21. Cavan, *op. cit.*, p. 23.

broad definition of delinquency includes conduct which violates the law only when committed by children, e. g., truancy, ungovernable behavior, and running away. Also included, but reported separately, are traffic violations whenever a juvenile court has jurisdiction in such cases.[22]

A distinction is made in some states between a juvenile delinquent (or a Delinquent Minor) and a Minor in Need of Supervision. The phrases a "delinquent minor," "delinquent juvenile," and "juvenile delinquent" are used interchangeably. A minor in need of supervision, however, usually refers to a child who has committed a strictly juvenile offense such as running away or truancy, or ungovernable behavior.[23]

The Juvenile Court Age. "Juvenile court age" is the age within which a child is subject to the delinquency jurisdiction of the juvenile court. Both a minimum and maximum age are involved.[24] Some states, such as Texas (where the minimum age is 10 years), have established a minimum age by statute,[25] but "under the great majority of laws it appears possible for a child to be found delinquent at any time from the day it is born *unless* there is some continued vitality to the common law rule of immunity below the age of seven."[26] California, for example, in holding that a child under seven was not within juvenile court jurisdiction found that the legislature did not intend to abolish this particular part of the common law when it established a juvenile court system.[27] This common law interpretation would not apply, however, to the situation in Texas where, though the minimum juvenile age has been fixed at ten years, the minimum age for criminal responsibility has been raised *by statute* to 15 years.[28] In this instance, juvenile court delinquency jurisdiction

22. Juvenile Court Statistics, 1966, Children's Bureau, Statistical Series, 90, Children's Bureau, Washington, D. C., 1967, p. 7.

23. Both New York and Illinois make this distinction.

24. There is customarily no minimum age limit to the dependency jurisdiction of the juvenile court.

25. Vernon's Ann.Civ.Stat. art. 2338.

26. Sanford J. Fox, The Law of Juvenile Courts in a Nutshell, St. Paul, Minn.: West Publishing Co., 1971, p. 5.

27. In re Gladys R., 1 Cal.3d 855, 83 Cal.Rptr. 671, 464 P.2d 127 (1970) (as cited *Ibid*).

28. No person may be convicted of any offense except perjury committed before he was 15 years of age, and for perjury only when it appears that he has sufficient discretion to understand the nature and obligation of an oath. Vernon's Ann.Texas Penal Code, Art. 30, § 1.

is apparently not seen to rest upon the attainment of the age of criminal responsibility. In New York, though there is a lower age limit for delinquency jurisdiction, "children in need of supervision" are subject to the jurisdiction of the juvenile court at any age.

The maximum age limit varies from state to state as fixed by statute. The upper age limit ranges from 16 in four states, to 21 in two states. In 33 states the upper age limit is 18. Age limits may be different for boys than for girls. In Illinois, for example, the upper age limit for boys is 17 and for girls is 18.[29]

In most states, the juvenile court age is determined as of the date of the offense; in other states, the jurisdiction of the juvenile court is determined by the age of the defendant at the time of trial (adjudication hearing). If the uppermost juvenile court age is 16, a boy who commits an offense the day before his sixteenth birthday would be tried in the one state in a juvenile court;[30] in the other state, since the case cannot be prepared for trial in one day, in an adult court.

The juvenile court age is not to be confused with the statutory age for acquiring adult status as to other privileges and responsibilities. In Georgia, for example, the age to be treated as a juvenile delinquent is 16; the voting age, 18; service in the armed forces, 18; marriage without consent of parents, 17 for boys and 18 for girls; end of compulsory education, 16; the right to purchase intoxicating beverages, 21; and the right to secure a drivers license, 16. The minimum age for executing a will is 14. In many states, few adult privileges and responsibilities are acquired prior to age 21, except, of course, for criminal responsibility which may attach at age seven.[31] (Do not confuse juvenile court age and the age of criminal responsibility. The fact that a juvenile court instead of a criminal court handles the juvenile offender does not amount to relieving him from criminal responsibility, and jurisdiction of the juvenile court may attach in the absence of criminal responsibility.)

29. You should refer to the statutes of your state to determine the juvenile court age in your state, or to a general reference work such as Wendell Huston, compiler, *Social Welfare Laws of the Forty-Eight States*, Seattle, Washington: Wendell Huston Company. The information is kept up to date in supplements.

30. Farrow v. State, 258 A.2d 276 (Del.1969).

31. Parnell Calahan, *Legal Status for Young Adults*, New York: Oceana Publications, 1958, pp. 8–81.

Exclusive Jurisdiction of the Juvenile Court. Whether or not the juvenile court has exclusive jurisdiction over offenders of juvenile court age depends upon the law of the state. In twenty-three states, the criminal courts have jurisdiction over some offenses, which means that the person committing that offense must be tried in the criminal court regardless of age and irrespective of the wishes of the juvenile court. Only three states, Oklahoma, Virginia, and New Hampshire give exclusive jurisdiction to the juvenile court for all offenses of all children within the juvenile delinquency age limits, and in many states traffic offenses by juveniles are heard in the regular traffic courts.

The Juvenile Court in the Court System. The founders of the juvenile court envisioned a separate, independent court, presided over by a judge specially trained in child psychology and with broad understanding of the problems of the young. The court would be separately housed, with its own trained staff. It would have facilities for temporary care of children awaiting disposition so that they could be spared the evil influence of being incarcerated in city jails with hardened criminals. The judge would have at his disposal psychologists and psychiatrists, and a wide choice of treatment facilities. Unfortunately, only a few of the larger metropolitan juvenile courts were able to even approach this ideal.

Although all of the states ultimately accepted the juvenile court philosophy, few made any real effort to establish a separate court with its specially trained judge in any but the largest cities. Instead, an existing trial court and its sitting judge was selected to become the juvenile court. This simply meant that the judge of the designated court was instructed to "wear two hats." When trying an adult offender, he was to wear the hat of a regular judge and follow the usual criminal court procedures; when hearing a case involving a juvenile, he was to put on his juvenile judge's hat and proceed according to juvenile court procedures. Thus, the same court might be a criminal court in the morning and a juvenile court in the afternoon, or change back and forth several times during the day according to the age of the defendant.

To make matters worse, in many cases the court chosen to be the juvenile court was a lower court, and one which did not require that the judge be a lawyer. In one state, for example, most of the juvenile courts are courts with misdemeanor jurisdiction only. In such courts, the judges need not have legal training. In the metropolitan areas of the same state, however, the juvenile courts are felony courts with general trial jurisdiction, presided over by lawyer-judges. Thus, though most of the juvenile *courts* are misdemeanor courts, most juvenile *cases* are heard at the felony court level.[32]

The statutes of most states give the juvenile judge authority to transfer a case to the criminal court if the offender is over a specified age and has committed a particularly heinous offense.[33] Such offenders can be both tried and punished as an adult. We will consider this and other procedural aspects of the juvenile court in the discussion of the juvenile court process.

With respect then to the system of criminal courts, the juvenile court, though not considered a criminal court, is nevertheless the court which hears and disposes of juvenile transgressors against the law, sometimes with exclusive jurisdiction to handle all offenses committed by juveniles of juvenile court age, sometimes with jurisdiction limited to certain offenses, and sometimes with concurrent jurisdiction with the criminal courts. Committing an offense which, if committed by an adult, would be a felony or a misdemeanor is sufficient to invoke the power of the juvenile court, and its jurisdiction also extends over offenses, such as truancy, running away, and the like, which are not offenses when committed by an adult. Since the incidence of juvenile offenses is very high, the juvenile court is one of the busiest courts in the criminal justice system.

YOUTH COURTS

A few states have youth courts which extend the juvenile court philosophy to the next age group above the juvenile court to age 21. The Boys' Court of Chicago is a part of the Municipal Court of Chicago and has jurisdiction of boys between the ages of seventeen and twenty-one. It operates under the criminal code that governs adults. The Philadelphia youth court is similar.

32. This is the situation in Texas.

33. This is sometimes called "certifying" the juvenile to the criminal court.

The New York youth courts have been established under the Wayward Minor statutes. In some of the courts, jurisdiction extends over youth between the ages of sixteen and twenty-one who have committed certain offenses, such as liquor or drug abuse, associating with prostitutes, being willfully disobedient, and morally depraved, but does not include felonies. The Youthful Offender Act of 1943 provided for a Youth Court in the criminal courts of New York, applicable to youth between the ages of sixteen and nineteen who have committed crimes not punishable by death or life imprisonment.

The youth courts, though classified as adult courts, use many of the techniques of the juvenile courts, and emphasize rehabilitation. However, it is not mandatory that youths be tried in youth courts even where they exist. As a result, the older youth who has committed even a minor offense is frequently tried in the adult criminal court.[34]

34. Cavan, *op. cit.*, pp. 418–420.

Chapter VII

INVESTIGATION AND ACCUSATION

We defined the criminal justice system as the system by which society identifies, accuses, convicts, and punishes offenders against the norms of the society expressed in the law. The criminal justice process is the sequence of steps taken from the initial contact of the offender with the law until he is released back into a free society. We established that the criminal justice system is characterized by the interdependency and interaction of its parts, and that the criminal justice process is a continuum along which the offender moves from arrest to release.

Traditionally criminal justice is studied as though it were made up of three independent sections or divisions—law enforcement, the judicial process, and corrections. Because by looking at one part of the total process at a time we can increase our understanding of the whole, we will divide the next three chapters into Investigation and Accusation, Adjudication and Conviction, Sentencing and Correction. These are roughly, but not exactly, equivalent to the traditional grouping and perhaps will be more appropriate to the systems approach we want to emphasize.

A precautionary word is in order. In an introductory text, it is impossible to dwell upon the "fine points" of the law, or to present the many sides of controversial questions. Neither is it possible to travel all the alternative paths that may be traveled by an offender who enters the criminal justice system. All we can hope to do is to become acquainted with the system and obtain an over-view of the process. This we will do by pausing at each major step along the criminal justice continuum to analyze what is happening; to identify if we can, how decisions are being made; and to consider their effect on the next step in the process.

In this chapter, we will start with the Constitutional protections against unreasonable searches and seizures, since these guarantees largely control law enforcement practices and procedures. We will identify the chief law enforcement officers at the city, county, state, and federal levels. Beginning with the steps leading up to arrest, we will proceed in sequence through arrest, booking, initial appearance before the magistrate (presentment), preliminary hearing, information or indictment, arraignment, and plea.

THE FOURTH AMENDMENT

The Fourth Amendment to the United States Constitution reads as follows:

> The right of the people to be secure in their persons, houses, papers, and effects, against unreasonable searches and seizures, shall not be violated, and no warrants shall issue, but upon probable cause, supported by oath or affirmation, and particularly describing the place to be searched, and the persons or things to be seized.

Since an arrest is a seizure of the person, a person is given the same protection against an illegal arrest as he is against an unreasonable search and seizure of his houses, papers, and effects. (An automobile has been held to be an "effect" within the meaning of this provision.) Similar provisions against unreasonable searches and seizures appear in the constitutions of all of the states.

The key word in the Fourth Amendment language is "unreasonable." The Constitution does not protect against all searches and seizures, but only against *unreasonable* searches and seizures. Though the Constitution speaks of "warrants" and the Constitutional ideal is obviously that no arrest or search will be made without a warrant, the truth is that the majority of arrests and a large proportion of searches are made without a warrant. In the case of arrests, the Constitutional requirement seems to be met by the issuance of a warrant after the arrest if the intention is to continue with the prosecution.

The requirement of probable cause must be met if an arrest, without or with a warrant, is to withstand the attack of habeas corpus. If evidence obtained from a search is to be admitted in evidence, the probable cause standards must likewise be met. Certain special pre-arrest procedures such as stop and question and stop and frisk are upheld as being reasonable and thus within permissible constitutional limits, though the level of certainty is somewhat below that of probable cause.

INVESTIGATION

Who Are Peace Officers. Law enforcement officers usually refer to themselves as "peace officers." Peace officers are public officials charged by the law with keeping the peace. For this purpose they are given general powers of investigation and arrest. Sheriffs and policemen are the best known peace officers, though other officials, such as liquor control officers, prosecuting attorneys, members of the Game and Fish Commission, park police, court attendants, and others are included in the definition of "peace officer" or are given special law enforcement and arrest powers.[1]

1. Peace officers are defined by the laws of each state. In New York, for example, the following persons are peace officers:

(a) A police officer;

(b) An attendant, uniformed court officer or an official of the supreme court in the first and second departments;

(c) An attendant, uniformed court officer or other official attached to the county courts of Nassau and Suffolk counties;

(d) A marshal, clerk or attendant of a district court;

(e) A clerk, uniformed court officer or other official of the criminal court of the city of New York;

(f) A uniformed court officer or an official of the civil court of the city of New York;

(g) An attendant, clerk or uniformed court officer of the family court;

(h) An attendant, or an official, or guard of any state prison or of any penal correctional institution;

(i) An officer of the staff of the board of parole in the executive department;

(j) A harbor master appointed by a county, city, town or village;

(k) An investigator of the office of the state commission of investigation;

(*l*) Onondaga county park rangers;

(m) An officer or agent of a duly incorporated society for the prevention of cruelty to animals or children;

(n) An inspector or investigator of the department of agriculture and markets;

(*o*) An employee of the department of taxation and finance assigned to enforcement of the tax on cigarettes imposed by article twenty of the tax law by the commissioner of taxation and finance;

(p) An employee of the New York City finance administration assigned to enforcement of the tax on cigarettes imposed by section D46–2.0 of the administrative code of the city of New York by the finance administrator;

(q) A constable or police constable of a city, county, town or village;

(r) Repealed.

(s) A probation officer;

(t) The sheriff, under-sheriff and deputy sheriffs of New York City. McKinney's N.Y.Criminal Procedure Law, § 1.20(33).

The New York Criminal Procedure Law makes a distinction between a peace officer and a police officer, and the authority given to a peace officer is somewhat less than that given to a police officer. (See for example, § 140.25). The following persons are police officers:

(a) A sworn officer of the division of state police;

A sheriff is an officer of the county. A police officer is an officer of a city or town. There may also be law enforcement officers of a state where a state has a state police force. The Texas Rangers are such a force. Highway police are also usually peace officers, though, as in Florida, they may not have general powers of investigation and arrest, being restricted in their exercise of such powers to traffic offenses. The chief peace officer of the United States is the United States Marshal.

The agents of the Federal Bureau of Investigation have power to investigate and arrest for federal crimes. Certain other agents of the federal government also have authority to arrest for federal offenses. Treasury Agents have authority in the areas of drug and liquor control, in counterfeiting cases, and in tax offenses. They also have the responsibility for the safety of the President, the Vice-President, and their families. Customs Agents have authority in immigration, border searches, and the like. Mail inspectors are charged with the safety of the United States mails, and investigate fraudulent use of the mails, mail theft, and

(b) Sheriffs, under-sheriffs and deputy sheriffs of counties outside of New York City;

(c) A sworn officer of an authorized county or county parkway police department;

(d) A sworn officer of an authorized police department or force of a city, town, village or police district;

(e) A sworn officer of an authorized police department of an authority or a regional state park commission;

(f) A sworn officer of the capital buildings police force of the office of general services;

(g) An investigator employed in the office of a district attorney;

(h) An investigator employed by a commission created by an interstate compact who is, to a substantial extent, engaged in the enforcement of the criminal laws of this state;

(i) The chief and deputy fire marshals, the supervising fire marshals and the fire marshals of the bureau of fire investigation of the New York City fire department;

(j) The chief of the bureau of law enforcement and field services, assistant superintendent of law enforcement, regional conservation officers, assistant regional conservation officers and conservation officers in the conservation department. McKinney's N.Y.Criminal Procedure Law, § 1.20(34).

The "geographical area of employment" of certain police officers is as follows:

(a) New York state constitutes the "geographical area of employment" of any police officer employed as such by an agency of the state or by an authority which functions throughout the state. McKinney's N.Y.Criminal Procedure Law, § 1.20(34–a (a)).

similar offenses. Other federal employees, such as Indian Agents and Park Rangers, have certain investigative and enforcement authority.

A law enforcement officer is charged with the prevention and control of crime and the apprehension of criminals. His jurisdiction (power) to act is generally limited by the geographical boundaries of the governmental unit to which he is attached. Thus, a city policeman has authority to act only within the city limits; the sheriff has no authority beyond the boundaries of the county; and a state police officer may operate only within his own state. Sometimes, by state law or working agreements between states, an officer "in hot pursuit" of a fleeing felon may be authorized to cross his usual geographical boundaries to effect an arrest. Whenever an officer crosses a state or county line "in hot pursuit," the first thing he does is to turn the offender over to the nearest local official authorized to take him into custody. The agents of the Federal Bureau of Investigation and other federal officers can, of course, cross state lines in investigation of federal offenses and may arrest an offender against the laws of the United States any place within the United States. Their authority in state crimes is solely to assist local officers upon request.

Field Interrogation. Arrest is the means by which most offenders enter the criminal justice system. In the usual case, the arrest is made by a law enforcement officer, though there is such a thing as a "citizens arrest."

Not all of the procedures taken by a police officer with respect to a citizen constitutes an "arrest." In the course of a general investigation of a suspected or reported crime, a police officer may stop and question any persons whom he believes may have information about the event. He may also demand their name and their business in the vicinity. If the answers given are unsatisfactory or if any of their actions give him reasonable cause to believe that they were involved in the planning or execution of the crime, he may pat down their outer clothing to determine if they have a weapon. These procedures are called "stop and question," "frisk," "stop and frisk," or "on the spot search," and come under the general titles of "field interrogation" or "detection." A writer on the subject of arrest defines arrest and distinguishes it from detection as follows:

> Arrest * * * is a distinct operational step in the criminal justice process, involving all police decisions to

interfere with the freedom of a person who is suspected of criminal conduct to the extent of taking him to the police station for some purpose.

A basic distinction * * * is that between actually taking a suspect to the station and the preliminary investigative devices of stopping and questioning, frisking, and conducting an on-the-spot search. The former is called an arrest * *.

In the usual case, the degree of interference is substantially greater when the suspect is actually taken to the station house. The stopping and questioning of a person on the street usually results in detention for only a few minutes, after which the officer decides that the suspect should either be taken to the station (arrested) or allowed to go his way. A frisk or search may take place during this brief detention. In contrast, the person who is taken to the station is ordinarily detained at least several hours. * * *

The person being dealt with also generally views the taking to the station as different from on-the-street investigation. For instance, if asked on a questionnaire whether he has ever been arrested, the person who was only questioned on the street, frisked, or searched would most likely answer no. The person who was taken to the station is more likely to answer yes, particularly if asked whether he has ever been "arrested or detained." [2]

Stop and Frisk. Stop and frisk is a special investigative procedure during which the officer with reasonable grounds to do so may make a limited search for weapons.

One of the first "stop and frisk" statutes was passed by the State of New York in 1964, with the title "Temporary questioning of persons in public places, search for weapons." It was immediately dubbed the "stop and frisk" law. The main provisions of this law now read as follows:

1. In addition to the authority provided by this article for making an arrest without a warrant, a police officer may stop a person in a public place located within the geographical area of such officer's employment when he reasonably suspects that such person is committing, has committed or is about to commit either (a) a felony or (b) a class A mis-

2. Wayne R. La Fave, *Arrest: The decision to take a suspect into custody*, Boston: Little, Brown and Company, 1965, pp. 4–5.

demeanor defined in the penal law, and may demand of him his name, address and an explanation of his conduct.

2. When upon stopping a person under circumstances prescribed in subdivision one a police officer reasonably suspects that he is in danger of physical injury, he may search such person for a deadly weapon or any instrument, article or substance readily capable of causing serious physical injury and of a sort not ordinarily carried in public places by law-abiding persons. If he finds such a weapon or instrument, or any other property possession of which he reasonably believes may constitute the commission of a crime, he may take it and keep it until the completion of the questioning, at which time he shall either return it, if lawfully possessed, or arrest such person.[3]

A draft of a model law to provide for similar procedures was set out in the *Model Code of Pre-Arraignment Procedures,* 2.02 (Ten. Draft No. 1, 1966). The Model Penal Code version provided that the procedure could not be used solely to aid in the investigation or prevention of the petty crimes (penalty no more than thirty days); loitering; and vagrancy.[4]

In a series of decisions entered the same day,[5] the United States Supreme Court upheld the right of the police to stop and frisk under severely limited circumstances. The Court did not pass upon the constitutionality of the New York law, though two of the cases arose in New York. In Terry v. Ohio, the Court announced the rule as to the right of an officer to stop and frisk as follows:

We merely hold today that where a police officer observes unusual conduct which leads him reasonably to conclude

3. McKinney's N.Y.Criminal Procedure Law, § 140.50.

Smith-Hurd Ann. Ill.Stat. ch. 38, Code Crim.Proc. § 108–1.01: *Search During Temporary Questioning.* When a peace officer has stopped a person for temporary questioning pursuant to Section 107–14 of this Code and reasonably suspects that he or another is in danger of attach, he may search the person for weapons. If the officer discovers a weapon, he may take it until the completion of the questioning, at which time he shall either return the weapon, if lawfully possessed, or arrest the person so questioned.

4. The Uniform Arrest Act also provides for Questioning and Detaining of Suspects. Uniform Arrest Act, Sec. 2, fn. 21, *infra.*

5. Terry v. Ohio, 392 U.S. 1, 88 S.Ct. 1868, 20 L.Ed.2d 889 (1968); Sibron v. New York and Peters v. New York, 392 U.S. 40, 88 S.Ct. 1889, 20 L.Ed.2d 917 (1968).

in light of his experience that criminal activity may be afoot and that the persons with whom he is dealing may be armed and presently dangerous; where in the course of investigating his behavior he identifies himself as a policeman and makes reasonable inquiries; and where nothing in the initial stages of the encounter serves to dispel his reasonable fear for his own or others' safety, he is entitled for the protection of himself and others in the area to conduct a carefully limited search of the outer clothing of such persons in an attempt to discover weapons which might be used to assault him. Such a search is a reasonable search under the Fourth Amendment, and any weapons seized may properly be introduced in evidence against the person from whom they were taken.

In the *Sibron* case, the search which had turned up a quantity of marijuana, the Court did not uphold the validity of the search, pointing out that the officer must be able to point to facts from which he reasonably inferred that the individual was armed and dangerous, which the officer could not do under the facts of that case.[6] A search by an off-duty police officer who saw two men furtively tiptoeing about the hallway of his apartment was upheld as reasonable,[7] though the Court tended to see the circumstances in the *Peters* case as giving rise to probable cause to arrest and not as a typical stop and frisk situation. The burglary tool which the officer found on Peters was admitted in evidence against him, and this was upheld in the decision of the Supreme Court.

Arrest on Suspicion. An arrest on suspicion is essentially an arrest for investigation. Since an arrest must be based on probable cause and be for a crime that there is reasonable grounds to believe has been committed, an arrest "on suspicion" or an "arrest for investigation" is of doubtful legality. Nevertheless, such arrests are frequently made and some state statutes specifically provide for them. What such arrests mean is that an arresting officer wants to take the suspect to the station house for further questioning or to have him available while additional outside investigation takes place.

Probable cause, we learned in a previous chapter, involves a level of belief greater than suspicion but less than certainty. This level of certainty must exist with regard to two facts: (1) that

6. Sibron v. New York, fn. 5, *supra*.

7. Peters v. New York, fn. 5, *supra*.

a crime has been committed, and (2) that the accused has committed it. Proof that probable cause did indeed exist must be based upon a showing of facts ascertainable through the use of the five senses, which can be articulated (explained, testified to) by the observer.

An arrest not based upon probable cause is an illegal arrest, and the person arrested is entitled to his immediate freedom. In some cases he has a cause of action for damages against the arresting officer. A search not based upon probable cause is an illegal search, and an arrest on suspicion will not support a search without a warrant. Any evidence obtained as a result of such a search cannot be admitted in evidence at the trial of the accused. Because of the "Exclusionary Rule," (See further discussion of the "Exclusionary Rule" in a following section) an "Arrest on Suspicion" may defeat successful prosecution.

ARREST AND SEARCH

Elements of Arrest. Four elements are necessary to constitute an arrest:

1. intention of the officer to make an arrest;
2. communicating this intention to the person arrested;
3. control by the officer of the person arrested; and
4. understanding by the person arrested that he is being arrested.

On occasion, of course, one or more of the elements may be missing, as when an officer arrests a person who has passed out from intoxication who is not capable of understanding that he is being taken into official custody.

No formal words are necessary to constitute an arrest, and no touching is required. If an officer, with the intention to arrest says, "Come with me," and the individual, knowing he is not free to leave the presence of the officer, quietly submits himself to the officer's custody and control, there has been an arrest.[8]

8. An arrest is defined in California as follows: West's Ann. Penal Code:

§ 834. **Arrest defined; persons authorized to arrest.** An arrest is taking a person into custody, in a case and in the manner authorized by law. An arrest may be made by a peace officer or by a private person.

The Purpose of Arrest. The purpose of arrest is prosecution. The issuance of the warrant of arrest prior to arrest usually, though not always, represents a decision to prosecute concurred in by the prosecutor. The issuance of the warrant of arrest after the arrest evidences in most instances a decision to continue with the prosecution.

There is a distinction between being arrested for a crime and being charged with a crime. A person may be arrested, taken to the station house, booked and released (or released without being booked) all without being charged. Charging implies a formal decision to continue with the prosecution. Traditionally, this decision is made by the prosecutor. Thus, it is said that the arrest decision is made by the police, while the decision to charge is made by the prosecutor.[9]

According to some authorities, a person is "charged" when the complaint is filed; according to others, a person is not charged until the warrant is issued. Because of this legal doubt about when the charging is actually accomplished, the practice is to issue a warrant of arrest though the accused is already in custody following an arrest without a warrant.

In practice, many arrests are made for reasons other than prosecution, and without intention to charge. Arresting a drunk

§ 835. **Method of making arrest; amount of restraint.** An arrest is made by an actual restraint of the person, or by submission to the custody of an officer. The person arrested may be subjected to such restraint as is reasonable for his arrest and detention.

Illinois sets out the *Method of Arrest* in § 107–5, Smith-Hurd Ann.Stat. ch. 38, Crim.Law and Proc.:

(a) An arrest is made by an actual restraint of the person or by his submission to custody.

(b) An arrest may be made on any day and at any time of the day or night.

(c) An arrest may be made anywhere within the jurisdiction of this State.

(d) All necessary and reasonable force may be used to effect an entry into any building or property or part thereof to make an authorized arrest.

In New York, "the sole function of a warrant of arrest is to achieve a defendant's court appearance in a criminal action for the purpose of arraignment upon the accusatory instrument by which such action was commenced." McKinney's N.Y.Criminal Procedure Law, § 120.10 (1).

In Texas, a person is arrested when "he has been actually placed under restraint or taken into custody by an officer or person executing a warrant of arrest, or by an officer or person arresting without a warrant." Vernon's Ann.Texas C.C.P., art. 15.22.

9. La Fave, *op. cit.*, p. 4.

to sober him up, or a prostitute to submit her to a medical examination are examples of this kind of arrest. Sometimes an arrest for investigation will be made of the suspect of a crime (often a sex crime) which rapidly inflame public passions, for the protection of the suspect, with the decision to charge depending upon developing circumstances.

Distinctions between detection and arrest, and between arrest and charging are not always clear. Sometimes stopping and questioning, arresting, and charging are so telescoped that it is impossible to separate them, and it is difficult to know just when arrest has taken place, or when the defendant has been charged. It is also difficult to determine sometimes just who makes the "charging" decision. We shall encounter some of these difficulties as we attempt to analyze the procedures for obtaining an arrest warrant, and the handling of the offender after arrest without a warrant.

Arrest With a Warrant. The process for obtaining a warrant of arrest may be initiated in several ways.[10] The victim, or

10. In California a complaint is filed before the magistrate under oath of the complainant. West's Ann.Penal Code, § 806.

In New York, when a criminal action has been commenced by the filing of an accusatory instrument, other than a simplified traffic information, if the accusatory instrument is sufficient on its face, the court may issue a warrant for the defendant's arrest. McKinney's N.Y.Criminal Procedure Law, § 120.20 (1).

The court has authority to issue a summons in lieu of a warrant of arrest based upon an accusatory pleading charging a misdemeanor. See *Ibid.*, § 130.30.

In Texas, an affidavit (also called a complaint) is filed. The requisites of the complaint are set out in Art. 15.05, Vernon's Texas Code Crim. Proc., Ann.

The Illinois statutes include in one section the pertinent provisions of complaint and the contents of the warrant. Smith-Hurd Ann.Stat. ch. 38, Crim.Law and Proc., § 107–9: **Issuance of Arrest Warrant upon Complaint.**

(a) When a complaint is presented to a court charging that an offense has been committed it shall examine upon oath or affirmation the complainant or any witnesses.

(b) The complaint shall be in writing and shall:

(1) State the name of the accused if known, and if not known the accused may be designated by any name or description by which he can be identified with reasonable certainty;

(2) State the offense with which the accused is charged;

(3) State the time and place of the offense as definitely as can be done by the complainant; and

(4) Be subscribed and sworn to by the complainant.

(c) A warrant shall be issued by the court for the arrest of the person complained against if it apother person having knowledge of the crime, (thereafter called the "complaining witness") may go directly to the prosecutor with his information. The prosecutor will prepare the supporting affidavit, (because it charges a crime, it is called a "complaint") which the informant will sign and swear to (thus providing the Oath or Affirmation required by the Fourth Amendment). The prosecutor and the complainant go before the magistrate who issues the warrant. The law may require that the complaint be sworn to before the magistrate, or it may be sufficient if it is sworn to before the prosecutor, a clerk, or a notary public.

Instead of going to the prosecutor, the informant may go first to the police. The police officer may take the complainant to the prosecutor, or will go himself to the prosecutor, who will prepare the complaint. The complaint will be signed by the complaining witness if present, or by the officer, or the prosecutor. The complaint is then taken to the magistrate, who issues the warrant. Or the police officer may go directly to the magistrate who will swear the police officer, have him sign the complaint, and issue the warrant.

If the police officer himself has witnessed the crime, or if his information is from an informer whose identity he does not wish to disclose, he may go to the prosecutor to file a complaint, or he may go directly to the magistrate. In such cases, the police officer becomes the "complaining witness."

pears from the contents of the complaint and the examination of the complainant or other witnesses, if any, that the person against whom the complaint was made has committed an offense.

(d) **The warrant of arrest shall:**

(1) Be in writing;

(2) Specify the name of the person to be arrested or if his name is unknown, shall designate such person by any name or description by which he can be identified with reasonable certainty;

(3) Set forth the nature of the offense;

(4) State the date when issued and the municipality or county where issued;

(5) Be signed by the judge of the court with the title of his office;

(6) Command that the person against whom the complaint was made be arrested and brought before the court issuing the warrant or if he is absent or unable to act before the nearest or most accessible court in the same county; and

(7) Specify the amount of bail.

(e) The warrant shall be directed to all peace officers in the State. It shall be executed by the peace officer, or by a private person specially named therein, and may be executed in any county in the State.

In some states a magistrate cannot issue an arrest warrant without the knowledge and concurrence of the prosecutor.[11] In other states, the consent of the prosecutor is not required. The decision to issue a warrant of arrest is a judicial decision, which should be made by a judicial officer. Furthermore, the warrant should issue after the judicial officer, in the exercise of independent judgment, decides that a showing of probable cause has been made. Thus, there is a requirement that the complaint filed must contain sufficient facts from which this independent judgment can be made. In practice, however, arrest warrants are sometimes issued by clerks, who treat the issuance of the warrant as a routine ministerial function. These may be county clerks, justice of the peace clerks, or in at least one state, specially designated police officers. Even when the warrant is issued by the magistrate, who is a judicial officer, he often has not made an independent decision as to whether the warrant should issue. Prior to recent decisions which have carefully scrutinized both arrest and search warrants, it was not uncommon for a magistrate to sign several blank warrants in advance. These warrants were kept in the police station and filled in by the police officers as needed.

A warrant of arrest is an order signed by a magistrate commanding the person addressed, usually "any person authorized to execute this warrant,"[12] to take a named person into custody and to bring him before the court to answer to the crime specified in the warrant.[13] The warrant issues in the name of the

11. The District Attorney or the Attorney General of the State must concur in California when the magistrate issuing the warrant is a Justice of the Peace. West's Ann. Cal.Penal Code, § 813.

12. In general, an officer can arrest only within his own jurisdictional limits, which may be state-wide or limited to a county or city.

Many states have adopted the Uniform Fresh Pursuit Act ("fresh pursuit" is sometimes called "hot pursuit") which extends the authority to arrest. As set out in the Iowa Code, for example, the Act reads as follows:

Any member of a duly organized state, county, or municipal law enforcement unit of another state of the United States who enters this state in fresh pursuit, and continues within this state in such fresh pursuit, of a person in order to arrest him on the ground that he is believed to have committed a felony in such other state, shall have the same authority to arrest and hold such person in custody, as has any member of any duly organized state, county, or municipal law enforcement unit of this state to arrest and hold in custody a person on the ground that he is believed to have committed a felony in this state. Iowa Code Ann. § 756-1.

13. A warrant of arrest is defined in Illinois and distinguished from

state. A magistrate, as we have said, is a judicial officer. Thus, all judges of courts of general jurisdiction are magistrates. The state law also usually makes justices of the peace and judges of municipal courts magistrates. A committing magistrate is a magistrate authorized to conduct a preliminary hearing and "bind over" a defendant for trial. In state court systems the committing magistrate is usually a justice of the peace. In the federal system, United States Magistrates and in some instances United States District Court Judges are "committing magistrates."

The warrant of arrest is then delivered to any officer authorized to execute the same, or in rare instances to a specially named individual who is not an officer. To execute the warrant means to implement its provisions by taking the named person into custody. The officer takes the warrant, locates the person accused, warns him of his rights, arrests him, and takes him to the station house. If requested, he reads the warrant to the person being arrested or hands him a copy. The officer notes the time and place of the arrest on the back of the warrant and takes it back to the magistrate. This is the "return" of the warrant. The warrant and the return become the permanent record of the arrest.

Arrest Without a Warrant. As we have said, in spite of the Constitutional preference for the use of a warrant to effect an arrest, not all arrests without a warrant amount to a prohibited "unreasonable seizure." Both an officer and a citizen have the right to arrest without a warrant for a felony committed in their presence. Both also have the right to arrest without a warrant for a misdemeanor committed in their presence which is a breach of the peace. A *breach of the peace* is any act which is a "violation or disturbance of the public tranquility and order * * * and includes all violations of public peace or order and acts tending to a disturbance thereof." [14]

other procedures in § 107–1, Smith-Hurd Ann.Stat. ch. 38, Crim.Law and Proc.: **Definitions.**

(a) A "warrant of arrest" is a written order from a court directed to a peace officer, or to some other person specifically named, commanding him to arrest a person.

(b) A "summons" is a written order issued by a court which commands a person to appear before a court at a stated time and place.

(c) A "notice to appear" is a written request issued by a peace officer that a person appear before a court at a stated time and place.

14. *Black's Law Dictionary, Revised 4th Edition.*

An officer has the right to arrest without a warrant for a felony reported to him by a reliable person where there is danger that the offender will escape or that evidence will be destroyed and there is no time to get a warrant. In many states, an officer can arrest without a warrant for any misdemeanor committed in his presence, whether or not the act constitutes a breach of the peace.[15] Thus, a reported misdemeanor which the officer does not witness is the offense for which the officer is required in most states to get a warrant before arresting the offender.[16] In practice, most officers arrest without a warrant for any offense committed in their presence, and often arrest without a warrant for reported misdemeanors, sometimes under special statutory authority granted for particular misdemeanors.

The same requirements of probable cause apply to an arrest without a warrant as to an arrest with a warrant. The arresting officer must be able to testify to the facts and circumstances upon which he based his belief that a crime had been or was about

15. The law concerning the authority of a police officer to arrest without a warrant can be generally summarized as follows. (It is beyond the scope of this book to consider minor variations between states.)

a. In every jurisdiction, a police officer can arrest without a warrant whenever he has probable cause to believe that a felony is being committed in his presence.

b. In all of the states except Mass. and Vt., a peace officer may arrest without a warrant when he has probable cause to believe that the person arrested is committing a misdemeanor in his presence.

c. A peace officer may arrest if he has reasonable grounds to believe a felony has been committed though not in his presence. This is the rule in Ala., Ariz., Ark., Cal., Colo., Conn., Del., D.C., Fla., Ga., Hawaii, Ind., Kan., Ky., La., Maine, Md., Mass., Mich., Mo., N.J., N.H., N.C., Ohio, Pa., R.I., S.C., Tex., Vt., Va., Wash., W.Va., Wisc., and Wyo. In Texas, the offender must be threatening to escape with no time to get a warrant. In Connecticut, the officer may act only "on the speedy information of others."

16. The Illinois statutes give a peace officer very broad powers to arrest. Smith-Hurd Ann.Stat. ch. 38, Crim.Law and Proc., § 107-2. The statute reads: **Arrest by Peace Officer.** A peace officer may arrest a person when:

(a) He has a warrant commanding that such person be arrested; or

(b) He has reasonable grounds to believe that a warrant for the person's arrest has been issued in this State or in another jurisdiction; or

(c) He has reasonable grounds to believe that the person is committing or has committed an offense.

The New York Criminal Procedure Law provides for the issuance of an "appearance ticket" in lieu of arrest whenever a police officer is authorized by law to arrest without a warrant for an offense other than a felony. See McKinney's N.Y. CPL 150.10-150.70.

to be committed and that the arrested person was involved in it. The officer cannot rely on a "hunch" or the fact that a person was acting "suspiciously" unless he can give *reasons* amounting to a belief and based on something he saw, heard, smelled, touched, or tasted. The officer's special training and competency to recognize the significance of certain behavior can be taken into account. Thus, facts and circumstances which to the untrained observer would not lead him to believe that a crime had been or was about to be committed may nevertheless be sufficient facts and circumstances to justify the officer's belief.

The detection techniques of stop and question and frisk often lead to an arrest without a warrant. If an officer in the course of the frisk finds a gun or other concealed weapon, he can arrest without a warrant, as an offense has now been committed in his presence. After an arrest an officer also has certain rights of on-the-spot search which we will discuss hereafter.

The Miranda Warning. As a result of two Supreme Court decisions, Escobedo v. Illinois,[17] and Miranda v. Arizona,[18] an officer must immediately inform an arrested person of his Constitutional rights. In fact, the Warning must be given even before an arrest at any time that an inquiry into a crime ceases to be a general inquiry as to the facts and circumstances, and suspicion begins to focus on an individual. This is sometimes expressed as "when the investigation shifts from the investigatory to the accusatory stage, The Warning must be given." The Warning must also be given at any time that an individual is under such restraint that he is not free to walk away from the scene, even though no formal arrest has been made.[19]

The required Warning is set out in detail in the case of Miranda v. Arizona, and is known as the "Miranda Warning." The officer must tell the person upon whom suspicion has focused the following: (1) You have a right to remain silent. (2) If you do not remain silent, what you say may be used against you. (3) You have a right to be represented by counsel during questioning and thereafter. (4) If you cannot afford to hire your own counsel, one will be provided for you at state expense. Sometimes the

17. Escobedo v. Illinois, 378 U.S. 478, 84 S.Ct. 1758, 12 L.Ed.2d 977 (1964).

18. Miranda v. Arizona, 384 U.S. 436, 86 S.Ct. 1602, 16 L.Ed.2d 694 (1966), reh. den. 385 U.S. 890, 87 S.Ct. 11, 17 L.Ed.2d 121.

19. Orozco v. Texas, 394 U.S. 324, 89 S.Ct. 1095, 22 L.Ed.2d 311 (1969), on remand 442 S.W.2d 376 (Tex.).

officer carries a small card upon which the Miranda Warning is printed. He may read from this card to be sure that he doesn't miss any of the points, and he may also hand a similar card to the person accused. In practice, the officers tend to make the warning even stronger than strictly required by the Miranda case as they have found that not all persons understand some of the words. So they say, "If you talk, what you say *will* be used against you at the trial," and they use the words "counsel, attorney, or lawyer," because the word "counsel" confuses some people.

If the officer fails to give the required Warning, no admissions or confessions made by the accused can be used in court.[20] Most people do not talk after receiving the Warning. If a person insists on talking, the officer will probably warn him at least once more to be sure there is no misunderstanding. If the accused continues to talk, any admissions he makes can be introduced into evidence at his trial.

In an effort to establish uniform arrest procedures, the Uniform Arrest Act was developed in 1947 by the Interstate Commission on Crime. It has been adopted in its entirety only by Delaware, Rhode Island, and New Hampshire. However, its provisions are making their way into the statutory law of many states. The Uniform Arrest Act is set out below.[21]

20. In the case of Viven Harris v. State of New York, 401 U.S. 222, 91 S.Ct. 643, 28 L.Ed.2d 1 (1971) a statement inadmissible in evidence because of failure to give the Miranda Warning was used for impeachment of a defendant who took the stand.

21. Uniform Arrest Act.

Section 1. Definitions. As used in this act:

"Arrest" is the taking of a person into custody in order that he may be forthcoming to answer for the commission of a crime.

"Felony" is any crime which is or may be punished by death or imprisonment in a state prison. Any other crime or any violation of a municipal ordinance is a misdemeanor.

"Peace Officer" is any sheriff, deputy sheriff, mayor, city marshal, constable, police officer or other officer authorized by law to make arrests in a criminal case.

Section 2. Questioning and Detaining Suspects.

I. A peace officer may stop any person abroad whom he has reasonable ground to suspect is committing, has committed or is about to commit a crime, and may demand of him his name, address, business abroad and whither he is going.

II. Any person so questioned who fails to identify hmself or explain his actions to the satisfaction of the officer stopping him may be detained and further questioned and investigated.

III. The total period of detention provided for by this section shall not exceed two hours. Such detention is not an arrest and shall not be recorded as an arrest in any official record. At the end of the detention period the person so detained shall be released unless arrested and charged with a crime.

Section 3. Searching for Weapons.

A peace officer may search for a dangerous weapon any person whom he is questioning or about to question as provided in section 2, whenever he has reasonable ground to believe that he is in danger if such person possesses a dangerous weapon. If the officer finds a weapon, he may take and keep it until the completion of the questioning, when he shall either return it or arrest the person. The arrest may be for the illegal possession of the weapon.

Section 4. Arrest—Permissible Force.

I. No unnecessary or unreasonable force of means of restraint may be used in detaining or arresting any person.

II. A peace officer who is making an arrest for any crime need not retreat or desist from his efforts by reason of the resistance or threatened resistance of the person to be arrested; nor shall he be deemed an aggressor or lose his right to self defense by the use of reasonable force to effect an arrest.

III. A peace officer, who has reasonable ground to believe that the person to be arrested has committed a felony, is justified in using force dangerous to human life for the purpose of making an arrest only when:

A. There is no other apparently possible means of effecting the arrest, and

B. The officer has made every reasonable effort to advise the person to be arrested that he is a peace officer and is attempting to make an arrest and has reasonable ground to believe that the person is aware of the fact.

Section 5. Resisting Arrest.

If a person has reasonable ground to believe that he is being arrested by a peace officer, it is his duty to submit to arrest and refrain from using force or any weapon in resisting it regardless of whether there is a legal basis for the arrest.

Section 6. Arrest without a Warrant.

I. An arrest by a peace officer without a warrant for a misdemeanor is lawful whenever:

A. He has reasonable ground to believe that a misdemeanor has been committed in his presence and that the person to be arrested has committed it.

B. He has reasonable ground to believe that a misdemeanor has been committed out of his presence whether within or without the state and that the person to be arrested has committed it and will not be apprehended unless immediately arrested.

II. An arrest by a peace officer without a warrant for a felony, whether committed within or without the state, is lawful, whenever:

A. A felony has actually been committed by the person to be arrested, although before making the arrest the officer has no reasonable ground to believe the person guilty of such offense.

B. The officer has reasonable ground to believe that a felony has been committed and that the person to be arrested has committed it.

Section 7. Arrest on Improper Grounds.

If a lawful cause of arrest exists, the arrest is lawful even though the officer charged the wrong offense or gave a reason that did not justify the arrest.

Section 8. Arrest by Virtue of a Warrant Not in Officer's Possession.

Search Incident to Arrest. The exact meaning to be placed upon the word "incident" in defining a search incident to arrest is a

An arrest by a peace officer acting under a warrant is lawful even though the officer does not have the warrant in his possession at the time of the arrest, but, if the person arrested so requests, the warrant shall be shown to him as soon as practicable.

Section 9. Summons Instead of Arrest.

In any case in which it is lawful for a peace officer to arrest without a warrant a person for a misdemeanor, he may instead issue to him a written summons in substantially the following form: (A variety of forms are used by different jurisdictions).

Upon failure to appear, a warrant of arrest may issue. Willful failure to appear in answer to such summons may be punished by a fine of not over one hundred dollars or imprisonment for not over thirty days.

Section 10. Release of Persons Arrested.

I. Any officer in charge of a police department or any officer authorized by him may release instead of taking before a magistrate any person who has been arrested without a warrant by an officer of his department:

A. When he is satisfied either that there is no ground for making a criminal complaint against such person or that such person has been arrested for drunkenness and no further proceedings are desirable.

B. When such person was arrested for a misdemeanor and has signed an agreement to appear in court at a time designated, if the officer is satisfied that such person is a resident of the state and will appear in court at the time designated.

II. A person released as provided in subsections A or B of this section shall have no right to sue any police officer on the ground that he was released without being brought before a magistrate.

Section 11. Length of Detention.

If not otherwise released, every person arrested shall be brought before any available magistrate within twenty-four hours of arrest, Sundays and holidays excluded, unless a judge of the (district) court of the (district) where he is detained or of the (district) court of the (district) where the crime was committed for good cause shown orders that he be held for a further period of not exceeding forty-eight hours.

Section 12. Identification of Witnesses.

Whenever a peace officer has reasonable ground to believe that a crime has been committed, he may stop any person whom he has a reasonable ground to believe was present thereat and may demand of him his name and address. If any such person fails to identify himself to the satisfaction of the peace officer, the officer may take him forthwith before a magistrate. If such person fails to identify himself to the satisfaction of the magistrate, the latter may require him to furnish (an appearance) bond or commit him to jail until he so identifies himself.

Section 13. Severability.

If any provision of this act or the application thereof to any person or circumstances is held invalid, such invalidity shall not affect other provisions or applications of the act which can be given effect without the invalid provision or application, and to this end the provisions of this act are declared to be severable.

matter of some controversy. A search made of an individual who is not arrested either immediately before or after the search, is clearly not a search "incident" to arrest;[22] nor is a search made at a place and time remote from the arrest. Some courts also hold that any search coming before the arrest, is not a search incident to arrest and is therefore invalid. A better view is stated in People v. Simon,[23] a California case:

> Thus, if the officer is entitled to make an arrest on the basis of information available to him before he searches, and as an incident to that arrest is entitled to make a reasonable search of the person arrested and the place where he is arrested [but see Chimel v. California which was decided after the *Simon* case], there is nothing unreasonable in his conduct if he makes the search before instead of after the arrest. In fact, if the person searched is innocent and the search convinces the officer that his reasonable belief to the contrary is erroneous, it is to the advantage of the person searched not to be arrested. On the other hand, if he is not innocent or the search does not establish his innocence, the security of his person, houses, papers, or effects suffers no more from a search preceding his arrest than it would from the same search following it.

Scope of Search Incident to Arrest. At the time of an arrest, the officer has the right to search the person arrested and his surroundings within "arms length." Prior to the decision in Chimel v. California,[24] a valid arrest gave an officer the right to search the "curtilage," which meant the nearby area customarily devoted to domestic pursuits. On a farm or ranch, for example, the "curtilage" included the house, the barn, the tool shed, and anything within the fence surrounding the farm house. In an apartment, it included the entire apartment. In a house in town, it included the house and the garage.

The *Chimel* case drastically limited the area which may be searched "incident" (in connection with, at the time of) an arrest. Since the purpose of the search is to locate weapons and prevent the destruction of evidence, the court said that once the "arms length" area had been searched, no additional warrantless

22. People v. Edge, 406 Ill. 490, 94 N.E.2d 359 (1950).

23. People v. Simon, 45 Cal.2d 645, 290 P.2d 531 (1955).

24. Chimel v. California, 395 U.S. 752, 89 S.Ct. 2034, 23 L.Ed.2d 685 (1969), reh. den. 396 U.S. 869, 90 S.Ct. 36, 24 L.Ed.2d 124.

search is justified. When the arrested person is under the control of the officer, he cannot reach a gun or destroy evidence; hence the search cannot extend beyond places the arrested person can reach when he is taken into custody. If an officer desires to search the entire premises, for example to locate concealed drugs which he believes to be in the house, he must first get a search warrant. Sometimes one officer stays on the premises while another gets the search warrant.

An officer may take into his possession anything that he finds in the search that is tools of a crime, or "fruits of a crime," or contraband. This evidence may be introduced against the defendant in the trial. However, evidence obtained in an illegal search is barred by the "Exclusionary Rule," made binding on the states in the case of Mapp v. Ohio,[25] which is discussed hereafter.

Search of the Person. Searches of the person are almost always made incident to arrest. A "frisk" is a search of the person which consists in patting down the outer clothing in search of a weapon and removing any object which might be a weapon or any contraband found in the course of a lawful frisk. A frisk usually takes place in a street encounter between the police officer and the person searched. A frisk has been held reasonable under certain circumstances, in Terry v. Ohio,[26] though it was pointed out that a frisk is a search that is protected by the Fourth Amendment. A frisk may take place on reasonable belief that a crime is being or is about to be committed and that the individual frisked may be armed and dangerous to the officer. This is a somewhat lower level of proof than probable cause required to make an arrest. A frisk may or may not be followed by an arrest.

A more complete search of the person usually follows an arrest. Such a search will be of the inner clothing, of pockets, handbags, and the like. In the station house, a strip search may be performed, and this may include search of the body cavities. As a matter of practice, a woman police officer conducts all station house searches of female offenders.

A special problem concerning searches is presented by the kind of search that takes place when a blood sample is used to determine drunkenness, or when a breathalizer is used, or when a suspect attempts to swallow the evidence. The question on such

25. Mapp v. Ohio, 367 U.S. 643, 81 S.Ct. 1684, 6 L.Ed.2d 1081 (1961), reh. den. 368 U.S. 871, 82 S.Ct. 23, 7 L.Ed.2d 72.

26. Terry v. Ohio, 392 U.S. 1, 88 S.Ct. 1868, 20 L.Ed.2d 889 (1968).

searches is not only the legality of the search but whether or not such searches amount to "self-incrimination." It was held in Schmerber v. California [27] that the taking of blood samples is not such an invasion of privacy as is protected by the Fourth Amendment and that the giving up of blood even when it proves to contain an illegal amount of alcohol for a driver is not self-incrimination. An officer may try to prevent a suspect from putting anything in his mouth, and even if he gets it in his mouth, may by force try to prevent him from swallowing it so long as the officer does not cut off the person's breathing. However, once the suspect has succeeded in swallowing whatever he puts in his mouth, it is unlawful to use a stomach pump or other means of forced vomiting. In general, any kind of body search that would "shock the conscience" of an ordinary citizen because of the method or amount of force used would be frowned upon by the courts.[28]

Automobile Searches. The great majority of automobile searches are made without a warrant. Because of the fact that an automobile is movable and may be quickly taken out of the jurisdiction, an automobile may be searched without a warrant under circumstances which would not support a warrantless search of a dwelling house or garage. Nevertheless, an automobile is an effect protected by the Fourth Amendment, and the search of an automobile incident to or after arrest must be "reasonable."

Many factors are taken into consideration in determining whether or not the search of an automobile is "reasonable." Among these are: the nature of the offense or violation for which the automobile is stopped, the prior information of the officer as to whether the car may be stolen or may contain contraband, whether the driver is arrested or merely given a summons or traffic ticket, whether the car is impounded by the officer under a state regulation requiring such impounding, whether or not contraband, or fruits, or instrumentalities of a crime are in "plain view," and what part of the car the officer searches. As a result, the law of searches and seizures of automobiles is complex. All we can hope to do here is to suggest some of the factors which may determine whether or not a search is reasonable (and hence

27. Schmerber v. California, 384 U.S. 757, 86 S.Ct 1826, 16 L.Ed.2d 908 (1966).

28. Rochin v. California, 342 U.S. 165, 72 S.Ct. 205, 96 L.Ed. 183 (1952); People v. Martinez, 130 Cal.App.2d 54, 278 P.2d 26 (1955); People v. Sanchez, 11 Cal.Rptr. 407, 189 Cal.App.2d 720 (1969); People v. Redding, 28 Ill.2d 305, 192 N.E. 2d 341 (1963).

legal) or unreasonable (and hence forbidden by the Fourth Amendment).

In the case of Carroll v. United States,[29] the United States Supreme Court announced the basic rule pertaining to the stopping of motor vehicles suspected of containing contraband. Federal prohibition agents had stopped a heavily laden car on the "rum-running route" between Detroit and Grand Rapids. Without specifically making an arrest, the officers searched the car and impounded the liquor which was being transported in it. The court said:

> [There is] a necessary difference between a search of a store, dwelling, house, or other structure in respect of which a proper official warrant readily may be obtained and a search of a ship, motor boat, wagon or automobile, for contraband goods, where it is not practicable to secure a warrant because the vehicle can be quickly moved out of the locality or jurisdiction in which the warrant must be sought.

The general rule then is that though there is no right to stop all travelers on the highway, law enforcement officials have the power to stop an automobile when they have probable cause to believe that it is carrying contraband. This rule extends also to the situation where the offender is stopped and arrested for a specific prior offense, as when he is fleeing from the bank with the loot, or is apprehended driving a stolen car which the officer has been requested to seize.

Routine stopping and searching of motor vehicles presents more complicated questions. Motor vehicles are stopped more often for traffic violations than because the officer suspects some violation of the criminal laws. In routine traffic regulation, officers frequently stop automobiles and trucks for traffic violations, failure to have a valid vehicle or operator's license, for defective equipment, weight inspections, and road blocks.

In most of the states, an officer has a right to arrest without a warrant a person who violates a traffic regulation. State law usually gives the officer the option to make a full arrest and take the violator before the magistrate or to give a summons or traffic ticket. The option chosen by the officer determines to a large extent the extent of his right to search the automobile or the person of the driver.

29. Carroll v. United States, 267 U.S. 132, 45 S.Ct. 280, 69 L.Ed. 543 (1925), cert. den. 282 U.S. 873, 51 S.Ct. 78, 75 L.Ed. 771.

In general, an officer who stops a motorist for a minor traffic violation and issues him a summons has no right to search either the car or the person of the driver. If some action of the driver or other evidence obtained by one of his five senses gives the officer grounds to believe that the driver possesses a weapon, the officer may search places where a concealed weapon might be within reach of the driver—the front seat, the glove compartment, over the rear-view mirror, under the seat, and so forth. If the driver is taken outside of the car (as for example, is over by the squad car) and cannot reach a weapon, then the officer has no right to search for the weapon since there is no longer danger that it may be used against the officer. To search the car, under such circumstances, the officer must either impound it under some state statute requiring this action, or obtain a search warrant to search it.

If the offender is stopped and arrested for drunken driving, the officer may search for liquor which is the "fruits of the crime," and his rights to search in such a case may extend to the back seat and the trunk. Or if, on a routine traffic stop, the officer smells liquor, or sees contraband liquor in plain view, he may search the entire car after arresting the driver.

Unless a car is legally impounded under a state statute requiring it, an officer must get a search warrant to search an automobile even if he has it in the police parking lot while he is interrogating the driver in the station house.

It is difficult to summarize the general rules relating to searches and seizures of automobiles. All of the variables must be taken into consideration, and a change of one of the circumstances may render a search either legal or illegal. If illegal, the evidence obtained would be excluded under the Exclusionary Rule as made applicable to the state by Mapp v. Ohio.[30]

In his book, *Constitutional Limitations on Evidence in Criminal Cases,*[31] B. James George, Jr., makes the following general observations as to searches and seizures of automobiles:

> *Routine search in traffic cases.* The weight of recent case law, though recognizing the right to stop cars and detain

30. Mapp v. Ohio, 367 U.S. 643, 81 S.Ct. 1684, 6 L.Ed.2d 1081 (1961), reh. den. 368 U.S. 871, 82 S.Ct. 23, 7 L.Ed.2d 72.

31. B. James George, Jr., *Constitutional Limitations on Evidence in Criminal Cases.* New York City: Institute of Continuing Legal Education; Practicing Law Institute, 1969.

their occupants temporarily, denies any right to the officer to make a routine search either of the driver or the occupant.

Search during equipment and weight check. Because the statutes authorizing the stopping and checking of vehicles for weight limitations or equipment are sustained as valid, an inspection conducted routinely by officers assigned to that duty should be considered to be valid. [The author believes this would extend to searches such as made by California and Arizona for plants or produce.]

Probable cause arrests and searches. If a vehicle is stopped on reasonable grounds to believe it may be carrying contraband, the right to search for contraband may be valid. If as he looks into the vehicle he sees material that cannot be legally possessed, the officer may make an arrest on the possession charge and seize the contraband. (If the encounter takes place at night, the defendant cannot object that the officer shines his flashlight into the car.) The officer may also have enough information as to the result of the lawful stopping and ensuing conversation to give him probable cause to believe that a felony has been committed out of his presence. He can then arrest, and conduct a search incident to that arrest, within the normal limitations on scope of incidental search.[32]

Search With a Warrant. A search warrant is an order issued by a magistrate which commands an officer to search the premises described, belonging to a person named, for articles which are listed in the warrant.[33] The description of the premises must

32. *Ibid.* pp. 70–72.

33. The New York Criminal Procedure Law defines a search warrant and sets forth the grounds upon which it may be issued as follows:

§ 690.05(2). A search warrant is a court order and process directing a police officer to conduct a search of designated premises, or of a designated vehicle, or of a designated person, for the purpose of seizing designated property or kinds of property, and to deliver any property so obtained to the court which issued the warrant.

§ 690.10. Personal property is subject to seizure pursuant to a search warrant if there is reasonable cause to believe that it:

1. Is stolen; or
2. Is unlawfully possessed; or
3. Has been used, or is possessed for the purpose of being used, to commit or conceal the commission of an offense; or
4. Constitutes evidence or tends to demonstrate that an offense was committed or that a particular person participated in the commission of an offense.

be sufficiently exact that the officer can distinguish the place to be searched from all other places. The articles must be described with as much certainty and in as much detail as possible, and the value given if the articles have a value. The person who owns the premises must be named. The reason for the search must be given—the articles were stolen, used in illegal gambling, to commit a homicide, or whatever. Sometimes a search warrant and arrest warrant are combined, in which case the date, place, and nature of the offense must be stated.

Four things are necessary for a valid search warrant: [34]

1. It must describe, with particularity, the place to be searched;
2. It must describe, with particularity, the things to be seized;
3. It must be based on probable cause; and
4. It must be supported by a sworn affidavit.

1. **Places Which May be Searched.** The place to be searched must be described in the warrant with sufficient certainty to enable the officer to distinguish the place from all other places. The description may be one used in the locality and known to the people there, as "the old Randolph house," and a technical description as by lot and block number is not required.

2. **Things Subject to Seizure.** In an early case in the United States Supreme Court, it was held that search warrants could be issued only for certain specified classes of things identified as fruits of a crime, instrumentalities of a crime, and contraband.[35]

§ 690.15.

1. A search warrant must direct a search of one or more of the following:
   (a) A designated or described place or premises;
   (b) A designated or described vehicle, as that term is defined in section 10.00 of the penal law;
   (c) A designated or described person.
2. A search warrant which directs a search of a designated or described place, premises or vehicle, may also direct a search of any person present thereat or therein.

The California Code defines a search warrant as "an order in writing, in the name of the people, signed by a magistrate, directed to a peace officer, commanding him to search for personal property, and bring it before the magistrate." West's Ann.Cal.Penal Code, § 1523.

34. Louis B. Schwartz and Stephen R. Goldstein, *Law Enforcement Handbook for Police.* St. Paul, Minn.: West Publishing Co., 1970.

35. Gouled v. United States, 255 U.S. 298, 41 S.Ct. 261, 65 L.Ed. 647 (1921).

This classification is carried into the statutes of many of the states. Under this rule, a search for "mere evidence" was invalid, at least in the case of searches based upon a warrant. In 1967, the Supreme Court changed the "mere evidence" rule, and held that a search incident to arrest or pursuant to a valid warrant may be for mere evidence or for fruits, instrumentalities or contraband. All that is required is that there be a *nexus* (a connection) between the item to be seized and the criminal behavior. "In the case of 'mere evidence,' probable cause must be examined in terms of cause to believe that the evidence sought will aid in a particular apprehension or conviction." [36] Whether or not a search for "mere evidence" is a valid search under state law depends upon the statutes of the state. The *Hayden* case decided that such a search is not in all cases prohibited by the Fourth Amendment.[37]

Fruits of a crime means material objects acquired by means of and in consequence of the commission of a crime, and sometimes constituting the subject matter of the crime. Thus, the stolen goods are fruits of the crime, as is the dead body in the case of a homicide.

36. Warden, Maryland Penitentiary v. Hayden, 387 U.S. 294, 87 S.Ct. 1642, 18 L.Ed.2d 782 (1967).

37. Illinois statutes provide for issuance of a search warrant for evidence. Smith-Hurd Ill.Stat. 38 Crim.Law and Proc., Ann., § 108–3: Grounds for Search Warrant. Upon the written complaint of any person under oath or affirmation which states facts sufficient to show probable cause and which particularly describes the place or person, or both, to be searched and the things to be seized, any judge may issue a search warrant for the seizure of the following:

(a) Any instruments, articles of things which have been used in the commission of, or which may constitute evidence of, the offense in connection with which the warrant is issued.

(b) Any person who has been kidnaped in violation of the laws of this State, or who has been kidnaped in another jurisdiction and is now concealed within this State, or any human fetus or human corpse.

New York includes personal property which constitutes evidence or tends to demonstrate that an offense was committed or that a particular person participated in the commission of the offense in property which may be seized. See fn. 33, *supra*.

In California, a search warrant may be issued "when the property or things to be seized consist of any item or constitutes any evidence which tends to show a felony has been committed, or tends to show that a particular person has committed a felony." West's Ann.Cal. Penal Code, § 1524(4).

In Texas, the search warrant may specify fruits or implements of the crime and contraband, but not "mere evidence." Vernon's Texas Ann.Code Crim.Proc., § 18.01.

Instrumentalities of a crime are the tools or instruments used to commit the crime, such as the murder weapon, the burglar's tools, the betting slips, the forged instrument.

Contraband is any material object which it is unlawful for a private individual to possess, as illegal drugs, untaxed liquor, gambling equipment, unlicensed guns, materials used for making bombs.

The general rule is that the goods to be seized must be described in the search warrant with such certainty that they can be identified. Thus, a description of items merely as "stolen goods" or "other articles of merchandise too numerous to mention" would be insufficient. Greater leeway in description is allowed if the articles to be searched for are contraband material, and some courts hold that contraband discovered in the course of a search with a warrant may be seized even though the articles are not described in the warrant.

3. **The Warrant Must be Based on Probable Cause.** We have previously discussed in some detail the meaning of probable cause. This level of belief must be reached by the magistrate before he issues a search warrant. The magistrate must believe that a crime has been committed and that there is reasonable grounds to believe that contraband, fruits or instrumentalities of the crime, or (in some states) evidence connected with the specific crime can be found in the place ordered to be searched.

4. **Affidavit for Search Warrant.** Since the Fourth Amendment says "No warrant shall issue except upon probable cause, supported by oath or affirmation," a search warrant, like an arrest warrant, must be based upon a formal affidvait or complaint signed and sworn to by a person with knowledge of the facts. Because it is sworn to, the affidavit constitutes the "oath or affirmation" required by the Fourth Amendment. This affidavit, like the arrest complaint, must state facts sufficient for the magistrate, in the exercise of independent judgment, to make a finding of probable cause.[38] Usually the prosecutor is informed

38. The requirement for the supporting affidavit is set out in the California statutes as follows:

West's Ann.Penal Code, § 1525. **Issuance; probable cause; supporting affidavits.** A search warrant cannot be issued but upon probable cause, supported by affidavit, naming or describing the person, and particularly describing the property and the place to be searched.

The New York statutory language is similar:

1. An application for a search warrant must be in writing and must

be made, subscribed and sworn to by a public servant specified in subdivision one of section 690.05.

2. The application must contain:

(a) The name of the court and the name and title of the applicant; and

(b) A statement that there is reasonable cause to believe that property of a kind or character described in section 690.10 may be found in or upon a designated or described place, vehicle or person; and

(c) Allegations of fact supporting such statement. Such allegations of fact may be based upon personal knowledge of the applicant or upon information and belief, provided that in the latter event the sources of such information and the grounds of such belief are stated. The applicant may also submit depositions of other persons containing allegations of fact supporting or tending to support those contained in the application; and

(d) A request that the court issue a search warrant directing a search for and seizure of the property in question.

3. The application may also contain:

(a) A request that the search warrant be made executable at any time of the day or night, upon the ground that there is reasonable cause to believe that (i) it cannot be executed between the hours of 6:00 A.M. and 9:00 P.M., or (ii) the property sought will be removed or destroyed if not seized forthwith; and

(b) A request that the search warrant authorize the executing police officer to enter premises to be searched without giving notice of his authority and purpose, upon the ground that there is reasonable cause to believe that (i) the property sought may be easily and quickly destroyed or disposed of, or (ii) the giving of such notice may endanger the life or safety of the executing police officer or another person.

Any request made pursuant to this subdivision must be accompanied and supported by allegations of fact of a kind prescribed in paragraph (c) of subdivision two. McKinney's N.Y.Criminal Procedure Law, § 690.35.

1. In determining an application for a search warrant the court may examine, under oath, any person whom it believes may possess pertinent information. Any such examination must be either recorded or summarized on the record by the court.

2. If the court is satisfied that there is reasonable cause to believe that property of a kind or character referred to in section 690.10, and described in the application, may be found in or upon the place, premises, vehicle or person designated or described in the application, it may grant the application and issue a search warrant directing a search of the said place, premises, vehicle or person and a seizure of the described property. If the court is further satisfied that grounds, described in subdivision three of section 690.35, exist for authorizing the search to be made at any hour of the day or night, or without giving notice of the police officer's authority and purpose, it may make the search warrant executable accordingly. McKinney's N.Y.Criminal Procedure Law, § 690.40.

The Illinois statute is quoted in fn. 37, *supra*.

The Texas law provides for several forms of search warrant with the supporting affidavit differing somewhat for each. The requirement for the affidavit when the place is known is set out in Art. 18.07,

of the request for a search warrant and gives his consent to its issuance. This is not always the case, particularly when the warrant is issued after regular office hours and time is important (as when the officer believes the stolen goods or contraband will be moved if he does not act quickly). Search warrants, like arrest warrants, are sometimes issued by clerks or other persons authorized to issue warrants who are not magistrates, though the practice is fraught with some dangers. Some magistrates issue the warrants as a more or less routine matter without making careful inquiry as to the facts and without forming an independent judgment as to the existence of probable cause.

A search with a warrant need not be connected with an arrest, and unlike the search incident to an arrest, does not depend upon the legality of the arrest for its own validity. A search with a warrant may take place before or after arrest, or there may never be an arrest, as when officers locate the stolen goods but never catch the thief.

Informers. An arrest without warrant may be made or an arrest or search warrant issued upon information furnished by an informer. Several legal problems arise, going particularly to the sufficiency of the affidavit or complaint for issuance of the warrant.[39] Though the words "informer" and "informant" are often used interchangeably, the word "informer" has taken on invidious connotation. Any person who reports a crime is an informant. An informer, however, is a person who reports a crime from motives other than his responsibilities as a good citizen.

Vernon's Texas Code Crim.Proc., Ann. (See generally Arts. 18.01–18.14, *Ibid.*) Art. 18.07 reads as follows:

A warrant to search for and seize property alleged to have been stolen and concealed at a particular place may be issued by a magistrate, whenever written sworn complaint is made to such magistrate, setting forth:

1. The name of the person accused of having stolen or concealed the property; or if his name be unknown, giving a description of the accused, or stating that the person who stole or concealed the property is unknown;
2. The kind and value of the property alleged to be stolen or concealed;
3. The place where it is alleged to be concealed; and
4. The time, as near as may be, when the property is alleged to have been stolen.

39. The affidavit must state facts showing the reliability of the informer. Aguilar v. Texas, 378 U.S. 108, 84 S.Ct. 1509, 12 L.Ed.2d 723 (1964), on remand 382 S.W.2d 480 (Tex.).

The Chicago Police Department once listed some different kinds of informers classified according to their motive for informing. The list included jealous wives, jilted sweethearts, and dismissed employees who want revenge; petty offenders who want to stand in well with the police; accomplices who want to keep all the loot or divert suspicion from themselves; a thief who is trying to find out what the police know about the offense and whether he is under suspicion; a person planning a crime who hopes to lead the officers in the opposite direction, and many others.[40]

The traditional informer informs for money or to escape responsibility for his part in an offense. Police pay informers, and depend upon them for valuable information about the offenses that are committed and the whereabouts of the offenders. Prosecutors dismiss cases or reduce charges against persons who "turn state's evidence." Officers, particularly narcotics officers or others on the vice squad, infiltrate groups and places where crimes are being planned or committed, for the purpose of informing on the transgressors, sometimes going to the extent of actually helping a guilty person to commit the offense. (An undercover agent buying narcotics from a pusher, for example).

A warrant for arrest or search may issue upon information furnished to a police officer by an informer. In such case the police officer signs and swears to the affidavit and recites in it that the information was derived from a "credible person," without, however, naming him. A credible person is a person worthy of belief. If the informer is the usual paid police informer, additional information must be included in the affidavit. The officer must show why the informer is worthy of belief. He does this by showing in detail, first, how the informer came by his information, being as precise as possible about persons involved, what the informer saw or heard, under what conditions, at what time; and second, he recites previous instances when information received from the informer has proved reliable.

40. The informants were classified into nine general types: The Anonymous Informant; the Self-Aggrandizing Informant; the Legitimate Informant; the Woman Informant; the Frightened Informant; the Rival Informant; the Mercenary Informant; the False Informant; the Double-Crosser Informant. *Investigators Notebook, Chicago Police Department*, August 21, 1961, as quoted in Melvin Gutterman, "The Informer Privilege," *The Journal of Criminal Law. Criminology and Police Science*, Vol. 58, No. 1 (1967) pp. 32–54.

If the affidavit is carefully drawn and contains all the required information to show how the informer got the information, and that past experience has shown that he can be relied upon, the warrant may issue without the name of the informer being disclosed. Depending upon the circumstances, the name of the informer may never be disclosed. The legal rules about when the identity of the informer must be disclosed to the accused are complex, and beyond the scope of this book. It is sufficient for our purposes to know that arrest and searches with a warrant may be based on information furnished by an informer. Such information will also support a felony arrest made without a warrant. In such case the police officer when called upon to show probable cause for the arrest must be able to make the same kind of showing as to the source of the informer's information and his previously established reliability as is required for the issuance of a warrant.

Electronic Surveillance. Electronic surveillance is a special kind of search based upon a special warrant accomplished by electronic eavesdropping or "bugging." Many law enforcement officers and others knowledgeable about crime in America, particularly those concerned with organized crime, believe that wiretapping and electronic eavesdropping are very important tools of law enforcement. Others point out the threat that such devices present to the privacy of the ordinary citizen.

The problem is made acute because of the sophistication of modern bugging devices. Devices exist which are capable of eavesdropping on anyone in almost any given situation. Some of the devices are no larger than a postage stamp and can pick up whispers in a room and broadcast them half a block away to a receiver.[41]

The federal Crime Control Act of 1968 [42] prohibited both wiretapping and eavesdropping except as specifically authorized by the Act. It gives a federal law enforcement officer the right to tap wires or eavesdrop only when authorized by a federal judge in certain types of serious criminal cases. The application to the judge must show probable cause to believe that a serious offense is being committed and that normal investigative pro-

41. Berger v. New York, 388 U.S. 41, 87 S.Ct. 1873, 18 L.Ed.2d 1040 (1967), conformed to 284 N.Y.S.2d 456, 20 N.Y.2d 801, 231 N.E.2d 132.

42. P.L. 90–351; 18 U.S.C.A. §§ 2510–2520.

cedures have been tried and are not likely to succeed. State officers have the same right only if the authority is given in state statutes.

American Bar Association Standards Relating to Electronic Surveillance. The American Bar Association *Standards Relating to Electronic Surveillance,*[43] prohibit the use of electronic surveillance techniques except on authority of the Attorney General of the United States and the principal prosecuting attorney of state and local government. Penalties are provided for wiretapping or eavesdropping by any other person. The wiretapping or eavesdropping can take place only upon application made to a judge which sets out in detail the identity of the prosecuting officer authorizing the application; the identity of the law enforcement office making the application; and a particular description of the type of communications sought to be or which were overheard or recorded. Probable cause showings are strict, and the use of electronic surveillance is restricted to situations of serious group criminal activity. A time limit is placed upon the use of the recording instruments, and a return on the order of authorization or approval must be made to the judge within thirty days. The recordings are then sealed until the time when they must be used in evidence.

Consent to Search. A search, with or without a warrant, to which consent is given is a reasonable search. Thus, a person who consents to a search waives any defenses he may have under the Fourth Amendment.

To constitute a waiver, a consent to a search must be knowingly and voluntarily made and must be given by a person authorized to give the consent. When the suspect himself consents to the search, the question is chiefly one of whether the consent was given understandingly and voluntarily. When someone else (as the suspect's wife, or his landlady, or the person to whom he has loaned his car) consents to the search, and it turns up evidence harmful to the accused, the question is not only whether the consent was voluntary but also whether the person consenting had authority to give the consent.

As to when a consent to search is voluntary, the courts have held that no consent is voluntary unless the person is adequately

43. American Bar Association Project on Standards for Criminal Justice, *Standards Relating to Electronic Surveillance,* New York: Office of Criminal Justice Project, January, 1971.

advised that he has a Constitutional right to refuse to consent to search, and that, if he does not consent, the officer will leave and not conduct a search. Silence in response to a request to search is usually not considered a valid consent. There must be some affirmative response indicating that the person understands the nature of his Constitutional rights and that he is consenting to waive them.

Basically, one person cannot waive the Constitutional rights of another. The apartment house manager cannot consent to a search of the tenant's apartment, even though the manager has a key to the apartment and a right of entry for purposes of cleaning or inspection. A hotel desk clerk cannot consent to the search of a guest's room; or an employee to a search of his employer's premises. However, a person who has joint occupancy or joint possession of the place or object to be searched, or has been put in possession by the owner, may sometimes give a valid consent. Under such circumstances, evidence found against the absent joint occupant or the owner could be introduced against him at the trial.

Do not assume from the discussion above that a person can prevent a search by merely refusing to consent to it. If an officer has a valid search warrant based on probable cause, or the search is incident to a lawful arrest and within the "arms length" limits set down by Chimel v. California,[44] no consent to search is required, and no refusal to consent can prevent the search. The importance of consent arises in situations where the officer has no warrant and the search is not incident to arrest.

The Exclusionary Rule. The Fourth Amendment guaranteed to the people the right to be secure in their "persons, houses, papers, and effects, against unreasonable searches and seizures." By implication, all unreasonable searches and seizures were prohibited by the Constitution and were therefore invalid. But very often, an illegal search or seizure turned up evidence of a crime and resulted in the arrest of the offender. The question then was whether or not the illegally obtained evidence could be introduced against the accused at his trial. The answer was an important one, because very frequently the illegally obtained evidence was the only evidence connecting the accused with the

44. Chimel v. California, 395 U.S. 752, 89 S.Ct. 2034, 23 L.Ed.2d 685 (1969), reh. den. 396 U.S. 869, 90 S.Ct. 36, 24 L.Ed.2d 124.

crime, and if its admission was denied, the case against the accused would fail.

The federal government and many of the states adopted the so-called "Exclusionary Rule" and decided to exclude from the trial any evidence against the accused illegally obtained. They argued that any other rule would render the Fourth Amendment guarantees almost worthless, and that excluding the evidence was the only way to discipline the police and prevent their violation of the Fourth Amendment prohibitions. Over half of the states, however, took the opposite view. Evidence illegally seized could be admitted against the accused at the trial in these states. They argued that excluding the evidence from the trial would result in letting a guilty man go free, and that there were other ways to discipline the police without subjecting the public to the future depredations of an offender set free because of a "technicality" in the law.

In 1961, the Supreme Court, in the case of Mapp v. Ohio,[45] imposed the Exclusionary Rule on the States, thus settling the controversy in favor of the states which refused to admit illegally obtained evidence to be used against the accused. The court pointed out that its ruling was both logical and made good sense:

> Moreover, our holding * * * is not only the logical dictate of prior cases, but it also makes very good sense. Presently, a federal prosecutor may make no use of evidence illegally seized, but a State's attorney across the street may, although he supposedly is operating under the enforceable prohibitions of the same amendment. Thus the State, by admitting evidence unlawfully seized, serves to encourage disobedience to the Federal Constitution which it is bound to uphold.[46]

Mapp v. Ohio is considered to be a landmark case not only because it imposed the Exclusionary Rule upon the States, but also because it decided that the Fourteenth Amendment "incorporated" the provisions of the Fourth Amendment, and thus made all

45. Mapp v. Ohio, 367 U.S. 643, 81 S.Ct. 1684, 6 L.Ed.2d 1081 (1961), reh. den. 368 U.S. 871, 82 S.Ct. 23, 7 L.Ed.2d 72.

(In New York, a summons is issued by the court, and may be issued in lieu of a warrant of arrest if the accusatory pleading charges a misdemeanor. The notice to appear issued by an officer is called an "appearance ticket.")

46. *Ibid.*

the provisions of the Fourth Amendment mandatory upon the States.

Summons. Before we leave our discussion of arrest, we must distinguish arrest from some procedures, such as stop and frisk and summons, which resemble arrest but do not constitute an arrest. A stop and question and a stop and frisk are not an arrest, because the intention of the officer is not, at this point, to take the accused into custody to answer to an offense. Neither is a *summons* an arrest. An officer may stop a person who has committed an offense and instead of taking him into custody merely serve him with a notice to appear in court to answer the charge. A traffic ticket is a summons, and in some states an officer is authorized to issue a summons in lieu of arrest for more serious offenses. Of course, a person who fails to obey a summons may then be arrested.

Persons who are not accused of offenses, but whose presence before the court is required (a witness, for example) can be brought into court on a capias or a bench warrant. The taking into custody under such an order is not an arrest. A person already arrested who is out on bail may also be brought again before the court on a capias, as when indictment is returned or an appeal denied. These subsequent appearances are not technically an arrest. Distinctions between arrest and other process are important. For example, the right to search incident to an arrest depends upon an *arrest,* and a person cannot sue for false arrest if he has not been arrested.

American Bar Association Standards Relating to Pre-Trial Release. The American Bar Association *Standards Relating to Pretrial Release* [48] would make mandatory the issue of summons rather than arrest in all cases in which the maximum sentence for the offense charged does not exceed six months, unless the judicial officers find that the defendant previously has failed to respond to a citation or summons for an offense other than a minor one such as a parking violation, or has no ties in the community, or cannot be found and an arrest warrant is necessary in order to subject him to the jurisdiction of the court.

The *Standards* also provide that when an arrested person has been taken to a police station house and a decision has been made

48. American Bar Association Project on Minimum Standards for Criminal Justice, *Standards Relating to Pre-trial Release.* New York: Office of Criminal Justice Project, Approved Draft, 1968.

to charge him with an offense for which the total imprisonment may not exceed six months, the responsible officer should be required to issue a citation in lieu of continued custody. Exceptions are recognized for an accused who fails to identify himself satisfactorily or refuses to sign the citation and where detention is necessary to prevent imminent bodily harm to the accused or another. In the case of an accused with no ties in the community or who has failed to appear in response to a citation for an offense other than a minor one such as a parking violation, the release on citation would not be required.

BOOKING

Making a Record of the Arrest. According to the chart of the Criminal Justice System on pages 168–169 booking is an administrative record of the arrest. The term is used to mean simply the station house record of the arrest or is expanded to include the procedures that take place in the station house after an arrest. In the smaller communities, the "station house" will be the sheriff's office or the city jail. In the usual case, booking is completed before the suspect is taken for his initial appearance before the magistrate. Sometimes, however, the suspect is taken directly before the magistrate after the arrest, and is then returned to the station house or the jail for the booking process. Or the practice may be to complete part of the booking procedures, take the accused before the magistrate, and return him to the station house or jail to complete the booking and jailing procedures. Within the same jurisdiction or the same police department, the booking procedures will vary depending upon the nature of the offense—felony or misdemeanor—whether the arrest was made with or without a warrant, and according to the time of the day or night that the arrest takes place. Often, too, the booking process is so telescoped with charging and the initial appearance before the magistrate that it is difficult to separate them.

Police officers working in a department are often not quite clear as to just what "booking" consists of. However, booking commonly includes a written report by the police officer of the time and circumstances of the arrest and the nature of the offense and may include a complete search of the accused, including in some cases a search of the body cavities. In the larger departments, the accused is fingerprinted and also photographed before a clock which shows the exact time and date the picture was taken. This is done to protect the police department from charges of using excessive force and also for purposes of identification. Booking procedures may, on occasion, also encompass a line-up, (line-ups also occur at later points in the proceeding) or the taking of the suspect before the victim in the hospital. If identification procedures can be carried out quickly, the necessary evidence of guilt may be preserved, or even more important, the innocent suspect may be promptly released. At some point in the booking process, the accused is given an opportunity to phone his family or an attorney.

Identification. The most common identification procedures are fingerprinting, voice and writing exemplars, photograph identification, line-ups, and, under special circumstances, breathalizer and polygraph tests. These procedures may take place as part of the booking process, or at any point before trial. None of these amount to "self incrimination," though this point is often raised. The Constitutional guarantee against self incrimination applies to evidence of a testimonial nature and not to the exhibition of the person for identification purposes.[48]

A decision by the United States Supreme Court, United States v. Wade,[49] has changed the rules concerning line-ups. At a line-up (also called a "show-up"), the accused is taken out on a stage or platform and is viewed by witnesses to the offense whom, because of the lighting arrangements, he cannot see. The line-up must include several persons who resemble the accused as to color, height, race, and so on. The accused may be required to speak words spoken by the offender, as "Put the money in a sack," or to wear a mask or other special article of clothing similar to that worn by the offender. The witnesses then attempt to identify the culprit from among those in the line-up. Since the *Wade* case, an attorney representing the accused must be present at the line-up, unless, after notice, he fails to appear or the accused waives the right. He does not participate in any way in the procedures; he is there merely as an observer to insure its fairness and to enable him to cross-examine about the line-up

48. Schmerber v. California, 384 U.S. 757, 86 S.Ct. 1826, 16 L.Ed.2d 908 (1966).

49. United States v. Wade, 388 U.S. 218, 87 S.Ct. 1926, 18 L.Ed.2d 1149 (1967).

if the accused objects to the introduction of a line-up identification at the trial.

Station House Procedures. In one police department with which the author is familiar, most of the persons arrested are taken to the central downtown police station. Persons picked up for a misdemeanor enter at the basement level into a large room where a battery of officers rapidly handle the booking process. The officer making the arrest gives his statement; a complaint is filled out and signed by the officer; the accused is asked his name, and told what he has been arrested for. He is then stripped and searched and his photograph and fingerprints are taken. If the accused desires, he can then make a phone call.

If the offense is a petty one, and the accused has cash on his person, the officers will accept a cash bail, and release him (after photographing him on the way out) with instructions as to when to return to trial. If the accused is in no physical condition to be released (as for example, is too drunk) his possessions are taken from him, his belt and shoelaces are removed, and he is taken to the jail. If the offense is a serious misdemeanor, the accused will be put in jail to await trial, or until he can furnish bail.

A person charged with a felony is taken by the arresting officer to one of the upper floors where the different felony "sections" are located. If the suspect has been arrested for a burglary, he goes to the burglary section; if the offense is a homicide, he goes to the homicide bureau, and so on. The arresting officer makes a brief report of the time, place, and circumstances of the arrest, and a brief statement of the offense. He then turns the suspect over to an officer in the section. The reports of the arresting officer are checked, usually by the section chief, to be sure that the facts stated constitute a felony offense, after which a "hold" is issued. A "hold" authorizes the keeping of the suspect in custody until the booking process is completed and the accused can be taken before a magistrate.

In this particular department, because of a special requirement of the law of the state, the accused is often taken before a magistrate for a special warning before the booking process is complete. The magistrate repeats to him the Miranda Warning already given to him by the arresting officer, and also informs him of his right to a preliminary hearing. This is an additional trip before the magistrate which is not required in other state procedures and is not to be confused with the "Initial Appearance

Before the Magistrate" which we discuss hereafter. The accused is then taken back to the section officer, who may question him briefly (again giving him the Miranda Warning) though the accused is not required to answer, and the questioning will cease whenever the suspect indicates that he wants to quit talking or wants an attorney present. The suspect is given a chance to call his family or an attorney, usually immediately after the officer's report has been made and the "hold" issued.

If the arrest has been made without a warrant, the arresting officer goes with the accused before the magistrate and fills out and signs the complaint, or if the arrest is made at night, leaves a report with the clerk of the Justice, who presents it the next morning to the magistrate. A warrant is issued by the magistrate when the complaint is filed, even though the defendant is already in custody. The officer endorses his return on the warrant—in this case reporting an arrest that took place before the warrant was issued. The reason for the issuance of the warrant is that there is some legal confusion as to just when an offender is "charged." Some authorities take the position that the complaint constitutes the charge; others insist that the warrant constitutes the charge, so the warrant is issued after the arrest to make sure of the "charge."

In the department in question, a juvenile who has been picked up by an officer is given the Miranda Warning and asked to give his name and his parents name and address. He is then put in a room by himself. As soon as possible, an officer takes the juvenile to the Juvenile Court. The arresting officer makes a memorandum of the time, place, and circumstances of the arrest, and furnishes this information to the juvenile court intake officer.

THE INITIAL APPEARANCE BEFORE THE MAGISTRATE

The decisions of the United States Supreme Court,[50] and the statutes of most states, require that a person who has been ar-

50. McNabb v. United States, 318 U.S. 332, 63 S.Ct. 608, 87 L.Ed. 819 (1943), reh. den. 319 U.S. 784, 63 S.Ct. 1322, 87 L.Ed. 1727. Mallory v. United States, 354 U.S. 449, 77 S.Ct. 1356, 1 L.Ed.2d 1479 (1957).

rested must be taken "immediately" or "with all possible dispatch" before a magistrate or, as in New York, before "the local criminal court." In other states, the accused is taken before the magistrate but not necessarily "with all possible dispatch." [51] The duties of the magistrate are to: (1) establish the identity of the accused, (2) inform him of the nature of the charges against him and, if he is charged with a felony, of his right to a preliminary hearing, and (3) fix bail. This appearance is called in some states the "presentment ," and in New York, an "arraignment."

If the arrest was with a warrant, the complaint has, of course, already been filed and the nature of the charge is stated in the complaint and the warrant. If the arrest was made without a warrant, the complaint is prepared, signed, and filed when the accused appears before the magistrate, and the usual practice is also to issue and endorse the warrant. Whether or not the prosecuting attorney is present depends upon state law and practice. The view in most states is that the decision to charge is a decision which should be made by the prosecutor. His assent to the issuance of the warrant is then required. In the states where the prosecutor's consent is not required, the police officer and the magistrate in effect make the decision to charge. In either event,

51. In Texas the words are "without unnecessary delay." Texas law requires an appearance before the magistrate for a warning similar to the *Miranda* Warning which must be given by the magistrate. This appearance is *in addition* to the appearance before the justice of the peace who can admit the defendant to bail. Vernon's Ann. Penal Code, Arts. 15.16, 15.17.

In Illinois, the words are "without unnecessary delay." Smith-Hurd Ann.Stat. ch. 38, Crim.Law & Proc., § 109–1. The Illinois law also requires the public posting in jails and police stations of notices advising the accused of his right to be informed of the charge against him, to remain silent, to be treated humanely, and provided with proper food, shelter and needed medical treatment; of his right to communicate with attorney and family, of right to a speedy trial (120 days; 180 if out on bail), and right to bail including release on his own recognizance. Smith-Hurd Ann.Stat. ch. 38, Crim.Law & Proc., § 103–7.

In California, the statutory language is that the officer must take the defendant before the magistrate "without unnecessary delay; and, in any event, within two days after his arrest, excluding Sundays and holidays." West's Ann.Penal Code, § 825.

In New York a police officer must "without unnecessary delay bring the defendant before the local criminal court in which such warrant is returnable." McKinney's N.Y. Criminal Procedure Law, § 120.90 (1). As to New York, the words "local criminal court" should be understood when the word "magistrate" is used herein.

the prosecutor is usually informed of arrests with or without a warrant, and he or his assistants appear at the time the accused makes his initial appearance before the magistrate. The prosecutor thus is in a position to make the decision whether or not to proceed with the prosecution.

If an offense is a petty misdemeanor, the case is often disposed at this initial appearance before the magistrate. The defendant pleads guilty to the offense charged in the complaint, judgment is rendered, and sentence (usually a fine) is pronounced. If the offense is a more serious misdemeanor which may involve a jail sentence, or the defendant does not desire to plead guilty, an information will be filed in the court where he is to stand trial. The date for the trial appearance will be fixed by the magistrate. If the offense is a felony, the date for the preliminary hearing is set by the magistrate. The preliminary hearing may be, and often is, waived by the defendant, particularly in those states where an indictment is necessary to bring an accused to trial on a felony. It may be waived also in states where the defendant is brought to trial for a felony on an information. (The difference between an indictment and an information will be discussed hereafter.)

Bail. Perhaps the most important duty of the magistrate at the initial appearance is to set bail. The amount of the bail is usually based on the nature of the offense—the magistrate often having a table showing the name of the offense and the bail usually required. Because the preliminary hearing comes so rapidly after arrest, information about the accused's prior criminal record and other factors which might affect the amount of bail is usually not yet available. All offenses are bailable, except, perhaps, first degree murder "where the evidence is clear and convincing" that the defendant is not entitled to bail. Bail may also be denied or revoked as to a defendant who is shown to have intimidated witnesses or attempted to bribe jurors.

Purpose of Bail. Bail is given to secure the release of a person from custody. It is an undertaking that the accused will appear at the time and place designated and submit himself to the jurisdiction and judgment of the court. The Eighth Amendment to the United States Constitution says, "Excessive bail shall not be required, nor excessive fines imposed, nor cruel and unusual punishments inflicted." Whether this provision, and similar provisions found in the Constitutions and laws of all the states, means that bail is a constitutional right, is the subject of some controversy. Some persons point out that the Constitution says nothing about a right to bail, it merely provides that it shall not be excessive; others maintain that there would be no point in providing against excessive bail if it could be denied altogether at the whim of the prosecution.

Forms of Bail. Bail can be furnished in cash, or by bond. A bail bond is an undertaking signed by the accused and other persons on his behalf guaranteeing that he will present himself for trial. The persons signing the bail bond are called the "sureties," and some showing must be made that they have property of a value at least equal to the amount of the bail (usually a greater value must be shown). If a defendant does not have friends or relatives who will "go his bond," he can get a bond from a person who writes bail bonds as a profession. He is called a bailbondsman, or a bondsman. He will become the surety on the bond for the payment of a fee, usually 10 per cent of the amount of the bail, though fees of 20 per cent are not uncommon. If the defendant does not appear in accordance with the agreement in the bond and the bondsman cannot produce him in court, the defendant is said to have "jumped bail." The bond is then forfeited, which means that the face amount of the bond is paid to the state by the sureties.

Release on Recognizance. When the premium on a bail bond is more than $500, most defendants are unable to make bail. A New York study showed that 25 per cent of all defendants failed to make bail at $500; 45 per cent failed at $1,500; and 63 per cent failed at $2,500.[52] Other studies showed that many people who fail to make bail are nevertheless persons with substantial ties in the community, who in all probability would appear for trial on the date set though no bail had been put up on their behalf. Courts which experimented with a form of release known as "release on his own recognizance" reported that the number of persons "jumping bail" did not perceptibly increase, and that the benefits of this form of release were great in that persons who had committed offenses did not have to spend long periods in jail awaiting trial, with consequent loss of jobs and hardship on their families. A person released on his own recognizance merely signs

52. Ares, Rankin and Sturz, "The Manhattan Bail Bond Project: an Interim Report on the Use of Pre-Trial Parole," *38 New York Law Review 67* (1963)

his own bond, agreeing to return for trial on the date set. No sureties are required. This procedure was introduced into the District of Columbia by the Bail Reform Act of 1966, and is also being used in some states, though it is by no means widely accepted. The New York Criminal Procedure Law sets up procedures for release on recognizance, and provides that a defendant who appears by counsel upon a summons or appearance ticket must be released on recognizance.

Preventive Bail. The question of whether bail can be used to keep dangerous offenders off the streets calls up deeply felt and divergent opinions. There is evidence that second, or even third and fourth crimes, are committed by persons already out on bail for a serious offense. The preventive bail concept is that upon a showing that a person is already out on bail, he may be denied bail for a second or subsequent offense if there is a finding made by the court that the defendant is a "dangerous offender." For example, the American Bar Association *Standards Relating to Pre-Trial Release* provide for a form of preventive bail in the right to exact special conditions before releasing a defendant when there is a showing that the defendant will commit a serious crime or will seek to intimidate witnesses. The defendant in such cases may be prohibited from communicating with certain persons; going to certain described geographical areas or premises; possessing any dangerous weapons; or indulging in intoxicating liquors or certain drugs; and may be required to report regularly and remain under the supervision of an officer of the court. If a defendant fails to keep these conditions, his release on bail may be revoked. To protect the defendant from long incarceration, accelerated trial is provided for all detained defendants.

Though the period of detention without bail is limited, and early trial is promised, many persons feel that preventive bail is not only unconstitutional but, because of the difficulty in defining and identifyng a dangerous offender, unworkable as well. The United States Supreme Court will ultimately decide the question.

The bail procedures at the initial appearance before the magistrate are important because they represent the first time after the arrest that the accused can obtain his release from custody. The bail set by the magistrate may be contested by a habeas corpus action, and if excessive, may be reduced. Bail is re-set at the preliminary hearing, and at the arraignment. A defendant may be released on bail even after conviction if an appeal is pending. The bond in this case is called an appeal bond.

The initial appearance before the magistrate, and in fact any appearance before a magistrate, is often called an "arraignment," and this is the terminology in New York. In other states an arraignment is the hearing before the court when the defendant enters his plea. In the case of a felony, this comes after indictment or the filing of the information with the trial court. In the case of a misdemeanor, it is after the filing of the information with the trial court. Except when referring specifically to the appearance before the local criminal courts in New York at which the defendant is not required to plead, in this book, by "arraignment" we will mean the appearance by the defendant before the court for the purpose of entering his plea. In ordinary talk by policemen and others in the criminal justice system, the appearance by the defendant before the magistrate for any purposes other than trial is called "arraignment." Thus, they speak of "arraigning" the defendant on the occasion of his initial appearance before the magistrate, though he is not technically "arraigned" until he enters his plea, except, as we have seen in New York where technically a defendant is "arraigned" at his first appearance in response to an accusatory pleading as well as at the hearing when he is required to plead to an indictment or information.

What happens to a defendant after his initial appearance before the magistrate depends primarily on whether or not he ends the case by pleading guilty to a petty misdemeanor, awaits trial on a serious misdemeanor, or is held for indictment or preliminary hearing on a felony. Whether or not he makes bail is also important. Unless he ends the case by pleading guilty and paying his fine, he is taken back to jail until bail is furnished or until he stands trial. When he makes bail, he purchases his right to freedom until he is tried and convicted or until his bail is revoked.

THE PRELIMINARY HEARING

The preliminary hearing is held before a committing magistrate, usually a justice of the peace.[53] (In New York the hearing

53. A preliminary hearing is also called a preliminary examination and an examining trial.

is conducted by a local criminal court). Though the preliminary hearing is of more importance in states prosecuting felonies on information than in those requiring grand jury indictments, the purpose is to make an additional judicial test of the existence of probable cause and to protect the accused from a totally unfounded prosecution. A Texas decision, in holding that return of an indictment lawfully terminated any right to have an examining trial (preliminary hearing), includes a good statement of the purpose of the preliminary hearing:

> While such a preliminary hearing can be a practical discovery tool, its primary justification is to protect an innocent defendant from confinement on a totally baseless accusation pending grand jury action, by determining if there is probable cause to believe that he committed the offense charged but not then made the subject of an indictment.[54]

Both the prosecution and the defendant appear at the hearing, and the prosecution must put on enough evidence to enable the justice to make an independent judgment that there was probable cause to arrest and charge the accused and that there is sufficient proof to support a continuation of the prosecution.[55]

54. Harris v. State, 457 S.W.2d 903 (Tex.Cr.App.1970).

55. The New York Criminal Procedure Law provides that a criminal action is commenced by the filing of an accusatory pleading. McKinney's N.Y.Criminal Procedure Law, § 100.05. With the exception of an indictment which may be filed by a grand jury directly in a superior court, all accusatory pleadings are filed in a local criminal court. § 100.05. Accusatory pleadings are: an indictment, an information, a simplified traffic information, a prosecutor's information, a misdemeanor complaint, and a felony complaint. § 1.20. Though the accusatory pleadings (except generally the prosecutor's information) serve to commence an action, prosecution of a misdemeanor must be upon information unless the defendant waives the filing of the information and consents to prosecution on the misdemeanor complaint, § 170.65; or unless the case is removed to superior court and prosecuted on indictment, §§ 170.20, 170.25. Prosecution of a felony must be upon indictment. § 210.05.

Except for an indictment filed directly in the superior court by a grand jury, whenever an accusatory pleading is filed, whether for a misdemeanor or felony, the accused must appear before a local criminal court to be arraigned. § 170.10. A defendant designated in an accusatory pleading charging a misdemeanor appears before the court for arraignment after arrest with a warrant, Art. 120; arrest without a warrant, Art. 140; in response to a summons, Art. 130; or in response to an appearance ticket. Art. 150. A defendant charged with a felony is arrested. Art. 120; Art. 140. (See also, Art. 110.)

If the accusatory pleading is a misdemeanor complaint, no plea is required, § 170.10(4) (d), unless the defendant waives prosecution on information and consents to be prosecuted upon the misdemeanor complaint. § 170.65. The defendant must, however, plead to an information, § 170.60, or an indictment. § 210.50.

The appearance before the local criminal court following the filing of an information, a simplified traffic information, or a misdemeanor complaint, is called an arraignment. § 170.10(1). The defendant must appear personally, § 170.10(1) (d), except where the offense charged is a traffic infraction or misdemeanor, § 170.10(1) (a), or defendant's appearance is required by summons or appearance ticket, § 170.10(1) (b), in which case defendant may appear by counsel instead of in person. The defendant has a right to counsel at every stage of the action, § 170.10(3), and to appointment of counsel if indigent. § 170.10(3) (c). The case may be immediately disposed of; if it is not, the court must issue a securing order either releasing defendant on his own recognizance or fixing the bail. § 170.10(7). If defendant appears by counsel in response to a summons or appearance ticket, he must be released on his own recognizance. § 170.10(7).

Provision is made for release on recognizance if an information is not filed within five days and the defendant is in custody. § 170.70. Provision is also made for moving the case to a superior court to be prosecuted, as a misdemeanor or felony, by indictment. §§ 170.20, 170.25.

The proceedings upon a felony complaint (called in New York an arraignment instead of a preliminary hearing or an examining trial) are set out in greater detail in the New York Criminal Procedure Law than in a typical criminal procedure code. The rights of the defendant are spelled out:

1. Upon the defendant's arraignment before a local criminal court upon a felony complaint, the court must immediately inform him, or cause him to be informed in its presence, of the charge or charges against him and that the primary purpose of the proceedings upon such felony complaint is to determine whether the defendant is to be held for the action of a grand jury with respect to the charges contained therein. The court must furnish the defendant with a copy of the felony complaint.
2. The defendant has a right to a prompt hearing upon the issue of whether there is sufficient evidence to warrant the court in holding him for the action of a grand jury, but he may waive such right.
3. The defendant has a right to the aid of counsel at the arraignment and at every subsequent stage of the action, and, if he appears upon such arraignment without counsel, has the following rights:
   (a) To an adjournment for the purpose of obtaining counsel; and
   (b) To communicate, free of charge, by letter or by telephone, for the purpose of obtaining counsel and informing a relative or friend that he has been charged with an offense; and
   (c) To have counsel assigned by the court in any case where he is financially unable to obtain the same.
4. The court must inform the defendant of all rights specified in subdivisions two and three. The court must accord the defendant opportunity to exercise such rights and must itself take such affirmative action as is necessary to effectuate them.
5. If the defendant desires to proceed without the aid of counsel, the court must permit him to do so if it is satisfied that he made such decision with knowledge of

the significance thereof, but if it is not so satisfied it may not proceed until the defendant is provided with counsel, either of his own choosing or by assignment. A defendant who proceeds at the arraignment without counsel does not waive his right to counsel, and the court must inform him that he continues to have such right as well as all the rights specified in subdivision three which are necessary to effectuate it, and that he may exercise such rights at any stage of the action.

6. Upon the arraignment, the court, unless it intends immediately thereafter to dismiss the felony complaint and terminate the action, must issue a securing order which, as provided in subdivision two of section 530.20, either releases the defendant on his own recognizance or fixes bail or commits him to the custody of the sheriff for his future appearance in such action. McKinney's N.Y. Criminal Procedure Law, § 180.10.

A defendant may waive the hearing on the felony complaint, in which case he is held for the action of the grand jury, § 180.30(1), or the court makes inquiry for the purpose of reduction of the charge. §§ 180.30 (2), 180.50. If the hearing is not waived, the proceedings on the felony complaint must be conducted as follows:

1. The district attorney must conduct such hearing on behalf of the people.
2. The defendant may as a matter of right be present at such hearing.
3. The court must read to the defendant the felony complaint and any supporting depositions unless the defendant waives such reading.
4. Each witness, whether called by the people or by the defendant, must, unless he would be authorized to give unsworn evidence at a trial, testify under oath. Each witness, including any defendant testifying in his own behalf, may be cross-examined.
5. The people must call and examine witnesses and offer evidence in support of the charge.
6. The defendant may, as a matter of right, testify in his own behalf.
7. Upon request of the defendant, the court may, as a matter of discretion, permit him to call and examine other witnesses or to produce other evidence in his behalf.
8. Upon such a hearing, only non-hearsay evidence is admissible to demonstrate reasonable cause to believe that the defendant committed a felony; except that reports of experts and technicians in professional and scientific fields of the kinds specified in subdivision two of section 190.30 are admissible to the same extent as in a grand jury proceeding.
9. The court may, upon application of the defendant, exclude the public from the hearing and direct that no disclosure be made of the proceedings.
10. Such hearing should be completed at one session. In the interest of justice, however, it may be adjourned by the court but, in the absence of a showing of good cause therefor, no such adjournment may be for more than one day. McKinney's N.Y.Criminal Procedure Law, § 180.60.

At the completion of the hearing, the felony complaint is disposed of as follows:

1. If there is reasonable cause to believe that the defendant committed a felony, the court must, except as provided in subdivision three, order that the defendant be held for the action of a grand jury of the appropriate superior court, and it must promptly transmit to such superior court the

The state does not have to prove the guilt of the defendant at the preliminary hearing—all that is necessary is that the state make out a *prima facie* case of guilt. *Prima facie* is Latin for "at first sight; on the face of it," and a *prima facie* case is such a case as will suffice until contradicted and overcome by other evidence. A *prima facie* case says one court is "one in which the evidence in favor of a proposition is sufficient to support a finding in its favor, if all of the evidence to the contrary be disregarded." [56]

Since the defendant seldom introduces any evidence in a preliminary hearing, it is not difficult for the state to make out a *prima facie* case. Of course, if the state fails to introduce sufficient evidence to support a finding that a crime was committed and that the defendant committed it, then the case against the defendant must be dismissed.

Many defendants waive the preliminary hearing, especially in states using the indictment to charge felonies. Defendants who are represented by attorneys request a preliminary hearing for the purpose of getting a look at the state's case, for the reasons set out in the decision in Coleman v. Alabama.[57] In deciding that

order, the felony complaint, the supporting depositions and all other pertinent documents. Until such papers are received by the superior court, the action is deemed to be still pending in the local criminal court.

2. If there is not reasonable cause to believe that the defendant committed a felony but there is reasonable cause to believe that he committed an offense other than a felony, the court may, by means of procedures prescribed in subdivision three of section 180.50, reduce the charge to one for such non-felony offense.

3. If there is reasonable cause to believe that the defendant committed a felony in addition to a non-felony offense, the court may, instead of ordering the defendant held for the action of a grand jury as provided in subdivision one, reduce the charge to one for such non-felony offense as provided in subdivision two, if (a) it is satisfied that such reduction is in the interest of justice, and (b) the district attorney consents thereto.

4. If there is not reasonable cause to believe that the defendant committed any offense, the court must dismiss the felony complaint and discharge the defendant from custody if he is in custody, or, if he is at liberty on bail, it must exonerate the bail. McKinney's N.Y.Criminal Procedure Law, § 180.70.

After an indictment has been filed with the superior court, the defendant is arraigned before that court, and must appear personally. § 210.-10.

56. Schallert v. Boggs, 204 S.W. 1061 (Tex.Civ.App.1918), motion den. 210 S.W. 601.

57. John Henry Coleman and Otis Stephens, Petitioners v. State of Alabama, 399 U.S. 1, 90 S.Ct. 1999, 26 L.Ed.2d 387 (1970).

a preliminary hearing is a critical stage of the criminal proceeding at which the accused is entitled to counsel, the Court first points out that the guiding hand of counsel is essential to protect the accused against an erroneous or improper prosecution, and goes on to say about the importance of his presence at the preliminary hearing to the accused:

> First, the lawyer's skilled examination and cross-examination of witnesses may expose fatal weaknesses in the State's case, that may lead the magistrate to refuse to bind the accused over. Second, in any event, the skilled interrogation of witnesses by an experienced lawyer can fashion a vital impeachment tool for the use of cross-examination of the State's witnesses at the trial, or preserve testimony favorable to the accused of a witness who does not appear at the trial. Third, trained counsel can more effectively discover the case the State has against the accused and make possible the preparation of a proper defense to meet that case at the trial. Fourth, counsel can also be influential at the preliminary hearing in making effective arguments for the accused on such matters as the necessity for an early psychiatric examination or bail.

In states which do not require an indictment in order to formally charge a person with a felony, the preliminary hearing serves as the forum for the determination of probable cause which is required before any information can be filed in the felony court. If the justice makes a finding of probable cause, the defendant is "bound over" for the trial. In states requiring that formal charge for a felony be by indictment, the preliminary hearing gives the defendant a look at the State's case and gives the innocent defendant an opportunity for early dismissal of the case against him, as was pointed out in the *Coleman* decision involving a state using the indictment procedure. If the defendant is out on bail, the bond already given may be kept in effect at the preliminary hearing, or a new bail may be set, higher or lower than the original bail. If the bail is changed, a new bond must be executed or the defendant returned to jail.

INDICTMENT AND INFORMATION

An indictment and information are alike in that both charge the defendant with an offense and are the documents upon which the defendant is brought to trial. Informations are used to charge both misdemeanor and felony offenses, except in some states and in the federal courts where an indictment is necessary to formally charge a felony.[58] An indictment differs from an information in that an indictment is returned by a grand jury. An information is signed and sworn to by a prosecuting attorney after a complaint is filed, and in the case of a felony, after a preliminary hearing has been held and the committing magistrate has made a finding of probable cause and "bound over" the defendant for trial in the felony court.

Indictments are necessary in criminal proceedings in federal courts because of the provision in the Fifth Amendment which reads, "No person shall be held to answer for a capital, or otherwise infamous crime, unless on a presentment or indictment of a Grand Jury * * *." A felony is an "infamous crime."

The Grand Jury. A grand jury is to be distinguished from a trial jury or petit jury.[59] The grand jury determines probable cause and returns an accusation (indictment). A trial jury decides on guilt or innocence. A grand jury is selected according to procedures set out in the statutes from among citizens of the county

58. In Texas, "* * * No person shall be held to answer to a felony unless on indictment of a grand jury." Vernon's Ann.Code of Criminal Procedures, Art. 1.05.

In New York, "The only method of prosecuting an offense in a superior court is by an indictment filed therewith by a grand jury." McKinney's N.Y.Criminal Procedure Law, § 210.05.

In California, offenses triable in the superior courts must be prosecuted by indictment or information * *. West's Ann.Penal Code, § 737. Before an information is filed there must be a preliminary examination of the case against the defendant and an order holding him to answer. * * * The proceeding for a preliminary examination must be commenced by written complaint. * * * § 738.

In Illinois, all prosecutions for felonies must be by indictment "unless waived understandingly by the accused, and unless the state expressly concurs on such waiver in open court. * * * If a prosecution of a felony is waived, such prosecution may be by information or complaint." Smith-Hurd Ann. Stat. ch. 38, § 111–2.

59. A grand jury is defined in New York as: "A body consisting of not less than sixteen nor more than twenty-three persons, impaneled by a superior court and constituting a part of such court, the functions of which are to hear and examine evidence concerning offenses and concerning misconduct, nonfeasance and neglect in public office, whether criminal or otherwise, and to take action with respect to such evidence as provided in section 190.60." McKinney's N.Y.Criminal Procedure Law, § 190.05.

where the trial is to be held. The statutes usually require, among other things, that the jurors be intelligent citizens of the county who can read and write the English language, that they be residents, and qualified jurors and free holders in the county, and have no suit in the court which requires intervention of the jury.

The jury commissioners, or other persons designated by law to select the grand jury, select a larger number of grand jurors than are required to make up a grand jury. Thus, a state which requires a grand jury of twelve may have twenty-three persons in the "array." The number of members of a grand jury varies from state to state. At common law, a grand jury consisted of not less than twelve nor more than twenty-three men, and this is still the rule in many states.[60] The number of grand jurors required to concur in an indictment may be less than the total number of grand jurors required to make up the grand jury. Thus, only nine members of a jury of twelve is required to return an indictment in Texas.[61]

A grand jury has authority not only to return indictments[62] in cases presented to them by the prosecuting attorney but to make independent investigation of any crimes coming to their knowledge. In New York, a grand jury may return an indictment directly to the superior court though criminal actions in that state are otherwise commenced in local criminal courts. If the accusation is a result of independent action by the grand jury, it is called a "presentment," instead of an indictment. The deliberations of a grand jury are secret, and in most cases the testimony given before a grand jury is also secret, although on

60. In Oregon and Utah, the grand jury is twelve men; in South Dakota, not less than six nor more than eight; in Texas, twelve; in Idaho, sixteen; in Washington, twelve; in California, nineteen; in New Mexico, twenty-one. In New York, the number is not less than sixteen or more than twenty. In Illinois, a grand jury consists of twenty-three jurors, of whom sixteen are necessary to constitute a quorum.

61. In New York and Illinois, at least twelve grand jurors must concur in the indictment. In California, fourteen out of nineteen must concur.

62. An indictment is defined in California as "an accusation in writing, presented by the Grand Jury, charging a person with a public offense." West's Ann.Cal.Penal Code, § 889.

In New York, a misdemeanor may be prosecuted on indictment. McKinney's N.Y.Criminal Procedure Law, §§ 170.20, 170.25.

occasion a defendant may have access to the testimony given by a witness before a grand jury.

Indictment. Where the grand jury indictment is routinely used in felony cases, or when, as in New York, prosecution of a misdemeanor may on occasion be by indictment, the case against the defendant is presented to the grand jury by the prosecutor who makes out a *prima facie* case, just as he would do before the justice of the peace in a state where the grand jury function is performed by a committing magistrate at a preliminary hearing. The grand jury may call additional witnesses, and on occasion, may call in the defendant. Usually, however, neither the defendant nor his attorney are present at the hearing before the grand jury. The votes of the jurors and other matters having to do with the way the jury arrived at its decision are protected by law from public disclosure.

When a grand jury makes its finding of probable cause, the foreman of the grand jury signs the indictment and presents it to the court which impaneled the grand jury.[63] This is called "indicting" the defendant or "returning a true bill" (the full name of an indictment is Bill of Indictment). If the grand jury does not find probable cause and decides against continuing the prosecution of the defendant, the jury does not return an indictment, in which case it is said that the defendant was "no billed." An indictment is a finding that the defendant committed a specified

63. New York law says the Indictment must contain:

1. The name of the superior court in which it is filed; and

2. The title of the action; and

3. A separate accusation or count addressed to each offense charged, if there be more than one; and

4. A statement in each count that the grand jury accuses the defendant or defendants of a designated offense; and

5. A statement in each count that the offense charged therein was committed in a designated county; and

6. A statement in each count that the offense charged therein was committed on, or on or about, a designated date, or during a designated period of time; and

7. A plain and concise factual statement in each count which, without allegations of an evidentiary nature, asserts facts supporting every element of the offense charged and the defendant's or defendants' commission thereof with sufficient precision to clearly apprise the defendant or defendants of the conduct which is the subject of the accusation; and

8. The signature of the foreman or acting foreman of the grand jury; and

9. The signature of the district attorney. McKinney's N.Y.Criminal Procedure Law, § 200.50.

offense at a named date and place "against the peace and dignity of the state."

When the trial court receives an indictment from the grand jury, a time and place for the arraignment is fixed by order of the court. Notice of the indictment is served upon the defendant, together with notice of the time fixed for his appearance. A certain amount of time must elapse (two or three days) from the date the indictment is served upon the defendant before he is required to appear for arraignment. If counsel is appointed, an additional time is usually allowed to counsel to prepare for the trial.

Information. Although the United States Constitution says that no person shall be held to answer for an infamous crime except upon indictment, it has never been the law that the states are required to follow this procedure.[64] Many states therefore prosecute felonies on information.[65] In those states, the prosecuting attorney makes out the information after the finding by the committing magistrate that the defendant be bound over for trial in the felony court. The information, like the indictment, is an accusation that the defendant, naming him, on such and such a date, at such place, committed the offense set forth in the information "against the peace and dignity of the state." The information is signed by the prosecuting attorney and filed in the court where the defendant is to be tried. The form of the information filed in the felony court is similar to the information which constitutes the formal charges for a misdemeanor to be tried in a lower court, except that the information cannot be filed for a felony offense until after the defendant has been "bound over" by the justice at the preliminary hearing.

Misdemeanors are tried on information even in states which require grand jury indictment in felony prosecutions.

THE ARRAIGNMENT

Entering the Plea. The arraignment on an information or indictment takes place in the court where the case is to be tried—in the case of a felony, a court having felony jurisdiction. The purpose

64. Hurtado v. California, 110 U.S. 516, 4 S.Ct. 111, 28 L.Ed.2d 232 (1884).

65. See fn. 58, *supra*.

of the arraignment on an information or indictment is to establish the identity of the defendant and take his plea. The magistrate reads the indictment or information to the defendant, asks him if the document states his correct name, and then inquires, "How do you plead?"[66] Since an arraignment is considered a critical stage in the criminal process, the defendant must be represented by counsel at the arraignment.[67]

The Forms of the Plea. In federal courts and in the courts of many states, the defendant may plead guilty, not guilty, or *nolo contendere.* Other states do not permit the *nolo contendere* plea. *Nolo contendere* means "no contest." In the criminal action itself, it is equivalent to a plea of guilty. However, the plea may spare the defendant from certain civil penalties that might follow a plea of guilty, and for that reason the plea is permitted in some states. As we have said, the plea is equivalent to a plea

66. The Illinois law defines the terms as follows: Smith-Hurd Ann. Stat. ch. 38, Crim.Law & Proc., § 102.9: "Complaint" means a verified written statement other than an information or an indictment, presented to a court, which charges the commission of an offense.

§ 102.11: "Indictment" means a written statement, presented by the Grand Jury to a court, which charges the commission of an offense.

§ 102.12: "Information" means a verified written statement signed by a State's attorney, and presented to a court, which charges the commission of an offense.

§ 102.8: "Charge" means a written statement presented to a court accusing a person of the commission of an offense and includes complaint, information and indictment.

§ 102.4: "Arraignment" means the formal act of calling the defendant into open court, informing him of the offense with which he is charged, and asking him whether he is guilty or not guilty.

The procedure on arraignment is set out in § 113.1: Before any person is tried for the commission of an offense he shall be called into open court, informed of the charge against him, and called upon to plead thereto. If the defendant so requests the formal charge shall be read to him before he is required to plead. An entry of the arraignment shall be made of record.

The arraignment procedures in Texas and California are similar.

In New York, we have seen (p. 119 *supra*) the word "arraignment" is given to any appearance before a local criminal court to respond to an accusatory pleading. A defendant is "arraigned" on a misdemeanor complaint though he is not required to plead thereto. McKinney's N.Y.Criminal Procedure Law, § 170.10(4) (b); and is arraigned on an information, to which he is required to plead. § 170.60. A defendant is "arraigned" on a felony complaint, but is not required to plead thereto, § 180.60; and he is arraigned on an indictment and must plead thereto. § 210.50.

67. Hamilton v. Alabama, 368 U.S. 52, 82 S.Ct. 157, 7 L.Ed.2d 114 (1961), on remand 273 Ala. 504, 142 So.2d 868.

of guilty in the criminal proceeding itself, and the court proceeds on that plea exactly as if the defendant had pleaded guilty. Some states permit additional pleas, such as former jeopardy and not guilty by reason of insanity.[68]

The plea of not guilty puts the state to the proof of all of the material elements of the offense. The plea is entered by the court on the back of the information or indictment. The time and place of the trial is then set. At this time, the bond given by the defendant may be continued, raised, or lowered as the judge shall see fit. If the existing bond is not continued, a new bond must be executed, conditioned on the appearance of the defendant for trial. The defendant who cannot make bail is returned to jail to await trial.

A plea of guilty is an admission by the defendant of every material element of the offense. The plea is entered on the back of the indictment or information. The court then sets the time for sentencing, usually a week or so in advance, or the sentencing may take place at the time the plea is entered. The plea of guilty is equivalent to a verdict of guilty.

We will discuss the plea in greater detail in the next chapter. The plea was mentioned here to show its position in the sequence of steps which constitute investigation and accusation, and which have moved the defendant from arrest to trial along the criminal justice continuum.

68. In Illinois, the defendant may plead guilty or not guilty, in Texas, guilty, not guilty, or *nolo contendere.* California permits six kinds of pleas—guilty; not guilty; *nolo contendere*; a former judgment or acquittal of the offense charged; once in jeopardy; and not guilty by reason of insanity. The effect of each plea is set out as follows: "A defendant who does not plead guilty may enter one or more of the other pleas. A defendant who does not plead not guilty by reason of insanity shall be conclusively presumed to have been sane at the time of the commission of the offense charged; provided, that the court may for good cause shown allow a change of plea at any time before the commencement of the trial. A defendant who pleads not guilty by reason of insanity, without also pleading not guilty, thereby admits the commission of the offense charged." West's Ann.Cal. Code, Penal, § 1016.

In New York, a defendant may plead guilty or not guilty to the entire indictment, or, with the permission of the court and the consent of the people, plead guilty to one but not all of the offenses charged; plead guilty to lesser included offenses with respect to any or all of the offenses charged; or plead guilty to any combination of offenses charged and lesser included offenses within the offenses charged. McKinney's N.Y.Criminal Procedure Law, §§ 220.10, 340.20.

Chapter VIII

ADJUDICATION AND CONVICTION

In this chapter we will deal with what is traditionally called the judicial process. Sentencing is correctly included as part of the judicial process. It is also accurate to say that sentencing is the beginning of the correctional process, though it would be better to recognize that arrest represents the real beginning of the correctional process. Since we are committed to a sequential presentation of the criminal justice process and one which emphasizes the inter-relationship of the steps in the continuum, we will focus here on the steps between arraignment and conviction, leaving sentencing to the next chapter.

THE RIGHT TO COUNSEL

We have introduced the question of the right to counsel in a previous chapter. Let us review it here. Right to counsel is guaranteed in the Sixth Amendment to the United States Constitution. *Miranda* requires counsel at interrogation after focus of suspicion,[1] and *Wade* requires counsel at the line-up.[2] The right to counsel at the preliminary hearing was decided in White v. Maryland and Coleman v. Alabama,[3] and representation is necessary at arraignment and plea. The right to counsel at a criminal trial was settled in Gideon v. Wainwright,[4] and this has been held to apply to representation at the time of entering a plea of guilty. The right to counsel at revocation of probation has been established,[5] and the right to representation at parole revocation

1. Miranda v. Arizona, 384 U.S. 436, 86 S.Ct. 1602, 16 L.Ed.2d 694 (1966), reh. den. 385 U.S. 890, 87 S.Ct. 11, 17 L.Ed.2d 121.

2. United States v. Wade, 388 U.S. 218, 87 S.Ct. 1926, 18 L.Ed.2d 1149 (1967).

3. White v. Maryland, 373 U.S. 59, 83 S.Ct. 1050, 10 L.Ed.2d 193 (1963), conformed to 231 Md. 533, 191 A.2d 237. Coleman v. Alabama, 399 U.S. 1, 90 S.Ct. 1999, 26 L.Ed.2d 387 (1970).

4. Gideon v. Wainwright, 372 U.S. 335, 83 S.Ct. 792, 9 L.Ed.2d 799 (1963), on remand 153 So.2d 299 (Fla.).

5. Mempa v. Rhay, 389 U.S. 128, 88 S.Ct. 254, 19 L.Ed.2d 336 (1967).

recognized in Michigan. The Supreme Court, since *Gideon,*[6] has extended the right to counsel, including the right of the indigent to appointed counsel, to all "critical stages" in the criminal justice process. As matters now stand, an accused may be represented by counsel of his own choosing from the time of arrest to conviction and through appeal. The Miranda Warning informs every accused of his rights to a lawyer, selected by him or appointed at state's expense, and in practice any defendant who wants counsel can have one from the time suspicion focuses upon him until conviction and on appeal. The trend is to make the indigent equal in all respects in the matter of representation.[7]

The accused, of course, may waive counsel, though proof of voluntary and intelligent waiver is required. Police and prosecutors are very careful to be sure that an accused understands his rights to counsel before any purported waiver is relied upon since the court puts on the state the burden of proving both the giving of the Warning and the sufficiency of any waiver.

THE GUILTY PLEA

The guilty plea is the most frequent method of conviction in most jurisdictions; in some, it accounts for 95 per cent of the criminal cases which result in a conviction. This means that an extremely high percentage of all inmates in our penitentiaries have arrived there after a voluntary plea and not after trial and verdict.

The Negotiated Plea. Except for minor misdemeanors, a substantial proportion of all guilty pleas have been negotiated. This is to say that the prosecutor and the defense attorney have talked the case over together and reached an agreement as to the nature of the plea and in many cases as to type and length of the sentence. A knowledge of this fact helps to explain why so many defendants plead guilty—in most cases, they have received an advantage from the plea. The prosecution, also, has received an advantage in that it does not have to go to the time and expense of a criminal trial.

6. Gideon v. Wainwright, 372 U.S. 335, 83 S.Ct. 792, 9 L.Ed.2d 799 (1963), on remand 153 So.2d 299 (Fla.).

7. Douglas v. California, 372 U.S. 353, 83 S.Ct. 814, 9 L.Ed.2d 811 (1963), reh. den. 373 U.S. 905, 83 S.Ct. 1288, 10 L.Ed.2d 200.

That many, if not most, of the guilty pleas in felony cases have been negotiated is a fact that has long been known to judges, attorneys, and to many offenders as well. However, this was not talked about openly, and many judges professed to be in complete ignorance of the practice. The problems which arose about negotiated pleas were as much a result of the secrecy which surrounded the process as of certain inherent dangers which must be carefully avoided. The American Bar Association in its *Standards for the Administration of Criminal Justice* has openly recognized the value and legitimacy of the negotiated plea of guilty, but has attempted to provide certain safeguards to insure its proper use.[8]

The advantages to the defendant in a guilty plea are of three major kinds (1) he is permitted to "plead down" to a lesser offense than he has actually committed, or (2) he is assured that the prosecutor will recommend to the judge a certain type and length of sentence, or (3) he is not charged with multiple offenses, or held to answer as an habitual criminal if he has two or three prior felony convictions. Sometimes benefits of all three kinds are obtained.

Let us take an example of a stituation in which a plea bargaining may take place. An armed robber with no prior felony convictions is caught red-handed when he robs the bank, which means that his chances of conviction are very good indeed. However, since this is his first offense, the prosecutor may feel that he does not want to "throw the book at him." The prosecutor and the defense attorney may reach a bargain that if the defendant pleads guilty, the charge will be reduced from armed robbery to unarmed robbery, which carries a lighter penalty. The prosecutor may also agree that if the defendant pleads guilty he will recommend a sentence which will permit probation. If the police suspect the defendant of previous offenses, he may be assured that in return for his plea of guilty, he will not be charged with them.

The question immediately arises as to why a prosecutor would enter into such a bargain. He, of course, wants to avoid the time and expense of trial. He may feel that the accused is a person who is entitled to a "break," and one who will benefit more from

8. American Bar Association Project on Standards for Criminal Justice. *Standards Relating to Pleas of Guilty*, New York: Office of Criminal Justice Project, Approved Draft, 1968.

supervision in the community on probation than from incarceration in the penitentiary. He may doubt that he can convict him of other offenses, as the evidence he has seen is very meager. Thus, the negotiated plea to unarmed robbery with a recommendation for probation is best for the defense and best for the prosecution.

The judge, of course, may not go along with the prosecutor's recommendation, either as to permitting the defendant to "plead down" or to letting him out on probation. In that case, the defendant will be allowed to withdraw his plea of guilty and stand trial. In other words, if the bargain is not fulfilled by the prosecutor, the defendant is no worse off than he would have been had he plead "not guilty" in the first place. The prosecutor never guarantees to the defendant what the judge will do, and the judge does not enter directly into the negotiations. However, in the great majority of cases the judge will follow the recommendation of the prosecutor, and according to the new American Bar Association *Standards Relating to Pleas of Guilty*,[9] he is to be openly informed that plea negotiation has taken place.

Responsibilities of the Court in Accepting a Plea of Guilty. The judge must determine three things about a plea of guilty before he accepts it: first, that it is voluntary; second, that it is knowingly made; and third, that it is accurate. The judge ascertains these facts in open court by questioning the defendant and his attorney and the prosecutor.[10] He takes particular care in cases

9. *Ibid.*

A practice is developing in California which involves the judge somewhat more closely in plea bargaining. At the time of the last pre-trial conference, the state is asked to give the defendant "its best offer." If the defendant accepts, the terms are put before the judge who may then commit himself to impose the agreed upon penalty. If the defendant refuses to accept the state's "last offer," he must go to trial on his plea of not guilty and a guilty plea will not be accepted thereafter.

10. In Illinois safeguards are set up as to the plea of guilty in addition to those set out in the general statute relating to pleas. (See § 113–1, fn. 66, *supra.*) The law provides: Smith-Hurd Ann.Stat. ch. 38, Crim.Law and Proc., § 115–2: Pleas of Guilty.

(a) Before or during trial a plea of guilty may be accepted when:

(1) The defendant enters a plea of guilty in open court;

(2) The court has informed the defendant of the consequences of his plea and of the maximum penalty provided by law which may be imposed upon acceptance of such plea.

(b) Upon acceptance of a plea of guilty the court may hear evidence of the charge.

where the defendant has waived an attorney and is entering the plea without representation.

To determine that a plea is voluntary, the court inquires of the defendant as to whether he has been threatened or coerced into entering it, and whether or not he has been given any illegal promises or inducements. If the prosecutor threatened the defendant or his family to get the plea, or illegally promised that the defendant would receive no penalty, the plea would be rendered invalid as not voluntary.

The defendant is said to have entered the plea knowingly only if he is fully informed as to the possible penalties he may suffer for the offense to which he pleads. The prosecutor never promises a defendant a specific number of years in prison or on probation, but only that the prosecutor will make the appropriate recommendation. The "bargain" then is that the prosecutor will recommend a certain penalty, but the defendant must take his chances on receiving a higher penalty up to the maximum provided by law, if the judge will not accept the prosecutor's recommendation. Therefore, the defendant must fully understand the

In Texas, the statute reads as follows: Vernon's Texas Code of Crim. Proc., Ann., Art. 26.13: *Plea of Guilty.*

If the defendant pleads guilty, or enters a plea of nolo contendere he shall be admonished by the court of the consequences; and neither of such pleas shall be received unless it plainly appears that he is sane, and is uninfluenced by any consideration of fear, or by any persuasion, or delusive hope of pardon, prompting him to confess his guilt.

In California, the plea of guilty must be made by the defendant himself in open court. Counsel must be provided in cases involving the death penalty or life imprisonment. Counsel may be warned in open court as to other felonies. West's Ann.Cal.Codes, Penal, § 1018.

In New York, a defendant may not plead guilty to an offense for which he could ultimately be sentenced to death without the permission of the court and the consent of the people. McKinney's N.Y.Criminal Procedure Law, § 220.10(4). The court may permit a defendant to withdraw a plea of guilty at any time before imposition of sentence. § 220.50(4). The plea to an indictment charging a felony must be entered orally by a defendant in person. § 220.50(1). Pleas to an indictment or information charging a misdemeanor may be entered by counsel upon written authorization of the defendant. §§ 220.50(1), 340.-20(2) (a). (An exception is made for certain traffic offenses.) One of the grounds for vacating a judgment is that "the judgment was procured by duress, misrepresentation or fraud on the part of the court or prosecutor or a person acting on behalf of the court or prosecutor. § 440.10(1) (b). A sentence may be set aside upon the grounds that it was "unauthorized, illegally imposed, or otherwise invalid as a matter of law." § 440.20(1).

highest possible penalty he could receive for the offense to which he pleads.

Many problems about negotiated pleas arise because the defendant misunderstands the prosecutor's promise to recommend a certain penalty and thinks it is a guarantee that he will receive that specific penalty and no more. When negotiations take place between two attorneys, this misunderstanding does not occur, though the defendant representing himself may reach the wrong conclusion. If the judge determines that the prosecutor has welshed on a bargain that was clearly made or concludes that the defendant really misunderstood, he will permit a withdrawal of the plea of guilty.

The judge must also determine that the guilty plea is accurate—in other words, that the defendant is guilty of a crime at least as great as the one to which he has plead guilty. To establish this fact, most courts, notwithstanding the fact that the defendant has plead guilty, require that the prosecutor put on a *prima-facie* case. In other words, the prosecutor must prove the crime and the defendant's participation in it to the extent that this will be believed if no evidence to the contrary is presented. The requirement that this presentation be put "on the record," i. e., taken down by a court reporter, is an additional safeguard to the defendant and to the prosecutor as well, though it is by no means the regular practice in some courts.

American Bar Association Standards Relating to Pleas of Guilty. The American Bar Association *Standards Relating to Pleas of Guilty* provide that the court should not accept a plea of guilty or *nolo contendere* from a defendant without first addressing the defendant personally and (a) determining that he understands the nature of the charge; (b) informing him that by his plea of guilty or *nolo contendere* he waives his right to trial by jury; and (c) informing him of the maximum possible sentence on the charge, including that possible from consecutive sentences, the mandatory minimum sentence, if any, on the charge, and any additional punishment authorized by the fact that the defendant has been previously convicted of an offense.

The court is also required to determine both the voluntariness and accuracy of the plea. The court may inquire of the defendant and prosecuting attorney if the plea is a result of plea discussions, and if the plea is a result of a plea agreement, what agreement has been reached. If the prosecuting attorney has agreed to seek charge or sentence concessions which must be approved by the court, the court must advise the defendant personally that the recommendations of the prosecuting attorney are not binding upon the court. The court must address the defendant personally to determine whether any other promises or any force or threats were used to obtain the plea. The court must also determine that there is a factual basis for the plea.

Plea withdrawal is permitted whenever the defendant proves that withdrawal is necessary to correct a manifest injustice, such as that he was denied effective assistance of counsel; that the plea was not entered by the defendant or a person authorized to act in his behalf; that the plea was involuntary, or was entered without knowledge of the charge or that the sentence actually imposed could be imposed. The guilty plea may also be withdrawn upon a showing by the defendant that he did not receive the charge or sentence concessions contemplated by the plea agreement and the prosecuting attorney failed to seek or not to oppose these concessions as promised in the plea agreement.

The *Standards* specifically recognize the propriety of plea discussions and plea agreements. The prosecuting attorney is authorized to make or not oppose favorable recommendations as to the sentence, dismissal of the offense charged if defendant pleads guilty to another offense reasonably related to defendant's conduct, and dismissal of other charges or potential charges against the defendant if the defendant enters a plea of guilty. The trial judge does not participate in plea discussions, but such discussions are disclosed to him.

THE PLEA OF NOT GUILTY

Speedy Trial. If the defendant enters a plea of not guilty at the arraignment, the court sets the date for trial.[11] As we have seen, the defendant has a Constitutional right to a speedy trial and this right is also granted in the constitutions of all of the states.

11. A plea of not guilty puts in issue every material allegation of the accusatory pleading (i. e., the information, indictment, or complaint). West's Ann.Cal.Codes, Penal, § 1019. Another statement is that the plea of not guilty "constitutes a denial of every allegation of the indictment." McKinney's N.Y.Criminal Procedure Law, § 220.40.

It is impossible to state in terms of days or months just what constitutes a "speedy trial." [12] Certainly the Constitutional provisions mean a trial without unnecessary delay, particularly for defendants in custody while awaiting trial. Unfortunately, the crowded condition of the court dockets in metropolitan areas, and the custom in smaller communities of holding a "jury term" only once or twice a year, have introduced considerable delay between the date of charging and the date of the beginning of the trial. In some instances, the delay has reached unconscionable proportions. The author knows of one county that finally got around to trying some criminal cases that had been on the docket for *twelve years*. It is only fair to point out, however, that in many cases the delay in the trial is due to the requests of the defendant who sees some advantage in postponing his trial as long as possible.[13]

The reasons for a speedy trial, as we have discussed previously, have to do with the preservation of testimony and the social desirability of settling disputes as promptly as possible. For the defendant who cannot make bail, a speedy trial prevents long periods of incarceration in jail, with the attendant loss of job, loss of family contacts, and the demeaning and degrading jail experience.

American Bar Association Standards Relating to a Speedy Trial. The American Bar Association Project on Minimum Standards for the Administration of Criminal Justice seeks to implement the Constitutional guarantee by requiring the courts to give priority in scheduling to criminal cases. Defendants in custody or defendants whose pre-trial liberty is reasonably believed to

12. See fn. 40, Ch. V, *supra*, referring to court rules in Florida and New Mexico establishing a time limit of approximately six months for trial of a felony.

13. In Illinois, there is a statutory requirement for a speedy trial—120 days for a defendant in custody, 160 days for a defendant out on bail. A 60-day continuance can be granted to the state if necessary to secure evidence. Failure to try the defendant within the time period results in a dismissal of the case for want of prosecution. Exceptions are recognized when the delay is caused by the defendant, for the need to determine defendant's competency to stand trial, an interlocutory appeal, etc. Smith-Hurd Ann. Stat. ch. 38, Crim.Law and Proc., § 103.5.

The New York Criminal Procedure Law includes the right to a speedy trial among the entitlements of the defendant. § 30.20, and provides for dismissal of an information or indictment upon failure to grant a speedy trial. §§ 170.30(1) (e), 210.20 (1) (g).

present unusual risks, (as for example, defendants denied bail or at liberty under restrictive conditions under provisions of a preventive bail act) are to be given preference over other criminal cases. The *Standards* [14] give control over the trial calendar (the setting of cases for trial) to the court and require the prosecuting attorney to file periodic reports with the court setting forth the reasons for delay as to any case for which he has not requested trial within a prescribed period following the charging. The speedy trial time limits are to be set by rules of court. A time limit of not to exceed six months is recommended by many students of the Criminal Justice Process as the time limit between charging and the beginning of the felony trial.

The *Standards* also set up procedures to insure the prompt trial of persons serving a term of imprisonment who are to be tried for another offense. The objective is to do away with the abuses of the "detainer system," which we will discuss hereafter in connection with the correctional problems detainers present.

The Effect of the Plea of "Not Guilty." The plea of "Not Guilty" puts into issue every material allegation of the charge as set out in the Information or Indictment. In contrast to the plea of "Guilty" which amounts to a confession of guilt in open court, the plea of "Not Guilty" is a "plea in bar" of the action, which means that it has as its object the defeat of the claim of the state that the accused is guilty of the offense. Thus, after a plea of "Not Guilty," the state is required to prove beyond a reasonable doubt against the defendant every material element of the offense charged.

Some states permit or require "double pleas" in certain instances. For example, to raise the defense of insanity in California, the defendant enters the double plea of "Not Guilty" and "Not Guilty by Reason of Insanity."

The "Not Guilty" plea puts in motion before judge and jury, unless a jury is waived, the entire criminal trial process which we will now consider in some detail.

14. American Bar Association Project on Minimum Standards for Criminal Justice, *Standards Relating to Speedy Trial.* New York: Office of Criminal Justice Project, Approved Draft, 1968.

JURY TRIAL

A trial in a criminal case will be before a jury unless the defendant waives a jury trial.[15] The defendant's right to a trial before an impartial jury is guaranteed in the Sixth Amendment. The right to waive a jury trial is optional with the defendant except in states which prohibit waiver in capital cases, or, as in some states, in capital cases in which the death penalty is requested by the state.[16] In some states, the procedure is for the defendant to file a request for a jury trial when he enters his plea or at some specified time prior to the beginning of the term of court at which a jury will be impaneled. (In small communities, as we have seen, a jury term may be held only once or twice a year.) A failure to file a request for a jury trial amounts to a waiver of the right to jury. In other states, an express waiver of jury trial is required. The waiver is in writing, or in open court and entered on the docket.[17]

15. When there is a jury trial, questions of law are decided by the court and questions of fact by the jury.

16. The defendant may waive a jury in any case in Illinois. Smith-Hurd Ann.Stat. ch. 38, Crim.Law & Proc., § 115.1.

This is also true in California. West's Ann.Penal Code, § 1167.

In New York, every trial of an indictment must be by jury trial. McKinney's N.Y.Criminal Procedure Law, § 260.10. Except where the indictment charges a crime for which a sentence of death may be imposed upon conviction, the defendant may, at any time before trial, waive a jury trial and consent to a trial without a jury in the superior court in which the indictment is pending. § 320.10. A person over sixteen years and less than nineteen years who is eligible for youthful offender treatment may waive a jury trial. § 720.40. Prosecution on information may be before a trial jury consisting of six jurors, (§ 360.10) and if he requests, the defendant must be accorded a jury trial. § 340.40(2). Request must be made prior to the entry of a plea of not guilty to the information, though the court may for good cause in its discretion grant a request for a jury trial made after the entry of a plea of not guilty but before the commencement of a single judge trial. § 340.40(6). The New York Law also provides for a three-judge trial in the New York City Criminal Court upon an information charging a misdemeanor (gambling offenses are excepted) upon timely request of the defendant or the people. § 340.40(3).

In Wyoming, a defendant must demand a jury or it is deemed waived.

In Texas, a defendant may waive the right to trial by jury except in capital felony cases in which the state has made it known that it will request the death penalty. Vernon's Ann.Code Crim.Proc. Art. 1.14.

17. There is no constitutional right to trial by jury in petty misdemeanor cases. The California Infractions Code, for example, specif-

The Jury Panel. The trial jurors are chosen from a group of potential jurors called the jury panel. A panel is selected, usually by lot, from a list of persons qualified for jury duty in the geographical area which corresponds to the jurisdiction of the court, or otherwise as provided by statutes in the various states. A trial jury in a federal case is selected from the district over which the district court trying the case has jurisdiction.

Certain persons are exempted from jury duty according to the law of the particular state. Usually excluded are persons over 65 years of age, persons with defects of sight or hearing, lawyers, police officers, and firemen. Other persons may be excluded upon request, as doctors, ministers, women with small children. No person may be excluded from jury duty solely on account of race or color.

The Trial Jury. The trial jury in a felony case usually consists of twelve jurors, though there is no Constitutional prohibition of a jury of less than twelve. Juries in misdemeanor cases frequently have fewer persons. Just why a felony jury is traditionally and by statute made up of twelve persons is not clear, though many persons relate it to the fact that Jesus had twelve Apostles. In the early law, jurors were witnesses who came to testify for or against the accused, but today jurors are required to be impartial persons who will render a decision on the facts presented before them in the course of the trial.

The trial jury is chosen from the jurors summoned to appear for the particular case (sometimes called the venire or the array). If the defense maintains that these jurors were improperly se-

ically provides that there is no right to trial by jury or to appointed counsel. West's Ann.Cal.Codes, Penal, § 19c.

In most states a defendant must be personally present during his trial for a felony. In Illinois, however, he can waive the right to be present. Smith-Hurd Ann.Stat. ch. 38, Crim.Law & Proc., § 115.3.

A defendant can lose his right to be present at a [felony] trial, if following the judge's warning that he will be removed if his disruptive behavior continues, he nevertheless insists on conducting himself in such a disruptive manner that his trial cannot proceed if he remains in the courtroom. He can reclaim the right to be present as soon as he is willing to comport himself with decorum and respect. Illinois v. Allen, 397 U.S. 337, 90 S.Ct. 1057, 25 L.Ed.2d 353 (1970), reh. den. 398 U.S. 915, 90 S.Ct. 1684, 26 L.Ed.2d 80.

There is usually no constitutional or statutory requirement that the defendant must be personally at a trial on a misdemeanor. He may appear by counsel, or, as in California, the trial may proceed in his absence. West's Ann.Cal.Codes, Penal, § 1043.

lected, it may challenge the "array," i. e., the whole group. This is seldom successful, but if it is successful, the first array is dismissed and a new group chosen. The veniremen are usually questioned as to their general qualifications before actual selection of the twelve members of the trial jury begins. Thus, the prosecuting attorney will question all prospective jurors in open court to see that they are citizens of the state, can read and understand the English language, that they have not been convicted of a felony (if according to law a convicted felon is prohibited from jury duty) and that there is no reason of health or hardship that will prevent them from serving throughout the case. The trial judge listens to any requests to be excused from jury duty, and excuses those who should not be required to serve.

After the qualification of the panel is completed, the name of one juror is chosen by lot. The Clerk of the Court often has a revolving drum with slips of paper in it on which are written the names of those summoned, from which he picks out one name at a time. The juror's name is read from the slip taken out of the drum, and he takes his place in the jury box. He is then questioned by both the prosecutor and the defense attorney.

A juror may be disqualified "for cause" if, among other things, he exhibits any physical infirmity which would disqualify him from serving, if he is related to the defendant, if he is a witness in the case, or if he has already formed an opinion about a case which will prevent his returning a verdict solely on the evidence. Prior to the *Witherspoon* case,[18] a juror who had conscientious scruples against capital punishment was excused from sitting in cases where the death penalty was requested. Now the prosecutor must show that the conscientious objections of the juror to capital punishment would result in his refusal to return a guilty verdict no matter what the evidence. If the juror can show that he would return a verdict on the evidence, though he is opposed to capital punishment, he cannot be excused for cause.

If a juror is excused for cause (a decision made by the judge), he leaves his seat in the jury box, and another name is drawn by the Clerk. This prospective juror takes the seat vacated by the excused juror and is examined by both the prosecution and the defense. This procedure continues until there are twelve persons sitting in the jury box who have not been successfully challenged for cause.

18. Witherspoon v. Illinois, 391 U.S. 510, 88 S.Ct. 1770, 20 L.Ed.2d 776 (1968), reh. den. 393 U.S. 898, 89 S.Ct. 67, 21 L.Ed.2d 186.

Each side now has what are called "peremptory challenges," which means that they have the right to ask that a juror be excused without giving any reasons for the request. The number of peremptory challenges is fixed by law; [19] Sometimes the state and the defense have the same number of peremptory challenges; in other states, the defendant may be given twice as many peremptory challenges as the state. When one attorney or the other desire to challenge a juror peremptorily, he writes the juror's name on a slip of paper and hands it to the judge. The judge calls out the name of the juror and excuses him. If the peremptory challenges are even, first the state and then the defense will give a name to the judge; if they are uneven, the state may submit one name and the defendant two, then the state one, and so on.

Whenever a juror is excused on peremptory challenge, another name is drawn by the Clerk. The person named takes the seat in the jury box vacated by the excused juror and is examined by prosecution and defense in the usual manner. This process keeps up until both sides have exhausted their peremptory challenges, or waive some of their challenges, and a jury of twelve persons is "accepted" by both sides.

In some courts, the custom is to select one or more additional jurors (called alternate jurors) if it is anticipated that the case

19. In Illinois, a defendant tried alone is allowed 20 peremptory challenges in a capital case, 10 in a case where imprisonment may be in the penitentiary, and 5 in all other cases. The number is reduced to 12, 6, and 3 if there is more than one defendant. The state is allowed the same number of challenges. Smith-Hurd Ann.Stat. ch. 38, Crim.Law & Proc., § 115.4.

In California the number is the same for state and defense—20 in capital or life imprisonment cases, 10 in all other offenses. West's Ann. Calif.Codes, Penal, § 1070.

In New York, (a) Twenty for the regular jurors if the highest crime charged is a class A felony, and two for each alternate juror to be selected; (b) Fifteen for the regular jurors if the highest crime charged is a class B or class C felony, and two for each alternate juror to be selected; (c) Ten for the regular jurors in all other cases, and two for each alternate juror to be selected. McKinney's N.Y. Criminal Procedure Law, § 270.25(2).

In Texas, the defendant in a capital case is allowed one extra challenge over the number allowed to the state (8 to the defendant, 7 to the state). In felonies where the death penalty is not sought, the state and defense are each allowed 10 (6 in cases involving multiple defendants). The number is reduced to 5 for misdemeanors tried in district court, and to 3 in misdemeanors tried in county court. Vernon's Texas Code Crim.Proc., Ann., Art. 35.15.

may take a long time to try. An alternate juror is chosen from the panel in the usual way,[20] and takes a seat to the side of the jury box. He hears all the evidence in the case, but participates in the deliberations of the jury only if one of the first twelve jurors is excused from the case before the trial is finished because of illness or family emergency. If one of the twelve jurors does become ill after the case has "gone to the jury," there is a mistrial, and the case must be re-tried.

The Order of Presentation of Evidence. After the jury is selected, the prosecution opens the case by explaining briefly to the jury what the case is about and what he hopes to show are the facts. This is called the "opening statement for the prosecution." The defense then has a chance to follow with its opening statement or may postpone it until later in the trial. The exact order in which the two sides present their case is fixed by the law in the state. However, the usual procedure is for the state to make its opening statement and present its witnesses, the defense then makes its opening statement and presents its witnesses, the state presents witnesses on rebuttal, and the defense presents witnesses on rebuttal. The judge then gives the instructions to the jury, and the prosecuting attorney gives part of the state's final argument to the jury. This is followed by the final argument of the defense, and usually, the state concludes the arguments. Because the state bears the burden of proving the case beyond a reasonable doubt, it is given the final word. However, in some states, the defense presents the last argument.

American Bar Association Standards Relating to Trial by Jury. The American Bar Association Minimum Standards for Criminal Justice [21] provide that in all criminal cases the defendants should have the right to be tried by a jury of twelve whose verdict must be unanimous *except* that, where not barred by constitutional provisions, the right to a jury trial may be limited in one or more of the following ways: (a) by denial of jury trial to those charged with "petty offenses;" (b) by requiring trial without jury for lesser offenses, provided there is a right to appeal without unreasonable restrictions to a court in which a trial *de novo* by a jury

20. The number of peremptory challenges allowed to an alternate juror may be fewer than for the regular jurors. See fn. 19, *supra*.

21. American Bar Association Project on Standards for Criminal Justice, *Standards Relating to Trial by Jury*, New York: Office of Criminal Justice Project, Approved Draft, 1968.

may be had; (c) by the use of juries of less than twelve, without regard to the consent of the parties; or (d) by permitting less than unanimous verdicts, without regard to the consent of the parties.

The federal rules of procedure already provide for the trial of minor offenses before United States Magistrates without a jury, and many states deny a jury trial in so called "petty offenses." As defined by the United States Code, a petty offense is "any misdemeanor, the penalty for which does not exceed imprisonment for a period of six months or a fine of not more than $500 or both * * *." [22]

The American Bar Association *Standards* would permit a state to deny a jury trial in misdemeanors above a petty offense if appeal procedures resulting in a trial *de novo* (a new trial) before a jury were provided for. They would also permit a state to use juries of less than twelve persons; or permit a verdict in a criminal case to be less than unanimous. Juries of six jurors are already common for the trial of misdemeanors, and a few states permit a felony verdict to be returned by less than a unanimous vote of the jurors. As we have seen, there is no provision in the United States Constitution that fixes the number of jurors, and the right of a state to reduce the size of the jury or permit a less than unanimous verdict would depend upon its own constitutional limitations. In view of the crowded dockets of the courts and the increasing length of jury trials, many states may pass legislation to modify the requirement of twelve jurors and permit less than unanimous verdicts.

THE RULES OF EVIDENCE

The presentation of evidence in a criminal or civil trial is governed by rules which are called the "rules of evidence." Since a trial in Anglo-American law is an adversary proceeding, the parties choosing up sides, the rules of evidence resemble the rules of a game, with the judge as the impartial umpire. Rules of evidence appear both in the statutes of the state and in rules made

22. 18 U.S.C.A. § 1(3).

by the court itself, but have developed principally in the case law.[23]

The purpose of the adversary proceeding is to get at the truth; the rules of evidence have been devised to assist in the attainment of that purpose. Since the rules of evidence are known in advance to all the parties, the procedures by which a man will be judged guilty or not guilty are known in advance. As we decided in the first chapter, this feature is what largely distinguishes decision making in the law from decision making in the social group.

We cannot hope in an introductory text to enter into an in-depth study of the law of evidence. All we can do is to get a general idea of the subject. Let us first, then define evidence.

Definition of Evidence and Kinds of Evidence. Evidence is every species of proof legally presented in a court of law through the medium of witnesses, records, documents, objects, etc., for the purpose of inducing belief in the minds of the court or jury on the issues in the case. Evidence can be classified as real evidence, testimony, direct evidence, circumstantial evidence, and in other ways. *Real evidence* includes objects of any kind (guns, maps, fingerprints, etc.) placed before the court or jury; *testimony* is the statements of competent witnesses. *Direct evidence* is eye-witness evidence; *circumstantial evidence* is evidence of circumstances which tend to prove the truth or falsity of a fact in issue. To be acceptable in court, evidence must be relevant, material, and competent.

Relevant Evidence. Relevant evidence means evidence which is related to the issue and which will tend to prove or disprove an alleged fact. Thus, if the defendant is charged with murder, and the issue is whether or not he killed the deceased, evidence as to his motive, his ability to commit the offense, his opportunity to commit the offense, and his intention to commit the offense, are all relevant evidence. His fingerprints on the murder weapon, his sudden wealth after the deceased was robbed, the threats he made against the deceased, his attempt to flee or commit suicide, are also relevant evidence, as the proof of these facts would tend to

23. Since the rules of evidence have been developed largely in the case law and are basically similar from state to state, no effort is made to point out differences between the law in the representative states whose statutory law we have discussed.

prove the guilt of the defendant. Lawyers often speak of the "chain of evidence," which refers to the fact that evidence tends to develop bit by bit with one piece of evidence supporting and tending to prove another.

Competent Evidence. Competent evidence means evidence given by a competent witness. Some evidence offered in court cannot be received for reasons of public policy or because it is patently unreliable. A person of unsound mind may not be a competent witness because it is apparent that he could not understand what he saw or heard or is not able to correctly relate it. Very young children are sometimes incompetent witnesses. However, there is usually no arbitrary age limit below which a child cannot testify. If it can be shown that the child was able to understand what he saw or heard, and knows the difference between right and wrong, he may be called as a witness and his testimony received. A convicted felon is a competent witness in most states, though the fact of his conviction may be shown to impeach (discredit) his testimony. Accomplices are sometimes declared by statute to be incompetent witnesses against their fellow conspirators, though the more common approach with reference to an accomplice is simply to require that his testimony be corroborated before it can serve to convict the defendant.

The mere fact that evidence is competent does not, of course, mean that the jury must believe it. Some competent evidence may be almost worthless in terms of inducing belief. A wife's alibi for her husband may be competent, but the jury may dismiss her testimony as not worthy of belief. As we shall see in a subsequent section, while competency of the evidence is for the judge to decide, the weight of the evidence is for the jury to decide.

Privileged Communications. According to the rules of evidence enacted into law in many states, certain witnesses are incompetent to testify as to conversations they have had with other persons, including the accused. The testimony is excluded not because the witness may be untruthful, but because the law puts the protection of secrecy around certain communications. Known as "privileged communications," the law protects them by prohibiting the person who heard them from relating them in open court unless the person who made the statements waives his privilege.

A wife cannot testify against her husband, though in some states she may testify for him.[24] A husband, in turn, may not testify against his wife though he may testify for her. (An exception is usually made to this rule in cases where the husband and wife are in a legal dispute with each other, or where it is claimed that one of them has mistreated their child or the child of either of them.) The law makes conversations between husband and wife privileged partly because the husband and wife were originally considered one, and thus to make one of them testify against the other would be equivalent to self-incrimination, but primarily because the law considers it very important to preserve the sanctity and privacy of the marriage relationship.

A lawyer may not be required to relate on the witness stand what his client told him, even if the client confessed his guilt to the lawyer. The statements made to a priest or pastor cannot be admitted in evidence over the objections of the penitent.[25] In many states, a doctor may not testify to anything told to him by his patient or observed by the doctor in the course of a medical examination, unless, of course, the patient himself first puts the doctor on the stand. Statements made to psychiatrists are similarly protected in many states.

Privileged communications must be distinguished from confidential communications. Privilege is a *legal right* based upon public policy which says that the person hearing the statement cannot be compelled to repeat it on the witness stand unless the person making the statement waives the privilege of secrecy given him by the law. Confidentiality is an *ethical principle* which requires that a person in a professional relationship with another shall not repeat to outsiders statements made to him in the course of the professional relationship. Many statements are entitled to the protection of confidentiality that have no protec-

24. In Illinois a wife may not testify for or against her husband in a criminal case. Bloomquist v. Rehnberg, 280 Ill.App. 1 (1935).

25. The common law notion of privileged communications extended only to the husband-wife, lawyer-client, and priest-penitent relationship. In 1828, New York extended the right to the doctor-patient relationship. California adopted the same rule in 1872. This is now the rule in about two-thirds of the states.

Texas is among the states which do not grant privilege to the doctor-patient relationship. The rules of privilege in Illinois follow the common law, and a wife may not testify for or against her husband in a criminal case. Bloomquist v. Rehnberg, 280 Ill.App. 1 (1935).

tion in the law of privileged communications. Thus, a welfare worker should not relate to others who have no reason to know matters told her by the client in the course of their interview; however, the court could compel the welfare worker to repeat the statements in court if they involved an issue before the court. Statements made by clients to welfare workers are not, in most states, privileged.

An otherwise privileged statement loses its privilege if made in the presence of other persons not in the privileged relationship. Thus, the lawyer may be required to testify to the admission his client made to him and several peace officers at the same time; or a pastor to a confession made in open church.

Weight of the Evidence. The competency of the evidence is for the judge to decide. The weight of the evidence is for the jury to decide. Weight means the most and the best evidence, both in quality and quantity. If a wife says her husband was spending the evening watching television when the murder occurred, she may very well be telling the truth. However, if the man's doctor says the defendant was in his office undergoing a physical examination when the event occurred, the doctor is more apt to be believed than the wife. Both the wife (because she is testifying for her husband) and the doctor are competent witnesses, but the weight of the doctor's testimony exceeds the weight of the wife's testimony in the usual case, though the jury is completely free to think the doctor is a liar or was mistaken and that the wife was telling the truth.

Judicial Notice. The course of a trial is affected by other rules of evidence, such as judicial notice and presumptions of both law and fact. Judicial notice means that the court will take as proved certain facts of common knowledge without requiring that witnesses or other evidence be produced to prove the fact in court. Thus, a court will take judicial notice of the days of the week, the months of the year, the properties of matter (gas explodes, a skidding car will leave skid marks, etc.), historical facts (the dates of all the wars, the names of the Presidents of the United States, etc.), the usual dimensions (12 inches to a foot, the number of pounds in a ton, etc.), and similar commonly known facts.

Presumptions of Law and Fact. There are also presumptions of law and of fact. A presumption of law is adopted as a matter of public policy, as for example, the presumption that a child under seven is incapable of committing a criminal act, or that a husband is the father of his wife's child. The law does not permit a presumption of law to be rebutted (shown to be untrue) except under the most unusual circumstances.

A presumption of fact can be rebutted but is taken as true until the contrary is shown. Thus, a man is presumed to be innocent, a woman is presumed to be chaste, and a person is presumed to intend the natural consequences of his act. There is a presumption that a person is sober, and that he will not commit suicide. There is also a presumption that a man who has not been heard from in seven years is dead. All of these presumptions of fact can be shown to be untrue. Though a man is presumed to be innocent, he can be shown to be guilty; a woman can be shown to be of ill-repute; a person may be shown to have been insane and hence did not comprehend the natural consequences of his act. A person may be shown to be drunk, or to have committed suicide. A man who returns after seven years is certainly not dead no matter what the law "presumed" about him.

Examination and Cross Examination. The adversary concept extends to the examination of each witness. A witness who is subpoened by the state (ordered by the court to appear as a witness for the state) is first examined by the prosecuting attorney; the defense attorney can then cross-examine him. If the witness is called as a defense witness, the prosecutor can cross-examine him. The purpose of examination is to present the witness' information before the judge and jury; the purpose of cross-examination is to test the witness' observation, recollection, and veracity, or to make it obvious that he is prejudiced against the side represented by the cross-examiner. Cross-examination will also bring out such facts as that the witness is a convicted felon (and for this reason presumably untruthful), that his opportunity to observe the events was insufficient, and that his memory is faulty. By getting him confused in his answer in cross-examination, doubt is cast upon the testimony he gave in direct examination. A cross-examiner can ask "leading" questions, which are questions suggestive of an answer. "Now on the night in question you left work early * * *". (Lawyers joke about a famous leading question: "When did you stop beating your wife?") Leading questions are not permitted in direct examination, but are permitted in cross-examination because they are helpful in getting at the truth.

Impeachment of Witness. To impeach a witness means to discredit his testimony. A witness may be impeached by the means suggested above and also by showing by other witnesses that the events were not as the witness related them. A rule of evidence says that a party to a criminal action may not impeach his own witness. That means, if one side or the other calls the witness, it must accept what he says and not try to make him change his testimony. The right to impeach is given the other side in cross-examination. The rule against impeaching your own witness does not mean, of course, that other witnesses on the same side may not testify differently. What it means is that a party may not call a witness to testify in his behalf and then make a direct effort to prove that he is a liar or mistaken, as is permissible in the cross-examination conducted by the opposite party. In New York, however, a party may introduce with respect to his own witness evidence that the witness has previously made a written statement or an oral statement under oath contradictory to his testimony.

Opinion and Expert Testimony. Another rule of evidence states that a lay (non-expert) witness may testify only to what he observed and cannot give his opinion on what happened. There are some exceptions to this. For example, a lay witness may testify that a man was drunk—which is an opinion—but will be required to tell how the man talked and acted that led him to believe that he was drunk. The right of the lay witness to express an opinion is limited to matters of common experience and must be based on observation.

An expert witness, on the other hand, may give an opinion even though he had not been present at the event. The basis of the expert witness testimony is that he is an expert in the field, and this must be shown before he can express an opinion. Though none of them were present at the event, a psychiatrist may give his expert opinion that the defendant was suffering from delusions at the time he killed the victim; a police officer may testify that skid marks of a certain length show the driver was driving at 70 miles an hour when he applied the brakes; a jeweler may testify as to the value of the property stolen; or a real estate agent to the value of the real property sold. A psychiatrist who has never even examined a defendant may be asked to give his opinion of his mental condition solely on the basis of what he has observed of the defendant in court and the testimony presented in court about the event. Expert opinion may be brought out by means of the hypothetical question, which must be based on facts in evidence. In effect, the expert witness is asked: "If so and so happened in such and such a way with this and that result, what is your opinion as to the mental condition of the defendant at the time?" An expert, but not a lay witness, is permitted to answer such a question.

Hearsay Evidence. The general rule is that hearsay evidence is not admissible (not competent evidence) to prove an issue in a court of law. Hearsay evidence is second-hand evidence in which a witness is telling not what he knows of his own knowledge but what somebody else told him. Since the person making the statement is not in court, there is no way that he can be confronted and cross-examined as to the truth of what he said. The law sees such evidence as denying the defendant the right to confrontation and also as unreliable. A woman may say, "I know the defendant was there that night because my brother told me he was there." If the defendant cross-examines only the woman, he can get no information as to when and under what conditions the brother saw the defendant, nor whether the brother had good eyesight, disliked the defendant, or any other fact that might discredit his testimony. The law therefore says that the woman's testimony is hearsay and not admissible. If the state wants the brother's testimony, it will have to call the brother to the witness stand, where he can be examined and cross-examined about the occasion when he saw the defendant.

There are many exceptions to the hearsay rule which we cannot consider here, except for the *res-gestae* exception, which is important to police investigation, and admissions and confessions which constitute important and sometimes crucial evidence against the defendant.

Res-gestae. The Latin phrase means literally "things done." It might be translated in modern terms as "the happening." If an event is under investigation, then the entire transaction and every part of it may be introduced into evidence even though some of the statements made at the time would ordinarily be barred by the hearsay rule. For example, if a police officer comes upon an accident which he undertakes to investigate, he can testify in court as to what happened and also as to *what was said* during the course of his investigation at the scene. A bystander may say to the driver of the car, "You were driving 80 miles an hour," and the driver not deny it. The police officer can testify to what the bystander said and that the driver did not deny it, though the statement is hearsay since the bystander is not in court to be cross-examined. Declarations uttered spontaneously and simultaneously with an act which is admissible in evidence may be admitted as an exception to the hearsay rule, provided the utterances are so closely related to the event that the probability of their truth is high. The *res-gestae* exception is thus strictly limited

Admissions Against Interest. Admissions against interest and confessions are also accepted into evidence as exceptions to the hearsay rule. An admission connects the accused with the act; a confession admits that he committed that act; a plea of guilty admits every material element necessary to make the accused criminally liable for the act. The defendant may say, "I was there when he was killed"—this is an admission which puts him at the scene, though it is not a confession that he killed the victim. A confession says, "I killed him"—but may go on to claim self defense or some other extenuating circumstance. A plea of guilty to second degree murder says, "I killed him, and I have no defense to the charge that I am criminally responsible for second degree murder"—at most, all that is then required is that the prosecution present a *prima-facie* case.

Confessions. The admission into evidence of confessions made by the accused presents many legal problems. Since the defendant cannot be compelled to take the stand at the trial, it is of great value to the state to have a confession which can be read to the jury. Sometimes in fact, the entire case for the state rests upon the confession. The defense is just as anxious to keep the confession out of evidence as the state is to get it in. It is very difficult to get a verdict of "not guilty" if the defendant has convicted himself out of his own mouth.

The legal rule has long been that a confession cannot be admitted in evidence unless it was voluntarily made, without threat, force, or coercion. Thus, before the judge will permit the confession of the defendant to be read to the jury, he carefully inquires into the circumstances under which the confession was made.

Since the decisions in *Escobedo* [26] and *Miranda*,[27] no admission or confession will be admitted into evidence unless the accused was given the Miranda Warning prior to making the admission or confession, nor will it be admitted into evidence if it appears that the accused was subjected to physical or psychological coercion to extract the confession or admission. In federal courts, and in many state courts, failure to take the accused promptly before the magistrate will invalidate any confession made in the interval between custody and first appearance before the magistrate. The McNabb-Mallory Rule [28] put an end to such practices as driving the defendant around in a squad car for several hours before taking him to the magistrate with the hope that during the interval he can be brought to confess or make damaging admissions. (The *Mallory* case is not binding on the states but many states by statute require prompt appearance before the magistrate, which amounts to legislative adoption of the *Mallory* rule. Of course, coerced confessions are inadmissible irrespective of statutory adoption of the McNabb-Mallory Rule.) [29]

In the *Escobedo* [30] case, the police officers refused to let the accused's attorney, who was outside the door, enter the interrogation room and as a result obtained damaging admissions from Escobedo. The decision in that case and the subsequent decision in Miranda v. Arizona [31] were intended to afford additional protections to the accused and to make it more difficult for the police officers to obtain admissions and confessions. In Texas, no oral confession may be admitted into evidence, and the procedures for obtaining a written confession are elaborate. Oral confessions are admissible in other states, however, if proper warnings are given and the confession is voluntary.

Many police officers understandably claim that the rules governing the interrogation of a person suspected of a crime are

26. Escobedo v. Illinois, 378 U.S. 478, 84 S.Ct. 1758, 12 L.Ed.2d 977 (1964).

27. Miranda v. Arizona, 384 U.S. 436, 86 S.Ct. 1602, 16 L.Ed.2d 694 (1966), reh. den. 385 U.S. 890, 87 S.Ct. 11, 17 L.Ed.2d 121.

28. McNabb v. United States, 318 U.S. 332, 63 S.Ct. 608, 87 L.Ed 819 (1943), reh. den. 319 U.S. 784, 63 S.Ct. 1322, 87 L.Ed. 1727. Mallory v. United States, 354 U.S. 449, 77 S.Ct. 1356, 1 L.Ed.2d 1479 (1957).

29. See fn. 51, Ch. VII, *supra*.

30. Escobedo v. Illinois, 378 U.S. 478, 84 S.Ct. 1758, 12 L.Ed.2d 977 (1964).

31. 384 U.S. 436, 86 S.Ct. 1602, 16 L.Ed.2d 694 (1966), reh. den. 385 U.S. 890, 87 S.Ct. 11, 17 L.Ed.2d 121.

much too stringent, and that police efforts to solve crimes are seriously hampered by the new requirements as to confessions and admissions. Defense attorneys reply that the rules are not stringent enough, that ignorant and poor defendants are still being forced or tricked into confessing to offenses they did not commit.

The effect of the *Miranda* ruling has been somewhat diluted by a Supreme Court decision which holds that a confession given without the warning may be admitted to impeach the testimony of a defendant who takes the stand in his own behalf and testifies on the stand in a manner to contradict the statements made in the confession.[32]

The truth seems to be that in spite of the *Mallory*, *Escobedo*, and *Miranda* decisions, confessions are still being made, though it is also true that additional safeguards have been set up by these decisions. Police officers for the most part are conscientious in following the new requirements, and in any event, all the circumstances are carefully scrutinized by a trial judge before the confession is admitted into evidence. If the trial judge makes an error in his ruling, the defendant has the chance to have the ruling reversed on appeal to the highest court of the state, and sometimes to the Supreme Court of the United States.

Objections to the Admission of Evidence. One of the main duties of an attorney in the trial of a case is to make a timely objection to the admission of evidence which, because of the rules of evidence, should not be heard by the jury. After the opposing side asks a question, and before the witness answers, the attorney will state his objections to the court. He will say, "I object to the admission of that evidence because it is irrelevant, or because it is hearsay, or immaterial, or because no proper foundation has been laid for its admission," and so on. The sing-song objection, "I object to the admission of the evidence because it is incompetent, irrelevant, and immaterial," is constantly heard in any trial. The court rules on the objection and thus permits the offered evidence to be admitted or refuses to permit its admission. If the attorney's objection is over-ruled by the court, the evidence is admitted; if the objection is sustained, the evidence is not admitted or must be admitted in some other fashion.

32. Viven Harris v. State of New York, 401 U.S. 222, 91 S.Ct. 643, 28 L.Ed.2d 1 (1971).

We have said previously, the admissibility of the evidence is for the court; the weight of the evidence is for the jury. This simply means that the jury doesn't have to believe or be persuaded by any evidence just because it is admitted. Thus, the court may admit the testimony of a child, but the jury may feel that the child did not have sufficient understanding about the matter. The court may even admit a confession, yet the jury decide that it was made under such circumstances as not to be believable. Some states specifically provide for this extra safeguard on confessions by first having a hearing before the court outside the presence of the jury, but then instructing the jury that even though the court had admitted the confession into evidence, the jury has the right to determine whether or not the confession was voluntarily made. A jury frequently hears the testimony of psychiatrists and expert witnesses which they simply do not believe, or disregard in whole or in part. This is their right. The moral judgment about guilt or innocence is made by the jury. In reaching that moral judgment, the jurors may put such weight on testimony as they please. The only requirement is that their decision must be made on the basis of evidence presented in court and not on the basis of prior beliefs or something heard outside the trial.

The Exclusionary Rule. We have previously discussed a rule of law known as the "Exclusionary Rule," which prohibits the admission in a court of law of any evidence obtained in violation of the Constitutional rights of the accused. Thus, the murder weapon seized in an illegal search, an admission made after an illegal arrest, or a confession obtained from a defendant who was not given the Miranda Warning cannot be admitted into evidence against the defendant.[33] A companion rule known as the "fruits of the poisonous tree" doctrine, prohibits the admission of evidence that was obtained *as a result of* an illegal or an initially "tainted" admission, confession, or search.

Let us suppose that the accused is not given the Miranda Warning and is induced by force and threats to make a confession. In the confession, he does not tell the officers where the murder weapon is but does tell them that he went to a certain empty building after the murder. On the basis of what the accused has told them about his movements, the officers go to the empty

33. Except for impeachment purposes after Viven Harris v. State of New York, 401 U.S. 222, 91 S.Ct. 643, 28 L.Ed.2d 1 (1971).

building and find the gun. The "fruits of the poisonous tree" doctrine decrees that the gun cannot be admitted into evidence against the accused since it was located by the officers as a direct result of an illegal confession obtained from the accused.

As we have seen, the Exclusionary Rule had long been the rule in federal courts, but not until the decision in Mapp v. Ohio [34] was the rule made mandatory on the states. In the *Mapp* case, which is often said to be the case that started the "Criminal Law Revolution," the court said that evidence illegally seized must be excluded from the trial in state courts.

The case changed law enforcement practices in a great number of states and gave rise to considerable criticism. Let us review the arguments. The critics of the *Mapp* decision point out that the rule has the effect of freeing a guilty man because the police officer erred in his duty. The police officer should be disciplined for dereliction of duty, say those who disagree with *Mapp*, but the public should not be endangered by turning back into society a dangerous felon. Supporters of the *Mapp* decision answer by saying that though methods of disciplining police officers exist on paper, they are seldom used. Thus the only way to control illegal police conduct is to make the police officer pay the penalty of a lost case. He will be more careful about the constitutional rights of the accused in the future, is the theory of those who approve of the Exclusionary Rule.

Cases are still reaching the higher courts involving application of the Exclusionary Rule. Whether it will be relaxed or strengthened will depend upon future court decisions. In the meantime, however, many states have enacted the Exclusionary Rule into statute, thus providing statutory guides for law enforcement officers and greater protection to the citizen against illegal searches and seizures.[35]

34. 367 U.S. 643, 81 S.Ct. 1684, 6 L.Ed.2d 1081 (1961), reh. den. 368 U.S. 871, 82 S.Ct. 23, 7 L.Ed.2d 72.

35. The rule is statutory in Texas. Vernon's Ann.Code of Crim.Proc., Art. 38.23:

No evidence obtained by an officer or other person in violation of any provisions of the Constitution or laws of the State of Texas, or of the Constitution or laws of the United States of America, shall be admitted in evidence against the accused on the trial of any criminal case.

In any case where the legal evidence raises an issue hereunder, the jury shall be instructed that if it believes, or has a reasonable doubt, that the evidence was obtained in violation of the provisions of this Article, then and in such event, the jury shall disregard any such evidence so obtained.

In California the defendant may move to suppress evidence obtained as a result of an unreasonable search or seizure. West's Ann.Penal Code, § 1538.5.

The New York Criminal Procedure Law defines "evidence" when referring to matter in the possession of or available to the prosecutor as meaning any tangible property or potential testimony which may be offered in evidence in a criminal case. McKinney's N.Y.Criminal Procedure Law, § 710.10(2). Concerning the suppression of evidence, the Law reads as follows:

Upon motion of a defendant who (a) is aggrieved by unlawful or improper acquisition of evidence and has reasonable cause to believe that such may be offered against him in a criminal action, or (b) claims that improper identification testimony may be offered against him in a criminal action, a court may, under circumstances prescribed in this article, order that such evidence be suppressed or excluded upon the ground that it:

1. Consists of tangible property obtained by means of an unlawful search and seizure under circumstances precluding admissibility thereof in a criminal action against such defendant; or
2. Consists of a record or potential testimony reciting or describing declarations or conversations overheard or recorded by means of eavesdropping, obtained under circumstances precluding admissibility thereof in a criminal action against such defendant; or
3. Consists of a record or potential testimony reciting or describing a statement of such defendant involuntarily made, within the meaning of section 60.45, to a public servant engaged in law enforcement activity or to a person then acting under his direction or in cooperation with him; or
4. Was obtained as a result of other evidence obtained in a manner described in subdivisions one, two and three; or
5. Consists of potential testimony identifying the defendant as a person who committed the offense charged, which potential testimony would not be admissible upon the prospective trial of such charge owing to an improperly made previous identification of the defendant by the prospective witness. McKinney's N.Y.Criminal Procedure Law, § 710.20.

1. Upon granting a motion to suppress evidence, the court must order that the evidence in question be excluded in the criminal action pending against the defendant. When the order is based upon the ground specified in subdivision one of section 710.20 and excludes tangible property unlawfully taken from the defendant's possession, and when such property is not otherwise subject to lawful retention, the court may, upon request of the defendant, further order that such property be restored to him.
2. An order finally denying a motion to suppress evidence may be reviewed upon an appeal from an ensuing judgment of conviction notwithstanding the fact that such judgment is entered upon a plea of guilty.
3. A motion to suppress evidence made pursuant to this article is the exclusive method of challenging the admissibility of evidence upon the grounds specified in section 710.20, and a defendant who does not make such a motion before or in the course of a criminal action waives his right to judicial determination of any such contention.

Nothing contained in this article, however, precludes a defendant

Right of Defendant Not to Testify. The Constitutional guarantee against self-incrimination protects the defendant from having to take the witness stand at a criminal trial. No comment can be made about the failure of the defendant to take the stand and no inferences drawn from the fact that he did not do so.[36] Thus, the state's attorney cannot say, before the jury, "If he is innocent, why doesn't he take the stand and say so?"

A defendant *may* take the stand in his own defense. If he does, he is subject to cross-examination just as any other witness and his testimony may be discredited in the same way.[37] Since cross-examination may be broader than direct examination, the defendant is unable to tell just the parts of his story he wants the jury to hear and conceal the rest. Once he takes the stand, the state can get all the facts surrounding the events that he has testified to.

PROCEEDINGS AT THE CLOSE OF THE EVIDENCE

Instructions to the Jury. The jury decides the facts, but the court decides the law. Therefore, the court must instruct the jury in the law applicable to the facts in the case. For example, if the defense is insanity, the judge must instruct the jury as to how insanity is determined in that state—whether by the M'Naghten Rule, the Irresistible Impulse Rule, the Durham Rule, or the Model Penal Code formulation. Of course, the judge does not just say, "You must follow the M'Naghten Rule,"—

from attempting to establish at a trial that evidence introduced by the people of a pre-trial statement made by him should be disregarded by the jury or other trier of the facts on the ground that such statement was involuntarily made within the meaning of section 60.45. Even though the issue of the admissibility of such evidence was not submitted to the court, or was determined adversely to the defendant upon motion, the defendant may adduce trial evidence and otherwise contend that the statement was involuntarily made. In the case of a jury trial, the court must submit such issue to the jury under instructions to disregard such evidence upon a finding that the statement was involuntarily made. McKinney's N.Y.Criminal Procedure Law, § 710.70.

36. Chapman v. California, 386 U.S. 18, 87 S.Ct. 824, 17 L.Ed.2d 705 (1966), reh. den. 386 U.S. 987, 87 S.Ct. 1283, 18 L.Ed.2d 241.

37. Including after admitting into evidence a confession given without the Miranda Warning which contradicts his testimony on the stand. See fn. 32 *supra*.

he carefully states the M'Naghten Rule as it applies to the facts in the case.

Instructions to the jury are prepared by the judge and the attorneys in the case after all the evidence has been received and both the prosecution and the defense have "rested," (i. e., completed the introduction of evidence). The prosecution and the defense each draw up the instructions that they want given to the jury, applying their theory of the case to the facts. The judge chooses from these offered instructions or may prepare his own. The instructions are written out, signed by the judge, and read by the judge to the jury. The jury later takes the set of written instructions into the jury room with them to guide them in their deliberations.

Arguments to the Jury. The arguments to the jury follow the giving of jury instructions by the court. The order of argument in a criminal trial is fixed by the law of the state; the usual sequence is for the state to present part of its argument, the defense to present its argument, and then the state to present the final argument. The argument of each side is an attempt to persuade the jury toward a favorable verdict. The state prosecutor will carefully sum up the facts and discuss the instructions of the court, giving them an interpretation favorable to the state. He may also call upon the jurors to do their duty as citizens and punish the defendant who committed such a heinous crime. The defense attorney will recapitulate the evidence favorable to the defendant, criticize the witnesses for the state and show how they should not be believed, and will interpret the facts and the instructions to the jury in the way most likely to result in a verdict of not guilty. The defense will almost surely call upon the jurors to do their duty as citizens and give this poor, erring defendant another chance to become a good citizen. Closing arguments to a jury can be works of art on both sides, and to many people, they constitute the high point of any criminal trial.

Charging the Jury. At the close of the argument, the judge charges the jury to retire to the jury room and well and truly consider the facts of the case, the instruction of the court, and the argument of counsel, thereupon to return a just verdict. The court will instruct the jury on the possible verdicts, and give them a written form for each verdict, the appropriate one to be signed by the foreman and returned to the court after agreement has been reached. The usual forms of verdict in a criminal case are "Guilty" and "Not Guilty," though the jury in a particular case may have an option of deciding on the degree of the offense. In such case it will be given alternative forms of the guilty verdict for Murder in the First Degree, Murder in the Second Degree, and Manslaughter, together with the form for the verdict of "Not Guilty." Again the foreman will sign the appropriate verdict. A verdict of "Not Guilty by Reason of Insanity" may also be a possible verdict in the case, depending upon the defense and the evidence introduced to support it. If this is true, the jury will be supplied a form for returning this verdict.

After the judge has charged the jury, the jurors are put into the custody of the bailiff, and will remain sequestered (isolated from other people) until they reach a verdict, or until it becomes apparent that they are not able to reach a verdict and are discharged by the court. Some juries are sequestered throughout the entire trial, depending upon the nature of the case; others are sequestered only after the close of the evidence. The jurors "retire" under the custody of the bailiff to a jury room to deliberate on their verdict. They take with them the pleadings in the case, the instructions to the jury, and usually any exhibits admitted into evidence. If at any time they want to refresh their memory about the testimony of any witness, they may ask the court reporter to give them a transcript of his testimony on the point in question. The jury sometimes asks for additional instructions, or asks the court to further explain instructions already given by the court. In such case, the judge and the attorneys work out a new set of instructions, which are taken to the jury by the bailiff.

All communications between the jury and the court are through the bailiff—no juror is permitted to leave the jury room. (In small towns, however, where there are no facilities for preparation of meals, the jury is taken at meal-time to a public restaurant. They remain in the custody of the bailiff, whose duty it is to see that they are not approached by any person not a juror and that they do not receive material or communications of any kind which might influence their verdict.) Jury quarters customarily provide sleeping arrangements for both male and female jurors in case their deliberations are prolonged.

The Deliberations of the Jury. The duty of the jury is to consider the facts and the law of the case and arrive at a verdict, which must be unanimous. The foreman of the jury, chosen by the jury itself (or sometimes automatically the first juror accepted by both the state and the defense) frequently begins the deliberation by taking a vote of the jury. The vote may on rare occasions result in an immediate unanimous verdict. The usual situation, however, is that the first vote discloses that the jury is divided; some voting "guilty" and some "not guilty." Discussions then go on back and forth between the members of the jury, with votes being taken periodically, until the jury finally votes unanimously one way or another. If the jury cannot reach agreement after prolonged deliberations, they report this fact to the court. The court usually instructs them to stay for another stated period and keep trying. If at the end of this time they still have not reached a verdict, there is a "hung jury." The members of a hung jury come back into court and are dismissed by the judge. If the defendant is to be convicted, he must be re-tried. Sometimes he is released after a hung jury because the state decides that if it couldn't convict him the first time, it probably can't do it the second time around. Jury deliberations, at least in theory, are secret.

In some states, juries are charged not only with deciding on guilt or innocence but also must fix the sentence. This practice is particularly wide-spread in capital cases where the death penalty may be imposed. We will discuss jury sentencing in a succeeding chapter.

The American Bar Association Standards Relating to Fair Trial and Free Press. The American Bar Association Project on Minimum Standards for Criminal Justice has developed standards[38] which seek to insure the defendant a fair trial by preventing the kind of news media coverage that "tries" a defendant in the press, intimidates or influences witnesses, or makes the selection of an impartial trial jury difficult, if not impossible. Restrictions are placed upon the attorneys and upon the law enforcement and judicial employees in criminal cases.

These restrictions severely limit the amount of information which can be released about a criminal case prior to or during trial. Information is not to be released about the prior criminal

38. American Bar Association Project on Minimum Standards for Criminal Justice, *Standards Relating to Fair Trial and Free Press*, New York: Office of Criminal Justice Project, Approved Draft, 1968.

record of the accused; the existence or contents of any confession or admission by the defendant; the results of any examination (as for example, a polygraph test); or about the identity, testimony, or credibility of a witness. A proposal to give the judge in the case the power to punish for contempt for improper disclosure of information about the defendant or the conduct of the trial is a matter of continuing controversy, particularly by reporters and other members of the news media who see the regulations set up as having a chilling effect on the "public's right to know" what is going on in law enforcement and in the courts of their community. As finally adopted, the *Standards* seek to strike a fair balance between the Constitutional guarantees of a free trial and a free press, one of the main objectives being to protect the jury from proper influences.

Return of the Verdict. After the jury has reached an agreement on the verdict, the jury comes back into the court room. The judge, the attorneys for the state and the defense, and the defendant must be present. The judge inquires of the jurors as to whether or not they have reached a verdict. The jurors nod or reply, "We have, your honor." The bailiff goes to the foreman of the jury, takes from him the written verdict, which has been signed by the foreman and brought into court, and presents the verdict to the judge. The judge reads the verdict, and hands it back to the bailiff to be read aloud in court, or reads the verdict himself from the bench. The verdict will say, "We, the jury, duly impaneled and sworn, find the defendant guilty as charged," or, "We, the jury, duly impaneled and sworn, do find the defendant 'Not Guilty,'" or whatever particular form of verdict has been agreed upon by the jurors.

If the verdict of the jury is "Not Guilty," the defendant is immediately released from custody. If the verdict is "Guilty," the defendant is kept in custody. Attorneys for a defendant found guilty customarily make certain motions to the court after return of the verdict which the court may take under advisement, or the judge may then and there set the time for sentencing. Sentencing takes place several days after the verdict, the exact time depending, among other things, on whether or not the court requires a pre-sentence investigation and the condition of the court docket. However, no prolonged period is permitted to elapse between return of verdict and sentencing.

Conviction. At the end of every criminal trial there are three separate and distinct steps—the verdict or plea of guilty, the judgment of the court, and the sentence. The verdict is returned by the jury; the judgment is the judgment of the court as to guilt or innocence based upon the verdict or plea; and the sentence fixes the punishment after a plea of guilty or finding of guilt.

Just which of these three steps constitutes "conviction" is a matter of some controversy. The problem is important because the defendant loses certain rights on conviction which he may never regain. At common law, the defendant was said to be "convicted" when the jury returned a verdict of guilty. Some authorities maintain that this is the rule today and that a man is convicted upon entry of plea of guilty or upon the return of the verdict of guilty. Other legal scholars maintain that there is no conviction until the verdict or plea are accepted and the judge makes a finding of guilt. Still others maintain that there is no conviction until sentence is pronounced.

The problem is related to the old common law "bills of attainder" which are forbidden in our Constitution. Under the bills of attainder, a man's property was taken when he was convicted of treason against the king. However, though guilt was decided by the verdict, attainder did not take place until the judge joined in the finding of guilt and ordered the attainder. Since many of the penalties for treason did not attach until after the court signed the bill of attainder, the reasoning was that the concurrence of the judge in the finding of guilt was necessary to constitute a conviction.

The question has arisen in modern times in cases where something interrupts the three-step sequence, as where the verdict is returned, but the judge postpones the adjudication of guilt and sentencing. For example, suppose a medical board attempts to revoke the license of a doctor who has plead guilty to a felony but who has not been sentenced, on the grounds that he has been "convicted" of the crime. The doctor may maintain that there is no "conviction" since the court order which adjudged him guilty has not been signed and sentence has not been imposed. Though the question does not arise frequently, the answer to it may be of considerable importance to the defendant.

APPEAL OF THE CONVICTION

Though there is no Constitutional right to appeal,[39] the laws of most states provide for an appeal of a conviction from the lower criminal courts to a court of general jurisdiction, and from a court of general jurisdiction to an intermediate appellate court or the highest court in the state. In the federal system, the appeal goes from the federal District Courts to the United States Courts of Appeals. Judgments of three judge District Courts declaring state laws unconstitutional go from the District Court directly to the United States Supreme Court. Certain cases may be appealed from the United States Courts of Appeals and from the highest courts in a state to the United States Supreme Court. As we have seen, however, the great majority of cases heard by the United States Supreme Court are heard on a writ of certiorari (writ of review) which is not, strictly speaking, an appeal. An appeal lies as a matter of right; whether or not the United States Supreme Court will review a case on application for writ of certiorari is discretionary with the Supreme Court.

The grounds and procedures for appeal of a conviction vary from state to state. Appeals from lower criminal courts to a court of general jurisdiction are characterized by the fact that on such appeals there is a trial *de novo*, which means that the court of general jurisdiction swears witnesses and hears evidence as though the case were before it on original jurisdiction. Appeals from courts of general jurisdictions to the higher appellate courts are on the record (this is why such courts are called "courts of record") and except in rare cases the appellate court does not hear witnesses and consider new evidence.[40]

39. Griffin v. Illinois, 351 U.S. 12, 76 S.Ct. 585, 100 L.Ed. 891 (1956), reh. den. 351 U.S. 958, 76 S.Ct. 844, 100 L.Ed. 1480.

This holding was applied to juveniles in the case of In re Gault where it was held that a juvenile did not have a Constitutional right to appeal. However, this right is granted to the juvenile in many states. Appeals from a judgment in juvenile court usually lie to a court of *civil* appeals.

40. In California, criminal appeals lie from the justice of the peace and municipal courts to the superior court. Appeals from the superior court go to the District Courts of Appeal, except in cases involving the death sentence, in which an appeal goes automatically to the Supreme Court. Appeal also lies from the District Court of Appeal to the Supreme Court of California.

In Texas, criminal appeals go from the justice and corporation courts

Higher appellate courts have authority to affirm the decision below, to reverse it, or to remand it back to the trial court for a new trial in accordance with the rules announced by the appellate court. The remand is the most frequent disposition by an appellate court. In a few states, the appellate court has a right to modify a sentence by changing the form (for example, from commitment to probation) or to reduce the term. The American Bar Association Standards for Criminal Justice recommend that this authority over sentencing be given generally to higher appellate courts.

Though there is no Constitutional right to appeal, if a state sets up appeal courts and procedures for appeal, the right must be available on an equal basis to all persons convicted in a lower court. Thus, it has been held that the state must furnish a free transcript and counsel on appeal to an indigent defendant.[41]

to the county courts. Appeals from the county courts and district courts go to the Court of Criminal Appeals, which is the court of last resort in criminal cases. The Supreme Court of Texas does not hear criminal appeals, but does hear appeals from a juvenile court.

41. Griffin v. Illinois, 351 U.S. 12, 76 S.Ct. 585, 100 L.Ed. 891 (1956), reh. den. 351 U.S. 958, 76 S.Ct. 844, 100 L.Ed. 1480.

Douglas v. California, 372 U.S. 353, 83 S.Ct. 814, 9 L.Ed.2d 811 (1963), reh. den. 373 U.S. 905, 83 S.Ct. 1288, 10 L.Ed.2d 200.

Anders v. California, 386 U.S. 738, 87 S.Ct. 1396, 18 L.Ed.2d 493 (1967), reh. den. 388 U.S. 924, 87 S.Ct. 2094, 18 L.Ed.2d 1377.

Chapter IX

SENTENCING AND CORRECTION

SENTENCING

No aspect of the criminal justice process is more crucial to the defendant than sentencing. It is the sentence that determines where and how long he will be under correctional supervision. As we shall see, his "real sentence" is a function of fixed legislative penalties, his individual sentence, and the operation of good-time statutes, and of suspended sentence and probation and parole laws.

Legislative Fixing of Penalties. We learned in Chapter II that if no penalty is provided for the commission of the prohibited act, there is no criminal offense. The illegal conduct is defined in the statutes passed by the legislature, and the legislature also fixes the permissible penalties. In the usual situation, the legislature does this by providing penalties for each offense as it is defined. Thus, the statutes defining burglary set out the permissible penalties for burglary, those defining arson set out the permissible penalties for arson, and so on.[1]

The legislature may fix only maximum penalties, in which case the language of the statute may be "Whoever shall violate the provisions of this act shall, upon conviction, be confined in the penitentiary for not more than ten years." Or the legislature may fix a minimum and maximum penalty. In this case the language may read: "One guilty of the offense defined herein shall be confined in the penitentiary not less than two nor more than twelve years," or "counterfeiting is punishable by imprisonment

1. This is the pattern in California, Texas, and Illinois.

New York classifies felonies into Class A, B, C, D, E felonies, with penalties ranging from a maximum of four years for a Class E felony to life imprisonment for a Class A felony. McKinney's N.Y.Penal Law, § 70.00.

Misdemeanors are classified as Class A and B misdemeanors, or are unclassified. A violation of an ordinance is punishable by fine only, and no term of imprisonment may be imposed. McKinney's N.Y.Penal Law, § 70.15.

in the State Prison for not less than one nor more than fourteen years."[2] The statute may provide that "the punishment shall be death or by confinement in the penitentiary for any term not less than five years," or state flatly, "One convicted of this offense shall be sentenced to a term of ten years in the penitentiary."

In the case of misdemeanors, the penalty may be fine, or a jail term or both, and a typical statute will say, "Misdemeanor theft shall be punished by imprisonment in jail not exceeding two years, and by fine not exceeding five hundred dollars, or by such imprisonment without a fine;" or it might read, "Misdemeanor theft shall be punished by imprisonment in jail not exceeding one year, and by fine not exceeding one thousand dollars, or both."

The exact language adopted with reference to each offense fixes the limits of the penalties for that offense. In some cases, the language will permit a judge to sentence for a term between the limits;[3] in other cases, the language is such that the judge must sentence for the exact limits stated in the statute.[4] Under this system the penalties are fixed crime by crime, thus will vary crime by crime. Also, penalty provisions are frequently changed. If a state is harassed by an extraordinary number of robberies, the penalty for armed robbery will be increased. If public opinion changes about an offense, as for example, the possession of marijuana, the penalties may be decreased, or the offense changed from a felony to a misdemeanor.

It is difficult to find a consistent pattern in sentencing provisions that are set out crime by crime. The Model Penal Code has adopted an altogether different system by classifying all offenses into first, second, or third degree felonies, misdemeanors or petty misdemeanors, and then providing penalties for each type of offense.[5] Thus, all offenses classified as first degree felonies

2. West's Ann.Cal.Penal Code, § 478.

3. In New York, the Court imposes a maximum term. A minimum term is at least one year. For Class A felonies, the minimum may be fixed by the Court between fifteen and twenty years. For Class B felonies, the Court may fix a minimum sentence at not more than one-third of the maximum. In all other cases, the minimum is fixed by the State Board of Parole. McKinney's Con.Laws of N.Y., Ann., Penal, § 70.00.

4. In California, the judge has no authority to fix the term or duration of a period of imprisonment. West's Ann.Penal Code, § 1168. See discussion of California sentencing practices, *infra.*

5. New York also classifies felonies and fixes penalties according to classification. See fn. 1, *supra.*

must be sentenced according to the penalty for first degree felonies (see table on Page 153), and for second degree felonies, according to the penalties for second degree felonies, and so on. Increased penalties are provided for in case of aggravated offenses, but these are uniform for aggravated offenses of the same classification. The virtue of this system is that all crimes of a similar degree of seriousness carry the same permissible penalties. If the legislature wants to increase or decrease the penalty for a specific offense, it must do so by changing its classification, not by just changing the specific penalty, unless, of course, it changes the penalties for all offenses of the same class. This keeps the general sentencing pattern consistent and prevents the distortions in penalties which occur when penalties are fixed crime by crime.

Enhancement and Habitual Criminal Statutes. The statutes of many states provide for enhanced (increased) sentences for offenders who repeat the same or similar offenses. An offense which is a misdemeanor may become a felony when repeated. In several states, D.W.I. (Driving While Intoxicated) first offense, is a misdemeanor; the second and subsequent D.W.I. offenses are felonies. The statutes may provide that the penalty for a second felony or misdemeanor shall be double that for the first offense, and an offense repeated a third time may carry triple the first offense penalty.[6] Many states have habitual criminal statutes which require mandatory life imprisonment for the offender who has been convicted of two or more felonies, or two or more felonies of a certain related type.[7] Studies show that habitual criminal statutes are not used as frequently as might be expected. Judges and juries are reluctant to send a man to prison for life. Thus, even when the indictment contains an "habitual count," this count may be dropped by the prosecution in return for a plea of

6. New York provides that the penalties for a Class A felony may be imposed on a persistent felony offender. McKinney's N.Y.Penal Law, § 70.10.

California requires life imprisonment of habitual criminals for a specified list of offenses. West's Ann. Penal Code, § 644.

Texas has mandatory life imprisonment upon the second conviction for a non-capital offense (Vernon's Ann.Penal Code, Art. 64) or third conviction on a non-capital felony (Art. 63). Penalties may be doubled for second convictions of certain offenses or quadrupled for third conviction of some misdemeanor offenses (Art. 61).

7. The exact combinations of repeated offenses for which penalties may be increased or habitual criminal sentences imposed differ from state to state.

guilty. "Pleading down" from "habitual" is a bargain most defendants are glad to make.

The Sentencing Authority. Sentencing is generally regarded as the province of the judge, and many judges consider this to be one of the most important (and most awesome) of their responsibilities. However, in some states, the duty to sentence is placed upon the jury; in others, the defendant may choose between judge and jury sentencing, or has a choice in all but capital cases. The law may permit the defendant to choose between judge and jury sentencing except in capital cases where the state has made known before the trial that it will demand the death penalty. Thus, in many states only the jury may sentence to death. A third type of sentencing authority is an administrative body, such as the California Adult Authority.[8]

Whatever the nature of the sentencing authority, all sentences imposed must be within the limits set by the legislature for the particular offense. The sentencing decision must fix both type and length of sentence. If probation is allowed for certain offenses, the judge or jury must decide whether to grant probation or to sentence to the penitentiary or jail. (The statutes in some states provide for misdemeanor as well as felony probation.) If probation is denied, then the length of incarceration in the penal

8. In California, a defendant is sentenced by the court to be imprisoned in a state prison and committed to the custody of the Director of Corrections. The court, however, does not fix the term or duration of the period of imprisonment. West's Ann.Penal Code, § 1168.

Sentence is fixed by the Adult Authority which exercises the powers and duties formerly exercised by the Board of Prison Terms and Paroles and the Advisory Pardon Board. West's Ann.Penal Code, § 3000.

The Adult Authority has powers to determine and redetermine sentences. West's Ann.Penal Code, § 3020:

> In the case of all persons heretofore or hereafter sentenced under the provisions of Section 1168 of this code, the Adult Authority may determine and redetermine, after the actual commencement of imprisonment, what length of time, if any, such person shall be imprisoned, unless the sentence be sooner terminated by commutation or pardon by the Governor of the State.

The term shall not exceed the maximum or be less than the minimum term of imprisonment provided by law for the public offense of which the person was convicted. West's Ann.Cal.Penal Code, § 3023.

Other sections of the statute provide for notices to and interviews with the prisoner when fixing sentence, and minimum terms are provided for armed or prior offenders. West's Ann.Cal.Penal Code, §§ 3022–3024.

institution must be decided upon. An administrative sentencing body such as the one in California usually has no power to grant probation, but is limited to fixing the length of incarceration between the maximum and minimum terms set by the court or by statute.

Definite and Indeterminate Sentences. A definite sentence (sometimes called a "fixed" sentence) is for a stated number of years. An indeterminate sentence has a maximum and minimum term. "Confinement in the penitentiary for a term of 10 years" is a definite sentence. A true indeterminate sentence would be from one day to life, but in practice, indeterminate sentences have minimum and maximum terms of years. "Confinement in the penitentiary for not less than two years nor more than twelve years" is a form of indeterminate sentence.

The definite form of sentence is used in the federal courts and in the courts of many of the states. The indeterminate sentence was adopted in other states as a means of making sentencing more flexible and to give the judge more leeway in individualizing sentences.[9] The theory was that sentences should fit the criminal, not just the crime. It was also assumed that the correctional authorities would know when a man had been "rehabilitated" and was ready for release. Under a fixed form of sentence he could not be released until the definite sentence had been served, a restriction which would not exist in an indeterminate sentence.

Many authorities believe that the indeterminate form of sentence has not worked out as anticipated. As a matter of law, the

9. Texas uses a form of indeterminate sentence that in legal effect is a sentence for the maximum term imposed. Vernon's Ann.Penal Code, Art. 42.09.

In New York, both indeterminate and fixed sentences are imposed. The commitment for a felony is by an indeterminate sentence to the state department of corrections (now the Department of Correctional Services). The commitment on a definite sentence is to the county or regional correctional institution. McKinney's N.Y.Penal Law, § 70.20. Definite sentences are used for Class A and B misdemeanors, § 70.15.

In Illinois, the sentence is to the Illinois State Penitentiary or to the Illinois State Reformatory for Women, except males under 17 and females under 18, who are committed to the Illinois Youth Commission. Smith-Hurd Ann.Stat. ch. 38, Crim.Law & Proc., § 119-2. All sentences to the penitentiary are for an indeterminate term; all sentences of imprisonment other than to the penitentiary are for a definite term not to exceed one year. Smith-Hurd Ann.Stat., ch. 38, § 1-7.

For California sentences, see fn. 8, *supra*.

indeterminate sentence is a sentence for the maximum term since a man may be incarcerated for the full term. Many judges impose a high minimum sentence to prevent parole, though this was not what was intended by those who support indeterminate sentences. Eligibility for parole in states with an indeterminate form of sentence is usually tied to the minimum sentence. Thus, by imposing a high minimum sentence, a man's eligibility for parole can be drastically postponed. In definite sentence states, and in some indeterminate sentence states, parole eligibility occurs after a fixed proportion of the maximum sentence has been served.

Concurrent and Consecutive Sentences. An offender may be charged and tried for more than one offense at the same time, or, as the lawyers express it, may be tried on more than one count. If found guilty, he must be sentenced on each count. In most states, the court has the option to make the sentences concurrent or consecutive.[10] Concurrent sentences run simultaneously; consecutive sentences must be served in sequence. (Inmates speak of concurrent sentences as "CC" and consecutive sentences as "stacked.")

Let us suppose that a defendant is sentenced on one count to a term of five years in the state penitentiary and is given a three year term in the penitentiary on a second count. If the sentences are concurrent, both will begin to run the day he is committed to the institution. At the end of three years he has served the shorter of the two sentences; at the end of two more years, he has served both sentences, and is entitled to release. If the sentences are consecutive, he will serve the full five year sentence first; when the sentence is served, the other sentence will begin to run and his total time in prison will be eight years. Understandably, prisoners prefer "CC" to "stacked" sentences. Correctional authorities strongly recommend concurrent sentences, and this is the position adopted by the Model Penal Code.

Section 7.06 Multiple Sentences; Concurrent and Consecutive Terms.

(1) *Sentences of Imprisonment for More Than One Crime.* When multiple sentences of imprisonment are imposed on a

10. In California, the length of time the prisoner must serve on cumulative or consecutive sentences is determined by the Adult Authority after he has served six months of his first sentence. West's Ann. Penal Code, § 3021.

defendant for more than one crime, including a crime for which a previous suspended sentence or sentence of probation has been revoked, such multiple sentences shall run concurrently or consecutively as the Court determines at the time of sentence, except that:

(a) a definite and an indefinite term shall run concurrently and both sentences shall be satisfied by service of the indefinite term; and

(b) the aggregate of consecutive definite terms shall not exceed one year; and

(c) the aggregate of consecutive indefinite terms shall not exceed in minimum or maximum length the longest extended term authorized for the highest grade and degree of crime for which any of the sentences was imposed; and

(d) not more than one sentence for an extended term shall be imposed.

(2) *Sentences of Imprisonment Imposed at Different Times.* When a defendant who has previously been sentenced to imprisonment is subsequently sentenced to another term for a crime committed prior to the former sentence, other than a crime committed while in custody:

(a) the multiple sentences imposed shall so far as possible conform to Subsection (1) of this Section; and

(b) whether the Court determines that the terms shall run concurrently or consecutively, the defendant shall be credited with time served in imprisonment on the prior sentence in determining the permissible aggregate length of the term or terms remaining to be served; and

(c) when a new sentence is imposed on a prisoner who is on parole, the balance of the parole term on the former sentence shall be deemed to run during the period of the new imprisonment.

Individualizing Sentences. As we have seen, there is conflict and inconsistency in our reasons for applying criminal sanctions because we attempt to achieve the objectives of revenge, incapacitation, deterrence, and rehabilitation all at the same time. Sentences for punishment should fit the crime; sentences for rehabilitation should fit the criminal—so the theories go. The problem is that even though the offense is the same, the circumstances vary, and devising a sentence that fits the criminal is an extremely difficult task.

Let us consider variations in the circumstances of the offense. In a single term there may be five defendants before the court charged with kidnapping. No. 1 is a woman whose baby died, and who took another woman's baby from the hospital. No. 2 is a young man whose girl-friend said she was breaking up with him. He put her in a car and drove her around for 24 hours trying to persuade her to change her mind, while her frantic parents tried to locate them and the girl did everything she could to get away. No. 3 is a divorced man who took his own child from its mother who had legal custody and refused to tell the mother where the child was. No. 4 is a kidnapper for ransom who kept a young woman buried in a box fitted with air tubes for breathing in order to make it impossible for searchers to find her, and who demanded $200,000 from her wealthy father. No. 5 is a woman accomplice of the kidnapper for ransom. She assisted in the kidnapping because she was in love with the kidnapper and was also threatened by him. She did everything she could to keep the kidnapped girl alive when it was possible for her to do so.

The offenses charged are identical—kidnapping. If the penalty must fit the crime, without any other consideration, all must receive identical sentences. Because of the heinousness of the crime of kidnapping for ransom, which is what the legislature had in mind when fixing the penalty, the sentence may be death or life imprisonment. However, by making the penalty section read, "Not less than four years nor more than life," the legislature itself recognized that not all kidnapping offenses look alike, nor should all kidnapping offenders receive the same penalty. A sliding scale of penalties requires that the sentences be individualized taking the circumstances of the offense and of the offender into consideration.[11]

11. Individualized sentences are of course different or "disparate." They are not, as a result, unjust. In fact, the contrary is true. The phrase "disparity of sentencing" is properly used to mean arbitrary and unjust sentences, or different sentences imposed for the same offenses, committed under similar circumstances, upon defendants of similar characteristics, particularly with reference to previous criminal history. See discussion of "disparity in sentencing," *infra.*

The Pre-Sentence Report. While the circumstances of the offense will usually be revealed in the course of the trial, this information will be limited after a plea of guilty. Also, because of the rules of evidence, essential data about the defendant is not admissible in the trial, as for example, his previous criminal record. This information is presented to the court in the form of a pre-sentence report (called the social history report in juvenile court).

Not all courts use a pre-sentence report, and a pre-sentence report is not prepared for a jury, though the jury may receive information about the defendant's criminal record for use only in the sentencing decision. The pre-sentence report is mandatory before sentencing for a felony in federal courts, and is required in many states. For example, in New York, a pre-sentence investigation must be made in any case where a person is convicted of a felony and also before sentencing on a misdemeanor if the sentence is to be probation, to a reformatory, or in excess of 90 days. In other states, however, the pre-sentence report is optional with the judge and its use may vary within a state from no use at all to careful investigation prior to every felony sentence. In some instances, the statute ties the pre-sentence report to probation, requiring that it be made before a felony offender can be placed on probation or, as in New York, before a misdemeanant can be placed on probation. In fact, the pre-sentence report has its historical origins in investigations in connection with probation decisions.

The contents of pre-sentence reports also vary. A good pre-sentence report will contain information about the defendant's age, education, physical and mental condition, previous employment record, his version of the offense (he may not have taken the stand during the trial), the version of the offense given by any accomplice, his family relationships, and the attitude of the community toward him and his offense. An important part of the pre-sentence report is a statement of the defendant's previous criminal record, particularly any prior convictions for felonies or serious misdemeanors. Arrest records and juvenile offense records are often included.

A pre-sentence report is made by a probation officer attached to the court. The probation officer interviews the defendant for basic data, and then checks school and employment records, and reports of any physical or psychiatric examinations. He talks to members of the defendant's family and persons in the community whose attitudes would be important in determining whether or not the defendant could succeed on probation, if that is being considered. The defendant's previous criminal record is checked through F.B.I. and state crime records, with questionable information verified as far as possible.

The Sentencing Decision. Many factors, both legal and extra-legal, enter into the sentencing decision. The legal factors include the nature of the offense; the number of counts with which the defendant is currently charged; his previous criminal record; and such factors as representation by counsel, whether guilt has been determined by verdict or plea, and the sentencing alternatives available to the judge. Extra-legal factors include race, age, sex, financial condition, and status in the community of the defendant, and the prejudices of the presiding judge.

Not all of the factors bear the same weight. Studies by Green [12] and others have shown that in determining type of sentence (probation or incarceration), the nature of the offense is of prime importance, followed closely by the number of counts and the previous criminal record, with prior felony arrests being the most important. The same legal factors affect length (minimum and maximum term) of sentence as shown in studies conducted by the Institute of Contemporary Corrections at Sam Houston State University.[13] As to the importance of non-legal factors, particularly race, on the sentence pronounced, there is much

12. Edward Green, *Judicial Attitudes in Sentencing*, New York: Macmillan & Co., Ltd., 1961.

13. Arland Rodney Allbright, "A Statistical Study of Sentence Disparity of Felons Convicted in District Courts in the State of Texas for Possession of Narcotics or Narcotic Drugs" (1969).

Bruce Alan Bales, "Factors Affecting Sentence Length of Convicted Burglars" (1970).

Robert Carl Jefferies, "A Statistical Study of Disparity of Sentence Among Robbers Received at the Texas Department of Corrections During 1965, 1966, and 1967" (1969).

Marcus E. Kenter, Jr., "Factors Related to Commutation of Sentences of Capital Cases" (1969).

James K. Pentico, "A Study of the Sentencing Factors Associated with the Offense of Rape" (1970). [Ethnic origin of the victim was found to be a significant factor in this study.]

Gerald Stewart, "A Statistical Study in Disparity of Sentencing in Cases of Forgery and Passing Forged Instrument in Texas" (1969).

All of the above studies appear in unpublished Master's Theses of degree candidates at Sam Houston State University in Huntsville, Texas.

controversy. The problem is referred to as "disparity in sentencing."

Disparity in Sentencing. Differences in sentences do not mean disparity in sentencing. Whether we believe the penalty should fit the offense or the offender, differing circumstances in the offense and different offenders of necessity result in different sentences—otherwise there is no such thing as individualized justice. However, differences in sentences which rest upon arbitrary and capricious grounds are unjust and are unacceptable in a democratic society.

Disparity of sentencing which is socially unacceptable means dissimilar sentences for defendants whose characteristics and crimes are similar. The extent of disparate sentencing in the sense of imposing unjust and arbitrary sentences for the same offense or similar offenders is a matter of some controversy. Many authorities maintain that matters of race, sex, social status and prejudices of the presiding judge produce wide variations in sentences that cannot be logically explained by the differences in the nature of the offense and the characteristics of the offender. Other more sophisticated studies, using the method of linear regression analysis, tend to show that if all other factors are kept constant, race, sex, and the sentencing judge have little or no significant impact on sentence.

Studies conducted by the Institute of Contemporary Corrections at Sam Houston State University [14] show, for example, that if offense, previous criminal record, number of counts, and some thirty-two other variables that may affect sentence are kept constant, no disparity of sentencing attributable to race alone can be shown. A similar result was obtained as to sex (which means that the shorter sentences received by women as a group is a function of less serious offenses and shorter criminal histories rather than the result of a sex differential in sentencing). The Institute studies were limited to length of sentence and to offenders in the Texas penitentiary system.

We cannot attempt here to completely analyze the problem of disparity of sentencing. Certainly to the degree that sentences are imposed for reasons other than the nature of the offense and the relevant characteristics of the individual offender, we must eradicate the practice in the criminal justice system. Race, sex,

14. *Ibid.*

social status, and financial condition of the defendant, and the prejudices of individual judges do not provide an acceptable basis for differences in sentences. However, it is equally important to understand that many factors enter into a sentencing decision and to have knowledge about these factors before judging the fairness of a particular sentencing decision, or sentencing decisions affecting a certain class or group of offenders.

If on the same day, a white man, a Negro, and a Mexican-American are sentenced for armed robbery, and the white man receives five years, the Mexican-American ten years, and the Negro fifteen years, it is a mistake to automatically assume that the Negro got a long sentence because he was a Negro, that the Mexican-American got a long sentence because he was Mexican-American, and that the white man got off easy because he was white. If the Negro had a longer criminal record than the Mexican-American, and the white man was a first offender, that fact alone could explain the differences in sentences. Many factors about the circumstances of the offense might also show that the different sentences were entirely just. It should never be assumed without investigation that arbitrary disparity of sentencing exists, and mere differences in sentences must not be taken to prove unjust disparity in sentencing. The criminal justice system does not aspire to uniform sentences for each offense and all offenders—the important consideration is that the sentences be individualized on a fair and just basis taking into account both the offense and the offender.

Sentencing Dispositions. The choices when sentencing an adult or juvenile offender are dependent primarily on the sentencing structure set up by the legislature and the sentencing alternatives available to the sentencing authority. With reference to adult offenders, the basic option is as to type of sentence, probation or incarceration, unless, of course, the defendant is by law not eligible for probation consideration because of type of offense, length of sentence fixed in the judgment, or previous criminal record. The second option is length of sentence, meaning in most instances, both minimum and maximum terms of incarceration. Here again, the options may be limited by mandatory minimum sentences, or mandatory maximum and minimum sentences, or other requirements in the legislative sentencing provisions.[15]

15. In California, as we have seen, the court does not fix the period of incarceration. This is done by the Adult Authority. See fn. 8,

The court's options may be also somewhat circumscribed because of agreements reached in plea negotiations, though as we have seen, the court is not bound to follow such agreements—the only requirement being that if it does not, the defendant has a right to withdraw his plea of guilty. Legal scholars and criminologists are urging that the court be provided with a wider range of sentencing dispositions, including the right to suspend sentence.

The American Bar Association Standards Relating to Sentencing Alternatives and Procedures. The problems of sentencing have long been of concern to judges, lawyers, correctional officials and legal scholars. The American Bar Project on Minimum Standards for Criminal Justice undertook a thorough study of present sentencing practices, and in the *Standards Relating to Sentencing Alternatives and Procedures* made far-reaching recommendations for changes in all aspects of sentencing. These *Standards* will not be immediately adopted by all of the states, but the recommendations made will gradually change sentencing law and practice. We cannot hope here to set out the *Standards* in detail, but we will consider some of the major provisions.

The *Standards* recommend that the authority to determine the sentence should be vested in the trial judge and not in the jury. All crimes should be classified for the purpose of sentencing into categories which reflect substantial differences in gravity; the categories, however, would be few in number. The sentencing court should be provided in all cases with a wide range of alternatives to permit a sentence appropriate for each individual case. The legislature should not specify a mandatory sentence for any sentencing category or for any particular offense, though the legislature would fix maximum penalties.

The sentence imposed in each case should call for the minimum amount of custody or confinement which is consistent with the protection of the public, the gravity of the offense, and the rehabilitative needs of the defendant. Thus, probation is the basic form of sentence. Revision of habitual criminal statutes is proposed, with sentencing under these statutes to be permitted under strictly limited situations. Jail time (credit on the sentence for time spent in jail after arrest and before trial) is to be allowed. Pre-sentence reports are to be used in all cases where incarcera-

supra. The court, however, has the authority to determine type of sentence by granting probation or committing.

tion for one year or more is possible, where the defendant is less than twenty-one years of age, or where the defendant is a first offender.

Sentencing is to be by the judge who presided at the trial or by the judge who accepted the plea. All outstanding convictions should be accommodated for sentencing at one time, and the defendant should be permitted to plead guilty to other offenses he has committed which are within the jurisdiction of the sentencing court. Duties of prosecution and defense attorneys do not cease upon conviction; the attorneys have the duty of assisting the court in the sentencing function.

Sentencing should be as soon as possible after the pre-sentence report is received; the defendant is to have his right to allocution (to speak to the sentence). A pre-sentence conference is provided for as is the right to offer additional evidence on the sentencing issue. A verbatim record of the entire sentencing proceeding must be kept. The sentencing judge is given authority to reduce or modify a sentence to time served, in appropriate cases.

In courts with more than one sentencing judge, meetings of the sentencing judges shall be held regularly to discuss the appropriate disposition of defendants who are then awaiting sentence and to assist the judge who will impose the sentence in reaching a decision. Sentencing institutes are to be held for the purpose of discussing problems related to sentencing, and to develop criteria for the imposition of sentences. New judges are to be given orientation training to familiarize them with sentencing alternatives, the purpose of sentencing and sentence procedures, and the nature of the non-custodial facilities which can be used in sentencing. Provision should be made for regular visits by every sentencing judge to each of the custodial and non-custodial facilities which may be utilized in framing a sentence, and the judge should regularly be informed as to the status of offenders whom they have sentenced.

Appellate Review of Sentences. The laws of most states make no provision for the direct, formal review by a higher court of sentences pronounced by a lower court, though this would provide a method of correcting unjust sentences. Legal practice has been that unless a sentence exceeded the maximum provided by law, or was so grossly inappropriate to the offense as to "shock the conscience" and require the application of the Eighth Amendment guarantees against cruel and unusual punishment, the sentence imposed by a sentencing judge would not be disturbed on appeal. Of course, if a defendant showed sufficient error in the record to require the case to be sent back for a new trial, re-sentencing took place after a second conviction. But absent errors sufficient to send the case back for a new trial, the appellate court would not disturb the sentence.

Scholars of the judicial process, including a great many sentencing judges, have long advocated the establishment in each state of a procedure on appeal which would lead to a review of the sentence alone, and which would permit modification of the sentence by the appellate court without going the route of sending the entire case back for a new trial. These scholars and judges point out both the need and benefits of appellate review of sentences. They note that a prisoner's appeal is frequently taken, not because of the lack of due process in his trial, but because of his dissatisfaction with the sentence. They also note the kind of disparity of sentence that amounts to injustice and arbitrariness. Of what use is it, they say, to give a judge a great many sentencing alternatives and never require him to state just why one alternative was chosen for the particular defendant in preference to another?

Judges of the federal courts, and judges of the state trial and appellate courts, have met together in groups and associations to discuss the problems of sentencing, and many have come to believe that a step forward in the administration of criminal justice would be taken by setting up the procedures for a higher court to review the sentences imposed by a lower one.

The Committee established by the American Bar Association to review sentencing practices and procedures recommended appellate review of sentences, and the *Standards Relating to Sentencing* were adopted in 1968 by the Association.[16]

American Bar Association Standards Relating to Appellate Review of Sentences. The *Standards* provide in principle that judicial review should be available for all sentences imposed where provision is made for review of the conviction. This includes

16. American Bar Association Project on Minimum Standards for Criminal Justice, *Standards Relating to Appellate Review of Sentences* (New York: Office of Criminal Justice Project, Approved Draft, 1968.)

review of sentence imposed after a guilty plea, and review of a sentence imposed by a trial judge, a trial jury, or the two in combination. The *Standards* contemplate that, at least for an initial experimental period, a reasonable limit should be imposed on the length and kind of sentence that should be subject to review. Thus, sentences imposing a small fine or a short jail period would not be subject to review.

The purposes of sentence review are stated in the *Standards* to be: (1) to correct the sentence which is excessive in length, having regard to the nature of the offense, the character of the offender, and the protection of the public interest; (2) to facilitate the rehabilitation of the offender by affording him an opportunity to assert grievances he may have regarding the sentence; (3) to promote respect for law by correcting abuses of the sentencing power and by increasing the fairness of the sentencing process; and (4) to promote the development and application of criteria for sentencing which are both rational and just.

As part of the sentencing procedure, the sentencing judge would be required in every case to state the reasons for selecting the particular sentence imposed. This would normally be done for the record in the presence of the defendant at the time of sentence.

Any court with power to review a conviction would have the power to review a sentence. Review of sentence would be available to the convicted person on the same basis as review of his conviction. The reviewing court would have the power to (1) affirm the sentence under review; (2) substitute for the sentence under review any other disposition available to the reviewing court (except that the sentence could not be increased), or (3) send the case back for further proceedings that could have been conducted prior to the imposition of the sentence (as for example, obtaining a pre-sentence report), and require that the trial court re-sentence the offender on the basis of such further proceedings.

Because of the increased attention being paid to sentencing problems, and the leadership provided by the Bar Association *Standards Relating to Sentencing Alternatives and Procedures* and the *Standards Relating to Appellate Review of Sentence*, many states will reform sentencing law and practice.

PROBATION

Probation is a sentencing alternative which permits the convicted offender to serve his sentence in the community under supervision. "Probation shall mean the release of a convicted defendant by a court under conditions imposed by a court for a specified period during which imposition of sentence is suspended."[17] Probation is in lieu of incarceration, except in a few states which require that the offender serve a short period in jail before probation officially begins. The federal government and almost all of the states provide for felony probation, and many also have provisions for misdemeanor probation.

Probation is a *judicial* act. Probation is granted by the court and can be revoked by the court. During the period of probation, the convicted offender is in the legal custody of the trial court granting probation under the supervision of a probation officer. *Parole,* on the other hand, is an *administrative act* and follows, not precedes, incarceration. The parolee is in the legal custody of the state during parole. Depending on the state law, this may mean in the legal custody of the Division of Corrections, of the sentencing authority, of the institution in which he has previously been incarcerated, or in legal custody of the Parole Board. He serves the remainder of his sentence in the community under the supervision of a parole officer. Parole is revoked by the paroling authority which granted parole. *Pardon* is an *executive act,* which may occur at any point in the criminal process, and does not involve supervision. The person pardoned is released from all legal custody.

Who is Eligible for Probation. The statutes of the state set up the basic eligibility requirements for probation.[18] In a few states,

17. This definition appears in the Uniform Adult Probation and Parole Act in Vernon's Ann.Texas Code Crim.Proc., Art. 42.12A, § 1 (b).

New York penal law provides for both probation and conditional discharge, which is a form of conditional release without supervision. Disposition cannot be made by conditional discharge for persons convicted of Class A or Class B felonies, nor of persons convicted of dangerous drug offenses. See McKinney's Con.Laws of N.Y., Penal § 60.10.

18. In Illinois, persons convicted of a capital offense, the sale of narcotics, or rape, are ineligible for probation. Smith-Hurd Ann.Stat., ch. 38, § 117-1.

In Texas, a person against whom a penalty in excess of ten years is assessed is ineligible for probation.

all defendants are eligible for probation. In others, defendants convicted of certain specified offenses, usually crimes of violence, are not eligible for probation. In still other states, eligibility depends upon the length of the term assessed. A prior felony conviction frequently bars an offender from probation; in other instances, the court has the authority to grant probation notwithstanding a prior felony conviction. In some jurisdictions, a jury may recommend probation and the judge must follow the recommendation; in others, the probation decision is made by the judge alone.

Vernon's Ann.Code Crim.Proc., Art. 42.12, §§ 3, 3b, 3c.

In California, probation cannot be granted to any person who has been convicted of burglary with explosives, rape with force or violence, murder, assault with intent to commit murder, train wrecking, kidnapping, escape from a state prison who was armed at the time of the offense, nor to a defendant who attempted to use a deadly weapon upon a human being, or inflicted great bodily harm or torture, or who has twice previously A persistent felony offender may been convicted of a felony, (or for offense of burglary by explosives, rape with violence, murder, assault with intent to commit murder, and other named offenses, if he has previously been convicted of a felony). West's Ann.Cal.Codes, Penal, § 1203.

In New York, the authorized dispositions include imprisonment or death for Class A felonies, McKinney's Con.Laws of N.Y., Penal § 60.05; probation, §§ 60.10 and 65.00; conditional discharge, §§ 60.10 and 65.05; and unconditional discharge, § 65.20. A narcotic addict or a prostitute may be sentenced to certification to the care and control of the narcotic addiction control commission, § 60.15. A persistent felony offender may be sentenced to imprisonment, § 70.10; young adults (16–21 years) may be given a reformatory sentence, § 75.00. Criteria for granting probation are set out as follows:

1. Criteria. The court may sentence a person to a period of probation upon conviction of any crime other than a Class A felony if the court, having regard to the nature and circumstances of the crime and to the history, character and condition of the defendant, is of the opinion that:

   (a) Institutional confinement of the defendant is not necessary for the protection of the public;

   (b) The defendant is in need of guidance, training or other assistance which, in his case, can be effectively administered through probation supervision; and

   (c) Such disposition is not inconsistent with the ends of justice.

Provided, however, that the court shall not impose a sentence of probation in any case where it sentences a defendant for more than one crime and imposes a sentence of imprisonment for any one of the crimes, or where the defendant is subject to an undischarged indeterminate or reformatory sentence of imprisonment which was imposed at a previous time by a court of this state and has more than one year to run. McKinney's Con.Laws of N.Y., Penal § 65.00(1).

Regardless of the wording of the statute, no defendant has an absolute legal right to receive probation—though he does have a right to be *considered* for probation. Thus, a judge who announced that he would "never grant probation to a drug pusher" was held to have illegally denied the man convicted of selling drugs of his right to be considered for probation on an individual basis. No defendant is required to accept probation.

Correctional authorities strongly recommend that an offender be given probation wherever possible. If he can serve his time in the community, he can continue to take care of his family. He does not lose his job, nor suffer the many harmful effects of incarceration. The Model Penal Code and the American Bar Association *Standards Relating to Sentencing Alternatives and Procedures* both make probation the preferred form of disposition after conviction, thus requiring an affirmative showing to justify incarceration. The criteria for granting and withholding probation as set out in the Model Penal Code are as follows:

Section 7.01 Criteria for Withholding Sentence of Imprisonment and for Placing Defendant on Probation.

(1) The Court shall deal with a person who has been convicted of a crime without imposing sentence of imprisonment unless, having regard to the nature and circumstances of the crime and the history, character and condition of the defendant, it is of the opinion that his imprisonment is necessary for protection of the public because:

(a) there is undue risk that during the period of a suspended sentence or probation the defendant will commit another crime; or

(b) the defendant is in need of correctional treatment that can be provided most effectively by his commitment to an institution; or

(c) a lesser sentence will depreciate the seriousness of the defendant's crime.

(2) The following grounds, while not controlling the direction of the Court, shall be accorded weight in favor of withholding sentence of imprisonment:

(a) the defendant's criminal conduct neither caused nor threatened serious harm;

(b) the defendant did not contemplate that his criminal conduct would cause or threaten serious harm;

(c) the defendant acted under a strong provocation;

(d) there were substantial grounds tending to excuse or justify the defendant's criminal conduct, though failing to establish a defense;

(e) the victim of the defendant's criminal conduct induced or facilitated its commission;

(f) the defendant has compensated or will compensate the victim of his criminal conduct for the damage or injury that he sustained;

(g) the defendant has no history of prior delinquency or criminal activity or has led a law-abiding life for a substantial period of time before the commission of the present crime;

(h) the defendant's criminal conduct was the result of circumstances unlikely to recur;

(i) the character and attitudes of the defendant indicate that he is unlikely to commit another crime;

(j) the defendant is particularly likely to respond affirmatively to probationary treatment;

(k) the imprisonment of the defendant would entail excessive hardship to himself or his dependents.

(3) When a person who has been convicted of a crime is not sentenced to imprisonment, the Court shall place him on probation if he is in need of the supervision, guidance, assistance or direction that the probation service can provide.

Length of Probation. The length of probation is determined by the legislative provisions.[19] Usually probation may not extend

19. In Illinois, the term of probation is not less than six months nor more than five years, which may for good cause be extended for not more than an additional two years. Smith-Hurd Ann.Stat. ch. 38, § 117.1.

In Texas, the term for felony probation may not exceed the penalty assessed. Vernon's Ann.Code Crim. Proc., Art. 42.12.

In New York, periods of probation are as follows:

Unless terminated sooner in accordance with the code of criminal procedure, the period of probation shall be as follows:

(a) For a felony, the period of probation shall be five years;

(b) For a Class A misdemeanor, the period of probation shall be three years;

beyond the time assessed against the individual defendant. However, in some states, and also in misdemeanor probation, the length of the probated term may exceed the term that the defendant would be required to serve if incarcerated, and may even extend to the maximum permissible term for the offense. The maximum term of probation in federal courts is five years. Convicted offenders sometimes refuse a probated term which extends beyond the term of incarceration or which imposes unusually stringent conditions.

Statutes frequently provide that the probation term may be reduced or terminated upon satisfactory performance by the offender for a number of years or a specific portion of the term.

Conditions of Probation. Minimum conditions or probation are set out in the statutes and commonly include requirements that the probationer shall obey all the laws of the United States, the state, and the municipality; that he support his dependents; that he avoid associating with criminals and other persons of ill repute; that he remain within the jurisdiction; and that he report regularly to his probation officer.[20] Other common provisions

(c) For a Class B misdemeanor, the period of probation shall be one year; and

(d) For an unclassified misdemeanor, the period of probation shall be three years if the authorized sentence of imprisonment is in excess of three months, otherwise the period of probation shall be one year. McKinney's Con.Laws of N.Y., Penal § 65.-00(3).

In California, misdemeanor probation may not exceed maximum term of permissible sentence, or for a period not to exceed three years. In felony cases, the term may not exceed maximum term fixed by law for the offense, except the term may be five years for offenses carrying a penalty less than five years. West's Ann.Penal Code, § 1203.1. The court may impose both a fine and a jail term as part of the conditions of probation. *Ibid.*

20. In the Texas law, the basic terms and conditions of probation are set out. The probationer shall: (a) commit no offense against the laws of this State or of any other State or of the United States; (b) avoid injurious or vicious habits; (c) avoid persons or places of disreputable or harmful character; (d) report to the probation officer as directed; (e) permit the probation officer to visit him at his home or elsewhere; (f) work faithfully at suitable employment as far as possible; (g) remain within a specified place; (h) pay his fine, if one be assessed, and all court costs whether a fine be assessed or not, in one or several sums, and make restitution or reparation in any sum that the court shall determine; (i) support his dependents; and pay a fee not exceeding $10.00 per month to be paid to the court by the probationer during the probationary period. Vernon's Ann.Code Crim.Proc., Art. 42.12, B. Sec. 6.

Known as the "Sec. 6 conditions," these are the only conditions that may be imposed if the jury recommends probation. Additional conditions may be added by the judge granting probation.

These conditions are fairly standard in the law of the representative jurisdictions. In California, as we have noted, a jail term may be made a condition of probation. West's Ann.Penal Code, § 1203.1.

This is also true in Illinois. Smith-Hurd Ill.Ann.Stat. ch. 38, § 117–2.

In New York, the conditions are fixed by the court, McKinney's Criminal Procedure Law, § 410.10, and may be modified or enlarged by the court at any time prior to the termination of the sentence. § 410.20. Action to modify or enlarge may not be taken unless the defendant is personally present. *Ibid.* Conditions of probation or conditional discharge may include:

1. In general. The conditions of probation and of conditional discharge shall be such as the court, in its discretion, deems reasonably necessary to insure that the defendant will lead a law-abiding life or to assist him to do so.

2. Conditions relating to conduct and rehabilitation. When imposing a sentence of probation or of conditional discharge, the court may, as a condition of the sentence, require that the defendant:

   (a) Avoid injurious or vicious habits;

   (b) Refrain from frequenting unlawful or disreputable places or consorting with disreputable persons;

   (c) Work faithfully at a suitable employment or faithfully pursue a course of study or of vocational training that will equip him for suitable employment;

   (d) Undergo available medical or psychiatric treatment and remain in a specified institution, when required for that purpose;

   (e) Support his dependents and meet other family responsibilities;

   (f) Make restitution of the fruits of his offense or make reparation, in an amount he can afford to pay, for the loss or damage caused thereby. When restitution or reparation is a condition of the sentence, the court shall fix the amount thereof and the manner of performance;

   (g) If a minor, (i) reside with his parents or in a suitable foster home or hostel as referred to in section six-f of the correction law, (ii) attend school, (iii) spend such part of the period of the sentence as the court may direct, but not exceeding two years, in a facility made available by the division for youth pursuant to subdivision two of section five hundred two of the executive law, provided that admission to such facility may be made only with the prior consent of the division for youth, (iv) attend a nonresidential program for such hours and pursuant to a schedule prescribed by the court as suitable for a program of rehabilitation of youth, (v) contribute to his own support in any home, foster home or hostel;

   (h) Post a bond or other security for the performance of any or all conditions imposed;

   (i) Satisfy any other conditions reasonably related to his rehabilitation.

3. Conditions relating to supervision. When imposing a sentence of probation the court, in addition to any conditions imposed pursuant to subdivision two of this section,

require the convicted offender to make restitution to his victim; pay his own bills; refrain from drinking intoxicating liquor; and not drive a car for a stated period if his offense had to do with vehicle operation. Keeping his probation officer informed as to his whereabouts, and obtaining his prior permission before changing jobs, getting married, or buying a car are frequently required of the probationer.

Other conditions such as regular church attendance and being at home by a certain time every night are often imposed, though they are of doubtful enforceability. The courts generally frown upon the imposition of any exotic conditions or any impossible of fulfillment—thus, a probation condition against drinking is sometimes held to be unreasonable if the defendant is an alcoholic.

The conditions of probation are determined and imposed by the court. The probationer and his supervisor are both given written copies of the conditions and of any amendments made thereafter by the court. Probation may be revoked for violation of any of the conditions of probation, though in practice not every violation by the offender results in revocation. Sometimes substantial violation may take place without the defendant's being removed from the community and incarcerated.

Probation Supervision. Probation officers are officers and employees of the court, except in states which have a state-wide probation and parole system. The qualifications of probation officers are stated in the statutes or in the regulations of the department.[21] Usual qualifications for adult probation are that

shall require as conditions of the sentence, that the defendant:

(a) Report to a probation officer as directed by the court or the probation officer and permit the probation officer to visit him at his place of abode or elsewhere;

(b) Remain within the jurisdiction of the court unless granted permission to leave by the court or the probation officer; and

(c) Answer all reasonable inquiries by the probation officer and promptly notify the probation officer of any change in address or employment.

McKinney's Con.Laws of N.Y., Penal § 65.10.

Conditions upon misdemeanant probationers are similar. All of the representative states, Ill., Texas, N.Y., and Calif., provide for misdemeanor probation. In California, the misdemeanant reports directly to the court and not to a probation officer.

21. In New York, California, Texas, and Illinois, the probation officer is appointed by the court. In all of the states, probation is a function of county government except that in New York a state Division of Probation exercises general su-

the officer be a college graduate and have had experience in working with people. Education in the behavioral sciences, in corrections, and in the techniques of social case work is required in some states and of considerable job value in all. State statutes and regulations commonly put a maximum limit on the case load of a probation officer; unfortunately, these limits are more often exceeded than observed.

A probationer must observe all the terms and conditions of his probation. It is the duty of his probation officer to assist him in every way possible to make a satisfactory and law-abiding adjustment to the community. If the probationer violates the terms of his probation, the probation officer must investigate and report the circumstances of the violation to the court, and in appropriate cases recommend to the court that probation be revoked. Some probation officers have power to arrest a probationer to bring him physically before the court. Probation officers also prepare pre-sentence reports and make recommendations about granting probation.

Because of excessive case loads, and in many cases because of inadequate training, few probation officers have an opportunity to give the kind of supervision envisioned by the proponents of probation. The supervision of some probationers is limited to once-a-month conference when the probationer comes in to report. If the probation officer feels that the probationer is "in trouble" and in danger of breaking the conditions of probation, more intensive supervision will be undertaken. One of the major tasks of a probation officer is to determine the right amount of supervision for each probationer on his case load. Some probationers do very well with a minimum of supervision; others require frequent contacts by the officer.

pervision over probation in the state.

In Illinois, a probation officer must be a "reputable person," and no police officer may be appointed. In Texas, the adult probation officer must have two years of college education and two years work with juveniles or adults, social welfare work, personnel work, or teaching, or be a licensed attorney with experience in criminal law (there are not statutory qualifications for juvenile probation officers). In New York, probation officers must be physically, mentally, and morally fit, and shall be selected because of definite qualifications as to character, ability, and training, and primarily with respect to their capacity for rightly influencing human behavior.

Age limits are frequently imposed for probation officers; in Illinois, a probation officer must be over 25 years old; in New York, between the ages of 21 and 55.

Discharge from Probation. When the probationer has successfully completed his term or probation, he is entitled to a discharge from probation.[22] Procedures for wiping out the conviction are included in many probation statutes.[23] The probationer sentenced under the Federal Youth Corrections Act receives a Certificate of Discharge and if he is discharged prior to expiration of the term of probation, the conviction is automatically wiped out.

Revocation of Probation. Probation may be revoked by the court if the probationer commits a new crime or violates a condition of his probation. Violations other than commission of a new crime are called "technical violations." The most frequent technical violations are for failure to report and removal from the jurisdiction. Some courts and probation and parole boards report all violations as "technical violations" unless the probationer is actually convicted of a new crime. Thus, the real reason for revoking probation may be that the defendant had committed, and often admitted, a new crime, but the probation report will reflect only a technical violation.

There are many reasons for this procedure, not the least of which is that the prosecutors are glad to be spared the expense of a new trial, and since revocation of probation effectively removes the probation violator from the society and brings about his incarceration, both the prosecutor and the offender are glad to forego the second trial, particularly if the permissible penalty for the new offense is less than the probated term. It is thus

22. In New York, the court may at any time terminate a period of probation or a period of conditional discharge. McKinney's N.Y.Criminal Procedure Law, § 410.90. In New York, the probationer appears before the court at the time of discharge from supervision to "be admonished or commended by the Court according to whether his conduct has improved or not." McKinney's N.Y.Code Crim.Proc., Ann., § 934.

23. West's Ann.Cal.Penal Code, § 1203.4: The guilty plea may be withdrawn, or the verdict is set aside, and the accusations and information dismissed, and "the probationer shall thereafter be released from all penalties and disabilities resulting from the offense or crime of which he has been convicted," except in case of a subsequent offense, the prior conviction shall have the same effect as if probation had not been granted or the accusation or information dismissed. The probationer is informed of these rights on the probation papers.

The Texas felony law is similar. Vernon's Ann.Code Crim.Proc., Art. 42.12. In misdemeanor probation, no conviction is entered on the records. Court initiates the proceeding to dismiss the information on its own motion. Vernon's Ann. Code Crim.Proc., Art. 42.13.

difficult to determine from many probation reports (this is equally true of parole reports) just how many probationers (or parolees) have actually committed new offenses while out on probation (or parole). Also, probation or parole is not always revoked for new infractions of the law if these infractions are minor. A probation officer has considerable discretion in deciding what violations to report to the court and when to recommend revocation of probation. The court has absolute discretion to revoke or not to revoke probation, irrespective of the recommendation of the probation officer. Usually, however, officer and court work in considerable harmony, with the court usually following the officer's recommendations.

When the probation officer recommends revocation of probation or a probation violation is otherwise brought to the attention of the court, the defendant is given a probation revocation hearing. A hearing is not a trial; it amounts to an appearance before the court at which the defendant is informed of the petition for revocation and of the reasons for it. He is usually given a chance to reply to the charge and in rare instances may summon witnesses in his behalf. A Supreme Court decision has held that a probationer is entitled to be represented by counsel on revocation of probation, unless counsel is waived.[24] Counsel is able to resist the application for the revocation by bringing to the attention of the court any factors bearing upon the allegations or that should be considered by the court before entering the order of revocation. Since the result of revoking probation is to deprive an offender who has not yet been incarcerated of his liberty, due process requires that counsel must be appointed for the indigent probationer.

Upon revocation of probation, a sentence of imprisonment is imposed upon the defendant. In some states, this sentence may not exceed that fixed in the judgment of the court or the verdict of the jury at the original trial or a plea of guilty; in others, the sentence may extend to the maximum provided by law for the offense.[25] In some states, the defendant receives credit on his

24. Mempa v. Rhay, 389 U.S. 128, 88 S.Ct. 254, 19 L.Ed.2d 336 (1967).

25. Illinois grants a hearing on revocation of probation. The court may modify the conditions of probation or the court may imprison the probationer for a term not to exceed the maximum penalty for the offense. Smith-Hurd Ann.Stat. ch. 38, § 117-3.

The New York law is similar. McKinney's N.Y.Criminal Procedure Law, Art. 410.

sentence for the time successfully completed on probation; in others, no credit is allowed, and the offender must serve the full term in the institution beginning with the date of incarceration.

COMMITMENT TO AN INSTITUTION AND INCARCERATION

Depending upon the organization of the state correctional system and the laws of the state, the court commits a felony offender to the director of the state department or division of corrections, or to the warden of a particular state penal institution.[26] In California, the commitment of adult felons is to the

The same rule prevails in California. West's Ann.Penal Code, § 1203.2.

In Texas, only the maximum sentence actually assessed may be imposed on a felon who violates probation. A sentence equal to the maximum permissible sentence may be imposed on a misdemeanant who violates probation. Vernon's Ann. Code Crim.Proc., Art. 42.12 and Art. 42.13.

26. In Illinois, all males over 17 are sentenced to and confined in the Illinois State Penitentiary; females over 18, to the Illinois State Reformatory for Women; custody is in the Department of Public Safety. Males under 17 and females under 18 are sentenced to the custody of the Illinois Youth Commission. The Department of Public Safety administers the correctional facilities in Illinois. Smith-Hurd Ann.Stat., ch. 38, § 119–2.

In Texas, commitment is to the Director of the Texas Department of Corrections. Vernon's Texas Civil Statutes, Art. 6166.

In New York, the commitment of a defendant is as follows:

1. In general. When a sentence of imprisonment is pronounced, or when the sentence consists of a fine and the court has directed that the defendant be imprisoned until it is satisfied, the defendant must forthwith be committed to the custody of the appropriate public servant and detained until the sentence is complied with.

2. Indeterminate sentence. In the case of an indeterminate sentence of imprisonment, commitment must be to the custody of the state department of correction as provided in subdivision one of section 70.20 of the penal law and the order of commitment must direct that the defendant be delivered to an institution designated by the commissioner of correction in accordance with section eight hundred one of the correction law.

3. Reformatory sentence. In the case of a reformatory sentence of imprisonment, commitment must be to the custody of the state department of correction as provided in section 75.05 of the penal law, and the order of commitment must direct, in accordance with section eight hundred one of the correction law, as follows:

(a) If the defendant is a male, the order must direct that he be delivered to the reception center at Elmira;

(b) If the defendant is a female, the order must direct that she be delivered to an institution designated by the state commissioner of correction.

4. Definite sentence. In the case of a definite sentence of imprisonment, commitment must be as follows:

(a) In counties contained within New York City or in any county that has a county department of correction, commitment must be to the custody of the department of correction of such city or county;

(b) In any other case, commitment must be to the county jail, workhouse or penitentiary, or to a penitentiary outside the county and the order of commitment must specify the institution to which the defendant is to be delivered.

5. Alternative local reformatory sentence. In the case of an alternative local reformatory sentence of imprisonment, commitment must be to, and the sentence must be served in, the local reformatory as provided in subdivision three of section 75.20 of the penal law.

6. Mentally defective defendants. In any case where the defendant may be committed upon a certificate of mental defect, as provided in sections four hundred thirty-eight and four hundred fifty-one of the correction law, the court may, notwithstanding any other provision of this section, commit the defendant to the custody of the state department of correction, and in such case the order of commitment must direct in accordance with section eight hundred one of the correction law that the defendant be delivered as follows:

(a) If the defendant is a male, to the Beacon state institution; and

(b) If the defendant is a female, to the Albion state training school.

7. Commitment for failure to pay fine. Where the sentence consists of a fine and the court has directed that the defendant be imprisoned until it is satisfied, commitment must be as follows:

(a) If the sentence also includes a term of imprisonment, commitment must be to the same institution as is designated for service of the term of imprisonment, and the period of commitment commences (i) when the term of imprisonment is satisfied, or (ii) with the approval of the state board of parole, when the defendant becomes eligible for parole, or (iii) when the defendant becomes eligible for conditional release, whichever occurs first; provided, however, that the court may direct that the period of imprisonment for the fine run concurrently with the term of imprisonment; and

(b) In any other case, commitment must be to the agency or institution that would be designated in the case of a definite sentence. McKinney's N.Y.Criminal Procedure Law, § 430.20.

In counties contained within New York City and in counties that have a commissioner of correction who is responsible for detention of defendants in criminal actions, it is the duty of the commissioner of correction of such city or county to deliver the defendant forthwith to the proper institution in accordance with the commitment. In all other counties it is the duty of the sheriff to deliver the defendant forthwith to the proper institution in accordance with the commitment. McKinney's N.Y.Criminal Procedure Law, § 430.30.

Director of Corrections, though the period of commitment is fixed by the California Adult Authority, an administrative body.[27] Misdemeanants are committed to a city or county jail, depending upon the offense and the jurisdiction of the sentencing court. Federal prisoners are committed to the Attorney General of the United States.

Once the convicted man is delivered to the state department of corrections or to the penal institution, the court loses all control over him. The decisions as to place and conditions of confinement are made by the correctional authority or by the warden of the institution to which he has been committed. States with state-wide correctional departments operate many different kinds of penal institutions for adult felons. Hardened professional criminals are placed in maximum security institutions; first offenders are placed in minimum security or open institutions; and specialized institutions may be provided for sexual offenders or the criminally insane.

The federal government operates both federal penitentiaries and federal correctional institutions; federal misdemeanants are placed in county or city jails with which the federal government has contracted for care for federal prisoners. The large states have a separate institution in which a newly convicted felon is kept for a certain period of time while decisions are being made as to the place and condition of his confinement. Some of these institutions, variously called Reception Centers, Diagnostic Centers, and the like, serve only to isolate the prisoner until danger of his carrying a communicable disease into the institution has passed. Other such centers carry on extensive diagnostic procedures to determine the best treatment plan for the prisoner in terms of his background and needs—the objective being, of course, to maximize his chances for rehabilitation.

During his stay at a reception or diagnostic center, a prisoner will be given complete physical and mental examinations, his educational level will be assessed, and his work skills inventoried. Extensive social histories are developed in some centers, with the pre-sentence report which has been sent to the institution with the prisoner being used as the base for additional investigation. The treatment plan for the prisoner provides that he be placed in

27. See fn. 8, *supra*, West's Ann. Cal.Penal Code, §§ 1168 and 3000.

a particular work assignment and that his special needs for educational opportunites, psychiatric treatment, or whatever, be taken care of. The federal government provides excellent plastic surgery at one of its institutions, since it has been found that the correction of physical deformities contributes greatly to an inmate's rehabilitation.

Some prisoners have brought suit in state and in federal courts claiming that the division of corrections has no right to make the decisions as to the place and condition of confinement. These petitioners claimed that the inmate is entitled to serve his time in the institution nearest his home, and that particular work assignments are not suitable. In one instance, the inmate claimed that he was being denied his constitutional right to rehabilitation. Up to the present time the courts have held that an inmate has no legal right to be incarcerated in any particular institution or to demand any particular work assignment unless the work assignment given him is manifestly beyond his physical abilities and threatens his health or physical well-being.

Institutional Units. At the end of his stay in the receiving center, the inmate is assigned to one of the units in the prison system. These units provide varying degrees of security and different work and educational opportunities. Women are housed in a separate institution, and frequently separate accommodations are provided for handicapped prisoners or prisoners with mental or physical problems. Where the state runs the correctional system, the inmate may be moved from institution to institution at the order of the director, and his assignments and treatment plan can also be changed as his well being and the welfare of the institution dictate. The Attorney General of the United States has the authority to assign and move federal prisoners in the same way. Where the court makes the assignment to a particular institution, transfer of the prisoner may be more difficult. In many states transfer between institutions presents no problem because the state has only one felony institution. Wyoming, for example, contracts with a neighboring state to house its female prisoners, and has only one penitentiary for males. Its two correctional institutions house juveniles and young first offenders. Transfers to and from the prison and the correctional institutions are permitted where necessary.

Deprivations Suffered by Inmates. Every incarcerated man suffers certain deprivations.[28] These include deprivation of right to freely contact the outside world; deprivation of sexual activity; deprivation of the right to carry on a business or profession; deprivation of certain rights of religious practice (but not of religious belief); and deprivation of the right to be litigious (to sue and be sued).[29] However, the inmate also has certain basic rights—to be properly housed and fed; to receive needed medical attention; to be protected in his personal physical security as much as possible; and to have access to the courts by way of appeal and habeas corpus. He also is protected by Eighth Amendment to the Constitution against cruel and unusual punishment.

The "Hands-Off" Doctrine. The concepts about inmate rights and the responsibilities of penal institutions toward the inmate are at the present time in a state of profound change. In the early development of Anglo-American law, the offender, upon conviction, became a kind of "legal outlaw." Though every safeguard and protection were give him prior to the determination of his guilt, once guilt was established his legal rights were minimal. Inmates who tried to change this state of affairs were met with a refusal by the courts to even hear their complaints. Known as the "hands-off doctrine," the position of the courts was that the judiciary had no authority to intervene in correctional decisions. Except in extreme cases involving the Eighth Amendment guarantee against cruel and unusual punishment, the courts would keep "hands-off" the administration of correctional institutions.[30]

The "hand-off doctrine" was first successfully challenged in cases involving the right of the Black Muslims to religious freedom in prison.[31] In a series of cases, the federal and some state

28. Price v. Johnston, 334 U.S. 266, 68 S.Ct. 1049, 92 L.Ed. 1356 (1948).

Pierce v. La Vallee, 212 F.Supp. 865 (N.D.N.Y.1962), aff. 319 F.2d 844, cert. den. 374 U.S. 850, 83 S.Ct. 1913, 10 L.Ed.2d 1070, cert. den. 376 U.S. 918, 84 S.Ct. 674, 11 L.Ed.2d 614.

29. Paul W. Tappen, "The Legal Rights of Prisoners," *The Annals of the American Academy of Political and Social Sciences, Vol. 293 (May, 1954)* pp. 99–111.

30. Banning v. Looney, 213 F.2d 771 (10th Cir.), cert. den. 348 U.S. 859, 75 S.Ct. 84, 99 L.Ed. 677 (1954).

31. The division of corrections of the following states recognizes the Black Muslims as a religion: Ark., Cal., Colo., Del., Mont., Md., Neb., N.M., Okla., Tenn., Wash., Wisc. Data obtained in response to a survey reported in Rabun C. Sanders, Jr., *Prisoners' First Amendment Rights Within the Institution*, an unpublished Master's The-

courts held that the Black Muslim has a right to have the Qúran or Koran (a form of Moslem Bible) in his cell if the right to have a Bible is accorded other inmates. The courts also held that whatever religious privileges were accorded other prisoners must also be accorded Black Muslim prisoners, and that the Black Muslims could not be segregated or subjected to special punishments solely because of their religious beliefs.[32]

The courts, however, made a careful distinction between religious beliefs and religious practices. Thus, the court denied the right of the Muslims to special diets prescribed by their religion, and to other religious observances that threatened institutional security or interrupted regular work and treatment programs of the institution. Similar restrictions on the religious practices of other denominations have also been upheld—the court pointing out the vital difference between freedom of religious *belief* and religious *practice*.[33]

The courts have also begun to inquire into the extent to which an inmate loses his First Amendment rights to freedom of speech and assembly, and the right to petition the courts for a redress of grievances.[34] The trend of the decisions seems to be that the inmate must be accorded all First Amendment freedoms in the institution unless sound reasons can be shown for their denial or restriction. The right to petition the courts has been held to include the right to consult with a "jail-house lawyer," if no other legal advice is available to the inmate who wants to file an appeal or an application for writ of habeas corpus, and according to a California decision, a penal institution must provide an attorney or a working law library.[35] But the courts have not held that an inmate is free to keep law books in his cell, or forego his work assignments to work on his "writ."

sis, Sam Houston State University, (1970) p. 43.

The states of Del., Idaho, Ill., Maine, Minn., N.H., Wash., and the federal institutions responding to the questionnaire (except the U. S. Army Discipline Barracks) give consideration to the dietary requirements of Jewish and Black Muslim prisoners. *Ibid.*, p. 48

32. Sewell v. Pegelow, 291 F.2d 196 (4th Cir. 1961).

33. Fulwood v. Clemmer, 206 F.Supp. 370 (D.C.C.1962).

Childs v. Pegelow, 321 F.2d 487 (4th Cir. 1963), cert. den. 376 U.S. 932, 84 S.Ct. 702, 11 L.Ed.2d 652.

34. Gitlow v. New York, 268 U.S. 652, 45 S.Ct. 625, 69 L.Ed. 1138 (1925).

Whitney v. California, 274 U.S. 357, 47 S.Ct. 641, 71 L.Ed. 1095 (1927), reh. gr. 269 U.S. 538, 46 S.Ct. 120, 70 L.Ed. 400.

35. Johnson v. Avery, 393 U.S. 483, 89 S.Ct. 747, 21 L.Ed.2d 718 (1969).

Gilmore v. Lynch, 319 F.Supp. 105.

Many forward-looking institutions are now employing full time attorneys to assist the inmates in their problems with the criminal courts and also to assist them in civil matters—such as divorce—which may come up during their period of incarceration.

The inmate's right to send and receive mail without restriction has been presented to the courts, and other institutional deprivations are also being challenged. As a result, prison administrators are carefully reviewing existing regulations in order to be able to show the court that those remaining are necessary and fairly imposed.

"Good Time" Allowances. To provide a tangible incentive to the inmate to conform to prison regulations and to take advantage of the opportunities offered him for rehabilitation, many states have passed what are known as "good-time" laws.[36] Though these laws vary in detail, they usually provide that an inmate who behaves well in the institution may serve his sentence at an accelerated rate.[37] In Texas, for example, an inmate who earns the status of State Approved Trusty is credited with two days time on his sentence for each calendar day actually spent in prison. The inmates call this "two for one." Inmates in another classification receive 40 days time credit on their sentence for each 30 calendar days in the institution, and still another classification provides for 50 days time credit for each 30 calendar days served.[38] Inmates who misbehave forfeit their good time allowances and serve their time day by day. The Texas inmates call this "one for one" or "doing it the hard way." "Good time" is credited in some states only to the maximum sentence. In other states it is credited to the minimum sentence and thus has the

36. The first Good Time Law was passed in New York in 1817. Connecticut passed a Good Time Law in 1821; Tennessee, in 1836; Ohio, in 1856. Only California and Pennsylvania have not made good time laws generally applicable to state prisoners.

37. The most common good time allowance is a reduction of one month for first year of sentence, two months for second year, three months for third year, four months for fourth year, and five months for fifth year and each year after that.

A federal prisoner earns good time at the rate of five days a month during the first year; six days a month after one year up to three; seven days a month between the third and fifth year; eight days a month during the years from five and ten, and ten days a month for the tenth and each succeeding year.

38. Vernon's Revised Civil Statutes of Texas, Art. 6184L.

effect of reducing the time necessary to achieve eligibility for parole.[39]

In some prison systems the inmates can also earn "points" for performing extra well on the job, participating in religious activities and in educational opportunities, attending group therapy sessions, or donating blood to be used in the prison hospital or other state hospitals. The earned points are called to the attention of the parole board when the time comes for the inmate to be considered for parole. Both good time allowances and points may be forfeited by the inmate for misbehavior in the institution. An inmate who tries to escape, for example, will assuredly forfeit his earned good time allowances and accumulated points. Further, he will probably be denied the opportunity for a considerable time to earn extra good time allowances; instead, he will be serving his time "one for one." Enlightened prison administrators provide for a special review board and special procedures for taking away an inmate's earned good time allowances. This gives the inmate a chance to justify and explain his conduct if he can and assures him of a group decision that protects him from arbitrary actions of a single correctional officer or warden.

Detainers. Detainers represent a considerable problem in correctional practice. As we have seen, a detainer is a kind of "hold order" against an inmate in which another jurisdiction requests that upon release the inmate be "detained" to answer to an offense committed in the requesting jurisdiction.[40] Almost any kind of informal request has been recognized as a "detainer." [41]

39. In New York, a person sentenced to a state prison or penitentiary, except one sentenced to a life sentence, receives credit on reduction of sentence of not to exceed ten days a month to be applied to the minimum sentence of an indeterminate sentence or term imposed by court if it is a definite sentence. The maximum reduction allowed is four months per year. No prisoner may be released until he has served at least one year. The allowance is two days per month for persons sentenced to other correctional institutions, with special allowances of three extra days a month, but not to exceed two months a year off the maximum sentence. McKinney's Correction Law, § 230.

40. The Attorney General of Georgia estimates that of the inmates released in any one year from the Georgia Department of Corrections, 25 per cent have at least one detainer against them. Many months, this percentage is doubled. *Defender Newsletter*, January, 1969.

41. "A detainer is a legal fiction. That is to say, it does not exist as a matter of law in this state, nor it is subject to any prescribed rules of definition." *Ibid.*

The practice has been for the director or warden having the inmate in custody to honor the demand of the requesting jurisdiction by notifying them when the inmate is due to be released. If the requesting jurisdiction wants to return him to answer to the offense, they have an officer waiting at the gates of the institution to pick him up.

A detainer has important negative effects on the incarcerated inmate. Customarily, an inmate on detainer cannot become a trusty or attain other position that permits him to earn maximum good time allowances. The prospect that he will be immediately re-arrested when he completes his present term of imprisonment gives the prisoner little incentive to take part in treatment programs and leads to discouragement and despair. Many parole boards won't "parole to a detainer," which means that they will not parole a man against whom there is an outstanding detainer. (The argument runs that there is no merit in releasing a man on parole only to have him immediately picked up by another jurisdiction.)

Over the years, many abuses have grown up around the detainer system. Law enforcement and prosecuting officers often file detainers for harassment purposes, with no real intention of bringing a man back for trial on the offense committed in their jurisdiction. Not infrequently, a man will spend his entire prison period under the handicaps of a detainer and upon release find no one interested in taking him back to the other jurisdiction. Studies show that detainers sometimes cannot be released because the officer filing them is dead or out of office. Sometimes the person filing the detainer proves to be a several-years-ago secretary in the prosecutor's office, or a temporary employee of the sheriff. Their authority to file a detainer is indeed questionable, but locating them to get the necessary information and release represents a difficult problem to the offender seeking to clear the detainer from his record.

Since the negative aspects of the detainer on the inmate in terms of his rehabilitation are considerable, and the law enforcement benefits of the detainer doubtful,[42] many persons have advocated that they be prohibited or the procedure be regulated.

42. "There is no proper criminological purpose served in holding several prosecutions over a defendant's head. Neither correction nor deterrence is thus served * * *." People v. Winfrey, 20 N.Y.2d 138, 281 N.Y.S.2d 823, 228 N.E.2d 808 (1967).

Some twenty states have agreed to a set of rules on detainers which require written notice, copies of formal documents setting forth the charge, and procedures for returning the inmate to the requesting state for trial. Known as the *Interstate Agreement on Detainers*, it standardized practices among the states who signed it. Unfortunately, no cooperative arrangements exist to aid the prisoners in the other thirty states.[43]

The Supreme Court of the United States began paying attention to the detainer problem in the early 1960s. In a series of cases based on the Constitutional right to a speedy trial, the Court handed down opinions which require that the jurisdiction requesting a detainer make a formal demand for a detainer and immediately request that the inmate be made available for trial. If a prompt trial is not afforded the inmate, the state loses its right to thereafter hold him to answer to the charge.[44]

As a result of these decisions and of procedures set up in the institutions, an inmate may now demand a prompt trial on a detainer.[45] If it is not forthcoming, the detainer is dismissed, and the prisoner can work toward his rehabilitation free of the handicaps previously imposed by the pending charge against him. Parole boards now "release to a detainer," particularly if there is reason to believe that the requesting jurisdiction has filed a "nuisance" detainer, but the important thing to the man "on detainer" is that his ability to force a trial in the other jurisdiction may result in a dismissal of the charge or a verdict in his favor.

American Bar Association Standards Relating to Speedy Trial. The American Bar Association Project on Minimum Standards

43. The following states have signed the Agreement on Detainers: Cal., Colo., Conn., Del., Hawaii, Iowa, Kan., Md., Mass., Mich., Minn., Mont., Neb., N.H., N.J., N.Y., N.C., Ohio, Or., Pa., S.C., Utah, Vt., Wash., Wis.

44. A leading decision involved a federal prisoner seeking relief from state detainers. Smith v. Hooey, 393 U.S. 374, 89 S.Ct. 575, 21 L.Ed. 2d 607 (1969).

Interstate detainers were involved in U. S. v. Provoo, 17 F.R.D. 183 (1955) where federal habeas corpus relief was granted the prisoner.

Florida was denied the right after eight years to try an inmate who had spent the time in a federal prison. Florida had made no attempt during that time to seek his return to Florida for trial. Dickey v. Florida, 398 U.S. 30, 90 S.Ct. 1564, 26 L.Ed.2d 26 (1970).

45. Some institutions make forms available to an inmate. A Request for Disposition of Pending Charges (or similar document) is sent to the district judge where the charge is pending, with copy to the prosecuting attorney. Trial within 90 days is requested.

for the Administration of Criminal Justice seeks to eliminate the abuses of the present detainer system by protecting the right of the prisoner to a speedy trial on other pending charges. The *Standards*[46] require that the prosecuting attorney who knows that a person charged with a criminal offense is serving a term of imprisonment in another jurisdiction must promptly undertake to obtain the presence of the prisoner for trial, or cause a detainer to be filed with the official having custody of the prisoner. The official having the prisoner in custody must inform him of his right to demand trial, and return a certificate to that effect to the prosecuting attorney who filed the detainer. The prosecuting attorney then requests the temporary custody of the prisoner for trial, and it is the duty of the official having him in custody to make him available for such purposes, subject to the traditional right of the executive to refuse transfer and the right of the prisoner to contest the legality of his delivery.

Failure to seek a trial in this manner would give the prisoner the right to raise his right to a speedy trial as a defense to the charge whenever he was brought to trial, and would also serve to remove the handicaps of an existing detainer during his period of incarceration.

Treatment Programs in Penal Institutions. The number, variety, and success of treatment programs vary widely from state to state and even from institution to institution within a state. Since statistics show that the average penitentiary inmate is apt to be a school drop-out and, in an alarming number of cases, is functionally illiterate, many institutions put special emphasis on providing the inmate with educational opportunities. A progressive department of corrections provides instruction at every grade level from the first through college. The students are taught in ungraded classes by certified teachers, and many institutions have highly trained professionals able to conduct remedial reading and other specialized classes. Some inmates actually attend college classes in the community. The Texas prison system constitutes an independent school district,[47] with authority to award

46. American Bar Association Project on Minimum Standards for Criminal Justice, *Standards Relating to Speedy Trial.* New York: Office of Criminal Justice Project, Approved Draft, 1968.

47. A unique feature of the Texas system is that the Superintendent of its Windham School District is a woman.

high school diplomas and General Educational Development Certificates (equivalent to high school diplomas).[48]

Opportunity for religious experience is also provided in most penal institutions. Catholic, Protestant, and Jewish chaplains are employed by the institution, and ministers of denominations not represented by the staff chaplains hold regular services in the prison chapel. Many chaplains are specially trained counselors and meet with inmates individually or in groups to assist them in their adjustment to prison life and to help prepare them for successful release. Specially trained psychologists and other counselors conduct group therapy sessions and provide individual counseling services.

Modern prisons have completely equipped hospitals with resident physicians and surgeons; psychiatric care is available though seldom on an adequate basis. Recreational programs are extensive, and inmate teams often travel to competitions held outside the prison walls. Depending upon the location and organization of the prison system, inmates have work assignments which vary from picking cotton, to making brooms and license plates, to operating sophisticated computed equipment. The Vocational Rehabilitation Service of the United States Department of Health, Education, and Welfare places full time vocational counselors in penal institutions to assist the inmate to prepare for and find employment upon release.

Pre-release Programs. Special pre-release programs are a part of some state correctional systems,[49] and there are privately operated "Half-Way Houses."[50] An inmate about to be released on parole or nearing the end of his sentence is transferred to a special institution where security measures are relaxed and pre-release programs help to prepare him for his return into so-

48. Juvenile institutions also often belong to a special school district or have arrangements with nearby school districts to issue the high school diploma earned by some of the boys and girls. Thus, there is nothing on the face of the diploma to indicate that the person "graduated" from a correctional institution.

49. *National Conference on Pre-Release, A Symposium on Adult Offender Programs.* Proceedings of a conference, published by Institute of Contemporary Corrections, Sam Houston State University and Texas Department of Corrections, 1967.

50. Saint Leonard's House is a center for work in corrections sponsored by the Episcopal Diocese of Chicago. In Minnesota, the Volunteers of America are active in correctional work. *Ibid,* pp. 23–30.

ciety.[51] At a typical pre-release center, the correctional officers and the inmates wear street clothes instead of prison uniforms; family visits and picnics are arranged; the inmate is taken to shows and sports events in a nearby city; and trained counselors help him with such things as straightening out his social security record (often very confused because he has worked under several different names), and obtaining a driver's license.

Improved Programs Needed. It must not be assumed, of course, that all prison systems provide these opportunities and services to an inmate. In at least one state, the prisons are run by the toughest inmates, who are given guns and life and death control over their fellow prisoners. In other prisons, the facilities are overcrowded, idleness is the rule, and no meaningful rehabilitation programs of any kind are carried on. Institutions of this kind are breeding grounds for continued criminality, and even the best-run prison systems fail in their rehabilitation efforts with many of the inmates. The truth is that proven techniques for changing human behavior are few, and lack of money and of trained personnel limit the use of even the most promising re-socialization programs.

Though many institutions for felons need improvement, the jails in the United States are a national disgrace. Filthy, overcrowded, with no pretense at providing work or rehabilitation programs, they condemn young and old alike to experiences both dangerous and degrading. The problem is made more serious by the fact that many persons being held in jails have not been convicted of a crime. Persons merely charged with a crime who cannot make bail, and material witnesses who have no charges against them are held in jails with convicted misdemeanants or felons awaiting appeal.

The *Manual of Correctional Standards* of the American Correctional Association[52] identifies and describes current standards for good correctional practices in twenty-seven subject areas. The *Standards* were first presented in 1946 to answer the requests of state governments and state legislatures for guidance in prison operations. The *Standards* are reviewed and up-dated

51. Community treatment centers for narcotics addicts are operated in many cities. The United States Bureau of Prisons inaugurated a Pre-Release Guidance Center program in 1961 in Los Angeles, Chicago, and New York, which were abandoned in favor of Community Treatment Centers. *Ibid*, pp. 49–58.

52. The American Correctional Association, *Manual of Correctional Standards*, Washington, D. C., 1959.

constantly. A major re-writing was undertaken after the 1970 Centennial Congress of the Association with assistance from the Ford Foundation.

The *Standards* cover the organization of a state department or division of corrections, personnel qualifications and personnel management for correctional officers, the proper fiscal management of correctional institutions, and the importance of research in corrections. Legal rights of probationers, prisoners, and parolees, the operation of voluntary service agencies in corrections, the proper operation of community detention (jail) facilities, and standards for camps, adult probation and parole, and for release procedures in a correctional institution, are included.

Standards are set for the physical plant with specifications as to cell size, recreation facilities, number of inmates housed in one unit, and protection of the inmate against fire or other physical hazard. Good food and adequate medical care are to be provided the inmate. A system of classification is recommended which will place each inmate in a job in accordance with his abilities and in accordance with the best program of rehabilitation that can be worked out for him on an individual basis. It is recognized that custody is an important aspect of prison administration, but emphasis is placed on providing employment, psychiatric care, and counseling services to the convicted man. The *Standards* also focus on the importance of providing education for the inmate, with access to library services and other means of self-improvement.

A program for institutional self-evaluation and certification is also being implemented by the American Correctional Association. In the self-evaluation, each correctional institution or department of corrections is given a means to rate itself, using the *Standards* as a guideline, and to make recommendations for its own improvement. Self-evaluation and certification are seen as important tools to bring about improvement in correctional treatment and administration in the United States.

PAROLE

Parole means the release of a prisoner from imprisonment but not from the legal custody of the State,[53] for rehabilitation out-

53. In New York, a parolee is in the legal custody of the warden of the prison from which he was paroled. McKinney's Correction Law, § 213.

side of prison walls under such conditions and provisions for disciplinary supervision as the Board of Pardons and Paroles may determine.[54]

Parole is an administrative act and comes after incarceration. The administrative body responsible for parole decisions and supervision in most states is a state-wide parole authority, usually called the Board of Parole, or, if probation is also administered state-wide, the Board of Probation and Parole. In a few states, the parole authority also has certain responsibilities with respect to pardons. The decision to grant parole is made by the parole authority, as is the decision to revoke parole.[55] In the early history of parole, the penal institution was the parole authority.

Purposes of Parole. A parole system has two purposes: first, to reform and rehabilitate the convicted prisoner so that, after he leaves the institution, he will be able to live a useful life in society; and second, to protect society from the criminal behavior of some of its members.[56] Students of parole point to the financial savings of parole, as it costs less to supervise a man on parole than to keep him in an institution. While on parole, the convicted man can support his family and assume other personal obligations which must be performed for him by others during his incarceration. Parole also serves the important function of providing the

In Texas, a parolee is under legal custody of the Parole Board. Vernon's Ann.Code of Crim.Proc., Art. 42.12.

In California, legal custody is in the Department of Corrections, subject to the rules and regulations of the Adult Authority. West's Ann.Cal. Penal Code, § 3056.

In Illinois, custody is in the Department of Public Safety or the Youth Commission. Smith-Hurd Ann. Stat., ch. 38, Crim.Law and Proc., §§ 123–1 and 123–2.

54. This comprehensive definition is contained in the Uniform Probation and Parole Act.

55. In California, the granting and revocation of parole and the fixing of sentences is determined by the Adult Authority. West's Ann.Penal Code, § 5077.

In New York, the Board of Parole in the Division of Parole in the Executive Department determines which prisoners serving indeterminate sentences may be released on parole, and the conditions of parole. McKinney's Corrections Law, § 210.

In Illinois, adult parole is granted and revoked by the Parole and Pardon Board of the Department of Public Safety. The Youth Commission is the paroling authority for persons in its custody. Smith-Hurd Ann.Stat. ch. 38, Crim.Law and Proc., § 123–1.

In Texas, the paroling authority is the Board of Pardons and Paroles. Vernon's Ann.Code Crim.Proc., Art. 42.12.

56. Rubin, *op. cit.*, p. 547.

convicted man with supervision and assistance during the painful and difficult transition from institutional life to job and family responsibilities outside the prison walls.

Parole Eligibility. The criteria for parole eligibility are set out in the statute. Some states prohibit parole to certain classes of offenders, as for example, those serving life terms or sentenced for certain kinds of felonies. Some parole boards refuse to consider sex offenders for parole.

According to the law of the state, eligibility for parole may be tied to the minimum sentence or to a stated proportion of the maximum sentence.[57] As we mentioned previously, where parole eligibility is attached to minimum terms, some judges impose high minimum sentences in an attempt to prevent parole for certain offenders. In states where parole eligibility occurs after a certain proportion of the maximum sentence one-fourth, one-third or other stated fraction, the minimum sentence has no effect on parole eligibility and thus little meaning in terms of time actually served.

No inmate has a legal right to parole, but, except as prohibited by statute, an incarcerated man has a right to be *considered* for parole. In some states the petition for parole is initiated by the inmate; in others, by the institution. Many parole boards provide for automatic consideration of an inmate whenever he

57. In Texas, a prisoner is eligible for parole after he has served one-third of his maximum term or twenty years. Time served is figured on calendar time less good time allowances. Vernon's Ann. Code Crim.Proc., Art. 42.12, C., Sec. 15.

In Illinois, parole eligibility is one-third of a determinate sentence, the minimum term of an indeterminate sentence, or twenty years. Good time is credited in determining parole eligibility. Smith-Hurd Ill.Stat.Ann. ch. 38, Crim.Law and Proc., § 123–2.

In California, a prisoner may be considered for parole at any time after he commences his term of imprisonment, West's Ann.Penal Code, § 3041, except for prisoners serving consecutive sentences; prisoners who attempt to escape, who must serve a two-year minimum; a prisoner under life sentence, who must serve a seven-year minimum; and habitual criminals, who must serve a minimum of fifteen years. West's Ann.Penal Code, §§ 3043–3049.

In New York, the prisoner serving an indeterminate sentence must serve the minimum sentence. McKinney's Correction Law, § 212. The minimum period of imprisonment for a Class A felony is not less than 15 nor more than 25 years; for all other felonies, the court fixes the minimum which must be at least one-third of the maximum term. McKinney's Penal Law, § 70.00.

has established parole eligibility, and for periodic regular review thereafter. No inmate is required to accept parole against his wishes, and many offenders prefer to serve out their terms in the institution in order to be free of supervision when released.

The Parole Decision. The parole authority sets its own procedures for obtaining information about the inmate being considered for parole. In some states, the parole board employs institutional parole officers who are assigned full-time to the penal institutions. Institutional parole officers interview new inmates and inform them of parole eligibility requirements. They also develop information on inmates to be considered for parole, which is presented to the parole board. The inmate's file will include a complete statement of his offense, his previous criminal record, his adjustment to prison, his health, aptitudes and skills, his family relationships, and the attitude of the community toward his release. The institutional parole officer also assists in the making of a parole plan, which must include arrangements for employment when the inmate is released, but is not the supervising officer after release. In other states, the parole officer is not assigned to the institution and works with the inmate only after he is considered for parole. In such states the parole officer who helps the inmate develop his parole plan may also be his supervising parole officer after release.

Except in a few states, when an inmate is being considered for parole he is granted a hearing before the parole board. The *Model Penal Code* requires this hearing, which is simply an appearance by the inmate before one or more members of the parole board where he is given an opportunity to state his own case for parole and to ask questions about the parole process. The rules of most parole boards exclude attorneys at this hearing, although an attorney may submit written arguments on behalf of his client. The United States Supreme Court has not yet held that there is a Constitutional right for representation by counsel at a parole hearing.

The members of the parole board review the file of the inmate both before and after the hearing, and make their decision to grant or deny parole. Some boards require a unanimous decision before parole can be granted. Other statutes require a stated majority of the board to concur in the decision to grant parole. Sometimes the inmate is told immediately after the hearing what the decision was; in most cases, however, he is notified several weeks later.

The practice in the federal system has been to send one or more members of the United States Board of Parole to the various federal institutions. The visiting member held hearings and made recommendations to the full board as to whether or not the inmate should be granted parole. As a result of recent changes in procedures, the members of the Parole Board no longer travel to interview the persons being considered for parole but sit *en banc* (in a group) in Washington to review applications for parole. Information for the use of the Board is developed by parole examiners employed by the Board.

An inmate granted parole is not immediately released. Final arrangements are made as to his employment and other necessary matters are taken care of. In states with pre-release centers, the inmate is sent to the pre-release center for several weeks before he is finally released from the institution to the supervision of his parole officer.

Parole Supervision. Supervisory parole officers are also employees of the parole board. Their function, like that of the probation officer (in many states and in the federal government, one officer supervises both parolees and probationers), is to assist the parolee in his adjustment into society and to see that he complies with the conditions of his parole. The supervisory parole officer recommends revocation of parole to the paroling authority and in many states has power to arrest the parolee and return him to jail or to the penal institution until the revocation hearing takes place.

Length of Parole. Parole is not a release from commitment but only from confinement. The parolee is released from the institution with permission to serve the balance of his sentence under supervision in the community. In a few states, the parole term may extend beyond the term fixed for incarceration, but generally the parole term represents the balance of the term remaining when the inmate is released on parole.[58] Good time allowances

58. In Texas, the length of the parole term may not exceed the sentence actually assessed. Vernon's Ann. Code Crim.Proc., Art. 42.12, C., Paroles, Sec. 22.

In Illinois, no person may be continued on parole beyond the maximum term provided by law for the offense for which he was convicted. Smith-Hurd Ann.Stat., Ch. 38, Crim. Law and Proc., § 123–4.

In New York, the parolee is in the legal custody of the warden of the prison from which he is paroled

are usually not earned by a parolee.[59] Time on parole is counted "one for one," though good time earned prior to parole will be credited on the sentence.

Parole Conditions. Parole conditions are similar to those imposed in probation. The parolee is required to be law-abiding, to support his dependents, to avoid the company of criminals and persons of bad repute, to remain in the jurisdiction, and to report to his parole officer regularly.[60] (However, a parole condition which required the parolee to leave the jurisdiction has been upheld.) Legal custody of a parolee remains in the director of the department of corrections, or the warden of the institution, or legal custody is vested in the parole board.[61] Federal parolees continue in the custody of the Attorney General of the United States.

Parole Revocation. Parole may be revoked for commission of a new offense or for violation of any of the conditions of parole. As in the case of probation, parole revocation records may reflect

until the expiration of the maximum term specified in his sentence. McKinney's N.Y.Con.Laws, Ann., Book 10B, Correction Law, § 213.

In California, the term may extend to the maximum term permissible for the sentence for which the parolee was convicted. West's Ann. Cal.Codes, Penal, § 3053.

59. If the statute applies to persons "confined," parolees are excluded; if allowance is on time served, parolees may earn good time allowance, as in Indiana. Woodward v. Murdoch, 124 Ind. 439, 24 N.E. 1047 (1890).

60. Conditions for parole are specified in writing in New York which may include, among other things, a requirement that the parolee shall not leave the state without the consent of the board, that he shall continue to his own support, and contribute to the support of his dependents, that he shall make restitution for his crime, that he shall take clinic treatment if he is addicted to the use of narcotic drugs, that he shall abandon evil associates and ways, and carry out the instructions of his parole officer. McKinney's Correction Law, § 215.

In Illinois, authority to make regulations not inconsistent with laws governing the issuance, supervision and revocation of parole of persons in the custody of the Department of Public Safety is given to the Parole and Pardon Board within the Department. Smith-Hurd Ann. Stat. ch. 38, Crim.Law & Proc., § 123.1.

In Texas, the Board of Pardons and Paroles imposes conditions similar to those for probation. Vernon's Ann.Code Crim.Proc., Art. 42.12.

In California, the authority is with the Adult Authority. West's Ann. Penal Code, § 3053. Conditions of parole are fixed by the parole authority who may require total abstinence from alcohol for a parolee who committed a sex offense where liquor was involved. *Id.* § 3053.6.

61. See fn. 53, *supra*.

only a "technical violation" unless the parolee is actually convicted of the new offense. The agency which granted the parole has the authority to revoke it.[62] Revocation may be recommended to the parole authority by the supervisory parole officer, or information about new offenses of the parolee may come to the parole board from law enforcement officers or the courts. In some states, the parole board must issue a warrant before the parolee can be taken into custody for violation of his parole; in others, the parole officer has authority to arrest without a warrant. (In some states, the parole officer has authority also to search the person and residence of the parolee without a warrant if a parole violation is suspected.)

The law is not clear as to whether or not the parolee is always entitled to a hearing on a charge of parole violation. Some court decisions mandate such a hearing, and some statutes require it. Most states provide a hearing as a matter of practice. A hearing is not a trial, and even when a hearing is provided for it may amount to little more than permitting the parolee to appear before the board and plead his case against revocation. There is as yet no Constitutional requirement that a parolee be represented by counsel at a parole revocation hearing,[63] nor does he have a right to summon witnesses on his behalf. The decision of a parole board to revoke parole will not be reviewed by the courts so long as the revocation was done within the scope of the legislative authority and was not on whim or caprice.

62. In Illinois the paroling authority may revoke the parole and return the parolee to custody to complete his sentence upon violation of any conditions of parole. Smith-Hurd Ann.Stat. ch. 38, Crim.Law & Proc., § 123-3.

In New York, parole may be revoked if the parolee has violated the conditions of his parole in any important respect. McKinney's Con.Laws of N. Y., Ann., Book 10B, Correction Law, § 216. A hearing before three members of the board of parole is provided for in New York.

In Texas, the parolee is granted a hearing on revocation within 45 days of arrest. Parole is revoked by the governor on recommendation of the Board of Pardons and Paroles. Vernon's Ann.Code Crim. Proc., Art. 42.12, C., Sec. 21.

In California, parole may be revoked by the Adult Authority if the prisoner breaks his parole, or violates any law of the state, or rule or regulation of the prison, or of the department [of Corrections], the director of the Adult Authority, or any of the conditions of his parole. West's Ann.Penal Code, § 3053. The Governor has like authority to revoke a parole and may issue a warrant for the arrest of the parole violator. *Id.* § 3062.

63. A parolee in Michigan has a right to an attorney at a parole revocation hearing. Warren v. Michigan Parole Board, 23 Mich. App. 754, 179 N.W.2d 664 (1970).

In some particulars the parolee's rights are fewer than those of a probationer. This is partly due to the differing ideas as to what parole actually is in a legal sense. Parole is considered by many as an act of grace, not a right; thus, the discretion of the board to grant or deny parole is not subject to judicial review and decisions to revoke parole need not guarantee the parolee a hearing. Probation statutes often provide for a suspension of imposition of sentence, but the parolee is in every sense a "convicted man," with a consequent loss of rights. Some authorities see parole agreements as a contract between the state and the parolee; if the contract provides for revocation of parole without hearing, then by accepting parole, the parolee has agreed to the terms and waived his right to a hearing. A few see parole as a "right," and argue for formal hearings and representation by counsel before revocation.

After revocation of parole, the parolee is sent back to the institution to finish serving his term.[64] In some states, he is allowed credit on his sentence for the time successfully spent on parole; in other states, no parole time is credited on the sentence if parole is revoked.[65]

Successful Completion of Parole. If a parolee successfully completes parole, he is discharged as a matter of law. Once a discharge has occurred, the parole authority has no jurisdiction over the parolee. Some states provide for a Certificate of Rehabilitation which the parolee, after a waiting period, sends to the Governor as the basis for a pardon.[66]

64. In New York, if a person violates or neglects to perform the conditions of his parole, he is remanded to the place of his former imprisonment to serve out the unexpired term for which he has been sentenced. McKinney's N.Y.Executive Law, § 18.

This is the practice in Illinois and Texas. In California, the practice has been for the Adult Authority to resentence a California parolee who breaks parole to the maximum term allowed by law. Hester v. Craven, 322 F.Supp. 1256 (S.D.C. 1971).

65. A Texas inmate does not receive credit on sentence for time spent on parole. Vernon's Ann.Code Crim. Proc., Art. 42.12. The sentence of a New York parolee continues to run while he is on parole. McKinney's Penal Law, § 70.40. In Illinois, the time served on parole prior to the violation is credited on the sentence. Smith-Hurd Ann. Stat. ch. 38, Crim.Laws & Proc., § 123–3.

The federal parole violator must serve the unexpired term of his sentence without credit for time served on parole. 18 U.S.C.A. § 4205.

66. In Texas, when any paroled prisoner has fulfilled the obligations of his parole and has served out his term, the Board makes a final order

Interstate Agreements on Probation and Parole. At one time, no method was provided for supervising a probationer or parolee outside the state where he was convicted, in spite of the fact that transient offenders are often arrested and convicted far from home where they have relatives and ties in the community. As a result, there was often no way to provide for supervision of the offender in the very place which would offer him the best chance for success on probation or parole.

Pursuant to the Crime Control Consent Act passed by Congress in 1936, a group of states entered into an agreement under which they undertook to supervise probationers and parolees for each other. This agreement, known as the Interstate Compact for the Supervision of Parolees and Probationers, had been signed by all of the states by 1951.

The act identifies "sending states" (i. e., the state where the offender was convicted and placed on probation or parole) and the "receiving state" (the state to which he wishes to return). Ordinarily the probationer or parolee must be a resident of the

of discharge and issues to the parolee a certificate of discharge. Vernon's Ann.Code Crim.Proc., Art. 42.12, C., Sec. 23. The certificate is in the form of a notice To Whom It May Concern, which sets out the name of the convicted person, his prison number, the date of conviction, the place of conviction and the sentence; the date he was received at the prison, the date of release on parole, and the date of discharge from parole. The same certificate is used to evidence discharge from the custody of the Department of Corrections. The Certificate is signed by the Director of the Texas Department of Corrections by the Chief of the Bureau of Records and Identification.

In Illinois, a person who has served not less than six months on parole may be discharged by the paroling authority. The paroling authority enters an order releasing and discharging the person from parole and his commitment on conviction. When approved by the Governor, the certificate operates as a commutation of sentence. The paroling authority forwards a copy to the clerk of the court in which the person was convicted, who enters on the record judgment that the sentence or commitment has been satisfied and released pursuant to the order. Smith-Hurd Ann.Stat. ch. 38, Crim.Law and Proc., § 123.4.

In New York, the board of parole may grant an absolute discharge from parole prior to the expiration of the full maximum term to any person sentenced for an indeterminate term having a minimum of one day and a maximum of his natural life, or to any person who has been on unrevoked parole for a minimum of five years. A discharge on parole constitutes a termination of the sentence on which the person discharged was released on parole. McKinney's Correction Law, § 220.

California has set up procedures under which a person who has successfully completed parole may apply for a Certificate of Rehabilitation and Pardon. See fn. 78 *infra*.

receiving state, or have relatives there, or have employment there. The receiving state agrees to accept the offender and give him the same supervision as is accorded a probationer or parolee in the receiving state. The sending state may enter the receiving state and take custody of the probationer or parolee who has violated the terms of his release without going through extradition proceedings, and a supplementary agreement even permits the violator to be incarcerated in the receiving state at the expense of the sending state, if both states consent.

Parole boards usually designate one member of their number to be the "Interstate Compact Administrator." He handles all the details of arranging the supervision of parolees who are either sent out of the state for supervision or received into the state after conviction in another state. Where probation is locally administered, the compact does not work as smoothly for probation supervision as for parole supervision. However, some exchanges take place and probation supervision is provided by the receiving state.

RELEASE

A convicted man who has successfully completed his term on probation or parole is entitled to his release from custody as a matter of law. A Discharge from Probation is noted on the court docket and may be followed by procedures to "wipe out" the conviction. A Parole Discharge Certificate is mailed by the parole board to the inmate, the parole supervisor, and to the department of corrections or warden of the institution of incarceration. Offenders being released from institutions are provided with a document evidencing their release, called a Discharge or Discharge Certificate.[67] If these documents are not furnished, the inmate is discharged by operation of law.

Over 90 per cent of convicted offenders are released from custody at some time, a fact which should be kept in mind in planning rehabilitation and resocialization programs. Rarely is a man locked up and "the key thrown away," no matter how serious his original offense. In most states, even "lifers" are eligible for parole after a stated period in the institution, though they are often barred from earning "good time." The actual date of re-

67. See fn. 66, *supra*.

lease of a convicted man from the institution depends both on the sentence imposed and the earned good time, the release date usually corresponding to the maximum term less good time.[68] This means that the time he actually spends in prison is considerably less than the maximum term fixed in the sentence pronounced by the court. Correctional authorities in general would prefer that a man always have a period of supervision to assist him in making the adjustment from institutional to community life, but this is not generally provided. However, a federal prisoner who can earn good time at a maximum rate of ten days per month after serving ten years of his sentence, must remain under supervision of a parole officer for the number of days his earned good time exceeds 180 days.

A few inmates are "released to a detainer," which as we have seen, is a kind of hold and means that the inmate is wanted to answer to offenses committed within or without the state for which he has not yet been tried or for which he has not completed the serving of his sentence (as where a man escapes from one prison and before he is caught is arrested and convicted of another offense, perhaps in a different state). The warden notifies the holder of the detainer and when and where the man will be released. If the officers from the other state or jurisdiction are on hand to take him into custody, the releasee is returned to that state or jurisdiction for trial or to complete a sentence.

Some institutions provide the newly released inmate with a new set of clothes, which he is permitted to select for himself from a supply kept in the prison. He is also given a bus ticket to his last residence within the state, and a small sum of money known as "gate money."

The Real Sentence. There is a difference between the *permissible* sentence for an offense (the minimum and maximum set by statute), the sentence *imposed* upon the offender (pronounced by judge or jury), and the sentence actually *served* (after reductions for good time and early release on parole). The important sentence to the defendant is, of course, the sentence actually served. The statute may provide a maximum sentence of twenty years, the particular defendant receive a maximum sentence of ten years, and the operation of the good time statutes result

68. Whether good time is applied to the maximum or minimum sentence depends upon the laws of the state.

in his release in a little over six years. The courts of some states tend to impose quite long sentences; yet because of the generous good time allowances, inmates actually serve shorter average terms than do offenders in states where the sentences imposed are not as long but the good time allowances are less generous. The *real sentence* of an offender is a function of the offense, the statutory penalty, the sentence imposed, the operation of probation and parole laws, the effect of good time allowances, and, as we shall see, of the continuing handicaps resulting from loss of rights upon conviction.

LOSS OF RIGHTS UPON CONVICTION

In all states of the Union, a conviction for a felony carries with it the loss of certain civil and political rights belonging to the citizens of the state. In some states, the rights are lost only upon conviction for an offense against the state; in others, rights are lost though the conviction is by another state or by the federal government.[69] The criminal statutes of the United States do not generally provide for forfeiture of civil rights upon conviction, but at one time citizenship itself could be lost if the offender was found to have deserted in the time of war from the military or naval service of the United States, or was convicted of treason against the United States. The decision in Trop v. Dulles[70] declared this to be cruel and unusual punishment prohibited by the Eighth Amendment. The court pointed out that there is no greater punishment than to render a man stateless.

Rights Automatically Lost Upon Conviction. The laws of each state list the rights that are automatically lost upon conviction. These may include the right to vote, the right to hold public office, the right to serve on a jury, and in a few states, the right to testify in a court of law. The armed forces of the United States refuse induction to a convicted felon and even to young men with a juvenile record. Seventeen states provide by statute that a defendant sentenced to a life term, or to death, suffers

69. In California, the Adult Authority may permit paroled persons civil rights, other than the right to act as a trustee, or hold public office, or exercise the privilege of an elector during parole. West's Ann. Penal Code, §§ 3054 and 3055.

70. Trop v. Dulles, 356 U.S. 86, 78 S.Ct. 590, 2 L.Ed.2d 630 (1958).

"civil death." In at least seven states the property of the man declared civilly dead may be distributed as though he were actually dead. His marriage is automatically dissolved and his children are subject to adoption as though he were dead.

Rights Which May be Lost Upon Conviction. Other rights which are not automatically lost may be lost by the convicted defendant by action of an individual or licensing board. Conviction of a felony is grounds for divorce in most states, though some require a certain period of imprisonment. Right to keep or obtain professional licenses of all sorts are extensively affected by a felony conviction. A convicted felon cannot obtain or keep a license to practice medicine; to practice law; to remain or become an architect; an engineer; an accountant; or even a barber or beauty operator. Convicted felons cannot obtain liquor licenses, nor run stores where liquor is sold (often they are not even permitted to work in them), and any employment requiring that a bond be furnished is out of the reach of the employee or prospective employee with a criminal record. In cases of existing licenses, the licensing authority may have to take formal action to remove the license, but when it does, removal is all but inevitable.

So extensive are the effects of the loss of rights on the convicted offender that many persons maintain that he suffers social banishment almost as severe as that suffered when specific sentences of banishment were handed down by the English courts. That the effects of a felony conviction are a life-long handicap cannot be denied, particularly in the matter of securing and keeping employment. Almost all applications for employment make inquiry of the applicant as to felony convictions; many inquire as to misdemeanor convictions and arrests as well. The problem is made more serious by the fact that there are few means established by law under which the rights can be restored and the felon be relieved of the handicaps which he incurs upon conviction.

PARDON

A pardon is a form of executive clemency used to correct mistakes in criminal justice as well as to restore rights lost upon conviction. Breaking the king's peace or otherwise violating his laws was deemed a personal affront to the king, which he could forgive. Thus, the pardoning power usually lies with the governor of the state,[71] though some of the early colonies gave the power to the legislature. The exercise of the pardoning power by the governor is restricted in some states. In Texas, for example, though only the governor has the power to pardon, he cannot issue a pardon until the action has been recommended by the Board of Pardons and Paroles. In some states, the pardoning power can be exercised only after conviction; in others, it may be used to free a man in any stage of the criminal justice process. Even in the states which require that the pardon must follow conviction, it may be exercised after verdict and before judgment, and while an appeal is pending.

Application for Pardon. In about half the states, the man desiring a pardon must publish a notice of his intention to apply for it and notify both the prosecuting attorney and the court. He may be required to also notify the chief of police in the town where the crime was committed. In other states, the convicted person petitions directly to the pardoning authority or to the governor, who may be required to notify the court, the prosecutor, and the police that the application has been filed. The pardoning body has authority to investigate the applicant's criminal and social background, medical and psychiatric examinations may be required, and employment records may be examined. Some states set hearings on the application at which persons in favor of or against the granting of the pardon are permitted to appear. Such a hearing is required for securing the Certificate of Rehabilitation which forms the base of a pardon in California.[72]

Granting the Pardon. When the required notices have been given and all necessary information developed, the pardoning authority will recommend to the governor that the pardon be granted or denied. In some states, the governor may act without recom-

71. In New York, the governor has authority to grant reprieves, commutations, and pardons for all offenses except treason and cases of impeachment, upon such conditions and with such restrictions and limitations as he may think proper. If a person violates or neglects to perform the conditions of a conditional pardon, the pardon is void and he is remanded to the place of his former imprisonment to serve out the unexpired term for which he had been sentenced.

72. See fn. 78, *infra*, where California procedures are set out in some detail.

mendation, or may grant a pardon notwithstanding a recommendation against it. In others, the governor may deny a recommended pardon, but cannot grant a pardon without recommendation.

The pardon is not effective until it is delivered, and prior to delivery, may be revoked. A pardon may be either full or conditional. A conditional pardon does not become effective until the condition (for example, that the offender return to his native country, or that he make restitution to the victim) has been fulfilled. Failure to fulfill the conditions renders the pardon void.

RESTORATION OF RIGHTS

For many years, restoring the rights of a convicted offender was not considered to be an important problem. The continuing handicaps suffered by an offender who had already "paid his debt to society" were overlooked or ignored. In recent years, however, the matter of restoration of rights has engaged the serious attention of legal and correctional authorities, and the National Council on Crime and Delinquency has proposed a uniform statute setting up legal proceedings to expunge a conviction and to remove the civil disabilities which result from it.

One state (Wisconsin) provides by statute that when a convicted felon has served his sentence, the rights he lost upon conviction are automatically restored. The pardoning power is frequently used to restore rights, though its original intent was only to correct legal mistakes and manifest injustices. Some states provide for petitions to the pardoning authority or to the courts for Certificates annulling the conviction and evidencing restoration of rights. The probation statutes in many states contain provisions for wiping out the conviction when the offender successfully completes his probation. Conviction of an offender sentenced under the Federal Youth Corrections Act is automatically set aside when the offender is unconditionally discharged prior to expiration of maximum sentence.

Rights Restored by Pardon. A full and unlimited pardon restores the ordinary rights of citizenship, such as the right to vote and eligibility to hold public office.[73] A full pardon removes the disabilities of "civil death" in some of the states with civil death statutes. A pardon is also used to restore other rights lost on conviction, being based in some cases, as we have seen, upon a Certificate of Rehabilitation received from a court.[74] It has been held that not even a Presidential pardon restores to a man his right to serve in the armed forces of the United States. Not all licensing bodies recognize a pardon when the regulations prohibit the granting of the license to a man who has been convicted of a felony offense.

Wiping Out a Conviction After Successful Completion of Probation. In an effort to mitigate the hardships caused by conviction of a felony, the probation statutes of many states provide that upon successful completion of the probation, the conviction may be expunged or "wiped out." In some cases, this includes setting aside the judgment, the verdict or plea of guilty, and the indictment, as well as bringing about a dismissal of the charge. If a sentence has been pronounced, it is also set aside, though the procedures on probation usually provide that if an offender is put on probation, imposition of sentence is suspended until probation is revoked.[75] Some misdemeanant probation statutes provide for removing the case from the court docket by action of the court, and specifically state that no conviction shall be entered until after probation is revoked.

Most of these statutes relating to wiping out conviction after successful completion of probation are relatively new and seem

73. A pardon does not actually restore a man to a particular office he lost when convicted.

74. In the federal system, a minimum waiting period of three years must pass before a pardon for this purpose will be considered; in bribery, narcotics, income tax, and some other serious cases, the minimum waiting period is five years. New Jersey will consider granting such pardon only upon proof of good behavior for two years after release. Rubin, *op. cit.*, p. 578.

See also California Restoration of Rights Procedures, fn. 78, *infra*.

75. There is a difference between suspending the *imposition* of sentence and suspending the *execution* of sentence. In the one case, the sentence is not pronounced and probation is granted instead (sometimes called a sentence to probation or a probated sentence). If probation is violated, the sentence is pronounced (imposed). In the other case, the sentence is pronounced but its execution suspended. Offenders with suspended sentences may be free in the community without supervision but may be taken into custody and imprisoned on the original sentence if they commit a new violation. Some states still use suspended sentences; in other states probation has been entirely substituted for the suspended sentence.

not to have been extensively used. Even when the procedures to wipe out the conviction have been successfully employed, the record of the conviction can be used against the defendant in a subsequent criminal case.

Certificates of Restoration of Rights. Some states provide that after the passage of a certain length of time (the time lapse being longer, the more serious the felony), a convicted felon may petition the convicting court for a certificate evidencing restoration of civil rights. Such certificates do not necessarily expunge the conviction, though some form the basis for a pardon.[76] These certificates are variously named—Certificate of Rehabilitation, Certificate of Adjustment, Certificate of Restoration of Rights, Certificate of Good Conduct, and so on.[77]

The procedure is for the petitioner to appear in court and demonstrate to the court's satisfaction that he has been living a law-abiding life for the period required, and in general make the case that he is entitled to restoration of his civil rights and that this restoration is in the public interest. (See fn. 78 below for a description of the comprehensive California procedures.)[78]

76. More than half the pardons granted in California are based on this procedure, set out in West's Ann.Penal Code, §§ 4852.01 to 4852.-2.

77. The California terminology is "Certificate of Rehabilitation;" New York issues a "Certificate of Good Conduct."

78. The procedure for Restoration of Rights and Application for a Pardon as set out in Secs. 4852.01 to 4852.21 of West's California Penal Code provides that a person at any time after discharge from custody or release on parole may file a notice of intention to apply for a certificate of rehabilitation and pardon. (The chapter does not apply to persons convicted of misdemeanors; to persons who have served time in county jails only; to persons serving a mandatory life parole; to persons committed under death sentences; or to persons in the military services.)

The notice is served on the chief of police of the city in which he resides, or upon the sheriff of the county. The petitioner gives to the peace officer his photograph and fingerprints, full information concerning his residence and occupation and any other information concerning his conduct and manner of living which the officer may desire, and agrees to submit to supervision of the peace officer during the period of rehabilitation. The period of rehabilitation begins to run when the notice of intention to apply for certificate of rehabilitation has been filed. At least three years residence in the county must pass, plus 30 days for each year of the term prescribed by statute as the maximum penalty of imprisonment (there are special provisions for persons who committed an offense carrying a life sentence or for persons convicted of multiple offenses).

During the period of rehabilitation, the person must live an honest

The uniform statute proposed by the National Council on Crime and Delinquency provides that the Certificate will also operate to expunge the record of the conviction. The NCCD Act has the additional unique feature of providing by law a form of question to be used on all employment application forms. The question is: "Have you ever been convicted of a felony, the record of which has not been expunged?" A "No" answer to this question protects the convicted felon from the necessity of revealing the conviction at all, and goes farther than do most existing procedures in an attempt to completely conceal the record of conviction. The NCCD Act, as do similar statutes, provides that the conviction may be used against the offender in a subsequent *criminal* action, as for example, to determine his right to probation or parole, or the right to subsequently charge him under habitual criminal statutes.

THE PROBLEM OF RECIDIVISM

The stated objective of the correctional process is to return the inmate to society as a law-abiding citizen. This proposition

and upright life, shall conduct himself with sobriety and industry, exhibit a good moral character, and shall conform to and obey the laws of the land.

At the expiration of the required period, the person files with the superior court of the county in which he resides a petition for ascertainment and declaration of the fact of his rehabilitation. Notice of filing of this petition is given to the district attorney of the county, to the chief of police and the sheriff, and a copy sent to the Governor. After 30 days, the petitioner appears (with counsel if he so desires), for a hearing and brings with him the records of his conviction and release. The supervisory officers, including the peace officers, report to the court. When the procedures are complied with, the court issues a Certificate of Rehabilitation which finds that the petitioner is fit to exercise all of the civil and political rights of citizenship. The court recommends to the Governor that a full pardon be granted the petitioner. Copies of the Certificate are sent to the Adult Authority and the Bureau of Investigation and in the case of persons twice convicted of a felony to the Supreme Court. The Governor may forthwith grant the pardon, except that in the case of a person twice convicted of a felony, the pardon must be granted upon the written recommendation of the majority of the judges of the Supreme Court.

The granting of the pardon restores the person to all civil and political rights of citizenship, including but not limited to the right to vote, the right to own, possess, and keep any type of firearm that may lawfully be owned and possessed by other citizens, except that this last provision does not apply to any person who was ever convicted of a felony involving the use of a dangerous weapon.

is so fundamental that the success or failure of a correctional system is almost entirely measured by the recidivism rate of the offenders who have been subject to its control. The sad truth is that, by this criteria, existing correctional procedures have proved to be extremely disappointing if not, for all practical purposes, almost worthless.

The words "recidivists" and "recidivism" come from a French verb meaning "to repeat." A recidivist is an offender who repeats his offense and thus passes more than once through the criminal justice system. The recidivism rate is an expression of the number of repeaters to the total number of convicted offenders, though methods used to arrive at the recidivism rate are by no means uniform.

General and Specific Recidivism Statutes. The statutes of most states provide for increased punishment for the repeating offender. Rubin distinguishes between "general" and "specific" recidivism statutes. The general statutes provide for increased punishment for the offender who is sentenced to a penitentiary term and has previously served a penitentiary term; or is convicted of a felony after having previously been convicted of a felony; or is convicted of a specified crime and has previously been convicted of a similar one or one of a list of crimes; and so on. Multiple offenders in one or more of these categories may also be subject to prosecution under habitual criminal statutes which mandate imprisonment for life. A specific recidivism statute provides for increased punishment if the crime of which the person is convicted is the same as the one for which he was previously convicted.[79]

Recidivism Rates. The statement is often heard that 60 per cent or more of the offenders are recidivists. Reported recidivism rates, however, vary according to the method by which they are calculated and generally suffer from the fact that they are based on a count of offenders already in custody. Thus, they do not take into account the offenders who have successfully completed probation and parole, and who have not been returned to custody. The figures on probation and parole revocation may themselves be reported in such a way as to conceal the true number of revocations based on the commission of a subsequent offense, as we have previously observed.

79. Rubin, *op cit.*, p. 392.

Whatever the shortcomings of the methods used to arrive at figures on recidivism rates, no informed person in the criminal justice field would deny that too many offenders pass clear through the criminal justice process, are released, and within a very short period are beginning the process all over again. Many released offenders commit several additional offenses before they are caught and returned to the system. Reports given by inmates in one prison system disclose that many of them have had five or ten or twenty previous felony convictions—one inmate admitted to over 100 arrests and said he could not remember all of the times he had been convicted of a misdemeanor. The total number of criminal *acts* represented in an inmate population is many times the number of the inmates.

Since we view the criminal justice system as a system, we cannot blame the high recidivism rate on the correctional process alone. Overcrowded court dockets, long delays before coming to trial, punitive bail procedures, incompetent lower court judges, and according to many, overemphasis on individual rights with little concern for the rights of society, all contribute to the breakdown in the system, dramatically spotlighted by the statistics on recidivism.

The human waste caused by repeated criminality, and its economic and social cost, put recidivism figures into a larger social frame. It is eminently clear that we must get about modernizing and improving our criminal justice system, adding strength and efficiency at every point from arrest to release.[80]

80. The Federal Judicial Center in Washington acts as a clearing house for proposals to modernize federal court operations. A national center for state courts was organized in 1971 upon recommendation of 600 lawyers, judges, and court administrators (including 40 of the 50 state chief justices) who met in Williamsburg, Virginia, in March of that year.

Chapter X

THE JUVENILE COURT PROCESS AND JUVENILE CORRECTIONS

THE JUVENILE COURT PROCESS

Jurisdiction of the Juvenile Court. The jurisdiction of the juvenile court is fixed by statute. As we learned in Chapter VI, the juvenile court is not, strictly speaking, either a civil or a criminal court, though it has attributes of both. Since there is no such thing as a juvenile court at common law, this court more than most courts is a creature of statute.

Juvenile court jurisdiction (which is always original jurisdiction) is basically of two kinds; jurisdiction over dependent and neglected children, and jurisdiction over delinquent children.[1] The court's dependency jurisdiction covers an age range from infancy to eighteen years, or otherwise as fixed by the statutes of the particular state. The delinquency jurisdiction, which is our only concern in this text, covers an age range also fixed by statute, which is characterized by the fact that the lower figure is seldom below the common law age of seven. You will remember that the courts at common law held that a child under seven was incapable of committing a crime after the Church decided that a child under seven was incapable of sin. In some states the minimum age corresponds with the minimum age for criminal responsibility.[2] In many states, however, a child may be subject to

1. The New York Family Court Act introduces an additional category. Both a delinquent and a "person in need of supervision" are subject to the jurisdiction of the court. In the case of a delinquent, the petition must charge that he "requires supervision, treatment, or confinement," while a petition to adjudicate a child to be in need of supervision must allege that he "requires supervision or treatment." N.Y. Family Court Act, §§ 731(c) and 732(c).

2. For example, in North Dakota, a "child" is defined as any person less than 18 years. A similar definition appears in the statutes of Kansas, Arizona, and Pennsylvania. In New York, the juvenile court has jurisdiction over children over seven and less than sixteen years of age. In Texas, the juvenile court age is between 10 years and 17 years for boys and between 10 years and 18 years for girls.

the delinquency jurisdiction of the court at an age when he is still exempt by statute from criminal responsibility.

The maximum age for juvenile court delinquency jurisdiction is also fixed by statute. It varies between 16 and 21 years, with the most common age being 18 years, and may be different for males than for females.[3] A characteristic of juvenile court jurisdiction, however, is that *once it has attached* it may continue until the juvenile reaches 21 years of age. Thus, a juvenile who is within the juvenile court age when he is adjudicated a delinquent may be held in the custody of the court or of the juvenile correctional authority until he is 21.[4] In most states, juvenile court jurisdiction is determined by the age of the offender at the time of the offense; in a few states, the jurisdiction is determined by the age of the offender at the time of trial.[5]

Delinquency Procedures. The *parens patriae* philosophy of the juvenile court had profound effect on juvenile court procedures. In its original conception, the juvenile court was a non-adversary court. The theory was that there is no one in the juvenile court "against" the juvenile; everyone, including the judge, the probation officers, and even the prosecuting attorney, are "for"

3. In Texas, the maximum age is 18 for girls and 17 for boys. Vernon's Ann.Civ.Stat., Art. 2338.

In Illinois, it is 17 for girls, and 16 for boys. Ill. Juvenile Court Act, § 702–2.

In New York, the delinquency age is the same for boys and girls (16 years) but for children in need of supervision (a non-delinquency category) girls are included until they are 18 and boys until they are 16. McKinney's N.Y. Family Court Act, § 714.

In California, the maximum age is 21; jurisdiction is exclusive in the juvenile court under age 18. West's Ann.Cal. Welfare and Institutions Code, § 603.

4. A juvenile in California who has been committed to the Youth Authority for a misdemeanor or felony may, under certain circumstances, be continued in custody of the Youth Authority until he reaches his 25th birthday or beyond. West's Ann.Welf. & Inst.Code, §§ 1770–1771 and §§ 1800–1803.

He ceases to be a ward of the juvenile court when he reaches the age of 21, or two years after adjudication of wardship if he has attained the age of 19 years or more at the time of the adjudication. West's Ann.Cal. Welf. & Inst.Code, § 607.

5. In Texas, the jurisdiction of the juvenile court is determined by the age of the juvenile at the time of trial.

A federal court has held that there was no juvenile court jurisdiction over a person who had reached the age of 27 although the offense was committed when he was under age 18. Application of Johnson, 178 F.Supp. 155 (D.C.N.J.1957). A different result was reached when the juvenile was 19 rather than 27. United States v. Johnson, 141 F.Supp. 641 (E.D.Va.1956).

the juvenile. Since the entire objective of the proceedings was to provide for the juvenile the kind of care and treatment that he would receive from a kind and loving father, juvenile court procedures were informal and protective of the juvenile. His identity could not be disclosed in the public press and an adjudication of delinquency was to cast no stigma upon him. Many juvenile courts took the position that there was no need for the juvenile to be represented by counsel since everyone in the court from the judge down was operating under the sole objective of doing what was best for the juvenile—an attorney would be superfluous under such circumstances.

Unfortunately, the noble objective of the juvenile court was not realized. Instead of protecting the juvenile, the informal non-adversary procedures served to deny him the fundamental rights of due process. So serious was the deviation from fundamental fairness that a Justice of the Supreme Court referred to juvenile courts as "kangaroo courts." [6] The decisions in Kent v. United States and In re Gault [7] required that the juvenile court accord to the juvenile sought to be declared delinquent the basic rights of representation by counsel; including counsel at state expense if necessary; notice of charges; confrontation of witnesses; and the right against self-incrimination. Since these decisions, delinquency proceedings more and more resemble the criminal court process, particularly prior to adjudication of delinquency. Dispositional proceedings which follow adjudication of delinquency remain informal, and certain non-judicial procedures taken at intake result in dispositions without a formal court hearing.

Grounds for Referral to a Juvenile Court. Since the purpose of the juvenile court is to give care and protection to the child, a juvenile may be referred to the court not only for offenses which would be crimes if committed by an adult but for a variety of behavior that in an adult would not be considered criminal. Thus, a juvenile may be taken into custody by the police for committing an offense which if committed by an adult would be a felony, for behavior constituting a misdemeanor, and for such things as truancy, drunkenness, rowdiness, fighting, frequenting

6. Kent v. United States, 383 U.S. 541, 86 S.Ct. 1045, 16 L.Ed.2d 84 (1966).

7. In re Gault, 387 U.S. 1, 87 S.Ct. 1428, 18 L.Ed.2d 527 (1967).

a place of ill-repute, being a runaway, or "engaging in any conduct harmful to himself or others."

Ruth Cavan, in her book *Juvenile Delinquency*,[8] lists some thirty-four types of behavior which may lead to an adjudication of delinquency in one or more states. In addition to behavior which violates a law or ordinance, a juvenile may be declared delinquent if he is incorrigible; is beyond the control of parent or guardian; is growing up in idleness or crime; absents self from home without just cause without consent; habitually uses vile, obscene or vulgar language in public places; wanders streets at night not on lawful business; engages in an illegal occupation; smokes cigarettes or uses tobacco in any form; is addicted to drugs; is disorderly; begs; uses intoxicating liquor; makes indecent proposals; loiters; operates a motor vehicle dangerously while under the influence of liquor; attempts to marry without consent in violation of the law; or is given to sexual irregularities. The juvenile court may exercise jurisdiction over a juvenile for a much wider span of misconduct than that which will give a criminal court jurisdiction over an adult.

Who May Refer a Juvenile to the Juvenile Court. Children of juvenile court age as defined by the statutes of the state are referred to the juvenile court by many different persons and agencies. The majority of referrals are by police officers who apprehend a juvenile in a delinquent act or pick him up after a report of such conduct. Juveniles are also referred to the court by parents, truant officers, school officials, victims of an offense, neighbors, and interested citizens.

Law Enforcement Officers and Juvenile Offenders. Not all juveniles apprehended by the police are referred to the juvenile court. The police perform an important screening process in deciding which juveniles shall be taken to court and which shall be returned to their parents after a warning. Some police departments have informal "rules of thumb" for making such decisions. A young child who has committed a felony or who has been guilty of several misdemeanors will usually be referred to the juvenile court. Sometimes police officers hold a child at the police station for a short period while they attempt to locate his parents or determine if he has previously been picked up by the police or handled by the court. In other cases, they release the

8. Cavan, *op. cit.*, p. 26.

child to his parents while they conduct a subsequent investigation.

Intake. If a child is referred to a fully developed and staffed juvenile court, his first contact in the court will be with an intake officer. Intake officers are on duty in large cities on a 24-hour basis. The intake officer hears the report of the arresting officer, which is usually reduced to writing, questions the child briefly to determine his identity and if possible to get the name and address of his parents, and makes a preliminary decision as to the nature of the child's misconduct and his need for the intervention of the court. Certain children are released, others are referred to other social agencies, and some are held for a hearing before the juvenile court judge.

The intake officer may refer the case to a probation officer, who will continue with the investigation of the case and locate the child's parents. The probation officer may completely release the child to the parents, or may work out with the parents some form of informal supervision with periodic reports of the child's progress to the probation officer. Approximately 50 per cent of the juveniles brought into juvenile court are handled "informally," i. e., non-judicially. No formal petition is filed and there is no adjudication of delinquency.

If the child is a runaway, or his parents cannot be located, or if located, they are obviously unable or unfit to take over the care of the child, the child may be placed in detention either by the intake officer or by the probation officer to whom the case has been referred.

Detention. Detention means holding a child in custody pending investigation or a court hearing. Detention will be in the juvenile detention facility if one exists; where no such facilities exist, children are often held in custody in county or city jails though this is customarily prohibited by law. Detention does not exceed 24 hours unless a court order is secured permitting detention for a longer period. Many juvenile courts have rules which limit this extended period to 72 hours, though as a matter of practice children are frequently held for longer periods when parents cannot be located or when releasing the child would constitute a danger to the child or to others.

Filing of Petition for Adjudication of Delinquency. The probation officer, as part of the intake process, makes a preliminary decision as to whether or not the child is to be "filed on," that is, whether or not he is to be held for a court hearing. The ultimate decision on this matter is usually made after consultation with the assistant prosecuting attorney attached to the court and by members of a special "court section" which has been set up in many juvenile courts since the *Gault* decision. Once a hearing is decided upon, the child may be continued in detention or released to his parents, who are required to bring him back into court on the date set for the hearing.

Preparing the Charges and Providing Counsel. When a court hearing has been decided upon, the charges against the child are reduced to writing and copies are served on the child and his parents. The child and his parents are informed of their right to counsel, at state expense if necessary. In some states, the parents of a child charged with delinquency are required by law to employ an attorney for the child and pay his fees. If the court suspects that the interests of the parent are adverse to the interests of the child, he will make sure that the attorney represents the child, or appoint an attorney in addition to the one chosen by the parents. Indigent parents may select counsel who will be paid by the state, or the court will appoint counsel.[9]

The Adjudicatory Hearing. The hearing before the court is set as soon as possible after the child has been charged, leaving a few days, however, for the defense counsel to prepare his case. The purpose of the hearing is to determine whether or not the child did in fact commit the delinquent act with which he is charged. In an adult court, this would amount to the determination of guilt or innocence.

Since the *Kent* and *Gault* decisions, the proceedings in an adjudicatory hearing in juvenile court closely resemble a trial in an adult criminal court. The adjudicatory hearing is before the juvenile judge and is attended by the child and his parents. A few states provide for juries in juvenile cases, though the United States Supreme Court has held that juveniles have no Constitutional right to a jury trial.[10] The witnesses against the child

9. A few juvenile courts are experimenting with juvenile public defender systems. A defense attorney is employed by the court, the county, or by a semi-public agency such as the United Fund.

10. In re Barbara Burrus, 403 U.S. 528, 91 S.Ct. 1976, 29 L.Ed.2d 677 (1971).

appear in court and testify on oath as in an adult court. An assistant prosecuting attorney or an attorney attached to the juvenile court represents the state and examines and cross-examines witnesses. The lawyer representing the child cross-examines the state's witnesses and presents witnesses on behalf of the child. The case against the child must be proved to the same level of proof required in criminal cases—beyond a reasonable doubt.[11]

After hearing all of the evidence, the court may dismiss or continue the case or make an adjudication of delinquency, which is a finding that the child is a delinquent child in need of the further supervision of the court. If the child is found to be delinquent, the court sets a date for the dispositional hearing or asks for the Social History Report and makes an immediate disposition of the case.

The Social History Report. The Social History Report is very similar to the Pre-Sentence Report used in adult criminal courts. The report is prepared by a Probation Officer who makes an extensive investigation of the child's background, family relations, mental and physical health, school performance, work record, and prior delinquent history. The Probation Officer starts the preparation of the report when the decision is made to file on the child, but the judge does not look at the report until after the adjudication of delinquency—this is to prevent information in the report from influencing the judge in his determination of guilt. Once the adjudication of delinquency is made, however, the judge relies heavily upon the Social History Report and upon the recommendations of the Probation Officer who has investigated the case in making his dispositional decisions.

The Dispositional Hearing. The dispositional hearing has retained many of the informal aspects that developed in the juvenile court prior to the *Kent* and *Gault* decisions. At no other point in the juvenile court process is the basic philosophy of the juvenile court more in evidence. The Judge, the Probation Officer, the Prosecutor, the Defense Attorney, and the child's parents, enter into informal discussions as to the best disposition

11. In re Winship, 397 U.S. 358, 90 S.Ct. 1068, 25 L.Ed.2d 307 (1970). The ruling was limited to the adjudicatory hearing, and did not affect the N. Y. procedures governing "children in need of supervision," where the level of proof required has been by a preponderance of the evidence.

for the child—the objective being not to punish him for his wrongdoing but to provide for his care and rehabilitation.

Depending upon community facilities, the judge may have a considerable range of dispositional alternatives. At this late date in the proceedings, he has authority to dismiss the case against the child. He may continue the case (i. e., postpone the order of disposition) or release the child into the custody of his parents. He may place the juvenile on probation, send him to a foster home, to a private institution for children, or as a last resort, commit the child to a state correctional authority or institution. A child may be removed from the custody of his parents without their consent only by court order, but the court has the authority to take the child from his parents if in his opinion this is best for the child.

Certifying a Juvenile for Trial in an Adult Criminal Court. The juvenile statutes of many states provide that juveniles over a certain specified age (usually 16 or 15) may under exceptional circumstances be sent to an adult criminal court for trial. Before this can be done, a hearing must be held before the juvenile court and a finding made that brings the case within the requirements of the statute. "Certification" is made in the case of juveniles who have committed a particularly heinous offense, such as cold-blooded murder, and who, in the opinion of the juvenile judge, can not be rehabilitated in the juvenile facilities. Certification is also used when an older juvenile commits a serious offense for which confinement until he is twenty-one would be a grossly inadequate penalty.

When a juvenile is properly certified to an adult criminal court, his trial will be held as though he were an adult, and the punishment imposed will be in accordance with the penalties fixed by statute for an adult committing the same offense. However, the imposition of the death penalty on juveniles is often specifically prohibited by statute.

Appeals. We have seen that there is no Constitutional right to appeal. This rule was applied to juvenile court proceedings in the case of In re Gault.[12] The juvenile in that case raised the question of his right to appeal, claiming that it was a due process right. The Supreme Court, however, refused to include the

12. In re Gault, 387 U.S. 1, 87 S.Ct. 1428, 18 L.Ed.2d 527 (1967).

right to appeal among the fundamental due process rights of juveniles.

Notwithstanding the fact that there is no Constitutional right to appeal an adjudication of a juvenile court, this right is granted by statute in many states. In some states, there is a *de novo* review. The decision of the juvenile court is given no weight and the whole case is re-examined from the beginning.[13] In New York, the appeal is to an intermediate appellate court.[14] This is also the situation in Texas where the appeal is to the Court of Civil Appeals, an intermediate appellate court below the Supreme Court of Texas.[15] A few states provide for a rehearing in the juvenile court before the case goes to the higher court,[16] and Florida provides for reconsideration under a special motion.[17] In California, there is an automatic review by the judge of any order of a referee that removes a child from his home,[18] or in any case a child may apply for a *de novo* hearing before the judge.[19]

The right to appeal is given in some statutes to "any party aggrieved," [20] which includes the child and his parents. Whether or not the state can appeal is unclear; the Uniform Juvenile Court Act gives the right to appeal to the state or a subdivision of the state.[21]

As a matter of practice, there are few appeals taken from the judgments of the juvenile court. "Sentences" are relatively short even when they involve commitment to a correctional institution. In many cases, both the child's parents and the attorney representing the child feel that the disposition by the court

13. Mass.Gen.Laws, Ann. c. 119, § 56.

14. McKinney's N.Y. Family Court Act, § 1101.

15. Vernon's Ann.Civ.Stat., Art. 2338–1.

16. Or.Rev.Stat. §§ 419.498, 419.561.

17. Sult v. Weber, 210 So.2d 739 (Fla.App.1968).

18. West's Ann.Cal.Welf. & Inst. Code, § 335.

19. *Ibid.* §§ 558, 560.

20. Vernon's Ann.Civ.Stat., Art. 2338–1.

21. Uniform Juvenile Court Act, 59 (a).

See generally on appeals of cases disposed of in juvenile court, Sanford J. Fox, *The Law of Juvenile Courts in a Nutshell*, St. Paul, Minn.: West Publishing Co., 1961.

is the best arrangement for the child, and do not want to prolong the proceedings.

JUVENILE CORRECTIONS

Probation. After a child has been adjudicated a delinquent, the most frequent forms of disposition are probation and commitment to a state correctional institution. A fully organized and staffed juvenile court has a probation department. Except in a few states, Juvenile Probation Departments are locally organized and financed. Typically, however, fully organized juvenile courts exist only in the metropolitan areas; in smaller cities and rural areas, no adequate supervisory services for juvenile offenders are available.

Juvenile probation, like adult probation, is a judicial function. The juvenile on probation continues in the custody of the juvenile court under the supervision of the probation officer. If there is a fully staffed Juvenile Probation Department, the probation officer will be a college educated professional with training and experience in social casework or in juvenile corrections. If there is no juvenile probation department, the probation officer may be the sheriff, an interested citizen, or the juvenile judge himself.

Terms and Conditions of Probation. The juvenile judge in the dispositional hearing sets the term and conditions of probation. Typical conditions require that the juvenile attend school regularly; obey all the laws; be at home every night by a certain hour; remain in a certain locality; and report regularly to the probation officer. Special conditions may prohibit the juvenile from driving a car, associating with the members of a juvenile gang, getting married without the consent of the probation officer, or require that the juvenile make restitution to the victim of his offense. The probation term may extend until the juvenile is twenty-one years old, though in practice probation terms usually do not exceed one or two years.

Probation Supervision. Ideally, the probation officer will have a case load not to exceed fifty probationers, and will have the time to give the juvenile close supervision. As a practical matter, most probation case loads are unrealistically high and the supervision given the juvenile is minimal at best. Some probation officers are beginning to work with probationers in groups, and group therapy for both probationers and their parents is provided in some areas. Some juvenile departments are also experimenting with forestry camps and other special work opportunities for probationers.

Revocation of Probation. Probation can be revoked by the court if the juvenile violates any of the terms of his probation. Typically, probation is not revoked for minor transgressions, but is usually revoked if the juvenile commits another offense, absconds from the jurisdiction, or fails to report regularly. The juvenile has a right to a hearing on revocation of probation and is also entitled to be represented by counsel at the revocation hearing. The juvenile whose probation is revoked is committed to the juvenile correctional authority, or, in some states, directly to a juvenile correctional institution.

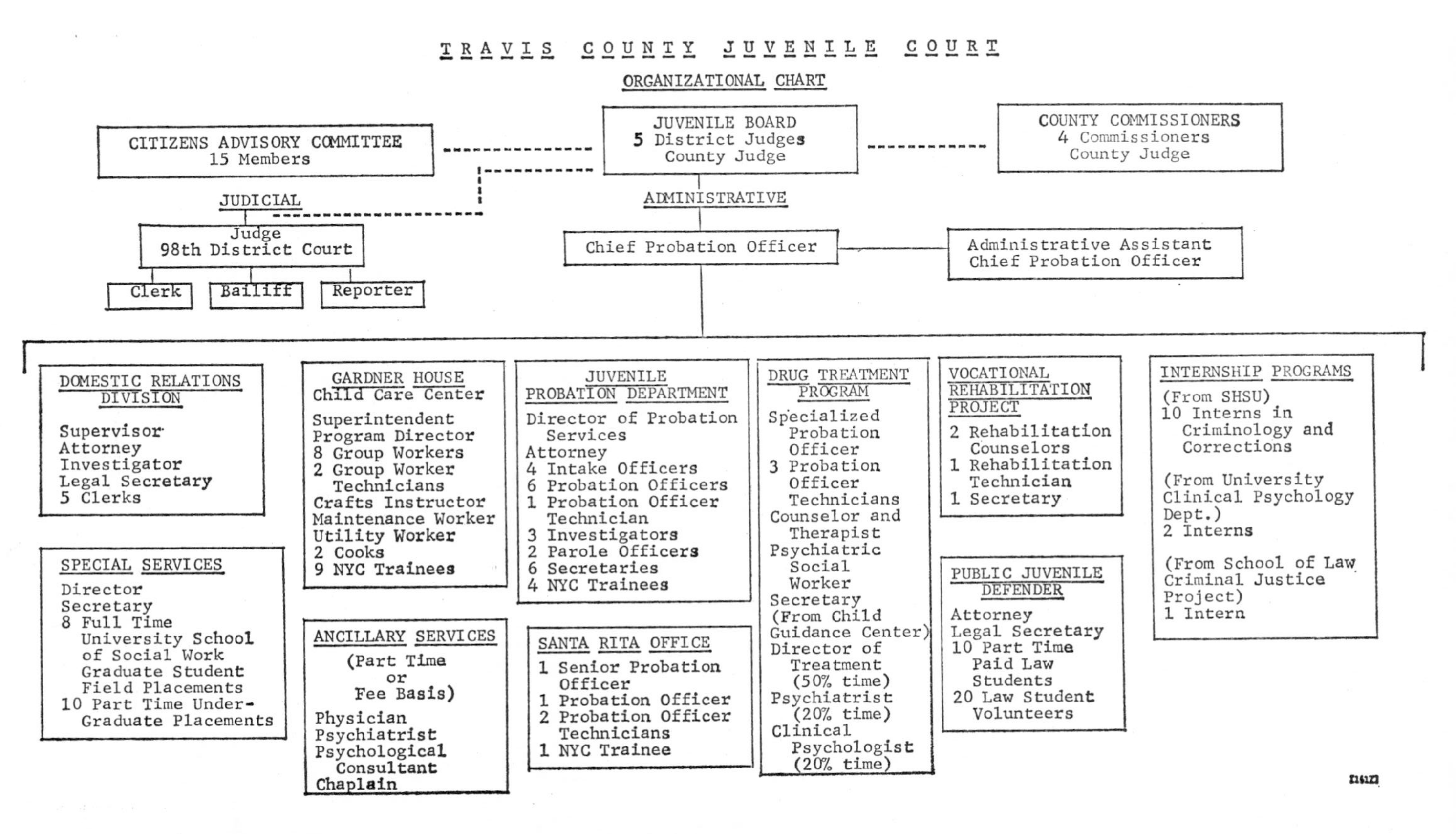
TRAVIS COUNTY JUVENILE COURT
ORGANIZATIONAL CHART
CITIZENS ADVISORY COMMITTEE
15 Members
JUVENILE BOARD
5 District Judges
County Judge
COUNTY COMMISSIONERS
4 Commissioners
County Judge
JUDICIAL
Judge
98th District Court
Clerk
Bailiff
Reporter
ADMINISTRATIVE
Chief Probation Officer
Administrative Assistant
Chief Probation Officer
DOMESTIC RELATIONS DIVISION
Supervisor
Attorney
Investigator
Legal Secretary
5 Clerks
SPECIAL SERVICES
Director
Secretary
8 Full Time University School of Social Work Graduate Student Field Placements
10 Part Time Under-Graduate Placements
GARDNER HOUSE
Child Care Center
Superintendent
Program Director
8 Group Workers
2 Group Worker Technicians
Crafts Instructor
Maintenance Worker
Utility Worker
2 Cooks
9 NYC Trainees
ANCILLARY SERVICES
(Part Time or Fee Basis)
Physician
Psychiatrist
Psychological Consultant
Chaplain
JUVENILE PROBATION DEPARTMENT
Director of Probation Services
Attorney
4 Intake Officers
6 Probation Officers
1 Probation Officer Technician
3 Investigators
2 Parole Officers
6 Secretaries
4 NYC Trainees
SANTA RITA OFFICE
1 Senior Probation Officer
1 Probation Officer
2 Probation Officer Technicians
1 NYC Trainee
DRUG TREATMENT PROGRAM
Specialized Probation Officer
3 Probation Officer Technicians
Counselor and Therapist
Psychiatric Social Worker
Secretary
(From Child Guidance Center)
Director of Treatment (50% time)
Psychiatrist (20% time)
Clinical Psychologist (20% time)
VOCATIONAL REHABILITATION PROJECT
2 Rehabilitation Counselors
1 Rehabilitation Technician
1 Secretary
PUBLIC JUVENILE DEFENDER
Attorney
Legal Secretary
10 Part Time Paid Law Students
20 Law Student Volunteers
INTERNSHIP PROGRAMS
(From SHSU)
10 Interns in Criminology and Corrections
(From University Clinical Psychology Dept.)
2 Interns
(From School of Law Criminal Justice Project)
1 Intern

The chart on the preceding page will help you to understand the juvenile court process and give you an idea of the number of people who are involved in helping the dependent or delinquent child who is referred to the juvenile court. The chart shows the organization of a juvenile court in a city of approximately 275,000 people. Not all juvenile courts have the same organization and few outside of large metropolitan areas provide the services that are offered by this progressive court. In smaller communities, as we have seen, the entire juvenile court may consist of one part-time judge.

Depending upon the offense and the needs of the child, services of any of the persons attached to the court can be called upon. Investigation will begin with intake and may involve detention in the child care center and examination by a physician, psychiatrist, psychological consultant or clinical psychologist. The chaplain acts as spiritual advisor and counselor to both the child and his parents.

Continued investigation and supervision on probation or parole requires the services of the Director of Probation Services and the probation officers. If the case is filed upon, the attorney for the court will present the case against the juvenile. This attorney acts in the same capacity as a prosecutor in a criminal court except that he is generally better informed about and more involved in the dispositional procedures (sentencing). A Public Juvenile Defender staff headed by an attorney and using the services of part-time paid and volunteer law students is a unique feature of this court which will be more and more frequently found in the larger juvenile courts.

The juvenile judge, in this case the judge of a district court, must approve the detention of children held in the Child Care Center for longer than 24 hours. He presides over all hearings in the court, and makes all of the decisions as to the disposition of children who are brought before the court. Only the juvenile judge may order a disposition which involves taking a child away from his parents.

The dispositional alternatives of the juvenile judge include placing the child in the custody of the Youth Council or putting him on probation in his court. The Youth Council may incarcerate the child in a juvenile correctional institution, and after a period in the institution, release him on parole. The juvenile on probation or parole is under the supervision of a probation or parole officer under the direction of the Director of Probation.

A juvenile with a drug problem would be assigned to the Drug Treatment Program under a specialized probation officer who could call upon the psychiatric social worker, the community worker, the counselor-therapist, and the community Child Guidance Clinic.

The Chief Probation Officer is the administrative head of the juvenile court and works closely with the juvenile judge. In this court, the Chief Probation Officer is employed by a Juvenile Board set up by statute and consisting of the county judge and the five district judges. Funds for the operation of the court are provided by the county commissioners. In this state, the county judge is chairman of the board of county commissioners. The Citizens Advisory Committee is a liaison between the juvenile court and the community.

The Internship and special programs bring young professionals into the court for training. The undergraduate interns work in the Court during the summer between their junior and senior years and have an opportunity to put into practice the theories they have learned in school. Graduate students are on supervised field placement assignments. Law students are learning about the legal procedure of the court, and young psychologists are given clinical experience.

As you can see, many highly trained people are involved in the juvenile court process, and many specialized services are available for the purpose of helping children in trouble.

Commitment to a Youth Authority or Institution. A delinquent juvenile who has violated the terms of his probation or who has not been placed on probation is committed to an institution for juveniles. If the state has a state-wide youth authority, the commitment will be to the authority,[22] who will then determine the place and length of confinement (which, however, cannot in most states extend beyond the juvenile's twenty-first birthday).[23]

22. In California, the Youth Authority; in Texas, the Texas Youth Council; in Illinois, the Illinois Youth Commission.

23. In Colorado, the maximum time the child may be held in custody in an institution is two years. Colo. Children's Code, § 22–3–14 (3); In New York, three years. McKinney's N.Y. Family Court Act, § 758(c).

California strictly limits the conditions under which a child may be

If the state has no state-wide youth authority, the commitment will be directly to a state institution for juveniles.[24] Once the juvenile court has committed the juvenile to a state youth authority or institution, the authority of the court over the juvenile is ended.

Treatment Programs in Juvenile Institutions. A large state will have many types of juvenile institutions and provide a variety of programs for the rehabilitation of delinquents. Early training schools focused on suffering and hard work; modern schools emphasize continued academic education and counseling. Work camps, often called forestry camps, have been found effective in many states, though the boys sent to such camps are usually carefully selected from the general training school population.

Parole. Some youth authorities provide for parole from a juvenile institution which is similar in all respects to adult parole. The juvenile is released into the community under the supervision of a parole officer who is employed by the youth authority or is sometimes a probation officer attached to a juvenile court.[25] He can be returned to the institution for violation of his parole conditions.

Aftercare. Many authorities working with delinquent juveniles believe that all juveniles need supervision when released from an institution. Aftercare supervision may be similar to parole supervision or may consist of assignment to a "halfway house." Halfway houses are located in the community, and provide a place where a boy may live while he is readjusting to life in a free society. Authorities in the halfway house assist the youth in obtaining a job which he may work at during the day, return-

removed from his home. One of three conditions must be found: (1) that the parent or guardian is incapable of providing or has failed or neglected to provide proper maintenance, training, and education for the minor; (2) that the minor has been tried on probation in the custody of the parent or guardian and has failed to reform; or (3) that the welfare of the minor requires that his custody be taken from his parent or guardian. West's Ann.Cal.Welf. & Inst.Code, § 726.

24. In some states, a juvenile may be transferred from the juvenile institution to an adult penal institution. This is the law in Wisconsin, Wis.Stat.Ann. § 48.

Placing a child in a penal institution is forbidden by the Uniform Juvenile Court Act, § 33(a).

25. In some states probation and parole officers supervise both adults and juveniles.

ing to the halfway house at night. When the boy and his counselors feel that he is able to "go it on his own," he is given his complete release from the youth authority and moves out of the halfway house.[26]

Release from Youth Authority or Institution. The juvenile may be released by the youth authority whenever in its opinion he has ceased to be a danger to the community and is ready to assume the responsibilities of a law-abiding citizen. All juveniles who have been committed to the youth authority or the institution by a juvenile court must in most states be released when they reach twenty-one years of age.[27]

The Effect of an Adjudication of Delinquency. The founders of the juvenile court took great precautions to protect the juvenile from any adverse effects from an adjudication of delinquency. Juvenile records were made available to authorized persons only; fingerprinting was forbidden, or if fingerprints were taken for identification purposes or to connect the juvenile with the offense, their later destruction was required. Publication of the names of the juveniles in the public press was forbidden, or the press agreed to refrain from such publication. Statutes provided that a juvenile record could in no way be held against a juvenile when he became an adult.[28]

In spite of the precautions, a juvenile record is a handicap in later life. The Armed Forces customarily refuse to induct an adjudicated delinquent; if he is accepted into the Armed Forces,

26. Juvenile and youth offenders committed under the Federal Juvenile Delinquency Act and the Youth Corrections Act were sent for a time to Pre-Release Guidance Centers. The new Community Treatment Centers chiefly serve the age group 20–35 as the Pre-Release Guidance Centers did not prove to be successful with younger juveniles. Gerald A. Collins, "The Changing Program of Pre-Release at the Federal Level," *Proceedings of National Conference on Pre-Release*, p. 49–58.

27. A juvenile in California who has been committed to the Youth Authority for a misdemeanor or felony may, under certain circumstances, be continued in custody of the Youth Authority until he reaches his 25th birthday or beyond. West's Ann.Welf. & Inst.Code, §§ 1770–1771 and §§ 1800–1803.

28. The Uniform Juvenile Court Act of 1968 and the Legislative Guide for Drafting Family and Juvenile Court Acts were prepared by the Children's Bureau in 1969. The Uniform Act has been adopted in North Dakota and several states contemplating revision of their juvenile court law are expected to incorporate many of the provisions of the Uniform Act.

it is after careful investigation of his success on probation and his subsequent conduct. A juvenile record increases the difficulty of obtaining employment, may result in the refusal of applications for licenses to engage in certain kinds of business, may make it impossible to secure a surety bond, and otherwise close the door to employment opportunities. However, the handicaps of a juvenile record are mild indeed when compared to those which follow a felony conviction. It is encouraging that efforts are being made to provide legal means to "wipe out" both a felony conviction and an adjudication of delinquency.

Chapter XI

HABEAS CORPUS AND EXTRADITION

HABEAS CORPUS

The writ of habeas corpus is referred to as the "Great Writ of Liberty." [1] Its purpose is to obtain the release of a person illegally confined or restrained of his liberty. The literal meaning of habeas corpus is "you have the body" and the writ commands the person "having the body" (i. e., restraining another) to bring the person into court and show cause as to whether or not the detention is legal.

The first Habeas Corpus Act was enacted in the reign of Caroline II (1689) and was amended in the reign of George III, who was the monarch at the time of the American Revolution. The Act was regarded as the great constitutional guaranty of personal liberty. It was provided for in the constitutions of the original colonies and is included in the constitutions of all of the states. Among the powers denied the Congress of the United States in Article I, Section 9, Clause 2 of the United States Constitution is the right to suspend the privilege of the writ except in cases of rebellion and invasion:

> The Privilege of the Writ of Habeas Corpus shall not be suspended, unless when in Cases of Rebellion or Invasion the public Safety may require it.

Technically the writ of habeas corpus is a civil and not a criminal remedy, but since it can in modern times be used in the federal courts and many state courts not only to deliver from illegal confinement but to test the conditions of confinement, the writ is closely associated with the criminal process.

What the Writ Is. The writ of habeas corpus is the remedy used when any person is restrained of his liberty. It is an *order* issued by a court or judge of competent jurisdiction, directed to

1. Ex parte Kelly, 123 N.J.Eq. 489, 198 A. 203 (1938).

anyone having a person in custody or under his restraint and commanding him to produce such person, at a time and place named in the writ, and show why he is held in custody or restraint.[2]

Who May Issue the Writ. The writ at common law could issue out of the courts of Chancery, King's Bench, Common Pleas, and the Exchequer. The writ, now as then, is issued by a great variety of courts. Most courts of record and of appeal in a state can issue the writ, as may any judge or justice of such a court. The Supreme Court and the lower federal courts, or any justice or judge thereof, can issue the writ. The writ issues day or night. It is usually given precedence on the docket, though this is not the case on reviews by the Supreme Court which originate in the application of a convicted prisoner for the writ.

Application for the Writ. An application for a writ of habeas corpus may be made by the person illegally confined or by any person on his behalf. The application sets out the name of the person being confined, the name of the person holding him in custody, or if unknown, the descriptions of the persons. The applicant then requests the writ of habeas corpus, and swears to the statements made by him. Inmates in penitentiaries speak of "writing a writ." What the inmates actually prepare is the application or petition for the writ—the writ itself, as we have seen, is an *order of a court.*

Issuance of the Writ. The judge or court may order a hearing on the application or issue the writ without delay. The writ is served upon the person charged to be illegally holding another, and if necessary, both the person being held and the person holding him may be arrested in order to insure their appearance before the court.

Return of the Writ. The writ must be immediately obeyed by the person on whom the writ is served, who must make a return setting out whether or not it is true that he has another under custody, by virtue of what authority he took and detains the person, and if he is holding the person under some legal authority, he must attach a copy of the document to the return of the writ. The person detaining another must also bring that person

2. West's Ann.Cal.Penal Code, § 1477. Vernon's Ann.Texas Code Crim.Proc., Art. 11.01.

before the judge unless it can be shown that by reasons of infirmity or sickness he cannot be removed. The person who is produced will be in the custody of the court until a hearing on the return can be made. Confinement may be in jail or otherwise as the court may direct.

Hearing and Order on the Return of the Writ. The court may set a time and place for a hearing on the return of the writ at which the person having custody must appear and show cause, if he can, why the detention is legal. After hearing all the facts and circumstances, the court may remand the restrained person back into custody of the person holding him, decree other provisions for his care or custody, admit him to bail, or discharge him. The court's decision is evidenced by a written Order which must be immediately obeyed by all parties.

Special Considerations Applicable to Prisoner's Writs. As we have seen, the writ of habeas corpus may be used by a person to secure his release from illegal arrest or from any other illegal confinement. The situation with respect to inmates of penitentiaries or other correctional institutions is somewhat different. They have been convicted of a criminal offense and are being held in custody under the authority of a judgment of conviction and commitment. A convicted man files the writ of habeas corpus to test the legality of the proceedings against him and, in some cases, in an effort to change the conditions of his confinement (to be released from solitary confinement, to be assigned to another institution, to receive certain privileges denied him by the prison authorities, etc.).[3]

3. The right to file a writ is a right guaranteed to the convicted man by the First Amendment. In re Ferguson, 55 Cal.2d 663, 12 Cal. Rptr. 753, 361 P.2d 417 (1961), cert. den. 368 U.S. 864, 82 S.Ct. 111, 7 L.Ed.2d 61.

Right to legal counsel is not guaranteed since the application is not technical and the writ is a civil remedy. Ex parte Hull, 312 U.S. 546, 61 S.Ct. 640, 85 L.Ed. 1034 (1941), reh. den. 312 U.S. 716, 61 S.Ct. 823, 85 L.Ed. 1146.

However, an illiterate Tennessee prisoner was held to be entitled to help from a "jailhouse lawyer," i. e., a fellow inmate, if no other assistance was available to him. Johnson v. Avery, 393 U.S. 483, 89 S.Ct. 747, 21 L.Ed.2d 718 (1969).

Progressive prison systems provide inmates with "writ-writing rooms," access to legal materials, and the assistance of an attorney employed by the department of corrections. Instructional manuals prepared by members of the Bar and the Division of Correctional Services are given to inmates in Minnesota.

In the case of federal prisoners, the writ is directed to the Attorney General of the United States. Writs issued on petition of state prisoners are directed to the director of the state department or division of corrections in the states where custody of convicted felons is placed in such a director or to the warden of the prison where the inmate is being held in the states without a central correctional organization. Writs may also be addressed to jailors holding misdemeanants or to superintendents of special correctional or treatment institutions. Juvenile offenders direct the writ to the state youth authority or to the superintendent of the institution where they are confined. As a result, the directors of the state departments of corrections are among the "most sued" members of the community.

The special procedures applicable to prisoners' writs have to do with the court in which the application for the writ may be filed, the provision for an evidentiary hearing, and the court which may actually order the release of the prisoner. An ordinary habeas corpus application may be filed in any court; the provision as to a prisoner may require that the application must be filed in the court of conviction. The trial judge may issue the writ of habeas corpus without a hearing, but is encouraged to provide a full evidentiary hearing at which the convicted prisoner is given every opportunity to prove the allegations of his complaint and the prosecutor permitted to justify his continued confinement. After hearing all of the facts and circumstances, the trial judge may issue or deny the writ. In the case of an ordinary habeas corpus writ, the writ is made returnable to the same court that issues the writ. In the case of prisoners' writs, however, the Texas law requires that the writ be made returnable to the Court of Criminal Appeals. The purpose of this is to restrict to the higher court the right to actually release a convicted prisoner from custody.

Federal and State Court Conflict over Prisoners' Writs. Applications for writs of habeas corpus filed by state prisoners in federal courts have been a source of considerable conflict between federal and state courts. As we have seen, only the Supreme Court can set aside a state prisoner's conviction on appeal or *certiorari* from the highest state court; lower federal courts have no such authority. However, Congress has given the lower federal courts jurisdiction in habeas corpus, which is a *civil* remedy. The result is that if a state prisoner claims that his *federal*

Constitutional rights were denied him in the state proceedings, he may obtain a review of those proceedings in federal District or Circuit Court, and by way of *certiorari* in the United States Supreme Court if the United States Supreme Court consents to review the case.

Prior to the "Criminal Justice Revolution," the practice was for the federal courts to require that the convicted man "exhaust his state remedies" before applying for federal habeas corpus. This meant that the federal courts would not hear the complaint of the inmate until it had been ruled upon by the highest court of criminal appeals in the state. In the last decade, however, federal courts have not adhered to this rule and have considered applications for habeas corpus filed by state prisoners who have not applied to the highest court of their state for relief. The lower federal courts have also frequently ordered the release of the prisoner after the highest state court has denied such release. The resulting conflict has strained federal and state court relations and inundated the federal courts, including the Supreme Court, with applications for writs of habeas corpus filed by state prisoners.

An effort is now being made to reduce this area of conflict between state and federal courts and to reduce the habeas corpus burden on the federal courts. The special procedures applicable to prisoners' writs have helped in this regard by setting up evidentiary hearings (a hearing where witnesses are heard) in the state courts. Such a hearing gives the convicted man his "day in court" and permits him to place before the court all of his arguments for release. Where such full hearings have been provided to the state prisoners, the federal courts tend to scrutinize the petitions filed in the federal court very carefully, and to grant an additional hearing in the federal court only when manifest error in the ruling of the state court can be demonstrated. The federal courts are also moving toward rules which will prevent the repeated filing of applications for the writ by prisoners, state or federal. The courts will hear a second application only if it can be demonstrated that it is based upon facts not included in the first application and not known to the inmate at the time of his first application. These changes will improve federal-state court relations and reduce the number of "frivolous" and repetitious applications for the writ of habeas corpus filed by convicted prisoners and other applicants as well. Justice Black remarked that the Supreme Court has more important things to do than decide on the length of a student's hair, particularly on an application alleging an "emergency."

The American Bar Association Standards Relating to Post Conviction Remedies. The American Bar Association Project on Minimum Standards for the Administration of Criminal Justice recommends a single or unitary remedy for post-conviction review to test the validity of judgments of conviction or the legality of custody or supervision based upon a judgment of conviction. The unitary remedy would encompass all claims whether factual or legal in nature and would take primacy over any existing procedure or process for determination of such claims.

Though, as we have seen, habeas corpus is a civil remedy, the *Standards* [4] recognize that it partakes of some of the attributes of both a civil and criminal proceeding, thus, the single unitary remedy would not be governed by characterizing it as either criminal or civil. There is recognition of the fact that the post-conviction stage is in a sense the extension of the original proceeding.

The *Standards* provide that the appropriate moving party in a post-conviction proceeding is the person seeking relief, proceeding in his own name. The respondent would be the entity in whose name the original prosecution was brought. Thus, the action would be entitled, John Doe v. the State, the People, the Commonwealth, or the United States of America, instead of being against the director of the department of corrections or the warden or superintendent of the correctional institution, as is the case in traditional habeas corpus proceedings.

The *Standards* suggest that original jurisdiction to entertain the application for post-conviction relief should be vested either in local trial courts authorized to try criminal cases, or in a single court of state-wide jurisdiction such as an appellate court. The most desirable venue is the court in which defendant's challenged conviction and sentence were rendered.

Grounds for relief are sufficiently broad to provide relief for meritorious claims, including claims that the conviction was obtained or sentence imposed in violation of the Constitution of

4. American Bar Association Project on Minimum Standards for Criminal Justice, *Standards Relating to Post-Conviction Remedies*, New York: Office of Criminal Justice Project, Approved Draft, 1968.

the United States or the laws of the state in which the judgment was rendered. Claims based upon the unconstitutionality of state statutes, the lack of jurisdiction of the court, or on the grounds that a sentence imposed exceeded the maximum sentence authorized by law, could also be raised. Claims based on retroactive decisions (as Gideon v. Wainwright)[5] would be heard. That a sentence has been fully served, or that there has been an unlawful revocation of probation or parole would constitute grounds for relief.

The *Standards* require that the applicant for relief be provided with certain minimum resources for the preparation of his application. These include stationery and supplies; the right to purchase and retain legal reference materials in reasonable amount; reasonable access to any legal reference material in the prison library; and uninhibited access to the courts and to private counsel.

It is stated as desirable for a prison to arrange for in-prison guidance and counselling of prisoners on the validity or invalidity of claims for post-conviction relief. Methods suggested are regular visits by lawyers or law students to the prison to discuss cases or problems on an individual basis, as arranged by an independent agency such as a local bar association or defender association or law school. The establishment of an adequate collection of legal reference materials in the prison library, and the distribution of specially prepared pamphlets to prisoners outlining the scope of post-conviction relief "in language understandable to the prison population" is also recommended.

The *Standards* recommend that no filing fees be required for filing the application, and that judges give personal attention to all applications for relief. The procedures set up in the *Standards* insure a fair hearing at which the applicant can present evidence. If an application proceeds beyond the preliminary screening stage, counsel would be provided the applicant who could not afford representation.

Appellate review of the decisions on the application are provided for, but repeated applications for post-conviction relief based upon the same facts and legal arguments can be denied by the court.

5. Gideon v. Wainwright, 372 U.S. 335, 83 S.Ct. 792, 9 L.Ed.2d 799 (1963), on remand 153 So.2d 299 (Fla.).

EXTRADITION

The Purpose of Extradition. Extradition is the method by which a fugitive from justice from one state may be returned from another state to stand trial in the state where the offense was committed, or if he has been convicted and escaped from custody, returned to the convicting state to complete his term of imprisonment. If D commits an offense in Wyoming and before he can be brought to trial in Wyoming flees to Colorado, extradition provides a method by which Wyoming may get him back from Colorado to answer to the charges in Wyoming. Extradition is necessary because, as we have seen, a criminal offense must be tried in the state where committed. Thus, Colorado cannot try the accused for the crime committed in Wyoming, and Wyoming can try him only if it has jurisdiction over his person. The obtaining of that jurisdiction over a fugitive from justice is the purpose of extradition proceedings.

Constitutional Provisions on Extradition. The Constitutional base for extradition is set out in Article IV. Section 1 of Article IV states that "Full Faith and Credit shall be given in each State to the public Acts, Records, and Judicial Proceedings of every other State. And the Congress may by general Laws prescribe the Manner in which such Acts, Records and Proceedings shall be proved, and the Effect thereof."

Section 2 of Article IV provides that "the Citizens of each State shall be entitled to all Privileges and Immunities of Citizens in the several States," and goes on to set out the basic provisions for returning a fugitive from justice from a sister state to the state from which he fled. The provisions are as follows:

> A person charged in any State with Treason, Felony or other crime, who shall flee from Justice, and be found in another State, shall on demand of the executive authority of the State from which he fled, be delivered up, to be removed to the State having Jurisdiction of the Crime.
>
> (No Person held to Service or Labour in one State, under the laws thereof, escaping into another, shall in Consequence of any Law or Regulation therein, be discharged from such Service or Labour, but shall be delivered up on Claim of the Party to whom such Service or Labour may be due.)

The Uniform Criminal Extradition Act. The method of obtaining extradition is set out in contracts between the states. Congress authorized the states to contract together for various purposes; cooperation in the matter of law enforcement was one of the first agreements arrived at between the states after Congressional approval for such contracts was given. The contracts between the states are, so far as possible, alike or uniform, and are evidenced by acts passed by each state legislature which authorizes the governor of the state to enter into the contract. These agreements are usually called "Interstate Compacts."

The compacts or contracts between the states are reciprocal, providing in the case of the Uniform Criminal Extradition Act that the state in which the fugitive is found will deliver him up to the state in which the crime was committed, and that the sister state will extend a like privilege to the other state. The basic provisions in the extradition law may read as follows:

> A person in any other State of the United States charged with treason or any felony who shall flee from justice and be found in this State, shall on demand of the executive authority of the State from which he fled, be delivered up, to be removed to the State having jurisdiction of the crime.[6]

The Uniform Criminal Extradition Act sets up the procedures between the states. The duty of the Governor is as follows:

> Subject to the provisions of this Article, the provisions of the Constitution of the United States controlling, and any and all Acts of Congress enacted in pursuance thereof, it is the duty of the Governor of this State to have arrested and delivered up to the Executive Authority of any other State of the United States any person charged in that State with treason, felony, or other crime, who has fled from justice and is found in this State.[7]

Demand for Extradition. The Uniform Act then sets out the method of extradition. It first provides that the governor of the state where the offense is committed shall demand in writing that the governor of the state harboring the fugitive return the fugitive to the state in which he committed the offense. Copies of the indictment or information and of warrants of arrest must

6. These provisions are quoted from Article 51 of Vernon's Ann.Texas Code Crim.Proc.

7. *Ibid.*

be attached. In case of a convicted felon who has escaped custody or violated the terms of his probation or parole, copies of the judgment of conviction or sentence authenticated by the governor of the state seeking the extradition of the fugitive must be attached. A complete set of the instruments must also be delivered to the defendant or his attorney.

Governor's Warrant of Arrest. The governor may investigate the case or call upon the Secretary of State, the Attorney General, or any prosecuting officer in the state to assist him in the investigation. If he decides that the demand should be complied with, he signs a warrant of arrest, sealed with the state seal, and directed to any peace officer or other person who may be entrusted with its execution. An interesting provision of the law is that the governor may *not* inquire into the guilt or innocence of the accused of the offense charged. The governor is properly concerned only with whether or not the demanding state shows a right to have the fugitive returned—the right to determine the guilt or innocence of the accused remains with the state where the offense was committed. The governor must also protect the rights of the accused in the extradition proceedings, but not to the extent of judging his guilt or innocence of the offense charged.

> The guilt or innocence of the accused as to the crime of which he is charged may not be inquired into by the Governor or in any proceeding after the demand for extradition accompanied by a charge of crime in legal form as above provided shall have been presented to the Governor, except as it may be involved in identifying the person held as the person charged with the crime.[8]

Execution of the Arrest Warrant. The arrest warrant is executed by taking the accused into custody, and the arresting officer may confine the person so arrested in jail. Under certain circumstances, a fugitive may be arrested without a warrant. Commitment under such an arrest may not exceed thirty days —the time given the governor to determine whether or not he will honor the request for extradition and issue the governor's warrant of arrest.

Rights of the Accused Person. The accused person must be taken before a judge of a court of record, who must inform him of the charges and of the demand of the requesting state for his sur-

8. *Ibid.*

render. Counsel is provided for, if the accused cannot hire his own. If the accused desires to attack the validity of his arrest, he must be given a reasonable time to file a writ of habeas corpus. When such a writ is applied for, notice must be given to the prosecuting officer where the arrest is made, and to the agent of the demanding state. Unless the offense charged is punishable by death or life imprisonment under the laws of the state where committed, the accused has a right to bail until arrested under the governor's warrant. The accused is also given certain immunities from service of civil process while awaiting extradition.

Waiver of Extradition Proceedings. Any person charged in one state with having committed a crime in another state or who has escaped from confinement in another state, broken bail or the terms of probation or parole, may waive the issuance and execution of the governor's warrant of extradition. In order to waive extradition, the fugitive must record a writing in a court of record in the state to which he has fled which states that he consents to return to the demanding state. The judge of the court is required to inform him of his rights to formal extradition proceedings evidenced by the governor's warrant, and if the accused stands by the waiver, to direct the officer having him in custody to deliver him up to the officer or agent of the demanding state. A great many fugitives waive extradition and voluntarily accompany the officer back to the state where they committed the offense to stand trial or be returned to confinement if the flight occurred after conviction.

Part Three

THE PROFESSIONALS IN THE CRIMINAL JUSTICE SYSTEM

INTRODUCTION TO PART THREE

A profession is characterized by organization, learning, and public service, and by a code of ethics by which the behavior of its members is judged and regulated. A spirit of public service distinguishes a profession from a trade or commercial activity.[1] In a fully recognized profession the following characteristics can be identified.

1. A recognized body of knowledge which is systematically transmitted to new members.
2. A professional organization to which the members belong or with which they identify themselves.
3. A Code of Ethics regulating the conduct of members.
4. Licensing, which grants the privileges of the profession to qualified persons and denies them to persons not licensed.
5. A spirit of public service.

Of persons working in the criminal justice system, the members of the legal profession belong to one of the great historical professions, which included the military, medicine, law, and the ministry. Legal knowledge is formally transmitted in approved law schools and tested in bar examinations. The American Bar Association and Bar Associations in each state, district, county or city are professional organizations of lawyers. Lawyers are bound by a comprehensive Code of Professional Responsibility, which is enforced by the organized Bar and by the courts. Only licensed lawyers may practice law. Lawyers perform and are expected to perform a variety of public service, including donation

1. Davis, Foster, Jeffrey, Davis, *op. cit.*, p. 313–314.

of legal services to indigents or others in need of such services and to public and civil organizations. The members of the legal profession associated with the criminal justice system are the prosecutor, the defense attorney, and the lawyer-judge.

While the lawyers are the only regular workers in the criminal justice system (except for the prison doctors and chaplains) who belong to one of the classic professions, other groups of workers in the system meet most, if not all the criteria which characterize a profession. They have specialized training and skills derived from a recognized body of knowledge which is systematically transmitted to new members; they have professional organizations and codes of ethics; members of some of the groups must be licensed or "certified," all demonstrate a spirit of public service. We have, therefore, elected to label as professionals in the criminal justice system not only the prosecutor, the defense attorney, and the lawyer-judge, but also the police officer, the correctional administrator, the probation and parole officer, the institutional correctional officer, and the court administrators. Because of their frequent close association with criminal justice, we have also included two related professionals—the psychiatrist and the social worker.

With respect to these professionals, we will explore their method of selection, their education and training, and their roles in the criminal justice process. We will also consider the inter-relationships among the professionals in the system. As we have pointed out in the Introductions to Parts I and II, understanding and cooperation among all persons associated with the criminal justice system is an imperative if criminal justice is to fulfill its crucial role in a modern society.

Chapter XII

THE POLICE

THE POLICE AGENCIES

In the United States, the police function is performed by a variety of agencies at all levels of government. According to the report of the *President's Commission on the Administration of Criminal Justice*, there were 40,000 law enforcement agencies responsible for enforcing the laws in 1966. Only 50 of those agencies were agencies of the federal government, and 200 were state agencies. The other 39,750 were dispersed throughout the counties, cities, towns, and villages of the United States. The police function is, therefore, primarily one of local government,[1] and the police officer's authority and responsibilities are confined to a single jurisdiction.

Federal Police Agencies. The people of the United States have never permitted the organization of a national police force with general investigatory and law enforcement powers. Such forces in pre-war Germany, in Russia, and in other totalitarian countries have provided examples which Americans have no intention of following. For this reason, even the Federal Bureau of Investigation has power only as to federal offenses and is primarily an investigating agency. The law enforcement powers of the other federal agencies are restricted to protecting the President and Vice-President and their families, and to federal tax, drug, currency, postal, and customs violations, and to interstate crimes. Park Rangers and Indian Agents operate in restricted areas, and the authority of the Military Police does not extend to civilians nor even to some non-military offenses committed by members of the armed forces.

State Police Agencies. The American reluctance to centralize police power has extended to state police agencies as well. Only

1. The President's Commission on the Administration of Criminal Justice, *Task Force Report, The Police*, (Washington, D. C.: Government Printing Office, 1967) p. 7.

a few states have state police agencies (such as the Texas Rangers) which possess general police powers. For the most part, state police are restricted to enforcement of the traffic laws and to providing state systems of communication and criminal investigation. Game wardens, officers of the liquor control unit, and similar state law enforcement officers have state-wide jurisdiction, but only over particular offenses.

Local Police Agencies. At the county level, the sheriff is the law enforcement officer. In rural areas he is the chief law enforcement officer. Constables and marshals may be county or precinct officers or officers of an incorporated town or village. The police officers attached to large, urban police departments are the officers largely responsible for law enforcement in the United States. In discussing the role of the police in the criminal justice system, we shall be referring chiefly to the city and the members of a large city police force.

THE POLICE OFFICER

The Complexity of the Police Role. Police are men charged with the duty of investigating crime and apprehending criminals. To fulfill the duty, they are given authority to invoke the criminal process—to arrest, to prosecute, and seek a conviction. As important as this function is, however, the average police officer spends a relatively small part of his time investigating and prosecuting serious criminal offenses. Most of his day is spent in keeping order, settling disputes, finding missing children, helping drunks, directing traffic, and monitoring parking meters. Because police are on duty 24 hours a day, the community sees them as a service agency to be called upon for an incredible number and variety of services. If a city gas main springs a leak, the police cordon off the area, go from house to house warning the residents, and re-light the pilot lights when the emergency is over. If a child's pet can't get down out of the tree, the police are called to help. They are supposed to prevent injury to children, drunks, mental patients, and naive citizens frequenting dangerous areas. They are called upon to deal with organized crime, sponsor sports programs for delinquent or threatened youngsters, conduct community relations programs, and deal with riots and other civil disorders.

Not only must the police officer keep the peace, investigate and prosecute crime, control traffic, protect children and needful citizens, and sponsor community programs of various kinds, he must also be aware of just how much law enforcement the citizens of his town desire or will tolerate. Any police officer who tried to enforce all the laws on the statute books would be out of a job overnight. Americans pass laws which they do not expect, and may not want, to be enforced. The speed limit may be 70 miles an hour, but the officer is not supposed to give a ticket to the substantial citizen doing 72 on the freeway. Gambling and prostitution are forbidden, but red light districts flourish and are tacitly accepted by the community. Stealing and public drunkenness are illegal, but the police officer is not supposed to arrest the conventioner who takes a couple of towels from the motel or is found on the street too drunk to get to his hotel room under his own power. The complexity and inconsistencies of the duties and services performed by the police make police role definition difficult and result in uncertainty and confusion among both the police and the citizens whose lives and property they are charged with protecting.

The Police Role in Handling Serious Offenses. While recognizing that the total police role is complex and confused, let us focus on the role of the police in the handling of the serious offenses against persons and property. The police officer is often called the "case finder" of the criminal justice system. Of the reported crimes, almost all are witnessed by or reported to the police. National statistics on the incidence of crime are based upon "crimes known to the police." Another set of statistics is based on "crimes cleared by arrest," which reflects crimes which the police have solved to the extent of making an arrest of one or more persons as perpetrators of the offense. The conviction of the persons arrested is not seen as a police responsibility though the police officer will testify as required and otherwise cooperate with the prosecutors in obtaining a conviction. Records kept by some police departments make no attempt to reflect the final disposition of a case—as far as the police are concerned the crime is "cleared" by the arrest, and their primary responsibility has been fulfilled.

The police officer's main duty in serious offenses is investigation and apprehension. To perform this job properly, he possesses a wide knowledge of the city, of the social conditions and incidence of crime in different areas of the city, and a great deal of information about individuals in his area prone to criminal acts. The police officer sets up relationships with people who, for a variety of reasons, will give him information about offenses and offenders and develops a system by which he keeps track of known offenders and troublemakers. In some areas, ex-convicts and offenders on probation or parole are required to register with the police.

The police officer has an important decision-making function. He by no means arrests every individual breaking the law, nor does he report every known offense to the prosecuting authorities. When he responds to a domestic dispute, he rarely arrests one of the spouses, though each may have inflicted substantial battery upon the other. He has learned from experience that the wife who wants her husband in jail will be as anxious to get him out in the morning as she was to get him in the night before. Prosecution would be useless—she will not testify against him. The patrolman on the beat, at least prior to the day of almost universal two-man squad cars, is typically watching over several juveniles, many of whom have already committed a juvenile offense. By means of talking with the child and his parents, and often by informal supervision, the officer attempts to keep the young person out of serious conflict with the society and out of juvenile court. The police officer also makes such decisions as whether or not to arrest the drunk or take him home to sober up; to grant immunity from arrest to a cooperative informer; to give a summons instead of making an arrest of the speeding motorist. He decides whether to make further investigation of the suspicious conduct of A, but to forego or postpone investigation of B. The police officer is also called upon to make some life and death decisions. He must decide whether or not to use force in making an arrest or apprehending a fleeing felon; perhaps he must decide to use deadly force to protect his own life or the life of another if the felon is resisting arrest.

Most police decisions must be made quickly and often under tense and rapidly changing conditions. Police officers resent the fact that an appellate court, by a 5–4 decision (five judges voting one way, four another) may overrule after months of study a decision that the police officer had to make in seconds, particularly when the majority opinion goes on to roundly castigate the police officer for his actions. Police opposition to civilian review boards rests largely on the proposition that no civilian, several days or weeks after the event, can correctly assess the forces operating upon the police officer which affected his on-the-spot decision and behavior. Education and training, experience, and clear administrative policy and directives help the police officer to make large and small decisions rapidly and correctly.

Once an arrest is made, police responsibility extends to booking, taking the accused before the magistrate, conferring with the prosecutor, appearing before the grand jury on request, appearing at the preliminary hearing, and testifying at the trial. Police investigation may continue up to the time and even during the trial. Police officers with special training and skills take fingerprints, and make scientific tests of all kinds. Investigations of physical evidence, such as footprints, blood stains, hair and skin under the nails of a homicide victim, and the like, are routine. Police officers are responsible for the preservation and proper handling of evidence and must be able to establish the "chain of possession" (i. e., show who has handled the evidence and that it has not been tampered with). If the police officer mishandles the evidence, it cannot be admitted at the trial against the accused. The criminalistics laboratories of the Federal Bureau of Investigation, of state criminal investigation agencies, and of metropolitan police departments are fully equipped, and staffed with highly trained professionals. Police departments maintain extensive communications facilities which are now being integrated into a national police communications network.

The decision to arrest is mainly a police decision, though the prosecutor and the magistrate are involved in the issuance of arrest warrants. Theoretically, the decision to prosecute is made by the prosecutor. In practice, however, the police officer often makes the decision to prosecute or has a great deal of influence on the decision. In spite of the fact that arrest by definition is for the purpose of holding the accused for prosecution, police make arrests for reasons other than prosecution. La Favre, in his study of arrest practices, sets out several circumstances under which arrests are made for purposes other than prosecution. These include detention for purposes of investigation; short detentions not considered to be an arrest; arrest of persons for their own protection (drunks in need of care, and suspected sexual offenders in danger from the community); and arrests to control prostitution, illegal gambling and other vice offenses. Some such arrests are immediately challenged by writs of habeas corpus, but the majority go unchallenged in the courts and are accepted as permissible, or even necessary police procedures.[2]

The Changing Role of the Police. Many factors are operating to change the role of the police. Supreme Court decisions have changed police practices in the areas of investigation and arrest. The *Miranda* Warning; mandatory legal representation of the accused in early stages of the investigatory process (during field investigation after suspicion has focused, and at the station house during the line-up or show-up) have brought about changes in police handling of the suspected offender. Whether or not these changes have seriously handicapped police investigation or have resulted in improved investigating techniques is a matter of considerable controversy in law enforcement circles. Studies made in the city of Dallas by the Institute of Contemporary Corrections and the Behavorial Sciences at Sam Houston State University were not able to demonstrate that the new procedures had significantly reduced arrests, indictments, or convictions over a two year period.[3] Other studies have reached similar conclusions.[4]

On the other hand, there is little doubt but that the average patrolman *feels* that the courts have given all the breaks to the offender—which may affect his performance as well as his morale.

Proposals are also being made to streamline and clarify the police role by making the police department a law enforcement

2. La Favre, *op. cit.*, pp. 483–489.

3. Wilburn Furn Foster, *Effects of Miranda Decision on the Grand Jury Process in Dallas County, Texas.* Unpublished Master's Thesis, Sam Houston State University, 1970.

William Scott, *The Effect of the Miranda Decision on Confessions in Dallas County, Texas.* Unpublished Master's Thesis, Sam Houston State University, 1970.

Richard M. Prather, Sr. *Effect of the Miranda Decision on Arrests in Dallas County, Texas.* Unpublished Master's Thesis, Sam Houston State University, 1970.

4. Evelle J. Younger, "Interrogation of Criminal Defendants—Some Views on Miranda v. Arizona," *Fordham Law Journal*, 35:255, December 1966. (Mr. Younger was District Attorney of Los Angeles County, California, when the article was written.)

Walter E. Meyer Research Institute, "Interrogation in New Haven," *Yale Law Journal*, 76:161a, July, 1967.

agency and not a community service organization. The suggestions are that offenses such as drunkenness and drug abuse be handled in detoxification centers and drug abuse clinics, removing the responsibility for these offenders from the police. It is also suggested that reports of domestic disputes be turned over to trained social workers, and that existing offenses such as homosexuality between consenting adults and abortion, be removed from the criminal code. Special traffic departments could be staffed with persons trained for traffic control but not trained for criminal investigation; only when a traffic offense required more than routine investigation would the fully trained police officer be called. Traffic meters could be monitored by meter-maids, and school crossings protected by men and women hired or even volunteering for the service. Reduction in the kinds of behavior constituting crime will reduce the number of criminals, and changes in the social definition of crime will have considerable impact upon the role of the police officer.

Education and Training of Police Officers. Police recruits in police departments at all levels of government have always had to meet certain physical standards as to height, weight, age, and visual acuity. Educational standards have been non-existent for one reason because police salaries have been so low that well-educated persons could not be attracted to police service. Only in the past few years have the larger departments required that the police recruit be a high school graduate; in smaller departments, even this standard is not met. However, this situation is changing rapidly. Partly as a result of the impetus furnished by the Omnibus Crime Control and Safe Streets Act, but mainly because of the leadership of police themselves, state and local educational standards require high school graduation for all police. In the future, this requirement will be raised to graduation from junior college and above. Many major metropolitan police departments now require recruits to have at least some college education, and are rapidly moving toward all-college-graduate police forces. By instituting incentive pay, giving academic leave, and co-operating with colleges and universities offering education to police, one city hopes to have a police department made up entirely of college graduates by 1975.

The emphasis in college education for police departs sharply from training offered in the traditional police academy. The college-educated police officer studies such subjects as causes of crime and deviant behavior, the psychology of youthful and adult offenders, minority group relations, urban sociology, social problems, probation and parole supervision, constitutional law, and community relations. He is also enrolled in courses in statistics, advanced management techniques, computer science, and research methods.

Police academy training, which has traditionally introduced the new officer to accident investigation, use of firearms, report writing, and laws of arrest and of search and seizure, will continue, but on an expanded basis. Under the impetus of standards set statewide by police standards commissions created by the state legislature, a minimum number of hours of classroom instruction in a variety of police related subjects is required of new and old officers alike, and academy training is scheduled to increase in amount and complexity.

The Specification for Awarding Law Enforcement Officer Qualification Certificate, as adopted by one Commission on Law Enforcement Officer Standards and Education, for example, makes provision for a Basic Certificate, an Intermediate Certificate, and an Advanced Certificate. Each of these certificates is awarded on the basis of the individual's length of service, police training, and higher educational pursuits at colleges and universities. The Commission also established specifications for the qualification of police instructors.[5]

The curricula for in-service police training places emphasis on the "how to do" police work; the education offered in colleges and universities, on the other hand, enables the officer to recognize the social and psychological significance of what he does. Police authorities believe that ideally an officer should first receive an education, because training goals can then be achieved with greater ease. But neither education nor training is labeled as most important, "for an officer needs to be adequately trained as well as adequately educated."[6]

5. Howard O. Benson, *Texas Law Enforcement Inservice Training—A Survey and Manual for Improvement of Inservice Training*, published as a *Monograph* by The Institute of Contemporary Corrections and The Behavioral Sciences, Huntsville, Texas, 1970.

6. *Ibid.* p. 39.

The Wyoming Law Enforcement Academy, sponsored by the Wyoming Peace Officers' Association and the University of Wyoming, with the cooperation of the Federal Bureau of Investigation has been training police officers from the Rocky

Some authorities are recommending a tri-level structure of programs in law enforcement education and training identified as follows:

1. **Junior colleges** to provide a basic professional education. They would serve as the springboard for entrance into four year colleges and universities. Officers, or potential officers will be given an understanding of the important role they play in the social order of the community, and in the welfare of the individual.

2. **Four year colleges or universities** offering professional programs leading to bachelor, masters, and doctorate degrees. This would be the primary setting for research and scholarship. From here would come the leaders of tomorrow, and the cadre of teachers for the profession.

3. **Law enforcement training schools** for vocational education. All phases of police training would be covered by both department training and outside agency schools and academies.[7]

Articles appearing in the professional journals of police, interviews with police chiefs of both large and small departments and with the police officer in the college classroom, are making it clear that police education is no longer seen as simply covering the laws of arrest and search, the rules of evidence, and legal basis for handling civil disorder. Police education of today must include in particular, says one writer, knowledge as "to the social

Mountain region since 1957. Officers from Wyoming, Colorado, Montana, Utah, New Mexico and Kansas have graduated from the Academy.

The courses are divided into classroom lectures and field problems and cover such subjects as burglary investigation, civil rights, basic sociology, accident investigation, psychology, homicide investigation, narcotics, counterfeiting, fraudulent checks, signed statements and confessions, sex crimes and assault investigations, jurisdiction of law enforcement agencies, laws of arrest, search and seizures, automobile theft, crime scene searches and laboratory examination, public relations in law enforcement, description and identification of persons, defensive tactics, testifying in court, handling of mentally disturbed persons, firearms training, game laws, records and crime reporting, and other technical subjects.

Resource personnel are provided by federal, state, and local law enforcement agencies. *University Reporter*, Vol. 1, No. 3, Febr., 1971; a publication of the Alumni Office, University of Wyoming, Laramie, Wyoming.

7. *Ibid.*, p. 42.

issues and behavior problems which confront the police every day."[8]

Though the police officer has only recently begun to admit it, not only is he a law enforcement officer, he is a correctional officer as well. One of the main objectives of the correctional process is to return the offender to society with respect for the law and the ability to stay out of trouble with the law. In almost 100 percent of the cases, the first contact of the offender with the law is with a police officer. The way the police officer goes about his business gives the offender his first impression of how the law operates. If the police officer is arbitrary, demeaning, or cruel, the offender forms a firm impression that the law is arbitrary, demeaning, and cruel—an impression which is seldom erased as he goes through the criminal justice process.

> Insofar as the goal of rehabilitation is respect for law and order, the granting to a parolee of what will *seem to him* a "fair deal" by giving him ample opportunity to present his side of the story will, of itself, increase that respect. An appearance of just dealing is as indispensable as justice itself.[9]

The highly educated and trained police officer of the future will recognize his correctional role in the criminal justice system.

The Police Officer in Relation to Other Professionals in the Criminal Justice System. The police officer is, of course, one of the most important professionals in the criminal justice system. Traditionally, however, his view of himself with respect to the rest of the system has been narrow and in some cases antagonistic. At the same time, other professionals in the system have tended to ignore or downgrade the role of the police officer and to blame him for circumstances and conditions beyond his control. Public support of police officers has in the past few years reached a new low, with police officers being labeled "pigs" and worse, and subjected to unprovoked verbal and physical abuse. One thing is true of the police officer—he doesn't like crime and criminals. He strongly resents what he calls the "do-gooder" approach to serious and persistent offenders. He will say with disgust that when he apprehends a juvenile and takes him to the

8. A. F. Brandstatter, "Education Serves the Police, the Youth and the Community," *The Police Chief*, August, 1966, p. 14.

9. In re Tate, 63 F.Supp. 961 (D.C. D.C.1946).

juvenile court, "the kid beats me home." By this he means that the youngster is released by the court so promptly that the investigation and arrest made by the police officer is made to appear useless. Even worse, the officer has the youngster right back on his beat to cause more trouble.

A moment's reflection will make it clear why the police officer, probably more than any other professional in the system, strongly dislikes crime and criminals. The police officer is the only criminal justice professional who regularly sees *the victim* and *the damage the criminal act has caused.* The police officer talks to the molested child, sees the results of a brutal beating, views the bloody dead body of the filling station operator who has been ruthlessly and unnecessarily killed by the robber. He must identify the young girl killed or mutilated by a drunken driver, and notify her parents. He listens to the heroin addict pleading for "a fix," and trys to comfort the old couple defrauded of their life savings. No other person in the criminal justice system comes into such constant direct contact with the victim. Actually, few other professionals in the criminal justice system ever see the victim, except perhaps as a witness in court many months after the happening. The rules of evidence require that gruesome pictures, particularly in color, that show the blood and gore of a brutal murder may not be admitted into evidence lest they "inflame the minds of the jury." No matter how professional he is, the policeman who has walked in on the bloody scene gets his mind "inflamed," and finds it hard to forget what he saw when he faces the offender. Other professionals in the system would do well to be sensitive to the police experiences at the scene of the crime, and appreciate the reasons for his "be tough on criminals" attitude. After he has arrested the same offender over and over, he should be forgiven his skepticism about the success of correctional programs. He should be consulted on penal reform, and be listened to when he talks about community problems. He should not be made the scapegoat for an antiquated and inefficient criminal justice system, and above all, he should receive the community support he deserves.

The police officer, on the other hand, should expand his knowledge of the other segments of the criminal justice system. It might help him to know that the juvenile court released the juvenile because the detention home was full and no foster homes were available. He should have an understanding of what the probation and parole officer is trying to accomplish, and realize that while incarceration may remove the offender from the neighborhood for a time, he will almost surely return, since few men are kept in prison for life. He can then support innovative and successful treatment programs which, hopefully, may change the offender's behavior, and lend his help to ameliorate the social conditions which are closely associated with criminality. The police officer can move from riot control to "confrontation management" and recognize that some traditional police methods in controlling civil disorders are counter-productive. He can see himself as the first—and a very important—cog in the criminal justice process; but only a part of the process, nevertheless. He will then realize the importance of interpreting the role of the police to others working in the system, and accept the fact that his own performance is related to and dependent upon his understanding of the criminal justice process as a whole.

Chapter XIII

THE JUDICIAL OFFICERS

Lawyers admitted to the Bar of the state become the prosecutors, defense attorneys, and lawyer-judges in the criminal justice system. Some non-lawyer judges serve in the lower courts and in the juvenile courts, but the felony and appellate courts and many of the juvenile courts are staffed with judges who have been legally trained.

Until recently, criminal law has been inadequately taught in law schools, and the Criminal Bar has not enjoyed a place of high prestige in the legal profession. The position of prosecutor has traditionally been used as the place where a young lawyer may gain trial experience before entering into private practice, or as a stepping-stone to higher political office. Except for a few attorneys who make national reputations as defense attorneys, representing defendants in criminal cases has never been a lucrative field of legal practice. Separate criminal courts exist only in the more populated areas. Since the majority of his case load will be civil cases, it is difficult for the average judge to specialize in criminal law.

Within the past few years, however, many changes have taken place that will raise the level of the Criminal Bar and result in impressive improvements in the operation of the courts and in the criminal justice process. Law schools are increasing their offerings in the criminal law, and the courses are attended by some of the brightest law students. The American Bar Association has sponsored a College for the training of prosecutors. Defender systems of various kinds are attracting able young lawyers to careers as defense attorneys. The lawyer is also finding a place in the juvenile court as prosecutor and defender, as well as judge.

Reform of the lower court system will increase the percentage of lawyer-judges in the courts and gradually eliminate the "barber-turned-judge" who is not unusual in justice, municipal, and even juvenile courts. The Chief Justice of the United States Supreme Court and the leaders of the Bar are calling attention to the need for court reform to speed up criminal justice and increase court efficiency. Penal Code reform has been completed or is going on in many states, which will eliminate the arbitrariness and inadequacies of Codes originally adopted for a sparsely populated and largely rural society. These reforms will bring about changes in the education and training of the professionals identified with the judicial process.

THE PROSECUTOR

The Importance of the Prosecutor. The Prosecuting Attorney is one of the most important professionals in the criminal justice system. His range of authority and the crucial nature of his decisions exceed those of any other person—with the possible exception of the judge. The prosecutor makes the decision to charge the suspect with a crime, which has obviously serious implications for the individual involved. The prosecutor determines the nature of the charge. He has authority to reduce the charge by negotiation or agree to a bargained sentence. He can dismiss the action once it has been filed, a decision he sometimes must make with the approval of the court, but which in many jurisdictions is his alone. The prosecutor conducts trials, appears before the courts of criminal appeal, represents the state in habeas corpus proceedings, is assigned to recommend the governor's action in extradition, and goes before the legislature to recommend or oppose penal reform. In the public mind, he is often the foremost law officer of the community. He makes innumerable decisions about the prosecution of offenses that largely determine the course of law enforcement in that community.

How Prosecutors are Selected and Trained. Prosecutors are attached to federal and state courts of all levels. The Attorney General of the United States represents the United States in the United States Supreme Court and in the Courts of Appeals. United States District Attorneys conduct trials in federal district courts. Attorneys General customarily represent their state in the criminal courts of appeal, both state and federal. In some states, the Attorney General is the chief prosecuting officer and appears in person or by deputy in all major criminal trials. In other states, the Attorney General appears only occasionally in a trial proceedings (as when the prosecuting attorneys of Marin County, California, withdrew from the prosecution of the Angela

Davis case because of their close association with the judge who was killed).

The Attorney General of the United States and the United States District Attorneys are appointed by the President. Attorneys General of the states are elected or appointed by the governor of the state. The prosecuting attorney of a district or county is usually an elected official; an appointed or elected City Attorney acts as the prosecutor in most municipal courts. The prosecutor in a juvenile court may be county or district attorney or an assistant assigned to handle juvenile cases, or he may be an employee of the court or its probation department. Prosecuting attorneys are variously called state's attorneys, county attorneys, district attorneys, prosecuting attorneys, and prosecutors.

One elected official will constitute the entire prosecuting attorney's office in small counties and rural districts. The prosecuting attorney of a large metropolitan area may employ a hundred or more assistants whom he selects, usually subject to the approval of the county commissioners or whatever governmental body authorizes the payment of salaries.

Until recently, few prosecuting attorneys had received any special training in the duties of the prosecutor prior to assuming office. In-service training was largely informal training received from older and more experienced prosecutors. Law schools are now introducing specialized courses for students interested in becoming prosecutors, and the National College of District Attorneys, sponsored by the American Bar Association, at the University of Houston College of Law is offering formal courses of instruction.

Particularly in smaller communities, the prosecuting attorney's job is more or less reserved for the young attorney who supports himself in the job while he builds up a clientele for private practice; in many areas, the prosecutor may engage in the general practice of law while holding the position of prosecutor. District Attorneys in metropolitan areas complain that the salaries offered prosecutors are so low that young attorneys stay as assistants only long enough to gain practical experience in the law and then go off to become defense attorneys or join private law firms. To be elected prosecuting attorney is often considered a stepping stone to higher political office. The career prosecutor is thus relatively rare.

Many of the proposed reforms of the criminal justice system are directed toward providing specialized education and training for prosecutors and encouraging career dedication to the office by able young lawyers.

The Role of the Prosecutor. The prosecutor is involved in the prosecution of criminal cases from the time of arrest to final conviction, and has considerable influence on the sentence. He is a party to the decision to issue a warrant of arrest, and in most instances, he participates in the decision to continue the prosecution after arrest without a warrant. Perhaps more than any other decision, the decision to charge has serious implications both for the individual involved and for the community.

Miller in his study of the decision to charge the suspect with a crime [1] points out that the decision to charge requires the resolution of three important issues; a determination of whether there is sufficient probability of guilt to justify subjecting the suspect to trial; a decision as to whether or not the prosecution is in the public interest; and a choice as to the specific crime to be charged.

The prosecutor typically charges the defendant with the highest offense which the evidence will support, viewing the evidence in the manner most favorable to the prosecution. This is because the charge of the highest offense permits a finding of guilt on lesser included offenses. If a prosecutor charges the higher offense, he may convict for lesser included offenses—or, to put it another way, he can convict the accused for the highest offense that can be proved at the trial. The reverse is not true—he cannot convict for a higher offense than the one charged. In order to be sure that he is able to convict on the highest possible charge, he starts out by charging the highest offense that he thinks he might be able to prove. The prosecutor then has wide authority to "negotiate down" to a lower offense and to file a *nolle prosequi*—i. e., dismiss the charges against the accused.

We have noted that as high as 95 per cent of the inmates of a state prison system are there on a plea of guilty. Thus, the authority of the prosecutor to decide upon the charge and to bargain with the accused and his attorneys to secure a plea of guilty puts in the hands of the prosecutor the disposition of most of the criminal cases. It is of course true that the judge does

1. Miller, Frank. *Prosecution: The Decision to Charge a Suspect With a Crime.* Boston: Little, Brown and Company, 1969.

not always follow the prosecutor's recommendations and that only the judge can actually fix the sentence. Nevertheless, the sheer volume of the prosecutor's decisions, the frequency with which the judge follows his recommendations, and the relative lack of control on the prosecutor's discretion make the prosecutor's decision a matter of prime importance. Many legal scholars view the role of the prosecutor with alarm, maintaining that uncontrolled discretion inevitably leads to arbitrariness, injustice, and sometimes to more serious evils.

The prosecutor is involved in all kinds of investigations that have a bearing on the decision to charge and the conduct of the prosecution. He talks with the arresting officer, interviews witnesses, goes to the scene of the crime, and studies ballistics tests, blood tests, and other physical evidence. He acquaints himself with the previous criminal history of the accused; makes recommendations on bail; maintains an action against the bail bondsman in case of forfeited bail; cooperates with law enforcement officers from sister states who seek to apprehend and extradite fugitives; and obtains extradition of fugitives from his own state who must be back for trial or imprisonment.

He prepares most of the legal documents—the arrest and search warrants, the grand jury indictments; the information; often the bail bond. He presents the case before the grand jury when he seeks an indictment; makes the *prima facie* case at the preliminary hearing; and appears for the state at the arraignment.

Not only must a successful prosecutor have skills in investigation and negotiation, he must be an able trial lawyer. In large prosecutor's offices, assistant prosecuting attorneys are given specialized assignments. Some will be assigned to the grand jury division; others to the misdemeanor division; others to the felony division, and so on. An attorney who is particularly successful with a certain type of case—homicide or robbery, for example—may try a majority of such cases that go to trial in a particular jurisdiction. Successful prosecutors become familiar with the abilities and also the prejudices and idiosyncracies of the trial judges, and keep close watch on the criminal dockets to get cases set before judges who they think will be most favorable to the case they intend to present. Both prosecutors and defense attorneys investigate members of the jury panel as to their profession, social status, and other matters that might make them an acceptable or non-acceptable juror to one side or the other at the trial. Prosecutors keep careful statistics on the number of cases handled; the number disposed of by plea of guilty; the number going to trial; the number of cases on appeal; and similar matters, as their budgets are often determined on the basis of such statistics.

Prosecutors also have many public relations duties. They are called on for speeches on crime and law enforcement to service clubs, civic organizations, schools, church groups, and for advice on drafting legislation affecting the prevention and control of crime.

The prosecutor in the juvenile court makes or participates in the decision on whether or not to file formal charges against the child; presents the state's case in the adjudicatory hearing; and makes recommendations as to the disposition of the juvenile. In the case of serious crimes committed by juveniles, the proscuetor may seek the transfer of the case from the juvenile to an adult criminal court.

The Prosecutor in Relation to Other Professionals in the Criminal Justice System. The prosecutor works closely with the police, with the judge, and with the public defender and defense attorneys. His relationships with the police are usually amicable, though he is very critical of police misconduct that keeps him from getting a conviction. A police failure to give the Miranda Warning, for example, brings the Exclusionary Rule into operation. As a result, a confession or other admissions against interest made by the defendant may be inadmissible in evidence. Moreover, evidence uncovered as a result of an illegal confession is also barred from evidence, under a doctrine which bars the admission of the "fruits of the poisonous tree." If an accused who has not been properly warned of his rights tells the police where to find the murder weapon, and the police go out and find the murder weapon, the statement and the weapon are both inadmissible in evidence against the defendant, since all evidence located as a result of an illegally obtained admission or confession is as "tainted" as the original illegally obtained statement.

A prosecutor understandably resents police failures which make evidence inadmissible—without such evidence he may be unable to convict the accused. Prosecutors are also often in conflict with police about arrests made for purposes other than prosecution, about any police action that smacks of harrassment, and about excessive use of force. Prosecutors expect police to successfully stay on the proper side of the sometimes narrow line that divides police assistance or encouragement in a criminal act from police entrapment, because a successful defense of entrapment precludes conviction of even a guilty defendant.

The police on their part have grievances against the prosecutor. They suspect that political reasons enter frequently into the decision of the prosecutor to prosecute or not to prosecute. They think that the prosecutor's acquiescence in the setting of low bail for dangerous offenders is unjustifiable, if not worse. They are contemptuous when "technicalities" of the law permit "obviously guilty" persons to go free. Police see some prosecutors as just plain incompetent, and believe that good police work is frequently frustrated by bungled prosecution. Many police also believe that plea bargaining works against the safety of the community and good law enforcement, and think that there is excessive use of probation, particularly of young offenders.

In general, however, police and prosecutor have a consistent and mutually supportive role as the public servants who stand between the people of the community and the criminal elements who threaten their lives and property.

Most judges and prosecutors work harmoniously together. Judges give serious consideration to the prosecutor's recommendations in sentencing, and will impose the bargained or negotiated sentence in a great majority of guilty plea cases. The judge does not enter directly into the plea bargaining process—in many jurisdictions there exists a kind of polite fiction that the judge doesn't know about the practice as we have seen, the American Bar Association Standards for the Administration of Criminal Justice recommend that plea bargaining be openly acknowledged as a necessary and valuable tool in the criminal justice process, and that the judge be told in open court the terms of the bargain.[2] The prosecutor should make it clear to the defendant that he cannot "guarantee" a sentence—all he can guarantee is that he will recommend the bargained disposition—and that if the judge chooses not to follow the recommendation, the plea of guilty may be withdrawn.

2. American Bar Association Project on Standards for Criminal Justice. *Standards Relating to Pleas of Guilty*. New York: Office of Criminal Justice Project, Approved Draft, 1968.

Prosecutors typically concern themselves very little with the correctional process, and usually have little knowledge about it. Their chief contact with a correctional institution is with the jail—they interview witnesses and talk with accused persons being held in the jail. Their contact with probation and parole officers is cursory; they recommend and request revocation of probation but know little about the supervisory functions performed.

The prosecutor's position in the juvenile court is a developing one, and relationships between the prosecutor's office and the juvenile probation department are apt to be characterized by considerable friction. The participation of the prosecutor in the decision to charge the juvenile is a recent development in many juvenile courts—formerly the decision was made by the probation officer to whom the case was assigned or by the probation staff. Probation officers complain that prosecutors do not understand the special purpose of the juvenile court, and insist on formal charges against juveniles who should be placed on informal probation. In a sort of reverse logic, probation officers criticize prosecutors who work out with the defense attorney and the child's parents agreements as to the disposition of the juvenile which turns the adjudicatory hearing into a formality. This deprives the juvenile of the therapeutic benefits of the full court hearing which many probation officers believe (though there is an almost complete lack of research on the fact) to be of value in changing his behavior.

Some prosecutors have considerable knowledge about community resources available to the offender and his family; others have almost no knowledge of such resources. Few prosecutors have an understanding of the case work method used in probation and parole and social case work, and many are actively antagonistic to its use with the offender. However, one prosecutor known to the author actively supported the hiring of a social worker in the city jail. The prosecutor, as other professionals in the system, needs to take the "systems view" of the criminal justice system and be more sensitive to the constant interaction among its parts.

American Bar Association Standards Relating to the Prosecution Function. The *Standards* define the role of the prosecutor and in its statements as to what constitutes unprofessional conduct set limits on the prosecutor's role and provide guidelines to the relationship of the prosecutor to other segments of the criminal justice system and the community. The office of the prosecutor, say the *Standards*, is an agency of the executive branch of government which is charged with the duty to see that the laws are faithfully executed and enforced in order to maintain the rule of law. The prosecutor is both an administrator of justice and an advocate; the duty of the prosecutor is to seek justice, not merely to convict. The prosecutor must exercise sound discretion in the performance of his function.

The prosecutor should be a public official who is a lawyer; authority for prosecution is properly vested in a district, county, or city attorney; in some states, conditions make it appropriate to create a state-wide system of prosecution in which the state attorney general is the chief prosecutor and the local prosecutors are his deputies; the office of the prosecutor should be a full-time occupation. The prosecutor should have full-time assistants and authority to appoint part-time assistants from the trial bar. The prosecutor should develop a statement of the general policies to guide his office and of the procedures of his office to achieve a fair, efficient, and effective enforcement of the criminal law.

The prosecutor should provide legal advice to the police concerning police functions and duties in criminal matters, and aid in training police in the performance of their function according to law; his relations with the court must be on the highest professional level; he must not intentionally misrepresent matters of fact or law to the court. The prosecutor should work for prompt disposition of criminal charges; he has affirmative responsibility to investigate suspected illegal activity when it is not adequately dealt with by other agencies. He must not use illegal means to obtain evidence, nor obstruct communication between prospective witnesses and defense counsel; he must not promise not to prosecute for prospective criminal activity except where such activity is an officially supervised investigative and enforcement program. He must not influence the testimony of an expert witness, nor pay an excessive fee for the purpose of influencing the expert's testimony.

The decision to charge a suspect with a crime should be initially and primarily the responsibility of the prosecutor; he must present to a grand jury only evidence which he believes is properly admissible at the trial, and disclose to the grand jury any evidence which he knows will tend to negate guilt. The prosecutor should explore the availability of non-criminal dispositions, including programs of rehabilitation, in deciding whether to press criminal charges, especially in the case of the first offender, and should be familiar with the resources of social agencies which can assist in the evaluation of cases for diversion from the criminal process.

The prosecutor should assist the accused in obtaining counsel at the first appearance before a magistrate, and cooperate in release on bail. The prosecutor should make known a general policy of willingness to discuss a possible guilty plea with defense counsel; it is unprofessional conduct for a prosecutor to make any promise or commitment concerning the sentence which will be imposed or concerning a suspension of sentence, but he may properly advise the defense what position he will take concerning disposition. If the prosecutor finds he is unable to fulfill an understanding arrived at in plea discussions, he should give notice to the defendant and cooperate in securing leave of the court for the withdrawal of the plea of guilty.

The *Standards* impose high professional conduct on the prosecutor in the matter of calendar control (which should be in the court with an obligation on the prosecutor to explain any reasons for delaying a case). He must act with dignity in the courtroom and support the authority of the court; he should take leadership in developing, with the cooperation of the courts and the bar, a code of decorum and professional etiquette for courtroom conduct. In the selection of the jury; his opening statements, in presenting evidence, in examining witnesses, and in the arguments to the jury, he must abide by the rules of evidence, truthfully relate the testimony of witnesses, and refrain from arguments calculated to inflame the jury. He should not make any public comments critical of a verdict, whether rendered by a judge or jury.

The prosecutor should not make the severity of the sentences the index of his effectiveness; he should seek to assure that a fair and informed judgment is made on sentence and to avoid unfair sentence disparities; he should assist the court in obtaining full and accurate information in the pre-sentence report and disclose to the defense and to the court at or prior to the sentencing proceeding all information in his files which is relevant to the sentencing issue.

The *Standards* recognize the importance of the prosecutor's role and the extent to which it involves the exercise of discretion. Instead of recommending the elimination or curtailment of this discretion, the *Standards* suggest that the safeguards to its arbitrary exercise be in the selection of highly trained prosecutors who see themselves as guardians of the rule of law, and whose duty it is "to seek justice, not merely to convict."

THE DEFENSE ATTORNEY

How Defense Attorneys are Chosen. An accused who can afford to do so selects and employs his own counsel. (It is said that the crime syndicates employ defense counsel on a retainer basis.) The usual situation for the person accused for the first time is to inquire of friends and relatives or of the attorney who represents him in civil matters the name of a competent criminal attorney. In large metropolitan areas there are members of the Bar whose chief practice is in criminal law and who have made impressive records in "getting their clients off;" the fees of such attorneys are generally beyond the person of average means. However, someone will know a defense attorney who represents less affluent clients from time to time in the interest of justice. In less populated communities, the defense attorney is apt to be a lawyer in general practice who perhaps has served a term or two as prosecutor and who regularly takes criminal cases. In states where parents are required by law to provide an attorney for a juvenile against whom a delinquency petition has been filed, the defense attorney is apt to be the family lawyer or an attorney known to the family. Attorneys who specialize in representing the accused juvenile are rare, and, in fact, many attorneys appear in juvenile court who have little knowledge of the court and its procedures.

Defender Systems in the United States. Indigents must be provided with counsel at state expense. Defenders are provided according to three basic methods: (1) appointed counsel, (2) full-time federal or state employees working as public defenders on a salary basis, and (3) by so called "mixed systems" which utilize the services of both appointed and salaried counsel.

Appointed counsel are selected in various ways. In smaller communities the judge may just appoint a member of the Bar who happens to be in the courtroom or whom he wants to favor by permitting him to earn the small fee provided by statute for defense of indigent defendants. In other courts, defense attorneys are appointed in rotation. In one county with which the author is familiar, the appointed attorneys are expected to turn their fees over to the Bar Association for the support of the county law library. In large metropolitan areas, the court may appoint defense attorneys from a roster of lawyers interested in criminal cases and who have also had some experience in the trial of criminal cases. This method probably provides the best representation to the accused, since a corporation or title lawyer seldom knows how to proceed when suddenly confronted with the duty to represent a felony defendant. Many appointed lawyers serve without fee; the statutes usually provide, however, for modest remuneration to be paid out of public funds.

Public defenders are employees of a public or private agency. They are supported out of private funds, out of funds raised for charitable purposes by public fund-raising drives such as the United Fund, out of county or state funds, or some combination of these. The Office of Economic Opportunity provides funds for legal aid to the poor, but at least in theory, these funds are allocated for civil representation and not for criminal defense.

The public defender is usually appointed by the agency or agencies providing the funds. He operates the public defender office alone, or may have assistants. Public defender offices are typically understaffed, with very restricted budgets. One state established a public defender system, did not fund it until a subsequent session of the legislature, and then provided funds for salaries only. The public defender was thus expected to do his work without money for office rent, telephone, or investigation. In time, public defender offices may be organized and staffed to compare with prosecutor's offices, although many taxpayers are reluctant, as they put it, to "pay for catching the criminal and then pay for getting him off."

The American Bar Association *Standards Relating to Providing Defense Services* recommend that a full range of defender systems be provided for in each state. Counsel would then be provided in a systematic manner in accordance with a widely publicized plan employing a defender or assigned counsel system or a combination of these. Publicity is recommended so that the indigent defendant may have prior information about his right to counsel and the manner of obtaining counsel.

The *Standards* provide for compensation for time and services necessarily performed in the discretion of the court and within the statutory limits.[3] The federal Criminal Justice Act of 1964 specifies an hourly rate not to exceed $15 for time in court and $10 for time spent outside of court, with a maximum of $500 for a felony and $300 a case for a misdemeanor, but permits the court to award larger fees for protracted representation.[4]

Certain safeguards are set up in the *Standards* to protect professional independence, but emphasis is upon the responsibility of the Bar to make defense services readily available to the poor.

The Role of Defense Counsel. Supreme Court decisions have greatly expanded the requirement for legal representation at successive stages of the criminal justice process. As the law now stands, an attorney must be present at the interrogation of the accused whenever the investigation has moved from the investigatory to the accusatory stage. The accused must also be represented at the line-up, at the preliminary hearing, at the arraignment, and at the trial. Counsel is required at a probation revocation hearing, and in some states at a parole revocation hearing. An attorney will be appointed to represent the indigent on appeal, but representation at state expense at the civil habeas corpus proceeding is not provided.

The defense attorney is an advocate. Guilty as well as innocent defendants are entitled to the representation under our system of law. The duty of the attorney is to safeguard his clients

3. American Bar Association Project on Minimum Standards for Criminal Justice, *Standards Relating to Providing Defense Services*, New York: Office of Criminal Justice Project, Approved Draft, 1968.

4. Nevada statutes provide for a $200 limit for Justice Court cases; $300 limit on non-capital District Court cases; $1,000 limit in capital cases. West Virginia provides $25 for misdemeanor, $50 for felony. Wyoming sets payment at $15–$50 for misdemeanor; $25–$100 for felony; and $50–$100 for a capital case. California and Wisconsin give the court discretion to determine the amount of compensation.

A statewide survey of the 19,773 members of the State Bar of Texas determined that on the average, each member of the bar gave $1,972 in time to court appointed cases during the year of the survey. This was in addition to $1,481 in free legal work to worthy organizations and $3,428 in service to civic and community projects. Morris Harrell [President of the State Bar of Texas], "$136 Million Worth of Justice," *Texas Bar Journal*, Volume 34 number 2, February 22, 1971, p. 99.

constitutional rights and to present his defense to the best of his ability.

The duty of counsel is to manage his client's case, which means that the lawyer, not the client, works out the courtroom strategy and makes the decision about the interrogation of witnesses. The attorney, not the client, is the professional. However, a Supreme Court decision has held that appointed counsel is required to present his client's case on appeal even when the attorney himself believes that the appeal is not well founded or is frivolous. The decision has caused much criticism in legal circles. The language of the court was that "the Constitutional requirement of substantial equality and fair process can only be attained where counsel acts in the role of active advocate in behalf of his client. * * * His role as advocate requires that he support his client's appeal to the best of his ability."[5]

The defense attorney has a particularly difficult role to play with reference to his own client. A study of over 2,000 applications for writs of habeas corpus filed by prisoners in the Florida prison system disclosed that offenders have very unrealistic notions about the role of counsel. Basically, the offender sees it as his lawyer's duty to "get him off," no matter how guilty he may be of the offense. In the process, the offender wants his attorney to act in a highly aggressive manner with which he can identify. The "fighting" criminal lawyer is the one who is appreciated by his clients, even when counsel's conduct may antagonize judge and jury and actually result in a more severe sentence. Offenders take literally the ethical admonition given to a lawyer to represent his client's interest "exclusive of all others." Lawyers interpret this to mean "exclusive of all others whose interests may be adverse to those of the client;" the offender insists that it means "exclusive of all others—period." Many an inmate complained in his application for writ that his lawyer was handling cases for other clients when he should have been devoting *full time* to *his* case, "as the Code of Ethics required." An attorney who fraternized with the prosecutor or spoke well of the judge was suspected by his client of a "sell-out." A substantial number of prisoners insisted that they were victims of a "frame-up," participated in by the prosecutor, the judge, and their own counsel. It was interesting to note that the inmates

5. Anders v. California, 386 U.S. 738, 87 S.Ct. 1396, 18 L.Ed.2d 493 (1967), reh. den. 388 U.S. 924, 87 S.Ct. 2094, 18 L.Ed.2d 1377.

complained as often of lawyers whom they had selected and paid as they did of appointed counsel.[6]

Defense attorneys generally tend to take a rather narrow view of their duty to their clients in sentencing. They present facts favorable to their client to the court during the sentencing hearing, but are not well informed as to sentencing alternatives and as to the requirements and importance of a good pre-sentence report. The counsel's role in the guilty plea case is to negotiate with the prosecutor and obtain for his client the very best possible bargain as to type and length of sentence. He also has a duty to safeguard the bargain during the sentencing hearing, or withdraw his client's plea of guilty.

Defense counsel's role in the juvenile court is a developing one. Many attorneys know little or nothing about juvenile court philosophy and procedures and approach the adjudicatory hearing in the juvenile court exactly as they would a defense in an adult criminal court. This of course ignores the fact that "getting him off" may be the very worst thing to do for the juvenile. More experienced counsel in the juvenile court see themselves as being there to safeguard the juvenile's constitutional rights, to be sure that only competent evidence is received against him, to assist him by presenting to the court facts favorable to the juvenile, and to challenge inaccuracies in the social history report. The best representation of a juvenile defendant is given by the lawyer who is well informed as to the dispositional alternatives available to the juvenile judge, who is able to suggest the alternatives, and who cooperates with the court, the juvenile, and the parents in securing the best possible placement for the long-range interests of the juvenile.

Many young attorneys see the role of defense attorney as including an attack on the conditions which cause or are associated with crime and delinquency. They promote and participate in different forms of social action, the purpose of which is the reform of the criminal justice system, particularly at the lower court level, and particularly as it deals with the offender who is poor or from a minority group.

6. Hazel B. Kerper. "Development of a Theoretical Foundation for the Use of 'Writs' in the Resocialization Process in the Correctional Setting." Unpublished Master's Thesis, Florida State University, December, 1965. Major Professor, Dr. Vernon Fox.

Hazel B. Kerper. "On 'Writs' and 'Resocialization'" *American Journal of Correction* (November/December, 1967).

The Defense Attorney in Relation to Other Professionals in the Criminal Justice System. The defense attorney often finds himself in conflict with the police and not infrequently with the judge. The conflict with the police has to do with what many defense attorneys call "police brutality," which in their view includes a great many forms of police action. The police understandably object to this characterization of their behavior, and wonder out loud as to how much the attorneys really know about offenders and their unhappy tendency to repeat their offenses. The police officer also objects to the defense attorney who "tries his case in the newspapers," though police chiefs frequently do the same thing. This tendency on both sides to attempt to use the news media as an aid to prosecution or defense particularly in cases which arouse great public interest, has resulted in the adoption by the American Bar Association of strict new rules about pre-trial publicity. The ABA effort is directed toward preserving the defendant's right to an impartial trial, a right which according to the news media, often conflicts with the right of free speech and the public's "right to know" about what is going on in its criminal process. The issues in this controversy involve basic Constitutional rights and will not be easily resolved.

Defense attorneys, particularly in the so-called "political trials," take umbrage not only with the police but with the prosecutor and the judge. The attack on Judge Hoffman in the "Chicago Seven" trial is without precedent in modern criminal practice, with many issues about the conduct of the trial to be resolved by the United States Supreme Court.

Not only defense attorneys but many other lawyers concerned with preserving the rights of the accused deplore the practices that develop in court and station-house after mass arrests during riots and other forms of civil disobedience. Normal procedures break down under the impact of large numbers of persons taken into custody within a short period of time. Charging, presentment, bail procedures, and even trials become perfunctory and arbitrary. This is particularly true when there has been little or no prior planning for such an emergency. Fortunately, the bench and the bar, as well as the police, are attempting to set up orderly procedures which will effectively preserve the Constitutional rights of the citizen caught up in a mass arrest during a period of high social tension.

American Bar Association Standards Relating to the Defense Function. The committee of the American Bar Association responsible for the preparation of the standards relating to the defense function introduce the proposed standards with this statement: "Few subjects in the administration of criminal justice are more in need of clarification than the role of the defense lawyer in a criminal case. Not only the public but also the legal profession itself—judges not excluded—at times manifest grave misconceptions and uncertainties as to the defense lawyer's function, the limits of proper conduct, and his relationship to the client." (We have already noted that the criminal defendant also suffers from grave misconceptions as to the role of his attorney.) The statement continues: "* * * news media and editorials sometimes have wrongly criticized lawyers who were performing their professional duties properly, and both editorials and news stories reflect confused ideas about the role and function of the lawyer for the accused."

The lack of interest in criminal law, the fact that the legal profession itself often looks down upon criminal practice, and the meager offerings of the law schools in the areas of criminal law, are commented on. "Happily," reports the committee, "this attitude is changing and the law schools and the organized bar are giving heightened attention to the criminal law."

The *Standards* state that counsel for the accused is an essential component of the administration of criminal justice. A court properly constituted to hear a criminal case must be viewed as a tripartite entity consisting of the judge (and jury, where appropriate), counsel for the prosecution, and counsel for the accused. The basic duty the lawyer for the accused owes to the administration of criminal justice is to serve as the accused's counsel and advocate, with courage, devotion, and the utmost of his learning and ability, and according to law.

As in the *Standards Relating to the Prosecution Function,* the role of the defense attorney is defined in terms of guidelines to honorable professional conduct and performance. The defense attorney is admonished to avoid unnecessary delay in the disposition of cases, to refrain from misrepresentations of fact on law, to avoid personal publicity connected with the case, and to put his client's interest paramount. He must seek to establish a relationship of trust and confidence with the accused, and obtain from him as soon as possible all relevant facts known to the accused. Fees must be set on the basis of the time and effort required by counsel, the responsibility assumed, the novelty and difficulty of the question involved, the gravity of the charge, the experience, reputation and ability of the lawyer, and the capacity of the client to pay a fee. The lawyer may not obtain literary rights from the accused to publish books, plays, articles, interviews, or pictures relating to the case.

The defense lawyer is required to conduct a prompt investigation of the circumstances of the case relative to guilt and degree of penalty, to keep his client informed of the developments of the case, and to take prompt action to preserve all the legal rights of the accused. Certain decisions relating to the conduct of the case are ultimately for the accused and others are ultimately for the defense counsel. The decisions which are to be made by the accused after full consultation with counsel are: (1) what plea to enter; (2) whether to waive jury trial; and (3) whether to testify in his own behalf. The decision on what witnesses to call, whether and how to conduct cross-examination, and all other strategic and tactical decisions are the exclusive province of the lawyer after consultation with his client.

The defense lawyer is instructed to explore the possibility of an early diversion of the case from the criminal process through the use of other community agencies; and if it appears desirable, secure the permission of his client and enter into plea discussions with the prosecutor. High standards of ethical conduct in the presentation of evidence, examination of witnesses, argument to the jury, and in all courtroom proceedings are imposed upon the defense attorney.

The defense attorney should be familiar with the sentencing alternatives available to the court and these alternatives should be fully explained by the lawyer to his client. Defense counsel should present in court any ground which will assist in reaching a proper sentence; should check the facts in the pre-sentence report and be prepared to challenge or supplement them if necessary. After conviction, the lawyer should explain to the defendant the meaning and consequences of the court's judgment and his rights to appeal; appellate counsel should not seek to withdraw from a case solely on the basis of his own determination that the appeal lacks merit. After a conviction is affirmed on appeal, appellate counsel should determine whether there is any ground for relief under other post-conviction remedies, such as habeas corpus, although he has no duty to represent his client in such proceedings unless he has agreed to do so.

The *Standards* place a duty on the bar to encourage through every available means the widest possible participation in the defense of criminal cases by experienced trial lawyers; lawyers active in general trial practice should be encouraged to qualify themselves for participation in criminal cases both by formal training and through experience as associate counsel; qualified trial lawyers should not announce a general unwillingness to appear in criminal cases, and law firms should encourage partners and associates to appear in criminal cases.

The duties of the lawyer to his client are said to be the same whether he is privately employed, judicially appointed, or serving as part of a legal aid system. Every jurisdiction should guarantee by statute or rule of court the right of an accused to prompt and effective communication with a lawyer, with reasonable access to a telephone and other facilities for that purpose. There should be a referral service which maintains a list of lawyers willing and qualified to undertake the defense of a criminal case which is organized to provide prompt service at all times. Personnel of jails, prisons, and custodial institutions should be prohibited by law or administrative regulations from examining or otherwise interfering with any communication or correspondence between a client and his lawyer relating to legal action arising out of charges or incarceration. The conduct of the defense of a criminal case requires trained professional skill and judgment; therefore the technical and professional decisions must rest with the lawyer.

The thrust of the *Standards* is to upgrade the defense function by encouraging better training in the criminal law, and high professional performance in all aspects of the defense role.

Law school internships in the office of the public defender, and early salaried employment as a defense attorney, may lead many more attorneys into a career in the criminal law. Dedicated young lawyers acting for the accused have much to contribute toward upgrading the criminal justice system. Many will find great personal (though probably no great financial) rewards in the process.

THE JUDGE

The lawyer-judges in the criminal justice system for the most part grace the benches of the federal courts, the state appellate courts, and the state trial courts of general (felony) jurisdiction. Many judges of juvenile courts and of lower state courts are also lawyers. Non-lawyer judges are in the majority in the justice of the peace courts, county courts with misdemeanor jurisdiction, and municipal courts. Judges of juvenile courts organized at the lower court level are frequently non-lawyers.

In some foreign countries, a law student decides upon a career as a judge early in his law school study and thereafter follows a special curriculum, and perhaps an extensive period of training as a law clerk. This has never been the practice in the United States. Judges in this country are drawn from the ranks of practicing lawyers, and learn the particular skills of their trade after, and not before, they take their place on the bench.

Specialization in the criminal law by a judge usually occurs only in large metropolitan areas where a judge is assigned to a court handling criminal cases exclusively. Again, the specialization occurs after elevation to the bench. Most trial court judges handle both criminal and civil matters, with civil litigation predominating, which mitigates against the development of special competence in the criminal law.

The Selection and Removal of Judges. Judges in the United States are both elected and appointed. The nine Justices of the Supreme Court of the United States are appointed by the President of the United States, with the approval of the Senate. There is nothing in the Constitution which says that a Justice must be trained as a lawyer, nor must he have had experience on the bench before being appointed to the Court. However, most modern Justices have been lawyers, and a previous distinguished career in law or in politics characterizes the majority of the appointees. A Supreme Court Justice holds his office "during good behavior"—which is not quite the same thing as "for life." In practice, however, appointments to the Supreme Court are for life. No Supreme Court Justices have been impeached, the only way they may be removed from office, though impeachment proceedings have been brought against a Justice. Judges of the United States Appeals and District Courts are also appointed by the President, the appointments being for life, unless the judge is removed by impeachment. Senate approval of the Presidential appointments is required.

Judges of state appellate courts are elected or appointed. The first elevation of the judge to the appellate bench typically occurs by appointment made by the Governor to fill a vacancy, after which the appointed judge must stand for election. The terms of appellate court judges are usually longer than those of trial court judges. As a result, the appellate court judge presents himself before the electorate less frequently than does a judge of a trial court. The majority of judges of the courts of general jurisdiction (district courts, circuit courts, superior courts) are elected, usually for a shorter term than judges of the appellate courts, but for a longer term than a county office holder. Again, the first elevation of the judge to the superior court bench is frequently by appointment to fill a vacancy, with the appointment being a form of promotion from a lower court or from the Bar membership. Judges are elected on a non-partisan ticket in many states, with partisan campaigning for the office forbidden or frowned upon.

Statistics developed in 1966 by the President's Commission on Law Enforcement and the Administration of Justice show that 80 per cent of the judicial positions in the United States are elective, with election by popular election in more than half the states, and partisan election in 19 of the states. One-half of the judges responding to the survey related that they were initially appointed to fill vacancies caused by death or retirement.[7]

Approximately ten states have amended their constitutions to provide for the merit selection of judges, according to what is known as the "Missouri Plan," because its method of selecting judges was first put into operation in the State of Missouri. Under the Missouri Plan, persons are nominated for judgeships by a non-partisan Commission, are appointed by the governor, and then face the voters in an election. The Commission carefully investigates all candidates for the office of judge (in Missouri the merit system applies to judges of the appellate courts, and the trial judges for Kansas City and St. Louis). The governor must appoint from the list of nominees submitted to him by the Commission. The judge runs at the next election without oppo-

7. The President's Commission on Law Enforcement and the Administration of Justice. *Task Force Report, The Courts*, p. 66.

sition, the voters being asked to indicate whether or not he should be continued in office. A vote of 50 per cent affirmative votes continues him in office until the end of his term. At the end of each term, the judge runs for re-election on the same basis, his re-election dependent upon his receiving a 50 per cent affirmative vote on the question of his remaining in office.

It is interesting to note that judges in the United States serve on the bench for an average of 25 years, though elective terms of six to nine years are common.

In the federal government, the only method for removing judges is by impeachment, although all cases were removed from one judge by the Judicial Conference of the 10th Circuit Court of Appeals under its supervisory authority over the courts in the circuit. Impeachment is also the only method for removing state appellate and trial court judges in many states. Impeachment is used so seldom, and is so expensive and cumbersome, that as a practical matter most states are without effective procedures to remove ill, senile, incompetent, or even dishonest judges. Some states provide for a fixed retirement age, others, as well as the federal government, encourage retirement by providing for the payment of almost full salary after retirement. About ten states have a procedure in which the houses of the legislature by concurrent resolution request the removal of a judge, and others provide for recall in a popular referendum. In New Jersey, the supreme court is given supervisory powers over other judges, and the supreme court may certify to the governor that they believe a judge is unfit to perform his duties and should be removed.

Texas and California have a Commission plan. A permanent Commission on Judicial Qualifications, composed of judges, lawyers, and non-lawyers, receive complaints on judicial unfitness. The Commission, after investigation, can recommend to the supreme court that a judge be removed from office or involuntarily retired. Many persons feel that some effective method of removing unfit judges must be found, the Commission system perhaps being one of the best methods used to date.

The Role of the Judge. The role of the judge varies according to whether he is a judge of a lower court, a court of general jurisdiction, or of an appellate court. A judge has a kind of special role when acting as a magistrate. The laws of the state define a magistrate by listing the persons who are included within the designation. Typically, all of the judges of the state are included in the list of magistrates, though in practice the justice of the peace is the "Committing Magistrate" and performs most of the duties assigned to magistrates. Non-judges may be included in the list of magistrates. In one state, for example, the mayors and recorders of incorporated towns and cities are magistrates.

The duties of the *magistrate* are judicial and usually include broad authority to preserve the peace and to issue all process intended to aid in preventing and suppressing crime. A committing magistrate is one authorized to commit the accused for trial. When a magistrate is inquiring into a criminal matter, he may be called an examining magistrate and his court an examining court.

Magistrates thus issue warrants of arrest and search, determine the identity of the accused and inform him of the charges against him at the initial appearance, fix bail, order release on bail, set the time for preliminary hearing, hold the preliminary hearing, and bind over for trial to a court of general jurisdiction or discharge the accused if no *prima facie* case is made by the prosecution. The magistrate may also be a trial judge, with authority to finally dispose of an action on plea of guilty or after verdict, his jurisdiction depending, of course, on the jurisdiction granted to the court in which he sits.

Lower court judges are trial judges with such authority as is granted to them in the legislation creating their court. As we learned in our discussion of jurisdiction, the power of a court to act may be limited in several ways, the main limitations being geographical, the nature of the offense, and the extent of the permissible penalty. Thus, a lower court may have county-wide jurisdiction in misdemeanors involving a fine over $200 and a jail sentence, while the justice of the peace court may have only precinct-wide jurisdiction and no authority to sentence to a jail or to a fine in excess of $200. Depending upon the state statutes, a municipal court may have jurisdiction to try all offenses committed within the boundaries of the municipality, including felonies. Other municipal courts are limited to the enforcement of municipal ordinances and may impose only small fines. Traffic courts usually handle traffic violations exclusively.

The majority of lower court judges are not legally trained, and personnel and facilities of the lower courts are grossly inadequate. Bribery and other forms of illegal inducement offered to judges and court personnel are often accepted. Some lower court judges quite regularly hand down sentences in excess of their statutory authority, yet because few cases are appealed, the practice can continue for years. The lower courts handle the drunks, the prostitutes, the vagrants, the drug addicts, the petty offenders, and the transgressors of the law at the bottom of the economic barrel. Court personnel become hardened and unfeeling. The role of the judges of such courts seems not to be to dispense justice but to pass as many people rapidly through the judicial mill as possible—group presentments and what almost amounts to group sentencing are not uncommon.

Since the offenders processed through the lower courts frequently end up for protracted periods in jails which are monuments to filth and brutality, the lower-court-jail system in the United States is an area that is crying for immediate and drastic reform. This is all the more true because many of the offenders being held in jails have not yet been convicted—they are awaiting indictment, or after indictment are awaiting trial. Since they cannot make bail, they are continued in custody. Federal jail statistics disclose that in one state 79 per cent of the jail population had not been convicted at the time of a United States Census Bureau survey.

Except in areas where lower court reform has been accomplished, lower court judges have limited skills, and no prestige in legal circles. All of them are assumed to be what many of them are—petty politicians exercising authority for which they are neither trained nor competent. This summation is, of course, unfair to a great many well-educated, community-minded men and women who serve as justices of the peace and municipal court judges in small towns and cities. Many, though they have no legal training, have a lot of good common sense and a keen sense of justice. They perform a valuable public service for which they are paid little or nothing, but which offers them a chance to help people, particularly young people, in trouble.

Superior court judges, or the judges of the courts of general jurisdiction, are lawyers, with all of the duties associated with a trial judge. In criminal matters, they preside over arraignments, fix bail, hear pre-trial motions, call the grand jury, oversee the selection of trial jurors, and act as umpires in the adversary system.

The trial judge does not normally participate in plea bargaining. When a defendant pleads guilty, as we have already learned, it is the duty of the trial judge to satisfy himself that the plea has been made voluntarily and without illegal promise or inducements. He must inform the accused of the maximum penalty that he may receive for the offense to which he pleads; require that the prosecution make a *prima facie* showing of the man's guilt, and listen to the recommendations made by the prosecutor and the defense attorney as to the proper sentence. If a bargain has been made, the court must honor the bargain or must permit the defendant to withdraw his plea of guilty.

The most awesome duty of the trial judge is in sentencing. He has the duty in federal court and in some states, and the authority in others, to request a pre-sentence report which will give him information not available at the trial about the defendant and his previous social and criminal history. The sentencing judge tries to arrive at a sentence which will fit the offense and the offender—not an easy task when the objectives of retribution and punishment cut up against the objective of rehabilitation.

The judges of the trial courts grant or deny applications for changes of venue, preside over habeas corpus hearings, inform fugitives of their rights in extradition proceedings, grant and revoke probation, and hear a variety of pre- and post-trial motions filed by prosecutors and defense attorneys. Judges also have general administrative duties over their courts. A judge may also be a judicial administrator for a number of courts in an administrative district, with authority to assign judges from one court to another for the more expeditious management of the trial dockets.

Appellate court judges hear cases on appeal which come up to them on the record. They study the voluminous transcripts of the proceedings in the lower court, set the cases for oral arguments, and render the decisions which "make" the case law. The decisions of the judges of the higher appellate courts of the United States, both state and federal, are regularly published in sets of books comprising the Reporter System.[8] The opinions written by both the majority and dissenting judges are set out in full.

8. See "How to Find and Cite the Law," Appendix A., *infra*.

Under the doctrine of *stare decisis,* the decisions of the highest court in the state are binding upon the courts of that state. The decisions of the United States Supreme Court are binding on all federal courts and, on federal questions including federal Constitutional rights, on all the states. The decisions of a United States Appeals Court are binding upon the federal courts in its circuit. Not infrequently an appellate judge of a state or federal court will write opinions of such outstanding logic and clarity that they are followed by other courts not bound to the decision by the doctrine of *stare decisis.* Chief Justice Traynor of the California Supreme Court obtained such prominence in the area of criminal law, as have judges of other courts.

Appellate courts are customarily given original jurisdiction as to the issuance of writs of habeas corpus, *mandamus,* and the like, but the work of appellate courts is primarily the review of decisions coming to them on appeal from lower courts and the writing of opinions which constitute the binding case law unique to the Anglo-American system or jurisprudence.

The Judge in Relation to Other Professionals in the Criminal Justice System. The position of judge of an appellate court or superior court is an honored one in the criminal justice system. Lawyers aspire to judicial appointments; a seat on the bench of a higher court is sought by ambitious and status-conscious members of the Bar. Lawyers consider the work of judges to be pleasant and financially rewarding, and the long terms offered in the higher courts are preferred over policital appointments that require frequent testing with the electorate. Lawyers customarily treat judges with deference and respect. The phenomenon of lawyers verbally abusing a judge during a trial is infrequent in the annals of American jurisprudence. The power of the court to hold in contempt is a persuasive deterrent to most lawyers. Thus, lawyers may disagree with decisions of higher courts but as a rule do not openly attack the court, the judge, or the criminal justice system.

Police officers, on the other hand, are openly contemptuous of court decisions which, in their opinion, hamper police investigation and give the offender what they consider an unfair advantage *vis a vis* the lawabiding citizen. Sentencing judges are criticized by police for being too lenient, and by offenders and their families for being too harsh.

Legal scholars and social scientists castigate judges and the judicial system for disparity in sentencing. Many of these critics of sentencing practices equate differences in sentences with disparity in sentencing which results in injustice, as we have seen. This criticism usually fails to take into account the many factors that influence the sentence in addition to the offense, the most important being the defendant's prior criminal record. Such criticism also fails to take into account the confusion which exists in the public mind as to the true objectives of punishment, as a result of which criminal statutes are inconsistent and tend to reflect recent public alarm over a certain type of offense, or great public sympathy for a particular offender. A Chessman case often brings about the abolition of the death penalty in a state or two; a Starkweather case will see it re-enacted. Chessman spent twelve years in the death row at San Quentin. During his incarceration, as a result of books and articles which he wrote in prison and the intervention on his behalf by prominent citizens, a great deal of public interest and sympathy were aroused, not only in the United States but abroad. (There were demonstrations in several countries on the day of his execution.) Starkweather and his girlfriend went on a killing spree in Colorado, Nebraska, and Wyoming, murdering several people almost at random. Of the states involved, the governors of all were happy to release him to the state whose laws permitted the imposition of the death penalty.

In spite of the fact that they send hundreds of convicted offenders to jails and penitentiaries each year, judges are poorly informed about the correctional process. When the judges of the Criminal Courts of Texas met in Huntsville in 1970 and toured the Texas Department of Corrections, this was the first time that most of them had ever been inside a penitentiary. The average judge tends to view the correctional officer, no matter what his training, as a sub-professional; at the same time, the judge's ignorance about correctional problems appalls and alienates the correctional officer.

It is a rare judge who can give a correct estimate of the average case load of the probation officers working in his own court. The situation reminded one observer of the old saw about why hospital corridors are wide—"so the doctors won't have to speak to each other in passing." Though the court corridors may not be wide, meaningful dialogue between judges and probation officers is rare. Judges who regularly use pre-sentence reports and depend upon their probation staff for their preparation tend to have better working relationships with the individual probation officers, though the judge's knowledge about the supervisory function performed by the probation officer remains woefully inadequate. The probation officer feels that he gets little understanding and support from the judge in the performance of his difficult task, and some judges are openly antagonistic to the social welfare concepts which form the basis for the case work techniques commonly used by the probation officer.

Juvenile probation officers often complain about new judges appointed to the juvenile court. Many come in with very unrealistic ideas as to what can be accomplished and surprisingly little prior understanding of the *parens patriae* concept of this special statutory court. Not infrequently new juvenile courts are created without any provision being made for even one additional probation officer. This creates additional tension between the judge and the probation staff, the judge because he can't get the help he needs, and the probation staff because all of them are already overworked.

Organizations of judges and individual judges are attempting to bridge the knowledge gap between the judicial process and corrections. Some judges have even had themselves committed to a penal institution to learn first-hand what happens to the convicted man. Such judges usually come out of prison with increased understanding of correctional problems and are ardent supporters of an improved correctional system.

Judges are perhaps the single most important group in the criminal justice system in bringing about legislative penal reform. Measures which the judges as a group oppose are difficult to get passed; proposals which they support tend to make their way into the criminal code. Judges as a group, however, are usually not in the forefront as promoters of penal reform, except as their decisions bring about change in the substantive and procedural law. There are exceptions, of course. Chief Justice Burger is taking leadership in the area of court reform, and there are always one or two judges in a state who are working to modernize and improve criminal justice administration.

THE COURT ADMINISTRATORS

Clerks of court, bailiffs, and court reporters are involved in the administration of criminal justice. The Clerk of Court is an appointed official when attached to a federal or appellate court. At the state superior court level, Clerks of Court are traditionally elected county officials. Clerks of Court in many areas are County Clerks as well, with duties in addition to those related to the court. A deputy is usually assigned the chief responsibility for acting as Clerk of Court where the two offices of County Clerk and Clerk of Court are combined.

The *Clerk of Court* is responsible for keeping all the records of the court. The returns on arrest and search warrants are made to the Clerk. In some courts the Clerks, either by law or in practice, issue such warrants. The indictment, the information, all of the pleadings filed by the prosecutor or defense attorney, the instructions to the jury, the verdict, and the sentence are kept in the files by the Clerk. Such documents are also transcribed into large bound volumes comprising permanent court records. Clerks of Court issue subpoenas for witnesses, notices about jury service, keep track of the fees due jurors and witnesses, and attend upon the court during trials to swear witnesses and produce court records needed by the judge or the attorneys in the case. Clerks keep a record of all cases filed, of all cases dismissed, of all cases tried, and of all cases appealed, having special responsibilities in the preparation of the record on appeal.

Clerks of Court also have duties in connection with the civil work of the court, receiving, filing, and recording documents in connection with divorce, adoption, settlement of decedent's estates, and civil proceedings of all kinds. Clerks have the duty to certify to the authenticity of copies of legal documents filed in the court, and some Clerks perform duties in connection with issuance of passports and filing of Workmen's Compensation claims.

There is a general lack of standardization of court records, which contributes to the inefficiency of the court system, but professional organizations of Clerks of Court often work toward more uniformity. (One state department of corrections regularly receives over twenty different forms of the judgment, sentence, and commitment, the basic document committing a man to prison. It is estimated that a standardized commitment form would save the department many thousands of dollars a year in record keeping expense.)

The wise young attorney just starting his practice does well to make a friend of the Clerk of the Court. He will receive invaluable advice and assistance in his early efforts if he does this. If he makes the mistake of "talking down" to the Clerk or attempts to impress her (many Clerks of Court are women) with his brand new Certificate of Admission to the Bar, he will have many things to learn—the hard way.

Clerks of Court frequently hold office for a great many years, being appointed for an indefinite period, or being elected to the office term after term. They seldom have had any special training for their jobs, except perhaps as a deputy or assistant in the office, prior to their being appointed or elected.

Bailiffs may be permanent court employees in large metropolitan courts that meet daily. In smaller communities, a bailiff is usually appointed by the judge for the duration of a trial, with one or two men making themselves regularly available for the post. The bailiff's duties are to see to the security and decorum of the court; he keeps an eye on the defendant after he has been delivered to the court, and summons witnesses when it is their turn to testify. He is responsible for the protection and care of the jury during the trial and during the jury deliberations. If the jury is sequestered (i. e. kept together under court rule) he goes with the jurors wherever they go, and reports to the court attempts by any person to contact a juror. He also watches for improprieties committed by a juror, as for example, making forbidden telephone calls, buying the daily newspaper which contains an account of the trial, and so on. The bailiff returns the jury into court when a verdict has been reached, and assists the judge in keeping order in the court if an unseemly outbreak is likely upon announcement of the verdict.

Court Reporters are highly paid professionals whose duty it is to take down, and when requested to transcribe, trial or other court proceedings. Some reporters use shorthand, others use stenotype machines. Experiments are being made with tape recorders, which have not to date worked out very well. In most courts, the court reporter draws a salary, and is also paid, usually by the page, for the preparation of the record on appeal. Some court reporters are permitted to hold other jobs while acting as court reporters. As a result, long delays often occur in the preparation of trial transcripts, to the detriment of both the appellant (almost always the accused, as the state's right to appeal in a criminal case is strictly limited) and the state, the appellee. Court reporters are also charged with the care and preservation of the physical evidence introduced during the trial, though permanent responsibility belongs to the Clerk of the Court. Guns and other such evidence are kept in a special safe provided for that purpose. Authority is given for disposal of the weapon after the time for appeal has passed or after a stated number of years. Some criminal lawyers have impressive collections of murder weapons.

The professional *Court Administrator* is a newcomer in the criminal justice system. The first class of Court Administrators graduated from the Institute of Court Management at the University of Denver in 1970. Their assignments were to highly paid positions with the federal courts.

The trained Court Administrator will take many of the duties of court administration off the shoulders of an over-worked chief justice or presiding judge. He is expected to bring up-to-date management techniques into the court and to greatly increase the efficiency of court operation. As more such Administrators are trained, they will be employed by state appellate and superior courts, which may expedite the reform which seeks to abolish the lower courts by merging them into courts of general jurisdiction. Some courts are already experimenting with the use of computers in selection of the jury panel and in the docketing of cases, with the computer preparing the notices which must be sent out to jurors, witnesses, and attorneys. Trained Court Administrators are expected to accelerate this trend and find additional uses for business machines in court management.

In the Congressional bill providing for the appointment of a circuit executive for each of the eleven federal circuits, the duties of the Court Administrators are set out as follows:

1. Exercising administrative control of all non-judicial activities of the courts of appeals of the circuit in which he is appointed.
2. Formulating and Administering a system of personnel administration.
3. Preparing a budget.

4. Maintaining a modern accounting system.
5. Establishing and maintaining property control records and undertaking a space management program.
6. Conducting studies relating to the business and administration of the courts within the circuit and preparing appropriate recommendations and reports to the chief judge, the circuit council, and the Judicial Conference.
7. Collecting, compiling, and analyzing statistical data with a view of the preparation and presentation of reports.
8. Representing the circuit as liaison to other courts and agencies.
9. Arranging and attending meetings of the judges and other officers of the circuit.
10. Preparing an annual report, including recommendations for more expeditious disposition of the business of the circuit.

The Bill also provides that "all duties delegated to the circuit executive shall be subject to the general supervision of the chief judge of the circuit."[9]

Upon the graduation of the class of the Institute for Court Management and the signing by President Nixon of the Circuit Court Executive Act, Chief Justice Warren E. Burger commented:

> I hope that from now on judges will encourage the more promising young people in court clerk's offices to secure special training. Only by this process is there any hope of escaping from the "management morass" that now afflicts most large court systems. No other course offers any hope of bringing court operations into the 20th century in terms of management that will match other developments in the law and the urgent needs of the courts.[10]

9. The Circuit Court Executive Act, HR 17906, The 91st Congress.

10. As quoted in *American Bar News*, Vol. 16, No. 2, February, 1971, p. 7.

Chapter XIV

THE CORRECTIONAL OFFICER

Almost any person working in a probation or parole department or in a correctional institution may be called a correctional officer. This includes correctional administrators and persons belonging to the recognized professions such as medicine, law, and the ministry, and the retired military personnel who work in correctional institutions. Many people would deny the title of "correctional officer" to the guard in the penitentiary, to the custodians and house parents at the juvenile institution, and to the teacher in the classrooms at the prison or boys' school. However, it is gradually being realized that these people can be among the most effective "agents for change" in the correctional system. For one thing, they have the most frequent contact with the inmate, with the greatest opportunity to help him change his attitudes and behavior. In-service training programs are beginning to focus on these employees. We will include them here, for they are indeed "correctional officers."

THE CORRECTIONAL ADMINISTRATOR

The correctional administrator holds a position as the director of a state department or division of corrections or of a statewide adult or youth authority. He is chairman of the state board of parole, or the superintendent of state institutions. He may be the director of public welfare if juvenile corrections, for example, are administered by this department. Correctional officers holding positions of this level must be men of outstanding administrative abilities. Their employees are numbered in the hundreds; the offenders under their care are counted in the thousands; the public property for which they are responsible is valued at many millions of dollars.

The chief administrative officer of a state-wide department or division of corrections or correctional services is usually a political appointee chosen by the governor of the state or by the official in charge of a major division or state government. One of his main duties is to prepare the budget for the operation of his department, which he must defend before the appropriate executive and legislative committees and often before the legislature itself. Since correctional budgets are notoriously inadequate, the director devotes a great deal of time in the effort to obtain funds for operation. In all probability, he must content himself with a grossly inadequate budget and continue to operate a department which is understaffed and which houses offenders in overcrowded institutions, many of them built before the turn of the century.

The administrator of a state correctional institution must be a public relations expert of high order. He is given the assignment of rehabilitating offenders, and meaningful work is an important rehabilitative tool. Yet the administrator may be prevented by state law from putting his men to any work which might be competitive with union labor, or permitting them to make any articles which would reduce the sales of the businessman who also makes and supplies such articles. If the director seeks to arrange college classes for inmates, he must be careful that their use of the science laboratories in a nearby school present no security threats to students or citizens. If he encourages use of parole, he must be able to defend his position every time a parolee commits a new offense, though the parolee is no longer in his custody. He must prevent escapes and control riots and disorders. (This includes keeping good relations with the news media reporting the disturbance.) He is expected to keep his difficult charges under control at all times, but is criticized for using solitary confinement or resorting to force. He is the defendant in every habeas corpus action brought by a convicted person who wants to test the legality or conditions of his confinement. (One director found himself unable to get credit because he had been sued so often.)

There are many outstanding men and women working under such conditions who seek by every means in their power to rehabilitate the offender, and who are outstanding not only for their abilities but for their humanity. True, there are cruel and vicious and stupid and dishonest correctional administrators, and prison conditions that are a disgrace to a nation. But there are also correctional administrators who run clean, humane, and progressive correctional systems, and who work constantly to upgrade correctional institutions and correctional practices.

At an administrative level slightly lower than that of the director of a state-wide department or division of corrections are the administrators of the sub-departments, usually chosen according to the function they perform, such as director of custody, director of treatment, director of records, the financial officer, and so on. Adult institutions are under the care of wardens and assistant wardens; juvenile institutions under a superintendent or director.

At the local level, the superintendent of a juvenile detention facility is an administrative officer, as is the chief probation officer of an adult or juvenile probation department. The local correctional administrator has the same problems with budgets as does his counterpart at the state level. He must go before a board of county commissioners or other local body responsible for allocating funds, whose interest in spending money on offenders is uniformly minimal. It is not unusual for a new juvenile court to be created because of the overcrowded dockets, with no provision whatsoever being made for the addition of probation officers, and the commissioners will object strenuously to providing funds to staff the new court. Depending upon the location of the court or agency, a local correctional administrator must supervise several employees. In metropolitan areas he may be responsible for several hundred children held in detention or for several hundred adults and juveniles on probation or parole. He must deal with judges, lawyers, and parents, and work closely with other welfare and service agencies. Too, he is held responsible for the success of his rehabilitative efforts, being expected to accomplish miracles of behavior change in juveniles or adults with a life-time history of trouble making and disturbance. That he succeeds as often as he does is a credit to his skill and dedication.

The local correctional administrator is chosen in many ways; typically, he is moved to an administrative position after serving as a probation or parole officer.

THE PROBATION AND PAROLE OFFICER

The probation and parole officer is distinguished from the institutional correctional officer in that he usually works with the offender in the community instead of in an institution. However, some parole officers are "institutional parole officers." In some states probation and parole is a state-administered function; in others, the parole department only is state-administered and probation is administered at the local (usually the county) level. In the states in this latter category, many communities are without probation services for either the juvenile or adult offender.

In some areas there is a distinction made between the parole officer and the probation officer; in the federal government and in many states one person may perform both functions. The United States Probation Officer, for example, works with both probationers and parolees. Distinctions are also commonly made between adult probation officers and juvenile probation officers. Juvenile parole is a small segment of probation and parole services. Few juveniles are committed for terms long enough to make parole an important factor and the trend is to develop after-care programs for juveniles which will be available for the juvenile who has served his full commitment in the institution as well as the one who secures an early release on parole.

In the discussion which follows we will assume a state-administered Board of Parole, and probation at the county level. This will enable us to draw contrasts between the two methods of providing probation and parole services.

Selection of the Probation and Parole Officers. The parole officer is an employee of the state-administered Board of Parole. State Boards are commonly attached to the executive department of state government, and the Board is given the authority to select the employees of the Department. A probation officer is an officer of the court but may be attached to a Probation Department organized at the county level.

Various methods are used to select probation officers. The County Commissioners or other governing board of the county may select and appoint all of the probation officers; or the Commissioner may appoint a Chief Probation Officer who has authority to employ other probation officers. A juvenile probation officer may be selected by a Juvenile Board organized in various ways but sometimes including all the judges in the county. A probation officer in a county with no probation department is selected by the judge and may be anyone from the sheriff, to the local minister, a concerned citizen, or the judge himself. Particularly in juvenile courts, judges often act as their own probation officers. One of the problems, of course, is that the number of persons on probation in smaller counties does not justify the employment of a full, or even part time, probation officer, and many states are without legislation to permit two or more counties to employ a single probation officer, each paying a portion of his salary.

Education and Training of Probation and Parole Officer. The state statute may set up the requirements for parole officers and also for probation officers. Adult probation or parole officers are usually required to be mature persons with a college degree who have had a stated number of years experience in positions of working with people prior to their employment in adult probation and parole. Oddly enough, a state which sets high standards for adult probation officers may have no statutory requirements for juvenile probation officers, though they must be the most skilled in the profession. Many states require that all the probation officers attached to a juvenile probation department must hold the Master of Social Work Degree and be experienced in case work techniques.

Until recently, there has been no consensus as to the kind of education and training needed by a probation and parole officer except in the states or courts which require the MSW degree. There is increasing agreement, however, that training for correctional work is properly grounded in the behavioral sciences, including the law. The areas of knowledge which the correctional worker needs include knowledge of his agency, of casework and group work techniques, of sociology, psychology, law, medicine, and public administration. Familiarity with community resources and skill in basic research are also deemed important.[1] It is also being generally accepted that persons other than those who have earned the MSW degree can be successful probation and parole supervisors—a rather necessary conclusion since there are not enough holders of the social work degree to go around. Also, many trained social workers have difficulty in working with the offender since they do not have the specialized skills required to work in the authoritative settings under restrictions imposed by the law.

1. George G. Killinger, Hazel B. Kerper, Charles M. Friel. *Job Obsolescence in the Law Enforcement and Correctional Field.* An exploratory study sponsored by the United States Department of Labor, Manpower Division, 1968.

Probation and parole officers are obtaining the necessary education in programs in criminology and corrections offered by several institutions of higher learning in the United States, or are preparing themselves with undergraduate training in psychology, sociology, law, government, and in social welfare. Master's degree programs in Criminology and Corrections are offered in several areas of the country. The University of New York at Albany, the University of California at Berkeley, and Sam Houston State University at Huntsville, Texas, among others, have degree granting programs at the doctoral level.

Probation and parole departments are also providing extensive in-service training for employees, with some departments having well-organized training sections. In-service training acquaints the new officer with the policies and procedures of the court or agency and instructs him how to prepare a pre-sentence or social history report and how to present a case in court. Group discussion of actual cases teach him techniques of case work and offer him help in problem solving by acquainting him with community resources available to the offender. Attendance at workshops and conferences dealing with crime and delinquency is encouraged and financially assisted by the agency. Thus, in-service training which has long been a feature of metropolitan police departments is now available to correctional officers working in the community and, as we shall see, to the institutional correctional officer as well.

The Role of the Probation and Parole Officer. The role of the probation and parole officer varies somewhat depending upon where he is employed; whether he is handling probation, parole, or both, and whether he is working with juveniles or adults. All probation and parole officers, however, are concerned with one basic problem—helping the offender to change his behavior—specifically to change his behavior in such a manner that he will avoid further conflict with the law. The probation and parole officer must accomplish this feat under limitations imposed by the conditions of probation and parole, including time limitations. With few exceptions, this behavior change must be accomplished by a probation officer who is working at a very modest salary, with an unrealistic case load, and with few community resources to fall back on in time of need.

The parole officer starts to work with the parolee as soon as he is being considered for parole, or sometimes much earlier.

An institutional parole officer interviews the prisoner within a week after his admission at the reception or diagnostic institution. The officer explains to the prisoner the provisions of the law and the rules concerning parole eligibility and the granting of parole. This helps the prisoner to make a satisfactory institutional adjustment and avoid the kind of conduct which will mitigate against his parole. When the inmate is being considered for parole, the parole officer assists him in the preparation of a "parole plan." Most Parole Boards require that an inmate must have a job lined up before he can be released. In working out the parole plan, the parole officer has frequent contacts with the prospective employer and also with the members of the inmate's family. The parole officer also gives help to the parolee as he attempts adjustment back into his family, or into a new community if he has no family or is not returning to his old neighborhood.

In the usual situation, the parole officer who helps the inmate work out his parole plan will be his supervising officer after his release. In some states, however, institutional parole officers work with the inmate only while he is in prison; the inmate is assigned to a different supervisory parole officer upon his release.

The role of the parole officer supervising the released inmate is to keep informed about his whereabouts and activities, to aid him find a new job when he loses his old one, and to provide him with counsel and advice which will help him make a satisfactory adjustment to the society.

The good parole officer is a friend to the parolee, but also maintains a proper professional distance, for if the inmate violates the conditions of his parole, the parole officer must make a decision as to whether or not to recommend the revocation of his parole. As we learned in an earlier chapter, a parole officer does not usually revoke parole for minor violations of the conditions of parole. A parolee may miss one reporting period, or violate restrictions on going into a bar or tavern, or fail to request permission to buy a car—such "technical" violations will not in most cases result in revocation of parole. Studies have shown that even the commission of petty offenses may not result in parole revocation, but the commission of any felony and of serious misdemeanors will bring about revocation. In some states, the parole officer has the authority to arrest the parolee who has broken parole, and he can be immediately transported back to the institution from which he was paroled. The authority to finally revoke parole is usually with the Parole Board.

The juvenile parole officer is commonly an employee of the youth authority in whose custody the juvenile has been placed. His duties of supervision are similar to those of the adult parole officer if no special after-care programs are involved. Many states are setting up "half-way houses" (half-way out—half-way in) to which juvenile parolees are released. The parolee lives in the half-way house while he looks for or holds down a job, coming back to the institution at night for both supervision and guidance. Some states place all juveniles being released into a half-way house for at least a short period—the theory being that the period in the half-way house increases the probability of satisfactory community adjustment. This theory, however, is hotly disputed by other correctional workers who believe that half-way houses are actually destructive of successful juvenile adjustment.

The probation officer attached to an adult probation department supervises offenders placed on probation by the court. Some authorities contend that it is easier to supervise a probationer than a parolee, since the probationer has not had such drastic "social surgery" and the long period of incarceration during which he has lost his job and his contacts in the community. Other authorities maintain that the techniques of supervision are so similar that no problems exist for this reason, and, as we have noted, many probation officers are also parole officers, and vice versa.

Except in a few areas, probation officers are overworked and underpaid. An excessive case load is common, even when the state statutes set a legal maximum on the number of cases to be assigned to the supervising officer. The locally-financed probation departments are almost always suffering from a severe lack of funds—maintenance of county roads and bridges is more important to the average county commissioner, and probably to the average citizen as well, than the supervision of offenders at liberty in the community. This lack of funds also characterizes juvenile probation departments in the metropolitan areas. Juvenile delinquents are not among the most popular persons in the community, and sufficient money to properly staff a juvenile probation department is seldom included in the budget appropriations.

Probation officers have the duty of preparing pre-sentence and social history reports, a job which entails quite extensive investigation of the offender's background. Not all adult criminal courts use pre-sentence reports, though they are required in federal courts before a felon can be sentenced. Juvenile judges, however, depend heavily on pre-sentence reports and the preparation of these takes up much of the time of the juvenile probation officer, which, of course, reduces the time he can spend in probation supervision. A good pre-sentence report gives information on the subject's offense, his previous criminal history, his education and work background, his physical condition, the results of any psychological testing, his family relationships, and how the community feels about him and his offense. It would be unwise, for example, to return the embezzler who had caused the little bank to fail back into the same community, at least until enough time had passed to dull community outrage and resentment.

Juvenile probation officers have special duties in intake and detention—many probation departments operate juvenile detention facilities. The juvenile probation officer also assists in the preparation of the case for court, and in making recommendations as to disposition of the juvenile—duties not performed by their adult counterparts. A common practice in juvenile courts has been for the juvenile probation officer to regularly testify in court as to the juvenile's offense, and give other information he has obtained about or from the juvenile. Since *Gault* [2] this practice is less frequent. It was also found that the probation officer who testified against the juvenile was in a very poor position to earn his cooperation and trust in the supervisory situation.

The Probation and Parole Officer in Relation to Other Professionals in the Criminal Justice System. Parole officers have relatively little contact with other professionals in the system except for the police. Relationships between the policeman and the parole officer are often fraught with dissension and misunderstanding. Many parole officers insist that the police harass parolees. The police practice of "rounding up" all ex-convicts in an area to question them about any serious offense that subsequently occurs is roundly deplored by parole officers. The po-

2. In re Gault, 387 U.S. 1, 87 S.Ct. 1428, 18 L.Ed.2d 527 (1967).

lice, whose use of this tactic has been somewhat curtailed by court decisions, reply that nine times out of ten the crime has been committed by an ex-convict. They point out the predilection of offenders to repeat their offense or commit new offenses, a fact which is supported by accepted figures on recidivism. Police officers also dislike programs which bring ex-convicts together and very frequently the conditions of parole will prohibit association with another convicted offender at a time when parole officers would like to try some of the new group therapy techniques in the management of their parolees.

Police and probation officers have similar areas of conflict, although the "round-up" does not usually gather in all the probationers in the area. Police officers tend to believe that probation officers have unrealistic notions about changing the behavior of the offender, and consider the "do-gooder" approach less than worthless. The police officer also tends to believe that probation officers ignore the welfare of the community and of law-abiding citizens when they fail to report minor violations of probation conditions, or "cover up" illegal behavior. Probation officers, on the other hand, stoutly defend their decisions on the basis that incarceration doesn't change the offender's behavior either, and that the offender's best chance for rehabilitation is in the community. They also point out that maintaining a probationer or parolee in the community is much less expensive than maintaining an offender in an institution.

We have previously touched upon the lack of understanding between the judge and even his own probation staff, a situation which is also characteristic of the prosecutor and the probation officer. In many cases, strained relations develop because of almost complete ignorance by the one of the other's job. When judges, prosecutors, police, and probation and parole officers are brought together at a workshop or conference and engage in frank discussions about their job responsibilities, it is not difficult to improve relationships. The participants in such dialogues discover their common goals and many common problems, and begin to realize the degree to which the criminal justice system functions as a system with interacting and mutually dependent parts. An even more dramatic change comes about when police, prosecutors, and judges begin to identify themselves as corrections officers and accept the fact that their actions and attitudes have profound effect on the rehabilitation of the offender.

THE INSTITUTIONAL CORRECTIONAL OFFICER

There is some disagreement as to just who is a correctional officer. In the broad sense, everyone who works in a correctional institution is a correctional officer. For that matter, almost everyone dealing with the offender as he moves through the criminal justice process can be said to be a correctional officer. Correctional purists reserve the name of correctional officer for the "treatment officers" in a correctional institution and refer to other employees as custodial officers, guards, cottage parents, cooks, gardeners and the like, according to their specific job assignment.

In terms of function, this author sees the correctional continuum as beginning with the first contact of the offender with the law and continuing until he is released back into a free society, and hence sees everyone who comes in contact with him in the process as a correctional officer. However, for the purposes of our discussion in this chapter we will limit the term "institutional correctional officer" to persons working in the penitentiaries and in the adult and juvenile correctional institutions who are assigned duties having to do with the rehabilitation of the offender as opposed to duties limited to the operation of the institution. The term "correctional officer" will not be limited solely to psychologists, counselors, chaplains, and others who in a penitentiary are traditionally under the direction of a "Director of Treatment," but will also include the house parents and custodial officers who come in daily contact with the inmate.

Adult Correctional Institution. Correctional institutions for adults are usually either penitentiaries or prisons, though some of the more open types of institutions are called simply "correctional institutions." Adult correctional institutions are traditionally classified as maximum, medium, or minimum security institutions. The average citizen who thinks of a penitentiary is usually thinking of the old-fashioned maximum security institution with high brick walls, barred windows and gates, and guard towers manned on a twenty-four hour basis. In such institutions, the inmates live in tiered cells made of steel and reinforced concrete, eat at long tables in a large dining room, and spend their days either in idleness or in such activities as making license plates and brooms, or in a variety of farming activities.

Unfortunately, this mental image of a penitentiary is all too true in the United States today. To call the brutal custodians (who are sometimes themselves inmates) in such institutions "correctional officers" is a contradiction in terms. In fact, it is a misnomer to call such institutions "correctional institutions," since men invariably come out of such institutions more brutalized and anti-social than before they went in.

A modern state-administered correctional system maintains institutions of various types to which inmates are sent after a stay at a reception or diagnostic center where an attempt is made to work out the treatment plan which will contribute the most to his rehabilitation. Such systems necessarily include a maximum security unit, since some offenders cannot be rehabilitated, or if they can, the techniques for doing so are not yet known. For the protection of society, such men need to be securely confined, many of them for life. Men whose chances of rehabilitation are somewhat better are sent to medium security units, where security considerations are important but the method of confinement is less severe. These institutions attempt to provide meaningful work, educational opportunities, and recreation facilities.

Young offenders and offenders serving their first term in an institution are assigned to minimum security institutions. These are often called "open" institutions since the grounds remain unfenced, prisoners are permitted to move freely from place to place within the institutional limits, and often are able to obtain the privilege of going into the nearby town or city. Institutions which have pre-release and work-release programs are of the minimum security type. Inmates from the federal correctional institution at Seagoville, Texas, for example, hold jobs in the nearby communities of Dallas and Fort Worth. They are transported back and forth to work in prison buses or may use public transportation. They spend evenings, nights, and week-ends at the institution.

Some states run work camps, often called forestry camps, which are minimum security units where the inmates are assigned jobs in land and forest conservation. These camps are a far cry from the old road camps, and the "chain gang" system under which private contractors bid for the services of the inmates and then were free to work them literally to death in forest clearance, road building, and the like. Modern forestry camps provide healthful surroundings, useful work, and counseling and guidance services. Camp programs are considered to provide advanced and effective methods of rehabilitation and inmates aspire to be assigned to them. At least one state, California, also has a special institution for the old, infirm, or handicapped inmate who cannot cope with the rigors of life in an ordinary penal institution.

Juvenile Correctional Institutions. Juvenile institutions are operated by the juvenile authority to whom the delinquent juveniles are committed by the court. These institutions are generally of the minimum security or "open" type, though an area on the grounds may be set aside for a maximum security type building in which intractable juveniles or juveniles who have committed serious felonies are confined. Some of the juvenile institutions are of the forestry-camp type. There are also privately operated institutions for juveniles, though such institutions for adults are a rarity in the United States. (In some foreign countries, it is not unusual for both adult and juvenile institutions to be privately financed.) In the United States, charitable organizations seldom operate adult penitentiaries. In the juvenile correctional field, however, programs for the rehabilitation of juveniles are supported by religious organizations and public donations. They include such well known places as Hifields in New Jersey and Boys Town near Omaha, Nebraska.

Juvenile correctional institutions were first called work houses, then industrial schools, now training schools, or just a school at such and such a place. (i. e., The Gatesville School for Boys.) These names reflect the changing focus of juvenile institutions from hard work to education as the main rehabilitation tool. In fact, the teacher in the institutional educational program may very well be the most successful professional in terms of ability to bring about behavior change in the institutionalized offender.

Specialized Treatment Institutions. Correctional workers are employed in specialized institutions such as those maintained for the treatment of the sexually deviant offender, the alcoholic, the drug addict, and the criminally insane. Some writers make a distinction between the criminally insane—by which they mean the person who was acquitted by reason of insanity and who will be sent back for trial in the event his sanity is restored—and the insane criminal, who is the convicted man who has become insane while in prison. Some institutions for the criminally insane (hereafter we will use the term "criminally insane" to include both the insane criminal and the criminally insane since the distinction is not an important one in practice) are maintained as a part of the state mental health program and the patients are confined to a maximum security type building which is far more restrictive than many such buildings on prison grounds. In some states, the division of corrections is responsible for the insane criminal, if not for the criminally insane, and may set aside a special building for housing such inmates together with inmates handicapped by physical disabilities. The United States maintains hospitals for the treatment of drug addicts, which are run by the Public Health Service, and detoxification and drug abuse treatment centers are being set up in many cities out of state or local funds.

Jails and Misdemeanant Institutions. The author has carefully refrained from characterizing the staff of jails and lock-ups as "professionals," which is unfair to some truly fine jail administrators. The Jail Administrator may be, but seldom is, a trained correctional officer. County jails are under the supervision of the sheriff, who may be a good law enforcement officer but whose knowledge of correctional administration often is zero.

As to jailors, who actually operate the jails, few can be called correctional officers by the widest extension of the meaning of the term. Jails are commonly "manned" by untrained, poorly paid men who see their entire responsibility as custodial, and who are often guilty of overlooking and condoning the most brutal and inhumane conditions.

In fairness, it must be pointed out that the jailor is usually in charge of an aged, filthy, run down institution, overcrowded with drunks, addicts, prostitutes, and offenders of all types, as well as with a great many underprivileged persons awaiting indictment or trial. Since even decent living accommodations are not provided, an attempt to develop in such a place recreational, educational, or rehabilitative programs of any kind would be useless, if not ludicrous.

The only ray of light in this picture is the increasing number of trained jail administrators who are making a career out of jail administration. These men bring about almost unbelievable changes for the better when they are given funds and at least a minimum amount of public support. Some states have established a state-wide, state-run, jail system and, with the availability of planning funds from Law Enforcement Assistance Administration, regional jails are in the planning stage in many states. The United States Bureau of Prisons has always been a factor in improving jail conditions, since inspectors sent out by the Bureau must inspect and approve all jails in which federal prisoners are housed. The federal government itself does not operate jails.

Education and Training of Institutional Correctional Officers. Education among institutional correctional workers runs from none (some jailors are functionally illiterate) to the highest degrees offered in the fields of education, law, medicine, psychiatry, psychology, the ministry, criminology and corrections, and social work. Chaplains have long been part of the correctional scene, and for a long time provided all the social services available to the inmate. Modern prisons are staffed with psychiatrists (few full-time, however), psychologists, and counselors who work with the inmates and assist in in-service training of the staff. Full time lawyers have been employed in some institutions to assist the inmates in writing applications for writs of habeas corpus and with other legal problems that arise during their incarceration (many inmates are divorced by their wives while in prison, for example, and arrangements have to be made for the care and support of the children).

Trained social workers offer all kinds of helpful services to the inmate in keeping him in contact with his family and helping to solve family problems which he is helpless to assume during his incarceration. As we have mentioned, a few jails are beginning to employ social workers who can help the jailed person in hundreds of ways. Trained vocational guidance counselors are being sent into prisons by the states. These programs are often subsidized by the Department of Health, Education and Welfare and the Department of Labor. The social handicaps associated with criminality and a prison record are now recognized as the vocational obstacles they are.

Graduates with bachelors and masters degrees in psychology, sociology, criminology and corrections, social rehabilitation, and related fields are appearing in substantial numbers on the staffs of penal institutions in a variety of positions. As students who planned careers in corrections, they have been educated in the behavioral sciences, with special courses in criminal law, abnormal psychology, sociology, social deviancy, criminology, juvenile delinquency, case and group work techniques, interviewing and counseling techniques, penology, and correctional administration. Many will have extensive research training and experience, for accurate evaluation of correctional programs demands the skills of the trained researcher.

Custodial officers, renamed correctional officers in recognition of their expanded role, attend classes in the behavioral sciences where they meet their peers from the police department and community-based correctional agencies. Cottage parents also attend classes and are the targets of intensive in-service training programs.

The Role of the Correctional Officer. It is obvious that the role of correctional officer will vary according to the type of institution in which he works and according to his particular job assignment.

In a treatment oriented institution attempting to maintain a "therapeutic community," his role is very different from the role he would play in a maximum security institution with little or no treatment program. His job title will also affect his role, as it usually reflects a job definition arrived at by the institution. Whether the institution houses adults or juveniles is also important in determining the character of the institutional officer's work and role, as will the nature of the institution, whether publicly or privately operated.

Many professionals from other fields work in correctional institutions, and are considered correctional officers. We have already mentioned the chaplains, doctors, lawyers, and psychiatrists, as well as the retired military officer. The American Correctional Association has admitted to associate membership in its organization some fifteen professional organizations whose members work regularly with the offender. These include the American Correctional Chaplains' Association; Association of Correctional Psychologists; Association of Paroling Authorities; Association of State Correctional Administrators; Correctional Education Association; Correctional Industries Association, Correctional Service Federation—U.S.A.; International Halfway House Association; National Council on Crime and Delinquency; National Jail Association; The Salvation Army; The Volunteers of America; Wardens' Association of America; and the Women's Correctional Association.

Whatever the type of institution or his title or job assignment, the institutional correctional officer, like his community based counterpart, is an agent of behavior change. He is charged with the duty of sending the inmate back into society as a law-abiding and contributing member of that society, as a person who will obey the law, not because he is afraid not to but because he wants to. Psychologists talk about helping the inmate to "internalize the values of the larger society," by which they mean accepting them as valid guides to his own conduct. To achieve this internalization of values is one of the goals of correctional treatment.

That the correctional officer fails in this task at least as often as he succeeds is by no means the sole fault of the correctional officer or even of the correctional system. Techniques simply do not exist that will insure change in the behavior of a 40 year old man who has spent his life in criminal pursuits, nor even in a 20 year old youth who is serving time for his first offense. If you will think how difficult it is for you to stop smoking or to stay on a diet, you will have some appreciation of the magnitude of the correctional task which often requires the restructuring of a man's personality and value systems.

Knowledgeable correctional administrators make the flat statement that from 25 to 50 per cent of their charges should never have been sent to prison—some form of supervision and treatment in the community would have been infinitely preferable and undoubtedly more successful. But those of us on the "outside" persist in seeing incarceration as a "cure all." What we really want many times, of course, is simply to hand the problem of criminal behavior over to somebody who will keep the offender out of our city and out of our neighborhood. The role of the correctional officer is badly in need of more precise definition.

On a somewhat less abstract level, the correctional officer in an adult institution is both custodial and treatment oriented, which brings about considerable role conflict. As one old-time warden remarked wryly, "You can't treat 'em if you can't keep 'em;" and a correctional officer often finds it difficult to decide whether he is "keeping 'em" or "treating 'em." This remark also illuminates the special problem of short-term correctional institutions such as jails and detention homes. Inmates are seldom in such institutions long enough to permit the development of meaningful education or even work programs. This handicap is faced to a less severe degree by juvenile institutions—the average length of incarceration of a juvenile in an institution is about 18 months.

Particularly in privately financed juvenile institutions, emphasis is being placed on developing what is known as the "therapeutic community." The objective is to bring everyone in contact with the child into a total treatment program designed for his particular needs. The professional staff of psychiatrist, psychologist, and social worker; the house parents even the cooks and gardeners are enlisted in a joint effort, and all cooperate to bring about change for the better in the attitudes, work habits, educational achievement, and behavior of the child. Even in such institutions, the long term results tend to be disappointing.

The Institutional Correctional Officer in Relation to Other Professionals in the Criminal Justice System. The role conflicts that plague the correctional officer are more apt to be in-house (i. e., within the institution) than with respect to non-institutional professionals. "Treatment personnel" and "custodial personnel" often constitute two separate camps within the institution. Some of the treatment staff profess to see no role for the custodial officer in the treatment program, and look down upon him as the poorly paid and untrained employee he often is. Some custodial officers believe that the treatment staff achieve few results except to add to the problems of the custodians. Inmates who attend group therapy sessions are frequently permitted to vent their grievances about the conduct of the custodial staff with, according to the custodians, resulting deterioration in their work habits and attitudes toward authority. The leaders of the group therapy sessions reply that the "catharsis" achieved by the inmate actually contributes to his institutional adjustment and reduces the problems of custody and security.

In juvenile institutions, the members of administrative and counseling staff are often viewed as "soft" on the inmates, and as refusing to back up the cottage parents in the discipline necessary to maintain order. The cottage parents, faced with belligerent youngsters, often privately complain about the rules which prohibit them from inflicting physical punishment.

The conflict between "professional staff" and house parents is exacerbated because the counselors and administrative staff are paid much more than the cottage parents, and work fewer hours. Cottage parents are often on duty twenty-four hours a day for six days a week. Also, it is not unusual for the cottage parents as a group to be considerably older than the administrators and counselors as a group, as many "retired" couples take jobs as cottage parents in publicly financed correctional institutions. The "generation gap" contributes to the misunderstanding.

Increased training and upgraded status for custodial officers and cottage parents serve to reduce the custodial-treatment conflict, and the "therapeutic community" concept brings all the groups into close working relationships.

The fact that correctional institutions, particularly penitentiaries, are traditionally located in remote areas in the state, at considerable distance from urban centers, increases the isolation of institutional correctional workers and contributes to institutional tensions. The maintenance of any kind of forward-looking treatment program is often impossible because of the difficulty in persuading either young or well-trained professionals to live where they have little or no social and cultural contacts. The United States Bureau of Prisons has announced that it is going to gradually phase out its large penal institutions such as the ancient prison at Atlanta. The Bureau intends to build small facilities in several cities which will provide easy access to the jobs and other opportunities offered in metropolitan areas. This will reduce staffing problems, and just as important, make it possible to institute work-release and similar programs for the inmates. It is probable that this trend will be followed by state departments of corrections.

The author thinks it fitting to close this chapter on the institutional correctional officer by setting out the Principles of the American Correctional Association adopted at their one-hundredth anniversary convention in Cincinnati in October, 1970. An interesting observation about these Principles is that they differ little from the first set of Principles adopted by the organization at its first convention, also held in Cincinnati, in 1870. The Principles state the goals which the correctional officers of this country have set for themselves. If they can be substantially realized in the next generation, they will bring about profound improvement in the American criminal justice system.

DECLARATION OF PRINCIPLES AMERICAN CORRECTIONAL ASSOCIATION

1970

Preamble. The Centennial Congress of Correction, to reaffirm the ideals and aspirations of its membership, to encourage a more enlightened criminal justice in our society, to promote improved practices in the treatment of adult and juvenile offenders, and to rededicate its membership to the high purposes stated by its founding leaders in 1870, does adopt this Centennial Declaration of Principles.

Principle I. The prevention and control of crime and delinquency are urgent challenges to society. The growing body of scientific knowledge, especially in the behavioral sciences, coupled with the practical wisdom and skill of those professionally engaged in society's struggle with the problem of crime, provides the soundest basis for effective action.

Principle II. The forces for the prevention and control of crime and delinquency ultimately must find their strength in the constructive qualities of the society itself. Properly functioning basic institutions—the family, the school and the church, as well as the economic and political institutions—and a society united in the pursuit of worthwhile goals are the best guarantees against crime and delinquency.

Principle III. Correction and punishment are the presently recognized methods of preventing and controlling crime and delinquency. The strengthening and expansion of the correctional methods should generally be the accepted goal.

Principle IV. In a democracy the success of any public agency, including that of corrections, depends in the final analysis on popular acceptance and support. An adequate financial base, emphasis on the adequacy of personnel, and insistence on an alert and progressive administration is the responsibility of the public and a function of its enlightened concern about crime and delinquency problems. This places on corrections the all-important burden of preparing and disseminating objective information needed for public policy decisions at all jurisdictional levels.

Principle V. The length of the punitive sentence should properly be commensurate with the seriousness of the offense and the extent of the offender's participation. Inequality of sentences for the same or similar crimes is always interpreted as an injustice both by the offender and the society. On the other hand, the length of the correctional treatment given the offender for purposes of rehabilitation depends on the circumstances and characteristics of the particular offender and may have little relationship to the seriousness of the crime committed. In a correctionally oriented system of crime control, statutes providing maximum flexibility in the determination of the appropriate release date can assure the optimal benefits of correctional treatment.

Principle VI. No law, procedure or system of correction should deprive any offender of the hope and possibility of his ultimate return to full, responsible membership in society.

Principle VII. The correctional process has as its aim the reintegration of the offender into society as a law-abiding citizen. In the course of non-institutional treatment the offender continues as a member of the conventional community. In the course of his institutional stay, constructive community contacts should be encouraged and maintained. The success of the correctional process in all its stages can be greatly enhanced by energetic, resourceful and organized citizen participation.

Principle VIII. Corrections, comprising both institutional and community-based programs, should be planned and organized as an integrated system responsible for guiding, controlling, unifying and vitalizing the correctional process.

Principle IX. The variety of treatment methods corresponding to the varying needs of the offenders suggests a diversification of correctional effort, resulting in a system of specialized agencies, institutions and programs. These should be so planned and organized as to meet the differential needs of the offender. The spirit of continued experimentation with new types of programs which show promise of more effective results should be encouraged and supported.

Principle X. The organization and administration of correctional agencies and institutions is a complex area of public administration and management, which deals with one of the most involved of social problems. It is essential that the administration of the correctional agencies meet the highest standards of public service, and that all employees be selected in accordance with the best criteria and serve on the basis of merit and tenure systems.

Principle XI. The special and complex problems in understanding and dealing with criminal and delinquent behavior imply the need for personnel possessing suitable personality traits and specialized skills and hence the need for special professional education and training of a high standard, including pre-service and continued in-service training at all levels. The potential contributions of ex-offenders as correctional workers should be recognized.

Principle XII. The collection and publication of criminal statistics designed to provide information on the extent and nature of criminality and juvenile delinquency and on the various phases of the correctional process is indispensable for the understanding of crime and for the planning and evaluation of correctional and preventative measures.

Such statistics are necessary and should be developed on national, state and local levels and should consist of statistics of the offenses known to the police, arrest statistics, judicial statistics, probation, institutional and parole statistics, as well as criminal career records.

Principle XIII. Research and the scientific study of the problems of criminal behavior and of the methods of dealing with it are essential prerequisites for progress. Through its educational and research institutions, society should sponsor, finance and carry out both basic and applied research in this area. The law enforcement and correctional agencies and institutions should lend their support, take initiative and engage in appropriate research as an indispensable part of their effort to improve their performance.

Principle XIV. Correctional agencies and institutions can best achieve their objectives by providing resources for the complete study and evaluation of the offender. Decisions determining the treatment design for the offender should be based on a full investigation of the social and personality factors. These investigations may be made at different levels, so long as the essential information is available at the proper step in the decision-making process.

Principle XV. To assure the eventual restoration of the offender as an economically self-sustaining member of the community, the correctional program must make available to each inmate every opportunity to raise his educational level, improve his vocational competence and skills, and provide him with meaningful knowledge about the world and the society in which he must live.

Principle XVI. Well-organized correctional programs will actively seek opportunities to collaborate with other public and private agencies to assure that the offender has access to a wide range of services which will contribute to his stability in the community.

Principle XVII. The criminal justice system should, insofar as possible, be relieved of responsibility for the care or treatment of persons who are charged with offenses which have their origins in the abuse of alcohol or drugs. Such persons are more appropriately the concern of community health and mental health services.

Principle XVIII. Community-based correctional programs are essential elements in the continuum of services required to assure the reintegration of the offender into the society. Probation, parole, residential treatment centers and other forms of conditional freedom such as work and study furlough programs provide important and necessary alternatives to imprisonment.

Principle XIX. Probations is the most efficient and economical method of treatment for a great number of offenders. To enhance the achievement of the full potentialities of probation, mandatory exceptions to the use of probation with respect to specific crimes or to types of offenders should be eliminated from the statutes.

Principle XX. All offenders should be released from correctional institutions under parole supervision, and parole should be granted at the earliest date consistent with public safety and the needs of the individual. Parole decisions should be made by a professionally competent board. The type and degree of supervision should fit the needs of the individual offender.

Principle XXI. Community-based correctional facilities, such as community treatment centers and half-way houses, provide important alternatives to more formally organized institutions and facilitate access to supportive community services.

Principle XXII. The transition of the offender from institutional life into the community should be facilitated wherever feasible by measures which permit his participation in normal community activities such as work and study furlough programs. Participants should be carefully selected and supervised and their economic exploitation scrupulously avoided.

Principle XXIII. The principles of humanity and human dignity as well as the purposes of rehabilitation require that the offender, while under the jurisdiction of the law enforcement and correctional agencies, be accorded acceptable standards of decent living and human dignity.

Principle XXIV. The architecture and construction of penal and correctional institutions should be functionally related to program designs. The variety of existing programs, to be further expanded in the future, indicates the need for similar variety and flexibility of architectural design and construction. The building standards and technological advances of the day should be reflected in these structures. The failure of large institutions indicates the desirability of institutions of moderate size, lending themselves better to fulfillment of the objectives of a good correctional program.

Principle XXV. New correctional institutions should be located with ready access to community agencies which provide services, such as mental health centers, and educational training institutions—all of which provide support to correctional programs and contribute to continuing staff development.

Principle XXVI. Except in most unusual circumstances, provision should be made for the separate housing of persons charged with crime and detained for court action and convicted prisoners who are under sentence.

Principle XXVII. Every effort should be made to establish, maintain, and develop local correctional facilities and programs which are designed to meet the needs of short-term offenders or offenders who are soon to be released from long-term imprisonment. Such facilities should work closely with and use the resources of local human service agencies, both public and private.

Principle XXVIII. Some criminal law violators who are found by the courts to be criminally responsible, but who, from the point of view of modern psychiatry and psychology are abnormal, need psychotherapy. Diagnostic and treatment facilities for such offenders should be provided at appropriate stages of the correctional process.

Principle XXIX. Control and management of offenders should be by sound scientific methods, stressing moral values and organized persuasion, rather than primarily dependence upon physical force.

Principle XXX. All employable offenders in correctional institutions should be given the opportunity to engage in productive work, without in any way exploiting the labor of prisoners for financial gain, or unduly interfering with free enterprise. It is imperative that all governmental jurisdictions, industry and labor, give full cooperation to the establishment of productive work programs with a view to imparting acceptable skills, work habits, and attitudes conducive to later gainful employment.

Principle XXXI. Religion represents a rich resource for moral and spiritual regeneration. Specially trained chaplains, organized religious instruction and counseling, together with adequate facilities for group worship of the inmate's own choice, are essential elements in the program of a correctional institution.

Chapter XV

RELATED PROFESSIONALS IN THE CRIMINAL JUSTICE SYSTEM

THE PSYCHIATRIST

The Conflict Between Law and Psychiatry. The role of the psychiatrist in the criminal justice process is the subject of considerable controversy in both legal and psychiatric circles. The highest tension seems to occur when the psychiatrist appears in the courtroom to testify on the question of criminal responsibility. At this point, basic philosophical differences between psychiatry and the law are exposed, and the conflict thus created is exacerbated by the barriers to understanding set up by psychiatric and legal language. The lawyers want the psychiatrist to testify in terms of "insanity"—a legal term. The psychiatrist wants to testify in terms such as "schizophrenia" and "psychosis"—psychiatric terms. The jurors want to understand in plain English the condition of mind of the defendant at the time of the offense, since it is their duty to decide whether or not he should be held criminally responsible.

The resulting confusion increases in direct proportion to the number of psychiatrists who testify. While most psychiatrists strongly object to the legal terms, no two of them can seem to agree on the meaning of the psychiatric terms. The "battle of the experts" rages on until the jury decides in its wisdom to ignore them all—an eminently sane decision under the circumstances.

Unfortunately the jury's rational decision does little to reduce the conflict. Psychiatry and the law seem to have an uneasy symbiosis—lawyers are forever seeking psychiatric testimony, particularly in capital cases, and psychiatrists who would not spend a single hour treating the offender, rise to the courtroom battle with zeal. Dr. Seymour Halleck, a psychiatrist, states the uneasy relationship between law and psychiatry in this way:

> Because our society cannot afford to redefine crime as an illness, criminology will not and should not become a sub-

> speciality of psychiatry. Still, the suffering of the criminal and the havoc he creates throughout the community will often call for the services of the psychiatric profession.[1]

Let us examine the roots of the controversy. C. Ray Jeffery, writing on "Criminal Justice and Social Change," states the psychiatric position as follows:

> The most recent development in Positivistic criminology has been the impact of psychiatry upon criminal law. The advocates of the psychiatric approach want therapy in place of punishment, mental hospitals in place of prisons; inmates are regarded as sick people, and crime is a social illness. The psychiatric approach is Positivistic—it focuses attention upon the criminal and not the crime; it seeks to rehabilitate rather than punish, and it wishes to individualize justice.[2]

The psychiatrist sees much criminality as the result of mental illness, and many criminals as mentally ill. Since the sick person must be treated instead of punished, mentally ill persons must be sent to hospitals and not to prisons. A test of criminal responsibility which has to do with knowledge of right and wrong (the M'Naghten Rule) strikes the psychiatrist as meaningless. He resents being forced to testify in terms of "insanity," a word which has meaning to the lawyer but little or none for the psychiatrist.

The lawyer replies that "mental illness" is much more difficult to define than "insanity," which over the years has proved to be a usable and reasonably precise concept. He also points out that the wide divergence of psychiatric opinion when presented with the same criminal defendant makes it eminently clear that the psychiatrists have not been able to reach any agreement as to the criteria to be used in determining which criminals are, and which are not, mentally ill.

At least in part because of the difficulty in devising criteria to determine which criminal is mentally ill and which is not, some psychiatric opinion reaches the point of declaring that all criminals are sick people and should be treated as such. Jeffery sees this as an attempt by the psychiatrist to get the community,

1. Seymour L. Halleck, M. D., *Psychiatry and the Dilemmas of Crime*, New York: Harper and Row, Publishers, 1967, p. 348.

2. Davis, Foster, Jeffery and Davis, *op. cit.*, p. 290.

through its legal agencies, to accept an unproven theory of behavior. In effect, the psychiatrists are saying, "We should be running things, and not someone else," though as many authors have pointed out, there is little or no evidence that psychotherapy can cure criminal behavior.[3] It is a matter of record, for example, that Monte Durham, whose troubles with the law lead to the famous Durham Rule (enthusiastically embraced by most psychiatrists; rejected by every court, state and federal, that specifically considered its adoption) had been in and out of mental hospitals at least as frequently as he had been in and out of jail. During that time he had received conflicting diagnoses as to the character of his "mental illness" and had on at least two occasions been released from the hospital as "cured" or at least sufficiently "cured" to stand trial.

That mental hospitals are much harder to get out of than prisons increases the lawyer's skepticism of the psychiatric approach. In a famous case in Washington, D.C., (The Durham Rule circuit) a man by the name of Lynch was arrested for passing a bad check. The offense was a misdemeanor carrying a maximum penalty of six months in jail. The prosecutor, as is permitted in that District, raised the question of his mental competency. After a psychiatric examination, he was sent to St. Elizabeth's Hospital. Five years later he was still there, though he had tried at regular intervals to secure his release. The doctors at the hospital refused to certify that if released he would not repeat his criminal behavior (the criteria for release being much more severe than the criteria for commitment).[4] The case ended when Lynch committed suicide by throwing himself under a truck on the hospital grounds.

Jeffery summarizes the criticism of the psychiatric approach to the problems of criminality under three main headings: (1) there is no evidence that mental disease causes criminal behavior; (2) there is no evidence that psychiatry can reform criminals or noncriminals; and (3) there is no evidence that psychia-

3. H. J. Eysenk, "The Effects of Psychotherapy," *Handbook of Abnormal Psychology*, New York: Basic Books, Publishers, 1961, pp. 697–725.

Halleck, *op. cit.*, p. 338–339—"It must be admitted that there are even less objective data to prove the effectiveness of psychotherapy with offenders than there are with the mentally ill."

4. Winfred Overholser, Superintendent, St. Elizabeth's Hospital v. Frederick C. Lynch, 288 F.2d 388 (D.C.C.A.1961).

try is a science or that it has incorporated within its thinking the findings and criticism of experimental psychology, sociology, and the law.[5]

The Role of Psychiatrist. In view of the criticism directed at the psychiatrist in the court room and in his role as the judge of mental illness and hence of criminal responsibility, is there a place for the psychiatrist in the criminal justice system? The answer is "yes," as some of the most vociferous critics of the psychiatric approach have pointed out. Halleck asserts that, "an enlightened correctional system would employ psychiatrists for only two purposes : (1) to help to diagnose, treat, and rehabilitate all classes of offenders; and (2) to help control dangerous offenders. Though he uses the words "*only* two purposes," the assignments he gives the psychiatrists are at the heart of criminal justice.[6]

The court clinic, staffed by psychiatrists, psychologists, and social workers could develop valuable information for the judge in the social history or presentence report. Sustained psychotherapy in the institution, particularly if augmented with family therapy, could very well bring about change in the behavior of the offender. (Since the inmates in United States prisons have an average of 82 seconds of psychiatric treatment per inmate per month, we really have not tested whether psychotherapy with the offender could be effective or not.)[7] The psychiatrist could also assist in training sub-professionals who could conduct programs of guided group interaction and provide counseling which, where it has been tried, seems to contribute to the inmate's institutional adjustment. As Halleck puts it, "Psychiatrists must learn that they do not have any monopoly on helping relationships, whether these are defined as psychotherapy or counseling." [8]

5. Davis, Foster, Jeffery and Davis, *op. cit.*, p. 292.

6. Halleck, *op. cit.*, p. 226.

7. Twenty-three full-time psychiatrists are employed to treat the 161,587 prisoners. Each psychiatrist is responsible for 7,026 inmates. If full-time employment for a psychiatrist means an eight-hour day and 160 hours a month, it would mean that there is not more than 82 seconds of psychiatric help available for each inmate during a whole month.

Alfred C. Schnur, "The New Penology: Fact or Fiction?" in Clyde B. Vedder and Barbara A. Kay, *Penology, A Realistic Approach,* Springfield, Illinois: Charles C. Thomas, Publisher, 1964, pp. 3–4.

8. Halleck, *op. cit.*, p. 347.

The problem of psychiatric testimony in the court room would be solved by Halleck by allowing the psychiatrist to testify as any other expert witness—presenting all the information available as to why the defendant committed the crime. The psychiatrist would not express an opinion on whether the offender knew right from wrong, but would describe in detail the emotional state of the offender at the time of the crime. The decision as to evil intent (*mens rea*) would be the responsibility of the judge or jury. Dr. Karl Menninger would keep the psychiatrist out of the court room, "where he makes a fool of himself," and put him to the task of diagnosis and treatment.[9]

The Committee on Forensic Psychiatry of the Group for the Advancement of Psychiatry suggests that:

> * * * the court, after determining the facts of the case, would proceed to the consideration of the way in which the offender should best be dealt with from the point of view of the merits of the case, the requirements of public morality and public safety and the chances of the offender's rehabilitation; and would dispose of each case by punishment, custody or treatment, or by a combination of these, or by release, as seems best fitted to the total situation.
>
> * * * Instead of the M'Naghten questions, the psychiatrist could be asked three questions which are equally meaningful to him and to an appropriate disposition of the case and which he frequently will be able to answer with reasonable estimates: *is the lawbreaker dangerous*, i. e., how likely is he to commit the same or another crime again; *is he deterrable*, is the motivation of his unlawful behavior such that anticipation of consequences can decisively influence his behavior; and *is he treatable* by medical or educational methods?
>
> The psychiatrist could try to answer these questions without *sacrificium intellectus* and without fear that the implications of his words may carry a jury of laymen in a direction which does not seem warranted in terms of the actual scientific meaning of his words. His answers could substantially assist the court in arriving at a reasonable decision

9. Karl Menninger, M. D., in an address at Sam Houston State University, April, 1970.

> about the disposition of the case through punishment, custody, or treatment * * * [10]

Psychiatrists have significant contributions to make to the scientific study of dangerous behavior, and the development of methods of early prediction and control. They can be in the forefront of the effort to convince the community that for its own protection, as well as for humanitarian reasons, society must demand humane and rational treatment of offenders.

THE SOCIAL WORKER

The trained social worker, who has earned the Master of Social Work (M.S.W.) degree, is a member of one of the principal helping professions. To earn the degree, a student must complete a two year graduate program which is designed to transmit the "body of knowledge" required for professional standing in social work. The typical curriculum includes courses in the social and behavioral sciences, but focuses on the development of skills in interpersonal relationships, including training in case work and group work. The M.S.W. degree is given only at institutions approved by the national Council on Social Work Education, and the Council keeps close check on the curriculum and teaching methods in approved institutions. Undergraduate training in social welfare is also supervised by the Council; the B.A. or B.S., however, does not confer professional status upon its holder.

The Role of the Social Worker. Since offenders are by definition problem people and typically come from problem families, the professional in the techniques of behavior change is of obvious value in the correctional process. The infusion of social workers into the criminal justice system proceeded at its most rapid rate in the juvenile courts. A helping court and a helping profession had a natural affinity for each other. The influence of the social worker in the court was so significant that the juvenile court was often characterized as "the illegitimate offspring of law and social work." In some juvenile courts, no one could be employed who did not possess the M.S.W. degree, and this re-

10. As quoted in Lawrence J. Friedman, M. D., "No Psychiatry in Criminal Court," *American Bar Association Journal*, March, 1970, Volume 56, pp. 242–243.

quirement was not infrequently written into the statutory law of the state.

In spite of philosophic compatibility between the objectives of the juvenile court and social work, fundamental areas of conflict existed in the juvenile court setting. The court, by definition, was a *court*; it was not a welfare agency. Social workers concerned with doing what was best for the child, began to ignore his constitutional rights of due process. The social worker in an agency setting may question the child in his own interests without concerning himself with his rights against self incrimination; he (or she, since the social worker is frequently a woman) can phrase the charges against him in vague terms without regard to the legal rule that requires formal accusation; and can rely upon hearsay evidence as to what occurred instead of proof beyond a reasonable doubt. Since the objective is to help the child, not to find him guilty of an offense, legal representation was in the view of the social worker, obviously unnecessary. The result (not, of course, to be entirely blamed upon the social worker, as lawyers and judges involved in the court were equally at fault) was that the juvenile court was called a "kangaroo court" by a justice of the Supreme Court of the United States.[11]

The decisions in Kent v. United States,[12] in In re Gault,[13] and subsequent cases restored the law-social agency balance in the juvenile court. It was established that a child in the custody of the court has the constitutional safeguards of right to notice of charges, right to counsel, and right against self-incrimination. He cannot be declared to be a delinquent child unless the delinquent act with which he is charged is proved beyond a reasonable doubt. In some juvenile courts the child has the right to a jury trial, the right to bail, and the right to appeal. Lawyers are not only admitted into the juvenile court, they are required in the juvenile court. As a result, the social worker is less and less involved in the adjudicatory hearing, but is fulfilling an expanded role in the making of informal dispositions, in preparing the social history report, and in all forms of counseling and supervision. His place in the correctional process in both juvenile and adult correctional institutions is assured.

In many private correctional institutions the professional staff is largely composed of psychiatrists, psychologists, and social

11. Kent v. United States, 383 U.S. 541, 86 S.Ct. 1045, 16 L.Ed.2d 84 (1966).

12. *Ibid.*

13. In re Gault, 387 U.S. 1, 87 S.Ct. 1428, 18 L.Ed.2d 527 (1967).

workers. Social workers attached to court clinics, or working in jails or correctional institutions, can provide a variety of very important services to both the court and the offender. Since he is skilled in getting the kind of information needed in a presentence report, he can provide the judge with an important sentencing tool. A social worker in a jail keeps the accused person in contact with his family and provides him with numerous essential personal services which he can obtain in no other way. Social workers in adult correctional institutions are a very important link between the inmate and the outside world. They contact his family and help with his personal and family problems, and thus keep the family in touch with the inmate. Offenders, by and large, are poor problem-solvers. As a group they are people who don't "cope" well. The social worker's problem-solving skills are above ordinary. He can thus give the offender both emergency assistance and important training in the techniques of "coping" with the daily problems of living in an institution or in the free society.

The social worker also plays an important role in the prevention of crime and delinquency, whether he is attached to a community social service agency or directly to the criminal justice system. Whatever he can accomplish in developing and maintaining family cohesion, ameliorating the effects of joblessness, reducing the school drop out rate, or increasing the participation in vocational training, helps to prevent crime and delinquency. While we probably cannot say that poverty and other social ills *cause* crime, that crime and delinquency are closely associated with poverty, joblessness, overcrowding in the central city, and the myriad other social ills that are characteristic of the urban ghetto, cannot be successfully denied. Thus, almost anything the social worker accomplishes in his attacks on chronic social ills helps to combat social deviancy, including the type of antisocial behavior characterized as crime and delinquency.

The Social Worker in Relation to Other Professionals in the Criminal Justice System. Interprofessional relationships between lawyers and social workers are difficult, whether the setting be the juvenile court, the legal aid bureau, or the correctional institution. Unfortunately, each profession has little understanding of the other's role, and lawyers are apt to compound the error by completely ignoring the professional status of the social worker.

Audrey D. Smith, who made a study of the social worker in the legal aid setting as part of the American Bar Foundation series on Legal Services for the Poor, sets out conclusions about the interprofessional problems of lawyers and social workers in legal aid agencies which apply with equal force to other areas of the criminal justice system where social workers are commonly found.

> Although practicing lawyers and social workers are both in helping professions which deal with conflict resolution, there are fundamental differences in their objectives and methodology. While one is specifically concerned with the individual's legal rights, the other is concerned generally with the welfare of the individual in relation to society. One appeals as a representative of the client to the adversary system of conflict resolution, while the other establishes and uses a professional relationship with the client to effect change in the client and/or his environment. When persons of two professions are working together in the same setting, these differences may be expected to create problems; hence some interprofessional conflict is inevitable.[14]

Miss Smith continues by pointing out that although the client (and probably the lawyer as well) sees the client's problems as legal, the legal problems are so interrelated with broader social problems that legal service alone may be only fragmentary and temporary. Social workers, she says, "through their skills in dealing with these broader social problems, can help maximize the legal services offered to make them more efficient."

The social work profession, like the psychiatric profession, tends to see itself as the only "helping profession." The professional organization of social workers lobbies in the legislature for statutory job requirements that reserve all supervisory positions in social service type agencies, including the juvenile courts, to holders of the M.S.W. degree. This approach is unfortunate. There are not enough trained social workers to staff other types of social agencies. The effort to pre-empt corrections is thus unrealistic, and in the long run self-defeating.

The social workers "me only" stance brings him into conflict not only with lawyers and judges, but with other persons specially trained to work with the offender. The graduates of pro-

14. Audrey D. Smith, *The Social Worker in the Legal Aid Setting*, Chicago: American Bar Foundation, 1970.

grams in criminology and corrections point out with considerable justification that the social worker is often handicapped by his training when he works with the offender. Offenders are people in trouble with the law and who are subject to its authoritative (and perhaps authoritarian) controls. The social worker performs best in a voluntary and more permissive relationship with the client, a relationship which cannot be readily developed or maintained with the offender. Moreover the offender's psychology may be such (as in the case of the psychopath) that the permissive relationship is contraindicated, in which case the social work approach will do more harm than good.

Halleck comments that "The average psychologist, sociologist, or social worker who is just out of graduate school is poorly equipped to treat anyone and is especially inept with the offender." [15] He recommends training in psychotherapy to begin the moment the non-psychiatric professional begins working in the correctional institution, and "before professional defensiveness and desperate withdrawal to administration and bureaucracy could develop." [16] He believes that if this suggestion were followed, the psychiatrists, sociologists, and social workers could constitute a sufficient resource to meet the therapy needs of most offenders.

Whether psychotherapy is the answer to the problems of the offender may be debatable, but the point Dr. Halleck makes about the persons who can become successful "agents of change" of the offender is a good one. As the old saying goes, "There is more than one way to skin a cat." The needs of the offender are so great, not to mention the equally great need of the society to be protected from his depredations, that use must be made of everyone whose background, education, and skills, equip him to make a contribution.

The social worker whose training is focused on developing techniques of behavior change has a particularly important contribution to make. To the degree that the criminal justice system is organized and recognized as a system, to the same degree will both the offender and society profit from maximum utilization of its resources, human and institutional.

15. Halleck, *op. cit.*, p. 347.

16. *Ibid.*

APPENDICES

Appendix A

HOW TO FIND AND CITE THE LAW

The law as we know it in the United States is derived principally from two sources (1) legislation (Constitutions, statutes, municipal ordinances, rules of court or administrative agencies, etc.) and (2) case law (the opinions of courts and decisions of administrative agencies).[1] Thus law can be defined as legislation plus case law. Under our system legislation is binding and must be obeyed. "Case law becomes binding authority by our doctrine of 'stare decisis,' which is the theory that a court should decide similar cases similarly."[2]

Federal Statutes. The basic law of the United States is, of course, the United States Constitution. It appears in many types of publications.[3] The acts of Congress appear as (a) Slip Laws; (b) Statutes at Large; (c) Revised Statutes; (d) United States Code. The United States Code is divided into 50 titles covering particular subject matter. For example, Title 18 covers Crime and Criminal Procedures, and Title 28 covers the Judiciary and Judicial Procedures. There is also an annotated set of the United States Code entitled the "United States

1. The terms "report," "case," "decision," and "opinion" are often used interchangeably in the study of the common law. In precise English, a "case" is a dispute brought to court for settlement, a lawsuit. The statement in which the court makes known its holding as to the rights of the parties is a "decision" or an "opinion." If the decision is in writing and published, the printed statement is a "report." We may refer to the "decision" in Gray v. Green as the "case" of Gray v. Green, or the "opinion" in Gray v. Green, or the "report" of Gray v. Green. This may be technically inaccurate, but does not appear to be in any way misleading. William R. Roalfe, Gen. Ed. *How to Find the Law, Sixth Ed.*, St. Paul, Minnesota, West Publishing Co. (1965) page 63, fn. 1.

2. *Ibid.* p. 10. Much of the material in this chapter is taken by permission from *How to Find the Law.* The student who wants to become proficient in legal research should acquaint himself with that publication.

3. A leading annotated copy is *The Constitution of the United States of America: Analysis and Interpretation*, prepared by the Legislative Reference Service, Library of Congress, 1964. The Constitution can also be found in U.S. Code Annotated, 1949, and current supplements.

Code Annotated" in which the text of the law is followed by an abstract of pertinent decisions.[4]

State Statutes. The Constitution of a State can be found in many forms. It may be set out in full in a separate bound volume, or it may appear as a volume of the statutes. Any beginning textbook on state government will have in it a copy of the State constitution.

The legislature passes laws (or statutes) as they come to them on the legislative calendar. At the close of a particular session of the legislature, the laws passed at that session are published in a bound volume (usually paperback) entitled "Session Laws." The Session Laws are identified by the name of the state and the year. Individual statutes are identified by number or by chapters. At a later date, the laws will appear in bound volumes arranged according to the subject matter. The Session Laws will first appear arranged according to subject matter as "pocket parts" to a set of laws already published. After a certain length of time the laws will be consolidated, compiled, revised, or codified. At that time new permanently bound volumes will appear incorporating all of the statutes to the date of publication. These bound volumes are called variously Statutes, Statutes at Large, Revised Statutes, Compiled Statutes, and Consolidated Statutes and Codes. (There are some technical differences in these terms which we will not consider here). Codes typically treat of broad subjects of the law such as Penal Code, Code of Criminal Procedure, Traffic Code, Juvenile Code, Corrections Code, and so forth. There are also sets of annotated statutes. An annotated set of laws or statutes are arranged in such a manner that the text of the statute is followed by notes concerning the cases which have decided something about the statute or referred to it. For example, a statute defining the crime of burglary as breaking and entering a building will be set out with all of the cases that decide what buildings may be burglarized.

Local Ordinances. Local law is to be found in Municipal Charters and County and Municipal Ordinances as well as Court Rules. There is usually a printed pamphlet of some kind setting out the Municipal Charter, or it may be found in the state laws. County and Municipal Ordinances are usually to be found in permanent or semi-permanent form. The most recent enactments can be found in the Minutes of the County Commissioners or the Municipal Council.

How Statutes are Cited

To "cite" a statute (or the decision of a court) means to give information as to where it can be found. Reference is made to the title of the volume (Session Laws, Revised Code, Consolidated Statutes, etc.), the article, section, and sub-section numbers. The sign § is used in some codes as either the article or section sign. The rule is to cite in the form of the original document.

4. A more detailed discussion of the statutes will be found in the section "How Statutes are Cited," *infra.*

The *United States Constitution* is cited to article and clause for which the § sign is used. Abbreviations are accepted. Thus

U.S.Const. art. 1, § 9

State Constitutions are cited in the same way. Thus

Const. Ore. art. 1, § 10

or

N.H.Const. art. 1, § 15

Federal Statutes are cited to the Statutes-at-Large, the Revised Statutes, or the United States Code. Since 1936, the *Statutes-at-Large* have been published at the end of each Congress. The Statutes-at-Large are arranged in chronological order by approval date and represent the official records of the laws contained therein. They are cited to the volume and section. Thus

40 Stat. 1551

The *Revised Statutes* consist of 74 titles and 5,601 sections and represent the first codification of federal law. They are cited by Section. Thus

Revised Statutes, Section 5596

or

Rev.Stat. Sec. 5596

A compilation of the laws of the United States was authorized by Congress in 1925, to be entitled the Code of Laws of the United States. It is referred to and cited as the *United States Code.* If the statute has been amended this fact is reflected in the citation. Thus

10 U.S.C. § 936 (1958) as amended
10 U.S.C. § 936 (1964) *or*
10 U.S.C. 936

A parallel citation to the Statutes-at-Large and the United States Code would read

37 Stat. 315 (1912),
7 U.S.C. §§ 151–154, 156–164–a, 167 (1958)

The *United States Code Annotated* is an annotated set of the United States Code. It is cited

26 U.S.C.A. §§ 5081–6300

or

U.S.C.A. Title 18 § 1081

The *Federal Rules of Criminal Procedure* are cited
Fed.Rules Crim.Proc. 46(f)

State Session Laws (sometimes called Acts, Statutes, Resolves, etc.) are cited by identifying the state, followed by the title, and the date. The particular statute is identified by chapter or section number. Thus

N.J.L.1964, ch. 75

In citing other *state statutes,* the Code, Statutes, Revised Statutes, Compiled Statutes etc. are identified by the name of the state and the title. The number of the particular statute is then given, followed by the article, section and sub-section numbers. The sign § is used in some codes to refer to the article or section number; in others they are labeled "Art." and "Sec." followed by a number. Again the rule is to cite in the form of the statute. Abbreviations may be used. Thus

Calif.Welf. & Inst.Code, § 564—sub. c
California Welfare & Institutions Code, § 564, sub. c
New York Penal Law, Sec. 1932
Ill.Rev.Stat.1957, ch. 38 §§ 666–668
D.C.Code, § 22–1301 (1951)
S.D.Code, § 34.3708–2
Public Laws of Vermont (1933) § 8878
N.Y.C.Cr.Proc. § 484
Ohio Gen.Code § 12447–1
Mich.Comp.Laws, § 28.1133
Texas Rev.Civ.Stat., Art. 2338

The date is given on statutes cited if this is necessary for identification. If the citation is to an annotated work, however, no date need be given since the annotations are kept up to date with pocket parts inserted at the back of the book. *Annotated statutes* may bear the name of the person or persons preparing the annotations whose name is set out in the title. Abbreviations may be used. Thus

McKinney's Con.Laws of N.Y., Ann., Penal § 15.05(2)
Smith-Hurd Ill.Ann.Stat. ch. 28, 81–2
West's Ann.Penal Code of Calif. § 1203.7
Purdon's Pa.Stat.Ann. tit. 19 § 1081

or

Fla.Stat.Ann. § 948.01
Ann.Pub.Laws of Md., 1957, art. 27 § 24
Vt.Stat.Ann. tit. 28 § 1010
Code of Ala.Ann. tit. 14, § 325(1)
Ann.Laws of Mass. ch. 272 § 16

Municipal charters and ordinances are cited by title, article and section number, the name and location of the city always being shown. Thus

Philadelphia (Pa.) City Charter § 10–107
Philadelphia (Pa.) Code § 10–819
Philadelphia (Pa.) Civil Services Regulations, § 29
Revised Code of the Civil and Criminal Ordinances of the City of Dallas, Texas, 1960, Chapter 37, Section 6, p. 883.

Case Law

Decisions of Federal Courts. The official reports of the decisions of the United States Supreme Court are published in the United States Supreme Court Reports, now designated the *United States Reports.* (Certain early decisions are in special volumes named after the reporter who compiled them, as Dallas, Cranch, Wheaton, etc.)

The decisions of the United States Supreme Court are also published in the *Supreme Court Reporter* and the *Lawyer's Edition of the Su-*

preme Court Reports. The Lawyer's Edition of the Supreme Court Reports contains selected cases which are fully reported together with the briefs filed by counsel.

The decisions of the United States Courts of Appeals (formerly United States Circuit Courts of Appeals) are published in the *Federal Reporter.* Selected decisions of the United States District Courts are published in *Federal Supplement,* and there is another set of books called *Federal Rules Decisions.* Prior to 1932 the decisions of the District Courts and of the Court of Claims and of Custom and Patent Appeals and of the Court of Appeals of the District of Columbia were included in the Federal Reporter. The Supreme Court Reporter, Federal Reporter, Federal Supplement, and Federal Rules Decisions are part of the *National Reporter System* which is explained in the discussion of State court decisions. A court decision is cited by giving the names of the parties, the name and number of the reporter, the page on which the case begins, and the date of the decision.[5] The names of the parties are often underlined or appear in italics.

Since the cases of the United States Supreme Court are reported in three series of reports—United States Reports, Supreme Court Reporter, and Lawyer's Edition of the Supreme Court Reports, a complete citation of a United States Supreme Court case would include all three reporters. Thus

Gideon v. *Wainwright,* 372 U.S. 335, 83 S.Ct. 792, 9 L.Ed.2d 799 (1963)

Some authorities maintain that citation to the United States Reports alone is sufficient. The system you will adopt will depend upon the use to which the citation is to be put. For your own notes, the United States citation serves to correctly identify the case. Thus

Gideon v. *Wainwright,* 372 U.S. 335 (1963)

The decisions of the federal courts, other than those of the United States Supreme Court, are published in two series known as the *Federal Reporter* and *Federal Supplement.* The *Federal Reporter* covers the decisions of the United States Courts of Appeals (formerly the United States Circuit Courts of Appeals). A correct citation to the Federal Reporter includes the name of the case, the volume and page of the Reporter, and identification of the circuit in which the case was decided, and the date. Thus

Smayda v. *United States,* 352 F.2d 251 (9th Cir. 1966)

The opinions of the District Courts which appear in *Federal Supplement* are cited the same way, except that the District Court is identified. Thus

Books Inc. v. *Leary,* 291 F.Supp. 622 (S.D.N.Y.1968)

5. If a second page number appears in a citation, the second number gives the page on which the matter quoted or under discussion can be found in the opinion. A citation written *Commonwealth* v. *Thomas,* 391 Pa. 486, 491 would indicate that the matter quoted or under discussion can be found on page 491.

The letters S.D.N.Y. stand for the "Southern District of New York," which means the case was decided by the United States District Court for the Southern District of New York.

Both state and federal decisions appear in sets of specialized reports. The *American Law Reports* are annotated and contain the full text of selected decisions under which cases on the same point are noted. The American Law Reports 2d contain a detailed treatise on a practical point of current law proceeded by a report in full of a modern case from a state or federal appellate court involving the problem annotated. When a case has been annotated in the American Law Reports, this information is given in the citation. Thus

> *Mosco* v. *United States,* 301 F.2d 180 (9th Cir. 1962), Annot. 89 A.L.R.2d 715

or

> *Mosco* v. *United States,* 301 F.2d 180 (9th Cir. 1962), 89 A.L.R.2d 715

Decisions of State Courts. Most of the decisions of the appellate courts of a state are written. The decisions of the highest court of the state are published in books known as the state reports, which bear the name of the state. In some states, decisions of an intermediate appellate court may appear in the same set as the decisions of the highest court, particularly if the intermediate appellate court is a court of last resort for a particular kind of action. In other states, the opinions of the intermediate appellate courts will appear in a separate set.

The great need for a comprehensive and unified system of reports lead to the development of the National Reporter System. The *National Reporter System* includes all the decisions of the highest court in each state published in the state reports. The Reporter System also includes the decisions of all intermediate appellate courts. These are usually incorporated in the regional reporters, except that there are separate units in the Reporter System used for the decisions of the lower New York and California courts.

The Reporter System reports the state decisions by regions. There are seven regional reporters, Pacific, North Western, South Western, North Eastern, Atlantic, South Eastern, Southern. The *Atlantic Reporter* covers the states of Connecticut, Delaware, Maine, Maryland, New Hampshire, New Jersey, Pennsylvania, Rhode Island, and Vermont. The *North Eastern Reporter* reports the decisions of the states of Illinois, Indiana, Massachusetts, New York, and Ohio. The *North Western Reporter* includes the decisions from Nebraska, North Dakota, South Dakota, Minnesota, Iowa, Michigan and Wisconsin. The *Pacific Reporter* reports the decisions from Arizona, California, Colorado, Idaho, Kansas, Montana, Nevada, New Mexico, Oklahoma, Oregon, Utah, Washington, and Wyoming. Alaska and Hawaii are also included in the Pacific Reporter. The *South Eastern Reporter* covers the states of Georgia, South Carolina, North Carolina, Virginia, and West Virginia. The *South Western Reporter* covers the states of

Arkansas, Kentucky, Missouri, Tennessee, and Texas. The *Southern Reporter* includes the approved decisions from Alabama, Florida, Louisiana, and Mississippi.

The *New York Supplement* contains reports from the New York Court of Appeals and decisions of the lower courts of New York. The *California Reporter* was founded in 1960 and includes all California Supreme Court decisions and the approved decisions of lower California appellate courts no longer published in the Pacific Reporter.

The volumes in each set of Reporters are numbered in sequence; as new decisions are announced, a new volume is published. In the Reporter System, and in some state reports, the consecutive numbers were ended at a certain point and a new set of numbers beginning with volume 1 were introduced. The volumes in the second series are identified by the use of "2d" following the name of the reporter. Thus, there is a volume 100 of California Reports and a volume 100 of California Reports 2d.[6] There is a volume 65 of the Pacific Reporter, and a volume 65 of the second series. All of the regional reports have begun a second series, as has the Federal Reporter.

As we have said, a case is cited by giving the name of the parties, the name and number of the Reporter in which it appears, the page on which the case begins, and the date of the decision.

The case of Commonwealth v. Thomas appearing in the Pennsylvania State Reports, would be cited as

Commonwealth v. *Thomas*, 391 Pa. 486 (1958)

The case of Commonwealth v. Thomas is also reported in the second series of the Atlantic Reporter. If only the National Reporter system citation is given, the state is identified. Thus

Commonwealth v. *Thomas*, 137 A.2d 472 (Pa.1958)

The better practice in reporting state decisions is to give both the state report and the National Reporter System citations. Thus

Commonwealth v. *Thomas*, 391 Pa. 485, 137 A.2d 472 (1958)

When a state decision has been presented to the Supreme Court of the United States in an application for writ of certiorari (writ of review), the disposition of that case in the Supreme Court is noted. Action by a higher state court is reported in the same way. Thus

People v. *Anderson*, 397 Ill. 583, 74 N.E.2d 693 (1947) certiorari denied 533 U.S. 833, 68 S.Ct. 485, 92 L.Ed. 1117

Fielden v. *People*, 128 Ill. 595 (1889) 21 N.E. 684, affirmed 143 U.S. 452, 12 S.Ct. 528, 26 L.Ed. 224

People v. *Tananevics*, 285 Ill. 374, 120 N.E. 766 (1918), affirming 208 Ill.App. 473; error dismissed 40, 252 U.S. 568, 40 S.Ct. 346, 64 L.Ed. 720

6. The California Reports are now into the third series, cited *Cal.3d.*

When a state court decision has been annotated in the American Law Reports this fact is indicated in the citation. Thus

Nuchols v. *Commonwealth,* 312 Ky. 171, 226 S.W.2d 796 (1950), 13 A.L.R.2d 1478

Legal Publications

It is beyond the scope of this introductory work to set out the many sources of legal materials. There are the encyclopedias, *American Jurisprudence* (Am.Jur. and Am.Jur.2d) and *Corpus Juris—Corpus Juris Secundum* (C.J.—C.J.S.). Each is made up of over 400 alphabetically arranged topics or titles designed to cover the entire field of American law. Many states have encyclopedias of state law, which contain a text statement devoted to the law of the particular state with supporting cases confined to those from that state or to federal court decision construing the state laws. *Texas Jurisprudence* (Tex.Jur.) is an example of a state encyclopedia.

State and local *Digests* are a device for isolating pertinent case law to be used as authority for any given legal proposition. In a set of books known as *Words and Phrases,* the word or phrase is set out alphabetically, and is followed by a list of state and federal citations defining it. *Blacks Law Dictionary Fourth Revised Edition,* published by West Publishing Company, is another source of definitions. Blacks also gives judicial definitions with citations to the appropriate case.

Shephard's Citations provide a "history" of each reported case, i. e., shows whether the case was affirmed, reversed, modified, or dismissed. To "Shephardize" a case means to locate it in one of the units of Shephard's Citations (developed for each state, and for each unit in the National Reporter System). The case is located by volume and page number. Under the page number will be found the citation of other cases which have dealt with the cited cases. Symbols indicate whether the case was affirmed, overruled, cited in a dissenting opinion, followed in another case, and so on. Only by "Shephardizing" a case can the legal researcher be sure that the rule announced in the case is still "the law."

Articles in law journals or law reviews are an important source of information for the student and legal researcher. *Law Reviews* are published by the leading law schools. The leading articles may be authored by judges, lawyers, or law professors, but a law review also contains articles researched and authored by law students as part of their educational program. The reviews are published as periodicals.

The reader who wants to adequately acquaint himself with the tools for legal research is again referred to William R. Roalfe, General Editor, *How to Find the Law, Sixth Edition* (1965) published at St. Paul, Minnesota, by the West Publishing Company.

Appendix B

GLOSSARY OF LEGAL TERMS

A

ACCUSATION. A formal charge against a person to the effect that he is guilty of a punishable offense.

ACCUSED. The generic name for the defendant in a criminal case.

ACCUSATORY INSTRUMENT. As defined in New York, an indictment, an information, a simplified traffic information, a prosecutor's information, a misdemeanor complaint or a felony complaint. Every accusatory instrument, regardless of the person designated therein as the accuser, constitutes an accusation on behalf of the state as plaintiff and must be entitled "the people of the state of New York" against a designated person, known as the defendant.

ACCUSATORY STAGE. In police practice, the investigation that occurs after suspicion has focused upon one or more particular individuals as being guilty of the offense. Distinguished from investigatory stage during which the offense is the subject of general investigation before suspicion has focused on a particular accused. Also used to mean the stages in a criminal prosecution from arrest to conviction or acquittal.

ACQUITTAL. A legal and formal certification of the innocence of a person charged with a crime.

ACT OF GOD. An act occasioned exclusively by violence of nature without the interference of any human agency; an act, event, happending or occurrence due to natural causes.

ACTUS. An act or action.

ACTUS REUS. The criminal act; the act of a person committing a crime.

ADJUDICATE. To determine finally; to adjudge.

ADJUDICATION. The giving or pronouncing a judgment or decree in a cause; also the judgment given. The equivalent of "determination."

ADVERSARY. An opponent. The opposite party in a writ or action.

ADVERSARY PROCEEDING. One having opposing parties, as distinguished from an *ex parte* proceeding.

ADVERSARY SYSTEM. The practice of conducting legal proceedings as a battle between opposing parties under the judge as an impartial umpire with the outcome determined by the pleadings and evidence introduced into court; in Anglo-American jurisprudence includes the presumption of innocence of the accused. To be distinguished from the accusatory system used in continental law where the accusation is taken as evidence of guilt which must be disproved by the accused.

ADVOCATE. One who assists, defends, or pleads for another.

AFFIDAVIT. A written or printed declaration or statement of facts, taken before an officer having authority to administer oaths.

AGGRAVATED ASSAULT. Assault with intent to kill or for the purpose of inflicting severe bodily injury; assault with the use of a deadly weapon.

ALIAS. Otherwise; in another manner; a fictitious name.

ALIENIST. One who specializes in the study of mental disease.

ALLOCUTION. The court's inquiry of a prisoner as to whether he has any legal cause why judgment should not be pronounced against him on conviction.

AMICUS CURIAE. A friend of the court. Also a person who has no right to appear in a suit but is allowed to introduce argument, authority or evidence to protect his interests.

APPEAL. The removal of a cause from a court of inferior to one of superior jurisdiction for the purpose of obtaining a review and retrial.

APPEARANCE BOND. A bail bond in which the only obligor is the principal.

APPEARANCE TICKET. In New York, a written notice issued by a public servant, requiring a person to appear before a local criminal court in connection with an accusatory instrument to be filed against him therein.

APPELLANT. The party who takes an appeal from one court of justice to another. In criminal law usually the defendant in the lower court.

APPELLATE JURISDICTION. The right of a court to review the decision of a lower court; the power to hear cases appealed from a lower court.

APPEARANCE. The coming into court as party to a suit.

APPELLEE. The party in a cause against whom an appeal is taken; in criminal law, usually the state or the United States.

ARRAIGN. To bring a prisoner before the court to answer the indictment or information. In practice, used to refer to any appearance of the accused before a magistrate, or before the trial court to enter his plea.

ARRAIGNMENT. See Arraign. The proceeding for arraignment of the accused at which he enters his plea to the charge. In New York, arraignment means the occasion upon which a defendant against whom an accusatory instrument has been filed appears before the court in which the criminal action is pending for the purpose of having such court acquire and exercise control over his person with respect to such accusatory instrument and of setting the course of further proceedings in the action.

ARRAY. The whole body of jurors summoned to attend a court.

ARREST. The taking of a person into custody to answer to a criminal charge.

ARSON. The intentional and unlawful burning of property. At common law, the malicious burning of the house or outhouse of another.

ASPORTATION. The removal of things from one place to another, such as is in some states required in the offense of larceny.

ASSAULT. The intentional unlawful use of force by one person upon another. If severe bodily harm is inflicted or a weapon is used, the offense is aggravated assault. The lesser degree of the crime is called assault or simple assault.

ASSAULT AND BATTERY. A battery is an unlawful touching of the person of another. See Assault.

AUTO THEFT. Stealing or driving away and abandoning a motor vehicle. May exclude taking for temporary use, or the taking for temporary use may carry a smaller penalty.

B

BAIL. To procure the release of a person from legal custody, by undertaking that he shall appear at the time and place designated, and submit himself to the jurisdiction and judgment of the court. In New York, cash bail or a bail bond.

BAIL BOND. A bond executed by a defendant who has been arrested, together with other persons as sureties, naming the sheriff, constable, or marshal as obligee, in a penal sum conditioned that the defendant shall duly appear to answer the legal process.

BAILMENT. A delivery of good or personal property by one person to another to carry out a special purpose and redeliver the goods to the bailor.

BAILEE. One to whom goods are delivered under a contract or agreement of bailment.

BAILOR. One who delivers goods under a contract or agreement of bailment.

BENCH WARRANT. Process issued by the court itself, or "from the bench," for the attachment or arrest of a person; either in case of contempt, or whether an indictment has been found, or to bring in a witness who does not obey a subpoena. So called to distinguish it from a warrant issued by a justice of the peace or magistrate. In New York, a bench warrant means a process of a criminal court in which a criminal action is pending, directing a police officer to take into custody a defendant in such action who was previously been arraigned upon the accusatory instrument by which the action was commenced, and to bring him before such court. The function of a bench warrant is to achieve the court appearance of a defendant in a pending criminal action for some purpose other than his initial arraignment in the action.

BEYOND A REASONABLE DOUBT. It is proof to a moral certainty, such proof as satisfies the judgment and consciences of the jury, as reasonable men, that the crime charged has been committed by the defendant.

BOOKING. The clerical process involving the entry on the police "blotter" or arrest book of the suspect's name, the time of the arrest, the offense charged and the name of the arresting officer. Used in practice to refer to the police station-house procedures that take place from arrest to the initial appearance of the accused before the magistrate.

BREACH OF THE PEACE. A violation or disturbance of the public tranquility and order.

BREAKING AND ENTERING. Any unlawful entry even though no force was used to gain entrance.

BURGLARY. Breaking and entering with intent to commit a felony or theft, or in some states, with intent to commit any offense.

C

CAPIAS. Lat. "That you take." The general name for several species of writs, the common characteristic of which is that they require the officer to take the body of the defendant into custody.

CARNAL KNOWLEDGE. Sexual intercourse; the slightest penetration of the sexual organ of the female by the sexual organ of the male.

CARRYING CONCEALED WEAPONS. All violations of regulations or statutes controlling the carrying, using, possessing, furnishing, and manufacturing of deadly weapons or silencers.

CASE. A general term for an action, cause, suit, or controversy in law or equity; a question contested before a court of justice.

CERTIORARI. To be informed of, to be made certain in regard to. The name of a writ of review or inquiry; a writ directed by a superior court to an inferior court asking that the record of a case be sent up for review; a method of obtaining a review of a case by the United States Supreme Court.

CHANCERY COURT. The court having the jurisdiction of a chancellor; a court administering equity. In some states in the United States, a court with equity power distinct from the courts of common law. Also called Court of Chancery.

CHANGE OF VENUE. The removal of an action begun in one county or district to another county or district for trial.

CHARGE. To impose a burden, duty, or obligation; to claim, demand; to accuse; to instruct a jury on matters of law.

CIRCUMSTANCES. Attendant facts. Any fact may be a circumstance with reference to another fact.

CIRCUMSTANTIAL EVIDENCE. All evidence of an indirect nature; the existence of a principle fact is inferred from circumstances.

CITIZEN. One who, under the constitution and laws of the United States, or of a particular state, is a member of the political community.

CIVIL ACTION. One brought to recover some civil right, or to obtain redress for some wrong not being a crime or misdemeanor.

CIVIL LAW. Having to do with the establishment, recovery, or redress of private and civil rights.

CIVIL COURT. Courts established for the adjudication of controversies between private persons, or the ascertainment, enforcement, and redress of private rights.

COERCION. Compulsion, constraint, compelling by force.

COMPLAINT. In criminal law, a charge preferred before a magistrate having jurisdiction that a person named has committed a specified offense. Usually the first document filed in a court charging the offense. In some states, the term complaint is interchangeable with information. See Information. It is also sometimes used interchangeably with Affidavit. See Affidavit.

CONCURRENT. Running together; contemporaneous. Concurrent sentences run at the same time and each day served by the prisoner is credited on each of the concurrent sentences.

CONSECUTIVE SENTENCES. Sentences which are served one after the other; inmates refer to such sentences as "stacked."

CONTEMPT. A willful disregard or disobedience of a public authority.

CONTEMPT OF COURT. Any act which is calculated to embarrass, hinder, or obstruct the court in the administration of justice, or which is calculated to lessen its authority or dignity. Direct contempts (also called "criminal contempt") are those committed in the immediate view of the court (such as insulting language or acts of violence) and are punishable summarily. Constructive (or indirect) contempts are those which arise from matters not occurring in or near the presence of the court, but with reference to the failure or refusal of a party to obey a lawful or decree of court.

CONTEMPT POWER. The power of a court to punish for contempt. A court of record has this power.

CONTRABAND. Any material object which is unlawful for a private individual to possess.

CONVICTION. In a general sense, the result of a criminal trial which ends in a judgment or sentence that the person is guilty as charged. In New York, conviction means the entry of a plea of guilty to, or a verdict of guilty upon, an accusatory instrument other than a felony complaint, or to one or more counts of such instrument.

CORPUS DELICTI. The body of the crime; the essential elements of the crime; the substantial fact that a crime has been committed. The actual commission by someone of the offense charged.

COUNT. The plaintiff's statement of his cause of action; also used to specify the several parts of an indictment or information each charging a distinct offense. Often used synomously with the word "charge."

COURT ABOVE, COURT BELOW. In appellate practice, the "court above" is the one to which a cause is removed for review, whether by appeal, writ of error, or certiorari; while the "court below" is the one from which the case is removed.

COURT OF APPEAL. An appellate tribunal. The name given to the court of last resort in several states; the court of last resort of a particular type of case; or in some states, an intermediate appellate court below the supreme court.

COURTS OF APPEALS. A system of courts of the United States (one in each circuit) created by act of Congress, composed of three or more judges (provision also being made for allotment of the justices of the Supreme Court among the circuits), and having appellate jurisdiction as defined by statute. Called the United States Courts of Appeals; formerly called the Circuit Courts of Appeals or United States Circuit Courts of Appeals.

COURT OF COMMON PLEAS. In English law, one of the four superior courts at Westminster. In American law, the name given to a court of original and general jurisdiction for the trial of issues and law. The superior court of the District of Columbia is called the Court of Common Pleas. The oldest court in the state of New York, the Court of Common Pleas for the City and County of New York is no longer in existence.

COURT OF COMPETENT JURISDICTION. One having power and authority of law at the time of acting to do the particular act.

COURT OF EQUITY. A court which has jurisdiction in equity, which administers justice and decides controversies in accordance with the rules, principles and precedents of equity. See Chancery Court.

COURT OF ERRORS AND APPEALS. The court of last resort in the state of New Jersey. Formerly, the same title was given to the highest court of appeal in New York.

COURT OF GENERAL SESSIONS. The name given in some states to a court of general original jurisdiction in criminal cases.

COURT MARTIAL. A military court convened under the authority of the government and the Uniform Code of Military Justice for trying and punishing offenses committed by members of the armed forces.

COURT OF QUARTER SESSIONS OF THE PEACE. A court of criminal jurisdiction in the state of Pennsylvania having power to try misdemeanors and exercising certain functions of an administrative nature. There is one such court in each county of the state.

COURT OF RECORD. A court the appeals from which are heard on the record. A court whose judicial acts and proceedings are recorded and which has the power to fine or imprison for contempt.

COURT OF SPECIAL SESSIONS. Courts of inferior criminal jurisdiction in New York. Jurisdiction roughly equivalent to that of a justice of the peace.

COURT OF STAR CHAMBER. An English court of a very ancient origin. Originally, its jurisdiction extended legally over riots, perjury, misbehavior of sheriffs, and other misdemeanors contrary to the laws of the land; afterwards stretched to the asserting of all orders of state; becoming both a court of law to determine civil rights and a court of revenue to enrich the treasury. It was finally abolished "to the general satisfaction of the whole nation."

COURTS OF THE UNITED STATES. Comprise the following: The Senate of the United States as a Court of impeachment; the Supreme Court; the courts of appeals, the district courts; the court of claims; the court of customs and patent appeals; the customs court; the tax court of the United States; the provisional courts; and courts of territories and outlying possessions.

CRIME. A positive or negative act in violation of penal law; an offense against the state.

CRIMINAL. One who has committed a criminal offense; one who has been legally convicted of a crime; one adjudged guilty of a crime.

CRIMINAL ACTION. The whole or any part of the procedure which law provides for bringing offenders to justice. In New York, a criminal action (a) commences with the filing of an accusatory instrument against a defendant in a criminal court, as specified in subdivision seventeen; (b) includes the filing of all further accusatory instruments directly derived from the initial one, and all proceedings, orders and motions conducted or made by a criminal court in the course of disposing of any such accusatory instrument, or which, regardless of the court in which they occurred or were made, could properly be considered as a part of the record of the case by an appellate court upon an appeal from a judgment of conviction; and (c) terminates with the imposition of sentence or some other final disposition in a criminal court of the last accusatory instrument filed in the case.

CRIMINAL CHARGE. An accusation of crime in a written complaint, information, or indictment.

CRIMINAL COURT. A court charged with the administration of the criminal laws and empowered to sentence the guilty person to fine or imprisonment. In New York, the criminal courts are comprised of the superior and local criminal courts. Superior court means the supreme court, or a county court. Local criminal court means a district court; or the New York City criminal court; or a city court; or a town court; or a village court; or a supreme court justice sitting as a local criminal court; or a county judge sitting as a local criminal court.

CRIMINAL HOMICIDE. All willful felonious homicides as distinguished from deaths caused by negligence.

CRIMINAL INFORMATION. A formal accusation of crime, differing from an indictment only in that it is preferred by a prosecuting officer instead of a grand jury.

CRIMINAL INTENT. An intent to commit a crime; malice, as evidenced by a criminal act; an intent to deprive or defraud the true owner of his property.

CRIMINAL LAW. That branch or division of law which treats of crimes and their punishment.

CRIMINAL PROCEEDING. One instituted and conducted for the purpose either of preventing the commission of crime, or for fixing the guilt of a crime already committed, and punishing the offender. In New York, a criminal proceeding means any proceeding which (a) constitutes a part of a criminal action or (b) occurs in a criminal court and is related to a prospective, pending or completed criminal action, either of this state or of any other jurisdiction, or involves a criminal investigation.

CRIMINAL PROSECUTION. An action or proceeding instituted in a proper court on behalf of the public for the purpose of securing the conviction and punishment of one accused of crime.

CRIMINAL JUSTICE PROCESS. The sequence of steps taken from the initial contact of the offender with the law until he is released back into a free society.

CRIMINAL JUSTICE SYSTEM. The system by which society identifies, accuses, convicts, and punishes offenders against the norms of the society expressed in the law.

CRIMINAL PROCEDURE. A method for the apprehension, trial, prosecution, and fixing the punishment, of persons who have broken the law.

CROSS EXAMINATION. The examination of a witness upon a trial or hearing, by the party opposed to the one who produced him, upon his evidence given in chief, to test its truth, to further develop it, or for other purposes.

CURFEW OFFENSES. Offenses relating to violation of local curfew or loitering ordinance which make regulations as to when a person (usually a juvenile) may be lawfully on the streets.

CURTILAGE. The enclosed space of ground and buildings immediately surrounding the dwelling house.

D

DAY IN COURT. The opportunity to present one's claim before a competent tribunal.

DAYLIGHT. That portion of time before sunrise and after sunset which is accounted as part of the day; usually one half hour before sunrise to one half hour after sunset.

DEALER. In the popular sense, one who buys to sell—not one who buys to keep.

DECREE. The judgment of the court; a declaration of the court announcing the legal consequences of the facts found.

DEFENDANT. The person defending or denying; the party against whom relief or recovery is sought in an action or suit. In criminal law, the party charged with a crime.

DEFENSE (old spelling, DEFENCE). In a criminal action, the answer made by the defendant to the State's case.

DEFENSE ATTORNEY. The attorney representing the accused in a criminal action.

DELIBERATE. As applied to a jury, the weighing of the evidence and the law for the purpose of determining the guilt or innocence of a defendant. In the case of jury sentencing, the deliberation may be for the purpose of fixing the sentence.

DELINQUENT CHILD. A person of no more than a specified age who has violated any law or ordinance or is incorrigible, a person who has been adjudicated a delinquent child by a juvenile court while of juvenile court age.

DETAINER. A kind of "hold order" filed against an incarcerated man by another state or jurisdiction which seeks to take him into custody to answer to another criminal charge whenever he is released from the current imprisonment.

DIRECT EVIDENCE. That means of proof which tends to show the existence of a fact in question without the intervention of the proof of any other fact. Is distinguished from circumstantial evidence, which is often called "indirect."

DIRECT EXAMINATION. In practice, the first interrogation or examination of a witness, on the merits, by the party on whose behalf he is called.

DISORDERLY CONDUCT. Conduct against public order. Sometimes used synonymously with Breach of the Peace, although not all disorderly conduct is a Breach of the Peace.

DISTRICT ATTORNEY. In New York, a district attorney or an assistant district attorney, and where appropriate, the attorney general or an assistant attorney general. See Prosecutor.

DOUBT. Uncertainty of mind; the absence of a settled opinion or conviction; the state of the case which, after the entire comparison and consideration of the evidence, leaves the minds of the jurors in such a condition that they cannot say to a moral certainty of the truth of the charge. If upon proof there is a reasonable doubt remaining, the accused is entitled to the benefit of an acquittal.

DRIVING UNDER THE INFLUENCE. See Driving While Intoxicated.

DRIVING WHILE INTOXICATED. Driving or operating any motor vehicle while drunk or under the influence of liquor or narcotics.

DUCES TECUM. From the Latin "bring with you." A subpoena duces tecum requires a party to appear in court and bring with him certain documents, pieces of evidence, or other matters to be inspected by the court.

DUE PROCESS OF LAW. The fundamental rights of the accused to a fair trial; the prescribed forms for conducting a criminal prosecution; the safeguards and protections of the law given to one accused of a crime. In substantive criminal law, the right to have crimes and punishments clearly defined in the law.

D.W.I. See Driving While Intoxicated. A first offense is sometimes referred to as "D.W.I. I" (one); a second offense as "D.W.I. II" (two).

E

EMBEZZLEMENT. Misappropriation or misapplication of money or property entrusted to one's care, custody, or control.

ET AL. And another; and others.

EVIDENCE. Any species of proof, presented at the trial for the purpose of inducing belief in the minds of the court or jury.

EXAMINING TRIAL. See Preliminary Hearing.

EXCLUSIONARY RULE. The rule which excludes from the trial of an accused evidence illegally seized or obtained.

EXPERT WITNESS. One who gives result of process of reasoning which can be mastered only by special scientists; one who has skilled experience or extensive knowledge in his calling or in any branch of learning; person competent to give expert testimony.

EXPERT EVIDENCE. Testimony given in relation to some scientific, technical, or professional matter by experts, i. e. persons qualified to speak authoritatively by reason of their special training, skill, or familiarity with the subject.

EX REL. By or on the information of. Used in case title to designate the person at whose instance the government or public official is acting.

EX PARTE. On one side only; by or for one party; done for, in behalf of, or on the application, of one party only.

EX POST FACTO. After the fact.

EX POST FACTO LAW. A law passed after the occurrence of a fact or commission of an act which retrospectively changes the legal consequences or relations of such fact or deed. Forbidden to both the states and the federal government by United States Constitution Art. 1.

F

FEDERAL QUESTION. A case which contains a major issue involving the United States Constitution or statutes. The jurisdiction of the federal courts is governed, in part, by the existence of a federal question.

FELONY. Generally an offense punishable by death or imprisonment in the penitentiary. At common law, an offense occasioning total forfeiture of either land or goods to which capital or other punishment might be superadded according to the degree of guilt. A crime of graver or more atrocious nature than those designated as a misdemeanor.

FELONY COMPLAINT. As defined in New York, a verified written accusation by a person, filed with a local criminal court, which charges one or more defendants with the commission of one or more felonies and which serves to commence a criminal action but not as a basis for prosecution thereof.

FELONY THEFT. See Larceny-Theft.

FORCIBLE RAPE. Rape by force, or against the consent of the victim.

FORGERY. Making, altering, uttering (passing) or possessing anything false which is made to appear true, with intent to defraud.

FRUITS OF A CRIME. Material objects acquired by means of and in consequence of the commission of a crime, and sometimes constituting the subject matter of the crime.

G

GAMBLING. Promoting, permitting, or engaging in gambling.

GOOD TIME. Credit allowed on the sentence for exemplary conduct in confinement.

GRAND JURY. A jury of inquiry authorized to return indictments.

GRAND LARCENY. Larceny of the grade of felony.

H

HABEAS CORPUS. Literally, "you have the body." See Writ of Habeas Corpus.

HEARING. In a broad sense, whatever takes place before a court or a magistrate clothed with judicial function and sitting without a jury. A trial is a hearing, but not all hearings require the formalities of a trial.

HEARSAY. Evidence not proceeding from the personal knowledge of the witness, but from the mere repetition of what he has heard others say.

HOMICIDE. The killing of one human being by another.

HUNG JURY. A jury so irreconcilably divided in opinion that it cannot agree upon any verdict.

I

INDEX CRIMES. The crimes used by the Federal Bureau of Investigation in reporting the incidence of crime in the United States in the Uniform Crime Reports. The statistics on the Index Crimes are taken as an index as to the incidence of crime in the United States.

INDICTMENT. An accusation in writing found and presented by a grand jury, charging that a person therein named has been guilty of a public offense punishable on indictment.

INDIRECT EVIDENCE. See Circumstantial Evidence.

INFAMOUS. Shameful or disgraceful. See Infamous Crimes.

INFAMOUS CRIMES. A crime which entails infamy upon one who has committed it; crimes punishable by imprisonment in the state prison or penitentiary. At common law, all felonies were considered to be infamous crimes.

INFORMATION. An accusation exhibited against a person for some criminal offense, without an indictment. An accusation in the nature of an indictment, from which it differs only in being presented by a competent public officer on his oath of office, instead of a grand jury on their oath.

INFORMER. A person who informs or prefers an accusation against another whom he suspects of the violation of some penal statute.

INFRACTION. The name given to minor offenses (chiefly traffic offenses) in the California Infractions Code.

IMPEACHMENT. A criminal procedure against a public officer to remove him from office. In the law of evidence, the adducing of proof that a witness is unworthy of belief.

IN FORMA PAUPERIS. In the form of a pauper; as a poor person or indigent. Permission to bring legal action without the payment of required fees for counsel, writs, transcripts, and the like.

INJUNCTION. A writ prohibiting an individual or organization from performing some specified action.

IN RE. In the affair; in the matter of; concerning. This is the usual method of entitling a judicial proceeding in which there are no adversary parties. For this reason, used in the title of cases in a juvenile court.

ISSUE. A single, certain, and material point, deduced from the pleadings of the parties, which is affirmed by the one side and denied on the other; a fact put in controversy by the pleadings; in criminal law a fact which must be proved to convict the accused, or which is in controversy.

INSTRUMENTALITIES OF A CRIME. Tools or implements used to commit a crime.

INTERMEDIATE APPELLATE COURT. In New York, any court possessing appellate jurisdiction, other than the court of appeals.

INVESTIGATORY STAGE. In police practice the stage of investigation during which the offense is the subject of general inquiry before suspicion has focused on a particular person or persons. Distinguished from the accusatory stage which covers the investigation that occurs after suspicion has focused upon one or more particular individuals as being guilty of the offense.

J

JAIL TIME. Credit allowed on a sentence for the time spent in jail awaiting trial or mandate on appeal.

JUDGE. An officer so named in his commission, who presides in some court. In New York, includes any judicial officer who is a member of or constitutes a court, whether referred to in another provision of law as a justice or by any other title.

JUDGMENT. In general, the official and authentic decision of a court of justice upon the respective rights and claims of the parties to the action or suit therein litigated and submitted to its determination. In New York, a judgment is comprised of a conviction and the sentence imposed thereon and is completed by imposition and entry of the sentence.

JUDICIAL PROCESS. The sequence of steps taken by the courts in deciding cases or disposing of legal controversies.

JURISDICTION. The power conferred upon a court to hear certain cases; the power of the police or judicial officer to act. The extent of the power of a public official to act by virtue of his authority. See also Original Jurisdiction, Trial Jurisdiction, Appellate Jurisdiction, and Preliminary Jurisdiction.

JURY PANEL. A list of jurors returned by a sheriff, to serve at a particular court or for the trial of a particular case. The word may be used to denote either the whole body of the persons summoned as jurors for a particular term of court, or those selected by the clerk by lot.

JUVENILE DELINQUENT. See Delinquent Child.

L

LARCENY. The taking of property from the possession of another with intent of the taker to convert it to his own use. Depending upon the value of the property taken, the offense is a felony or a misdemeanor. See Theft.

LAW. Law is the formal means of social control that involves the use of rules that are interpreted, and are enforceable, by the courts of a political community.

Law is the effort of society to protect persons, in their rights and relations, to guard them in their property, enforce their contracts, hold them to liabilities for their torts, punish their crimes, by means of remedies administered by government.

LAW OF THE LAND. See Due Process.

LEADING QUESTION. A question which is suggestive of the answer; one which instructs witness how to answer or puts into his mouth words to be echoed back; one which suggests to witness the answer desired.

LEGAL. Conforming to the law; according to a law; required or permitted by law; not forbidden or discountenanced by law; good and effectual law.

LEGAL DUTY. That which the law requires to be done or foreborne.

LEGAL ETHICS. Usages and customs among members of the legal profession, involving their moral and professional duties toward one another, toward clients, and toward the courts.

LEGAL PROVOCATION. Provocation sufficient in law to be a defense to the act.

LEGISLATION. Legislation is rules of general application, enacted by a law-making body in a politically organized society. Included in legislation are constitutions, treaties, statutes, ordinances, administrative regulations, and court rules. Distinguished from case law, common law, and "judge-made law."

LESSER INCLUDED OFFENSE. When it is impossible to commit a particular crime without concomitantly committing, by the same conduct, another offense of lesser grade or degree, the latter is, with respect to the former, a "lesser included offense." In New York, in any case in which it is legally possible to attempt to commit a crime, an attempt to commit such crime constitutes a lesser included offense with respect thereto.

LESSER OFFENSE. Sometimes used synonymously with a "less serious offense," or "minor offense."

LIMITATION OF ACTIONS. The time at the end of which no action at law can be maintained; in criminal law, the time after the commission of the offense within which the indictment must be presented or the information filed.

LINE–UP. A police identification procedure during which the person of a suspect is exhibited to witnesses to the crime to determine whether or not they can connect him with the offense. Also called a "show-up."

LOCAL CRIMINAL COURTS. In New York, a district court; or the New York City criminal court; or a city court; or a town court; or a village court; or a supreme court justice sitting as a local criminal court; or a county judge sitting as a local criminal court.

M

MALA IN SE. Wrong in themselves; acts immoral or wrong in themselves.

MALA PROHIBITA. Crimes *mala prohibita* embrace things prohibited by statute as infringing on other's rights, though no moral turpitude may be attached, and constituting crimes only because they are prohibited.

MANSLAUGHTER. The lowest degree of culpable homicide; death caused by culpable recklessness or negligence.

MATERIAL ALLEGATION. One essential to the claim or defense, and which could not be stricken from the pleading without leaving it insufficient.

MATERIAL FACT. One which is essential to the case, defense, application, etc. and without which it could not be supported.

MENS REA. A guilty mind, a guilty or wrongful purpose, a criminal intent. Guilty knowledge and wilfulness.

MINOR. A person or infant who is under the age of legal competence; one under twenty-one.

MIRANDA WARNING. The warning which must be given to the suspect whenever suspicion focuses upon him. The officer must warn the suspect (1) that he has a right to remain silent; (2) that if he talks, anything he says may be used against him; (3) that he has a right to be represented by counsel and the right to have counsel present at all questioning; and (4) that if he is too poor to afford counsel, counsel will be provided for him at state expense.

MISDEMEANOR. Any offense which is not a felony.

MISDEMEANOR COMPLAINT. As defined in New York, a verified written accusation by a person, filed with a local criminal court, which charges one or more defendants with the commission of one or more offenses, at least one of which is a misdemeanor and none of which is a felony, and which serves to commence a criminal action but which may not, except upon the defendant's consent, serve as a basis for prosecution of the offenses charged therein.

MISDEMEANOR THEFT. See Larceny-Theft.

MOOT. A subject for argument; unsettled, undecided. A moot point is one not settled by judicial decision.

MOOT CASE. One which seeks to get a judgment on a pretended controversy, or a decision in advance about a right before it has been actually asserted and contested, or a judgment on some matter which, when rendered, for any reason, cannot have any practical legal effect upon a then existing controversy.

MOOT COURT. A court held for the arguing of moot (or pretended) cases or questions. Students in law school participate in "moot courts."

MORAL TURPITUDE. An act of baseness, vileness, or depravity in the private and social duties which man owes to his fellow men, or to society in general, contrary to the accepted and customary rule of right and duty between man and man.

MURDER. The highest degree of culpable homicide.

N

NARCOTIC OFFENSES. Offenses relating to narcotic drugs, such as unlawful possession, sale or use. Also used to describe any substance abuse offense.

O

ORDER OF RECOGNIZANCE OR BAIL. In New York, a securing order releasing a principal on his own recognizance or fixing bail.

ORIGINAL JURISDICTION. Jurisdiction in the first instance; jurisdiction to take cognizance of a case at its inception, impanel a jury, try the case, and pass judgment upon the law and the facts. Distinguished from appellate jurisdiction. See Trial Jurisdiction.

P

PARDON. An act of grace, proceeding from the power entrusted with the execution of the laws, which exempts the individual on whom it is bestowed from the punishment the law inflicts for the crime he has committed.

PARENS PATRIAE. Literally, "father of his country." The doctrine that the juvenile court treats the child as "a kind and loving father."

PAROLE. The release of a prisoner from imprisonment but not from the legal custody of the State, for rehabilitation outside of prison walls under such conditions and provisions for disciplinary supervision as the Board of Parole may determine. Parole is an administrative act and follows incarceration.

PER CURIAM. By the court. An opinion of the court which is authored by the justices collectively.

PER SE. By himself or itself; in itself; taken alone.

PEREMPTORY CHALLENGE. Self determined, arbitrary, requiring no cause to be shown. As applied to selection of jurors, challenges allowed by law to both the state and defense to remove a prospective juror without cause from the panel of jurors.

PETIT JURY. A trial jury as distinguished from a Grand Jury; an ordinary jury of twelve men (or less) for the trial of a civil or criminal action.

PETTY LARCENY. Larceny of the grade of misdemeanor.

PLEA OF GUILTY. A confession of guilt in open court.

PLEA OF *NOLO CONTENDERE*. One which has the same effect in a criminal action as a plea of guilty, but does not bind the defendant in a civil suit for the same wrong. Literally, "No contest."

PLEA OF NOT GUILTY. A plea denying the guilt of the accused to the offense charged and putting the state to the proof of all of the material elements of the offense.

POLITICAL COMMUNITY. A political community involves forcible maintenance of orderly dominion over a territory and its inhabitants.

PRECEDENT. An adjudged case or decision of a court of justice considered as furnishing an example or authority for an identical or similar case afterwards arising on a similar question of law. See *Stare Decisis*.

PRELIMINARY EXAMINATION. Same as Preliminary Hearing.

PRELIMINARY HEARING. The examination of a person charged with a crime before a magistrate.

PRELIMINARY JURISDICTION. As defined in New York, a criminal court has "preliminary jurisdiction" of an offense when, regardless of whether it has trial jurisdiction thereof, a criminal action for such offense may be commenced therein, and when such court may conduct proceedings with respect thereto which lead or may lead to prosecution and final disposition of the action in a court having trial jurisdiction thereof.

PREPONDERANCE. The larger part of; the most, in quality or quantity.

PREPONDERANCE OF THE EVIDENCE. Greater weight of evidence: the preponderance of the evidence rests with the evidence which produces the stronger impression and is more convincing as to its truth when weighed against the evidence in opposition.

PRESENTMENT. The initial appearance by the accused before the magistrate after arrest. Also, a written notice taken by a grand jury of any offense, from their own knowledge or observation, without any bill of indictment laid before them at the suit of the government. See Indictment.

PRESUMPTION OF FACT. An inference affirmative or disaffirmative of the truth or falsehood of any proposition or fact. Presumptions of fact are not the subject of fixed rules, but are merely natural presumptions such as appear from common experience to arise from the particular circumstances.

PRESUMPTION OF LAW. A rule of law that courts and judges shall draw a particular inference from a particular fact, or from particular evidence, unless and until the truth of such inference is disproved; an inference which the court will draw from the proof which no evidence, however strong, will be permitted to overcome.

Presumptions of law are reduced to fixed rules and form a part of the system of jurisprudence to which they belong. Presumptions are evidence, or have the effect of evidence.

PRIMA FACIE CASE. A case developed with evidence such as will suffice until contradicted and overcome by other evidence.

PRIMA FACIE EVIDENCE. Evidence good and sufficient on its face; such evidence as in the judgment of the law, is sufficient to establish a given fact, or the group or chain of facts constituting the party's claim or defense, and which if not rebutted or contradicted, will remain sufficient.

PROBABLE CAUSE. Reasonable cause. Having more evidence for than against. An apparent state of facts which would induce a reasonably intelligent and prudent man to believe, in a criminal case, that the accused person had committed the crime charged. More than suspicion, less than certainty.

PROBATION. The release of a convicted defendant by a court under conditions imposed by the court for a specified period during which the imposition of sentence is suspended. Probation is in lieu of incarceration and is a judicial act.

PROCEDURAL LAW. Machinery for carrying on a suit or action.

PROCEDURE. The mode of proceeding by which a legal right is enforced as distinguished from the law which gives or defines the right; the machinery, as distinguished from its product. A form, manner, and order of conducting prosecutions.

PROSECUTOR. One who prosecutes another for a crime in the name of the government.

PROSECUTOR'S INFORMATION. As defined in New York, a written accusation by a district attorney filed with a local criminal court, which charges one or more defendants with the commission of one or more offenses, none of which is a felony, and which serves as a basis for prosecution thereof.

PROSTITUTION. Sex offenses of a commercialized nature.

PROVOCATION. The act of inciting another to do a particular deed; that which arouses, moves, calls forth, causes, or occasions.

PROXIMATE CAUSE. That which, in a natural and continuous sequence, unbroken by any efficient intervening cause, produces the injury, and without which the result would not have occurred.

PUBLIC DEFENDER. An attorney designated by law or appointed by the court to represent indigent defendants in criminal proceedings. A public defender is paid by the state or by a private agency, or serves without fee.

R

RAPE. The unlawful carnal knowledge of a woman by a man forcibly and against her will. See also Statutory Rape.

REAL EVIDENCE. Evidence furnished by things themselves on view or inspection, as distinguished from a description of them given by a witness.

REBUTTAL. The introduction of rebutting evidence; the showing that a statement of witnesses as to what occurred is not true; the stage of a trial at which such evidence may be introduced; also the rebutting evidence itself.

REBUTTING EVIDENCE. Evidence given to explain, repel, counteract, or disprove facts given in evidence by the adverse party.

REBUTTABLE PRESUMPTION. A presumption which may be rebutted by evidence; a species of legal presumption which holds good until disproved.

RECEIVING STOLEN PROPERTY. Buying, receiving, and possessing stolen property with knowledge that it is stolen, or under circumstances requiring inquiry as to its origin.

RECORD. A written account of some act, transaction, or instrument; a written memorial of all the acts and proceedings in an action or suit, in a court of record; the official and authentic history of the cause, consisting in entries in each successive step in the proceedings. At comon law, a roll or parchment upon which the proceedings and transactions of a court are entered.

RELEASE ON OWN RECOGNIZANCE. A court releases a person on his own recognizance when, having acquired control over his person, it permits him to be at liberty during the pendency of the action upon his own agreement and without furnishing sureties for his appearance.

RELEVANT. Applying to the matter in question. A fact is relevant to another fact when, according to common course of events, existence of one taken alone or in connection with the other fact renders existence of the other certain or more probable.

RES GESTAE. Things done. The whole of the transaction under investigation and every part of it. *Res gestae* is considered an exception to the hearsay rule, and is extended to include not only declarations by the parties to the suit, but includes statements made by bystanders and strangers under certain circumstances.

RESPONDENT. The defendant on appeal; the party who contends against an appeal.

REUS. A person judicially accused of a crime; a person criminally proceeded against.

RIGHT OF ALLOCUTION. See Allocution. The right of the convicted person to speak in his own defense before judgment is pronounced.

ROBBERY. Stealing or taking anything of value from the person by force or violence or by putting in fear.

RUNAWAY. A juvenile offense; also a juvenile offender who has run away from home without his parent's permission.

S

SCIENTER. Knowingly, with guilty knowledge.

SECURING ORDER. In New York, an order of a court committing a principal to the custody of the sheriff, or fixing bail, or releasing him on his own recognizance.

SENTENCE. The judgment formally pronounced by the court or judge upon the defendant after his conviction in a criminal prosecution awarding the punishment to be inflicted.

SERVICE OF PROCESS. The service of writs, summonses, rules, etc. signifies the delivering or leaving them with the party to whom or with whom they ought to be delivered or left; and when they are so delivered, they are then said to be served.

SEQUESTER. To keep a jury together and in isolation from other persons under charge of the bailiff during the pendency of a trial, sometimes called "separation of the jury." To keep witnesses apart from other witnesses and unable to hear their testimony. In the case of witnesses sometimes called "putting the witness under rule."

SEX OFFENSES. Rape, prostitution, commercialized vice, statutory rape, offenses against chastity, common decency, and morals.

SHOW CAUSE. An order to appear as directed and present to the court reasons and considerations as to why certain circumstances should be continued, permitted, or prohibited, as the case may be.

SHOW–UP. See Line-Up.

SIMPLE ASSAULT. Assault which is not of an aggravated nature. See Aggravated Assault.

SIMPLIFIED TRAFFIC INFORMATION. As defined in New York, a written accusation by a police officer filed with a local criminal court which charges a person with a traffic violation or misdemeanors relating to traffic, and which may serve both to commence a criminal action for such offense and as a basis for prosecution thereof.

SOCIAL CONTROL. Social control is the process by which subgroups and persons are influenced to conduct themselves in conformity to group expectations.

STANDING. The qualifications needed to bring legal action.

STAR CHAMBER. See Court of Star Chamber.

STARE DECISIS. To abide by, or adhere to decided cases; doctrine that, when a court has once laid down a principle of law as applicable to a certain state of facts, it will adhere to that principle, and apply it to all future cases where facts are substantially the same, regardless of whether the person and property are the same.

STATE. The supreme political community. Also a state of the United States.

STATUTORY LAW. See Legislation.

STATUTORY RAPE. Carnal knowledge of a female child below the age fixed by statute. Neither force nor lack of content are necessary elements of this offense.

SUBPOENA. A process issued by a court to cause a witness to appear and give testimony for the party named.

SUFFICIENT PROVOCATION. See Legal Provocation.

SUMMONS. A writ, directed to the sheriff or other proper officer, requiring him to notify the person named that an action has been commenced against him, and that he is required to appear, on a day named, and answer the complaint in such action. In New York, a summons means a process of a local criminal court, requiring a defendant to appear before such court for the purpose of arraignment upon an accusatory instrument filed therewith by which a criminal action against him has been commenced.

SUPERIOR COURTS. Used generally to denote courts of general trial jurisdiction. The name given to the felony courts in California and Illinois. In New York, a superior court means the supreme court or a county court with criminal jurisdiction.

SUPERIOR COURT WARRANT OF ARREST. In New York, a process of a superior court directing a police officer to arrest a defendant and to bring him before such court for the purpose of arraignment upon an indictment filed therewith by which a criminal action against him has been commenced.

SUPREME COURT. The highest court of the United States, created by the Constitution. The name given in most states to the highest court of appeals, the court of last resort.

SUSPECT. To have a slight or even vague idea concerning; not necessarily involving knowledge of belief or likelihood. Is sometimes used in place of the word "believe." Also, a person who is suspected of having committed an offense, or who is believed to have committed an offense.

SUSPICION. The act of suspecting; or the state of being suspected; imagination; generally of something ill, distrust; mistrust; doubt. The apprehension of something without proof or upon slight evidence. Implies a belief or opinion based upon facts or circumstances which do not amount to proof.

T

TESTIMONY. Evidence given by a competent witness, under oath or affirmation; as distinguished from evidence derived from writings, and other sources. Testimony is one species of evidence, but the words "testimony" and "evidence" are often used interchangeably.

THEFT. A popular name for larceny. See Larceny.

THE GREAT WRIT. A name given to the Writ of Habeas Corpus.

TORT. A private or civil wrong or injury; a legal wrong committed upon the person or property independent of contract which is redressed in a civil court. A personal tort involves or consists in an injury to the person or to the reputation or feelings as distinguished from an injury or damage to real or personal property, called a "property tort."

TORT FEASOR. One who commits a tort.

TRANSCRIPT OF RECORD. The printed record as made up in case for review by a higher court; also a copy of any kind. In referring to the written documents on appeal the words "transcript" "record" and "Record on Appeal" are used interchangeably.

TRIAL JURISDICTION. In New York, a criminal court has trial jurisdiction of an offense when an indictment or an information charging such offense may properly be filed with such court, and when such court has authority to accept a plea to, try or otherwise finally dispose of such accusatory instrument. See Original Jurisdiction.

V

VAGRANCY. Vagabondage, betting, loitering. Soliciting for prostitution is sometimes included in the definition of vagrancy.

VANDALISM. Willful or malicious destruction, injury, disfigurement, or defacement of property without consent of the owner or person having custody or control.

VENIRE. From the Lat. to come, to appear. The name given to the writ for summoning the jury, and also to the body of jurors summoned.

VENIRE FACIAS. In practice, a judicial writ directed to the sheriff of the county in which a cause is to be tried, commanding him that he "cause to come" before the court, on a certain day therein mentioned, twelve good and lawful men of the body of his county, qualified according to law, who are in no way kin to the plaintiff or to the defendant, to make a jury of the county between the parties in the action.

VENIREMAN. A member of a panel of jurors; a juror summoned by the writ of *venire facias.*

VENUE. A neighborhood; the neighborhood, place, or county in which an injury is declared to have been done, or fact declared to have happened. "Jurisdiction" of the court means the inherent power to decide a case, whereas "venue" designates the particular county or city in which a court with jurisdiction may hear and determine the case.

VERDICT. The formal and unanimous (or one concurred in by the majority of jurors required by law) decision or finding made by a jury, impaneled and sworn for the trial of a cause, and reported to the court (and accepted by it) upon the matters or questions duly submitted to them upon the trial. From the Latin "veredictum," a true declaration.

VIOLENCE. Physical force.

VOIR DIRE. Literally "To speak the truth." The preliminary examination of a witness or juror as to his competency, interest, etc.

W

WARRANT OF ARREST. A written order issued and signed by a magistrate, directed to a peace officer or some other person specially named, and commanding him to arrest the body of a person named in it, who is accused of an offense. In New York, a warrant of arrest means a process of a local criminal court, directing a police officer to arrest a defendant and to bring him before such court for the purpose of arraignment upon an accusatory instrument filed therewith by which a criminal action against him has been commenced.

WRIT OF *CERTIORARI.* See *Certiorari.*

WAIVE. To abandon or throw away; in modern law, to abandon, throw away, renounce, repudiate, or surrender a claim, a privilege, a right, or the opportunity to take advantage of some defect irregularity, or wrong.

WRIT OF *HABEAS CORPUS.* A writ directed to a person detaining another and commanding him to produce the body of the prisoner or person detained.

Appendix C

SELECTED SECTIONS UNITED STATES CONSTITUTION

Preamble

We the People of the United States, in Order to form a more perfect Union, establish Justice, insure domestic Tranquillity, provide for the common defence, promote the general Welfare, and secure the Blessings of Liberty to ourselves and our Posterity, do ordain and establish this Constitution for the United States of America.

Article I.

Section 6. The Senators and Representatives shall receive a Compensation for their Services, to be ascertained by Law, and paid out of the Treasury of the United States. They shall in all Cases, except Treason, Felony and Breach of the Peace, be privileged from Arrest during their Attendance at the Session of their respective Houses, and in going to and returning from the same; and for any Speech or Debate in either House, they shall not be questioned in any other Place.

Section 9. The Privilege of the Writ of Habeas Corpus shall not be suspended, unless when in Cases of Rebellion or Invasion the public Safety may require it.

No Bill of Attainder or ex post facto Law shall be passed.

Article III.

Section 2. The Judicial Power shall extend to all Cases, in Law and Equity, arising under this Constitution, the Laws of the United States, and Treaties made, or which shall be made, under their Authority;—to all Cases affecting Ambassadors, other public Ministers and Consuls;—to all Cases of admiralty and maritime Jurisdiction;—to Controversies to which the United States shall be a Party;—to Controversies between two or more States;—between a State and Citizens of another State;—between Citizens of different States;—between Citizens of the same State claiming Lands under Grants of different States, and between a State, or the Citizens thereof, and foreign States, Citizens or Subjects.

In all Cases affecting Ambassadors, other public Ministers and Consuls, and those in which a State shall be a Party, the supreme Court shall have original Jurisdiction. In all the other Cases before mentioned, the supreme Court shall have appellate Jurisdiction, both as to Law and Fact, with such Exceptions, and under such Regulations as the Congress shall make.

The Trial of all Crimes, except in Cases of Impeachment, shall be by Jury; and such Trial shall be held in the State where the said Crimes shall have been committed; but when not committed within any State, the Trial shall be at such Place or Places as the Congress may by Law have directed.

Article IV.

Section 2. The Citizens of each State shall be entitled to all Privileges and Immunities of Citizens in the several States.

A Person charged in any State with Treason, Felony, or other Crime, who shall flee from Justice, and be found in another State, shall on Demand of the executive Authority of the State from which he fled, be delivered up, to be removed to the State having Jurisdiction of the Crime.

No person held to Service or Labour in one State, under the Laws thereof, escaping into another, shall, in Consequence of any Law or Regulation therein, be discharged from such Service or Labour, but shall be delivered up on Claim of the Party to whom such Service or Labour may be due.

The Bill of Rights

AMENDMENT [1.]

Congress shall make no law respecting an establishment of religion, or prohibiting the free exercise thereof; or abridging the freedom of speech, or of the press; or the right of the people peaceably to assemble, and to petition the Government for a redress of grievances.

AMENDMENT [II.]

A well regulated Militia, being necessary to the security of a free State, the right of the people to keep and bear Arms, shall not be infringed.

AMENDMENT [III.]

No Soldier shall, in time of peace be quartered in any house, without the consent of the Owner, nor in time of war, but in a manner to be prescribed by law.

AMENDMENT [IV.]

The right of the people to be secure in their persons, houses, papers, and effects, against unreasonable searches and seizures, shall not be violated, and no Warrants shall issue, but upon probable cause, supported by Oath or affirmation, and particularly describing the place to be searched, and the persons or things to be seized.

AMENDMENT [V.]

No person shall be held to answer for a capital, or otherwise infamous crime, unless on a presentment or indictment of a Grand Jury, except in cases arising in the land or naval forces, or in the Militia, when in actual service in time of War or public danger; nor shall any person be subject for the same offence to be twice put in jeopardy of life or limb; nor shall be compelled in any criminal case to be a witness against himself, nor be deprived of life, liberty, or property, without due process of law; nor shall private property be taken for public use, without just compensation.

AMENDMENT [VI.]

In all criminal prosecutions, the accused shall enjoy the right to a speedy and public trial, by an impartial jury of the State and district wherein the crime shall have been committed, which district shall have been previously ascertained by law, and to be informed of the nature and cause of the accusation; to be confronted with the witnesses against him; to have compulsory process for obtaining witnesses in his favor, and to have the Assistance of Counsel for his defence.

AMENDMENT [VII.]

In Suits at common law, where the value in controversy shall exceed twenty dollars, the right of trial by jury shall be preserved, and no fact tried by a jury, shall be otherwise re-examined in any Court of the United States, than according to the rules of common law.

AMENDMENT [VIII.]

Excessive bail shall not be required, nor excessive fines imposed, nor cruel and unusual punishments inflicted.

AMENDMENT [IX.]

The enumeration in the Constitution, of certain rights, shall not be construed to deny or disparage others retained by the people.

AMENDMENT [X.]

The powers not delegated to the United States by the Constitution, nor prohibited by it to the States, are reserved to the States respectively, or to the people.

Other Amendments

AMENDMENT XIV.

SECTION 1. All persons born or naturalized in the United States and subject to the jurisdiction thereof, are citizens of the United States and of the State wherein they reside. No State shall make or enforce any law which shall abridge the privileges or immunities of citizens of the United States; or shall any State deprive any person of life, liberty, or property, without due process of law; nor deny to any person within its jurisdiction the equal protection of the laws.

TABLE OF CASES

References are to Pages

INDEX

References are to Pages

References are to Pages

References are to Pages

WEST PUBLISHING CO